CHINA
MARCHES
WEST

CHINA MARCHES WEST

THE QING CONQUEST OF CENTRAL EURASIA

Peter C. Perdue

THE BELKNAP PRESS OF
HARVARD UNIVERSITY PRESS
Cambridge, Massachusetts
London, England
2005

Library of Congress Cataloging-in-Publication Data

Perdue, Peter C.
China marches west : the Qing conquest of Central Eurasia / Peter C. Perdue.
p.   cm.
Includes bibliographical references and index.
ISBN 0-674-01684-x (alk. paper)
1. China—History—Qing dynasty, 1644–1912.   2. Russia—History—1613–1917.
3. Mongols—History.   I. Title: Qing conquest of Central Eurasia.   II. Title.

DS754.P47   2005
951′.03—dc22   2004059472

To Linda, Kay, and Alex, and the memory of my parents

Contents

Maps

Preface

I began the research for this book in more peaceful times, purely out of intellectual curiosity about a little-known region of the world and a neglected topic in Chinese imperial history. Today, the issues raised by this study have come all too close to home, both for the Chinese and for us. The PRC government has now convinced the UN Security Council to classify the East Turkestan Independence Movement as a terrorist organization. At the same time, the PRC has launched a visionary project to "develop the West," so as to bring the Central Eurasian and interior regions of China firmly into the economic web generated by the reform program of the last two decades. Although I believe that China will maintain control over this region for the foreseeable future, I make no predictions. But the imperial legacy of conquest still hangs heavy over the future of the Chinese nation-state.

Specialists have, for disciplinary convenience, usually divided the region in two. "Inner Asia," conventionally defined as modern Mongolia (Inner and Outer), Manchuria, Xinjiang, and Tibet, has historically been primarily the province of those knowledgeable in Chinese, Mongolian, and Manchu languages. "Central Asia" generally refers to the area of Turkic peoples bounded by the former Soviet Union, and much of its scholarly literature is in Russian. But we cannot let a simple Russian–Chinese divide define a cultural arena, especially for the early modern period, centuries before either nation existed. "Inner Asia" has its uses as a subdivision of Asia setting it off from East, Southeast, and South Asia, but it is misleading to set its boundary simply along the former Sino–Soviet border. "Asia," a European concept not embraced by any indigenous peoples of the region until the twentieth century, has fairly clear maritime borders to the east and south (ignoring the problematic status of Australia, New Zealand, and Polynesia) but no clear borders on the northwest.

These geographic descriptions reflect a binary division which has now vanished. I prefer the term "Central Eurasia," now used by the U.S. State Department and by the only Department of Central Eurasian Studies in the United States, at Indiana University. It is a less familiar term, but it lacks the historical baggage of other words. It also reminds us of the artificiality of the distinction between "Europe" and "Asia," and the awkward status of Russia in this definition. Without being foolishly consistent, I have used "Central Eurasia" most of the time in this book, and have used "Inner Asia" only when the discussion clearly refers to the Chinese side of the border.

I chose the title of this book carefully. "China marches west," because this is the story of a conquest endorsed by the Chinese nation-state today. But it is the "Qing Conquest," not the "Chinese Conquest," because many of the major participants were not Han Chinese, and "Central Eurasia" instead of more common terms like "Inner Asia," "Central Asia," "Mongolia," or "Xinjiang" in order to indicate the large scale and blurred boundaries of the territory the empire gained. Chinese historians would prefer a title like "The Unification of the Mongolian and Uighur Peoples under the Qing Multinationality State"; Russians and Mongolians might choose "The Invasion of the Mongolian Peoples by the Aggressive Manchu Qing." Every choice of words has political implications; none is neutral, but some can be more detached than others. Throughout, I try to stress the pre-national character of the processes described here. The warriors and traders of the eighteenth century did not think in terms of nation-states; they pursued their own interests as they saw them, and we should both recover and respect their views. Nevertheless, they laid the necessary groundwork for nationalism by their actions. This study both critiques nationalism and demonstrates the continuity between empire and nation.

Its dates are indefinite. We might begin with the birth of Nurhaci in 1559, the first Russian penetration of Siberia in 1582, the first declaration of an empire in Manchuria in 1616, or the launching of the wars against Galdan in 1690. Likewise, this story could end with the death of Amursana in 1757, the final suppression of rebellion in Turkestan in 1765, the "return" of the Torghut Mongols to Qing territory in 1771, or extend through the final Russian conquest of Central Eurasia in the mid-nineteenth century. History being a continuous flow, all periodization is inevitably Procrustean. I indicate significant turning points throughout.

This is a long book, to be sure. If I had found an adequate study of this topic, I would not have gone on at such length. And yet it falls far short of being a comprehensive analysis of Qing China's relations with Central Eurasia, or even of the Zunghar campaigns alone. To my surprise and horror, what seemed to be a manageably focused study of a "peripheral" subject soon revealed vast seas of archival and published documents and secondary research. There still remain huge numbers of documents and questions which I have not had the time or energy to study in depth. I have ended with many more questions unanswered than resolved. I only hope that by insisting on the importance of China's northwest campaigns I can stimulate others to follow the frontier trail.

Although this is a large, sprawling book, it has a simple format. It alternates between structural analysis and narrative. Part One sets the stage, looking at the ecological conditions under which the contests took place and the background to dynastic decision making up until the seventeenth century. Part Two follows the basic story from the rise of the Qing in Manchuria, the establishment of the Mongol state, and the arrival of the Russians in the early seventeenth century, through the consolidation of control at the end of the eighteenth century. Part Three turns back to a structural analysis of the economic and environmental constraints which the conquerors and their rivals had to overcome. Part Four looks at the cultural performances and symbolic representations that legitimated the conquest and left a legacy to the future. And Part Five sums up the implications for modern China and modern theorists about state building in China and elsewhere. I have tried to give a balanced account of the motives of all the major parties involved in the conflict, but since the bulk of the sources are in Chinese, biases are unavoidable, even if we read texts against the grain. This is primarily a book about the Qing rulers and the world they made, but it tries to rescue from "the enormous condescension of posterity" (to quote E. P. Thompson) many others who played their parts in the drama. I take no position on whether the empires described here were good or evil: that kind of judgment is not the historian's role. But I do insist that their conquests were not inevitable, that resistance and accommodation both deserve their story, and that the course of this struggle left traces that persist today.

Acknowledgments

This study has taken far too long for me to be able to thank adequately everyone who has contributed to it. Joseph Fletcher, with whom I studied Manchu at Harvard, died in 1984 while I was in the archives in Beijing completing my first book and exploring a new topic on northwest China. I and many others have tried to carry on the work that he so heroically pioneered. I received valuable help from the staff at the Number One Archives in Beijing, the Palace Archives in Taiwan, the Archive of Foreign Policy, and the State Archive of Ancient Acts in Moscow. Galina Khartulary and Valerii Klokov were invaluable guides to the mysteries of Moscow. In Beijing, I would like to single out Cheng Chongde, Director of the People's University Qing History Institute, and his colleagues, and Li Bozhong, an old friend and colleague, among many others. Back home, I am especially grateful to Dean Philip Khoury for his constant support, and to all my colleagues on the MIT History Faculty for comments and encouragement. Anne McCants, Pauline Maier, Harriet Ritvo, and Elizabeth Wood offered especially valuable reactions to an early chapter. John Dower has been a constant source of sagely wisdom. I could make progress on this book even while serving as department head only because of their goodwill and dedication. Many parts of this text have been presented at seminars at the Fairbank Center for East Asian Studies at Harvard University, Columbia University, the University of California, Irvine, the California Institute of Technology, the Institute for Agrarian Studies at Yale University, the University of Kansas, and annual meetings of the Association of Asian Studies, the American Historical Association, and seminars as far-flung as Istanbul, Taibei, Beijing, and Japan. I greatly appreciate all the helpful reactions received from those who attended, especially Tim Brook, Pamela Crossley, Nicola Di Cosmo, Philip A. Kuhn, Robert Marks, Ken Pomeranz, James C. Scott, Carl Strikwerda, Charles Tilly, Frederic Wakeman, Joanna Waley-Cohen, R. Bin Wong, Alexander B. Woodside, Donald Worster, and many others. My deepest regret is that Benjamin Schwartz, a model of scholarly rigor and personal engagement, died before this manuscript was finished. I would have loved to hear his reactions. I deeply appreciate the tireless labor of the research assistants at MIT and Harvard who helped with the preparation of the book: Cherng Chao, He Wenkai, Jiangti Kong, Ellen McGill, Nana Okura, Helen Tang, and Angela Xiang. I am also grateful to the many scholars who have gone before me in this field. For centuries, in many languages, often without knowing of one another's existence, they accumulated an invaluable fund of synthetic and documentary knowledge. If we see a bit further, it is because we stand on their shoulders.

I must also offer special thanks to the Chao family, whose endowment of the T. T. and Wei Fong Chao Professorship helped substantially in providing the resources to prepare this manuscript for publication, especially the beautiful artworks included in it. I thank Lin Man-houng of Academia Sinica, Taiwan, for her invaluable help in obtaining artworks from Taiwan. My editors, Kathleen McDermott and Elizabeth Gilbert, have been particularly generous, firm, and efficient in bringing this book into its present form. Amanda Heller meticulously edited the final copy, and Phil Schwartzberg drew the elegant maps.

In mostly unconscious ways, many environments have influenced the perspectives of this book. Travels to Beijing, Japan, Mongolia, Moscow, and Xinjiang have helped to ground the abstractions of ancient texts with contemporary experience and the natural world. I am grateful to all those whom I met there and who helped me on the way. More locally, I reflect on Jamaica Pond, the Arnold Arboretum, the Charles River, Dorchester, MIT, and Harvard Yard, where many of the ideas in this book were generated.

Some chapters draw on previously published material in revised form: "Boundaries, Maps, and Movement: The Chinese, Russian, and Mongolian Empires in Early Modern Eurasia," *International History Review* 20 (June 1998), pp. 263–286; "Empire and Nation in Comparative Perspective," *Journal of Early Modern History* 5, no. 4 (2001), pp. 282–304; "The Agrarian Basis of Qing Expansion into Central Asia," in *Papers from the Third International Conference on Sinology: History Section (Zhongyang Yanjiuyuan Disanzhou Guoji Hanxue Huiyi Lunwenji Lishizu)* (Taibei: Institute of History and Philology, Academia Sinica, 2002), pp. 181–223; and "A Frontier View of Chineseness," in *The Resurgence of East Asia: 500-, 150-, and 50-Year Perspectives,* ed. Giovanni Arrighi, Takeshi Hamashita, and Mark Selden (London: Routledge, 2003), pp. 51–77.

Note on Names, Dates, Weights and Measures, and Chinese Characters

Names

Achieving consistency in the romanization of personal and place-names has caused me constant headaches. I have tried wherever possible to write each person's name in the romanized version of the language of his primary ethnic group. Alternative romanizations are given in parentheses, preceded by an indication of the language (Ma. for Manchu, Mo. for Mongolian, Ch. for Chinese, and T. for Tibetan). For Chinese names, I use *pinyin* romanization; for Manchu names, the spelling used in Jerry Norman, *A Concise Manchu-English Lexicon* (Seattle: University of Washington Press, 1978). Russian names generally follow the Library of Congress system. Mongolian names come in many flavors, reflecting differences of dialects and different romanization systems. Foolish consistency being impossible, I have used spellings that, I hope, will be at least pronounceable by those unfamiliar with the subtleties of Altaic languages, and at least recognizable by those who care about philological accuracy. For Tibetan, I give a pronounceable version following R. A. Stein, *Tibetan Civilization* (Stanford: Stanford University Press, 1972), with the original spelling in parentheses. Turkic names and places usually follow James A. Millward, *Beyond the Pass: Economy, Ethnicity, and Empire in Qing Central Asia, 1759–1864* (Stanford: Stanford University Press, 1998). See Appendix A for the names and reign years of the major Central Eurasian rulers discussed here.

I use different romanizations to distinguish Soochow, the great textile city of the lower Yangzi, from Suzhou, the garrison town in western Gansu.

Dates

All dates in the text are given in the Julian solar calendar; Chinese references in the notes follow the Chinese lunar calendar with reign name (KX: Kangxi; YZ: Yongzheng; QL: Qianlong). An asterisk indicates the lunar intercalary month following the numbered month.

Weights and Measures

1 *jin* (catty) = 1.3 pounds or 0.6 kg
1 *li* = 0.36 miles or 0.576 km
1 *mou* = 0.1647 acre or 0.0666 hectare
1 *shi* = 103.5 liters or 2.9 bushels (23.5 gallons). One *shi* of milled rice
weighed approximately 175–195 pounds (80–89 kg).
1 *patman* (Ch. *bateman*) = a Turkestani land and grain measure, equivalent to 4.5–5.3 *shi* of grain, or 26.5 *mou* of land (from Millward, *Beyond the Pass,* p. 54).

Chinese Characters

Because I wrote this book for readers who may not know Chinese, it does not contain Chinese characters. A character list is available on the Web site *dspace.mit.edu*; search for "Perdue."

The conquest of the earth, which mostly means the taking it away from those who have a different complexion or slightly flatter noses than ourselves, is not a pretty thing when you look into it much. What redeems it is the idea only.

Joseph Conrad, *Heart of Darkness*

You have conquered the empire on horseback; but can you rule it on horseback?

Lu Jia (ca. 228–140 BCE) to Emperor Han Gaozu

Introduction

FROM the seventeenth to the mid-eighteenth century, three great empires—the Manchu Qing (1644–1911), the Muscovite–Russian (1613–1917), and the Mongolian Zunghars (1671–1760)—contended for power in the heart of Eurasia. The distances were vast, communications slow, military campaigns extended and costly, and cultural alienation was huge. By the end of this epic confrontation, an early version of the "Great Game," only two empires were left standing.[1] The Qing and Russians faced each other along an extended border. They had become two of the largest empires in world history.[2] The Zunghars had vanished. Despite nineteenth-century upheavals, this binary division of Eurasia lasted until the collapse of the Soviet Union in 1991.[3] This book examines the division of the continent between the two empires, emphasizing the Qing empire's conquest of Mongolia and Xinjiang. (See Maps 1 and 2.)

No one could claim that the Qing campaigns in Central Eurasia have been ignored. Every textbook mentions them. This is not the recovery of a long-forgotten event. And yet, there has never been an adequate full-length study of them in English.[4] Studies in other languages also have their limitations. This book, based on primary sources, archival and published, in several languages, tells a dramatic story almost unknown to English-language readers.

It also critiques some of the dominant paradigms of modern Chinese historiography, most prominent in the work of Chinese scholars but also implicitly adopted by many in the West. In brief, most historians, supported by the prevailing nationalist ideology that reigns on both sides of the Tai-

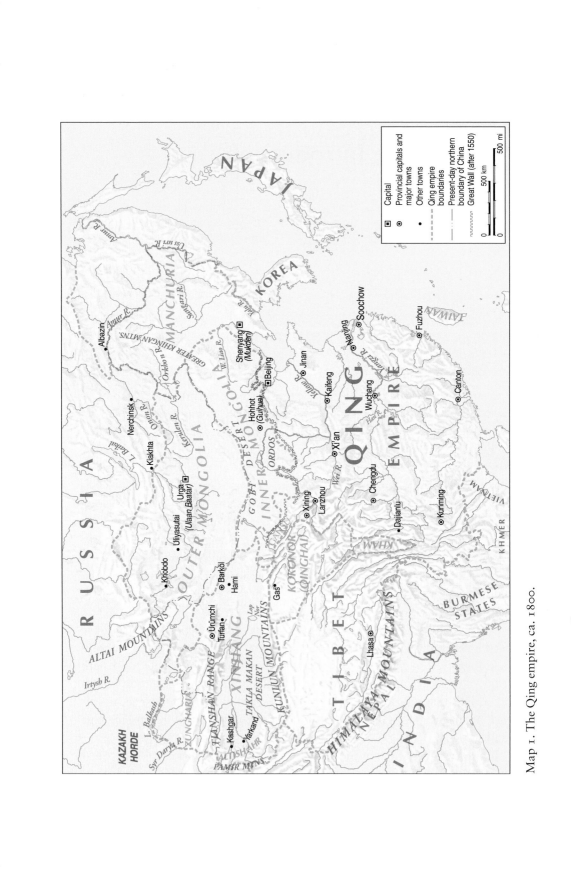

Map 1. The Qing empire, ca. 1800.

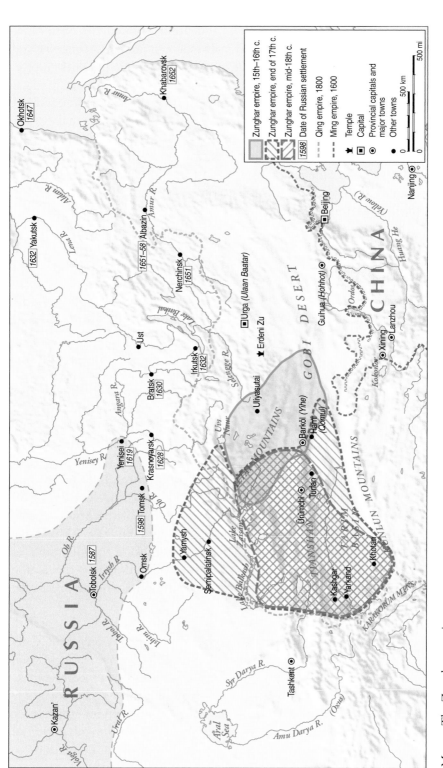

Map 2. The Zunghar empire.

wan Strait, take the current territorial and cultural boundaries of the Chinese nation-state for granted. They view the conquest of Mongolia and Xinjiang as the fulfillment of a development that culminates with the Republic of China in the twentieth century, or, in Chinese terms, the "unification" of the peoples of Central Eurasia in the multinational Chinese nation-state. These historians view the Qing expansion at its maximal extent, around 1800, as the end of this process. Since then, in the nineteenth century, the empire declined from its peak of glory until it recovered sovereignty over much of the region by 1949. Mongolia, of course, and much of Manchuria north of the Ussuri River still remain outside the People's Republic, as does Taiwan. In the ideals of Chinese nationalists, all these regions should be part of the modern nation-state. Indeed, from time to time the mainland Chinese leaders have indicated that they still see these regions as part of the nation. They of course strongly insist that Taiwan belongs to one China. Even though nationalists rejected the Manchus as an obstacle to China's modernization, the Chinese nation-state derived its concept of its ideal boundaries from the maximal expansion of the Qing empire in the eighteenth century. Like other nationalists, the Chinese built on the past they rejected.

From this perspective, the conquest of Xinjiang and Mongolia was important but not epochal. But what if we reject the view of the conquest as merely one link in a chain that inevitably led to the nation-state? What if it was a contingent product of the crosscutting wills of many players, only some of whom were Han Chinese, and none of whom had modern nationalism in mind? The security threat from the northwest was indeed long-lasting, in every imperial ruler's mind. What emperor did not wish to rid himself of the damned nomads who harassed the northwest frontier? All previous efforts, however, with the brief exception of the Mongol-ruled Yuan dynasty (1279–1368), were unsuccessful, until the Qing achieved the final solution in the mid-eighteenth century. Why were the Qing able to eliminate the Mongol threat once and for all, and to dominate this region ever since, when no previous dynasty succeeded? That will be one of the central questions of this work.

Specialists in Central Asian history have generally ignored this period. The entire era from the fall of the Mongol empire to the present day, regarded as the "Époque de la Décadence," accounts for only 30 pages out of over 350 in Denis Sinor's introduction to the field. They have emphasized philology over ethnography (only 8 pages in Sinor) or other social scientific perspectives.[5] Luc Kwanten's survey of steppe empires stops at the year 1500, because he, like many others, regards the Mongol empire of Chinggis Khan as the culmination of the steppe imperial tradition, followed by centuries of decline.[6] Many historians have used the paradigm of a classical age of florescence and expansion, followed by a period of "decline," to structure their accounts. Historians of the Ottoman and other empires have grown increasingly critical of this perspective.[7] The main defect of this paradigm is that it takes the end for the beginning by reading history backward from a time of weakness to its origins in an "era of decadence." Like nationalist historiography, the paradigm of decline forecloses consideration of roads not taken, crucial decisions, and contingencies, and denies agency to the actors. We need to reintroduce independent agency to the Central Eurasians in this story, without taking for granted either the hostile perspectives of their Manchu rivals or nostalgia for the days of Chinggis Khan.

A careful examination of these events raises many questions about the predominant historiography both of China and of Central Eurasia. The best overview in a western European language is still that of Maurice Courant, a French diplomat who in 1912 wrote *L'Asie Centrale aux 17e et 18e siècles: Empire Kalmouk ou Empire Mantchou?* It relies almost entirely, however, on a single Chinese source. I. Ia. Zlatkin's *Istoriia Dzhungarskogo Khanstvo, 1635–1758* (History of the Zunghar Khanate, 1635–1758), the best survey in Russian, uses Manchu and Russian but not Chinese sources. Chiba Muneo provides an extended Japanese narrative, and a number of Japanese scholars have written relevant works.[8] Chinese scholars have produced an enormous secondary scholarly literature and a major synthesis. But each of these scholarly traditions has deficiencies, which reveal particular cultural and national characteristics. In the final section of the book, I briefly review the historiography of the conquest in order to indicate how historians of this topic, like all historians, have reflected the concerns of their time.

The study of modern Chinese history has increasingly turned inward. Early works focused on China's international position and included study of the Manchu nature of the regime, the military institutions, and the security considerations of the center.[9] The rise of the Fairbank school shifted interest toward diplomatic relations with maritime Western powers, the central civil institutions of the Qing, and intellectual history. The influence of G. William Skinner's regional systems model led scholars to turn toward intensive socioeconomic studies of single provinces or sub-regions. Much was gained from the turn inward, but something was lost, too. Particularities of individual variation overrode wider contexts. Placing China in world history should be a priority today, and study of the frontier is a promising way to integrate China with the wider Eurasian world. This study of Qing expansion offers points of comparison with studies of frontiers elsewhere in the world. It also questions the rigidity of Skinner's regional systems model.

Instead of fitting our regional analyses into a prescribed geophysical framework, we must recognize that often political and social processes moved fluidly across regional boundaries, driven by considerations of military security, economic gain, or cultural transmission.

History, Time, and Memory

As well as reshaping conceptions of space, this study aims to adjust our views of Eurasian time. Historians have often viewed Chinese and Central Eurasian history in terms of cycles. The dynastic cycle paradigm has provided a convenient explanation of the rise and fall of Chinese imperial regimes ever since the Zhou conquered the Shang in 1045 BCE. The repeated unification and collapse of steppe empires has also inspired cyclical explanations. Although many scholars see repetitive patterns in the state formations of both China and the steppe, they find widely divergent causes for them. We may roughly classify these causes as moral and material. Moral explanations look for the essence of change in human psychology. China's dynastic cycle theorists attributed the rise and fall of empires to the moral characteristics of the ruler. If he governed wisely, he made his people happy and attracted others to support him. If he was debauched, the peasantry suffered, the soldiers rebelled, and officials deserted his cause. Updated versions of the dynastic cycle paradigm, by contrast, focus on material bases of imperial rule, such as maintenance of irrigation works, equitable tax collection, or famine relief. In this perspective, if bureaucratic management of these key social institutions failed to meet the social challenges, mass rebellion or external invasion brought the dynasty down.

For steppe empires, the predominant material explanation has invoked climatic determinism, assuming that cycles of desiccation inevitably drove nomads out of their steppe homelands to invade the settled societies around them. By contrast, Ibn-Khaldūn, the great Islamic historian and social theorist, outlined a theory based on social solidarity, or 'asabiyya, arguing that the collective unity generated by tribal societies created a form of power which allowed them to conquer decadent urban civilizations. After the conquest, as the moral codes generated in the steppe-desert environment decayed under the influence of urban ways, the tribal conquerors lost their solidarity and became victims of new invaders. Ibn-Khaldūn's theory shows striking similarities to the Chinese dynastic cycle model, even though he applies its moral definitions not to "civilized" Confucianized rulers but to nomadic warriors.[10]

The cyclical models have the advantage of highlighting common patterns that transcend the narrative of particular events. They thus point toward generalizations about broad processes of social change. Long before the rise of Western sociology, both Chinese and Middle Eastern social theorists had begun to analyze the long-term evolution of their societies in comparative terms. The danger of cyclical theorizing, however, lies in its denial of human agency and its neglect of linear change. Strict adherence to cyclical explanation implies that people do not learn from experience. They are doomed to follow in the same tracks as their ancestors. But we know well that no social process ever perfectly repeats the past, for two reasons. First, technological advances greatly altered the kinds of conflicts that tore societies apart and the pressures that held them together. New weapons, reductions in transport costs, or new forms of communication, for example, all transformed the means of integration and disintegration of Chinese dynasties. Second, both Chinese and nomadic peoples learned from history. They knew the precedents set by their ancestors, and they constantly used their knowledge to build on past experience or to learn from their mistakes. Hence the writing and rewriting of history formed a key element in shaping the strategies of empire builders, officials, and ordinary social interactions.

The geographical and strategic environment of Chinese–nomadic interaction created recurrent situations, but those involved dealt with these situations in different ways, depending on their historical and technological resources. I describe in the chapters that follow examples of frontier trade, horse breeding, and the use of gunpowder weaponry to indicate how the Qing–Zunghar conflict partially followed old paths but often broke new ground.

It is particularly important to stress innovation by steppe empire builders, since settled observers have so often viewed nomads as doomed to stay in the same tracks forever. The striking continuities in nomadic life from the creation of pastoralism to the present often inspired images of monotony, repetition, and stagnation. The settled observers who provide nearly all of our sources usually saw the nomads as catastrophic eruptions into their civilizations, comparable even, in Braudel's words, to biblical plagues.[11] Mechanical theses of environmental determinism likewise deprived the Central Eurasians of any agency, tending to reduce them to mere biological actors. We shall see biological, naturalistic analogies invoked repeatedly by the enemies of the Zunghars, so as to exclude them from the human world and justify their extinction.

During the age of high imperialism, in the nineteenth century, Westerners likewise portrayed Chinese as victims of natural forces, or as liable to sudden inexplicable outbreaks of violence. They applied simple stereotypes of determinism and Asian autocracy to explain China's persistent resistance to

Western intrusion. Our perspectives on China have changed considerably in recent years. Serious scholars have abandoned old stereotypes of "Oriental Despotism." The "Naito hypothesis" and the "early modern hypothesis" both hold that decisive socioeconomic changes occurred in China during the ninth to tenth or late sixteenth century, respectively. In the last section of this book, I support the "Eurasian Similarity Thesis," which argues that Chinese empires were just as economically dynamic as European ones up to the end of the eighteenth century.[12] By giving China an internal dynamic of its own, comparable to but separable from that of the early modern West, these analyses point toward the true incorporation of China into world history.

Only recently, scholars have also argued for substantial historical change in pastoral societies. Thomas J. Barfield's model of nomadic state building recognizes linear evolution, but his theory makes nomadic state builders dependent on the changes in Chinese empires and does not allow them much agency of their own. Nicola Di Cosmo has made the most cogent argument for autonomous dynamics in the formation of steppe empires. He argues for freeing our study of Inner Asian peoples from biological imagery and mechanical causation, and develops a periodization of state formation based on the means by which state builders obtained revenue from external actors. From the second century BCE to the eighteenth century CE, revenue extraction developed from tribute extraction, to trade-tribute partnerships, to dual administration of settled and nomadic peoples, to fully developed procedures for taxing an agricultural base.[13]

Our story finds the Zunghars making use of all of these methods as they attempted to support their expanding state. They exacted tribute from their neighbors, traded extensively with the Qing, Russians, and Central Eurasians, practiced a form of dual administration in Turkestan, and developed fiscal structures in the Ili valley. As Di Cosmo notes, however, they lacked the "breathing space" to consolidate their state because of the simultaneous expansion of the Qing and the Russians against them. Hence, I see the seventeenth and eighteenth centuries as the decisive turning point in steppe-settled interactions, determined by the actions of both the agrarian empire builders and the nomadic state makers. The closure of borders created by the concurrent expansion of the Qing and Russian empires substantially increased the constraints on the peoples in between. The Zunghar leaders did, as Barfield argues, try to use whatever resources they could get from their imperial neighbors, Russian and Chinese, to support their state, but they also tried to develop internal resources from the oases of Turkestan and the Eurasian caravan trade. Material resources mattered, but simple desiccation had little to do with state formation. Attacks of drought could just as easily drive Mongols to seek refuge under Qing protection as to attack the empire. How nomads reacted to drought was a product of personal and diplomatic negotiation between the Qing and the Khans.

Throughout this discussion I stress the multiple opportunities available to all the actors and the indeterminacy of the outcome. The Qing conquest and elimination of the Zunghars was never inevitable. Some environmental factors favored the Qing, but others favored the Zunghars. Personal decisions, accidental deaths, misunderstandings, and deceit all played important parts. This story would have no drama if Heavenly mandates, environmental conditions, or teleologies of the nation predetermined the outcome. Instead, I place this story in its broadest context while keeping in the foreground the contingent results of human decisions.

The Qing Conquests as a World Historical Event

Two contradictory paradigms have shaped our general outlook on the significance of Central Eurasia. Many theorists have described it as the region least prepared for modernization. In their view, its isolation from global trends, its political and cultural fragmentation, and its poverty of natural resources gave it few of the prerequisites for rapid development.[14] For these theorists, universal processes of economic growth, political and social integration, and communication inevitably drag backward, traditional societies into agonizing transformations. The backward societies have little or nothing to offer to the advanced societies. Sooner or later, in this linear, railroad track view of history, they follow the leaders.

An alternative perspective is one we may call the "world historical" point of view. Rejecting the automatic classification of societies by nation-state units so characteristic of modernization theory, it denies that national units can develop in isolation from one another. Often major civilizational units transgress contemporary nation-state boundaries, and all these regions constantly interact. Central Eurasia, in this view, was not a remote, isolated region but the crossroads of the Eurasian continent, and it had a decisive impact on all the settled societies around it. A current of historical interpretation from the Russian Eurasian school, to the geopolitics of Halford Mackinder and Owen Lattimore, to the contemporary world historians and theorists of world systems has viewed Central Eurasia as a key region of the Eurasian world system.[15]

In the early modern period, Central Eurasia was indeed the crossroads of the Eurasian continent. Every major religion reached it. Trade routes between China, the Middle East, Russia, India, and Europe crisscrossed the region. Up until at least the sixteenth century, the caravan traders following the old Silk Routes played a major part in global trade. Even in the seventeenth and eighteenth centuries, as the old Silk Route trade declined, the Russo-Chinese tea and fur trade remained important. Religious diversity, linguistic pluralism, and cosmopolitanism characterized the oasis cities. More than anything else, it was the conquest of the region by the "modern" empires of China and Russia that relegated it to backwardness in the nineteenth century, not any essential features of the region. Scholars critical of the modernization paradigm have blamed imperial conquest for causing backwardness in other parts of the world. Perhaps conquest had the same effect here. At least we can say that the Qing and Russian conquest of the region strongly affected the potential of Central Eurasian peoples for development in the nineteenth and twentieth centuries.

The Qing conquests, then, were a major world historical event in three senses. First, for the empire's rulers and subjects, these victories fundamentally transformed the scale of their world. By vastly expanding the territorial reach of the state, the conquests opened up new terrain for colonial settlement, for trade, for administration, and for the literary imagination. Second, the expansion of the Qing state formed part of a global process in the seventeenth and eighteenth centuries. Nearly everywhere, newly centralized, integrated, militarized states pushed their borders outward by military conquest, and settlers, missionaries, and traders followed behind. Western European historians often characterize this period as that of the "seventeenth-century crisis" of state formation followed by eighteenth-century stabilization, and other historians have found parallel processes around the globe.[16] Treating China's imperial expansion as part of a global process helps us to view China in a broader perspective instead of seeing everything about its imperial experience as unique. Third, China's expansion marked a turning point in the history of Eurasia. Across the continent, the great empires founded by Central Eurasian conquerors in the wake of the disintegration of the Mongol empire had captured the heartlands of densely settled regions, used the resources of these regions to supply military forces, and pushed back from the heartlands into the core of the continent. When their borders met, they negotiated treaties that drew fixed lines through the steppes, deserts, and oases, leaving no refuge for the mobile peoples of the frontier.

The closing of this great frontier was more significant in world history than the renowned closing of the North American frontier lamented by Frederick Jackson Turner in 1893.[17] It eliminated permanently as a major actor on the historical stage the nomadic pastoralists, who had been the strongest alternative to settled agrarian society since the second millennium BCE. Many Inner Asianists regard the decline of the nomadic warrior as having been completed in the sixteenth century because of the diffusion of gunpowder or shifts in the Central Asian caravan trade.[18] One last major nomadic state, however, held out against the military forces closing in on the steppe. These Mongols battled vigorously against the Manchu Qing armies. They adopted gunpowder weaponry in response to the military threats around them, and the caravan trade remained a significant source of revenue for all the contending parties. Thus the true world historical transformation that tipped the balance against unfettered nomadism happened from 1680 to 1760, and the Qing rulers were major forces in this momentous change.

PART ONE

The Formation of the Central Eurasian States

1

Environments, State Building, and National Identity

THREE theoretical perspectives inform this work: frontier environments, state building, and the construction of national and ethnic identities through historical representation. Many historians, recognizing the critical role of the environment in shaping human affairs, have focused on the interaction between man and nature. Western writers have, however, inflicted a debilitating environmental determinism on the analysis of Asian history that reflected nineteenth-century European assumptions of racial superiority. In the eighteenth century, Baron de Montesquieu contrasted the flat, monotonous plains of Asia with the varied landscape of Europe to explain the contrast between Asiatic despotism and European freedom. Karl August Wittfogel's *Oriental Despotism* carried on the same style of analysis by connecting Chinese imperial autocracy and Soviet communism alike to state control of hydraulic works.[1] Both used grossly oversimplified contrasts between European and Asian environments to undergird ideological arguments protecting Western liberties against threats from the East. Responsible environmental history has to shake off this tainted legacy and look at much more nuanced relationships between humans and their natural surroundings without political preconceptions.

The American geographer Ellsworth Huntington drew a direct connection between environmental change in Central Eurasia and the evolution of civilization. As he stated in *The Pulse of Asia*, after travels through Chinese Turkestan from 1903 to 1906:

In relatively dry regions increasing aridity is a dire calamity, giving rise to famine and distress. These, in turn, are fruitful causes of wars and migrations, which engender the fall of dynasties and empires, the rise of new nations, and the growth of new civilizations. If, on the contrary, a country becomes steadily less arid, and the conditions of life improve, prosperity and contentment are the rule. There is less temptation to war, and men's attention is left more free for the gentler arts and sciences which make for higher civilization.[2]

He found the same "parallelism between climatic changes and history" from Turkey to China, in Europe, and in the New World. For Huntington, desiccation processes, most visible in Central Asia, repeatedly forced nomads out of the center of the continent, causing everything from the barbarian invasions of Rome to the rise of Islam, and even threatening a potential invasion of the United States by starving hordes of Chinese in the twentieth century.[3]

Arnold Toynbee used Huntington's findings to support his claims that nomads were trapped by climatic conditions in a stagnant way of life, leaving them a "society without history."[4] Only environmental changes could alter their inevitable submission to the cycle of seasons, when droughts forced them to invade settled civilizations. Toynbee, like his predecessors, based his definitions of civilization on a contrast between the creative mastery of nature in the settled agrarian realms and the animalistic vulnerability of nomads to cycles of desiccation.

Despite Huntington's blatant, naïve racism and his almost laughable crudity, he did correctly single out aridity as an important defining characteristic of Central Eurasia. In his travels he observed carefully the local geology and the relationship of the local people to their environment, mixing sensitive description with vast biased speculations on human character. His analysis alerts us to the inevitable political contamination of all efforts to link human and natural history. Owen Lattimore at first endorsed Huntington's and Wittfogel's views, but in his later work he argued for the greater importance of social over geographical causes. He found "mechanical explanations, in the form of climatic cycles or progressive desiccation [accounting] for the 'blind' eruption of nomad hordes" too crude, because they ignored the "dynamics of social groups." More recent work has tried to shake off its imperialist traces by placing European and American developments in a broader global context.[5]

Most of this new work has concentrated on the impact of Europeans on the North American frontier, and of Americans on the western United States during the nineteenth century. We need to see, however, the American expansion westward across the continent as part of a worldwide expansion of agrarian frontiers in the eighteenth and nineteenth centuries.[6]

Both the Russian and Chinese empires pushed from opposite directions across Eurasia beginning in the sixteenth and seventeenth centuries. The natural environments of North America and northern Eurasia, in fact, have many similarities. Both include temperate forests which are home to fur-bearing animals, which are trapped by native peoples; both have grasslands where nomadic peoples roam; and both have deserts and arid regions as well as fertile agricultural zones. The Chinese reached no Pacific coast, of course, and found no gold (although the Russians prospected for gold in southern Xinjiang), but like their American counterparts, they moved west in search of land. The Russians reached the Pacific and beyond to Alaska in their inexorable quest for furs. In all three cases, the interlocking environments of forests, deserts, steppes, and agrarian settlement shaped their histories. Natural forces beyond human control and organized efforts to tap the environment for human livelihood drove the settlers onward.

Environmental historians have closely examined settlement on new frontiers. William Cronon's work, for example, has progressed from a study of the impact of English settlers on seventeenth-century Massachusetts, to the takeover of the Great West by the forces of capitalism centered in Chicago, to the exploration of the mining frontiers of Alaska.[7] In each case he has focused on the interplay between indigenous peoples, the natural environment, and the disturbance created by intrusive aggressive settlers from western Europe. Alfred Crosby's studies of the "Columbian exchange" likewise followed in detail the ecological disruption brought by European settlers to the New World. Recent work on Oceania likewise demonstrates the devastating impact of European biota on the ecosystems of the Pacific Islands. There is thus a close link between environmental and frontier history.[8]

Students of America's frontiers inevitably have to refer to Frederick Jackson Turner's famous thesis about the formation of the American character by pioneer settlement.[9] Critics of Turner's excessive Anglocentrism aim to offset his biases by exploring the histories of the other peoples who inhabited the American West before the arrival of English settlers, Native Americans, Hispanics, and Chinese among them. Others promote a separate regional history of the West, autonomous of the forces of eastern capitalism, with its own special identity.[10] Most of the participants in this debate, however, do not examine North American frontiers comparatively. On the Eurasian frontiers, Chinese and Russians also viewed their settlement programs as the penetration of civilization into wilderness, ignoring or repressing the independent histories of other inhabitants. The national histories of both countries are intimately bound up with their expansion into the Eurasian interior. Although they have maintained national states, unlike the indigenous Americans, Mongols and other Central Eurasian peoples likewise still find much of their history written in terms of penetration of their territory by expanding empires. Neither China nor Russia produced as prominent a figure as Turner to epitomize its national character, but each country's experience demonstrates useful analogies to the North American process. The Eurasian frontiers, because of their remoteness from western Europe, are much less well known than those of America, but they deserve to be included in any comparative study of frontier settlement.

Similarly, theorists of state building have aimed primarily at explaining the rise of European states from the sixteenth century forward.[11] Some theorists explicitly exclude "empires" like the Qing from their analysis, putting them in a different category from "states."[12] Here, however, I argue for resemblances among the three major competing agrarian empires in Eurasia—the Zunghar Mongols, the Russians, and the Chinese—and the European states. All three, driven by geopolitical competition, mobilized their resources for war, trade, and diplomacy against one another. In order to compete with its rivals, each regime strove to increase its "stateness"—its "formal autonomy, differentiation from nongovernmental organizations, centralization, and internal coordination"—by extracting resources from its subject peoples and from its neighbors.[13] These efforts led to substantial social and institutional reforms. The self-interest of state rulers and their officials led them to develop bureaucratic methods to tap agrarian and commercial production all across Eurasia. Western Europe did not follow a special path.

The collapse of the Soviet Union and the resurgence of nationalism in eastern Europe and elsewhere have nurtured a new crop of theories of nationalism and national identity.[14] These new theories argue that nations, as "imagined communities," are created, not born. Nationalist ideologies claim two contradictory positions at the same time: that their nation has deep roots in land, language, and culture, and that it is a new creation, rejecting the stagnant legacy of the past. The contemporary study of nationalism highlights this contradiction, stressing the artificial, constructed nature of every nation, including China.[15] Language and subjective identity count for much more than the "objective," nearly timeless features of land and race in defining the boundaries of the modern nation-state. Ideologues mobilize particular interpretations of past events as tools for constructing new national identities. As Eric Hobsbawm has remarked, "History is the raw material for nationalist or ethnic or fundamentalist ideologies, as poppies are the raw material for heroin addiction."[16] History becomes a weapon, easily turned into myth, appropriated for the purposes of nation builders and citizens. The real events of the past are viewed indirectly, mediated by memory. But Europe was not the only nationalist construction site, and "geobody building" did not begin in the nineteenth century.[17]

The historian's task is to recognize both the falsity and the effectiveness of myth.[18] As soon as the battles for territory ended, the battles for control over the historical meaning of conquest began. The conquest of Eurasia played a critical role in the national conceptions of all three of the competitors, but it was interpreted in strikingly different ways. Thus our story begins with nature, continues with individual actors, and ends with the historians. After a long excursus through the events, we return, in a cycle of recapitulation, to examine how myth making, which began under the Qing empire, created the elements that composed the nationalist histories of the twentieth century. The conclusion returns to the perspectives sketched here, to address the implication of this story for general paradigms of Chinese and world history.

The Unboundedness of Central Eurasia

Central Eurasia has never coincided neatly with national boundaries. Only under the brief rule of the Mongols was the region united under one imperial ruler. Until 1991, China, Mongolia, and Russia or the Soviet Union controlled the bulk of the region, with other parts in Iran, Afghanistan, and the Ottoman empire. Today, eight independent nations (the five former Soviet Central Asian Republics, Russia, Mongolia, and China) divide up most of the territory. Fragmentation has been by far the most common experience of Central Eurasians. The bipolar Soviet–Chinese split turns out to have been a brief interlude.

Most broadly defined, Central Eurasia extends from the Ukrainian steppes in the west to the shores of the Pacific in the east, from the southern edge of the Siberian forests to the Tibetan plateau. But all of its borders are so ambiguous that endless disputes arise. If Central Eurasia includes all grasslands and steppes, it extends through the Ukraine into the Hungarian plains. By cultural and linguistic criteria, including the Ural-Altaic language family, Turkic and Mongolian peoples are found as far afield as Finland, Manchuria, and, arguably, Japan and Korea. Steppe nomadism alone is not sufficient as a defining feature, because all across the region nomads coexisted with settled agriculturalists; and other nomads, of the Middle East, or reindeer herders of Siberia, are omitted.

Almost every scholar defines the boundaries of the region differently. Cyril Black includes the five Central Asian Republics, Iran, Afghanistan, Tibet, Xinjiang, and Outer Mongolia in "Inner Asia," but not Manchuria or

Inner Mongolia, because Chinese dominated these areas in the twentieth
century. He estimates a total area for this region in 1989 of 4.9 million
square miles (12.7 million square kilometers), with a population of 135
million.[19] Joseph Fletcher divides the region into the "desert habitat characteristic of Central Asia (a region that includes, roughly, present-day Afghanistan, Soviet Central Asia—which does not include Kazakhstan—and
Sinkiang [Xinjiang] south of the Tianshan mountains)" and the "steppe
habitat" which "covers a wide zone running from Europe to Manchuria
along roughly the fiftieth parallel north latitude, its main regions being
the south Russian steppe, Kazakhstan, Zungharia, much of Amdo (present-
day Tsinghai [Qinghai] province), and Mongolia north and south of the
Gobi."[20] He omits Tibet. Denis Sinor's organization of the region, primarily
linguistic, includes the speakers of Finno-Ugric, Altaic, Manchu, Mongolian, and Turkic languages.[21] Finns, Lapps, and Hungarians enter the picture, but Chinese, Russians, Tibetans, Arabs, and Iranians are omitted, except as the writers of sources. Richard Frye confines himself to Indo-Iranian
language speakers.[22]

Rather than choosing among these disparate definitions, I would stress
the great indeterminacy of the cultural characteristics and territorial borders of this zone, which resulted in constant competition by empires, religions, and cultural groups to define and control it. No simple myths of
well-bounded space could ever confine it: no imaginary hexagon of France,
no sceptered isle of England, no manifest destiny stretching between two
ocean coasts. The huge flatlands offered no decisive barriers to invaders,
and the mountain ranges left large gaps through which conquerors could
pour their troops. The bewildering fluctuations of a multitude of empires,
each ruled by different peoples with different boundaries and institutions,
demonstrated the great plasticity of the landscape.

I shall try to avoid anachronistically imposing definitions from the age of
nationalism on the region, focusing on the critical importance of the conquests of the seventeenth and eighteenth centuries for the evolution of the
Chinese and Russian empires. Manchuria, Mongolia, and Tibet cannot be
excluded from this story, but Iran and Afghanistan played very small roles.
I view the conquest not as the "Chinese" conquest of "Xinjiang," but as the
expansion of a Central Eurasian state that used the massive resources of the
Chinese bureaucracy and economy to bring as much as possible of Central
Eurasia and the Chinese core under its rule.

The main actors in our drama, in fact, covered nearly all the major zones
of classical Central Eurasia, from the south Russian steppes in the west,
where the Volga Kalmyks settled, to Manchuria in the east. Siberian native

peoples in the north provided the furs that drew Russia to the region, and
Tibetan lamas to the south provided religious, bureaucratic, and clerical expertise critical for the formation of the Zunghar state. Caravan traders of
many nationalities linked all these territories together. This story encom-
passes a vast scale, not neatly bounded by national territories. The end of
the nomadic empire builders meant the end of unbounded space and the
clear demarcation of the region into mutually exclusive agrarian empires,
soon to become even more exclusive nation-states.

To free ourselves from national divisions, it is best to begin by looking at
ecological zones, starting with the largest scale and then narrowing down.
(See Map 3.) Central Eurasia contains forests and fields, oases and deserts,
grasslands, rivers, and mountains. Its inhabitants include pastoral nomads
roaming the grasslands, traders in the oasis towns, and the agriculturalists
surrounding them. The homogeneity and uniformity of the ecological zones
of the region make it quite distinct from other, more fragmented parts of
the world. Very high mountains surround its periphery, but the great majority of the territory is broad and flat. Climate and precipitation determine
the basic characteristics of vegetation and animals in four broad horizontal
strips, defining tundra, forest, steppe, and desert. It is not the absolute
amount of precipitation but the ratio of precipitation to evaporation that is
decisive. Very low rainfall in the cold tundra still produces wet soil, while
more rain in the southern deserts yields no moisture. South of the Arctic
tundra, where only reindeer herders can find subsistence, are the forests of
Siberia, which overlap with the steppe grasslands. The grasslands shade
into steppe desert and large expanses of pure desert in the south.[23]

Change did occur in Central Eurasia, but outside observers often missed
its signs. On the one hand, the uniformity of the ecological zones allowed
easy movement east and west, which especially suited the herding and nomadic peoples who flourished there. On the other hand, the lack of diversity within the zones limited possibilities for greater development. The
Chinese and other sedentary peoples incorporated diverse agricultural and
maritime production areas within their borders, and used the variegated
products of their different zones to build up complex civilizations and empires. The Central Eurasian peoples often seem to have repeated the same
adaptations to the monotonous environment without change for millennia.
Grazing animals, the tent, the mounted warrior, and his mobile but precarious existence recur in the descriptions of the many different peoples of Central Eurasia from the Scythians to the last of the Mongols. The "civilized"
writers who provide our sources tended to regard the Central Eurasian peoples as universally greedy, primitive, and poor, and identified them almost

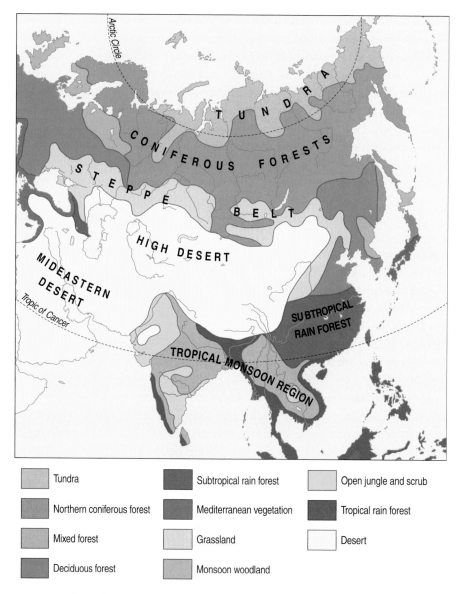

Map 3. Ecological zones of Eurasia.

exclusively as nomads. They ignored the different ways of life in the region and neglected its possibilities for technological development. They "allow[ed] the assumed Nomad to obscure the living man."[24]

The substantial uniformity of climatic zones from east to west also made it impossible to draw sharp boundaries across the region. Since no obvious divisions marked the end of one culture and the beginning of another, all sorts of travelers and warriors could move freely back and forth. The greatest problem of empire builders was to define their stopping point, and, once they had stopped, to make provisions for security along their frontier. Basic natural features such as rivers, mountains, and settlements did not define well-enclosed spaces but tended to create centrifugal patterns. As Justin Rudelson writes, "The historical focus of the Xinjiang oases was not inward, toward each other, but outward, across borders."[25] Empires and their borders shifted constantly across the region because no natural boundaries existed.

For the most part, the rivers of Central Eurasia flow inward, or into frozen Arctic seas. They do not link the region to the world around it. The Amu Darya and Syr Darya flow from the high Pamir and Tianshan Mountains into the Aral Sea, embracing a desert, and no fertile crescent, between them. Far to the west, only the Volga connects via the Caspian Sea with the Middle East, and to the east, the Liao River of Manchuria supported agrarian settlement. The other main rivers are not very effective transport arteries. The major Siberian rivers, like the Ob, Yenisei, and Lena, flow north into the Arctic Sea. The Russians were able to cross Siberia by following their tributaries as they branched out to the east and west, but at the cost of many difficult land portages. The lakes, too, though very large, isolated among deserts and high mountains, generally lead nowhere. But along stretches of certain rivers, agrarian settlers could interact with nomads. The location of these rivers had the greatest effect on the builders of the Zunghar empire, who had to obtain agricultural resources from small river valleys and oasis production. The Ferghana valley supported sizable cities, such as Kokand and Andijan. Farther north, the Ili River valley connected with Lake Balkash, which linked the Zungharian steppe with the Kirghiz-Kazakh steppe. In Mongolia, from the region of modern Ulaan Baatar, the Orkhon and Selengge rivers flowed north into Lake Baikal, and the Kerulen River flowed east into Hulun Lake in modern Inner Mongolia.

Each of the major steppe empires put its political and spiritual base in one of these river valleys.[26] The Selengge and Orkhon rivers served as the headquarters for the Eastern Turks, the Uighur empire, and the later Mongol empires of the Oirats. Ögödei, son of Chinggis Khan, built the Mongol empire's central capital at Karakorum on the Orkhon River. After the capital collapsed, the site still remained sacred to the Mongols. The monastery of Erdeni Zu, built in 1586, became the headquarters of the chief Buddhist cleric of Mongolia. The Liao River valley was the core region of the Manchurian-based empires of the Khitan Liao, the Jurchen Jin, and the Manchu Qing. The northwest Gansu corridor (especially the irrigated lands of the Yellow River around Yinchuan) served as a base for the Tangut Xixia kingdom.

Vast distances separated all of these small valleys, and they pointed in different directions. Except for Chinggis Khan, no steppe ruler ever controlled all of them simultaneously, nor did any single settled empire until the Qing. For would-be empire builders, the Liao River was the most promising, both because of its fertile agricultural lands and because there were few physical barriers to moving south into the North China plain. The Selengge-Orkhon region was the farthest removed from any settled empire. Empires here benefited from isolation, but they had few available resources beyond the steppe to draw on nearby, except for the fur hunters of Siberia. The Zunghars, when they were based here, had to expand in all directions at once: east and south toward Manchuria, north to Siberia, and southwest across the Mongolian steppe, aiming for Ferghana.

Ferghana, or ancient Turkestan, had been the site of many oasis kingdoms, periodically overrun by steppe conquerors like the Qaraqanids and Timur. Prosperous both in agrarian resources and in caravan trade, it linked directly east to the cities around the Tarim basin and west to Iran and the Silk Road. Naturally it was an attractive target, and the Zunghars early on made attempts to extract wealth from it. The Qing conquerors, however, after defeating the Zunghars, took the east Turkestan Tarim basin cities of Kashgar and Yarkand, but did not immediately push over the Tianshan-Pamir Mountains to the richer settlements of Kokand, Ferghana, Bukhara, and Samarkand. Qing armies invaded Kokand in 1830, but then withdrew, because in the eighteenth century the Qing court had made a decision to stop at this point. The ancient links between these cities, and their unified integration in previous empires, reminds us that there were no "natural" limits to Chinese expansion in this direction, despite the towering peaks dividing east and west Turkestan. Manchu, and later Chinese, rulers consistently tried to keep control of Xinjiang, despite huge costs, but limited China's borders to those defined in the mid-eighteenth century. They stopped their advance not because of inevitable geographic constraints or the expression of essential Chinese territorial claims, but for contingent political and cultural reasons.

Richard Frye writes that "the history of [Central Asia] is primarily one of oases, large and small."[27] He overstates the case, but oases undeniably provided the primary resources for the settled populations of the region. Oasis settlements are "perpendicular civilizations."[28] They are settled societies, but very different from those of great agrarian civilizations, where village populations spread across a broad landscape. The Turkestan oasis towns were independent, self-sufficient units. Their irrigation water came from melting snow in the Tianshan Mountains, which also contained small pastures. Agriculture in the valley depended on channeling the snowmelt down to fields below, where high temperatures allowed a long growing season. These prosperous farmers could support an urban population, but trade and contact with the outside world were extremely difficult. Only the passing caravans of the Silk Road traders, a completely distinct society, linked the oasis communities with one another and with the outside world.

The oasis communities were stable but fragile. Prolonged drought dried up the river sources, forcing valley people to move up into the mountains. Drought that killed mountain pastures prompted mountain pastoralists to raid the towns below. Such disturbance of this miniature pastoralist–settled symbiosis quickly allowed the desert sands to move in. The abandoned cities of Turkestan and Zungharia that litter the desert testify to the vulnerability of the oasis communities to political and ecological change.

Nevertheless, the oasis dwellers accounted for the primary concentrations of agricultural and commercial wealth in this vast landscape, focal points of attention of all empires, nomadic and settled. When possible, they sought protection and support from powerful neighbors. Turfan and Qomul (Hami) in the east, the closest major oases to China, often entered into tributary relations with the empire. The presence in Turfan of two abandoned garrison towns from the Han and Tang dynasties reflects Chinese imperial interest in controlling the region. As a gateway to the steppe, far beyond the Great Walls, Turfan was a valuable security resource for expanding Chinese dynasties.

Other oases, farther away, could not count on China's protection. They entered into relations with nomadic conquerors, often serving as their major tax base and administrative center. Khocho, near Turfan, and Beshbalik, near modern Ürümchi (Ch. Wulumuqi, Urumqi), became Uighur principalities after they lost Mongolia. Timur made Samarkand into one of the most flourishing urban centers of the fifteenth-century world. The symbiosis of nomadic warriors and oasis cultivators benefited both when the warriors brought their wealth back home and attracted merchants to their base. But when the nomadic empires contracted, the oases could easily revert to isolation, or abandonment. We seldom learn the fates of the people who left their oasis homes, but we know that nearly the entire Turfani population sought refuge within Qing borders for several decades in the eighteenth century. They were, fortunately, able to return, but other peoples disappeared into the sand.

For Fernand Braudel's Mediterranean, "mountains come first," but the mountains of Central Eurasia do not determine its borders or its overall climate.[29] The distance of the entire region from the ocean creates its continental climate, with extreme temperatures in summer and winter. Precipitation and evaporation define the east-west climatic zones. Mountains, by blocking moisture-bearing winds, create regional features, like deserts and oases, but no single mountain barrier marks off the region.

One great series of mountain chains runs northeast to southwest from Lake Baikal and Manchuria to the Hindu Kush.[30] Although some of the ranges are 3,000 to 4,000 meters high, with peaks over 5,000 meters, there are large gaps between them, especially from east to west. Along the Ili River valley, nomads and travelers moved freely back and forth, and farther north the Zungharian gate opened into the Kazakh steppe. The mobility of nomad armies for a long time frustrated the efforts of the Qing empire to confine them or hunt them down. Mountains and forests offered them refuge but did not block their movement. The Zunghars learned how to use forests to blunt the impact of Qing artillery fire.

Mountain ranges delimited the southern boundary of the region more closely, dividing it into fragments. The great ranges of the Caucasus, the Elburz of northern Iran, the Pamirs, and the Tianshan, marked off the steppe to the south. Farther east, the Tianshan range divided Xinjiang into two very distinct sections. The Kunlun Mountains sealed off Tibet from the north, and the Himalayas sealed it off in the south. The Altai and Sayan ranges divided Mongolia from Xinjiang to the south and Siberia to the north. The Khingan range marked off Manchuria from Mongolia. The Urals, perhaps the range best known to Europeans, were the least significant physical barrier; only by cultural convention did they become the line demarcating European from Asiatic Russia. Nevertheless, each of these ranges contained passes and gaps. India, Afghanistan, and Iran maintained constant cultural connections with the Central Eurasian peoples.

A huge zone of deserts stretches from the Caspian Sea to the Gobi and Ordos in Mongolia.[31] These deserts, too, break up the region. Their extreme aridity eliminates inhabitants from the core, allowing settlements only on the periphery. The Taklamakan desert makes life possible in southern Xinjiang only on the oases on the rim of the Tarim basin, as the Gobi divides Mongolia in two. The deserts did not, however, block movement entirely. They could all be crossed by caravans linking the oasis towns; so they did not form impassable barriers, but they did prevent close integration of the settlements on their edges.

These physical barriers broke up the unity of culturally similar peoples, although they were not the sole determinant. The Mongols of Inner Mongolia and the Khalkhas of eastern Outer Mongolia were drawn ever closer into the Chinese orbit, while the Oirats in the west, separated from them by vast empty spaces, never succeeded in re-creating the Mongol empire of Chinggis. Cultural unity and disunity were, however, a product of political strategy, not geographic determinism. Manchu frontier officials especially knew how to exploit divisions among the Mongols. By selectively tying the Eastern Mongols closer to the Chinese economy, they promoted increasing development of trade and settlement in Mongolia from the seventeenth through the nineteenth century. Geography yielded to commercial penetration.

Forests extended for 6,000 miles across northern Eurasia, from Manchuria through Siberia. The coniferous forests of the taiga "form the most extensive tree cover in the world." The climate is subarctic, and much of the soil is permafrost. Although elk, deer, bear, lynx, and other large animals live in the forest, the small fur-bearing animals—sable, fox, ermine, marten, and squirrels—proved to be the most valuable forest product for the Russians who moved there.[32]

In the prehistoric past, large forest zones covered much of the North China plain during warmer and wetter climatic periods; but since the deforestation of the plain in the Han dynasty, large extensive forests remained for the most part confined to Siberia and Manchuria.[33] The peoples of the forests practiced small-scale hunting and gathering or agriculture with primitive tools, and remained "on the margins of world history," primarily because of the low productivity of farming in such a cold climate.[34] Other forests on mountain uplands provided shelter for pastoralists who moved to higher altitudes with their herds in the summer. Like the oasis peoples, the forest peoples remained confined to small horizons; they never built big political structures on their own, and they were victims of pressure from the expanding empires around them.

Although the forest peoples do not figure as major actors in this story, they provided the resources for the state builders who contended over the Eurasian steppe. The native peoples of Siberia, who paid tribute in furs, attracted all three greedy empires, who demanded *iasak,* or tribute, from them. Without the fur-bearing animals of Siberia and Manchuria, the Russian adventurers, traders, and military colonists would never have been interested in expanding to the east, and the Manchus themselves, expert hunters in their own right, could never have built a state.

We may divide the steppe into three horizontal bands: wooded or forest steppe in the north, pure grasslands in the middle, and desert steppe in the south. The central grasslands extend from the Ukraine, the northern Caucasus, southern Urals, and Kazakhstan through eastern Mongolia and Manchuria, including the high grasslands of Zungharia and the valley of the Ili River. Rich black soil under the continuous belt of grass supported its annual regrowth, despite the cold and arid climate. The grass belt allowed fluid movement by the nomads across the vast distances east and west. Thus, in the early seventeenth century the Torghuts could break off from the Western Mongols and move 3,000 kilometers west to the banks of the Volga without ever leaving the steppe. They undertook an extremely difficult return to their homeland in the late eighteenth century for political, not environmental, reasons.

Over five thousand species of plants grow in the Central Eurasian steppe. All of them must withstand aridity and violent climatic changes. They ripen early and quickly in the spring, and usually go into dormancy in the summer and winter. Not all of them are suitable for grazing animals, of course, and the short blooming season means that much of the grazing must be done in the spring. "Livestock are always moved toward a perpetual spring": pastoralists drive them up to alpine meadows in the summer and down to lower elevations in fall and winter.[35] The rigid restrictions of climate and pasture defined tight limits on nomadic mobility, despite the appearance of freedom. Access to pasture required close attention to weather, geography, and the needs of animals, as well as enough organization to ward off invaders of the tribal pastures. Pastures left dormant could easily be raided by others.

The boundaries between grasslands and forests shifted north and south over prehistoric time in tune with the changing climatic parameters of temperature and moisture. Tundra, desert, grassland, and forest-steppe dominated northern and northwest China during the first half of the Wurm glaciation (70,000 BP–40,000 BP), but as the climate warmed from 40,000 to 25,000 BP, forests spread into Manchuria and the North China plain. Colder, drier climate from 25,000 to 15,000 BP drove the forests out, replacing them with treeless dry steppe. Warming followed again around

Grasslands of Mongolia. One of the photos taken by Frederick Wulsin during his expedition of 1923, and colorized in Beijing.

12,000 BP, and broadleaf forest spread once more through North China, but a drier climate after 11,000 BP brought back grassland to replace forest in parts of northern and northeast China. Clearly the ability of agriculture to flourish in the borderland forest-steppe zone depended heavily on the climatic conditions, and the frontier was always much more vulnerable to dryness than the North China plain.

The earliest agricultural sites in eastern Inner Mongolia date from 5300 BCE, during another warming period, following cold conditions from 8000 to 6000 BCE. Forests spread through the Western Liao River area, and three successive Neolithic agricultural regimes followed, each increasingly linked to developments in North China. Agricultural tools, ox and sheep bones, and finally the appearance of foxtail millet, the main grain of the northwest around 2000–1000 BCE, indicate the culmination of agriculture in this region during a time when mild winters and moist, temperate climate flourished.

Around 1000 BCE the climate turned cooler and drier, agriculture declined, and a pastoral nomadic culture displaced the settled farmers in the Western Liao River. Pottery declined in quality, horses appeared, and pigs disappeared. Cultural influences now came from the north and west instead of from the south and east. Hunting and fishing cultures may also have evolved toward mobile hunting and animal husbandry. The shift in cultures in this region corresponds to the appearance of references to the Rong and Di tribes in historical sources.

Asian nomadism first evolved in the thirteenth century BCE in the Upper Yenisei River, north of the Altai Mountains. From there it moved southeast and southwest into China's borderlands and across Central Eurasia. Colder, drier climates disfavored agriculture in marginal areas but favored mobile pastoralists living off grasslands and herds. Thus, over the long term, ecological forces underlying two sharply distinct cultural regimes pushed nomads and settlers back and forth.

The steppe nomads originated at the margins of the steppe, not in the heart of it. Owen Lattimore argued that some may have come from reindeer herders and seed gatherers in the Lake Baikal forest region who moved south, shifting from dependence on reindeer to the steppe assemblage of sheep, cattle, horses, and camels. Others might have originated in oasis peoples who went hunting in nearby mountains and grasslands, eventually domesticating animals at the outer edges of oases. A third source was Chinese peasants at the edge of the loess soil region in Gansu-Shaanxi, who eventually gave up on farming and turned to pastoralism.[36]

Harold Peake and Herbert Fleure have noted the contrasts between the northern steppe (the grasslands extending from Hungary to eastern Manchuria) and the southern steppe (from western India through Persia and Arabia to North Africa).[37] The inhabitants of the southern steppes, from prehistoric times, had been in contact with irrigated agriculture and the earliest urban civilizations. They raided the settled cultivators, but just as often traded goods with the towns, where they picked up the central religious ideas of the region, especially the belief in a supreme deity. Their primary animal was the one-humped camel, not the horse, whose great demand for water limited its spread through the desert.

By contrast with the south, in the north nomads had less contact with settled cultivators and traded less with cities. The northern steppes are walled off from the ancient Middle East by the linked mountain ranges of the Sayan, Altai, Tianshan, Elburz, Pamir, and Hindu Kush. Much of the

Camel caravan crossing Mongolia. Photo taken by Frederick Wulsin, 1923.

land to the south is high plateaus, 500 to 1,000 meters in altitude. For the people of the north, the horse was far more important than the camel because of its ability to endure cold. Its demand for water was not such a problem in colder climates. The two-humped Bactrian camel became the main pack animal of the Silk Road for the caravan traders but not the animal of the nomad.

Peake's division of northern and southern steppe resembles Joseph Fletcher's distinction of "desert" and "steppe" nomadic habitats. As Fletcher writes, "The desert nomad understood agrarian cultivation and urban society." When the Turks moved across Eurasia, they followed paths prepared previously for them by the Arabs. They came in gradually, in small groups, and did little damage to the settled societies. They soon assimilated and adopted Islam. The (northern) steppe nomads, the Mongols, lived apart from settled peoples. Geography here separated the two worlds instead of uniting them. On the Chinese end, "the steppe-sown dichotomy was sharper than anywhere else in the Eurasian steppe," and "Mongolia and China confronted one another throughout much of history as worlds apart."[38] The great ecological separation, along with the suddenness of the Mongol conquest, explains the tremendous destruction inflicted by

Chinggis compared to other steppe invasions. Eastern Eurasian nomads and Chinese, for much of their history, regarded each other with mutual contempt, literally as animals: the Chinese used "pig" radicals on the characters for barbarians of the northwest; the Mongols, when they conquered the North China plain, regarded Chinese peasants as "herds" to be driven out.

Farther east, however, Manchuria linked the steppe and settled worlds. Although the region was mainly populated by hunters and fishermen, nomads repeatedly conquered the region to use its resources for their state. In the thirteenth century, the Jurchens extended their control south to the Chinese settled population, combining both the settled and nomadic worlds under a dual administration.[39] The Qing rulers drew explicitly on the experience of these ancestors for administering both steppe and settled worlds.

In sum, in the northern grasslands, and especially in eastern Eurasia, the focal point of our story, the steppe and the sown diverged sharply, and the nomads remained for a long time quite isolated from both settled agricultural and urban civilizations. Their main contact with them was through raiding. Conversely, the settled Chinese peasant and urban-centered official alike often saw the nomad as utterly foreign and hostile, not a dynamic element in the civilizational complex, but an alien threat to be bought off, walled off, or driven out. The Manchus, like their predecessors the Jurchen, occupied the key bridge between the two worlds.[40]

What we now call "Xinjiang" is a recent creation. The Qing created the name "Xinjiang" (New Frontier) during their eighteenth-century conquests. It did not become a province of the empire until the late nineteenth century. It has no essential geographical unity; as noted earlier, its topography fragments the region. It was a conglomerate of different cultures, ecologies, and peoples, mostly separate and oriented toward their local environments. Yet this region is at the center of our story.

Xinjiang lies directly across both northern and southern steppe zones. North of the Tianshan, the Zungharian steppe acts as a gateway connecting the plateaus of Mongolia with the lowlands to the west. The Altai Mountains bound it on the north and northeast, but a corridor leads east into Mongolia north of the Gobi desert. The center of Zungharia is desert, but grasslands ring it on the North and South. The Ürümchi oasis, now the capital, but always an urban center under different names, lies at the southern end of the basin, on the northern edge of the Tianshan. The northern branch of the old Silk Road leads from here east via Hami to Jiuquan in

Gansu province, and west through the Ili valley to Kuldja (modern Yining). To the west, the Tarbaghatai Mountains and Zunghar-Alatau ranges run east and west, leaving an opening into the Kazakh steppe. Major nomadic empires always tried to occupy the Zungharian basin because of its large expanse of grasslands and its productive oasis towns. The Zunghars, who gave their name to it, were only the last in a series. Conversely, until Qing armies could reach the Zungharian basin, they could not destroy the Zunghar state.[41]

Trade, Transport, and Travel

Humans learned to domesticate the horse around 4000 BCE in the southern steppes of Russia.[42] By 1950 BCE the first horse-drawn chariots appeared in western Asia, and by 1200 BCE the Chinese were using chariots in warfare. Riding on horseback took longer. The first mounted warriors, the Scythians and Cimmerians, appeared in the ninth century BCE, and soon invaded Assyria but diffused only slowly to China and Mongolia. Large horses derived from Arab stocks were bred in northern Iran, Kazakhstan, Turkmenistan, Uzbekistan, Tajikistan, and Kirghizstan in the first millennium BCE, but the basic stock of the east Eurasian warriors, the small pony or "Przewalski's horse," did not appear in Mongolia until the fifth century BCE. Within a century, these horsemen had become a powerful presence on China's northwest frontier.[43] Possession of the horse turned the pastoralist from a mere herder into a powerful predator. He could raid sedentary societies for other goods, or simply use the threat of raids to extort better terms of trade.[44] Horses demanded greater areas of pasture than the other grazing animals; acquiring them was an investment in a capital good, which brought greater returns by enabling conquest of other pasturelands and better terms of trade from settled societies.

When horse-riding nomads entered regions without sufficient pasture, they dismounted. Their use of the horse demonstrates adaptation to different environments. The Huns, for example, once they crossed the Carpathian Mountains, found a terrain lacking the large pastures of Central Eurasia. By the fourth and fifth centuries CE, their battles with the Romans were more like pitched infantry battles than swift cavalry raids. The Hungarian Alföld, by Lindner's estimate, contained 42,400 square kilometers, which could support at least 320,000 horses, assuming that one horse requires 25 acres (10.1 hectares) of pasture. But allowing for the presence of other grazing animals, as well as the presence of forests and marshes mixed with pasture, limits the number of horses to about 150,000, enough to sup-

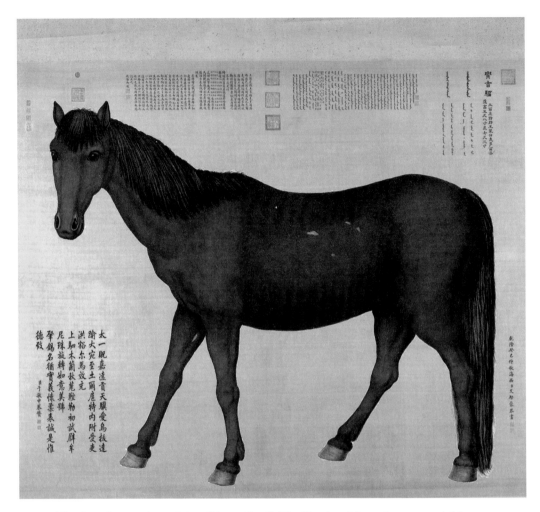

The "precious and auspicious" horse Baoji. The Torghut Mongols presented this horse to the Qianlong emperor after their return from Russia, and the Czech court painter Ai Qimeng (Ignatius Sickeltart) painted it in 1773.

port at most 15,000 mounted warriors—less than two Mongolian divisions. As Rudi Lindner writes, "Hungary is not Mongolia. To expect the Huns to have retained the domestic economy of the steppe once they had reached the Danube is to reject the role of ecology in history." Thus the Huns turned sedentary when they entered Europe, and "the Carpathians mark the far western frontier of the history of nomadism."[45]

The horse was both the mainstay of the nomadic economy and the one essential element in warfare which the sedentary civilizations could not breed in sufficient numbers for their own needs. Thus it was the key linchpin linking steppe and sedentary peoples. Ever since Herodotus commented on the Scythians, historians have realized that "in combat the [nomadic] horse always puts to flight the horse of the enemy."[46] Although, in principle, the nomads could be a self-sufficient society, they rarely chose to live solely off the steppe. They wanted to trade with settled peoples for luxury goods, but they often traded in more common products such as linen, tea, and grain.[47] Likewise, the settled peoples could do without steppe trade only if they were willing to endure constant raiding. The trade of rare products for horses seemed advantageous to both sides. Sechin Jagchid argues that peace was always possible with the nomads when the Chinese satisfied their needs for trade, but the Chinese often "failed to discover that poverty and famine caused the nomads to invade China to supply their needs by force."[48] But several factors made the negotiation of trade precarious. Repeatedly the Chinese dynasties set up markets for trading tea for horses, but all were problematic.[49] First, not only in China but also in Europe and the Byzantine empire, critics found it humiliating to pay extortionate prices to the barbarian raiders.[50] Second, on the nomadic side, stable trade relations required a leader who could negotiate and enforce agreements to prevent border raids while ensuring a reasonable supply of horses.[51]

The Chinese learned very early the critical importance of the supply of horses to military success. The first clear account of the use of mounted men in China appears in the story of Zhao Wuling's adoption of nomadic cavalry warfare in 320 BCE.[52] Efforts to obtain horses by other means than trade with the nearest enemy account for the first major Chinese expedition into Central Eurasia. Han Wudi in 104 BCE sent an army of thirty thousand men to Ferghana to capture the famous "blood-sweating horses" of the Ferghana valley. This first expedition failed, returning with only 10 to 20 percent of its men. The second expedition, with sixty thousand men, succeeded in getting the horses, but again the cost in men and resources was high. Only ten thousand men returned home.[53]

Later dynasties tried to breed horses within the empire but succeeded only briefly. The Tang were able to build a supply of up to 700,000 horses through an extensive breeding program but still had to rely on extensive imports from Samarkand. They traded large amounts of silk with the Turks to obtain them.[54] The rebel military governor An Lushan had much greater success than the Tang central government in supplying his forces, because he could pick the best cavalry horses available on the northwest frontier. After An Lushan's rebellion in 755 blocked Tang access to the northwest, the rising price of horses drove the government deep into debt. The financial crisis created by the closing of the Silk Road brought attacks on Buddhism in the ninth century, including the melting of statues for coin. Thereafter the Chinese always depended heavily on Mongolia for their horse supply. The Song and Ming mainly used the officially supervised tea-for-horse trading markets, even though these produced poor-quality animals at exorbitant prices. Chapter 3 describes the difficulties with frontier trade in the Song and Ming. This experience informed the very different approach of the Qing.

The Manchus were well aware of their predecessors' dilemmas. They took special care to develop close relations with the Eastern Mongols because of their desperate need for reliable horse supplies for the northwestern campaigns. Inducements of trade, titles of nobility, and grain for famine relief all served to bring over cooperative Mongol Khans to the Qing side. In return, they owed levies of horses, men, and supplies when demanded by the Qing. The 1757 rebellion of the Eastern Mongols is the clearest demonstration of the heavy burden placed by the Manchus on their Mongol subordinates and of the critical importance of allied Mongols in the campaign.

We know much less about the role of the other four essential domesticated animals in nomadic society: sheep, goats, camels, and cattle. None of them had the prestige of the horse, because none of them were suited for warfare, but they were economically much more fundamental. Owen Lattimore in the 1940s found that pastoralists in Xinjiang owned 11.7 million sheep and goats, 1.55 million cattle, 870,000 horses, and 90,000 camels.[55] Sheep and goats were the essential animals for subsistence, and the nomads stripped them of everything they produced. They put a heavy burden on the grasslands: one sheep needs 5 to 10 hectares (twelve to twenty-five acres) of pasture, and consumes a harvest of 45 to 180 pounds of dry matter per acre.[56] Sheep and goats monopolized their pastures because they grazed the grass too close to leave anything for horses. Horses had to graze separately.[57]

Even if horse-riding warriors looked more dashing, any ruler aiming to increase his influence had to pay attention to his sheep. Batur Hongtaiji, the founder of the Zunghar state, became known as the "sheep-raising king" because of his efforts to build up his herds.[58] Since the Qing armies and settlers also needed sheep, the Zunghars were able to sell them profitably at regulated markets.[59] Sheep were the basic source of meat for frontier settlers and nomads alike. The severe overgrazing which has now damaged many of Inner Mongolia's grasslands has long historical roots. The size of herds began to increase when the Zunghar state and the Qing armies fought each other in the eighteenth century.[60]

The two-humped Bactrian camel, the chief transport animal of the desert

Goats in a village in Gansu province. Photo taken by Frederick Wulsin, 1923.

caravans, also served the military and diplomatic missions. The huge caravans crossing the Gobi desert were essential to the tea trade with Russia.
Camels brought coal to Beijing from the northwest.[61] The emperors' military campaigns depended heavily on camels to bring supplies to distant
outposts. Camels were, however, cantankerous animals, difficult to control
and difficult to breed. Qing armies had to employ specialized personnel to
rear young animals and to drive them across the desert. The Qing con-

quests, a multicultural venture, depended on Turkic camel drivers as much as Mongol horsemen and Chinese infantry. Camels could even carry artillery between their humps and, when they sat down, provide a platform for firing the guns. This use of camels in warfare, depicted clearly in eighteenth-century engravings of Qianlong's expeditions, persisted through the nineteenth century in Persia, Bukhara, and Turkestan.[62]

Travel across this great land mass was arduous, dangerous, and slow. In the 1920s, Lattimore obtained detailed figures on rates of travel from Guihua (modern Hohhot) to Guchengzi, just southeast of Ürümchi, via the Great Road. To travel this distance of 1,800 miles took 120 days for heavy caravans, 90 days for express freight, and 70 days for travelers going by forced march, a rate of 15 to 25 miles per day. Kangxi's army in 1690 crossed the Gobi at a rate of fifteen miles per day. On the difficult desert road from Guihua to Morhgujing, north of Baotou, it took 100 days to cover 285 miles.[63] We might take these as the maximum and minimum rates of travel across the Chinese steppes and deserts. Camels, the main beasts of burden in desert territory, could travel only two to two and one-half miles per hour. It was possible to travel rapidly on the Yellow River, as the Kangxi emperor did on his return from one of his military campaigns. The unique *pifazi,* or rafts supported with inflated hides, could transport up to twenty-five tons of goods from Lanzhou to the upper bend in the river, but this river passed only through the Ordos region. The other steppes and deserts had little river transport.[64]

Animals, of course, had to carry most of their fodder with them when crossing deserts. This in turn limited the quantity of goods they could carry and raised the cost of equipping a caravan. Nevertheless, the caravan trade routes, some of the oldest long-distance trade routes in the world, endured for millennia. Caravan traders could profit only from the exchange of lightweight and valuable commodities, carried peripherally to the main bulk of the caravan's animal and human supplies. Chinese silk, of course, was the preeminent commodity in value of the Old Silk Road, but China also exported porcelain, metalware, and jade. Caravan trade was tightly confined by the ecological parameters set by the desert, steppe, and oasis environment. Three institutions were critical to it: garrisons and watchtowers manned by soldiers to keep the peace; postal relay stations, originally established by the Mongol empire, for rapid communications; and caravanserai, to provide lodgings and trading places in the oases. Traders formed a small group of sixty to one hundred men with a minimal number of animals and a small load of highly valuable goods. They could not afford to travel with large defense forces. This made them perfect targets for bandits and nomadic raiders. Only in times of relative peace could the trading cara-

Raft on the Yellow River. Wulsin, like the Kangxi emperor and many others, used this traditional form of raft to travel down the river.

vans move unhindered. Trade waxed and waned, depending heavily on the ability of settled and nomadic rulers to establish minimal order. This trade, more than any other, was extremely vulnerable to changes in the surrounding political environment. Many scholars have argued that the caravan trade declined in the sixteenth century because of new competition from European overseas trade, but this inverts the relative importance of politics and economics. It was rising political and military instability in Eurasia during the sixteenth and seventeenth centuries, not European competition, that killed the long-distance trade. In fact, the trade did not disappear but moved north to a new secure channel, carrying furs and silk directly between Russia and China. Commerce was much more dependent on political power than vice versa.[65]

One of the most important transport routes led from Gansu province to the northwest, through a narrow corridor between deserts, to the oases of

Turkestan.[66] This "Imperial Highroad," as Lattimore called it, was much more stable than a caravan route. All Chinese dynasties which could control the region maintained this road, but its final form was a product of Qing security needs, a major highway built to provide supplies for the garrisons conducting campaigns on the frontier. Wheeled vehicles could travel part of the way faster than camels and donkeys; military quartermasters brought large numbers of carts here from interior China. Transport costs still remained extremely high: shipping grain from Hexi, the agricultural regions in Gansu west of the Yellow River, to Hami, the nearest oasis, raised its price by a factor of ten.[67] Road construction helped to reduce transport costs, but efforts to increase agricultural production in the oases themselves worked better. The difficulty and cost of land transport thus stimulated efforts to develop the local agrarian economy.

Military expeditions by settled regimes into the steppe could defend themselves easily against nomadic raiding, but at heavy cost. Their structure was the inverse of the merchant caravans. They proceeded more slowly, but with large numbers of men and animals, including replacement transport. Often they brought sheep and cattle with them for meat supplies. They valued neither profit nor speed but the presence of numbers. Usually they followed the existing trade routes, but sometimes they had to leave the main roads in pursuit of nomad enemies, leading them into difficult desert crossings. Military supply demands overwhelmed the modest merchant caravanserai, so they had to pitch separate camps. From the Han dynasty up to the mid-Qing, no Chinese army could last more than ninety to one hundred days in the steppe. This logistical barrier established a fundamental limit on the ability of Chinese expeditions to penetrate Central Eurasia. Until the Qing, almost none of these aggressive campaigns succeeded. As we shall see, nomad military strategy took advantage of the logistical limitations of Chinese steppe incursions.

Pilgrims, ambassadors, spies, diplomatic envoys, and marriage partners (generally Chinese women sent as spouses to win over nomad rulers) also traveled these arduous routes. Even though they were not the dominant political or economic actors, many of them left valuable accounts about Central Eurasia. Chinese emperors are another special kind of steppe traveler. The best known are the Yongle emperor (r. 1402–1424), who conducted five campaigns in Mongolia; the hapless Zhengtong emperor, captured by Mongols in 1449 near Datong after the failure of his military expedition; and the much more successful Kangxi emperor. Kangxi's letters to his son while he was on campaign deserve to be included among the most striking and vivid travel narratives in Chinese literature.

The Frontier Zone

Fernand Braudel writes: "The question of boundaries is the first to be encountered; from it all others flow. To draw a boundary around anything is to define, analyse, and reconstruct it, in this case select, indeed adopt, a philosophy of history." To which David A. Hollinger would add: "But not all exclusions are bad, the conventional wisdom of our time will be quick to remind us, and we are all left with the responsibility for deciding where to try to draw circles, with whom, and around what."[68]

The borderlands between the core of China and the farthest nomadic pastures were a zone of frontier interaction, a "middle ground" where peoples following radically different ways of life adapted to one another and to the environment.[69] Because the steppe was filled with people constantly on the move, all those moving through it had to adopt to some extent the customs of the nomads, those best suited to life in the steppe. Chinese armies ate more meat than they would at home and got used to traveling with herds of animals. They had to leave their forts and stay in tent encampments. They used horses and cavalry forces much more than in the interior and had to deal with recalcitrant camels and mules instead of docile oxen pulling carts. Merchants and other professional caravan men likewise changed their ways on the frontier. As Lattimore noted during his trip through Mongolia in 1926–27, 90 percent of the caravan men were Chinese who had cut their links to settled fields, ancestral homelands, and heartland customs. On the caravan routes, they made offerings to gods of fire and water, not ancestral deities; for clothing, food, and drink, they relied on sheep, not pigs and chickens.[70] The trade frontier was a social space in which core ethnic identities had to bend to fit rigorous geographical conditions. Mongols on the caravan routes had to put up with more restricted mobility than they could gain in the broad pasturelands; Chinese became accustomed to a life of much greater wandering than their settled peasant confrères in the interior.

The frontier zone was a liminal space where cultural identities merged and shifted, as peoples of different ethnic and linguistic roots interacted for common economic purposes. Most Han Chinese officials found this environment hostile, abhorrent, and alien. Their Manchu and Mongol colleagues did not find it so strange. The idea of Chinese turning native, abandoning the essential elements of civilization and preferring a mobile life, shocked established powers but attracted others. The story of the eighteenth-century Qing empire is of an effort to seal off this ambiguous, threatening frontier experience once and for all by incorporating it within the fixed boundaries of a distinctly defined space, and by drawing lines that clearly demarcated separate cultures.

North Americans and Europeans had similar experiences. The peoples on either side of an ambiguous border often have more in common with each other than with the heartland of the nations they belong to. Frontier peoples have ambiguous loyalties; they share a resentment of the economic and political advantage of the centers that rule them.[71] Frederick Jackson Turner saw frontier settlement as the penetration of empty space by Anglo-Saxon settlers, a process that reaffirmed the quintessential Americanness of the pioneers. By contrast, new historians of the American frontier emphasize the special regional characteristics of the West, the persistence of the indigenous inhabitants in the face of the Anglo-American invasion, and the formation of new hybrid identities with ambiguous loyalties to the metropolitan centers of the East. In both China and the New World, powerful empires based in eastern metropolises incorporated large, sparsely populated arid western zones. Although the conquerors pretended that the newly conquered regions were empty of civilized peoples, contact transformed both the metropole and the frontier.

The most conspicuous display of demarcation in China's frontier zone, of course, is the "Great Wall," or more accurately translating the Chinese word *changcheng*, the "Long Walls" that many Chinese dynasties built on the northwestern frontier. Arthur Waldron has shown that, contrary to Western and Chinese myth, the "Great Wall" is not thousands of years old. Not until the sixteenth century did the Ming dynasty construct a single, nearly continuous defensive barrier.[72] Yet for many centuries the goal of cutting off the steppe from the settled zone inspired Chinese frontier policy. In Lattimore's interpretation, the Great Wall was built not to keep the nomads out but to keep the Chinese in. It "was an attempt to establish a permanent cultural demarcation between the lands of the nomad tribes and the lands held by settled people."[73] No other settled empire on the periphery of the steppe ever tried to create such a sharp demarcation between the steppe and the sown, although there is a partial Russian analogue in the seventeenth century.[74] For most of Chinese history these efforts, in fact, failed militarily. Since Chinese efforts to demarcate the frontier never succeeded, the zone was never stabilized. It always contained transitional social groups—sinicized nomads, semi-barbarized Chinese, Tibetans, Muslims, and other non-Han peoples—mixtures of merchants, nomads, oasis settlers, and peasants. In Lattimore's words, "China could never put an end to the ebb and flow of frontier history and maintain the civilization of China in the closed world that was its ideal."[75]

Only after the mid-Qing, when the wall became militarily irrelevant, did it acquire effective symbolic value as a cultural marker among both Chinese and Westerners.[76] The history of China's Long Walls highlights the interaction between cultural definition and geography on the frontier. The Qing conquest likewise relied on both symbolic and ecological manipulation to define its achievements. As Qing officials cleared land, settled peasants, and drew maps, they moved both real sand and lines in the sand.

Even the Qing conquests did not settle things for long. Stabilization of the frontier zone has never proved permanent. The Sino-Russian treaty negotiations of 1689 seemed to demarcate a clear boundary across the Eurasian continent. But in the mid-nineteenth and early twentieth centuries, when China's defenses weakened, the Russians transgressed the border line in the Ili crisis and built the Far Eastern Railway through Manchuria. Concurrently, the British pushed their interests in Tibet, motivated by fear of Russian expansion. Strategic analysts dubbed this geopolitical competition the "Great Game." By the early twentieth century, however, the exaggerated British fears that Russia intended to threaten India seem to have subsided, and the frontier stabilized again. Treaties included the Anglo-Russian settlement of the Pamir boundary in 1895, the Anglo-Russian convention of 1907, by which both parties agreed not to penetrate Tibet, and Russian agreements with China over Outer Mongolia in 1911, in which, like the British in Tibet, the Russians agreed to representation in Mongolia but not occupation.[77]

The "second thirty years'" war of the twentieth century, however, from 1914 to 1945, destroyed this and all other colonial agreements. When the dust settled, Central Eurasia still was divided in two, now by the cold war. Although for a short time Eurasia seemed to fall under a monolithic communist bloc, by the 1960s the Sino-Soviet split established a line across the continent not too different from the border of 1689, except that Outer Mongolia, part of the Ili valley, and northern Manchuria now belonged to the Soviet Russian sphere. This division, in turn, lasted only thirty years. With the collapse of the Soviet Union, five independent states in addition to Russia and Mongolia now occupy Central Eurasia. Although the borders of China with Russia and Central Asia have not changed, unrest in Tibet and Xinjiang calls into question any assumptions about permanence and stability. Instability, indefiniteness, and physiographical unboundedness still challenge the unceasing efforts of nation-states to draw lines and settle their peoples in immobile, fixed territorial and psychological sites.

Fixing people in place territorially requires material and organizational resources: armies, border guards, passports, visas. Fixing people psychologically requires intellectual and cultural resources: nationalist symbols, rewritten history. Both strategies contest natural human urges to move, to change, and to evolve, but they are supported by equally natural human urges for security, fixity, and stability. Excessive stabilization can bring repression and stagnation, but excessive fluidity means chaos and anarchy. All states, including the Qing and modern China, struggle to find the appropriate balance between stability and freedom.

Isolation and Integration

David Christian has outlined how these distinct ecological zones and their frontiers shaped the states and societies of Russian Eurasia. The two geographic features of Central Eurasia that define it as a distinct unit in world history are its low natural productivity and its "interiority," or distance from oceans. Northern latitude and continental climate patterns meant cold weather, low rainfall, and poor agricultural productivity. Five distinct ecological adaptations in succession responded to these ecological and geographic characteristics: hunting, pastoralism, pastoral nomadism, agrarian autocracy, and command economy. Each was designed to achieve the maximum possible concentration of resources from a region where these agricultural and human resources were few and highly dispersed. Each form, in turn, marked off Central Eurasia as very distinct from the richer settled societies around it, and these societies often regarded the natives of Central Eurasia as utterly alien. Each of the civilized societies had its alien other in Central Eurasia, and each evolved as a reflection of the other.[78]

Systematic, specialized hunting, beginning with the mammoth hunters of the Upper Paleolithic, divided early humans from the specialization in gathering on the periphery. The rise of agriculture in the Neolithic period had its contrasting counterpart in the rise of pastoralism from 6000 BCE. Pastoralism based on grazing herds allowed population growth and required military mobilization to defend the herds. The warrior chieftains of the *kurgan* (burial mound) cultures from the fourth to the third millennium BCE developed into full-fledged nomadic warrior societies by the second millennium BCE. As the nomads mastered the horse, settled societies, unable to pasture horses, had to trade with nomads to obtain horses from the steppes. Even the first agrarian empires of Mesopotamia and Egypt had to contend with constant raids from 2600 BCE.[79] After 1000 BCE, nomadic military superiority, based on rapid mobility and universal use of the horse, dominated the steppes until 1500 CE.

Agrarian autocracy was a product of the forest at the western periphery of the steppe. The rise of Muscovy from a conquered subject of the Mongol empire to a powerful independent state by the seventeenth century rested on its ability to exploit brutally but effectively the extensive low-productivity agricultural regime of the forest and steppe. The steppe environment, and the constant interaction of Russians with nomadic states to their east, accounts for many of the military and cultural similarities between Russians and the nomads they fought. They learned much from their enemies, as we shall see. When nomadic warriors conquered China, they brought Central Eurasian institutions with them, mixing with those of the settled core. By contrast, when Han Chinese from the core ruled China, especially under the Ming dynasty, they showed very little respect for or willingness to learn the lessons of the steppe nomads, even when these lessons could have brought them military success. This accounts for the general impression of a gradual shading off of Russian into nomad, as opposed to the sharp delineation of Han from non-Han that is characteristic of China. As Lord Curzon put it, in typically British terms, "The Russian fraternizes in the true sense of the word. He is guiltless of that air of conscious superiority and gloomy hauteur, which does more to inflame animosity than cruelty may have done to kindle it, and he does not shrink from entering into social and domestic relations with alien and inferior races."[80]

As mentioned earlier, the modernization paradigm regards Central Eurasia as an especially isolated region, cut off from the major trends of the modern world by physical and cultural barriers. By contrast, in the "classical" early modern perspective it is seen as the "crossroads" of Eurasia, linked to all the sedentary societies around it through long-standing networks of trade, conquest, and religious and cultural exchange. We will face this dual paradox repeatedly. Settled civilizations on the periphery regarded Central Eurasia as remote, peculiar, hostile, and threatening; within the region, Central Asians came in contact with outsiders from the entire Eurasian continent: travelers, pilgrims, missionaries of different religions, conquerors, traders, and explorers. The same ambivalence characterizes descriptions of Central Eurasian ecology: we can view it as an extremely isolated region, or one of the most integrated with the rest of the continent, depending on our perspective.

The impact of smallpox in Central Eurasia illustrates its paradoxical ecological position. According to John R. McNeill, the isolated biota of the Pacific Islands were unusually labile: that is, subject to sudden and unpredictable change when they came into contact with outside forces. Pacific Island biota had developed few defenses against the common predators of the Eurasian and North American continents; hence the newly arrived rats, deer, snakes, cows, pigs, and sheep devastated the existing populations of birds and plants. Dramatic changes occurred with the first arrival of humans in the islands; even more dramatic change followed the era of Cap-

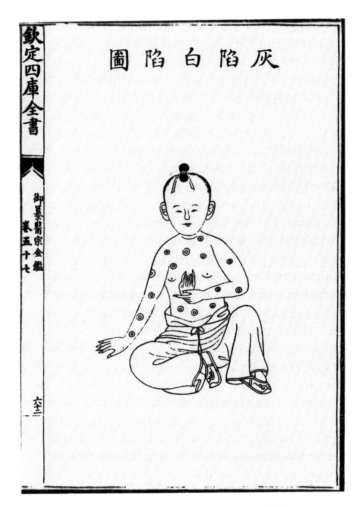

Smallpox victim, one of numerous illustrations of the disease in
a Qing imperial medical encyclopedia.

tain Cook after his Pacific voyage of 1769. In many places, like New Zealand, European portmanteau biota nearly completely overwhelmed native
plants and animals and people; on other islands, native peoples and plants
recovered, but in constant competition with the aggressive European,
American, and Asian invaders.[81]

By contrast, no ocean barriers cut off Central Eurasia from the outside
world. Humans, animals, and other hitchhiking biota have for millennia
crisscrossed its land routes. Still, the common analogy of the grasslands to a
great internal sea does hold up in the ecological sense to some degree.
Deserts and high mountains block passage of many organisms, and ex-

treme heat and cold kill off temperate zone organisms. Most notably, Central Asians remained nearly isolated from the European and Asian disease pools until the eighteenth century. Then smallpox, among other diseases, decimated the Mongolian population when it came into contact with Chinese settlers, just as Native American and Oceanic populations died off after the European conquests of the New World.

Mongols knew in the mid-fifteenth century that they could catch smallpox from the Chinese, and the Chinese in turn warned them not to settle too close to the border to avoid spreading it. The Ming dynasty held only sporadic horse fairs where Mongols and Chinese mingled; then Chinese bans on frontier trade in retaliation for nomadic raids had as a by-product the effect of protecting the Mongols from infection.[82] Chinese migrants who went beyond the Great Wall, however, could also spread the disease, and there were more than 100,000 of them in southern Mongolia by 1590. Still, few Mongols caught the disease under the Ming.

The Manchus, before the founding of the Qing, also rarely encountered smallpox, but they knew of its danger. Mongols and Manchus who had not been exposed to the disease were exempted from coming to Beijing to receive titles of succession. The main response of the Mongols and Manchus to those who did fall ill was quarantine. Li Xinheng commented that if anyone in a tribe caught smallpox, his relatives abandoned him in a cave or distant grassland.[83] Seventy to 80 percent of those infected died. The German traveler Peter Simon Pallas, who visited the Mongols three times from 1768 to 1772, commented that smallpox was the only disease they greatly feared. It occurred very seldom, but spread rapidly when it struck: "If someone catches it, they abandon him in his tent; they only approach from the windward side to provide food. Children who catch it are sold to the Russians very cheaply."[84] The Mongols whom Pallas visited lived far from the Chinese border, but they knew well that smallpox was highly contagious and nearly fatal.

The Chinese discovery of variolation—a method of inoculation—was of great aid in reducing the severity of attacks. The Kangxi emperor himself was selected as heir in part because he had survived the disease in childhood; his father had died of it. In 1687 he inaugurated regular inoculation of the royal family, and his successor extended mandatory inoculation to all Manchu children.[85] The Manchus adopted this Chinese medical practice in order to protect themselves against the virulent strains that were absent from the steppe. Only Manchus who had survived the disease were allowed to be sent to the Mongolian steppe. Mongols close to the Manchu and Chinese border gradually grew immune, but those farther away suffered great losses in the nineteenth century when Chinese penetration increased.

Disease determined critical turning points in the conflict between the Manchus and Zunghars. Ligdan Khan, the first major Mongol rival to Manchu rule, died of smallpox.[86] In 1745, when the Zunghar Khan Galdan Tseren died, outbreaks of smallpox caused upheaval among the Zunghars; one report stated that 30 percent of them died.[87] Another epidemic struck Zungharia in the 1750s, just as the Qianlong emperor launched his final campaign. The last rebel against Manchu domination, the young prince Amursana, died of smallpox at the age of thirty-five, opening the way to the complete conquest of Xinjiang. Wei Yuan estimated, after the Zunghars had vanished as a people, that 40 percent of them died of smallpox—more than lost their lives in battle or fled to Russia.

The Mongols for their part tried to avoid contact with Han Chinese as much as possible. Apparently they never learned the variolation techniques, so their only recourse was isolation. When negotiating licensed trade with the Qing in the 1740s, Galdan Tseren feared that his envoys would catch the disease when they passed through Chinese territory, so he asked for permission to avoid the northwestern towns of Hami and Suzhou and instead go direct to Dongkeer. Tibetans also tried to avoid traveling in the Chinese interior: the Panchen Lama used his lack of immunity to smallpox as an excuse to avoid an audience with the Kangxi emperor in Beijing. The Manchus themselves often tried to accommodate the Mongols in order to spare their lives. The Kangxi emperor noted that many surrendered Mongols living in the capital were dying of diseases. He pitied them because "the capital's food and drink are against their nature," and they were "like caged birds and animals," so he provided them with tents and settled them beyond the wall in Zhangjiakou and Guihua. When Mongol children flocked to Kangxi's military camp in the Ordos while he was on campaign, he called in a special doctor to inoculate them.[88]

So in respect to certain disease vectors, the pathogens of Eurasian settled regimes hit Central Eurasia with devastating impact by the eighteenth century. The vulnerability of the Mongols to smallpox is eloquent testimony to their isolation from the germ pools of dense populations. At the same time, their constant contacts with the Manchus and Chinese made them aware of the danger, even though they could not prevent its incidence. The Manchus, by contrast, could take active measures against the disease, having closer regular contact with the Chinese, greater medical knowledge, and greater acquired immunity. They in turn used this knowledge to inoculate Mongols who surrendered to them, leaving those who resisted them to face the ravages of the disease. The disease environment itself significantly affected the outcome of the conflict, but the disease vectors acted through human agency.

Another conspicuous ecological impact was the invasion of the grasslands by the agricultural regimes of Chinese and Russian settlers. Here ecological integration brought more ambiguous results, in one sense following the inverse cycle to that of disease, in another sense similar to it. From the smallpox bacterium's point of view, the eighteenth century brought successful colonization of new human and animal territory, followed by eventual adaptation and acquisition of immunity by the hosts and a slowing down of new colonization—a typical logistic curve. From the human point of view, severe population decline from the new diseases was followed by slow recovery after several centuries. Similarly, the new crops introduced by agricultural settlers, especially wheat and millet, had great initial success, pushing back the grassland frontiers and greatly expanding the cultivated area. This benefited peasant cultivators, whose population grew, at the cost of pastoral nomads and their grassland-dependent animals. But by the twentieth century, at the end of the logistic curve, excess cultivation in arid regions without sufficient irrigation brought the desert back. The remaining grasslands are still under severe stress, but agriculture is not prospering either.[89]

The difference between the spread of disease vectors and the spread of agriculture is that agriculture always required heavy subsidies from outside to succeed. In such a hostile host environment, only greater investments in water supplies, seed, animals, and tools from the state could make it work. A glance at Central Eurasian agriculture evokes strong analogies to the settlement of the American West, where the arid region west of 100 degrees longitude could never support settlement without heavy subsidies from the government back east.[90]

Thus we can view Central Eurasia in the same light as other formerly remote, forbidding frontiers invaded by aggressive European biosystems. The main incursion began in the eighteenth century, but the actors were primarily Chinese, and secondarily Russian. Analyses that focus only on western European and American examples of cultural, ecological, and political imperialism need to pay more attention to the other expanding empires which concurrently marched their agrarian frontiers across the eighteenth-century world.

In short, David Christian's analysis of Russia fits the Manchus too. The parallels are striking. In the late sixteenth century two forest peoples—the Russians and the Manchus—began to build strong states and to expand until they divided the northern steppe. In both cases, organization and political structure had to make up for demographic inferiority. The lands of western Europe and south of Manchuria were far more favorable to dense agrarian settlement than were the heartlands of Muscovy and the Manchus. Yet both states expanded. Kinship networks bound together the ruling elites; serfdom, or bond servitude, tied the agrarian producers to the militarized state. "Autocracy, then, was a response to the difficulties of creating a powerful agrarian state in Central Eurasia."[91] Both empires had greater resources than the nomadic peoples of the interior, but both were on the periphery of the settled agrarian civilizations to their west and south. Both extracted resources from agrarian producers and used them to dominate both the steppe and the agricultural zones. Both used military aristocracies effectively to concentrate the limited resources of the agrarian periphery. The "Manchurian solution," in Barfield's terms, had been tried twice before by the Khitans and Liao in East Asia, with only partial success.[92] Manchus and Russians found parallel solutions to the problem of mobilizing the resources of the northern forests and fields to dominate the Eurasian continent.

2

The Ming, Muscovy, and Siberia, 1400–1600

EACH of the central players in our drama—the Manchu Qing empire, the Zunghar Mongolian state, and the Muscovite–Russian empire—had long experience with the steppe. Although they did not directly confront one another until the seventeenth century, the previous century set the stage and provided the ideological, material, and political resources with which they conducted their geopolitical game. This chapter briefly summarizes the story that led up to the seventeenth-century conflict and highlights some of the major issues confronting these Central Eurasian regimes in their efforts to dominate the steppe.

All narratives are selective. I begin with a brief discussion of the Ming dynasty background to the clash over the steppe, focusing on themes relevant to later analysis: the logistics of military supply, especially the interrelationship between frontier trade and horse purchases; the strategic decisions for attack and defense; and the consequences of these decisions for the structure of the state and for relations between the Han and Mongols.

The Ming rulers inherited problems with frontier defense faced by earlier Han-ruled dynasties. They practiced two different strategies, neither of which succeeded for long, and neither of which was imitated by the Qing. For the first half of the fifteenth century, they led aggressive campaigns against the Mongols, as far as the Orkhon, Onon, and Kerulen rivers. The military campaigns ended with the embarrassing capture of the Zhengtong emperor by Esen Khan in the Tumu incident of 1449. Parallel to the military campaigns, the Ming rulers launched logistical efforts to obtain adequate supplies of horses for the frontier garrisons. They promoted govern-ment-supervised trade in the form of horse and tea markets. As in the Song programs of Wang Anshi, their goal was to exchange products of the Chinese interior for the one necessary product the Han Chinese could not produce internally: militarily capable horses. This new institution also collapsed by 1449, undermined by both military failure and the internal pressures, ecological and commercial, on the tea-producing regions.

The early Ming experience highlights the same problems and advantages that would be faced by the Qing during their expansive period. Negative factors for Chinese rulers included the limitations of supply in the steppe, the unreliability of Mongol allies, and the constant instability of steppe politics. In the favor of the Chinese was the poverty of the steppe and the Mongols' dependence on Chinese goods, the rising importance of trade relations for the Mongol chieftains, as well as their interest in gaining Chinese legitimation of titles, useful in the constant succession struggles. Divisions among the Mongols helped the Ming rulers most. As the split between Eastern and Western Mongols (Oirats) became the fundamental dividing line in the steppe during the fifteenth century, China's ability to ward off attacks on the frontier depended on careful manipulation of the fears of each group of Mongols about the other.

The Ming and the Mongols

Our story begins around the year 1400 CE, shortly after the collapse of the Great Mongol empire founded by Chinggis Khan. Peasant rebellions in China against Mongol rule brought down the Yuan dynasty when the Mongol invaders fled without putting up a fight. Zhu Yuanzhang, peasant leader and former Buddhist monk, captured Beijing in 1368, but he established his main capital at Nanjing, close to his hometown of Fengyang in Anhui.[1]

The early fifteenth century was a critical turning point in the history of both China and Central Asia. In 1399 Prince Di of Yan rebelled against his nephew, the reigning Jianwen emperor. His successful military coup brought him to power as the Yongle emperor (r. 1403–1424) and initiated the series of aggressive military campaigns, led personally by the emperor, against the Mongols. In 1405 the death of Timur just before launching an invasion with 200,000 men spared China the devastation he inflicted on the Middle East. China no longer faced a major threat from a consolidated empire led by a conqueror with the ambition of Chinggis Khan.[2] Henceforth,

China's Mongol rivals for power over the steppe divided into eastern and western groups bitterly at odds with each other.

The first reference to the western Mongolian tribe known as Oirats (Oyirad) occurs in Rashid ad-Din's description of the rise of Chinggis Khan. In 1201, under their chief Khudukha-beki, they joined in a military alliance with their neighbors, the Naiman and Merkid, to fight a losing battle with Chinggis. The Oirats were called the "forest people" (perhaps from Mongolian *oi*, "forest"), living in the upper reaches of the Yenisei River near Lake Baikal.[3] Their main occupation was hunting and fishing, not pastoral nomadism. To their north and south lived the Turkic Kirghiz and Naiman. To their east and west were the Mongolian Merkid and Tumad. They formed a distinctive group speaking a different dialect from neighboring Mongol peoples. Among them the political power of shamans was especially high: the term *beki* (shaman) indicates that their ruler, Khudukha-beki, was one of the leading priests.[4] In the great battle of 1201, Khudukha-beki tried to use his shamanic powers to stir up a storm against Temujin, but he failed:

> The Oyirad Khudukha Beki [and three others] . . . these four men [led] Jamugha's forces to battle . . . Just as the two armies began to charge one another . . . Buyirugh Khan and Khudukha, who were great shamans, began to conjure a storm of darkness. They began to raise winds and darkness in order to blind us, when suddenly the storm turned. Instead of striking our army their storm blinded their own men. Their soldiers fell into ravines on the mountainside unable to see, crying: "Heaven's turned against us!" and their army dispersed . . . Khudukha Beki ran back to the forests as far as the Shisgis.[5]

Khudukha fled back to his forests but soon after surrendered to Temujin with his four thousand households of followers. In 1217 he aided Chinggis Khan's son Jochi in an expedition to subdue the other forest peoples of the region. In return Khudukha was allowed to marry the women of his tribe to Chinggis's descendants.[6] When Chinggis created his organizational system of thousands and myriads *(tümen)* designed to undercut tribal ties, he offered the Oirats along with the Ongguts the exceptional privilege of maintaining their tribal affiliations within the *tümen* units.[7]

After Chinggis's death, the Oirats occupied an important strategic position at the juncture of the four giant appanages *(ulus)* belonging to his sons: Tolui to the southeast, Ögödei to the southwest, Chagatai to the west, and Jochi to the northwest. This four-way division of Chinggis's conquests became the basis for the four great successor Khanships of Eurasia: the Yuan, Il Khan, Kipchak, and Chaghatai Khanates. The Oirats supported the 1260–1264 rebellion of Arika Buga against Khubilai, and their "Waila" army helped in the attacks.[8] After their defeat by Khubilai, the Oirats disappeared from the historical records for over a century, but they reappeared in 1388 as opponents of the last Yuan emperor, Toghon Temur, the direct descendant of Khubilai.[9] The year 1399, when an Oirat commander killed the successor to the Mongol Khan, marks the decline in independence of the Eastern Mongol Khans and the rise of Oirat hegemony over the Mongolian steppe.

Zhu Yuanzhang had ordered, but not led personally, nine campaigns against the remnants of the Mongol empire in China, and his fourth son, Prince Di of Yan, the future Yongle emperor, had participated in two of them.[10] He was an experienced military commander, very familiar with steppe conditions, and determined to eliminate Mongol power from the northwest. He also knew well how to manipulate divisions among the Mongols to China's advantage. During the military campaigns within China against the Jianwen emperor and his supporters, he made sure to keep on friendly terms with the Mongols, avoiding a two-front war. He gave several chieftains high ranks, and when Mongols in the Northeast, suffering from famine, requested permission to barter horses for grain in 1407, he opened the first of the horse markets on the frontier that would later become an important trading link between Chinese and Mongols.

The Mongols had suffered continual anarchy for two decades, but in 1408, the Eastern Mongol chieftain Arughtai killed the Khan and recalled Bunyasiri, a direct descendant of Chinggis, from Beshbalik to become a new Khan of the Eastern Mongols. Arughtai, the real power, never claimed the Khanship for himself, but worked behind the scenes as the Khan's assistant. Although Yongle at first tried to conciliate the new leaders, he broke with the Mongols when the Khan killed his emissary in 1409. Yongle then turned to the Oirats to offset the rising Eastern Mongol power. He granted Chinese titles to the three Oirat chieftains, of whom the most important was Mahmud. Mahmud cooperated by launching an attack against Bunyasiri while at the same time Yongle sent out 100,000 men under his best general, Qiu Fu, against him. Qiu Fu, unwisely advancing too far, found himself surrounded by a Mongol army near the Kerulen River. Qiu Fu was killed and the Chinese army destroyed. Vowing revenge, Yongle personally planned a major campaign against Bunyasiri, the year after he definitely decided to move the capital of China north to Beijing.

In this first great campaign he assembled at least 100,000 men (the *Mingshi* figure of 500,000 must be exaggerated) and 30,000 carts for transport, leaving Beijing on March 15, 1410. The army went from Xinghe, 50 kilometers northwest of Kalgan, north to Mingluanshu, where the emperor held a great military parade to impress the Oirat envoys, thus ensuring their neutrality. Although Bunyasiri wanted to flee, Arughtai disagreed, so the two leaders separated, each acting in effect as head of a separate tribe, fatally weakening their strength. Yongle first attacked Bunyasiri to the east, pursuing him to the Onon River, where he defeated Bunyasiri's troops. Bunyasiri in flight was killed by the Oirat Mahmud. The emperor then turned east against Arughtai, who fled with remnants of his army. Yongle returned in victory to Beijing on September 15 after six months on campaign.

The wily Arughtai then presented tribute and proposed to surrender, if the emperor would make him overlord of all foreign barbarians—much the same proposal that would be presented by the Mongol prince Amursana in the mid-eighteenth century. Yongle, now needing the Eastern Mongols on his side, granted Arughtai the title of Hening Wang and enrolled him as an ally. The new threat came from the rising power of the Oirat Mahmud, who had named Bunyasiri's son Delbek (Ch. Daliba) the new Mongol Khan and besieged Karakorum, the old Yuan capital. In 1413 Mahmud, fearing the new alliance of China and the Eastern Mongols, began his attack on China, sending thirty thousand troops to the Kerulen River. This attack instigated Yongle's second personal campaign. He left Beijing on April 6, 1414, marching to Xinghe, then through the steppe on the same route up to the Kerulen and beyond to battle the Oirats at the upper Tula River. An innovation in this battle was the Chinese use of cannon, which the Mongols could not resist. Although Yongle forced Mahmud to retreat, he could not pursue him. Delbek Khan and Mahmud escaped, and the emperor returned to Beijing on August 15. Arughtai, supposedly the emperor's ally, begged off participating in the campaign because of illness.

Mahmud sought reconciliation after his defeat. Although the emperor was suspicious, relations might have warmed up, but then Arughtai in 1416 attacked and killed Mahmud and Delbek Khan. The emperor enfeoffed Mahmud's son Toghon with his father's title of Shunning Wang and tried to establish peace between the two Mongol groups, but the incessant seesaw of Mongol politics was to a large extent a result of deliberate Chinese policies of divide and rule. Each time one ruler grew stronger, China supported the other, thus preventing the unity of the Mongols while ensuring continual conflict. Still, Yongle had achieved temporary success. No further attacks by the Oirats ensued for six years.

During the last years of Yongle's reign, however, the emperor campaigned three more times against the same players as before. Now the growing power of Arughtai led him to pillage caravans on the way to Beijing, and in 1422 he overrran Xinghe, the outpost fortress north of Kalgan. Yongle now prepared his largest army to date, spurning the advice of important officials, who urged him not to launch another campaign. Just as in the Qing, a classic conflict between a remonstrant official and an autocratic emperor focused on the issue of supplies for a northwest campaign.

These officials were well worth listening to. They included Xia Yuanji, Minister of Revenue for sixteen years, a man who "was noted for his ability to know exactly what funds and grain supplies were held anywhere in the empire"; Wu Zhong, the Minister of Works; and Fang Bin, the Minister of War. They argued that the empire could not afford to supply such a massive campaign. When Fang Bin committed suicide to demonstrate his commitment, the furious emperor imprisoned Xia and Wu and confiscated Xia's estate. Both men survived torture in prison until they were released by the next emperor after Yongle's death in 1424. Xia earned a legendary reputation as an upright, forceful Confucian official, although his main talent was as an efficient if unoriginal administrator (somewhat like Chen Yun in the PRC). Xia, notably, also criticized the extravagance of Zheng He's maritime treasure fleets and was mainly responsible for their abolition.[11]

Supplies for the third expedition included 340,000 donkeys, 117,573 carts, 235,146 men, and 370,000 *shi* of grain. In addition, Shandong, Henan, and Shanxi provided 200,000 donkeys for officers and men, which must have been a tremendous burden on these provinces. On April 12, 1422, the emperor left Beijing and headed for Kulun. When Arughtai fled, the Chinese took booty from his camp in typical steppe fashion. The frustrated Yongle then took out his anger on three Urianghai Mongol tribes not involved in Arughtai's attack, plundering them mercilessly. After this unedifying looting expedition, he returned to Beijing on September 23. The final two campaigns generally repeated this frustrating pattern of futile pursuit of Arughtai, followed by supply shortage and ruthless plunder of any available Mongols along the route. In the final campaign of his life, the emperor was forced to turn back, fearing the approaching winter. He died on the return journey on August 12, 1424.

Yongle was the last aggressive emperor of the Ming. His Qing successors uncannily repeated his experience, with similar campaigns over much greater distances. Each time he faced serious supply shortages; although he won several decisive battles, his enemies escaped to fight again. Mongol allies proved unreliable, just as likely to raid and plunder after submitting tribute as before. By setting Eastern and Western Mongols against each other, Ming rulers warded off the unlikely threat of a unified Mongol alliance. The great campaigns were far more expensive than the intermittent raiding they were supposed to prevent. They seem to reflect a thirst for personal vengeance more than rational calculation of strategic necessity. The route to controlling the Mongols via trade had not yet been discovered. Far-sighted officials who advised against the heavy expense of these campaigns suffered imperial censure. Yongle's aggressive campaigns did not even provide a temporary solution to the problem of frontier defense.

Nevertheless, Yongle left important lessons for his followers in the Qing. He truly loved campaigning in the steppe. In his *Beizhenglu*, an account of his campaign travels similar to Kangxi's letters, he insisted on the bracing effect of personal experience of the grasslands: "Scholars see only what's on paper; this cannot compare with what you see with your own eyes."[12] His failure to capture Arughtai demonstrated that a single army setting out from China could not track down the swift Mongol formations. Kangxi, by contrast, adopted the Mongol tactic of using multiple armies converging on one objective. Most important, Yongle reoriented the empire institutionally toward the north and northwest. From 1407 to 1421 he constructed China's new capital at Beijing, where it has remained ever since.[13] His successors rebuilt the Grand Canal to supply Beijing and focused much of their fiscal and agrarian policy on maintaining the large state presence in North China, far from the most productive agriculture in the south.

For the Mongols, this was an unsettled time. No leader emerged to rival the stature of the Yuan emperors or of Timur. No Mongol really aspired to rule the entire steppe. China was a target for raiding and plunder, but not a genuine goal of conquest. The only Chinese territories seriously attacked were border outposts. Unification of the Mongols required a convincing leader of the Chinggisid line; this is why Arughtai supported Chinggis's descendants while working behind the scenes. But the Khans remained weak and incapable of rallying all the Mongols behind them.

After Yongle's death, the Oirats became the aggressive party. Reunited under their new leader, Toghon, who had killed two rival chieftains, they named Toghto-buqa their Khan, defeated Arughtai in 1431, and killed him in 1434. But the great new leader of the Mongols, who was to lead the Oirats to dominate the greatest portion of the steppe since Timur, was Esen, the son of Toghon. Peace had reigned on the northern frontier under the Xuande emperor (r. 1426–1435), but with the rise of Esen, the new

Zhengtong emperor (r. 1436–1449), enthroned at the age of eight, faced a vigorous rival.[14]

Esen in 1443 took over his father's title of Tayisi, or military assistant to the Grand Khan. He quickly overshadowed Toghto-buqa, the Chinggisid Khan, who was far more inclined toward peaceful relations with China. Esen first focused on the Prince of Hami, who was a Mongol normally loyal to China. Repeated raids and threats by Esen and Chinese lack of support forced him to submit in 1448. Esen then took Gansu, proclaiming his own provincial government there. Mongols fleeing Gansu appealed to the Chinese emperor for aid but received none. Once Esen had secured his rear, he could now prepare for a major attack on China. He plundered the Urianghai Mongols on China's northeastern frontier, forcing their submission. At the same time, he used tributary missions to China to build up his economic resources, expanding the number of envoys to over two thousand in the 1440s, and three thousand in 1448, despite Chinese complaints about the great cost of feeding such huge numbers. The refusal of the Chinese to allow even greater tribute missions and complaints about plundering by Mongol envoys on their way to Beijing served as the pretext for Esen's invasion, but Esen could also raise legitimate complaints about being cheated by Chinese merchants when conducting trade in the capital. Yet despite warnings of Esen's preparations for attack, the Ming court made few preparations. The young emperor was completely dominated by his eunuch tutor, Wang Zhen, a man with no military experience, interested more in his private wealth than in the empire's security. Finally, when Esen moved against Datong, the key strongpoint of the Great Wall in Shanxi, Wang Zhen persuaded the emperor to lead personally a huge army, said to be 500,000 men, against Esen. Hostile sources claim that the only reason Wang Zhen insisted on the emperor's personal leadership was to ensure that the emperor would visit Wang's hometown in Shanxi.

Thus began the process leading up to the "ridiculous" Tumu incident of 1449, when the "foolish, incompetent" Zhengtong emperor succeeded in getting himself captured by Esen.[15] Despite constant warnings by competent officials about the danger of being stranded in the steppe without adequate provisions, the massive army began to run short of supplies almost as soon as it left the walls of Beijing. Eunuch advisers to military officials prevented adequate preparations along the march to Datong. The Mongols fell back as the army approached the city, waiting for the chance for an ambush. Only after reaching Datong did Wang Zhen recognize the danger and decide to turn back. On the return journey, following classic nomadic strategy, Esen first attacked and destroyed the Chinese rear guard. The starving

troops sought shelter at the border outpost of Tumu. Wang refused to advance to the nearby walled city of Huailai, not wanting to leave behind his
personal baggage train. So the emperor and his exhausted troops were surrounded and captured at Tumu, and Wang Zhen and the eunuchs were
killed.

Esen failed to follow up his amazing windfall victory with an immediate
attack on Beijing. Instead he first extorted payments of 20,000 taels from
the garrison commander at Datong and then returned with the emperor to
the steppe. This behavior should make us doubt whether Esen really intended to reconstruct the empire of Chinggis Khan or to conquer China. By
the time he turned back to lay siege to Beijing two months later, Yu Qian,
the very capable finance minister ruling as regent in the emperor's absence,
had placed the emperor's younger brother on the throne and organized a
tough defense. Esen quickly gave up the siege, returned to the steppe, and a
year later sent the emperor back. Negotiations with two envoys sent by the
new Jingtai emperor demonstrate that the new emperor was not particularly eager to have his brother back, since he gave no instructions for the return of the emperor to either mission.[16] The captive emperor, desperate to
return, guaranteed that he would not seek to recover his throne. Esen himself was quite anxious to unload his illustrious captive, now useless to him.
The emperor upon his return was held under close house arrest until his
supporters staged a coup in 1457, killed the reigning emperor, and restored
him to the throne as the Tianshun emperor (r. 1457–1464).

After the emperor's return, Esen briefly reached his height of power, once
again subduing the Eastern Mongols and the Khan Toqtobuqa near Turfan
in 1451. Toqtobuqa was killed in 1452. At its peak, the Oirat empire extended from Urianghai and the Jurchens in the east to Hami in the west. But
his fatal step was to proclaim himself Khan in 1453. Even though the Chinese emperor approved his designation, Mongols still expected leadership
only by legitimate descendants of Chinggis. Revolts by his military commanders forced him to flee, until he was killed in 1455.

Esen's conflict with the Ming can easily be misinterpreted. Frederick
Mote argues that the Mongols, remembering their unification under the
Yuan, had achieved new self-awareness of themselves as a "Mongol nation" under Esen and that Esen effectively appealed to all Mongols to reconstruct the empire of Chinggis Khan.[17] Little evidence supports this interpretation, and much makes it implausible: Mongol chieftains in Hami and
Urianghai submitted to Esen only reluctantly, under threat of force, and reverted to Chinese alliances when possible. Esen could hardly have had un-
equivocal designs on conquering the Chinese empire, since he did not fol-

low up his capture of the emperor with an immediate attack on Beijing. Instead, he engaged in the typical raiding and extortion, and quickly gave back his captive when he found him of no immediate use.

The dialogue between Esen and Yang Shan, the second envoy sent to retrieve the captive emperor, is a very revealing account of a nomadic ruler's attitudes toward China, one of the few examples we have of direct dialogue between a steppe ruler and Chinese representatives. It is, however, reported only through Chinese sources. (Later, we shall examine a similar conversation of a Western Mongol leader with a Russian envoy in the eighteenth century, in which the Russian sources give a different impression.) When Yang Shan accused Esen of "black ingratitude," Esen replied, "Why did you lower the price of horses and why did you often deliver worthless and spoiled silk? In addition, many of my envoys disappeared without a trace and never returned home . . ." Yang Shan blamed Esen for supplying too many horses, thus lowering the price, and blamed "government contractors" *(tongshi)* for supplying "worthless silk." He claimed that many of Esen's three to four thousand envoys were "thieves and brigands" who feared returning home. Threatening Esen with great losses if he conducted further attacks, he offered him great profits if he resumed trade: "If you now return the emperor, and make peace as before, the riches of China will arrive daily, and both countries will be happy."[18] Yang Shan had a weak hand to play, since Ming forces were weak, and the court gave Yang no valuable gifts to present; but in the end, Esen sent back the emperor in return for resumption of trade in silk and horses.

The incompetence of Chinese policy in this period highlights the requirements for success. Arrogance toward "barbarian" nomads, failure to pay attention to military logistics, clumsiness in managing diplomatic alliances with Mongols, and mismanagement of tribute trade by eunuchs in search of profit all greatly facilitated Esen's rise to power. Yet the Mongols' desire for trade induced them to make peace in the end. The Qing combined trade, diplomatic, and military pressures much more effectively.

After Tumu, the Ming rulers abandoned forward campaigns into the steppe. They found themselves on the defensive on all fronts, constantly warding off repeated attacks by many autonomous Mongol chieftains. The period from 1450 to 1540 marked an inconclusive shift to a full-fledged Great Wall strategy. Even though no single unifying leader arose among the Mongols, the ability of Ming frontier commanders to protect the border declined even further. Since Arthur Waldron's excellent study of the Great

Wall focuses on this period, I will only highlight the issues of frontier military supply and nomadic diplomacy and trade, which are somewhat underplayed in Waldron's account.[19]

Waldron divides the strategic history of the Ming into three periods: the first, from 1368 to 1449, a time of an open frontier, with no major wall building; the second period, 1449 to 1540, a time of inconclusive shift from offensive to defensive strategies, with great controversy and the beginning of major wall based defenses; and the third, from 1540 to the end of the dynasty, marked by reinforcement and consolidation of settled garrisons at large fortifications and the completion of the full Great Wall complex.

The Oirats withdrew to the Orkhon River after Esen's death in 1455 but continued raids on the northwest border. Now, however, the Eastern Mongols gained strength under Bolai, who attacked and plundered Shaanxi and Gansu. In 1461 General Li Wen, angry at being refused promotion, refused to mobilize his troops, causing the Chinese to suffer a great defeat.[20] The Chinese aimed to buy peace by establishing tribute trade with the Mongols, allowing them to choose their own routes and plunder along the way. Censor Chen Xuan delivered a devastating report on the laziness of the border commanders, the lack of supplies, and the mistreatment of poor soldiers, but his insistence on wholesale replacement of commanders was not heeded.[21]

More ominously, in the 1470s Mongols began to move into the fertile steppes of the Ordos, inside the Yellow River bend, a strategic salient of the steppe held by the Chinese. Debates over the defense of the Ordos raged for the rest of the century.[22] Wang Yue, the most capable military commander of the time, realized that an army of 150,000 would be necessary to defend the Ordos, but that it would be impossible to supply such a huge number in the steppe. The Chinese were forced to withdraw their outposts to the south and tacitly agree to the loss of the Ordos, while Mongols used the region as a base for raids to the south and west. Yu Zijun proposed the building of major defense fortifications in 1471 and 1472, and after gaining the support of Wang Yue against considerable opposition, succeeded in 1474 in carrying out his plan. The wall he built ran 600 miles from northeastern Shaanxi to northwestern Ningxia, using a labor force of forty thousand men at a cost of over 1 million taels. The wall also provided a shelter for military farms which yielded sixty thousand bushels of grain per year. It proved its effectiveness in 1482 when the soldiers at the wall held off a major Mongol offensive. This project began the first serious Chinese effort to link economic rehabilitation with a defensive strategy. Instead of an aggressive "extermination campaign" (jiao), Wang supported "restoring the people's livelihood" (shao su min lao).[23] Wang Yue's famous victory over the

A Russian delegation passes through the Great Wall.

Mongols at Red Salt Lake in 1473, the first in half a century, did not initiate further forward moves into the steppe; instead it bought time for Yu to complete his wall. Wang Yue was the last Ming commander in the northwest who could effectively manage both supply and mobilization. Many believed, mistakenly, that serious problems with supply shortages and corruption of frontier commands began only after his death in 1499.

China was still partly protected as long as the Mongols remained divided into eastern and western groups, but in 1483 Batu Möngke (Dayan Khan) again unified the Mongols. He conducted raids every year against Liaodong, Gansu, Datong, Xuanhua, and Yansui. Small detachments of swift Mongols routed incompetent Chinese military officials, who reported false victories to the court. Wang Ao reported at a court conference in 1501 on the desperate situation of the frontier, where commanders quarreled with one another, no one dared fight nomads openly, officials were lazy, and the troops showed no courage.[24] In 1513 Batu began building fortified camps in the Xuanhua and Datong areas, from which he staged increas-

ingly dangerous incursions with up to fifteen thousand cavalry even closer
to Beijing.[25] At the same time, internal succession struggles were tearing
apart the principality of Hami, a useful buffer for China against the western steppe. Turfan conquered Hami in 1513. The high point of Mongol
power came in 1517, when Batu moved on Beijing itself. Although the Chinese held him off in a major battle, he continued to threaten the capital
until 1526.

The issue of the recovery of the Ordos still dominated Ming strategy discussions in the early sixteenth century. Hard-liners regarded trade or negotiation with the irredeemably violent Mongols as impossible. They continually advocated unrealistic plans to drive the nomads out of the region.
Advocates of compromise had to consider soberly the relative costs and
benefits of major military expeditions compared to trade, but no one could
actively advocate trade relations with the Mongols in this period. Wall
building emerged as a second-best policy, approved by neither side but acceptable to both. At the same time, the links between economic develop-

ment and frontier defense grew more apparent. Qiu Jun's highly regarded manual of historical statecraft, the *Daxue Yanyibu*, published in 1487, contained a chapter on the Ordos question that stressed the importance of concurrently strengthening defense and the local economy. Zeng Xian, the great proponent of both recovery of the Ordos and of wall building in the 1540s, relied on Qiu Jun's work to argue for the connection between economic development and military defense, first in building walls at Linqing around the Grand Canal, and later in the northwest.[26]

At the same time, the increasing unreality of court politics undercut frontier defense. The Zhengde emperor (r. 1506–1521) purported to love military affairs, and he frequently wore Mongol dress. He liked to tour the frontier, built a palace there, and defeated Mongol raiders in 1517, but failed to develop a coherent strategy.[27] In some ways his behavior curiously foreshadows that of the Qianlong emperor. He took a Uighur concubine, he set out on a costly southern tour despite official protest, and he enjoyed promoting the image of a vigorous martial emperor, but in fact he did no serious strategic planning. Qianlong, however, surrounded by able Grand Councilors and vigorous Manchu, Mongol, and Chinese commanders, could afford his indulgences much better than could his Ming predecessor.

In 1506 Yang Yiqing began to increase fortifications along the frontier, but eunuch interference thwarted his plans after only thirteen miles were built.[28] The Jiajing emperor's reign (1522–1567) featured further factionalism at court and rising contempt for Mongols. Officials ordered, for example, that in documents the character *yi* for "barbarian" be written as small as possible. In 1551 the emperor prohibited all trade with the Mongols on pain of death. But in the 1540s a second major debate over the Ordos marked a significant turning point in frontier policy.

Altan Khan (1507–1582), the grandson of Batu, had risen to power in the mid-sixteenth century as the next great Mongol raider of the Chinese empire. He never unified all the Mongols, but he led the twelve Tümed (ten thousand–man units) under his control north of Shaanxi and Shanxi in continuous attacks along the frontier, followed by requests for permission to conduct tribute trade—requests which the Chinese nearly always rejected. This repeated cycle of "request, refusal, raid" continued for forty years until 1570.[29] Once again debates raged about defense strategy at court. Weng Wanda proposed major wall-building projects in Xuanfu and Datong to block the most accessible points and the erection of permanent watch posts. The emperor gave him 600,000 taels, with which he repaired fortifications and helped to restore the local economy, but he rejected Weng's proposal to allow Altan to send tribute. Zeng Xian submitted detailed reports in 1547–48 proposing an aggressive campaign to drive the Mongols out of the Ordos, but Weng pointed out that it would be impossible to support the huge baggage trains necessary in this desert-steppe environment.

Zeng proposed an attack by 300,000 men by land and water routes, including the use of firearms, at a cost he estimated at 2 million *shi* of grain and 3,000 taels of silver. Zeng estimated a total cost of over 300,000 taels, but the real costs would be much larger, up to 1.3 million taels. Waldron estimates that including transport costs would drive up the total to 3.75 million taels.[30] The Ministry of War, stressing the difficulties of finance, urged the need first to rebuild the border economy. Zeng nevertheless began his preparations, stirring up the hostility of the local population by corvée impressment, and by requisitioning cooking pots and farm tools to cast into weapons.

Both Weng and Zeng had close advisers of the emperor to support their case, but the eunuchs lobbied against Zeng. In 1547 the emperor ordered Zeng executed, permanently rejecting the idea of a recovery campaign.[31] Zeng Xian and Xia Yan later won reputations as patriots, despite the unrealism of their recovery project. Further raids ensued, and cowardly border commanders concluded that it was better simply to surrender to the Mongols and then buy them off than to resist. Now the Mongols gained the support of many Chinese, including deserters from the army, criminals, refugees, and agricultural settlers in the Ordos region. Chinese military advisers pointed out the weak points of the Ming defense lines and the best places to attack. Altan began building a new city, Köke Khota, or Guihua (present-day Hohhot), under their influence as he moved toward a more settled way of life.[32] The Chinese denounced these traitors in Mongol service, and demanded their heads, but continued to refuse trade. One attempt to open horse markets in 1551 was quickly shut down after Mongol raids, and the emperor prohibited all trade with the Mongols on pain of death.

Only under the next emperor's reign (Longqing, 1567–1572) could the Ming, in a brilliant stroke of frontier diplomacy, bring itself to negotiate peace on the frontier. The genius behind the successful policy was Wang Chonggu, Governor-General of Shaanxi, who realized that all the elements for a settlement were in place. He was supported by the vigorous Grand Secretary Zhang Juzheng, Ming China's most illustrious high official, who took a great interest in frontier affairs.[33] Altan Khan wanted peaceful trade relations; he raided only if tribute was refused. The Ming had reinforced its walls and mainly needed horses from the Mongols for the mobility of the garrisons. The Chinese wanted their deserters back, and the Mongols were willing to surrender them for a price. The opportunity for a settlement appeared when, in 1570, one of Altan Khan's grandsons, feuding with his chief, surrendered to the Chinese. Wang Chonggu recommended accepting his surrender and exchanging him for the Chinese deserters, promising trade relations with Altan if he swore to cease his attacks.

Wang's report is a good outline of future Qing policy. He recommended giving honorary rank and official degrees to selected Mongol chieftains, regulating the time and size of tribute embassies, limiting them to 150 men once per year, and limiting frontier horse markets to eight hundred men from the nomads, supervised by five hundred troops.[34] After stormy discussions at court, the Ming emperor and Zhang Juzheng squelched cries for Wang's impeachment and accepted the new policy, opening frontier horse markets and overturning the trade prohibition of 1551. Altan was given the honorary rank of Shunyi Wang, sixty-three other chieftains received appropriate titles, and frontier trade was tightly regulated at fixed dates and restricted, unlike other tributary missions, to the frontier. Merchants flocked to the frontier to sell silk, fur, grain, and cooking pots to the Mongols; the government collected taxes on the trade and used the income to buy poor horses at high prices from the nomads.

The Lama Buddhist church began its rise to influence in Mongolia in the late sixteenth century as well. The first Mongol contact with Tibetan Buddhism since the thirteenth century occurred in 1566, when the Ordos Mongol Khutukhtai Secen Hongtaiji (1540–1586) traveled to Tibet, offering to protect the church if the Tibetans submitted to him. Secen converted to Buddhism and brought with him over 100,000 Mongolian, Tibetan, and Chinese converts. In 1576 he advised Altan Khan to use the religion to strengthen his position among the Mongols.[35]

After the peace settlement, Wang Chonggu encouraged the emperor to promote Buddhism among the Mongols, and Mongol princes hired Chinese craftsmen to build temples in Mongolia and Kokonor. The Mongols agreed to donate horses and camels to monasteries instead of sacrificing them to their ancestors. Altan invited Sodnam Gyamtsho (bSod-nams-rgya-m-ts'o) of the Gelugpa (dGe-lugs-pa) sect in Lhasa to visit him at the first major temple built in Kokonor. In 1578 Altan gave him the title of "Dalai Lama" (Oceanic Teacher in Mongolian), and the Dalai Lama declared Altan to be the reincarnation of Khubilai Khan. The grandson of Altan Khan became the first Mongol to take the post of Dalai Lama in 1586.

Many scholars argue that Altan Khan's invitation marked the first introduction of Tibetan Buddhism into Mongolia, but Henry Serruys has shown that "all the facts point to an uninterrupted Lamaist tradition in Southern Mongolia going all the way back to Mongol Lamaism of early Ming times and in final analysis to the end of the Yuan period." The close and continuous association of the Mongols with the Tibetan Buddhist establishment had begun centuries earlier, but the sixteenth-century situation allowed the "expansion and consolidation of something that had never completely disappeared from Mongolia and was only waiting for the right opportunity to reassert itself."[36] Later the Qing would try to cut these ties to Tibet but keep the Mongols focused on Buddhism centered in Beijing.

The late sixteenth century was also the heyday of wall building along the Ming border. The Nine Border Garrison system reached its highest elaboration, existing walls were strengthened with brick and stone, and the walls were linked together with watchtowers, all at heavy cost in silver. Most of the present-day Great Wall dates from these sixteenth-century works. All of these elements—controlled trade and tribute, patronage of Buddhism, grants of titles, defensive strengthening, and investment in the local economy—became key points of Qing strategic policy.

Conversely, the Mongols also exhibited debilitating signs of division which plagued their efforts to unite against the Ming. Altan was not a would-be unifier of all the Mongols. Unlike in the northwest, the tribes of the northeast frontier refused to make peace with China, even after Altan's submission. The Mongols in the northwest only temporarily followed Altan's lead. As Dmitrii Pokotilov puts it, "they collaborated only as long as there existed a common interest and the chance of easy and quick plundering, but when it became necessary to intercede for the interests of some individual prince with the risk of strong resistance, all solidarity immediately disappeared, even among near relatives."[37] Only in the late sixteenth century did the Ming finally succeed in exploiting these divisions among Mongol tribes. This divide-and-rule strategy, which, as mentioned earlier, became the cornerstone of Qing policy, kept peace along the northwest frontier until the end of the dynasty. The new threats to the Ming arose from domestic social disturbances within northwest China and elsewhere, and from the rising Manchu state in the Northeast.

Ming strategy thus evolved from unsuccessful efforts at military penetration of the steppe to costly defensive walls and garrisons, supported by the acceptance of limited trade with the tribes in the guise of tribute missions. The trade lever proved to be the least costly and most effective in removing the threat of raids. Sechin Jagchid has argued that it was only Chinese mis-

understanding of the need of nomads for trade that prevented peaceful relations with the steppe. In his view, once emperors accepted regular trading
relations, they faced little military threat:

> For a period of two thousand years, trade was the chief determinant of
> peace and war between the nomadic and the Chinese peoples along
> China's northern border. The nomadic peoples were dependent on a
> few key products produced by the agriculturalist Chinese, particularly
> grain and cloth. When they were able to obtain these goods peacefully
> through the mechanisms of trade, bestowals, and court-to-court inter-
> marriage arrangements, stability along China's frontiers was possible,
> but when they were denied ready access to these essential commodi-
> ties, war was almost a certainty.[38]

Trading relations, however, did not by themselves necessarily weaken
the strength of nomadic state builders. A far-sighted challenger to Chinese
power could use trading privileges to build up the resources of his state.
This was the strategy pursued by Nurhaci, the founder of the Manchu
state, in his early years. In order to reduce the threat, Chinese dynasties had
to combine peaceful trading relations with efforts to ensure that the steppe
tribes remained disunited. This meant gathering intelligence and gaining allies among nomadic tribes to balance against rising powers. When Chinese
rulers could take advantage of the "fatal individualism" of the Mongols to
keep them weak, they reduced their defense costs by diverting nomads from
raids on the frontier toward attacking one another. The Ming court partly
succeeded in this strategy in the late sixteenth century in Mongolia but
failed to recognize the significance of the growing strength of the Manchus
in the Northeast.

I have described the evolution of Ming strategy from military offense to
trade and defense in terms of the recognition by the Ming of the value of
trading relations to the nomads of the frontier. Frontier trade, however, was
equally important for the Ming court itself. A Han-ruled dynasty like the
Ming, which did not control the steppe, faced the same problem as its predecessors: an inability to produce within its borders sufficient numbers of
militarily capable horses to supply its army. Even for defensive warfare, domestic Chinese horses were inadequate against the tough, swift ponies of
the Mongols. Matteo Ricci noted in the late sixteenth century that most
Chinese army horses were "so degenerate and lacking in martial spirit that

they are put to rout even by the neighing of the Tartars' steeds and so they are practically useless in battle."[39] Well aware of this problem, the first Ming emperor established two organizations to breed horses for battle: the Yuanmasi (Pasturage Office) and the Taipusi (Court of the Imperial Stud) under the Ministry of War. But domestic pasture was hopelessly inadequate. "Horse households" in North China were supposed to provide horses to the Taipusi in Beijing, but by the end of the fifteenth century, the government had to allow them to buy replacements. Nearly all of the replacements were "western horses" *(xima)* obtained from private traders who had bought them at frontier markets in the northwest. The traders charged the horse households very high prices and gave them horses nearly useless for warfare.[40] So efforts to provide horses from inside the Great Wall once again ended in failure.

The only option was to obtain horses by trade with the nomads. This required two basic elements: the Han Chinese had to produce a product the nomads wanted, and they had to find nomads who would cooperate in providing horses to be used in military activity against other nomads. Diplomacy and trade had to work together. For about a half century, from 1393 to 1449, the "gold tablet system" *(jinpai xinfu)* seemed to provide the answer. Chinese officials believed that the nomads had a desperate need for tea. As one official put it, "All the barbarians need tea to survive. If they cannot get tea, they become ill and die."[41] This delusion supported a policy of large-scale shipments of tea to the frontiers, with the conviction that China could use the supply of tea to control nomad attacks. Every three years, 1 million *jin* of tea from Sichuan was to be traded with specially licensed nomads for fourteen thousand horses at three principal designated frontier "tea–horse markets" *(chamasi)* in Hezhou, Daozhou, and Xining (in present-day Gansu and Qinghai).[42] Hezhou was the largest market. The success of this system depended on Chinese government monopsonistic control over the purchasing of tea and monopolistic control over its exchange at the markets, as well as the ability to designate acceptable nomadic horse traders. Only a limited number of tribal chieftains could receive one of the forty-one coveted gold tablets that entitled them to trade with government representatives. The Ming also attempted to fix the price of horses, first at the level of 30 to 40 *jin* per horse, but later at prices ranging from 50 to 120 *jin* depending on quality.

The gold tablet monopoly system at first dramatically raised tea production and the horse supply, but Sichuan was too far away and transport costs too high to make this effort successful for long. In 1397 the state obtained 13,518 horses in exchange for 500,000 *jin* of tea. Sichuan's quota of tea rose to 1 million *jin* every three years, but by 1444 it was reduced to

420,000 *jin,* until abolition of the quota in the 1450s. Sichuan tea planta-
tions declined in importance as Hanzhong *fu,* in southern Shaanxi, became
a much more adequate source. Sichuan's production used to be three times
that of Hanzhong, but the proximity of Hanzhong to the frontiers favored
it, and the government's promotion of refugee settlement in the region encouraged land clearance for planting tea.

While Yongle's aggressive campaigns succeeded, the tea monopoly system provided him the necessary logistical support, but his demands expanded as the campaigns proceeded. The total number of horses possessed
by the army increased from 310,617 in 1415 to 1.2 million in 1422. With
the end of the campaigns, the gold tablets held by friendly nomad horse
traders were lost, scattered by hostile attacks. Famine struck Shaanxi in
1450, requiring local officials to sell their tea stocks for grain. Military officials were too busy fending off attacks from Esen Khan to transport the
tea, so they used 10,000 taels from the treasury to buy horses.

External attacks from Western Mongols were, however, only one cause
of the system's demise. The internal challenge from private commerce was
just as serious. From the beginning, Ming rulers tried to stamp out private
trade in many commodities, driven by an ideology of agrarian self-sufficiency. Private trade in tea was especially threatening, because merchants
could link up with unauthorized horse traders, driving up the official tea–
horse exchange ratio, which was set below the market price. But given the
inadequacy of the official trade, Yongle himself had to rely heavily on private traders for his horses, paying high prices for them (80,000 *jin* for seventy horses). After 1450, when officials shifted their attention from Sichuan
to Shaanxi, they were forced to recognize the usefulness of private trade.
They also shifted from levying tea taxes in kind to collections in currency.
In the fifteenth century a new merchant contracting system, "Equitable Exchange" (of grain for salt), or *kaizhongfa,* had developed, at first in the salt
monopoly, to provide grain supplies to frontier garrisons. The state gave
salt merchants monopoly licenses to trade in salt in exchange for providing
designated amounts of grain to the northwest frontier.[43] In 1505 the Ming
initiated a similar tea merchant contracting system *(kaizhongcha)* in response both to repeated famines in Shaanxi and to the need for horses.
Merchants who contributed grain for famine relief received licenses to
trade in tea, which they could exchange for horses at the frontier. They
were obliged to provide the state with a fixed number of horses, and trade
outside these channels was prohibited.

The effect was to stimulate greatly tea production in Hanzhong, and to
promote tea trade as far away as Hunan and Guangdong. Merchant profits
rose dramatically; by 1501 Shaanxi had obtained 9 million *jin* of tea. But

the officials soon noticed that they received very few horses, and those they did obtain were of the poorest quality. In 1503 the government's share of the trade was 33 percent; it obtained only 10,000 horses at a cost of 500,000 to 600,000 *jin*. Calls rose to abolish private markets again.

Yang Yiqing, who directed the horse administration in the northwest, analyzed the critical situation in great detail and recommended drastic reforms.[44] He proposed yet another system, called "Equal Cooperation of State and Merchant" *(guanshang duifen)*. He recognized that tea production had grown rapidly, stimulated by private commerce, but the state received only 10 to 20 percent of total production. Private tea traders were driving up the fixed official prices for horses but provided only the worst-quality horses as their quota to the state. In principle, Yang wanted to revive the government monopoly gold tablet system, yet he knew that banning private trade would only leave the tea plantation workers without a livelihood and dry up supplies to the frontier markets, while failing to relieve the shortages of horses. Reviving the trade and ensuring profit for the state required incentives for both officials and merchants. In 1505 he proposed and implemented a policy of "Summoning Merchants to Purchase and Transport" tea to the frontier *(zhaoshang maiyun)*. Selected merchants were invited to purchase up to 10,000 *jin* of tea each for a total of 500,000 to 600,000 *jin*, transport the tea to the frontier markets, and sell 33 percent of the tea to the garrisons at a price of 50 taels per *jin* (25 taels for production costs, 25 taels for transport). They could keep half of the tea for their own trade. Unlike the previous *kaizhong* system, this allowed the government to keep control of the exchange of tea for horses with the nomads so it could profit by fixing prices, and illegal smuggling was strictly prohibited.

Anyone aware of the course of the economic reforms in China of the past two decades will recognize remarkable parallels here. Sixteenth-century China was a halfway house in the movement toward reform; the state could not yield entirely its monopoly control of strategic trade but recognized the importance of providing incentives to merchants and tea producers. The state held on to what modern socialist governments call the "towering heights" of the economy, closely tied to security needs, while encouraging private trade in less strategic commodities. This reform, however, worked no better than the earlier ones. Frontier officials accumulated large stocks of tea but found no horses they could buy, because merchants persisted in the private tea–horse trade, cleaning out all the good horses from the market. In 1532 the three *chamasi* held 870,000 *jin* of tea but could not buy horses. By the mid-sixteenth century, Ming officials tried to limit merchant-contracted tea to 500,000 to 600,000 *jin* and the number of merchants to 150. By 1586 the Hanzhong tea tax had been completely commuted to silver. Merchants bought the entire local tea supply, and they went down the Han River to Xiangyang in northern Hubei, which had become a major tea entrepôt. The state could not stop illegal trade with the nomads of the northwest, but by the end of the sixteenth century their strategic importance had declined.

Perhaps the most basic factor underlying the increasingly defensive strategy of the Ming in the northwest during the sixteenth century was the shortage of horses and grain on the frontier. When the *kaizhongfa* merchant contracting policy failed to attract enough supplies to the frontier, the Ming allowed merchants to establish their own merchant colonies *(shangtun)* near the garrisons.[45] On these agricultural settlements, merchants with salt licenses paid tenant farmers to produce the grain for shipment to the garrisons. But by the late fifteenth century, excessive state demands from the merchants caused them to abandon the colonies on the border and return home. By 1530 there was not enough mercantile capital in the frontier region to make colonies feasible.

The Ming experience demonstrates the very precarious balance of commercial and strategic interests that the court had to pursue on the frontier. Three different systems of horse–tea trade evolved over two centuries, from complete government monopoly of both products in the early fifteenth century, to nearly complete private contracting for purchase, transport, and sale in the late fifteenth century, to a mixed government-merchant contracting and transport system in the sixteenth century. None worked for long. None provided critical strategic goods in sufficient quantities to meet immediate military needs. But the principle held: the only way Chinese rulers could obtain the two crucial logistical components of preindustrial warfare—horses and grain—was to link state requisitions to the developing commercial economy of the interior, then devise means of transporting supplies to the northwest.

The steppe barrier proved a major obstacle to Chinese expansion. Frontier markets under government control had many advantages. On the one hand, they kept out foreign merchants from the center of the empire; they lowered transport costs for horses obtained from the steppe (but raised them for tea produced in the interior); and they were small in number and kept under close military control. On the other hand, the state could never entirely prevent private trade. The frontier in the sixteenth century became a classic "borderland," only weakly patrolled, where powerful officials and military officers diverted supplies of tea and horses for their own profit. Yang Yiqing recognized that people on the border "could speak the barbarian languages, and soldiers from many provinces collect there to trade horses with the barbarians. They hire local people as guides, and penetrate far into barbarian territory." Cultures were mingling, despite imperial efforts to keep them apart, but Yang's reforms could not impose authority over these local frontier profiteers.[46]

The sixteenth century marked a new high tide in the advance of commercial relations throughout China.[47] The influx of silver, first from Japan and later from the New World, provided the medium for expanding long-distance monetary exchange. It made possible the nearly complete monetization of the tax system, known as the Single Whip reforms, throughout the century. Military defense needs played just as important a role as private trade and taxation in spreading silver around the empire. In the late sixteenth century, Beijing sent over 4 million taels of silver per year to the northwest garrisons for purchasing goods from local peasants and frontier merchants.[48] These garrisons formed a vast consumer belt demanding constant replenishment of grain rations and textiles. Their demands fostered the growth of a trading system that linked the northwest to the lower Yangzi, through merchant contracting with the state and through private networks. The military and civilian distribution systems were intertwined through mechanisms of silver payment. The key challenge for Ming frontier officials was to tap enough of this flow of goods to supply their garrisons, and to limit the profits scooped up by the aggressive Shanxi merchants. Because they failed to ensure an adequate supply of grain and cloth at reasonable prices, the troops remained poorly fed and clothed, inciting them to desert their posts at the end of the dynasty. Ming rulers had shut down the great Southeast Asian voyages in the early fifteenth century because they put greater priority on northwest defense, but they still had to rely on the commercial resources of the southeast to supply the defensive wall on the northwest.

Tea, horses, grain, and silver remained vital components of Qing frontier trade, too. The Qing also established frontier markets, mainly with the Russians at Kiakhta, where tea exports were a valuable item of trade. But they solved the horse problem differently. Unlike the Song and Ming, the Qing did not try to establish either a monopoly or a subcontracted tea-for-horses trade. It obtained its horses on private markets with government funds, or it requisitioned horses from surrendered Mongols.

What accounts for the Ming difficulties on the frontier? Ray Huang traces Ming strategic failure to the fundamental weaknesses of the Ming garrison, or *weisuo*, system.[49] These hereditary military forces always suffered from inadequate funding, even as expenses rose. Ming fiscal institutions could not efficiently gather revenue from the interior and ship it to the frontier. Revenue management was fragmented, and there was no centralized auditing. The Ming founder designed his empire's fiscal structure for a small-scale village economy; it could not accommodate the expanded and commercialized revenue needs of the sixteenth century.

Although Huang blames Ming fiscal structures, three other factors had greater weight. First, the Ming economy put limits on the empire's defense. Before the sixteenth century, Ming China lacked a sufficiently commercialized economy to make possible fully monetized acquisition of strategic goods. Even 4 million taels of silver was still inadequate to meet the annual needs of the northwest garrisons. Second, the Han ethnicity of the rulers and officialdom isolated them from the steppe environment. Ming Taizu, his successors, and his officials came predominantly from southern China, far from the frontier. The Manchu Qing rulers, by contrast, knew Mongols well. Mongols and Manchus intermarried and cooperated on military campaigns. Third, the Ming state lacked essential tools of communication and administration that would be much more highly developed in the Qing. Thus ecology, ethnicity, and state structure interacted to produce different results.

Still, the Ming did last over 250 years. For part of this period it established a stable defensive relationship with the steppe. It, more than any other dynasty, relied on the Great Wall for real defense. In this sense it was the true culmination of a Han-centered strategic polity that had begun with the Qin dynasty of the third century BCE. Although it began as a severely agrarian regime, hostile to commerce, and repeatedly shut down promising moves toward commercial developments by calling off the Southeast Asian naval expeditions and campaigning against the seaborne traders along the southeast coast, it also attempted in two major institutions, the *kaizhongfa* and *shangtun*, to mobilize mercantile incentives in the interests of strategic defense. As Mark Elvin notes, this effort to combine commerce and defense, even though unavailing, left a valuable repertory of experience for its successors, who built on the Ming logistical framework.[50]

State Formation in Muscovy and Russian Expansion

Let us now introduce the third major player in the Central Eurasian Great Game: the expanding state of Muscovy, which became the Russian empire. Russia's entrance into steppe politics is conventionally dated from the mid-sixteenth century, after the takeover of Kazan' and the beginning of the Siberian expeditions; but Muscovy was an active player on the steppe a century earlier, when it emerged from the breakup of Chinggis Khan's empire.

Mongolian rule had strongly shaped the Muscovite state, and its foreign and military policies derived first from steppe conflicts and only later from contact with western Europe.

The Kipchak Khanate, better known by the anachronistic term "Golden Horde," was the portion of the Chinggisid empire that included the Russian steppe. It originated as the *ulus*, or personal territory, of Jochi, the eldest son of Chinggis Khan. By the late fourteenth century the Khans' control of the *ulus* had severely weakened. Leadership struggles between rival successors divided authority at the center, while several new states formed in eastern European and Russian territory to challenge the Khans' rule. The Grand Duchy of Lithuania, Moscow, Tver', and other states competed with one another and with the successor Khans for local control. Moscow, located at a strategic point in command of the major trade route of the Volga, was in an excellent position to play off rival Khans against one another. The rise of Timur (Tamerlane) to power in eastern Eurasia in the 1360s further weakened the ability of the Khans to control Muscovy. Dmitri Donskoi, declared the ruler of eastern Russia in 1375 after crushing efforts of Tver' and Lithuania to invade Moscow, then moved down the Volga River. His most famous battle with the Mongol ruler Mamay, at Kulikovo field on September 8, 1380, forced the Mongol ruler to flee. But Tokhtamysh, who had taken over Jochi's *ulus,* attacked and looted Moscow in 1382. Only the clash between Tokhtamysh and Timur in the 1390s saved Moscow from once again being subordinated to Mongol rule.

Timur crushed Tokhtamysh's independence, but he did not challenge Muscovite resistance when he prepared to storm the city. By the time Timur died in 1405, he had fatally undermined the trade of the Golden Horde by disrupting the caravan routes and destroying its cities, and had made it impossible for later Mongol rulers to subordinate the newly autonomous Russian states. It was in the first half of the fifteenth century that "East Russia, actually, if not yet formally, emancipated herself from Tatar domination."[51] Muscovites made only token tribute payments to the Khans, and there was no real interference by the Khan in Moscow's affairs. When Moscow beat back Tatar efforts to storm the city in 1451, many Tatars subordinated themselves to Moscow's ruler. Thus the rising Muscovite state included a mixed population of Russians and Tatars in the service of the Grand Duke.[52]

Russian historians have debated for centuries the influence of the Mongols on Russia. The eighteenth-century historian N. M. Karamzin declared that "Moscow owes its greatness to the Khans," recognizing both the heavy debt owed by Muscovite rulers to the Chinggisid empire along with the severe impact of Mongol oppression on political liberties and the "deterioration of morals." Nineteenth-century nationalist historians like S. M. Solov'ev and V. O. Kliuchevksy tended to play down Mongolian influence, although others, like Prince Nicholas Trubetskoy, insisted that an understanding of the Mongol empire was essential to understanding the Muscovite state. The twentieth-century historian George Vernadsky argues that the greatest influence of the Tatars on Moscow came only with the breakup of the Horde and the incorporation of Mongols into the service of the Grand Duke after 1480. Donald Ostrowski, however, has argued for a much greater direct influence of Mongolian traditions on the formation of the Muscovite state during the period of its rise to independence. He suggests that the Muscovite princes created a "sharp rift in institutional continuity" in the early fourteenth century by introducing Mongol political and military institutions on a wide scale.[53]

The major institutions of fourteenth-century Muscovy paralleled very closely those of the Kipchak Khanate. These included the dual administrative structure, dividing authority between the chief military commander (Kipchak *bekalribek*, Russian *tysiatskii*) and the chief controller of the treasury (Kipchak *vizier*, Russian *dvorskii*); the use of Mongolian and Turkish terminology for taxation and currency (*tamga*, "commercial tax"; *kazna*, "treasury"; *den'gi (tengge)*, "money"; etc.); the elaboration of a sophisticated postal system for transmission of documents and information (Mongol *jam*, Russian *iam*, Chinese *zhan*); the use of petitions to the prince (*chelom bit'e*, derived via Turkish from the Chinese *ketou*); and the creation of a "clan polity," in which only one family could produce the ruling prince or Tsar, and the heads of other leading clans were ranked in a strict hierarchy (the Mongol *ungu bogol*, Russian *mestnichestvo* system). Russian military institutions, strategy, and tactics also were derived from the Mongol system. Finally, the principle of "lateral succession," dubbed "bloody tanistry" by Joseph Fletcher, allowed all the brothers and uncles of a ruler to compete for succession, leading to violent internecine warfare during succession conflicts. This principle competed with the vertical succession by the ruler's son, introduced from Byzantium, until 1425.[54]

Muscovy's military formation also clearly reflects its steppe origins.[55] It did well in resisting Tatar attacks because it recognized how Mongolian military formations worked. Once Muscovy freed itself formally from the Mongols in the 1460s, it became a contender for power over the other succession states of the steppe. This was the process that led to the dramatic expansion in the mid-sixteenth century of Muscovy eastward against Kazan' and Astrakhan and into Siberia. Muscovy, like Kazan', the Crimea, and others, was a succession state of the Golden Horde, and it raised itself to power by deploying the familiar techniques of steppe politics: using support from the Khans to legitimate its rulers' local authority while manipulating the Khans against one another to create maximum autonomy.[56]

Such striking similarities between two very disparate societies, nomadic and settled, demonstrates the power of cultural borrowing and the great influence a conqueror can have on the subjugated society. Muscovy's close contact with the steppe led it to adopt steppe institutions in order to strengthen the rulers' power. Ming China, more closed off from the steppe by the defensive barrier of the Great Wall and the ritualized tribute system, did not adopt nearly so many Mongolian institutions, but its successor, the Manchus, would use methods similar to those adopted by Muscovy two centuries earlier.

The general trend in recent historiography of this period is toward a more polycultural analysis, one that does not try to make a rigid separation between essentially "Russian" and "Mongolian" elements but recognizes the creative role of cultural mingling in the transformation of states. It attempts to avoid the Eurocentric and colonialist premises of nationalist historiography that saw the Mongols as nothing more than cruel Asiatics or a gang of bandits.[57] Certainly the initial impact of the Mongols on all Eurasian states was destructive, but after the conquest, the Mongols promoted the revival of the caravan trade, from which Russian princes profited greatly.

The Mongols ruled Russia indirectly, by staying in the steppe to preserve the classic nomadic warrior's way of life. In China and Iran, where they occupied settled regions, the urban garrisons lost their dedication to the military discipline of the grasslands. Furthermore, since pasturelands were scarce in agrarian China, the Mongol military machine decayed from within as urban warriors began to assimilate to Chinese ways. The indirect rule over Russia meant that Mongol domination lasted a century longer there than in China or Iran. It also meant greater Mongol influence on Muscovite institutions than in China or Iran. This happened despite the "larger social distance" between Mongols and Russians created by the separation of Mongolian steppe dwellers and Russian settled agriculturalists.[58]

The Mongol solution to the dangers of assimilation as practiced in the Kipchak Khanate required separation of the realm into two spheres, one nomadic and one settled. Periodic raids and invasions of the settled zone, with limited official representation and intervention through tribute collection, kept the settled area intermittently quiescent, while the nomads could maintain their pastoral way of life relatively undisturbed. The Chinese-Iranian solution brought greater administrative elaboration in the settled

region, closer contact of conquerors and conquered, and in the end undermined the basis of Mongolian domination. In the centuries that followed,
these two basic choices—separation or assimilation—faced the Manchus
as well.

Muscovy began its great expansion eastward by conquering the steppe
state of Kazan' in the mid-sixteenth century. The prevalent nationalist historiography of this conflict depicts a rising Christian Muscovite state struggling to overcome the united opposition of the "remnants of the Golden
Horde" composed of Turkish and Mongolian tribes together with Islamic
merchants. As Edward Keenan and Jaroslaw Pelenski argue, this ideology
is a later creation of Russian Orthodox priests, legitimating Muscovy's conquests as a combined religious and military crusade.[59] It does not represent
the actual relations between Muscovy and the steppe polities in the sixteenth century. Rather than depict Muscovy as a separate state struggling
against "remnants of the Horde," it is better to see Muscovy along with the
Tatar Khanates as a group of successor states to the Chinggisid empire,
each seeking a modus vivendi in new conditions.

The Eurasian steppe has often been called a "land sea," whose cities
are its ports and caravans its convoys.[60] But the nomadic inhabitants of the
steppe are the third crucial element that distinguishes land from water. The
catastrophic decline in importance of the steppe began with Timur's destruction of its economic bases in the 1390s. Until the 1460s centrifugal forces directed power to peripheral states, which struggled to consolidate their rule. Then these rival states (Moscow, the Crimea, Kazan', Siberia)
aimed to stabilize their relationship as they cut back the Great Horde's central power. Finally, from 1520 to the 1550s, the three states contended with
one another over the power vacuum left by the collapse of the Horde, and
Moscow emerged as the dominant force in the western steppe.

Muscovy was far more closely linked to steppe politics than its contemporary, the Ming dynasty. The Muscovite rulers knew intimately the game
of nomadic politics, and they effectively exploited divisions within the
steppe polities for their own ends. But in general, they did not seek military
conquest of the steppe. Muscovy's main strategic concerns lay to the west,
against the Polish-Lithuanian state. They tried to keep peace in the east in
a situation of divided and confusing allegiances, as they also tried to use
the commercial resources of the steppe to build up the state treasury in
preparation for war in the west. The major activities of Muscovite state

builders in the sixteenth century foreshadowed those of Peter the Great and
his successors.

The Khanate of Kazan' (1445–1552) was a confederation of agricultural
and nomadic peoples whose nucleus on the Volga River included Tatars,
Turks, and Muslims. Princes of dominant clans administered peasant com-
munes headed by elders, and these groupings were collectively called the
"Land" (Zemlia). Above them, the Khan, a descendant of the Chinggisid
Jochi, conducted diplomacy and war, collecting his revenues from personal
landholdings, levies on the local aristocracy, and taxes on trade. The opposition between the Khan and his court on the one side and the "Land" on
the other was common to all Turkic polities, the Muscovite state, and the
Manchu Qing empire. Succession practices, too, showed commonalities deriving from the Turkish tradition, following the "bloody tanistry" of passing the throne first through all the brothers, then to the eldest son of the eldest brother. This pattern ensured frequent instability and power struggles
upon the death of each Khan. The divisions within the polity created open-
ings for exploitation by rival states that could back contending parties to
ensure their dominant influence. The Muscovite play within Kazan' again
mirrors the play of the Manchus within the Zunghar state on a much
grander scale in the eighteenth century.

Kazan' was not technically a state. It was formally a *iurt*, or territory
of the Golden Horde. In fact, however, as a major trade entrepôt on the
Volga, it collected significant revenues from both riverine and overland
trade with nomadic regions. Muslim merchants controlled the main Volga
River routes, but Russians gained rising influence. Merchants and the Land
generally favored peaceful trade, while the Khan and his court might seek
to expand the territory by war.

Other actors in this steppe political game included the Nogai confederation of nomads, the Crimea Khanate, and the Ottoman empire. The Nogai
were a purely nomadic confederation, extending east from the Volga to the
Irtysh River in Siberia. They had no fixed capital, and were ruled by a council led by a Grand Prince. They, not Muscovy, were the decisive forces in
Kazan's foreign policy. For Muscovy, the Nogai were most important as the
main source of horses for riding, just as Muscovy was the Nogai's main
source of income. The horse drives to Moscow in the sixteenth century
brought as many as thirty to forty thousand horses to the capital annually.[61] This was three times as many as the Ming usually obtained. Here is

another indication of Muscovy's intimacy with and Beijing's distance from the steppe: Russians secured their main military mounts in the capital itself; Chinese confined horse trade to the frontiers.

Early encounters of Muscovite princes with the Khans of Kazan' were pragmatic and cooperative. Each of the principalities tried to outbid the others for a *iarlyk,* or Khan's charter.[62] Vasilii Vasilevich of Moscow was granted a *iarlyk* by the Khan Ulu-Magmet investing him as Prince of Moscow. Even though Ulu-Magmet later attacked and defeated Vasilii, they negotiated a peace which lasted until Vasilii's death in 1462. Commerce between Moscow and Kazan' flourished. Ivan III (r. 1462–1505), Vasilii's successor, focused his attention on his main enemy to the west, the Grand Prince of Lithuania, and strove to keep stability to his south and east through an alliance with the Khan of the Crimea. Stability on this frontier left him free to attack Novgorod, the great northwestern trading city, and force it into submission in 1478.[63] Despite sporadic raids by Akhmed Khan from Kazan', Ivan kept good relations with him, and the necessary horse drives by the Nogai continued. Akhmed's desperate attack on Moscow and its failure in 1487 "marked the entry of Muscovy as an important force in the political dynamics of Volga and steppe politics."[64] The collapse of the Golden Horde had left a power vacuum which would eventually bring all the successor states into conflict with one another.

Nevertheless, stability lasted from 1480 to 1510 based on the Moscow Crimean alliance balanced against Kazan'. The final remnants of the Great Horde were mopped up when Mengli Girei, the Crimean Khan, captured Astrakhan in 1502. After this, hostility between Moscow and the Crimea grew. The Crimean Khan broke with Moscow and allied with Lithuania. When Vasilii III (r. 1505–1533) succeeded Ivan, he increased Muscovite intervention in Kazan' against the wishes of the Crimean Khan. A contested succession to the Khanate in Kazan' led certain groups to invite Moscow's intervention on one side and others to invite Crimea to intervene on the other. The Land invited the Crimean candidate to become Khan in 1521, but aggressive moves by Kazan' against Moscow were defeated when princes in Kazan' deposed their Khan with Moscow's support. The main point is that internal Kazan' politics drove developments in this period, and Kazan' did not take direction from either Moscow or the Crimea. By the 1540s Moscow mobilized against Kazan', but also aimed to reach accommodation with the princes of the Land in Kazan'. Notably, nationalism or religious loyalty played very little role in these alliances: Tatars, Muslims, and pagans fought on Moscow's side, and Kazanians failed to get support from their fellow Muslims. There never was a united Turkic-Muslim front against Orthodox Moscow.

Moscow's siege of Kazan' in 1545 brought the collapse of political institutions in Kazan'. Ivan IV came of age in 1547 and was crowned Tsar. When he left on his campaign against Kazan' in 1549, he gained considerable support from Kazan's people and was prepared to enter the city peacefully, when certain groups within the city rebelled against the arranged intervention. Ivan finally had to assault the city, which fell to him in October 1552.

In sum, Kazan' fell primarily because of internal divisions. It was unable to balance the differing interests of nomadic Nogai, Siberian, and Mongol military aristocracy, Muslim merchant classes, and Muscovite agents. The Muscovite agents knew well how to maneuver these factions in their own interest, just as the Manchus used their close relations with the Mongols to prevent a united front against them. Like that of the Manchus, "Muscovy's participation in steppe politics was not that of an outsider or intruder, but that of friend and brother, i.e. a participant in a system to which it owed its political origins and traditions."[65] Both Muscovy and the Qing grew out of the traditions of Central Eurasian state competition but learned to adapt their institutions so as to make maximum use of the settled societies they ruled. At the same time, they used their knowledge of the steppe to ensure that no future rivals would unite against them. Both succeeded brilliantly in this double expansion into settled and nomadic realms.

The conquest of Kazan', however, marked the end of Muscovy's active participation in steppe politics. For the next century, it turned gradually westward to nourish its growing empire, and it expanded across Siberia, north of the steppe, seeking the wealth to support its territorial and administrative ambitions. Siberia was to Muscovy what Russia had been to the Mongols: a peripheral region to be ruled indirectly at low cost, yielding as much wealth as possible from the native population for the purposes of the Khan or Tsar.

"There was from the beginning, the Russian land . . . always one Russian land, where now the city of Kazan' standeth."[66]

We continue the story of Muscovite expansion across Siberia, but let us first examine how the Tsars justified their conquests. Accounts of Moscow's relations with Kazan' before the conquest diverge considerably from the justification of the conquest by chroniclers after the event. As we have seen, diplomatic and archival sources provide a picture of Muscovy and Kazan' as common but rival successor states within the world of the Mongol Horde. They conducted commercial and diplomatic relations with each other on pragmatic and friendly terms. Divisions within the Khanate some-

times led to Muscovite interventions on one side or the other, but for most
of the period from 1450 to 1550, the dominant rulers in Kazan' acted independently of Moscow. Religious or cultural differences were not the fundamental driving forces of the relationship. In the end, Moscow intervened at
the invitation of elements within Kazan' to protect them against rivals supported by the Crimean Khan.

Russian chroniclers, however, depicted a world of sharp, irreconcilable
struggle between two forces alien to each other: the barbarian pagans of
Kazan' and the virtuous Christians of Russia. They separated radically the
two regimes, stressing the national, cultural, and religious differences. They
also provided spurious legitimations for the conquest based on claims of
continuous Muscovite rule from the antique past.

The ideological history of Muscovite-Kazanian relations produced by
clerical chroniclers in the late sixteenth and early seventeenth centuries
demonstrates strategies of legitimation that would be used to justify other
conquests of Central Eurasian states by settled agrarian regimes. First was
the false legal claim that the Muscovite ruler had an established right to
grant investiture to the Kazan' Khans ever since 1487, when Ivan III had intervened on one side of a dynastic struggle in the Kazan' Khanate.[67] Later,
the Russian rulers made a second legal claim, that Kazan' was a patrimony
(*votchina* or *otchina*, i.e., *iurt*) of the Muscovite Grand Princes. Muscovy
also invoked the "right of conquest" derived from its victory in war, and
the idea of continuity of the Russian princes, claiming that they had ruled
over the Tatar Khanate lands since antiquity.

The *Kazanskaia Istoriia* of the 1590s, more historical fiction than chronicle, incorporated these ideological arguments into a very widely read version of the struggle that was taken as fact by many successive historians.[68]
This retrospective justification rested on two central themes: the prominence of territory (the land) and the claim to unity (*one* Russian land). Both
of these themes fit much better into the new territorial states built after
the conquest than into the fluid personal relations before it. Only careful
study of archival sources and diplomatic documents independent of the
Kazanskaia Istoriia has reconstructed the truly complex intercultural negotiations that marked this and other encounters on the steppe.

The remarkable similarity of arguments in the Russian chronicles to later
nationalistic justifications of conquest, and to nationalistic Chinese interpretations of the Qing conquest of Central Eurasia, demonstrates two important conclusions:

- The ideological reconstruction of the history of the encounter of settled
  and Central Eurasian regimes displays remarkable similarity at both
  ends of the steppe.

- In both cases ideological reinterpretation began soon after the completion of the conquest; it did not have to wait for nineteenth-century nationalists.[69]

Instead of depicting a complex process of pragmatic negotiation, in which Moscow or Beijing often compromised and often acted by norms well understood by parties in the steppe and in the settled regime, the chroniclers substituted a much simpler opposition of "barbaric" Tatars, or nomads, and "civilized" rulers. The victors claimed to have held continuous control since antiquity over the territories they had just recently conquered. With this claim, those who resisted could be classified as "internal" rebels, not autonomous state powers. The expansion of the state appeared as a continuous, organic process of incorporation of peoples who naturally belonged to its dominion. Both China and Russia built on this ideology of incorporation to create their modern nationality policies.

One element notably different in the Russian ideology from the Chinese was the stress on religious opposition. Russian clerical chroniclers naturally brought Providence into their accounts of battles, describing them as God-inspired conflicts between pagan forces of darkness and Christian forces of light. The sins and vices of Christians explained Russian defeats, and God's grace and intervention in a just cause explained Russian victories. Chinese legitimation did not invoke sharp religious oppositions between victors and vanquished, because the Qing incorporative religious policy accepted Buddhism as part of the system. Nevertheless, Chinese official writers still saw Heaven's hand behind the emperor's victories, casting out the opponents as "bandits" who defied Heaven's will.

Chinese legitimation also invoked long-standing continuities with previous imperial regimes that claimed sovereignty over Central Eurasia. It too treated the resisting autonomous Mongol states as "internal" rebels on what was essentially Chinese territory. It drew a sharp cultural boundary between the "raw" barbarian Zunghars, who deserved extermination because they did not belong to the civilized realms, and the "cooked" Mongols, who had voluntarily submitted to Manchu rule. Although direct intervention by an active Providence was not invoked, the Chinese emperors did claim that their successful conquest reflected the natural order of the cosmos, and they inscribed this view on stelae all over the empire.

This effort to turn the unpredictable, mixed, pragmatic interactions of armies, states, and people into foreordained binary conflicts is of course common to many other rewritings of history. In the settled–Central Eurasian encounter, however, the inequality of resources makes it especially difficult to recover a genuinely polycultural perspective. The vast majority of surviving documents come from the victorious Chinese and Russian states. These states created themselves and constructed their own histories through their archives and through suppressing the archives and accounts of alternative versions.

Thirty years after the taking of Kazan' and Astrakhan, Russia began its second great eastward expansion.[70] The Cossack Ermak's defeat of the Khan of Kuchum in 1582 opened up the forests of Siberia to Russian settlement. Fortress by fortress, Russians established strongholds on the major rivers, moving steadily eastward until they reached the Pacific, and across the Bering Strait to Alaska.

The motives and process of this second Asiatic expansion differed greatly from those of the first. No major nomadic state ruler blocked the way. There was no need to play intricate diplomatic games in the style of steppe politics. The Tsar himself was not directly involved. Merchant-entrepreneurs *(promyshlenniki)* and Cossacks, semi-independent representatives of the state under the incomplete supervision of governors *(voevody)*, pushed the frontier forward and conducted the negotiations with local tribes. Extraction of wealth, not security, was the main goal. Furs, "soft gold," had provided critical sources of income for the Muscovite state since medieval times.[71] Exhaustion of nearer territories drove the Russians to pursue sable, otter, mink, and other fur-bearing animals farther eastward. Like slash-and-burn agriculturalists or Canadian and American pioneers, Russian tribute collectors drained a region of its surpluses, then moved on to exhaust new regions.

Expansion altered the identity of the emerging empire. The image of Siberia as a land of abundance under colonial domination, a Russian equivalent of El Dorado, grew firmly established in the seventeenth and eighteenth centuries. Peter's declaration in 1721 that Russia was now an *imperii* (empire), no longer a Tsardom, placed Russia in the European balance of power as an expanding empire with its own distinct Asiatic domains. The geographer Vasilii Tatishchev created the conceptual division of Russian Europe from Asia at the Ural Mountains, inspiring the cartographic delimitation of the border by the Swedish officer Philipp Johann von Strahlenberg.[72] Often neglected in Russian scholarship, the Siberian expansion into Asia shaped Russia's fate just as much as its better-known moves westward into Europe.

In its early stages, the Siberian expansion was linked to the struggle with Kazan'. The Principality of Novgorod had profited from trade in gray squirrel furs with Siberia since the twelfth century. Muscovy crushed Nov-

City of Tobolsk.

Tobolsk, the headquarters of the Russian administration of Siberia.

gorod in 1471, taking over its fur-bearing tributaries, but it expanded farther to the northeast to acquire the much more valuable sable furs. In 1483
and 1499 the Muscovites attacked to the northeast, crossing the Urals, past
Tiumen' to the Ob River, and subordinating the Iugri and Voguly tribes.
Moscow traded the luxury furs—sable and ermine, especially—with European and later Ottoman merchants. It also used the furs as diplomatic gifts
for the Crimean Khan, who in turn allowed Muscovite caravans to cross
the steppe and trade at his Black Sea ports. Moscow's expansion had two
goals: to acquire sables as tribute by directly subordinating the northeastern tribes, and to control the trade route bringing commercial furs to market at Ustiug. When Muscovy and Kazan' were at peace, Moscow's northeast aggression slackened, because it could rely on the Kazan' market for
furs; when hostility grew, Moscow pressed northeastward to secure its fur
supplies. The early sixteenth century saw reduced expansion to the northeast, but after the conquest of Kazan', Moscow resumed its Siberian attacks. The Siberian expansion continued and followed on the long-standing
Muscovite drive to gain economic resources from the eastern steppe and
forest zones at the expense of the formerly dominant Khanates of the region, Kazan' and Sibir'.[73]

Until the mid-sixteenth century, a Central Eurasian Khanate blocked direct Russian access to Siberia. It was founded in the late fifteenth century by
Nogai Tatars fleeing north from the Russian expansion south of the Urals.
Its capital was at the town of Sibir', or Kashlyk, near the future Russian city
of Tobolsk. Under Ediger Taibugid, the Khanate paid tribute to Muscovy,
but Khan Kuchum conquered Sibir' from Ediger in 1563, rejected tribute
payments, and gained control of a large expanse along the Tura, Tobol, and
Irtysh rivers. He then aimed to establish friendly relations with Ivan of
Moscow, sending tribute missions in 1570, but Russian settlers had already
begun moving into his territory. Gregory Stroganov had established a tax-
exempt settlement on the Kuma River in Perm in 1558. In 1579 a nephew
of Gregory's hired the Cossack *ataman* (headman) Ermak Timofeevich to
protect his possessions from Kuchum's raids. Ermak until this time had led
a freebooting pirate's life plundering caravans and Tsarist officials along
the Don and Volga rivers. Ermak, leading 840 men, in 1582 defeated Khan
Kuchum's forces at the Tura River and forced the local Ostiak and Vogul
tribes to pay tribute. He captured the Khan's capital, and the Khan fled
south. He offered the newly conquered lands to Tsar Ivan IV and begged
the Tsar to forgive his past crimes. By 1583–84 he reached the mouth of the
Tobol River, but in 1584 or 1585, besieged by Tatars, he drowned in the
river, and his troops retreated.[74] Part bandit, part folk hero, Ermak opened
up Siberia to Russian colonization.

Consolidation of the Siberian holdings continued under the reign of Boris Godunov (regent 1584–1598, Tsar 1598–1605), with the founding of the first major fortresses *(ostrogi)* at Tiumen in 1586 and Tobolsk in 1587. Tara, founded in 1594, became the main base for operations against Kuchum, driving him into the Nogai Horde in 1598, where he was put to death. According to George Lantzeff and Richard Pierce, the founding of Tara, designed to secure the safety of the trade route used by Bukharan merchants, "might also be considered the first step of the Russians toward central Asia."[75] Step by step the fortresses marched eastward—to Narym in 1596, Eniseisk in 1619, Yakutsk in 1632—reaching the Pacific coast in 1649.

The Russian strategy of conquest was based on rivers, portages, and the *ostrog* (fort).[76] First, Cossacks explored the river valleys, then *voevody* followed with soldiers who built a fort as a base to annex further territory. The dispersed tribal peoples of the north could not offer any systematic resistance, much as they detested the inexorable tribute exactions. The Tsars were mainly preoccupied with Russia's frontiers to the west or south, so they left the local *voevody* alone.[77]

Supplying even these small garrisons was difficult, since the Siberian forests produced low agricultural yields. The native peoples could live off meager agriculture because of their active hunting and fishing, but the Cossacks, ignorant of local resources, could not manage to support themselves. Desperately short of food, they plundered native villages to find caches of grain, dried meat, and fish. Permanent garrisons could only survive on regular shipments of supplies from Moscow and the west. During the "Time of Troubles" in the early seventeenth century, "hungry, without supplies and reinforcements, the garrisons dwindled from death and desertion."[78]

Vasily Poyarkov's expedition to the Amur in the 1640s excited great interest when he claimed to have discovered broad river valleys with fertile fields, a large population growing crops, and an abundance of sable and fish. He boldly proclaimed, "The warriors of the Sovereign will not go hungry in this land."[79] Before they discovered the Amur, his expedition spent a horrible winter eating bark and roots, during which forty of his men died of starvation. It was their own fault, because they had plundered the local Daur people to relieve their grain shortages, causing the natives to flee from the Russians and abandon their fields. The Amur promised great riches that could feed the other Siberian garrison towns, obviating the need to import supplies from faraway European Russia.

This was the main motivation behind the fortification of Albazin by Erofei Pavlovich Khabarov in 1650. When Khabarov discovered that the local Daurs paid tribute to China, he drew up grandiose plans, supported by Moscow, to attack the Chinese empire and seize its large supplies of gold and silver. Manchu troops attacked in 1652, but temporarily withdrew, convincing the Russians that they could occupy the region successfully. Wild rumors spread about the wealth of the Amur, leading farmers, *promyshlenniki*, and soldiers to desert their fields and garrisons and rush to the region.

But the Russians were soon disappointed. After further clashes with the Chinese troops, the expedition leader Onufry Stepanov reported, "As for grain, there is very little of it on the Amur because the Bogdoi Tsar [Chinese emperor] has forbidden the natives to sow grain and has ordered them to move into his territory."[80] In 1658 the Manchus surrounded and destroyed Stepanov and his men and killed him. From 1658 to 1672 the Amur became a no-man's-land, to whose defense Moscow was not committed. Caught in a freebooters' camp beyond Moscow's control, settlers suffered food shortages, because the desperado Russians had driven away the native peoples.

By the time of the Nerchinsk negotiations in 1689, Moscow had willingly given up the region, realizing that the Amur could not provide food for the Siberian centers of the fur trade. In short, food shortages in Siberia drew the Russian state to the Amur, but the primary importance of the fur trade led them to give it back to the Chinese. Contrary to many accounts, the Russians had no consistent commitment to territorial aggrandizement. Their drive east was in pursuit of trade and food, not land. Regional ecology determined the Siberian expansion, as the exhaustion of furs in one area of the north drove the traders and Cossacks farther east. Once the fur trade was exhausted on land, the fur drive continued to the Pacific, relying on sea otters as the main source. By the nineteenth century, when profits from fur declined, Siberia's image had changed from a land of abundance to a land of desolation. Once the seductive target of traders, adventurers, natural scientists, and runaway serfs, it became the land of exile, frost, and backwardness.[81]

In Alan Wood's words, "It was, after all, the conquest and settlement of Siberia in the late sixteenth and seventeenth centuries which more than anything else . . . originally transformed the land-locked medieval Tsardom of Muscovy into the mighty Russian Empire."[82] The conquests of Kazan' and Siberia played a crucial role in establishing the most distinctive feature of the Russian state: Its vast territorial expanse. The autocratic power of the Russian Tsar was the second feature most noted by European observers. But this aspect is easily misinterpreted. Although from the days of Ivan IV the Tsars claimed total authority over their dominions, in practice their control was much more limited. Likewise, it is misleading to interpret Russian state building as solely a coercive process.[83] The conquest and rule of Siberia involved a motley collection of different groups, none of which was completely under the thumb of the Russian state, and it was not part of a "master plan" conceived in an ambitious Tsar's head. Siberia contained a "complex symbiosis" of many participants, including "military servicemen, hunters, merchants, officials, Orthodox clergymen, fugitive serfs, entrepreneurs and tradesmen *(promyshlenniki)*, convicts, religious dissidents, foreign prisoners of war, cossacks, artisans, adventurers and vagrants." An "intricate web of mutual dependency existed between state and private individuals, military, hunters, peasants, craftsmen, merchants."[84] Even the provincial governors *(voevody)* dispatched by Moscow had great independent powers. They combined military and civil authority in their hands, they enjoyed great personal wealth from compulsory "gifts" and bribes extracted from their subjects, and they acted with almost autocratic power. But they too did not control entirely the influx of "wandering people" *(guliashchie liudi)*—who could be runaway serfs, deserting soldiers, or criminals fleeing the law—into these vast spaces. This great influx of voluntary fugitives in the eighteenth century increased the Russian population of Siberia from 169,000 adult males in 1719 to 412,000 in 1792.

Siberian and Chinese Frontiers

The Chinese and Russian frontier settlers expanding into Central Eurasia resembled each other in many ways. Both faced an alien presence, but not an entirely incomprehensible one. In this respect, they differed from the conquistadors of the New World. The Russian explorers of Siberia were not like their western European counterparts, who returned from the New World across the Atlantic Ocean with tales of wondrous discoveries and "marvelous possessions."[85] Seventeenth-century Muscovites seem to have had no real interest in the curious customs of other peoples. They did not try to incorporate them into elaborate schemes of classification, some of which included foreign peoples in the same category as animals. Muscovites stood out by virtue of their single-minded devotion to profit and lack of missionary zeal, quite different from the Spanish and Portuguese. Furthermore, because there were no "wide seas, high mountains, or other symbolically significant divides" between Russians and the Siberian peoples, the Cossacks, again unlike the Spanish conquistadors, moved only gradually into the territory. They "never entered a new world because . . . they had not been sent to a new world and because they had no 'public' that wanted to hear about new worlds."[86]

For the Chinese on the northwest frontier, Mongolia was not a new world either. Chinese rulers and soldiers had been familiar with nomads on the steppe for centuries. They certainly regarded them as an alien race, and often explicitly compared them to animals, but they did not regard entrance into the frontier in the seventeenth century as an exotic, radically new experience. Neither the Ming soldiers camped along the Great Wall nor the Manchu warriors on campaign felt the need to increase their store of knowledge about the exotic peoples of the steppe, except for immediate security needs. Whereas the Russians sought profit, and took interest only in places that held fur and ivory, the Chinese sought security, and focused only on immediate threats.

To be sure, the Chinese had a much longer experience with their frontier than the Russians did. Discussions of steppe peoples in China went back to the formation of the first states in the first millennium BCE. Frontier defense and diplomacy deeply influenced Chinese political philosophy from then on. Russian state creation came much later, in the ninth century CE. One could argue, on the one hand, that the Chinese frontier experience was deeper and more influential than the Russian one because of its prominence over time and in political debate. On the other hand, the continual gaze of Russians toward western Europe since the eighteenth century has led many historians to neglect Russia's equally important Central Eurasian roots. If we compensate for the neglect of the subject in Russian historiography, one could argue that frontier relations were just as significant for Russians as for Chinese.

Both Cossacks and Ming soldiers camped in static fortresses in remote locations, but the Cossacks were much more isolated. The Russian government mostly left the fortresses to their own devices, separated by hundreds of miles of forest. Each fort created its own self-sufficient community, based on extraction of tribute, small amounts of arable cultivation, and trade with local peoples. The Chinese forts, by contrast, were in constant contact by way of the sentry posts and signal fires along the Great Wall. Shipments of salt came from the interior in exchange for tea. Paradoxically, greater connection of the Chinese fortresses with the interior meant less integration with the steppe, while the greater isolation of the Siberian fortresses forced their occupants to adapt to their new environment. Trade with northern peoples was a necessity for survival in Siberia. Thus, despite oppressive relations of exploitation, the Russians did not view the Siberian peoples as utterly incomprehensible aliens. The Ming Chinese, by contrast, shored up their defenses to sharpen the differences between themselves and the alien, threatening nomads. Both empires, expanding on land frontiers, faced much more blurred boundaries between themselves and the natives than did the maritime empires, but their reactions differed. While the Chinese attempted systematically to integrate their defensive frontier regions with the core of the empire, the Russians left the garrisons to fend for themselves.

The eighteenth century marked a shift in the perspectives of both empires. Under Peter the Great, ideas of civilization defined by the Enlightenment entered Russia. Peter promoted scientific investigation of the minerals and birds and other curiosities of Siberia. Officials who described and classified its flora, fauna, and peoples began to realize that the Enlightenment ideals of rationality, cleanliness, and social graces excluded the natives. Now terms like "alien" and "wild men" *(dikii)* entered the Russian vocabulary. As the fur tribute declined, the Russian state took a greater interest in the region and concluded that the timid, helpless, *iasak*-paying people must be separated from the Russian middlemen and *iasak* collectors. The interest in classification, the replacement of a focus solely on trade with a view of native peoples as humans in their own right, and the effort to separate them from the destructive impact of commerce by state controls all have parallels to eighteenth-century Chinese frontier policies. The use of Siberia as an exile colony also parallels the Chinese use of Xinjiang.[87]

In sum, Siberia offers many points of comparison with China's colonial domains in Central Asia, particularly Mongolia and Xinjiang. Both regions mixed multiple ethnic, economic, and social categories. The conflict between native peoples and conquering settlers, the lure of trade, the promise of freedom combined with the enforcement of exile, and the predominance of military rule based on isolated garrison islands in the midst of a sea of desert or forest form common background conditions. The native peoples of Siberia were much smaller in number than those of Chinese Central Asia, and they offered only sporadic resistance. The Mongolian and Turkic peoples fought back much more stubbornly. Both in the end lost to the pressure of the armies and settlers of the expanding empires.

Disease, too, played an important role in weakening native resistance on both frontiers. Smallpox epidemics appeared in western Siberia in the 1630s, reducing one native group's population by half. Spreading east of the Yenisei in the 1650s, the disease wiped out 80 percent of the Northern Tungus and Yakuts. By the mid-eighteenth century, it reached the Buriat Mongols. The timing of the spread westward from China to the Mongols is very similar, and the effects on the Mongols were nearly as devastating. In addition to their superiority in arms and wealth, the Russians and Chinese had the great advantage of centuries of exposure to the germ pools of Eurasia, which had become increasingly united by the development of maritime trade. Like the Native Americans and Hawaiians, the isolated terrestrial inhabitants of Central Eurasia received this massive biological shock at the same time that they encountered superior weaponry and the lures of gold, tobacco, and alcohol.

Conquest and settlement influenced the state structure of both empires even before they came into contact with each other. The Russians faced only minimal opposition as they moved east, so they could easily control huge expanses with scattered fortresses and small garrisons up to the mid-seventeenth century. Their first contact with the congealing Mongolian state to the southwest led them to recognize that they had encountered a much more formidable foe. The building of Kuznetsk in 1618, the southernmost outpost of Siberian expansion, responded to Mongol raids and rival claims for tribute from the Kirgiz Kazakhs of the steppe.[88] During the eighteenth century, beginning with Peter the Great's ambition to systematize Russian domination, the Russians began building a fortified defense line against nomadic raids, stretching from Ust-Kamenogorsk in the west to Kuznetsk in the east. Every 100 kilometers they set up two defense positions with two hundred soldiers. The aim was to fortify the watersheds of all major rivers. Kuznetsk was rebuilt in stone in response to the threat of the Zunghar state, but with the decline of the Zunghars after the mid-eighteenth century, its significance diminished. This great wall-building campaign of the eighteenth century repeated the goals of Muscovy's seventeenth-century defense line in many aspects, as it also echoed the Ming defense line strategy of the sixteenth century.[89] In each case, the expanding state attempted to defend against repeated raids from a consolidating nomadic state by investing large amounts of resources in static fortified positions closely connected with one another. The Russian and Ming states resembled each other in this respect more closely than the Qing, who undertook an aggressive campaign to destroy the Mongol state at its source in the steppe.

Yet the curious combination of extreme autonomy with extreme autocracy distinguishes Russian state building from that of both Ming and Qing China. Although Tsar Ivan IV became notorious for the brutal terrorism of his private security force, the *oprichnina*, he also designated the powerful mercantile Stroganov family as nearly independent landowners on the eastern frontier, and implicitly permitted them to hire the bandit Cossack Ermak to create their own autonomous army. This form of "contract colonialism" has more in common with European maritime colonial empires than with Chinese practices. Europeans often delegated the initial conquest, by default or explicitly, to missionaries, adventurers, and trading companies. In one sense, the Stroganovs were the most businesslike of all colonial enterprises, nearly completely uncontaminated by rival impulses of religious conversion. Ming and Qing China, by comparison, mobilized merchant capital to develop its frontiers but always maintained official control of trading licenses. When private traders threatened the tea–horse trade, Ming officials shut down the system. Russian expansion into Siberia thus combined features of absolutist western European regimes, Central Eurasian political formations, and responses to nomadic state formation in the steppe analogous to those faced by Chinese dynasties.

3

Central Eurasian Interactions and the Rise of the Manchus, 1600–1670

As the Russians moved east, approaching Lake Baikal, they came into contact with groups of Mongolian nomads, who proved to be much more formidable adversaries than the Arctic peoples of western Siberia. The Mongols had last been united under Dayan Khan in the mid-sixteenth century. By the early seventeenth century they had fragmented once again into independent tribes, each under its own leader. In succession, from west to east, the Russian Cossacks and *voevody* came into contact with each of these major tribes during the early seventeenth century: first the Oirats (later known as Zunghars), then the Altyn Khans around the Altai, and later in the 1640s the Eastern Mongol (Khalkha) leaders, the Chechen, Tüsiyetü, and Jasaktu Khans.[1] (See Map 4.)

The Western Mongols during the Ming had been known as the Derben Oirat (Four Oirats), designated variously as including the Khoshot, Zunghar, Derbet, Torghut, and later Khoit and Choros tribes. In fact the term "Four Oirats" rarely indicated any formal confederation of these tribes, who spent most of their efforts fighting one another. In the sixteenth century some of the Oirats had moved west and subordinated themselves to Kuchum Khan of Siberia. The collapse of Kuchum's dominion under Russian attack set many Central Eurasian peoples in motion, some of whom sought protection from the Russians, while others aimed to maintain independent domains. The extension southward to the edge of the steppe of the Russian fortresses, particularly Tara, Tobolsk, Tomsk, and Kuznetsk, increased contacts between the two disparate ecological zones of the taiga and the steppe. Tobolsk was the town most constantly in contact with the

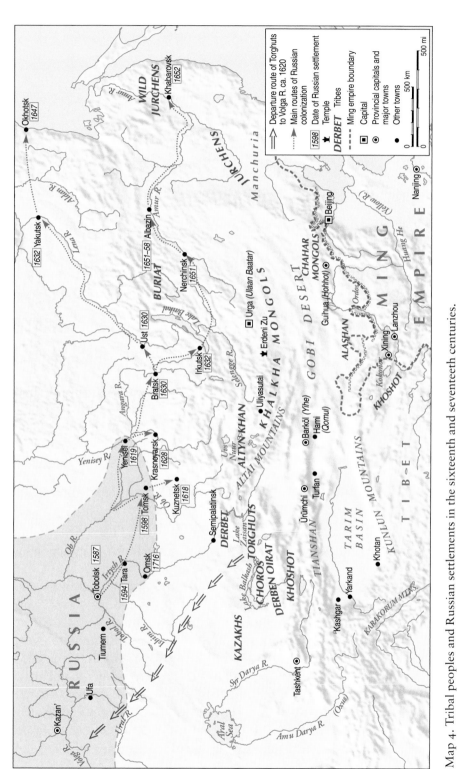

Map 4. Tribal peoples and Russian settlements in the sixteenth and seventeenth centuries.

Mongol family in the eighteenth century. The woman is preparing *kumyss*, a fermented drink, for a visiting lama.

Oirats. Tara, the farthest south of the Russian *ostrogy*, reported the first contacts with Oirats in 1606. Russian military expeditions against the Mongols in 1607 pushed them back in order to secure Russian monopoly of *iasak* payments.[2]

The Russians soon realized that with so few military forces facing the steppe warriors, they had to act carefully. The Mongols began to send embassies to explore negotiated relationships. The first Oirat embassy to Moscow in 1607–8 requested rights to pasture along the Irtysh and Ob rivers and to trade in Siberian towns in return for an alliance against their Mongol rival, the Altyn Khan. The first Altyn Khan (r. 1567–1627) had built a powerful state just south of the Mongolian Altai Mountains, which exerted pressure on the Oirats to the west.[3] The Russians granted pasture rights but refused to commit themselves to an alliance unless the Mongols swore allegiance to the Tsar and paid *iasak*. This became the constant refrain of

Encampment of the Derbet Mongol *ulus* near the Volga in the eighteenth century. The memorial in front was built to honor a deceased lama in 1772.

Russian–Mongol relations: Mongols aimed to use Russian backing against their rivals, Mongolian, Manchu, or Chinese, and to gain the benefits of trade at Russian fortress towns, while the Russians steadily pushed for the subordination of individual tribes to the Tsar.

In their dealings with the Oirats, Russian officials used the terms they inherited from their relations with the western steppe. They referred to the oaths of submission as *shert'*, a term derived from the Turkish and Arabic words *shart*, meaning a clause of a treaty.[4] From Moscow's point of view, these were not equal relations but the submission of non-Christian peoples to the Orthodox Tsar. Russians called offers of negotiation *chelobit'e,* or "petitions," literally "knocking of the head (on the ground)," derived from the Chinese term *ketou* transmitted through the time of Mongol rule. In Russian accounts, the Mongols begged officials to "allow them to be under our Tsar's lofty hand."[5] Whatever words they used, the Mongols' intentions were quite different. Mongols generally saw the Russian demands for oaths and tributes as temporary expedients, indicating alliances between equal powers, while the Russians saw these signs of allegiance as permanent recognition of subordination. Very few Mongolian leaders ever accepted permanent subordination to the Tsar, the one exception being the

An *obo*, or sacred Mongolian site, usually marked by a pile of rocks and prayer flags. This monument honors a deceased Khoshot prince.

Torghuts of the Western Mongols, who moved thousands of miles west to settle on the Volga River. Most maintained the essence of freedom in the steppe by preserving their rights to mobility.

In 1608 the Oirats defeated the Kazakhs and drove the Altyn Khan off to the southeast, so they no longer needed Russian protection. They rejected Russian demands for submission, but they increased trade activity at the fortresses of Tomsk and Tara. Mongols brought 550 horses to Tara in 1607 in exchange for money, writing paper, and cloth. Thus was established the essential basis of commercial exchange between Siberia and the steppe. The Siberians, like the Chinese, suffered most acutely from a shortage of horses, very difficult to raise in the forests. The Mongols supplied these essential transport animals from the grasslands in exchange for the manufactured products of settled civilization. Later there appeared the other essential source of Mongol revenue, furs, which they controlled as intermediaries in the trade between Russia and China.

The Russians nearly succeeded in obtaining the genuine submission of an

The Tibetan Buddhist deity Yamantaka embraces his consort. Mongolians and Tibetans respected the terrifying power of this manifestation of Buddha.

important Mongolian leader in 1614, when the Oirats suffered heavily from a cold winter that killed their herds and from losses to Altyn Khan which obliged them to pay him tribute. The governor of Tobolsk offered peace to the suffering Oirats if they would submit to the Tsar, and sent the embassy of Ivan Petrov and Ivan Kunitsyn to stay for two months with leading Mongol princes. Dalai Taisha, the strongest leader of the Derben

Oirats, claimed to be willing to submit to the Tsar, and offered ten thousand warriors to serve in attacks on the Nogai. When Dalai reneged on his offer, the governor prepared military expeditions to enforce his subordination, but he was rebuked by Moscow, which ordered him to maintain peace with the Mongols. Russia in the early seventeenth century, weakened by wars with the Poles and Swedes, wanted to avoid military action in the east.

During this mission, the Russian envoys tried to learn as much as they could about the fabled Chinese empire. They asked about its size and population, its allies, and the beliefs of its people. They obtained some valuable though misleading information from their Mongol hosts, who told them that the Chinese lived in brick cities, on large rivers, whose names they did not know, and their ruler (the Wanli emperor) was called "Taibykankan" (Da Bogda Khan?). According to the Oirats, the Altyn Khan and the Chinese shared the same language and beliefs. Clearly, all they knew of China were the Mongols settled near the Ming dynasty frontier.[6]

Khara Khula (d. 1634/35?), the Zunghar prince, also sought Russian aid. In 1620 he sent an embassy to Moscow and received in return the first edict of a Russian Tsar to a Mongol leader, stating, "You, Khara Khula, will submit yourself to Russia and gain our protection from your enemies."[7] But relations between Russia and the Oirats were broken off for fifteen years as Khara Khula began his wars with the Altyn Khan Ombo Erdeni to his east.

Meanwhile, to escape civil war, the Torghut Mongols (known to the Russians as Kalmyks) began moving west, toward the Russian fortresses of Ufa and Tiumen. The Torghuts also refused genuine submission to the Tsar, but they wanted to trade horses at Siberian towns for furs, rifles, and iron. Moscow rejected their demands. When, after 1623, they began raiding Russian territories and *iasak* peoples, Moscow ordered renewal of regular trade if the Kalmyks would maintain their distance from the Russian towns and cease their raids. In the 1630s the Torghuts began their great migration across the Kazakh steppe to their ultimate settlement on the banks of the Volga.[8] Other groups continued to migrate there through the end of the 1640s, and they kept up ties with their tribesmen back in Mongolia. Thus one part of the Oirat confederation became a genuine dependent of the Russian Tsar as the remaining tribes unified under Zunghar leadership in western Mongolia.

Next to the Torghuts, the early Altyn Khans were the most active of the Mongols in seeking Russian aid. Russian relations with the Altyn Khan, who ruled northwest Khalkha Mongolia, differed from those with the Oirats, because of the Khan's proximity to China. In 1616 the Khan enticed a Russian embassy with the offer of access to the China trade, one month away through his territory, in return for supplies of rifles and furs. The embassy of Ivashko Petlin, Russia's first major embassy to China, did pass through Altyn Khan's territory unobstructed, but when the Khan asked for military aid against his Oirat rivals, the Tsar, angered, cut off relations through the 1620s. Here too the Russians followed a consistent approach, aiming to stay out of internecine conflicts while securing access through Mongolian territory to China. Likewise, the Mongols, for their part, aimed to draw the Russians to their side through tactical declarations of submission to the Tsar. The new Altyn Khan in 1631 renewed relations with Russia, offering to swear an oath of allegiance, in order to gain aid against his new rivals to the south. He also sent the first tea caravan to Russia from China in 1638. By the end of the 1640s, however, the Altyn Khan had allied with the rising Manchu power, and his successors refused to recognize previous oaths sworn to the Tsar. Interestingly, in the 1660s, the last Altyn Khan, Luvsan, asked for Russian aid to help him build a fortress on the Khemchik River at Tuba, but he was refused. His submission to the Qing in 1681 and his death in 1682 ended the autonomous power of the northwest Khalkhas.

The Russians entered the Mongolian steppes just as the fragmented tribal heads were beginning to unify themselves under Oirat leadership, and as the Ming dynasty was in decline. China had little political influence in the region, but the lure of its market for furs drew the Russians steadily eastward. Even in this early period it became clear that Russo-Mongol relations would be tense, because Mongols refused to submit unconditionally to the Tsar, and Russians mainly considered Mongolian territory a way station to China. Chinese nationalist historiography to the contrary, the Russian Tsar never allied with the Oirat–Zunghars against the Chinese state, but despite claims of Russian and Mongolian historians, their relations were not uniformly harmonious.

Building the Zunghar State

While the Ming fell and the Russians encroached, from the late sixteenth to late seventeenth century the Western Mongols tried to create a unified state, against great odds. The Oirats in the late sixteenth century were extremely fragmented. After individual chieftains lost battles with Eastern Mongolian chiefs, they were driven west to the Altai Mountains. At the same time they were attacked from Kazakhstan and from Turfan. By the 1590s some Oirat princes had been forced to submit to the Kazakhs in order to keep their pastures.

Altyn Khan began a major drive against the Oirats in the 1580s. When he sent an army searching for their leader, he found no one unified confederation but instead autonomous princes scattered along the Irtysh River. In 1616 Russian envoys who contacted the Oirats learned that they were divided into four tribes: the Derbet, led by Dalai Taiji; the Zunghar under Khara Khula; the Khoshot under Baibagas; and the Torghut under Kho Urluk. Dalai Taiji was the strongest among the four, but he was not the Khan. Baibagas of the Khoshot was called Khan, since he was descended from the Khans who founded the Oirats in the thirteenth century.[9] Although Baibagas Khan (d. ca. 1630) served as the leader of the assembly of princes (*chulgan dargi*, Ch. *qiuergan*), he had no real independent power.[10] Each of the Khans controlled his own people autonomously. In response to Altyn Khan's threat, however, Baibagas Khan was able to collect a joint army of thirty thousand Khoshot, eight thousand Derbet, six thousand Choros, four thousand Khoit, and two thousand Torghuts.[11] Although this was a first step toward united action, the Oirats remained divided by constant rivalry between the princes, especially between Baibagas Khan and the Zunghar chief Khara Khula. Internal struggles over pasturelands countered by efforts to unify in response to outside threats would sharpen considerably in the early seventeenth century.

At a general assembly in 1616–17 the Oirats agreed to establish internal peace and not to help those who attacked fellow Oirats, but the rivalry of the princes continued. At the same time certain tribes began to establish relations with the Russians moving across Siberia. Kho Urluk of the Torghuts had begun negotiations for submission to the Tsar with the governor of Tara in 1607.[12] When the great war with Altyn Khan broke out in 1608, most Oirats lost interest in Russian ties, as they briefly achieved unity against the threat from the east. But in the 1620s both Khara Khula and the Altyn Khan sent embassies to Moscow seeking aid against each other. Khara Khula, notably, expressed his need for iron weapons. Moscow accepted Khara Khula's submission, as noted in the edict quoted earlier, but refused to intervene on either side. By 1622 the dissatisfied Khara Khula and other Oirats were raiding Kuznetsk for weapons.[13]

During the 1620s the Oirats succeeded in putting together a coalition of the four tribal leaders to march against the Altyn Khan. In the unified Oirat army, Baibagas Khan commanded sixteen thousand troops, Khara Khula led six thousand troops, and three other leaders commanded a total of fourteen thousand men.[14] In 1623 the combined forces attacked the Altyn Khan, with indecisive results. They took many captives, but Khara Khula lost many of his own men. Further battles led to victory over the Altyn Khan in 1628–29. Oirats who had fled for protection to the Siberian fortresses were now able to move back into their homelands in Zungharia and eastern Turkestan.

Khara Khula tried to increase his influence by mediating disputes over in-heritance, but he remained only one of the prominent leaders within the Oirat confederation. A major civil war then tore the Oirats apart in 1625. When one Khoshot prince died, his brothers Baibagas Khan and Chokur quarreled over the division of his inheritance. Khara Khula and Dalai Taiji of the Derbet both tried to mediate, but the dispute was resolved only after Chokur mobilized a ten thousand–man army against his brother and de-feated him.[15] Even when the Oirats faced a serious threat from Altyn Khan, they could not restrain themselves from internecine conflict. Both Khara Khula and Dalai Taiji tried to strengthen their unity, but the tribal structure remained unstable.

At the same time, Kho Urluk began the negotiations that would lead his Torghuts across the steppe to the Volga.[16] Most of the Torghuts had left for the Volga with about fifty thousand families (200,000 to 250,000 people), removing the major source of division within Zungharia. The Torghuts' emigration reduced the Oirats' total strength but aided their unity by re-moving the most disgruntled tribes from Khara Khula's control.

Tibetan Buddhist influence in western Mongolia proceeded more slowly than in the east but became a powerful force in the late seventeenth century. Baibagas was dissuaded from entering a monastery, but many Mongol aris-tocrats offered their sons to the monasteries. Zaya Pandita (1599–1662), the adopted son of Baibagas, strengthened the Western Mongols' unity through a close alliance with Tibet.[17] In 1616 he was sent to a monastery in Tibet, where he studied Buddhism and tantric arts for twenty-two years. When he attended the installation of the seventeen-year-old Dalai Lama in 1635, the Panchen Lama gave him the mission to spread Buddhist teach-ings among his Mongol people through translations of Tibetan texts. On his return home in 1639, he first went to Baibagas's son Ochirtu Taiji, who became the Chechen Khan, but soon received invitations from the other top leaders of the Mongols, the Jasaktu and Tüsiyetü Khans, and visited the pastures of the four chief Oirat leaders, including the leader of the Torghuts. He spent nearly every year of his life traveling from one tribe to another, in each place conducting funerary and matrimonial rituals, found-ing temples, preaching, fasting, and translating Tibetan texts. In 1648 he devised the Todo script, a variant of the Mongolian script designed spe-cially for the Western Mongolian dialect. During his life, he translated over 177 valuable Tibetan Buddhist texts into Mongolian. In 1650, on one trip to Tibet, he brought 110,000 taels of silver, which he donated for the pro-duction of statues and gave in support of the Tashilumpo monastery. He also asked the Dalai Lama his opinion of the new Qing emperor.

Impressed by his great knowledge of Tibetan Buddhism, the Khans gave him disciples, servants, and large herds of horses and cattle. In return, he was able to exert considerable political influence. Zaya Pandita was the key mediator between the left and right wings of the Oirats when they went to war against each other after 1657, and he attended the large assembly *(chulgan)* held in 1660 to reconcile the opposing factions. When he died on his return from Tibet in 1662, his disciples brought his ashes back to Lhasa, where he was honored by both the Red Hat and Yellow Hat lamas, and the Dalai Lama had a large silver statue made of him. Zaya Pandita founded the Oirat literary tradition, kept the Mongolian Khans linked to one another with his constant traveling and preaching, and ensured the dominance of Buddhism in western Mongolia. Although he failed to prevent the Mongols from fighting one another, he kept the rival Khans in contact, constantly emphasizing their common bonds as patrons of the Buddhist church.

The nineteenth-century Russian explorer Nikolai Przewalski found Buddhism to be a "religion that sapped vitality and hindered progress" in Mongolia, as did Owen Lattimore, who thought that Buddhism withdrew the most productive Mongols from pastoralism and paralyzed the nobility by fixing their territories around monastic settlements.[18] But Buddhism did not have the same effects in the seventeenth century, when the Oirats were building their state. Zaya Pandita offered the Khans their strongest legitimating force beyond the claim to military superiority and descent from Chinggis Khan. Lamas offered important resources to the Mongolian chiefs, giving them legitimacy as reincarnated Khans, providing them with a writing system, and linking them to a cultural system distinct from that of either the steppe or China. Although Ming officials found Buddhism useful among the Mongols, they could not control what the Mongols made of it. Only the Manchus, in the eighteenth century, devised methods to ensure that Mongols and Tibetan lamas subordinated themselves to the Qing state.

Most scholars of this period, from Peter Simon Pallas in the eighteenth century to I. Ia. Zlatkin and Hiroshi Wakamatsu more recently, have argued that when Khara Khula died in 1635, he passed on a legacy of progress toward unification that allowed his son Batur Hongtaiji (r. 1635–1653) to declare himself sole leader of the Oirats, and the founder of the Zunghar Khanate. Miyawaki Junko, however, has severely criticized this interpretation. In her view Batur never became Khan, because only patrilineal descendants of Chinggis Khan could assume this title.[19] The true unification of the Oirats as a "Khanate" occurred only in 1678, when Galdan received the title of Boshoktu Khan from the Dalai Lama after killing his father-in-law and rival, Ochirtu Chechen Khan. In her view, the erroneous interpretation of the Zunghars as having created a "nation-state" under Batur as Khan derives from reading sources created in the eighteenth century instead of looking at the seventeenth century itself.

Miyawaki's interpretation fits well with our project of reconstructing the contingencies of state formation in this period, and her critique of retrospective application of inappropriate concepts is well founded. Even though Batur's power has been exaggerated, however, we may still at least credit him with an incomplete state-building *project,* one that aimed at further centralization and stabilization of the Oirat community under Zunghar rule.

The title of Khan was held by the Khoshot leader Gush Khan, who took it on the death of Baibagas in 1630. Gush Khan married his own daughter to Batur Hongtaiji, so their family relations were close. But Batur, as Miyawaki notes, could not be the undisputed leader of the Oirats because he had no direct Chinggisid ancestors and could only name himself "Hongtaiji," second in command to the Khan. Gush Khan, Batur, and Ochirtu Taiji marched together in a military alliance against the Kazakhs in 1634–35. Gush Khan also led an expedition to Lhasa in 1636 and Batur accompanied him in expeditions to Kokonor in 1637.[20]

Batur invites comparison to his Manchu contemporary Hong Taiji. Like the Manchu leader, he tried to centralize power among the tribal chiefs, although, unlike the Manchus, he could not claim the supreme title of Khan. (Among the Manchus, the title did not require descent from Chinggis.) Circumstances favored him, but his legitimacy was never secure. Threats from the divided Kazakhs in the west and from the Altyn Khan in the east declined. The departure of the Torghuts had reduced population pressure on the grasslands. In 1635 the Khoshots, 100,000 of them, had moved to Kokonor to create their own state. Those who did not want to subordinate themselves to Batur chose exit over resistance. Batur aimed to induce the breakaway groups to return to a united Zunghar leadership, along with the Eastern Mongols, but he could not conduct military campaigns against them.

Instead, he strengthened ties with the Russians, renewing diplomatic relations after a hiatus of fifteen years. He sent thirty-three embassies to Moscow during his reign, and received nineteen in return from Siberia.[21] By arranging for the return of Cossack war captives and the settlement of border conflicts, he competed with the Altyn Khan for the favor of the Tsar. Two major sources of conflict were at least temporarily resolved: the access to salt sources and the allegiance of the Kirgiz. Rivalry over the Kirgiz tribes living on the Yenisei River grew in 1641 when Batur claimed the right to collect tribute from them, rejecting the claim of the *voevoda* of Tobolsk likewise to collect tribute. War was avoided by an ingenious device, the recognition of dual sovereignty, obliging the unfortunate Kirgiz to pay *iasak* to both the Russians and the Zunghars.[22] At the same time, Batur was allowed to expand duty-free trade in Tobolsk, Tara, Tiumen, and especially Tomsk. A separate quarter of Tobolsk grew up, called the Tatar Settlement. Trade was mostly conducted under the name of diplomatic gift giving, in which the Zunghars exchanged their horses, cattle, sheepskins, and furs for handicrafts made of cloth, leather, silk, silver, walrus ivory, and metal.[23] "Bukharan" merchants from Turkestan prospered as the intermediaries in this new Central Asian trade. The Russians, by now well aware that the trade route to China passed through Zunghar territory, favored the growth of peaceful trade relations with the Mongols.

Batur demonstrated a clear goal of accumulating resources of trade, agriculture, and population in order to build his state's power. In 1638 he asked the Siberian *voevoda* to provide pigs and chickens to be raised on Zunghar farms in newly annexed areas of Turkestan. In 1639 he asked for guns, armor, and bullets. Told that it was impossible to obtain these items in Tobolsk, he sent a mission to Moscow for them. In 1650 he demanded greater "gifts" from the Tobolsk governor in order to ensure the continuation of peaceful trade relations. At the same time he asked for Russian artisans, including stonemasons, carpenters, blacksmiths, and weapon makers, to be sent to Zungharia.[24] Russia agreed to send pigs and chickens but refused to supply weapons makers, consistently avoiding the promotion of arms flows out of Russia to Mongolia. From 1636 to 1638 Batur did, however, begin building his capital, a stone fortress and monastery at Kubak Zar between Lake Yamysh and the Irtysh River.[25] At first it was a small city with only around three hundred people. Russian emissaries reported that Chinese and Mongol artisans built it of stone, with walls 100 meters around and 6 meters high. Chinese, Mongols, Bukharans, and lamas lived in separate districts. Batur had Turkestani peasants brought in to cultivate the fields. Fortresses surrounded the capital, containing four cannon brought from China. Batur Hongtaiji himself pastured about seven days away and visited the town from time to time. He asked the Russians to send him more artisans, and he built several other towns in the next four years. Like Altan Khan before him, Batur had begun to lay the foundations of a settled regime, but his city did not last long. After his death, it decayed, and now no traces are left.

Salt became another key resource for the growing state. It was perhaps the scarcest essential nutrient on the northwest frontier, and its supply had been a major focus of Ming frontier policy. Siberian settlers also needed salt in their diet, and there were no sources of it in the forest zone. The Russians and Mongols had clashed over access to salt since the early seventeenth century. In 1611 the Mongols had captured some sources near Tara, forcing the Russians to mount a military expedition to drive them off. In 1613 Siberian settlers arrived at the great salt lake of Yamysh. This lake, however, lay in a region under Zunghar domination. Until 1620 the Russians developed the lake and extracted major supplies of salt with no opposition. Then the Mongols arrived and blocked further production. As armed conflicts broke out, the Russians planned to build a fortress at the site, but they gave up the idea, realizing that the difficulty of access and the lack of pastures and fields prevented support for resident troops. Instead they sent periodic military detachments to collect salt as needed. But in 1634, two thousand Mongols attacked the Russian military expedition. Batur offered to replace armed conflict with peaceful trade. In 1635 the Tsar agreed to allow Mongol salt mining at the lake, while Batur approved regular salt caravans traveling from Lake Yamysh to Russia in exchange for increased trade. Around Lake Yamysh grew a mercantile settlement, which became the largest trading center in Siberia until the designation of Kiakhta as the China trade center in 1689. Fairs lasting two to three weeks attracted merchants from all over Central Eurasia, who sold horses, Chinese goods, and slaves (despite prohibitions) to Russia in return for metals, textiles, and glass. The Russians promoted the growth of civilian trade but strictly forbade the export of weapons and gunpowder.[26]

The great assembly *(khuriltai)* of 1640 represented the high point of efforts to gather the Mongols together in a loosely united confederation.[27] It gathered the Khans of the Khalkha Mongols, Kokonor, the Volga Kalmyks, and representatives of the Tibetan church in Tarbaghatai to discuss ways to avoid internecine conflict. Only the Chahars, already subordinate to the Manchu state, were excluded. The assembly agreed on a code, which aimed to regulate disputes, unite the Mongols against outside threats, and increase the powers of Khans and princes.[28] Attacks by one tribe against another would be punished by fines, tribes would aid one another against outside attack, and each prince would protect his own pastures and return fugitives from other tribes who fled to him for protection. Tibetan Buddhism was declared the official church of the Mongols.[29]

Most historians credit Batur Hongtaiji and Zaya Pandita with bringing together this great alliance of Khans and princes, but Miyawaki demonstrates that the leading force was the Jasaktu Khan of the Khalkhas, and that the assembly was held in Khalkha, not Oirat, territory. The Jasaktu Khan faced the most imminent threat from the rising power of the Manchus and had the greatest incentive to form an alliance against them. The Mongol-Oirat code, however, did not create a founding law of a new Mongol or Zunghar state; like earlier Mongol laws, it applied only to relations between tribes and left each Khan autonomous in his own domains.[30]

In 1640 the Manchus were not yet a serious enough threat to most of the Mongols to provide a strong stimulus for a united front. Although some of the southern Mongols had submitted to them, the Manchus were still building their state in Manchuria and concentrating on the battle with the Ming. The code's provisions were also internally directed. The code strengthened the powers of individual Khans to settle disputes within their domains but left them completely sovereign and took no steps toward a larger confederation. Just at the time when the Manchus were building a powerful centralized state based on a banner system that crosscut tribal allegiances, and Japan's unifiers were beginning to combine a strengthened feudalism with a centralized military regime, the Mongols achieved only partial internal consolidation without creating an even loosely united confederation. In the 1640s serious internal wars broke out among the Oirats, and a decade later the Khalkhas and the Khoshots of Kokonor were cooperating with the new Qing state.

Although the *khuriltai* of 1640 could have been an important step toward the institutionalization of the Mongol state, it lagged far behind its rival states in formation in Russia, Manchuria, and Japan. Early modern states were built in two stages: first, by a local prince who attained supremacy over his military followers, and second, by a federation of the princes under a recognized military leader. In Japan, for example, Tokugawa Ieyasu consolidated his shogunate by combining strong local *daimyō* power within the domains with a careful balancing of *daimyō* forces against one another. The Manchu leaders created new organizations, the banners, that incorporated some of the tribal leadership in non-tribal organizations. They borrowed the idea from Chinggis Khan's ten thousand–man units *(tümen)*. The Mongol successors to Chinggis, however, in the much vaster spaces of Central Eurasia could not join under one recognized leader. Instead they remained divided into several rival groups that could at best join in temporary alliances with one another, but could just as easily ally with non-Mongol neighbors on all sides.

Batur could not be Khan, but he could build a city, increase his people's prosperity through trade, and participate in efforts to construct a coalition against the Qing. On his death in 1653, however, all his efforts fell apart. One of his nine sons, Sengge, succeeded him, but Sengge's brothers disputed his control over half of his father's people. They killed him in 1670. One brother, Galdan, who had been sent to a Tibetan lamasery, returned to take charge during this succession crisis. Galdan became the great unifying leader the Mongols needed, as he expanded the Zunghar state into the largest power in Central Eurasia.

The Rise of the Manchus

Many historians have described the astonishing conquest of the Chinese empire by the Manchus, a tribal people dispersed through the forests and fields of China's northeast frontier. Here I concentrate on three themes that will recur throughout our story: the struggle between clan-based organization and bureaucracy, the exploitation of an agrarian base, and the role of Manchu–Mongol relations in forming the early Manchu state. Each of these themes highlights the interactions between the growing Manchu state and its neighbors in Central Eurasia while emphasizing similarities of the challenges faced by all three.

The predominant theme in most studies of the rise of the Manchus has been the transformation of the clan society of the Manchu tribes into a centralized bureaucratic state. Franz Michael attributed this change from "feudal" to bureaucratic relations to the influence of Chinese advisers and classical texts. In his view the Manchus, like previous conquerors, needed to adopt Chinese ways before the conquest in order to succeed: "There was no essential difference between conquest from outside and from inside the country . . . [A]s a general system (the Manchus) had to accept the Chinese way of life and Chinese civilization."[31]

Unlike later scholars, Michael argued that "the Manchus never became completely absorbed into the Chinese culture. They remained the privileged group of conquerors; the group which retained part of the military and feudal past all through its history." Yet he still believed that "it was the Chinese civilization which had to be recognized as [the Manchus'] political and ideological standard." For Michael, the Manchuness of the Qing derived only from the early years of conquest; it was not embedded in the permanent institutions of the state.[32]

Michael's main source was the *Kaiguo Fanglue*, published in 1789 under the Qianlong emperor's aegis, but this text was selectively edited in order to produce a spurious impression of a Confucianized Qing regime that was the legitimate successor to the Ming. It fails to reveal evidence of conflicts between the state founder, Nurhaci, and his nobles and family, and it provides little evidence of the economic crises that plagued the early Manchu state. More recent studies, relying on the valuable Manchu language records in the Old Manchu archive, give a very different picture. They carry on the tradition of "Altaic" interpretations of the Qing established by Japanese scholars in the early twentieth century.[33] The Manchu state builders did not smoothly acculturate themselves to Chinese ways as they built their state; there were major internecine conflicts within the elite over this wrenching transformation. Chinese influence in the form of printed texts was negligible in the early years, because very few texts were translated into or published in Manchu, and most of them were not philosophical classics. Instead, the bureaucratization of the state must be seen as a pragmatic, contingent reaction to the conquest process itself, influenced by advice from surrendered Chinese of the frontier regions, but also from Mongolian allies, Manchu nobles, and bicultural "transfrontiersmen" (in Frederic Wakeman Jr.'s term) who spanned the cultural gaps among the three peoples. The state lurched from brilliant military victories to severe subsistence crises; much of the discontented Chinese population under its rule revolted, but other Chinese officials supported the Manchus against the Ming. Succession crises threatened to dismantle it, but centralization overcame factionalism in the end.

Bloody tanistry plagued the Manchu state from its origins. Under Ming influence, the Manchus could also invoke the principle of primogeniture, but not as a regular practice. Nurhaci (1559–1626), the founder of the Manchu state, began his career of military conquest in 1583 in alliance with a few hundred men of his tribe, a confederation with his eldest son, Cuyeng, and his younger brother Shurhaci. By 1609 the three men had fallen out; Nurhaci had Shurhaci killed in 1611. Nurhaci at first felt obliged to appoint Cuyeng his successor, but he later denied the succession to Cuyeng and had him killed in 1615. Nurhaci named no successor on his death in 1626. Like the Mongols and their ancestors the Jurchens, the Manchus found it difficult to agree on the uncontested rule of a single leader.[34]

Military conquest, however, reduced internecine wrangling as it brought more people under the military state's control and provided the human resources for further expansion. As Nurhaci and his army subjugated the rival tribes of the Northeast, they incorporated them as companies (niru) of three hundred men each within the army-state.[35] The Hada tribes, defeated in 1599, became some of the first companies that went into the formation of the banners, the most vital institution of the Manchu state. The banner system began to form as early as 1601, derived primarily from the Manchu practice of organizing military maneuvers as hunting expeditions. The Eight Banners (Ch. Qi, Ma. gûsa), created in 1615, laid the basis for the multiethnic coalition that Nurhaci proclaimed as the Latter Jin empire in 1616. As Mark Elliott points out, the banner companies (niru) maintained ethnic homogeneity, even though the banners *(gûsa)* mixed Mongol, Chinese, and Manchu companies together. Thus the banners flexibly incorporated members of several different ethnic groups while maintaining their distinctiveness. The banners cut across kinship connections within the Manchus, tying them together in a new military and civil organization that owed total loyalty to its commander.[36]

The banners fixed new ties of solidarity at the base of the new state, overriding the kinship loyalties of the early tribes of Manchuria and Mongolia. Yet each banner commander remained nearly autonomous, a powerful warlord with loyal troops under him. To create a centralized state, Nurhaci still needed to unify it at the top. In 1615, along with the banners, he established the *sunja amban* (Five State Councilors), vesting leadership in the hands of Nurhaci and five of his sons-in-law. He named his four remaining sons Hosoi Beile (Senior Chieftains). Although Nurhaci appointed the rulers of each banner, these men had the power to choose the leader's successor, and commanders "held [the banners] virtually as private property."[37]

As the Manchus conquered Liaodong and incorporated Chinese into their state, Nurhaci used his new subjects to limit the power of the Manchu nobles, or *beile*. The *beile* were either relatives of Nurhaci or rulers of independent tribes before the conquest. They controlled their own people and captives, but the Chinese were directly subordinated to Nurhaci as Khan, not to the *beile*. Nurhaci kept moving his capital farther westward and southward toward the Chinese border and away from the *beile*'s territory, against their resistance. The *beile* Adun was killed in 1621 for defying the "order of the state" *(gurun i doro)* by sowing discord, probably for refusing to accept the move of the capital. Nurhaci also selected eight scholars, called *baksi*, as his principal advisers.[38] These men, like Dahai (d. 1632) and Erdeni Baksi (d. 1623), were fluent in Manchu, Mongolian, and Chinese. Some may have been originally of Han origin, but their ancestors went native and joined Manchu clans on the frontier. They wrote proclamations in Chinese and translated Chinese classical texts. As "transfrontiersmen," they were multicultural in their background, not simple agents of sinicization. By offsetting the power of the *beile*, they served as crucial aids to reinforcing the Khan's central power.[39]

Nurhaci had recommended collective rule by the senior *beile* in his last testament: "The one who succeeds me should not be one who relies on force. If this type of man becomes ruler, I fear that by relying on the power of his position he would offend Heaven. Furthermore, one man's wisdom is no match for the wisdom of many. You eight men are the leaders of the Eight Banners, and if you can rule the nation with a common purpose, then nothing will be lost."[40]

His eighth son, Hong Taiji (1592–1643), however, as commander of both the Bordered Yellow and White Banners, had a decisive advantage in the succession struggle. He probably usurped power by force after Nurhaci's death and soon took immediate steps toward autocratic rule, contravening his father's intentions.[41] He eliminated Amin, Daisan, and Manggultai, three of the senior *beile* who had ruled with his father. Amin, for example, who attacked and looted Korea against his orders and massacred Chinese in Yongping, was indicted for crimes and imprisoned in 1629.[42] By 1636 Hong Taiji had enlarged the Chancellery, which originated in his father's eight *baksi,* set up the Six Boards and the Three Courts, recruited more Chinese scholars, and dismissed the *beile* from the boards. The Deliberative Council of Ministers (Yizheng Wang Dachen Huiyi), created in 1622 and expanded in 1637, derived from Nurhaci's collective advisory bodies. But Nurhaci's councils included the eight highest-ranking *beile,* while Hong Taiji excluded Manchu princes from his council. He included only the direct administrators of the banners.[43]

Hong Taiji's Chinese advisers urged him to invade China quickly, and they supported the concentration of power in his hands. Newly acquired wealth from conquest, they argued, should go directly to the Khan, to be distributed by him to the *beile.* They rejected the collective rule of the *beile* and the principle of each *beile* passing out his loot autonomously to his followers. As one memorialist put it, "Ten sheep with nine shepherds will create disorder and disunity."[44] This move toward authoritarianism clearly benefited the Chinese advisers, who expected large material rewards from conquest of the rich lands to the south in return for their loyalty to the Khan, at the expense of *beile* who wanted to maintain autonomy.

In short, Hong Taiji, at his death in 1643, left a seemingly permanent legacy of a strong authoritarian state. He had named the Manchus as a single people, elevated himself to supreme leader above the nobility, created new governmental institutions, and announced the Manchu "historical mission," the creation of a new dynasty, named Qing, to replace the Ming. Rejecting the earlier designation of the state as the Latter Jin, Hong Taiji deliberately signaled a break in continuity both from Ming to Qing and from his Jurchen ancestors, stating openly: "The Ming is not a descendant of Song and I am not descendant of Jin; times are different."[45]

The new state was, however, still fragile. Quarrels over the succession under the regency that followed Hong Taiji's death could easily have led to its collapse. From the death of Hong Taiji in 1643 to the Kangxi emperor's

---

Hong Taiji (r. 1627–1643), the second ruler of the Manchu state.

assertion of his personal rule in 1669, six factions ruled successively as regents over the fledgling state.[46] Except for the Shunzhi emperor's personal
rule from 1653 to 1661, these groups were dominated by Manchu noble
banner commanders. These nobles had varying policies toward the adoption of Chinese ways or the incorporation of Chinese into high-level positions. Dorgon (r. 1643–1651) was the first to introduce Chinese officials
into high administrative posts, but the regency led by Oboi (r. 1661–1669)
promoted a return to old Manchu ways, downgrading Chinese institutions
and officials.

The Manchu reaction, however, did not imply the reassertion of *beile*
control. In fact, the regents also promoted the ascendancy of the central
ruler over his Manchu nobles, and they helped to institutionalize emergent
bureaucratic organizations whether derived from Ming precedents or new
creations of the rising state. Bureaucratic and autocratic supremacy over
collective noble rule was a continuous trend during this period, but it was
not a smooth course toward "sinicization." The drive to autocracy was
powered by the military and administrative demands of the expanding
state, and not by any growing acceptance of the superiority of Chinese civilization. Attitudes toward the role of Chinese institutions in the state could
change, but the progressive ascendancy of the Khan and his advisers over
the *beile* could not easily be reversed.

Dorgon, as regent for the five-year-old Shunzhi emperor, completed the
conquest of Beijing in 1644.[47] He began the "dyarchy" policy of having former Ming and Manchu officials serve together in high administrative posts.
("Dyarchy" is in fact a misnomer, since Chinese bannermen were a third
significant group of officials who fit neither category.) He also abolished the
assignment of Manchu princes to the Six Boards. Upon Dorgon's death in
1650, factional rivalry between the Manchu regents, led by Jirgalang, ensued for two years, until the Shunzhi emperor took personal control from
1653 to 1661. Shunzhi relied heavily on non-Manchu groups to offset
Jirgalang, encouraging contacts with the Jesuits, Buddhists, and eunuchs.
He supported the right of Chinese to memorialize with scathing attacks on
the corruption of the Manchu noble elite.

The state seemed to be heading in a strongly Chinese direction under the
young emperor, but on his death in 1661, the Empress Dowager in alliance
with the Manchu nobles supported a reactive move. They put the new emperor, Kangxi, at age eight *sui* (seven Western years), on the throne under
the supervision of four powerful Manchu regents: Oboi, Soni, Suksaha,
and Ebilun.[48] Stressing the need for a new reign of virtue, they forged the
will of the Shunzhi emperor, putting in his mouth severe criticism of his attachment to corrupt non-Manchu practices. The regents purged the eu-

nuchs and Buddhists, severely interrogated the Jesuit astronomer Adam Schall, and executed many other Christian followers. They claimed to be returning to the idealized, militarist, pure Manchu state of Nurhaci and Hong Taiji, although in fact both these leaders had skillfully blended multiple cultural elements. The Council of Ministers was cut back in size but expanded in its functions, while the influence of Ming institutions—the Neisanyuan, Six Boards, and censorate—declined.[49]

The regents became notorious for their harsh policies toward local Chinese officials. Their support of a crackdown on tax deficits in Jiangnan touched off a revolt by students and officials, who were subjected to mass execution in 1661. They introduced the systematic evaluation *(kaocheng)* of local officials in order to root out corruption and ensure prompt tax collection. The regents did not, however, restore the principles of collective rule or local *beile* autonomy, even in Manchuria. Southern Manchuria became a new province, Fengtian, under the rule of a military governor, and a military governor took over control of northern Manchuria when it was threatened by Russian incursions. Only in one respect did the regents allow excessive autonomy: they permitted Wu Sangui and the other military commanders of feudatories in southwest and South China to expand their military power and administrative independence. In foreign policy, they were cautious and not expansive when facing the Mongols, the Russians, or Zheng Chenggong's regime on Taiwan.

Overall, the regency period did not undermine the stability of the state, despite its apparent reassertion of Manchu traditional values. Further centralization and military authoritarian rule increased, but we cannot attribute this centralization very much to Chinese influence. In seventeenth-century Russia, during the Time of Troubles (1602–1613), the Muscovite state had collapsed, and local barons strongly attacked the claims of the centralizing Tsars. Succession struggles, foreign invasion, peasant revolt, economic decline, and assertion of baronial autonomy all nearly destroyed the state, until the advent of the new Romanov dynasty in 1613. The Manchus faced all of these challenges as well. The two founders of the state had created it as pragmatic military administrators using the most promising of the diverse cultural elements of their frontier environment. The Manchu reaction failed because it aimed to "purify" the state of contamination from Chinese practices, without understanding that many of these elements were integral parts of the state, and without producing a successful alternative model.

The regents, notably, were never able to produce a "Sacred Edict" announcing the fundamental principles of their emperor's rule, as the Kangxi emperor did in 1670. The Sacred Edict spelled out the "bare bones of Confucian orthodoxy as it pertained to the average citizen."[50] Later versions fleshed out the emperor's maxims and delivered elaborations of them orally to villagers across the empire. Unlike the Kangxi emperor, the regents did not have enough confidence in a coherent program to address the Han population so directly. Nevertheless, the regents did promote the fundamental objectives of the founders, as they too were driven by their environment toward greater centralization and authoritarian control.

Only when the Kangxi emperor finally asserted his personal power in 1670 were his clan members permanently excluded from all administrative posts. Thus the seesaw struggle between clan and bureaucracy followed no simple line toward growing sinicization, but moved back and forth depending on contingencies of personality and the progress of the military and economic resources of the state.

By comparison with the Russian and Mongolian states, the Manchus faced a simpler geopolitical situation. They maintained a clear focus on a single enemy: the Ming dynasty to the south. On their other borders they faced mainly sympathetic Mongols to the west, inoffensive tribal peoples to the north, and the relatively weak Korean king to the southeast. They had defeated one rebellion by the Sunid Mongols allied with the Khalkhas in 1646.[51] Russian incursions into northern Manchuria had not yet become a serious threat in the 1660s. The focus on a single front gave a clear structure and purpose to the state leader's goals, and the demands of military expansion drove consistent projects of administrative and cultural reform. After they moved south of Beijing, from the 1640s to 1660s, the rulers continued to drive the Ming holdouts south, as they established local institutions for governing the huge Chinese subject population. Even after the strong leadership of the two founders, the regents, who practiced a cautious foreign policy, followed the momentum established in the early years. They put down local rebellions and evacuated the southeast coast in order to isolate Zheng Chenggong and his Ming supporters on Taiwan. They elevated the status of the Lifanyuan, which became the core institution for dealing with northwestern affairs, separated off from the Libu, which dealt with tributaries to the east and southeast.[52] This decision institutionalized the bifurcated foreign policy of the Qing and ensured that the northwest border received a distinctive kind of attention. But the Manchus deferred the subjugation of most of the Mongols until they had secured the south. The Oirat Mongols, by contrast, constantly alternated between different fronts, confronting Mongols to their east, Russians and Kazakhs to the west, and Tibet to the south. By 1670 the leaders were embroiled in fratricidal strife, and no one could claim the legitimate title of Khan. The Manchus' steady centralization under both emperors and regents laid the foundation for the expansive ambitions of the Kangxi emperor after he took personal power.

Centralized power, however, could not by itself obtain enough resources to sustain the growing state. Manchuria has a deceptive ecology. Viewed from the forests of Siberia, or from the deserts and steppes of Central Eurasia, its rivers appeared to be filled with fish and bordered with rich agricultural lands, and its forests abounded in game, forest products, and minerals. So the Russian settlers thought as they pushed east across Siberia, hearing tales of the riches of the region. But they were soon disappointed. The local tribes looked poor, the fields provided very little grain for the armed garrisons, and the fortresses soon found themselves short of food. As noted earlier, the Russians ran into food supply problems even before they knew that they were trespassing on the territory of the new Manchu state.

When the Manchus were a dispersed tribal population, they could support themselves at a low level of subsistence without too much difficulty by practicing a mixed economy that combined hunting, fishing, and small amounts of agricultural production. They also prospered from trade in forest products, particularly jinseng root, sold to Koreans and Chinese, and furs. Ming officials had effectively used this Manchu desire for trade to divide the tribes by granting each of them separate patents that allowed participation in tribute missions. They could thus use the rivalry over patents to play the tribes against one another. Nurhaci, in order to centralize his power, had to take control of all the patents himself. This meant depriving the other tribes of their access to tribute resources.

Only after Nurhaci began building his military machine designed for state unification and ultimately for conquest of China did the logistical bottlenecks become severe. As he defeated rival clan leaders and incorporated them into banners, he incurred responsibilities for provisioning these troops. The best available sources for new provisions were the neighboring peoples of Korea and Liaodong, so his first moves were to plunder them in time-honored Central Eurasian fashion. Nurhaci also promoted economic development from the earliest years, as the Manchus used Chinese artisans to smelt iron, mine gold and silver, and develop sericulture and cotton production.[53] But the Ming responded by cutting back tribute income after 1609 and closing down the profitable border markets. By 1615, before he declared his new dynasty, Nurhaci was already admitting that his state lacked enough food to feed its own people, and it could not fight neighboring Mongolian tribes. He urged the clearance of more land to fill the granaries.[54] From this time until the conquest of Beijing, the urgent need for grain supplies became a major factor in the expansion of the state. In 1619

Nurhaci conquered the Yehe clan in order to get more food. At the same time that he was encouraging the Mongols to join him in the conquest, he told them that they had to bring their own provisions when they marched against the Ming, and they could not steal food from the local population.[55]

After the declaration of the Latter Jin dynasty in 1616, Nurhaci faced the dual problem of feeding his own population and winning over the Chinese of Liaodong to the south. He promised to "nourish the begging poor" and to overcome the disparities of wealth created by the corruption of Ming officials.[56] Newcomers to Manchu rule were guaranteed grain rations in 1623, and the allocations were made equal for Chinese and Manchus. Conquered Chinese households could be incorporated in a range of statuses, from free to slave. In 1624 Chinese households who had 5 to 7 Manchu *sin* of grain (equal to 9 to 13 *shi*, or about 800 to 1,000 kg) were given land and houses, while those with less were made into slaves.[57] But the status of *boo-i niyalma,* or *aha,* did not correspond exactly to the Chinese category of "bondservant-slave" *(nupu)* or to that of "free man" *(zhuangding).* It was a relationship of personal dependency on a master which in theory guaranteed close personal relationships and equal treatment. As the Khan stated, "The Master should love the slave and eat the same food as him."[58] By insisting on the paternalism of the relationship, notably through guaranteeing food supplies, the Manchu ruler aimed to convince the Chinese of Liaodong that they could gain security and overcome unjust disparities of wealth under the new state.

But the conquest of Liaodong in 1621 led in practice to much sharper conflicts between Manchus and Chinese and much more severe subsistence crises. Rebellions by the Chinese against unequal treatment also focused on food supplies: Manchus had to fear poisoning of wells by their new neighbors and beware of eating pigs, salt, chickens, eggplant, and other products.[59] Nurhaci promoted co-occupancy of households, whereby Manchus and Chinese lived and worked together, in order to overcome antagonism, but food shortages as well as cultural differences made this experiment a failure. The Manchus had no grain reserves of their own in the winter of 1621–22, so they had to extract food from the Chinese, who tried to conceal it, and institute general grain rationing as an emergency measure.[60] They ordered equal distribution of land the next year, at 5 *cimari* (30 *mou*) per adult male, but it is not clear if this was ever carried out. The expanding state tried to resolve the logistical crisis with new corvée and grain taxes levied on the larger Chinese population, but free land was scarce in Liaodong, and grew even scarcer as Chinese fled the fighting in Liaoxi to the west. The refugees found that they had "not enough grain or salt to eat."[61]

Manchus under economic pressure exploited the Chinese in their households, treating them as slaves and stealing their possessions. The Chinese of Liaodong openly rebelled in 1623, setting fire to buildings, poisoning Manchu associates, and stealing grain from the granaries. Although the rebellion was easily suppressed, the Khan heard repeated reports that his people ignored edicts commanding fair treatment of the Chinese. An even more serious uprising in 1625 exposed further abuses by local Manchu officials and commanders.[62]

Hong Taiji listened to newly enrolled Chinese advisers against the wishes of some of the Manchu nobility. The Chinese urged further centralization of power and greater leniency toward the subject Chinese population, convincing him that social unrest was undermining the Khan's authority and favored the interests of his unruly clan nobility, the *beise*. Those who resisted undue favoritism toward Chinese advisers in the state, like Amin, wanted to return to the good old days of plunder and raiding. Amin invaded Korea in 1627 and pillaged the territory, defying the Khan's orders, and massacred and looted the Chinese town of Yongping in 1629. Hong Taiji, declaring him an enemy of the state, had him thrown in prison in 1633, where he died in 1640.

The social and economic crises of the state led Hong Taiji to abandon Nurhaci's fruitless attempts at Manchu–Chinese integration. He instituted a strict segregation policy that attempted to create separate but equal domains. The co-occupancy of households was abolished, and a new organization, the *tokso*, enrolled Chinese into units of thirteen households under a single headman, who served under a Manchu banner commander. Chinese were to hand in all weapons, while all Manchus had to be armed.[63] Stricter controls over mobility, including rewards for returning fugitive bondservants, curiously parallel the contemporaneous effort of the Russian state to tighten up the bonds of serfdom.

But the Manchu state was "on the brink of economic disaster" in 1627.[64] The first major defeat of the Manchu army by the Ming in 1626 exposed the state's great vulnerability. The marginal economy of Manchuria could only barely support its growing population, but to provide in addition for a large army on a military campaign, the army had to gather booty from its victories. This was exactly the dynamic of the typical steppe nomadic federation, which expanded explosively when it succeeded in gathering enough loot from victory to reward its supporters but collapsed implosively at the first signs of defeat. The food crisis of 1627, the most severe yet, drove up grain prices eightfold over 1623, to 8 taels per *sin* (1 Manchu *sin* = 1.8 *shi*), and brought tales of cannibalism and robbery. There was no grain for newly surrendered subjects, and the granaries were empty. Nor was there land for newly arrived Chinese.[65] Other food crises struck in 1635 and

1637. The lack of provisions for the army weakened the Manchus' military power considerably. Their horses could not pursue the enemy because they were too tired and weak.[66] Efforts to raise agricultural production in Liaoxi failed; exhortations to rich landowners to provide for the poor fell, as usual, on deaf ears, and the Manchus could not afford to alienate them by forcing them to sell at low prices.[67] Korea again offered a tempting target. The Manchus forced Korea to provide grain under threat of military invasion, and cut off its profitable tribute trade with China so that they could monopolize it for themselves. Relations with the Mongols, crucial to Manchu military strength, also threatened to turn sour if the Manchus could not provide enough grain in exchange for Mongol horses. They had to prevent the Mongols from selling horses to China and repressed the secret Mongol trade in grain with Chinese.

Thus, despite conventional impressions, the Manchu state and army were in a weakened condition in the 1630s. Although the Manchu archival documents do not provide detailed information on this period, the repeated pattern from 1636 to 1644 of Manchu attacks on Chinese cities followed by harvesting of the fields and withdrawal indicates that the Manchus were not strong enough to pursue a plan of direct conquest.[68] They were in danger of reverting to the old raid and extortion policy instead of creating a viable new state, let alone conquering a Chinese dynasty.

Hong Taiji was firmly on the throne by 1635. He had overcome his Manchu rivals and declared the new Qing dynasty in 1636. Having captured a Yuan dynasty seal from the Chahar Mongols, he could style himself the rightful successor to Chinggis Khan as well. But his weakening army was opposed by the Chinese commander of the pass, Wu Sangui, whom he could not defeat. He was saved only by the fortuitous events of 1644: the conquest of Beijing by the rebel Li Zicheng, the death of the Ming emperor and the flight of his court, and Wu Sangui's decision to leave his defensive position to attack Li Zicheng, allowing the Manchus to pour through the pass.[69]

Severe logistical constraints on the new Manchu state, then, nearly caused it to collapse. In fact, the Manchus were not alone. All major agrarian states in the sixteenth and seventeenth centuries stretched their state-building ambitions far beyond their means. The multiple crises that struck the globe in the seventeenth century in England, France, Russia, Germany, China, and the Ottoman empire, among others, have been traced to the excessive burdens placed on agrarian economies with limited productive potential by burgeoning state and military apparatuses. Population growth also increased demands for subsistence on limited agrarian production systems in western Europe and China. Fiscal exactions ran up against the barriers of agrarian production and local elite resistance. Ming surtaxes to support military defense touched off the rebellion in the northwest that brought down the dynasty, and French noble resistance to royal taxation likewise tore the country apart in the Fronde civil wars of the seventeenth century.[70]

In this context, the Central Eurasian states occupied a special niche. On the one hand, unlike the western European states, they were not burdened by growing populations within a limited territorial area. There was still plenty of room for peasants to move across the steppes and open lands of Russia. The main problem for Russian state builders was to tie the peasants to the land in order to extract labor dues and taxes from them. On the other hand, the rate of agrarian production was so low that only small amounts over subsistence could be extracted. Extensive agriculture was accompanied by extensive state extraction. Russians also discovered a second lucrative source of state revenue in the Siberian fur trade. Exploitation of the northern forest peoples, which had begun as early as the twelfth century by Novgorod, brought in valuable fur-bearing animals at relatively low cost.[71] The Manchus likewise could rely on the forest resources of their region as the main base for the early stages of state building. Nurhaci was, in effect, a forest tribal leader who conquered his fellow tribespeoples and used their production as the basis of his military regime.

But both Manchus and Russians faced severe strains when they moved into more densely settled regions. Conquering these regions required negotiations with local elites much more securely based than the forest peoples of Siberia or Manchuria. In Poland–Lithuania, the Ukraine, or Liaodong, these frontiers required major military siege campaigns and adroit negotiations before they could be incorporated into the new state. The conquerors had to support the subject peoples and ward off subsistence crises to avert social disorder. Both states nearly collapsed in the mid-seventeenth century. The Manchus avoided failure only when the Ming court abandoned Beijing, while Muscovy survived only after the citizens of Moscow rallied an army to drive off Polish invaders, put down peasant revolts, and elect a new Tsar.[72] A breakthrough to new sources of economic wealth and technology by the end of the century provided new expansive powers for both regimes: Peter the Great turning decisively toward the West but building on the Muscovite legacy; the Qing rulers taking over China's abundant agricultural wealth in the south but also not abandoning their strategic goals in the northwest. In the early to mid-seventeenth century, by contrast, the survival of both states seemed precarious. In the stability of leadership and logistics, the Russian, Manchu, and Mongol states were close rivals.

Mongolian Influence on the Manchu State

The Manchus' relations with the neighboring Mongol tribes were crucial to the strengthening of the state from its earliest years. Kinship and ideological intimacy tied them closely together. Nurhaci had exchanged wives and concubines with the Khalkha Mongols since 1594, and he received the title *Sure kündulen Han* from them in 1607, replacing his clan title of *sure beile* (wise prince), thus raising his claims from that of a local clan leader to the level of a Central Eurasian Khan. In 1616 he gave himself the title *Geren gurun be ujire genggiyen han* (the radiant emperor, whom Heaven has designated to nourish the many countries), consolidating his claim to the Mongolian traditions of leadership.[73] The ideal of a multinational ruler, or universal Khan (Mo. *gür qan, dalai-yin qaghan*), derived from the Buddhist "wheel-turning king" *(chakravartin)*, had been transmitted through Tibet to Mongolia in Yuan times. Tibetan lamas gave sacral character to Chinggis and Khubilai Khan in their writings, regarding them as incarnations of powerful boddhisattvas and tutelary deities.[74] The last claimant to this ideal rulership in the seventeenth century was the descendant of Chinggis Khan, Ligdan (Linden) Khan, of the Chahars. Any Inner Asian claimant to imperial power had to link himself to this ideological tradition.

Other concepts of imperial rule, according to David Farquhar, derived not from Chinese but from Mongolian sources. The Manchus had not yet begun, in this early period, to translate basic Chinese classical texts. As mentioned previously, the earliest literate advisers to Nurhaci were men like Dahai and Erdeni Baksi, who had grown up with Mongolian connections. Dahai and Erdeni were probably Chinese in origin, "transfrontiersmen" in Liaodong whose ancestors had changed their cultural identity, adopting Manchu names and cultural traditions.[75] Dahai (1592–1632) was in charge of all official communication with the Koreans, the Mongols, and the Ming court. He conducted peace negotiations with Ming commanders during the Manchu military campaigns, and he read out the emperor's proclamations in Chinese in 1629–30. He also translated military books and the Ming penal code into Manchu. Erdeni Baksi (d. 1623) knew Mongolian and Chinese texts from his early youth and could speak with both Chinese and Mongols in their native tongue. Erdeni told Nurhaci that omens in the sky (the northern lights), so conspicuous in the years 1612, 1614, and 1615, indicated that the Mandate of Heaven was due to be changed soon. This interpretation, combining Central Eurasian reverence for Heaven with Chinese mandate theory, induced Nurhaci to proclaim the Latter Jin dynasty in 1616.[76]

These tricultural men were the key brokers who synthesized the essential elements of the Manchu state from diverse roots. They were later given bi-ographies in the *Baqi Tongzhi* (Eight banner gazetteer) as the first "Confu-cians" *(ruren)*, even though their backgrounds were more Central Eurasian than Chinese. The later generations of literati given biographies in this text have very little Mongolian background; their chief contributions came from the translation of Chinese texts into Manchu. They performed a dif-ficult and dangerous cultural straddling act, one which made them vulnera-ble to attacks from rivals. Dahai was dismissed from office in 1623, and Erdeni was executed in 1623 for unspecified crimes. They may have been the victims of false rumors spread by *beile* who resented their intimacy with the rising Khan.[77]

The concept of "Heavenly destiny" (Ch. *tianming*, Ma. *abka-i fulingga*: the first reign title of the Manchus, declared in 1616), if it ultimately had Chinese origins, had been transmitted to the Manchus from Mongolia. Khubilai Khan had claimed this mandate for his empire in 1272.[78] The Manchu *beile*, who combined the roles of hereditary princes and officials, corresponded exactly to their Mongolian counterparts, the *noyan*. The idea of a dual nature state (Mo. *qoyar yosun*) divided between secular and reli-gious spheres derived from sixteenth- and seventeenth-century Mongolian theories of the "nature of the state" (Mo. *törö sajin*, Ma. *doro sajin*). Thus the "higher" concepts of a state that transcended clan leadership, even though they looked similar to Chinese classical concepts, came to Manchu-ria "through a Mongolian strainer."[79]

Even the Manchus' most distinctive innovation, the banner organization, had just as strong Mongolian roots as Chinese. Franz Michael argued that the banners were modeled directly on the Ming *weisuo*, or hereditary mili-tary garrisons, but the original banner model had nothing in common with the decimal organization of the Ming *weisuo*.[80] It was based on a division into two *geren* (hordes), each *geren* divided into four *tatan* (camps) of sev-enty-five men each, but each banner also contained cavalry *(uksin)* and foot soldiers *(yafahan)*. Only later did the banner assume a more decimal form of organization. In any case, the Ming *weisuo* themselves originated from Yuan dynasty decimal military formations.[81] The other distinctive features of the banners also had common Mongolian origins: the combination of military and civil administration, the use of sacred flags, and the appoint-ment of hereditary officers, for example.

By its final form in 1623, the banners were based on the *niru* (arrow, company) which was originally a hunting and fighting unit of the Manchus, very similar to the *qosighun* of the Mongols in the thirteenth and four-teenth centuries. The *gûsa* (banner), like the *qosighun*, was based on "the able-bodied men of a tribe or other autonomous political unit when considered as a military force."[82] Its head was a hereditary prince, and its official titles were modeled on the Mongolian ones. Thus the central institution that provided the backbone of the Manchu conquest could be traced to Mongolian roots.[83]

Just as in the Russian case, it is less important to prolong the argument over the relative importance of Chinese or Mongolian sources of the banners than to recognize the creative synthesis produced by the Manchus out of their frontier location. The fluidity of institutional and personal identities characteristic of the region, the mixing of peoples and ecologies and social structures, provided the cauldron in which innovative social formations could be brewed, which led to a military and social structure of irresistible force. For Roberto Unger, "the Mongols' experience in the steppe and the borderlands and the problems they had to face as a conquest elite prepared them . . . for the role of teachers of statecraft. They taught the lesson of continued mobilization, of hostility to vested rights and local prerogatives, and of insistence on insulating at least parts of governmental power from the influence of local landowners and notables." The Mongolian patterns, adopted by the Qing, prevented China from falling back again into "reversion cycles," in which local landowners took over control of agrarian resources, starving the central state and shutting down commercial exchange networks. The Qing banner system "kept the conquest elite ready for service and prevented it from sinking into a class of landowners anxious about their local interests."[84]

The banners and other Manchu institutions are examples of productive hybridity, combining "pure" Mongolian elements (the script, for example) with Chinese elements transmitted through Mongolian filters, and, later on, purely Chinese elements that entered the state as it expanded to the south.

Intermarriage with Mongolian noble families further cemented the alliance between the two peoples. In 1612 Nurhaci himself married the daughter of the chief of the Khorcin Mongols. From 1612 to 1615 Nurhaci and his sons together married six Mongolian women. After 1617 other Manchus married into the Mongolian nobility, and surrendering Mongol tribes enrolled in Manchu banners provided significant numbers of women to marry the Manchu elite.[85]

Hong Taiji expanded the marriage alliance policy, marrying twelve of his daughters to Mongolian chieftains. He used marriage ties to draw in more of the twenty-one southern Mongolian tribes that joined the Manchu alliance. The Manchu–Mongolian alliance became even more systematized and regulated after the Qing conquered the rest of China. Special annual subsidies of silver and silk, elaborate funerals, and the granting of high rank to sons all encouraged intermarriage. At the same time, restrictions on visits to the capital kept the Mongolian nobles under control. Manchu women married to Mongolians could come to the capital, their home-town, only once every ten years, and they could stay for only sixty days. But young Mongolian boys were selected as consorts for the princesses, brought to the capital for education in Manchu and Chinese culture, and sent back to their tribes suitably acculturated. The Qianlong and Jiaqing emperors expanded the system to encompass thousands of marriages be-tween all levels of the Manchu and Mongolian noble classes. At the same time, commoners of both sides were kept rigidly segregated, and intermar-riage was banned.

This highly regulated, large-scale kinship creation program differed sub-stantially from previous dynasties' uses of occasional marriage alliances to ensure peace with northwestern frontier peoples, the so-called *heqin* policy, which went back to the Han dynasty.[86] Han and Tang use of *heqin* alliances was intended only to ward off frontier threats, but the Manchus aimed at intimate linkages with their fellow Central Eurasians—linkages that did not, however, obliterate boundaries between the two peoples. Marriage al-liances were used alongside other techniques—gifts, stipends, tax exemp-tion, education, access to official posts—to provide strong incentives for Mongols to cooperate with the rising Manchu power. In 1689 the Kangxi emperor boasted, rather prematurely, that because of his intimate ties with the Mongols beyond the wall, he had brought peace to the northwestern frontier, eliminating the constant menace of nomadic raids that plagued the Ming dynasty.[87]

Despite the growing intimacy of Manchu–Mongol ties, one major Mon-gol leader, Ligdan (Linden) Khan of the Chahars, resolutely opposed the growing Manchu power. As the last descendant of Chinggis Khan, he held an official Yuan seal and viewed himself as the legitimate representative of the Mongolian imperial tradition. But after his losses in battle to the Man-chus in 1628 and 1632, the Manchus took over the Yuan seal and enrolled the Eastern Mongols as a whole in the banner system. Ligdan Khan's son married a Manchu princess after Ligdan died of smallpox in Qinghai. The Chahar and Khalkha Mongols comprised 384 *niru* with 19,580 families, the Khorcin 448 *niru* with 22,308 families.[88] Only after this definitive vic-tory could Hong Taiji proclaim the genuine three-nationality empire, which he named Da Qing in 1636. No longer did the Manchus need to hark back to their Jurchen predecessors of the twelfth century, the regional state of the Jin (1115–1234 CE); now they could legitimately claim to be building a uni-versal empire.

Ligdan Khan played another important function in the Manchu state. He had translated the large Tibetan Buddhist canon, the Kanjur, into Mongolian during his rule. The Manchus were introduced to Tibetan Buddhism through this channel, preparing the way for the visit of the Dalai Lama to Beijing in 1652.[89]

The successful incorporation of the Eastern and Southern Mongols during the early conquest period provided a substantial fund of experience that the Manchus could use when they confronted the more isolated, hostile, and autonomous Mongolian tribes farther west. Over the century and a half following the conquest, in their extension of the empire, they returned to the techniques of seduction, threat, personal ties, and authoritarian bureaucratic regulation that they had used successfully in the relations between Mongols and Manchus during the first fifty years of building the state.

The greatest gift of the Mongols to the Manchus, of course, was the Mongolian script.[90] In 1599 Nurhaci ordered Erdeni Baksi and G'ag'ai to create a script for the Manchu "national language" *(guoyu)*. They objected that the Manchus had long used the Mongolian script and language, and they could not create a new one. Nurhaci then said, "When the Chinese read out their writing, people understand it, whether or not they can read Chinese; likewise for Mongols; but our words must first be translated into Mongolian; then [the Manchus] don't understand it."[91] He then ordered them to create a new alphabetic script, using the Mongolian script as a model:

> Taizu [Nurhaci] asked, "Why is it difficult to write down our language, but easy to learn the languages of other countries?" G'ag'ai and Erdeni replied: "It would be best to create a script for our country's language, but we do not know how to transcribe the sounds." Taizu said: "If you put a letter for 'ma' after a letter for 'a,' is this not 'ama' [father]? If you put a letter 'me' after a letter for 'e,' is this not 'eme' [mother]? My mind is made up; you just try it out." Thereupon they took the Mongolian script and wrote the Manchu language. The creation of the Manchu script began with Taizu.[92]

So Erdeni and G'ag'ai, following Nurhaci's orders, created the new writing system, and soon began to translate Chinese texts into Manchu, as well as using Manchu in imperial proclamations. Dahai, in 1632, added the diacritical marks to distinguish different Manchu vowels, along with extra symbols for particular Chinese consonants; this "pointed" script became the standard Manchu writing system for the rest of the dynasty.

Nurhaci was, of course, wrong to assume that classical literary Chinese could be understood when read out loud. His advisers, well acquainted with Mongolian imperial language, resisted the introduction of Manchu writing probably in order to maintain ties to the Mongolian institutional tradition. To judge from his discussion, Nurhaci had in mind a syllabic script (like Japanese *hiragana* and *katakana*), not the actual Mongolian or Manchu scripts, which were alphabetic. Nurhaci's motives were political, not linguistic. What he stressed was oral communication of written commands by the ruler to the entire Manchu population, literate and nonliterate. He needed a scriptural apparatus to bolster his new state because he, like all previous Central Eurasian rulers, needed to communicate his personal will beyond the boundaries of person-to-person contact. His edicts could now be read out in their own language to all his Manchu subjects, and texts could be translated into their native language for their own education. In effect, by creating a distinctive script, Nurhaci broadened the cultural horizons of his people, allowing them to adapt non-Manchu ideas but maintain their distinct identity. The new technology of writing made possible the expansion of the state to cover all the Manchu people. But it also allowed the introduction of large quantities of Chinese classical literature through translation into the Manchu literate world, which had formerly been much more closely tied to Mongolia and the Buddhist world of Central Eurasia.

In short, the Mongols contributed a great deal to the early Manchu state. They provided military allies, horses, and a tradition of legitimation reaching back to Chinggis Khan. Along with the Yuan seal came the concept of a universal empire encompassing many peoples, an ideal of rulership that vastly transcended either the state of the Manchus' ancestors, the Jurchen Jin, or that of the Ming. Personal connections through kinship and literary connections through the script bound the two peoples together. Nurhaci often invoked the common heritage of the Mongols and Manchus when promoting alliances, although at other times he stressed their differences. Not all the Mongols accepted the supremacy of the young Manchu state; only decisive victory in war persuaded them to submit. From its origins, the rulers of the Manchu state learned how to devise interrelated strategies of war, diplomacy, and economic inducement to ensure the loyalty of their critical allies in the northwest.

Early Modern State Building Compared

The Chinese and Russian empires displayed many common patterns as they expanded over Eurasia. They both grew explosively in size, in little over

fifty years spreading from small tribal kingships to domination of vast forests, fields, steppes, and deserts. At about the same time, the three Middle
Eastern "gunpowder empires," the Mughals, Safavids, and Ottomans, also
expanded. Even though gunpowder was not the primary factor, new military organizations partially based on gunpowder weaponry vitally aided
their conquests. The Manchus, Russians, and Mongols also relied on new
military organizations to bind their states together. They shared a basis of
common interactions with peoples of the steppe, from whom they learned
the importance of rapid mobility and careful attention to military logistics.
They sought the easiest sources of wealth from the settled peoples nearby,
in oases, paddy fields, or fur trapping villages, but they went beyond raiding and rapid extraction by using these resources to build new states.

In this chapter, the Central Eurasian steppe has been the element linking
the three states together in the early period of their formation. After their
success, however, the conquerors attempted to disguise the complex processes that generated their new states. Russian clerical chroniclers created a
simple dualism of struggle between Christianity and paganism to legitimate
the new Tsars, while Chinese historians inserted the Manchus into the orthodox doctrine of inheritance of the Mandate of Heaven and sinicization.
In fact, the conquerors succeeded not because they followed rigid religious ideologies and cosmological precepts, but because they pragmatically
mixed together multiple traditions. Russian Tsars relied on astute steppe diplomacy, horsemanship, and many Mongolian heritages as well as Orthodox Christianity and subordination of Slavic peasantry. Manchus mingled
Mongolian rulership, horsemanship, and language with Chinese classical
texts and Manchu kinship connections. The Zunghar Mongols adapted Tibetan Buddhist practices to Mongolian clan connections and oasis cultures.

The Ottoman empire provides another example of such creative mingling. Historians for a long time interpreted the rise of the Ottomans as the
product of a tribe of righteous warriors for Islam *(ghazi)* on the fringes of
the Byzantine and Turkish empires. But Cemal Kafadar has recently shown
that the early Ottomans grew out of a fluid frontier environment where
identities and loyalties constantly shifted. Rudi Lindner has also pointed to
the important role of nomads in the early Ottoman state. Later, in the seventeenth century, the Ottomans were challenged by armed groups, called
celali, or "bandits." Many historians viewed the *celali* as outright opponents of the Ottoman state, but Karen Barkey has shown that they were in
fact products of the Ottoman regime, mainly demobilized soldiers who
sought higher positions within the state. The Ottomans once again successfully negotiated with multiple armed groups in ceaselessly competitive
frontier conditions to keep their state alive.[93] The Ottoman state endured

for so long because its rulers knew how to negotiate with diverse groups within the polity.

If we examine each of these empires in isolation, we tend to see only the apparently distinctive features that mark them as most innovative. Considering the rise of three or four empires together reveals instead substantial resemblances in the role of nomads, the relations between central state structures and local nobilities, and negotiations with rival state builders. Some of these techniques were borrowed from neighbors; others evolved as common responses to a similar frontier environment. But the Central Eurasian connections of the state founders marked all of them and left a permanent legacy.

PART TWO

Contending
for Power

4

Manchus, Mongols, and Russians in Conflict, 1670–1690

I N the late seventeenth century, the vigorous young ruler of China, known as the Kangxi emperor, took decisive action to expand and strengthen his new empire. In an astonishingly short period of time, a mere thirty years from taking personal power, he decisively imposed his will on the regents— his own uncles, the generals ruling the southwest, Taiwanese aborigines, and, most impressively, the free nomadic military leaders of Mongolia. By 1700 it seemed that no one could resist the imperial command. None of these achievements was determined in advance, and victory was never certain. The emperor had to overcome substantial opposition from his closest advisers, and his troops battled incessantly against immense human and natural obstacles. Although the structure of the emerging Qing state, including its Central Asian elements, supported Kangxi's vigorous campaigns, we cannot ignore the sheer force of personal will that so strongly marked these critical years. Kangxi's dynamic intervention transformed the Qing from a promising but limited enterprise into an unprecedented project of expansion. The Mongol campaigns signaled most definitively this transformation of the Qing into a Central Eurasian empire with world significance.

Kangxi the Ruler

Aisin Gioro Xuanye (1654–1722) was the third son of Fulin, the Shunzhi emperor. His grandmother and the four Manchu regents selected him to be-

come emperor, with the reign name Kangxi, when his father was dying of smallpox.[1] Fear of smallpox, a virulent disease among both Manchus and Mongols, played an important role in the choice of Xuanye, who had survived exposure to it as a boy. By the 1630s, Manchu generals, believing that Mongolian territory was an especially dangerous site of the disease, tried to ensure that only officers already exposed to smallpox could lead expeditions through this region.[2]

The new emperor combined the blood of the three ruling peoples in his veins. His ancestry was in fact less than half Manchu, since his father and paternal grandfather were sons of Mongol princesses. He was one-fourth Chinese on his mother's side, although she belonged to the Manchu imperial clan.[3] Eight years old at his succession, the boy emperor grew up under the supervision of his uncles. When he reached the age of fourteen *sui* in 1667, a Chinese censor urged him to take personal power.[4] Although he formally assumed personal rule in that year, he did not move actively against the constraints of the regency until June 1669, when he arrested Oboi, the chief regent, and had him prosecuted for a detailed list of crimes. Oboi soon died in prison. The new emperor then proceeded to purge all the Six Board presidents and major banner officials to assert his undisputed power.

Kangxi's first task was to eliminate the factionalism at the top levels of government, which, he believed, had brought about the downfall of the Ming dynasty and also plagued the regency. He needed to alleviate the severe tensions between Manchus and Chinese caused by the harsh Manchu nativism of Oboi, and to convince the Chinese literate class that only his rule would bring peace. He also needed to complete the unfinished tasks of gaining military control of Taiwan and southwest China. By suppressing the Three Feudatories revolt (1673–1678), the new emperor demonstrated dramatically that he would reject the cautious, vacillating policies of his regents. Kangxi's personal will injected a new dynamism into Qing expansionism that brought back the spirit of the early days of the growth of the state.

The Chinese generals Kong Yude, Shang Kexi, Geng Zhongming, and, most important, Wu Sangui had crucially aided the Manchu conquest. The defection of Chinese officials and generals to the Manchu side was essential in winning the battle against the holdout forces of the Southern Ming dynasty. As a reward for their services, these generals had been given nearly total autonomous power over southern and southwest China. In 1660

The Kangxi emperor (r. 1662–1722), in a scholarly pose.

Shang Kexi ruled Guangdong, Geng Jimao controlled Fujian, and Wu Sangui controlled Yunnan.[5] Wu, the strongest of them, commanded 65,000 troops and held high noble rank. Central government support of his army cost 9 million taels, two-fifths of state revenue in the Shunzhi period.[6] The regents did not challenge the growing independence of the feudatory generals, nor did they expand their own banner forces to balance them. Kangxi would expand the banners by 179 more companies from 1667 to 1675, to a total of 799 companies.

Once the Southern Ming forces abandoned South China, the military services of the feudatories were no longer needed, but they aimed to preserve their power base. Wu Sangui offered his retirement to Kangxi in 1667 to test Kangxi's will, but Kangxi, not ready to challenge him, kept him on. When Shang Kexi offered to retire in 1673, the time for the true test had come. The key issue was whether or not the central government would allow these territories to become hereditary family possessions of the founding generals. The Deliberative Council agreed to accept his retirement, but they would not allow his son to inherit his command. When Wu and Geng offered their retirements, the majority of Kangxi's councilors advised against accepting them, because the court was not prepared to face a military challenge from these strong regional powers. Kangxi, however, overruling his advisers, accepted Wu's retirement, thus touching off the revolt by Wu Sangui in December 1673. Shang Kexi and Geng Jingzhong, Geng Jimao's son, joined Wu's revolt, thus throwing all of southern China into rebellion. Kangxi won this difficult campaign for several reasons: the feudatories could not cooperate effectively with one another; Wu Sangui was discredited as a defender of Chinese interests because he had collaborated with the Manchus; and Kangxi's expanded banner troops were still the most effective fighting force in the empire. But the fortuitous death of Wu Sangui in 1678 put a quick end to what could have been a very drawnout conflict.

Kangxi's successful suppression of the southwest secessionists had consequences for Qing attitudes toward control of other parts of the empire. No subsequent ruler would ever allow any region the degree of autonomy that the feudatories had attained. Even though the other frontier regions, after their incorporation by conquest, maintained distinctive and somewhat autonomous local administrative systems, the Manchus, by controlling titles, succession to power, lands, and taxation, ensured that breaking away would be difficult.

The Kangxi emperor wearing armor.

Kangxi's first military campaign set the tone for the later northwest campaigns. Kangxi developed a long-standing suspicion of the Dalai Lama during this period. The emperor wanted the Dalai Lama's support for crushing the revolt, but he knew that Wu Sangui, whose territory bordered Tibet, had also been making overtures to the lama. Even though the Dalai Lama denied supporting Wu, the emperor remained suspicious. He received excellent support from the Chahar Mongols during the campaigns, which justified further efforts to mobilize surrendered Mongol forces in military expeditions. Overall, however, the emperor was very dissatisfied with the performance of his field generals, whom he regarded as excessively cautious and untruthful.

By 1678 Kangxi already had reason to suspect that the Western Mongols under Galdan, unlike the eastern tribes, would not docilely accept subordination to Manchu rule. But in the 1680s his main goal in the northwest was to ward off the increasing Russian penetration of northern Manchuria. Kangxi's forward moves culminated in the attacks on the Albazin fortress in 1684 and 1686, and the negotiations leading to the Nerchinsk treaty of 1689. Preventing the Russians from supporting the rising power in western Mongolia was one of the main motivations for the treaty.

By 1684 or 1689 Kangxi could regard his consolidation of Manchu power as complete.[7] He had won over the Chinese scholar elite to his rule and successfully incorporated nearly all the Ming elite with the *boxue* special doctoral exam of 1679. He had secured the boundaries of the state on all its frontiers and defeated major opposition from Ming loyalists, the maritime fortress base of Zheng Chenggong on Taiwan, the fortress commanders in Siberia, and the powerful regional generals controlling the southwest. He had ensured the supremacy of the emperor over rival Manchu magnates and established stable institutions of bureaucratic rule. Why, then, ten years later, did this secure ruler launch another series of extremely risky campaigns of expansion, again defying his cautious advisers, and even participating in the campaigns personally? There was no strategic imperative for the Qing empire to expand further; it already exceeded the size of the Ming empire by 1678, and the Zunghar Mongols arguably did not constitute a serious threat to the core of Chinese rule. We will explore later how the campaigns against Galdan developed out of the contingent interaction of Russians, Mongols, Manchus, Tibetans, and other actors in the fluctuating environment of the steppe.

Relations between Galdan and Kangxi began amicably, following precedents set by Galdan's ancestors. In 1653 Gush Khan had been allowed to send tribute missions to Beijing, and received an imperial seal and title from the Shunzhi emperor. Ochirtu Khan, the Chechen and Tüsiyetü (Ch.

Tuxietu) Khans, and other Mongols stationed near the Gansu border had also been accepted as tributaries. The Qing accepted Galdan's request in 1677 to offer tribute. The court knew something of Galdan's character: that he was "rough and crafty and likes fighting," that he had made himself a leader by executing his vow of vengeance against those who had killed his brother Sengge, and that he had quickly achieved dominance over many of the Western Mongols.[8] His rapid rise from small chief to a great prince entitled him to present tribute on an equal level with the other Khans. The Qing aimed to ensure peace among the quarreling Mongol tribes by appealing to them as tributaries, equally subject to the emperor's benevolence or wrath. In 1655 eight of the Khalkha leaders were granted the title of "Jasak" and provided with fixed tribute allowances. They had to present annually eight white horses and one white camel—the "Nine Whites" *(jiubai)*. In return they received silver, tea, brocades, and other textiles—all profitable items of trade.[9] These Mongols from beyond the pass could enter the empire only on strictly regulated tributary missions.

The expansion of Galdan's power, however, disrupted Qing goals of maintaining peace among the tributaries and of keeping them confined to regions beyond the passes. By the end of 1677, Ölöd (Western Mongol) leaders defeated by Galdan had begun to cross the border illegally, stealing horses from border guards and local people.[10] The most powerful among them were Erdeni Qosuuci (Ch. Erdeni Heshuoqi) with over ten thousand tents and Morgen Alana Dorji with several thousand. Threatened by winter famine, these invaders crossed the border, killing and plundering for food and animals. The emperor, realizing that they were driven by desperation, ordered border troops not to kill them but to attempt to drive them out. Above all, he preferred a defensive policy: strengthening the alertness of border guards to prevent the Mongols from crossing the border in the first place.

In 1676 or 1677 Galdan had defeated and killed his father-in-law, the Khoshot leader Ochirtu Khan. He tried to recruit Ochirtu's men to join him, but many fled.[11] Major attacks were reported on the Mongols in the Ordos region by the remnants of Ochirtu's defeated bands in early 1678. At the same time, panicked Mongol loyalists reported rumors that Galdan was planning to attack the Qing borders himself. His own headquarters were at Jinshan, two months' march from Jiayuguan, but he had called for an assembly of the Mongols in the Ordos, intending, they said, to plan an invasion.[12] Meanwhile, through 1679, Erdeni Qosuuci continued his plundering, while the emperor tried to get Erdeni's lord Dalai Batur Taiji and Morgen Taiji to control him. Kangxi, who needed Galdan's aid in resolving the border troubles, since he was preoccupied with the Three Feudatories war, asked Galdan to capture Erdeni Qosuuci's band. Galdan replied that Erdeni now "roamed with the wild animals" and could not be found. The emperor responded that Galdan must capture Erdeni and return the plundered goods, or else the Qing would take their own measures.[13] By fall of 1679 Galdan had ten thousand troops prepared to invade Turfan, and he was sending scouts farther east to Hami, only 525 kilometers, or ten days' march, from the Suzhou garrison in Gansu. Still, General Zhang Yong concluded that the news about Galdan's intentions was not reliable and sent men to Jiayuguan to investigate.[14]

Galdan did take Hami and Turfan, and he had already conquered the rich oasis towns of eastern Turkestan. In October 1679 Zhang Yong received a message from Galdan, along with gifts of horses and furs for the emperor. Galdan stated, "The northwest area I have now entirely taken. Only Xihai [Qinghai], which was divided between my ancestors and your ancestors, now you control alone. I want to take it back." Zhang Yong's Mongol spies had learned a few more details about Galdan: he was born in 1644, so was now age thirty-six *sui*; he was "violent and evil, and addicted to wine and sex." The previous year he had mobilized troops to invade Xihai, marched toward it for eleven days, and then dispersed his army. He had sent troops to Turkestan (the "turban-headed Hui territory"). He did not yet dare to challenge the imperial troops on the border.[15]

We have only the (hostile) Chinese sources' version of Galdan's message, but even in this version, Galdan claimed only the right to partition the steppe along the lines of the Ming dynasty. The Ming rulers had never controlled Mongolia or Qinghai, and they extended only a thin strip into Gansu along the Great Wall. He himself did not appear to threaten the Qing's borders; the main disturbance came from the other defeated Mongols seeking refuge within the passes. Zhang Yong concluded that Galdan had no intentions of invading, and there was no need to worry about Gansu.

Meanwhile, Galdan took advantage of Kangxi's involvement in the southwest to increase his scope of action. With the Dalai Lama's approval, he took the title of Bushuktu Khan. *Bushuktu*, derived from the Mongolian "Boshugh" (decree of Heaven, fate, destiny, command) has very similar connotations to the Chinese concept of the "Mandate of Heaven."[16] In October 1679 he sent an envoy with tribute gifts to Beijing, announcing his new title. The Lifanyuan (Court of Colonial Affairs) noted that never before had a Mongol Khan simply announced a new title to the Chinese emperor without first obtaining imperial approval and an official seal. In this case, however, the court recommended that Galdan's embassy be accepted, because he seemed to be submitting to the Qing. Galdan, however, had clearly marked himself as determined to act more autonomously than the other Khans, who first requested seals from the Qing emperor before they assumed titles.

Kangxi's Mongol policy was to limit Qing intervention on the frontier by encouraging his tributaries to police themselves. He rejected a request by the Khalkhas to increase Qing guards at border posts, instead urging the Khalkhas to maintain control of their followers to prevent them from pillaging the frontier.[17] After the suppression of the Three Feudatories revolt in 1681, he summoned his Mongolian envoys to a banquet and instructed them in the general rules of Mongolian policy. Taking with them imperial orders and gifts, they would urge the Mongols to make peace among themselves. All officials who did not speak Mongolian should have their discussions translated by interpreters, and all discussions should be recorded. They should respect Mongolian customs and not be excessively concerned with following Chinese ritual. They must keep tight control of their embassies to prevent causing disputes with the Mongols. This was a comprehensive effort by the Qing ruler to establish contacts with all the Mongolian Khans on a basis of mutual understanding.

The emperor sent an embassy to Galdan in response to his request to offer tribute. It reported back to Beijing in the fall of 1683. Galdan, who had never before received imperial envoys, had been delighted to hear of their arrival. He insisted on selecting an auspicious day to receive the imperial orders, and he was concerned to follow the correct rituals. As he said: "Chinese customs are complicated. Our country's customs are simple and easy. When Chinese board officials receive an imperial order, the banquet is held only a month later. Although our country does not have boards, we have zaisang [ministers]. If a zaisang receives the order, this follows Chinese custom. If we follow our custom, the Khan himself receives the order and gifts directly." He decided to receive the imperial gifts and orders directly. Interrogating the envoys, he said, "I've heard you recently had a rebellion, which has now been suppressed." The envoys replied, "There were rebels recently, but our emperor did not want to disturb the people with arms, so he gradually induced them to surrender. Some surrendered, some were exterminated, and now all is settled." Galdan was also impressed that the Qing had sent Tibetan-speaking envoys to Tibet. He demonstrated his Tibetan connections by making the embassy watch lamas doing ritual dances and chanting scriptures. He offered them numerous banquets and sent them off with lavish gifts, including four hundred horses, sixty camels, three hundred sable and five hundred ermine pelts, and, interestingly, "four Ölöd fowling pieces [niaoqiang]." The envoys agreed that Galdan would attempt to capture Batur and Erdeni if possible, and both sides would observe the two chiefs' activities until the fourth month of 1685. Even if he could not capture and punish them, Galdan promised to prevent the two from attacking the Qing frontier.[18]

This first embassy to Galdan indicates the flexibility of both sides and their mutual interest in good relations. Each side was aware of the cultural differences between them, and neither one wanted to let ritual details interfere with communication. Galdan was seen as less threatening than the Russians, and a useful resource for the Qing in maintaining control over the less powerful Mongolian tribes who raided the border. As so many previous dynasties had done, the Chinese emperor helped one steppe leader to secure preeminence in the hopes of winning him over to establish stable tribute relations.[19]

Tribute presentations served as a flexible means of using economic incentives to secure border control. The Qing envoys pressed Galdan to assert tighter authority over his tributary envoys. Many envoys had come purporting to be Galdan's men, but without carrying any official credentials. Galdan noted that his direct envoys all carried his official seal, but the allied tribes—Derbets, Torghuts, Khoshot, and others—lived too far away to be provided with official credentials. Also, Galdan's own kinsmen carried no papers when they crossed the border. The looser, more casual controls of the Mongolian Khans clashed with the demands of Chinese bureaucratic paperwork. When the Qing envoys insisted, "If you send sons and nephews without credentials, we will not allow them to cross the border. Do you understand?" Galdan replied, "Whether or not they cross the border is your emperor's decision."[20]

Only two months later the emperor cracked down more severely on abuses by Galdan's missions. The embassies were getting too large—up to several thousand men—and the members were committing crimes along the route to the capital: "They loot and plunder the horses of Mongols beyond the pass, and pasture them at will after they enter, trampling fields, and plundering people's goods."[21] Kangxi had previously set no limits on the size of Galdan's missions, but now he restricted them to two hundred men. Others would have to trade at the border towns. Reliable headmen (toumu) were to watch carefully over the actions of all who entered the pass. Although he had pardoned the crimes of the previous embassies, in the future all who committed crimes in the interior would be punished by Chinese laws. Extraterritoriality, the right of foreigners to be tried by their own legal codes, was not part of the emperor's thinking for these missions.

Nevertheless, the next year Galdan sent an embassy of three thousand men to test Kangxi's order. All but two hundred were turned back at the border.[22] Galdan disputed the emperor's restrictions, arguing that since ancient times, trade with the Ölöd had followed fixed regulations, which did not limit the size of missions; but the Lifanyuan responded that the rules had changed, and Galdan's "claim from tradition" was rejected. Galdan, like so many nomadic state builders, clearly needed the tribute trade to obtain resources, and the emperor, while supporting Galdan's claim to preeminence over the Western Mongols, used the tribute lever to restrain his demands. This was one of the issues that lay behind Galdan's more aggressive moves eastward three years later. But the Qing did not cut off all access to the capital by Galdan, and in fact backed up his exclusive rights in 1686, declaring that only Galdan and the four great (Khalkha) princes had rights to trade in the capital; all others must trade at the border.[23]

Trade restrictions did put pressure on Galdan's authority. His kinsmen blamed Galdan, not the emperor, for their loss of opportunities to trade independently.[24] Indirectly, making Galdan the sole authority entitled to send missions to the capital and requiring all Western Mongol traders to obtain seals from him created tensions within the Mongolian tribes—tensions that could be used by the Qing to pit them against one another.

As Galdan expanded, he forced other Western Mongolian tribal leaders to attack the Chinese frontier to survive. When Galdan killed Ochirtu Khan, he took over his possessions and territory, but Ochirtu Khan's son Lobzang Gunbu Labdan and his nephew Batur Erke Jinong fled to seek aid from the Dalai Lama. The Dalai Lama found a place for them to settle at Alake Shan. In 1683 reports came from the Ordos chief that Batur was pasturing along the shores of the Yellow River. He asked that Batur be sent back to his tribal territory. The emperor sent a letter to Galdan saying, "This [Batur] is one of your Ölöd people. If you want him back then take him; otherwise we will take measures." Galdan replied that he would deal with Batur the year after next. Kangxi declared that the Qing could absolutely not accept Batur, although he knew that Galdan's people were said to be so poor that "anyone who owned one horse is considered very wealthy there." Expecting internal divisions to break out soon in Galdan's reign, he decided to wait before taking action.[25]

Prince Gandu had also been roving along the frontier ever since Galdan killed his grandfather. In 1684 Batur, Erdeni, and Gandu requested the emperor's pardon in return for swearing loyalty to the Qing.[26] The emperor made it clear that he could have sent troops to exterminate *(jiaomie)* them as criminals, but he pardoned them because of the long-standing presentation of tribute to the Qing by Ochirtu Khan. He decided to settle Batur's people together with those of Lobzang Gunbu in a convenient place. Stressing that Galdan had refused to accept Batur's people, he proclaimed his merciful acts to an assembly of Jasaks, lamas, and representatives of the

Dalai Lama: "You lamas constantly plan for the common people with merciful hearts. All the Ölöd nobles present gifts to the lamas and follow respectfully their laws. I know that Lobzang Gunbu Labdan and Batur Erke Jinong are descendants of Ochirtu Khan, and Ochirtu Khan long protected the laws of the lamas. How can you bear to watch silently as his descendants are driven into poverty!"[27]

Kangxi thus launched an effective propaganda campaign to persuade the lamas to settle Batur's and Lobzang's people under the emperor's protection. These were the first Western Mongols to seek Qing protection. Negotiations ensued to establish clear boundaries for their settlement. The emperor held the power to eliminate the tribes, as he made clear, but gained a reputation for mercy which would suit him well in the future, and his appeal to shared values between the Buddhist lamas and the Qing regime was a step toward drawing the Tibetan Buddhist church away from support of the Mongols and toward the Manchus.

Galdan's Intervention

A major split between the two "wings" of the Eastern Mongols drew both Galdan and Kangxi into conflict. On the "right" (western) wing were the Jasaktu Khan and Altyn Khan; on the "left" (eastern) wing were the Tüsiyetü and Chechen Khans.[28] Their dispute went back to the "Lobzang incident" of 1662, the first year of Kangxi's reign, when Lobzang, of the Altyn Khan lineage, attacked and killed the Jasaktu Khan, Wanshuke.[29] The Kangxi emperor reprimanded Lobzang for violating one of the Qing's tributaries. The left-wing Tüsiyetü Khan also came to the aid of the Jasaktu Khan and crushed Lobzang, who fled across the Russian border. The Jasaktu Khan's rule was saved, but during the chaos many of his people had fled to the Tüsiyetü Khan's lands and remained there. After the Tüsiyetü Khan installed Chengun, Wanshuke's brother, in the Jasaktu Khan's position in 1670, peace returned to his lands, but the Tüsiyetü Khan refused to send back his people who had fled to him for protection. Galdan had himself been involved in the dispute as a mediator, trying to draw in the Dalai Lama to support the Jasaktu Khan.

By 1684 the Jasaktu Khan was still seeking the return of many of his people from the Tüsiyetü Khan, with no result, and he appealed to Kangxi and the Dalai Lama for help. The emperor was inclined to have the Dalai Lama settle the matter:

You, Dalai Lama, are compassionate . . . all respect you, Khalkha lords worship you, respect your teachings and laws, and you are sincerely

Portrait of the Lcan-skya (Ch. Zhangjia) Hutukhtu, dated 1693. The high lama is flanked by Tsongkhapa, founder of the Yellow Sect, on the left, and Shakyamuni, the historical Buddha, on his right. Below are the demon Demchog with his partner, White Tara, and the four-headed Mahakala.

Engraving of the Potala, the Dalai Lama's central temple in Lhasa.

obedient to this dynasty. I am distressed that the Jasaktu Khan's people cannot gather together; this will create mutual killing and war, then how can the two Khans coexist? You must have the Jasaktu Khan's people return and make peace between them, following my impartial benevolence. You can send a high lama to meet my high official on the Khalkha border, and set a time to meet.

But the Dalai Lama's representatives were unable to get the two sides to make any agreements that year. On the death of the Jasaktu Khan, Kangxi confirmed his successor. By 1686 he heard that battles had broken out between the two wings, with "brothers and kinsmen attacking one another," and men were fleeing from the left wing to the right wing and vice versa.[30]

Arni, the emperor's envoy, met at Kuleng Barqir (Mo. Küriyen belciger) with the collected Khans and nobles of the two wings and the Dalai Lama's envoys to urge the battling Khalkhas to make peace. Also present was the brother of the Tüsiyetü Khan, titled the Jebzongdanba Khutukhtu, the leading Buddhist cleric of Mongolia, who claimed equal and independent authority with the Dalai Lama in Tibet. Arni passed on the emperor's words: "You are all descendants of the same ancestor. If you continue fighting, you will all be eliminated. There is no profit in peace for me; there is gain in war for me." The emperor implied that although he and the Qing would actually profit from the division of the Khalkhas, their real interest was in a unified, peaceful Mongolian people. The Mongolian princes expressed their appreciation for the efforts of the emperor and Dalai Lama to bring them together, but noted that "whether we make peace is up to us two Khans." On October 10, 1686, before the Jebzongdanba Khutukhtu and the Dalai Lama's envoys and Buddha's image, the Khans, princes, and over sixty ministers swore oaths of eternal peace, and each promised to return to his own lands.[31]

The compilers of the official history of Kangxi's campaigns commented on the emperor's activities here, demonstrating the difference between the contemporaneous Qing view and the retrospective view developed at the time of compilation in 1708. They noted that "state builders" (liguozhe) are threatened primarily by internal dissension, and secondarily by external threats. Because the Ölöd and Khalkhas were close neighbors, any weakness among the Khalkhas would lead "the strong to gobble up the weak." When brother fought brother among the Khalkhas, with "the roots torn up the leaves would wither," and the Khalkhas were threatened with extinction.[32] In the compilers' view, Kangxi's intervention thus persuaded them to make peace before they were destroyed by Galdan's invasion. But the emperor at the time made no reference to Galdan, nor did he indicate that Galdan was a major threat to either the Khalkhas or the Qing. He was still setting Galdan up as the official tributary trader of the Western Mongols. Kangxi's border policy continued to be defensive, aiming to ward off refugees from the Qing borders by trying to establish peace among the Khalkhas. Only after the defeat of Galdan was history rewritten to suggest that he had always been an implacable enemy of the Qing.

The next year the emperor confirmed the succession of the Chechen and Tüsiyetü Khans with imperial seals and congratulated them for making peace. In the second month, however, he received a communication from Galdan complaining about a violation of ritual propriety at the 1686 meeting. The Lifanyuan, reporting that the rituals of the Yellow Hat sect, the Dalai Lama's sect, had been followed properly, regarded the matter as closed. But Galdan could not let it rest. He sent letters to Arni, the Jebzongdanba Khutukhtu, and the Tüsiyetü Khan spelling out his complaint: at the Kuleng Barqir meeting, the Jebzongdanba Khutukhtu, a subordinate of the

Dalai Lama, had sat directly across from the Dalai Lama's representative, violating the clerical hierarchy.

By July 1687 Galdan had moved his headquarters eastward from the Altai and summoned the followers of Jasaktu Khan to meet with him. The Tüsiyetü Khan feared an immediate attack, but Kangxi did not respond quickly. By October the Tüsiyetü Khan was reporting definite evidence that Galdan planned to attack by two routes, and his followers were urging him to meet Galdan in battle. The emperor only continued to urge the two sides to make peace, and issued a remarkably conciliatory edict to Galdan. He once again repeated his intention for all his tributaries to live in peace, allowing that he might have heard false rumors that Galdan was preparing an attack: "You, Galdan, have been obedient and presented tribute. I may not have reliable information because the distance is so far, or some followers may be stirring up trouble."[33] He denied permission to Batur Erke, the refugee Mongol leader settled in Qing territory, to take his men to support the Tüsiyetü Khan by the shortest possible route.

At the end of 1687 the Tüsiyetü Khan invaded the Jasaktu Khan's territory, killed the Khan, and scattered his people. Galdan's younger brother, who had led four hundred troops against the Tüsiyetü Khan, was killed in the attack. In revenge for the loss of his brother, Galdan's troops crushed the Tüsiyetü Khan and invaded Erdeni Zu, the great monastery built during the Ming dynasty at the old Yuan capital of Karakorum.[34] Galdan remained in the rear while six thousand men plundered the Erdeni Zu region, destroying temples and scriptures of the Jebzongdanba Khutukhtu. Thus they took their revenge for his insolence toward the Dalai Lama.

Galdan's attack shattered the Khalkha confederation. As the Chinese chronicle puts it, everywhere the Khalkhas "abandoned their tents, possessions, horses, sheep and fled south, day and night without stopping."[35] Other Khalkha tribes fled north. They besieged the new Russian envoy, Fedor Alekseevich Golovin, at Selenginsk, until he drove them off. Several chieftains offered to swear oaths of submission to Russian rule in return for protection from Galdan. Golovin, however, demanded "eternal loyalty" to the Tsar, while the Mongols sought only temporary alliances. Some of them rejected the Russian demands and turned to join the rising power of Galdan, while others maintained Russian connections until Galdan's defeat. The Khalkha tribes split in three directions—Russian, Chinese, and Zunghar—finding no unity while they were under attack.[36]

What were Galdan's motivations for these attacks? Most Chinese historians treat his bringing up the issue of ritual propriety toward the Dalai Lama as a mere pretext for his plan to destroy the Tüsiyetü Khan. But Galdan, raised from youth under the shelter of the Tibetan lamas, had strong feelings about proper deference toward the Dalai Lama. The restriction of tribute trade opportunities by the Qing also forced him to make a decisive move. A true peace among the Khalkhas would have blocked Galdan's expansion to the east and thwarted his ambitions to dominate all the Mongolian peoples—if he had such ambitions. And finally, the desire for personal revenge for the death of his brother led him to order an orgy of destruction of the temples belonging to his enemy. We need not assume any single consistent plan behind the tempestuous Galdan's actions, but only an accumulation of economic, cultural, and personal slights.

The pro-Manchu Eastern Mongol and banner commander Lomi, author of the *History of the Borjigid Clan [of Chinggis Khan] (Mongghol borjigid obogh-un teüke)*, written from 1732 to 1735 based on contemporary sources, believed that Galdan's motive for attacking the Khalkhas was simply to avenge the death of his brother. The Jesuit Jean-François Gerbillon (1654–1707), who accompanied the Kangxi emperor on his campaigns, agreed. These views differ from later accounts, which ascribe to Galdan much more ambitious aims. If Lomi's account reflects "the general understanding of the class of his time," it probably best represents Galdan's immediate views when he invaded.[37]

At first, Kangxi again reacted defensively to Galdan's invasion. He sent 2,500 troops to the border, who soon had to hold off defeated Khalkhas in flight. The Tüsiyetü Khan and the Khutukhtu first fled to the Chechen Khan's territory, but even though the Khan offered the refugees support, their people continued to flee south, crossing the Qing border at the Sunite guard post *(kalun)*. Investigators found six hundred lamas and two thousand families, a total of twenty thousand individuals, desperately seeking Chinese protection.[38] The emperor ordered a full discussion by the Deliberative Council on whether to drive the Khalkhas away from the border or protect them from Galdan's pursuit. The council advised that it would be impossible to drive the desperate refugees away, but if they stayed long in the area, they would destroy the local grazing supply. The emperor still temporized, deciding to wait another month to see how the situation developed.

Meanwhile, Galdan sent a letter explaining that he was punishing the Khan and the Khutukhtu for violating the respect due the Dalai Lama, saying he had "fought for the Dalai Lama's soul by destroying their dwellings."[39] He told the Qing ruler to refuse to accept the Khutukhtu's surrender and instead arrest him. Again the emperor was remarkably noncommittal, refusing to blame either Galdan or the Khan and Khutukhtu. But by the next month, as further flights by defeated Khalkhas increased pressure on the border region, the Qing had to send troops to protect the Khutukhtu.

Galdan had now reached Hulunbeir (Mo. Külün bayir), seven to eight days' march from the border. The emperor prepared ten banner companies, a total of ten thousand men, for defensive action on the border under the command of the Khorchin Tüsiyetü prince Shajin.[40] Emissaries sent to Galdan heard him say, "If I make peace with the Tüsiyetü Khan, who will recompense me for [the loss of] my brother Dorjizhabu? If I put out all my effort, in five to six years, I can destroy the Khalkhas, and capture the Jebzongdanba Khutukhtu."[41] When Galdan withdrew from the Qing border to attack the Tüsiyetü Khan, however, the emperor declined to pursue him. Then, when the Tüsiyetü Khan desperately appealed for military aid from the Qing to attack Galdan, Kangxi laid down his conditions: the Khan could retain his title, but he must surrender to the Qing and agree to be settled under Qing supervision. On August 28, 1688, the Tüsiyetü Khan and Galdan fought a pitched battle for three days. Galdan crushed the Khan, who fled, isolated and weak, across the desert to the Khutukhtu's territory. Kangxi took further defensive measures, sending two thousand troops to guard the Ordos.

Two months later the emperor ordered a partial withdrawal. The border troops lacked clothing for the oncoming winter, their horses were worn out, and they were running out of supplies of rations and fodder. Much of the available grain at the border had been distributed to the refugee Tüsiyetü Khan's people.[42] By the spring of 1689, over twenty thousand starving Khalkhas had come to request relief, and supplies were low. The emperor was now inclined to agree with Galdan's version of events: it was the Tüsiyetü Khan who had violated the oath of peace, killed the Jasaktu Khan and Galdan's brother, and first launched the invasion of Mongolian territory. The Tüsiyetü Khan had "brought on his own destruction" (*ziqu miewang)*, and Galdan was not to blame.[43] Gerbillon also believed that the Jebzongdanba Khutukhtu, the younger brother of the Tüsiyetü Khan, had "ruined his family by his arrogance, because he put himself on a par with the Grand Lama of Tibet."[44] The emperor did not even blame Galdan very much for destroying the Buddhist temples and images in Khalkha territory. Nevertheless, the emperor pardoned the Tüsiyetü Khan's crimes and refused to surrender him and the Khutukhtu to Galdan for punishment. Once again he urged the Dalai Lama to intervene to make peace between the contending parties, proclaiming his disinterested benevolence: "I do not rejoice at the defeat of others as my own profit. But if they surrender to me, I am Lord of Heaven, and must take care of them, else who will? I will give to all who seek help; just as you lamas will not let people die, you will take care of them too. My goal is to dissolve the contention between Khalkha and Ölöd, and create peace. If you can send lamas to Galdan, urging him to make peace, he will follow your laws."[45] At the same time, he threatened to cut off all of Galdan's trading privileges if he did not abandon his vows of revenge.

While Galdan was moving east to meddle in Khalkha affairs, conflict was brewing back home in Zungharia. Tsewang Rabdan, the son of the assassinated Sengge, had grown to maturity and become a threat to Galdan, who tried to have him killed in 1688. Tsewang Rabdan escaped, but his brother was killed, and when Galdan left to march against the Khalkhas, he attacked Hami with his own men. This forced Galdan to move back to meet Tsewang Rabdan and relieved the pressure on the Eastern Mongols, allowing the Qing to reduce their troop allotments by one-half. Arni's interview with Galdan in the fall of 1689 indicated that the Mongol leader was still determined to avenge his brother's death, even though his people were confronting famine, "eating human flesh," and facing a hard battle.[46] Galdan also indicated his suspicions that the Qing were about to forge an alliance with the Russians and the Khalkhas against him, since Arni had just returned from Selenginsk with two thousand troops. Arni assured him that he had only negotiated border issues with the Russians, and the troops he brought with him were not to be used to support the Khalkhas. Kangxi's edict to the Dalai Lama at the end of the year reflected his understanding that Galdan had been defeated by Tsewang Rabdan and was in desperate straits. Asking the Dalai Lama for confirmation, he offered to accept Galdan's surrender to the Qing. Within less than a year, in the emperor's eyes, Galdan's forces had been reduced from a serious military threat to a starving remnant band deserving of pity.

Qing officials proceeded to organize the Khalkhas into banners and settle them temporarily on the border. The emperor told the Khalkhas that they had no discipline *(fadu)*; they needed a strong hand of supervision to prevent them from dispersing. Governors (Jasak) were appointed to collect the remnant Mongols, assign them to banners, and allot them fixed pastures. But the emperor also promised that they could return to their old homes when the Ölöd conflicts were settled.

Through the winter of 1689–90 Galdan remained in Khobdo to resist the rebellion by Tsewang Rabdan, at the same time collecting troops for a move east against the Khalkhas. Although he had a few thousand followers, many of them were tempted to desert him for Tsewang, unless there was promise of significant booty from attacking the Khalkhas.[47] Kangxi continued to send small detachments to the border for defensive measures: 500 to Guihua, 1,500 to the Ordos. At the same time, he established contact with Tsewang Rabdan to find out the reason for his rebellion. The Chechen Khan promised to attack Galdan with 10,000 troops if the em-

peror gave his backing. For the first time, the emperor now allowed the
sale of Qing military supplies to the Khalkhas. He doubled the number of
troops heading to the Tula River and specified that they should bring cannon with them.[48]

Meanwhile, the Dalai Lama appeared to diverge from the Qing emperor's goals. The regent (T. sDe-pa, Ch. Diba), the highest-ranking official
in Tibet, told the emperor's emissary that he must arrest the Tüsiyetü Khan
and Khutukhtu and deliver them to Galdan. This new support for Galdan
aroused suspicions about the Dalai Lama. What Kangxi did not know was
that in fact the fifth Dalai Lama had died in 1682 and that real secular
power was then assumed by the sDe-pa, who refused to announce the death
of the Dalai Lama or to install a new one. The sDe-pa was an active supporter of Galdan's campaigns and an enemy of the influential Khoshot
princes in Tibet and of the Khalkhas. Kangxi, however, continued to appeal
to the Dalai Lama as his ally in making peace among the Mongols.[49]

On June 9, 1690, Galdan led thirty thousand troops across the Urja
River to attack the Kundulun, Chechen, and Tüsiyetü Khans.[50] Reports indicated that Galdan intended to meet up with supporting Russian troops.
Songgotu (Ch. Suoetu), the Manchu envoy to the Russians at Nerchinsk,
quickly delivered them the message that Galdan was threatened with internal revolt, his troops lacked food, and the Russians should not intervene.
Qing generals sent more troops and cannon to the frontier. The Russians
denied Galdan's request for twenty thousand troops.[51]

Kangxi's First Personal Expedition

On July 27, 1690, the emperor announced that he would personally lead
the expedition against Galdan. Kangxi's first personal campaign (qinzheng)
was now under way. Three armies would converge on Galdan's camps: one
led by Prince Fuquan, the emperor's brother, leaving from Gubeikou, one
led by Prince Changning from Xifengkou, and one led by the emperor himself. He invited the Jesuits Gerbillon and Pereira to accompany him. Probably sixty thousand troops participated in the campaign.[52] This sudden shift
from defensive measures to a personal campaign remained without justification at the time by the emperor. Clearly it cannot be explained, as later
historians did, as a response to a growing threat from Galdan's rising
power, for Kangxi knew that Galdan was in desperate straits. Galdan's
march to the east was primarily a plundering expedition to support his
starving troops. Although he had a large army, many of them would
quickly desert him if they did not get their loot, and Tsewang Rabdan still

threatened to his rear. By the end of the fifth month Galdan was camping on the lower Kerulen River with his supporters, who had dwindled to ten thousand men. Their food was nearly gone, and they were consuming their horses to survive. Yet Kangxi proceeded cautiously. He did not expect a long campaign. He issued four months' rations to the troops, half of which they would carry with them, the rest to be bought on the way.[53] But he ordered the advance troops to wait until the main army had arrived with sufficient supplies of cannon and men and to avoid battle at all costs. Other reports from fleeing Khalkhas put Galdan's strength at (an exaggerated) forty thousand men, but no one knew exactly where he was. Kangxi told his Mongolian allies to mobilize ten thousand men from the Khorchin banners.

Galdan, by contrast, continued to believe in making peace with the Qing, and tried to confine his conflict to internal Mongolian matters. Meeting several of the Mongolian bannermen, he told them, "We are of the same tribe [buluo]; why do you fight us? The Khalkhas are our enemy," not the Mongolian bannermen of the Qing. Galdan's younger brother, who commanded the troops, assured the Qing that his men would not cross the border. But meanwhile, Kangxi was preparing his full-scale expedition. He set the date of departure of the main army from Beijing for August 8, 1690, followed by the emperor himself two days later. He paid special attention to providing cannon for the army. In his edict to Galdan, he accused him of violating the empire's frontiers and refusing to return imperial envoys, and he claimed that Qing troops were acting purely for defensive purposes. Envoys to Galdan were not to inform him that the emperor and his princes were personally leading the campaign. In fact, Kangxi made clear his intention to destroy Galdan only in secret instructions to the armies on the frontier: "Have one man take a clerk to the armies, and secretly tell them: 'The emperor has sent us to tell you to advance slowly, because the great army will soon arrive. Prepare your troops, but do not engage in battle. Every night send out patrols, and wait for reinforcements. If Galdan receives orders and retreats, then stop him and tell him not to retreat. If he does not stop, have the armies attack immediately.'" In other words, the goal was to keep Galdan from fleeing, and to avoid battle until the main body of the army could arrive.[54]

Military operations seldom proceed according to plan. As Galdan continued to pursue the Chechen and Tüsiyetü Khan's men along the Khalkha River, Arni, the Qing commander, instructed to observe but not to fight, got into battle unintentionally when he ran across Galdan at the Urhui River. Arni's two hundred crack Mongolian troops and five hundred Khalkha raiders could not withstand Galdan's twenty thousand men drawn up in battle formation. Galdan had both fowling pieces and cannon, but Arni's cannon had not yet arrived. The Zunghar attack drove the Qing troops into ignominious retreat.

Now Kangxi had to salvage the situation from Arni's blunder. First he stripped Arni of his position and degraded him by four ranks. Then he tried to persuade Galdan that it had never been his intention to attack the Mongolian leader, putting all the blame on Arni's illegal action. His thoroughly disingenuous edict stressed the common interests of Zunghars and Qing and the purely defensive nature of the Qing mobilization, and evaded Galdan's main demands: the extradition of the Tüsiyetü Khan and Khutukhtu. Once again, the envoy to Galdan indicated vaguely that Qing troops were moving to the frontier but concealed the presence of the emperor and the high princes.[55]

By the seventh month there were already problems with supplying the troops beyond the passes. Reports indicated that the horses were tired, the sheep worn out, and rations scarce, requiring more grain shipments. The Qing strategy was still to advance slowly and wait until the Great Army had arrived. Galdan, it was feared, would retreat in the face of such large forces, making it impossible to crush him in battle. The first army was expected to arrive at Galdan's camp in ten days, so it was necessary to stall him with the false offer of peace talks. Thus the Qing would "use these diplomatic messengers going back and forth to delay him and wait for the Great Army." Galdan indicated genuine interest in peace negotiations; he claimed that he never intended to violate the Chinese frontier, but was interested only in taking revenge on those responsible for his brother's death. Kangxi, in reply, reproached Galdan severely for raiding the Qing border posts, but offered to discuss peace under the Dalai Lama's auspices. He again claimed that the again huge army he was assembling was "not to punish you, but to establish discussions." The emperor invoked his recent experience with the Russians, in which troops were sent to the frontier to establish peace negotiations and withdrawn when the treaty was concluded. He neglected to mention the siege and destruction of the fortress at Albazin.[56]

Even though Galdan had now moved away to the north, the emperor was determined to persevere with his personal expedition. It seems that the emperor was looking for pretexts to continue his personal campaigns in the face of criticism. Instead of justifying his campaign as a personal drive against Galdan, he claimed that he needed to accompany the troops in order to put down disturbances among the Khalkhas.[57] The Khorchin prince, whose supplies were running out, had already given up the pursuit of Galdan, so he returned to his pastures, despite the emperor's severe criticism. As Galdan continued to indicate interest in peace talks, the emperor asked,

"How can we rein in [*jimi*] Galdan so as to wait for the Shengjing army to arrive?"[58] He sent Galdan sheep and set a time and place to meet for talks.

At this critical juncture, in late August, the emperor was forced to return to the capital at the urging of his ministers. "Hot weather," probably the cause of an illness lasting through the month of September, prevented him from spending a long period beyond the passes. His ministers also had feared unrest when the Chinese in the south learned that the emperor had left the capital.[59] Galdan, at the same time, supported by the Dalai Lama's envoy, requested a meeting at Ulan Butong (350 kilometers north of Beijing) to discuss the return of the Tüsiyetü Khan and Jebzongdanba Khutukhtu. He was only 40 *li* (23 km) away from the Qing army.

Fuquan, the Prince of Yu, then reported a crushing defeat of Galdan. Having advanced to Galdan's camp at Ulan Butong, he saw the enemy at noon on September 3, 1690. The Qing fired their "deerhorn cannon" and ordered an attack. The Zunghar troops protected themselves in the forest at the foot of the mountains and used their camels to shield themselves from artillery fire. As Maska, an officer in Fuquan's army, described it, the enemy "bound the feet of ten thousand camels, covered them with felt, and lay down behind them, spread out like a wall. We called it a 'camel wall' [*tuocheng*]. They shot arrows from slits in the wall."[60] The left wing of the Qing army was able to surround the Mongol troops in the mountains and inflict great casualties on them, but the right wing, blocked by a great marsh, had to return to its original position by nightfall. Although Fuquan reported that Galdan had suffered heavy casualties, in fact he had not driven him from his position, and he knew that Galdan was prepared to resist strongly the next day. Gerbillon did not witness the battle but heard reports of it immediately. Although he described the battle as a "defeat" for Galdan, he knew that the Qing troops had retreated to their camp after the first day's fighting, and neither side was prepared to fight further. The Russian envoy, Kibirev, who was with Galdan's forces, did not see the battle as a Qing victory.[61] The emperor, however, was highly optimistic, and for the first time publicly announced his goal of a "final solution": "We must now consider how to pull up the roots entirely [*qiong qi genzhu*], wipe out the remaining followers, and clean up everything permanently with one blow [*yiju yongqing*]."[62]

His optimism was premature. Both Fuquan and Galdan knew that the Qing might win a second battle, but the outcome was uncertain. Qing troops suffered severe supply difficulties; Galdan had lost many men and horses but remained encamped securely in the forest. Qing artillery could not ensure victory, as the Mongols were protected by both camels and trees. When Galdan sent emissaries to talk peace on September 7, the field com-

The battlefield of Ulan Butong, where Qing forces fought the Mongol leader Galdan in 1690. Contrary to later accounts, this was not an overwhelming victory for the Qing. Galdan escaped, and Commander Tong Guogang, the Kangxi emperor's uncle, was killed in the battle. According to legend, Tong's cannon sank into the marshy ground, and spring water gushed out to form a lake, now called the General's Lake.

manders considered it best to hold off the attack. Galdan now conceded the main issue: he did not demand the immediate return of the Khan and Khutukhtu, but asked only that the Khutukhtu be sent to his superior, the Dalai Lama, for investigation. The generals told Galdan that he must move far away from the Qing borders and promise never to raid the frontier again. Their troops were prepared to advance and exterminate *(jiao)* Galdan if he did not agree. In their thinking, they should not further weary the troops with an unnecessary battle; either Galdan would withdraw to a remote region, or, if he remained nearby, they could wait for the planned meeting in four to five days with the advancing troops to strike the decisive blow.

The emperor, highly suspicious of the crafty Galdan, urged the generals into rapid pursuit, but he implicitly had to accept the logistical limitations of the frontier. He allowed his son Yinti to return to the capital, under the assumption that there would be no further attacks. Galdan, meanwhile, having successfully stalled for time, fled as fast as he could to the north under cover of darkness. The generals wanted to pursue him, but "the horses' strength did not allow [them] to advance." On the ninth, as planned, they met with the Shengjing Ula and Khorchin troops; the Great Army was still 100 *li* (58 km) away. Galdan's envoys, who had promised to obtain an oath of allegiance from Galdan, were sent after him to get his written commitment. Galdan, in the course of flight, plundered twenty thousand sheep and over one thousand horses to replenish his army, but the generals continued to wait for his answer. Although the emperor urged a quick advance, he realized that "the princes and generals are with the army, and they personally see the situation."[63]

By the middle of September, troops had begun to withdraw to defensive positions. Frontier garrisons provided for returning troops who lacked food and horses. Galdan's official oath arrived on September 20. He had set up a Buddhist statue in his camp, bowed low before it, and asked forgiveness for his crimes. He promised to withdraw far from the Qing frontier in search of a place with "good water and grass, and no people." After discussion with the Deliberative Council, the emperor, still distrustful, accepted Galdan's oath. Once again he proclaimed his common interest with the Dalai Lama in peace between the Zunghars and Khalkhas. Galdan had violated the Dalai Lama's teaching by entering Qing territory and plundering the frontier Mongol tribes, and the proper Qing policy would be to pursue him "across steep mountains, to remote frontiers" and to execute him as a rebel. The emperor made the extraordinary claim that his princes and ministers all urged a second battle but he alone had stopped them. (On the contrary, the emperor had urged battle against his generals' resistance, but by distorting the facts, the emperor could pose as a peacemaker.) In return, Galdan must not only withdraw from the frontier but cut off all contact with other Mongolian tribes as well. The emperor promised to destroy him mercilessly if he violated his oath.[64]

Even allowing for normal diplomatic duplicity, Kangxi's craftiness certainly exceeded that of Galdan. The emperor was in fact furious at Galdan's escape, and he took his revenge on his generals. But the brute facts of distance, food, and horses made his most desired goal, the elimination of an autonomous Mongol leader, impossible.

At the end of the year, trials determined punishments for the generals who had failed to destroy Galdan. Fuquan, the emperor's elder brother, was pardoned because of inexperience in combat. Although other high-ranking Manchus accused Fuquan of negligence, the emperor's son would not criticize his uncle's conduct on the campaign. Fuquan was stripped of his rank and forced to remain on the frontier for several months. Other officers received whippings and imprisonment, notably the artillery captains who had abandoned a heavy cannon on the battlefield.[65]

The aftermath of the abortive campaign revealed clearly the severe supply problems that had already begun to plague the Qing troops from the first days of mobilization. Until the Qing army overcame fundamental supply constraints in the mid-eighteenth century, this pattern repeated itself. Apparent smashing victories were followed by rapid abandonment of the frontier, allowing the nomadic rival to revive. As soon as Galdan fled beyond reach, the Qing generals began their withdrawal. The first troops to withdraw did not even have horses; camels loaded with food supplies had to be sent to meet these starving soldiers on their return.[66] Violating regulations, Duke Zhuoketuo and Vice Minister Alami of the Board of Revenue had illegally advanced to the Shengjing army two months' extra rations and five months' extra salary because they knew that official rations could not meet the urgent needs of these soldiers about to go out on campaign.[67] The emperor pardoned these officials because they had been moved by the troops' poverty and hunger. Two months after Galdan's flight, troops were still waiting on the frontier for word of Galdan's oath of submission, but this army needed an immediate shipment of four hundred camels with supplies to sustain itself. Instead, the emperor ordered a full withdrawal back to the border posts, including cannon, leaving only four hundred men. Even before securing Galdan's official submission, the Qing armies could not support their expensive campaign beyond the wall.

But supply costs had dogged the expedition from its earliest days. Maska, a Manchu general who wrote a diary of his experiences with the army he accompanied from Beijing, described vividly the climatic extremes beyond the wall.[68] After crossing the Great Wall at Zhangjiakou, the soldiers first had to traverse the Dabaghan mountain range in cold, drenching rain on narrow paths under steep cliffs. Beyond the mountains they entered the steppe, which was so dry that they had to dig wells to find water, even though they were pelted with "hailstones big as peaches." Once they entered the Gobi desert, the only water they found "stank of rotting flesh" and made them vomit because of the infestation of tamarisk roots, and they found no animals or birds except for small marmots.[69] Good drinking water lay five feet deep under the sand. Having crossed the desert, they once again were struck by heavy rains, which nearly drowned both men and horses, and by now their grain supplies had run out, leaving them unable to advance. The exhausting struggle with the elements made it difficult for men and horses to move at more than a crawl. It took twelve days to cross the Gobi, a distance of 300 kilometers. Only when they met up with other troops could they proceed into battle against Galdan.

Horses were costly to purchase and to feed. Before the campaign, the emperor had caused a riot in Beijing when he set a price of 12 to 20 taels per horse, probably because the excessively low price induced officials to seize horses from local people, including high-ranking literati.[70] During the preparations for the campaign, each captain took charge of pasturing ten horses, which he would turn over to the Ministry of War when they were strong and fat. Nevertheless, inspectors constantly reported thin, starving horses at frontier garrisons.[71] No unit could remain long in a fixed location without quickly running low on supplies for both horses and men. The emperor had expected a short campaign of only two months, but as soon as he announced his personal expedition, he started to hear of exhausted troops and horses. Tired men could only travel slowly, and they were forced to depend on the local population to "help" them with supplies. He had to prohibit soldiers from selling weapons to the Mongolians in exchange for food and horses. Troops carried both grain and silver with them, but silver purchases drove up prices on local markets, and many soldiers were reluctant, or unable, to carry two months' worth of rations on their backs. Even though the furious emperor wanted to punish his generals who retreated, he recognized that they had suffered severe shortages, stressing that "China cannot rest in levying troops and planning supplies."[72]

Even after the campaign, supply costs took their toll in the form of heavy debts. As noted earlier, the emperor spared from punishment two officials who had illegally lent official funds to their deeply indebted soldiers. After indebted soldiers threatened to riot in the capital, and several even tried to force their way into the palace, the emperor announced that he would take responsibility for their debts, at a total cost of 16 million taels.[73]

Qing officials, despite their intentions, had to supply not only their own troops but also those of their Mongolian allies. For a while they refused the military aid offered them by the Khorchin prince, until he promised to provide his own grain and horses. Even after accepting the alliance, they at first refused to allow him to purchase supplies on local markets, but finally relented. The next month the prince had to return home when his supplies were exhausted. Even though he "deserved execution" for his betrayal, the emperor had no choice but to pardon him.[74] When the Khalkha Mongol refugees fled across the border, however, the Qing had to provision over twenty thousand starving people immediately. Commander Fiyanggû sold his stocks of tea and cloth and used silver to buy them animals and several months' worth of grain.[75] Refugee demands for subsistence pushed the emperor to attempt to finish Galdan once and for all.

Even though the compilers of the campaign history fulsomely praised the emperor for sparing the common people the burdens of supplying his campaigns, imperial demands strained the edges of the local economy and central resources. Chen Feng estimates the total cost of the first Zunghar campaign at 3 million taels, or 6 percent of treasury holdings in one year.[76] The Qing armies had proved that they could confront and drive off a Mongolian force in the steppe, but they learned that the logistical costs of such expeditions were high and the economic burdens heavy. Galdan lost many men and horses but survived to fight another day. Exterminating the rival state required more than ambitious military plans; the Qing rulers needed allies, both Mongolian and Russian, to achieve their goal, and they needed economic development to support military mobilization.

The Treaty of Nerchinsk and the Excluded Middle

The Chinese emperor's successful campaigns against Galdan would have been impossible without Russian acquiescence. China and Russia signed the Treaty of Nerchinsk in 1689 and the Kiakhta trade treaty in 1727. These treaties had decisive consequences for Central Eurasian power relations. Their most important effect was to reduce the ambiguity of the frontier by eliminating unmapped zones. Peoples in between the two expanding agrarian empires took advantage of the fluidity of this zone to protect their identities through shifting allegiances. After 1689, refugees, deserters, and tribespeople had to be fixed as subjects of either Russia or China. Maps, surveyors, border guards, and ethnographers began to determine their identities and their movements. The treaties served both empires internally and externally by stabilizing movements across borders and enabling the suppression of groups who did not fit into imperial definitions of space.

Many scholars have examined the diplomatic negotiations that led to

THE CITY OF NERZINSKOI IN DAURIA

1 The wooden Castle in: habited by the Governor. 2 The Church. all
The Inhabitants soldiers which trade to China, and have great immunities.

Nerchinsk, site of the treaty negotiations between Russia and China in 1689.

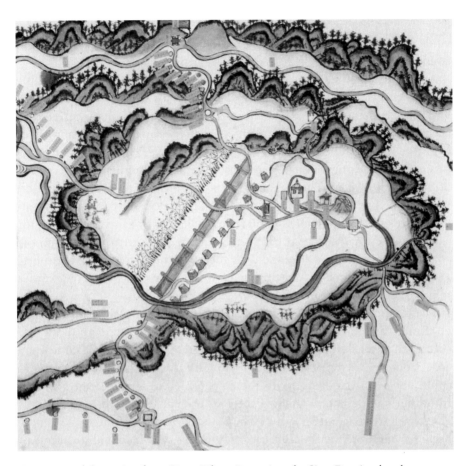

Qing map of the region from Urga (Ulaan Baatar) to the Sino-Russian border at Kiakhta. North is at the top, with Kiakhta at the extreme top center. The large temple on the center right is the residence of the Khutukhtu, high lama of Mongolia. Walls, guardhouses, and a willow palisade guard the city on the west; the circles with yellow labels are watchtowers *(karun).*

these treaties, but most of them concentrate on the bilateral Russo-Chinese relationship. The success of these frontier negotiations, however, depended on the relationships among four parties—Russians, Mongols, Manchus, and Jesuits—each of whom had separate interests. In this section I focus on the importance of the Mongolian connection for both the Russians and the Manchus. The two empires had gradually groped toward each other across vast underpopulated spaces in the seventeenth century. Both sides came to realize initially that they had a common interest in fixing the allegiances of the tribal peoples on their borders, and, later, that they needed to prevent each other from allying with the rival Mongol state to their west. The lure of trade with the rich Chinese market drew the Russians to the Qing side, while the Russians' control of the northeast border attracted their Qing counterparts. Mongol efforts to find allies proved unavailing.[77]

As the Russian settlers moved east across Siberia, they soon became aware of the riches of China. Siberia contained "an inexhaustible supply of what had constituted Russia's chief marketable commodity—her gold in short—namely the fur-bearing animals, such as ermines, black and silver foxes, beavers, otters, mink, but best of all, sables."[78] Furs provided a significant amount of revenue to the Muscovite state, and Beijing offered the best market for them. The Russians knew very little in detail about the Chinese empire but saw it as a profitable trading opportunity from the beginning. After an unsuccessful attempt to reach Beijing by caravan in 1608, for example, they had learned that "[the Chinese] use firearms, and people come from many lands to trade with them. And they wear golden robes, and to him [the emperor] they bring all kinds of precious stones and other things out of many countries."[79]

The diplomatic mission of Ivashko Petlin and Ondrushka Mundoff in 1618–19 was the "first European mission to [China] in modern times that succeeded in reaching Peking and returning in safety," but the Tsar learned little from it. Because they had no tributary gifts to present, the envoys could not get an audience with the emperor. (They had received a letter from the Wanli emperor inviting them to present tribute, but no one was able to translate it until 1675.)[80] The Russians knew the Great Wall well, because they had traveled along it for ten days, but they had no access to the court in Beijing. Russians had much more contact in this region with Mongols, especially the Altyn Khan, than with either Manchus or Chinese, and they had no real knowledge of the Manchus' powerful state until they ran directly into them on the Amur River in 1644.

Russian Cossacks had begun to move into the Amur watershed in 1632, when they founded Yakutsk, but Vasily Poyarkov's expedition of 1643–1646 was the first to provide detailed information about the resources of the region. Poyarkov's arrival alerted the Manchus to Russian expansion, stimulating them to take defensive measures. When Erofei Pavlovich Khabarov returned on his second expedition in 1650, he defeated tribes who were vassals of the Manchus, but he was surprised by the arrival of a Manchu force in 1652. The Manchus, unaware that Khabarov represented a serious attempt at colonization by the Russians, did not try to destroy the Cossack force, but instead retreated. In 1654 and 1658, however, Manchu troops decisively defeated the Cossacks and drove them out of the Amur back to Nerchinsk. The Qing did not follow up this action, however, so outlaws and Cossack bands filtered back eastward. In the 1660s a Polish exile and some Cossack criminals built a fortress at Albazin, which grew to hold three hundred people.[81]

Meanwhile, Russian embassies continued to pursue the prospects of trade in Beijing. The embassy of Fedor Isakovich Baykov in 1653 had a directly commercial purpose, since the Russians were now desperate to develop the fur trade. Because he refused to perform the *ketou,* Baykov's gifts were rejected, but he gathered important information. In 1658 and 1668 the embassies of Setkul Ablin, a Bukharan dispatched by Baykov to trade in furs, demonstrated that selling furs to Beijing could be very profitable. In 1672 Ablin returned to Russia with an 18,700 ruble return on an investment of 4,500 rubles.[82] Since Ablin was designated only a "messenger" of Baykov and not an official envoy, he could avoid the restrictions of tributary ritual and concentrate on trade. By now fur had become the dominant element in the Russo-Chinese trade, exchanged in Beijing mainly for silk and other textiles. Russian hopes for profit rose.

Conflicts over the allegiance of the tribes of the Amur valley, however, blocked trade relations for the next twenty years. Gantimur, for example, a Tungusic chieftain who left Manchu control to become a Russian subject, exemplifies the opportunities available before the closing of the frontier.[83] The defection of Gantimur caused intense diplomatic conflict between the two empires but ultimately led both to realize that they shared an interest in establishing a well-defined border. Gantimur had fled from his homeland in Siberia to avoid Russian demands for tribute in 1653. The Russian commander Khabarov built the fortress of Nerchinsk in Gantimur's territory in 1654. Gantimur received a mandarin rank and led troops against the Russians but then came back under Russian control in 1666–67. The Russians aimed to attract local tribes to Albazin by offering military protection and food supplies, while the Manchus ordered Tungus tribal leaders to move away from the border, closer to Qing control.

Gantimur and his powerful warriors were an attractive resource for both sides. The Kangxi emperor demanded Gantimur's return, fearing that others would follow his example, but the Russian governor, in turn, demanded that the Qing emperor declare himself a vassal of the Tsar. Such an outrageous demand was too shocking even to be translated from Russian. Fortunately, in 1675, the Tsar in Moscow, determined to promote the fur trade, sent a major embassy to Beijing, led by Nikolai Milescu Spathary, to negotiate diplomatic relations and trade. Spathary's embassy failed, primarily because he refused to send Gantimur back. The Qing feared that Gantimur would aid Siberian Cossacks who were raiding their frontiers, while the Russians feared that returning him would encourage other tribes to refuse *iasak* tribute payments on which they relied to support their garrisons. Yet both sides gained valuable information from this encounter. Kangxi realized that raids on the border could be stopped by offering trade prospects to the distant Tsar, and the Russians confirmed the power of the new dynasty and the attractiveness of the China market.

Both sides now agreed that clarifying the ambiguous border was crucial to trade and security on the frontier. By the 1680s they were ready to negotiate. Kangxi had repressed the Three Feudatories uprising in 1678 and taken Taiwan in 1683. He sent two letters in May 1683 offering negotiations if Albazin were evacuated. By the time the letters arrived in Moscow in November 1685, Qing troops had destroyed the fortress, and would besiege it again after Russian reoccupation in 1686. In response, the Tsar dispatched Golovin from Moscow in January 1686 as plenipotentiary ambassador to negotiate a demarcated frontier and to establish commercial relations. He arrived in Selenginsk in October 1687. Golovin first intended to invite the Khutukhtu of Mongolia to act as mediator between Russia and China, but then he received an invitation to write to the Kangxi emperor directly. Kangxi agreed with the Russian proposal to meet in Selenginsk in 1688, but the Qing officials called off the meeting when Galdan began his attack on the Khalkhas in the same year.

The primary Qing concern became preventing the Russians from supporting Galdan, whose power was growing. The Russians likewise realized that turmoil in Mongolia threatened a resolution of border conflicts with China. Galdan had driven the Khalkhas into flight both north and south. Some sought shelter on the Qing border; others moved north against Selenginsk, first besieging Golovin in the fortress and then forcing him to flee to Udinsk. By March 1689 he had defeated these Mongols and recovered Selenginsk. The Qing officials now agreed to his suggestion to meet at Nerchinsk farther east, freer from Galdan's disruption. Envoys from both sides arrived there in July 1689. Golovin, with his entourage of about one thousand, met with seven ambassadors, led by Songgotu, and a supporting cast including the two Jesuits Gerbillon and Pereira, military regiments, and Buddhist clergy numbering at least ten thousand.[84] The Qing representatives were all high Manchu officials, including Tong Guogang, the Chinese uncle of the Kangxi emperor, and Sabsu and Langdan, who had led the troops that demolished Albazin.

No Mongol princes attended the meeting at Nerchinsk, but their hidden presence affected two critical issues of the negotiations: the means of communication and the delineation of the border. The delegates first had to choose a language of discussion. Neither side could use its native language, because preserving the illusion of equality was essential to success at the negotiating table. Both parties had open tents side by side, with equal numbers of men. The Qing officials did have Russian translators available but did not use them. As high-ranking Manchus, they excluded participation by any Chinese in border negotiations. Tong Guogang had argued for the presence of Chinese in 1688, but his proposal was rejected. The Russians had tried to obtain Manchu translators from their Daur tributaries but could not find any competent ones. Both the Russians and the Manchus, however, were quite familiar with Mongolian, which had been the most common language of communication among different peoples in this frontier region. And yet the primary language of the Treaty of Nerchinsk became not Mongolian but Latin, a language known to only one or two Russian representatives and the two Jesuits serving the Qing.

Because the Jesuits had inserted themselves as crucial mediators, they could decide the terms—and the language of communication. On the first day of the meeting, August 22, the envoys agreed in principle to communicate in Latin.[85] According to Golovin's report, they believed that there were not enough Mongolian translators, and these were not reliable, so both sides agreed that it would be more "objective" to rely on the Jesuits' Latin. The Pole Andrei Belobotskii acted as the Russians' Latin translator. Discussions, however, soon became hung up on the question of where to draw the border. (See Map 5.) At first, the Manchus claimed all the territory up to Lake Baikal, basing their claim on the fact that all the Mongolian tribes of this region had paid tribute to the Yuan empire. The Russians held out for preserving Albazin and Nerchinsk, suggesting that the border be drawn along the Amur River. They heard the Manchus threaten them with military strikes if they did not concede immediately. When they realized that the Jesuits were "inserting words" in their translations, they asked to communicate with the Qing envoys in Mongolian. After a long discussion among themselves in Manchu, the Qing envoys said that they had "only directed the Jesuits to speak of the border issue, and not of military matters."[86]

Each time discussions deadlocked, the Russians tried to communicate directly with the Manchus, using Mongolian translators, but the Jesuits opposed them on the pretext that the translators were incompetent. The Jesuits also told the Russians not to speak to the Manchus in between negotiation sessions, and they told their own interpreters and Manchu official assistants (jargochi) never to speak to the Russians alone in Mongolian.[87] Mongolian could certainly have served as a bridging language just as easily as Latin; by excluding it, the Jesuits put themselves in the position of getting better terms for the propagation of their religion from both sides. They enticed the Russians into promising favorable treatment from the Tsar by pretending to be able to dissuade the Kangxi emperor from war, and they

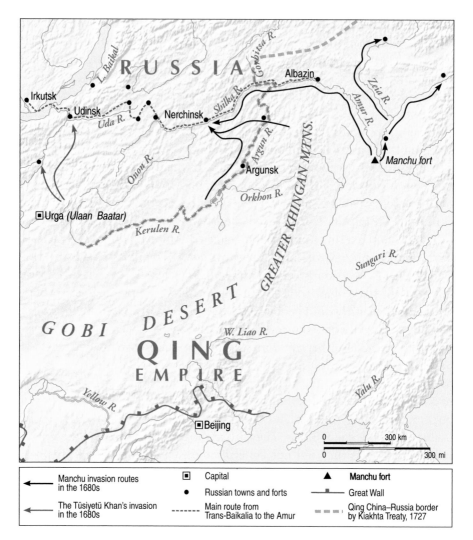

Map 5. The Sino-Russian frontier.

obtained an Edict of Toleration from Kangxi in 1692 by taking the credit for successful treaty negotiations. In the time-honored tradition of powerful mediators up to Henry Kissinger in our own day, they were determined to exclude any communication channels outside themselves.[88] Monopolizing the language and the access of each side to the other, they successfully kept any Mongolian interests out of the negotiations.

The conflict over where to draw the border line was ultimately settled by the threat of force and by the ambiguous loyalty of the Mongols between the two empires. On the second day, Golovin agreed to allow the border to run along the Bystry, or Burei, River, a small tributary of the Argun, if the

Qing would pay compensation for the destruction of Albazin. Songgotu then proposed that the border should run along the Shilka River, following its course into the Amur. This line would leave the Russian fortress of Argunsk in Qing territory, along with a valuable salt lake and mines. Golovin rejected Songgotu's proposal to adjourn the conference until both sides had submitted letters outlining their demands to their emperors; he suspected that the Manchus would only use the time to move troops into the frontier region. He also tried to win over the Jesuits to his side by promising them favorable treatment for proselytizing in Siberia.

Golovin then learned that the Qing were inducing at least two thousand Buriat and Onggut Mongols near Nerchinsk, who had paid *iasak* to the Russians, to desert to the Qing. Songgotu offered to set the border at the Gorbitsa River, south of the Shilka, if the Russians would agree to determine a border with the Khalkhas along the Selengge River. Since the Khalkhas had not yet submitted to the Qing, Golovin rejected the authority of the Qing to determine the borders. Songgotu then mobilized an army of 12,000 men, plus the Buriat and Onggut deserters, to surround Nerchinsk, while Golovin with his 1,500 men prepared a last-ditch defense. Two days later, knowing that his position was hopeless, Golovin gave in to most of the Qing demands. Reasoning that there were few settlements and few furs between the Gorbitsa River and Albazin, and his Mongolian tributaries were deserting in increasing numbers, he abandoned his claims to Albazin but retained access to the salt and mines north of the Argun. Under the final terms of the treaty, the fortress of Argunsk would be moved to the north side of the river, into Russian territory; the Qing would pay no compensation for Albazin but would allow traders access to the regions; and the border would be drawn north of the Amur River along the nearest mountain range, determined by stone markers. A stele at the mouth of the Argun gave the text of the treaty inscribed in Russian, Chinese, Manchu, Mongol, and Latin. Other parts of the border would be delimited later.

Golovin thus succumbed to an adroit use of military threats and enticements by the Manchus. Losing his Mongolian tributaries would have cost him nearly all control of the Transbaikal region. At the price of giving up Albazin, he preserved access to lands north of the Argun, and he kept control of the tributaries currently under Russian control. The Qing gave up claims to land which it never controlled in the first place, and by offering trading access ensured that the Russians would not support Galdan. Today, nationalist historians on either side argue that the other side got the better deal. They reduce the treaty to a bipolar Sino-Russian confrontation, neglecting the significance of the other two parties affected by the negotiations.

The Russian and Qing officials calculated their positions not just in terms

Boundary markers between Russia and China determined by the Nerchinsk treaty. A Russian Orthodox cross is atop the left marker; the Manchu writing on the right says "border" *(jecen i ba)*.

of the effect on the other party but in light of the consequences for all participants in the steppe power struggle. It was the Jesuits who clearly got the most out of Nerchinsk, gaining great credit with Kangxi, who allowed them free access for missionary activity. The Jesuits had already gained the trust of the emperor by providing him with weapons, teaching him geometry, and informing him about the wider world. Now they showed their diplomatic skills as well. In the end, however, they never succeeded in converting the Manchus or the Chinese to Christianity, and they lost influence

A detail from the *Jilin Jiuhetu* (Map of Nine Rivers of Jilin), a large map of the Man-churian–Russian border region used by Qing negotiators at Nerchinsk. All rivers and villages are labeled in Manchu.

when Kangxi left the throne. The Qing rulers had used them for their own purposes and then cast them aside. The Mongols, both Galdan and the frontier tribes, lost the most because the settlement locked them on one side of the border and deprived them of the ability to find allies.

Galdan discovered the effects of the Nerchinsk treaty immediately. In early 1690 he sent an envoy to Golovin in Irkutsk seeking Russian military support for his planned attack on the Khalkhas.[89] Since the Russians them-selves had been attacked by the Tüsiyetü Khan, Galdan expected an alli-ance against their common enemy. Golovin replied that he had tried to con-tact Galdan in 1688 to discuss an alliance, but his messengers had been unable to get through. Now, however, he was unable to join forces with

Galdan. He did, however, send an envoy to inquire about Galdan's troop strength and to find out how many Russian traders were in Galdan's territory. After signing the treaty with the Manchus, Golovin no longer had an interest in a Zunghar alliance. His main concern was to protect Russians in Galdan's territory and to prevent the defection of Mongols who were paying tribute to the Tsar. Golovin's envoy told Galdan to allow free trade at Irkutsk and to send back the brother of the Altyn Khan, who had rejected his tribute obligations to the Tsar and sought protection from Galdan.

As soon as he heard of Galdan's approach to the Russians, the Kangxi emperor reminded the Russians that aiding an attack on the Khalkhas, who were subjects of the Manchus, would violate the Nerchinsk treaty.[90] Nerchinsk now served as the model for defining obligations on the frontier, and the Qing had defined the terms. Galdan was too late. He continued to send embassies to the Russians in Siberia throughout the rest of the decade, but they refused to allow him to appeal to Moscow. In the end the lure of the China trade was much stronger than any prospects for gold exploration in Zunghar territory. The Qing's greatest gain from Nerchinsk was thus to deprive the Zunghars of a potential ally.

At Nerchinsk and Kiakhta the Qing signed their first treaties with a Western power, the only ones for over two centuries negotiated on a basis of relative equality. Yet neither empire's rulers believed in equal-status negotiations between sovereign states. Both acted from hierarchical assumptions of tribute, vassalage, and deference. How could these treaties be negotiated under such contradictory understandings? Negotiations succeeded only because two other parties intervened as vital cultural intermediaries. The hidden presence of the Zunghar Mongol state induced both empires to adjust conventional diplomatic rituals. The Jesuits and their Latin language were the last survivals of the fluid intercultural communications of the vanishing frontier, before formal state-to-state contact took over. In order to secure their monopoly, however, the Jesuits had had to exclude the ability of the rivals to communicate in Mongolian.

Unlike McCartney's experience in the late eighteenth century, the issue of kowtowing to the emperor did not ultimately derail these negotiations. As in the later negotiations with other European powers, the two sides had very different goals. The Russians wanted trade, while the Chinese wanted security. But unlike in the nineteenth-century "unequal treaties," each side gained what it needed without inflicting unacceptable costs on the other.

Each side found the other both culturally familiar and alien. Both Chinese and Russians had been accustomed for centuries to diplomacy with Central Eurasians, but for the most part they had dealt with nomadic tribal confederations that were militarily powerful but institutionally unstable.

Now each confronted a large, established imperial rival. Norms of protocol had to change. The Russians took a pragmatic view of frontier expansion: they had moved into Siberia not for glory but for profit. Territory and imperial honor took second place to promotion of the fur trade. The Qing, for its part, compromised on ritual propriety in order to secure Russian neutrality in the coming conflict with the Zunghars.

Nationalism and contemporary politics have strongly influenced interpretations of Nerchinsk and Kiakhta.[91] Until the Sino-Soviet split of the 1960s, Russian and Chinese historians interpreted the treaties as the roots of the "fraternal alliance" of the 1950s, the only successful equal treaties between China and the West. Since the 1960s, however, Russians have viewed them as "unequal" treaties forced on a weakened Russian empire by aggressive Manchu expansion. Chinese historians regard the Russians as treacherous imperialists who signed the treaties but continued to give significant aid to the Mongol state. Most recently in China, nationalists have claimed that the treaties themselves were "unequal" to China's disadvantage, because China gave up claims to large parts of eastern Siberia purportedly occupied by "Chinese" (i.e., Tungusic) peoples. Both sides construct the other as ineradicably "aggressive" in order to shore up their own insecure national communities. Like the military campaigns, diplomatic history too has become a tool of nationalist ideology.

5

Eating Snow: The End
of Galdan, 1690–1697

URING the six years between his first and second campaigns, the emperor shored up his defenses and planned to isolate Galdan from potential allies. Galdan, for his part, aimed to win back the Khalkhas who had surrendered to Kangxi, recover his strength far from the border, and ensure support from the Dalai Lama. Tibet became a primary focus of rivalry. The emperor tried to cut off communication routes between Galdan and Tibet running through Hami and Xining. Galdan, in turn, tried to cut contact between Kangxi and Tsewang Rabdan, because the emperor aimed to use Galdan's nephew against him at his rear. Both rulers publicly professed their dedication to peaceful relations while each plotted against the other.

Kangxi began to recognize the severe supply problems that prevented him from pursuing Galdan to his lair. He had vowed to "exterminate Galdan root and branch," but he could not reach him in distant Khobdo. He could only act defensively, until either his logistical foundations were more secure or Galdan could be lured into a closer attack. The first steps toward building the giant logistical network that culminated in Qianlong's campaigns of the 1750s began during this period. Likewise, the "fatal individualism," or divisions between the Zunghar and Khalkha Mongols, and within the Zunghars themselves, prevented any joint action by them against the Qing regime.[1] These divisions, arising in the 1690s, ultimately caused the destruction of the Zunghar people in the mid-eighteenth century.

The Dolon Nor Assembly

Although angry at Galdan's escape, the emperor realized that Galdan's absence offered him an opportunity to extend his influence over all of the Khalkha tribes. Soon after his victory at Ulan Butong, he made plans to establish "order and discipline" among the Khalkhas.[2] He convened a great meeting of the Khalkha Khans at which he would organize them into banners like their fellow Chechen Mongols in the Forty-nine Banners, and settle them permanently in designated territories. The emperor once again faced opposition to a dangerous trip beyond the wall.[3] Censor Shen Kaizheng urged him to delay the meeting because of bad weather and risks to his health, but the emperor insisted that these major issues could be settled only with his personal presence. Leaving Beijing on May 9, 1691, he first conducted a great hunt, laid out as a military campaign, then set out for Dolon Nor.

Kangxi knew that the primary cause of disorder in Khalkha Mongolia was the internecine warfare among the Khans, stemming from deeply rooted personal feuds. These rival parties had drawn Galdan and the Qing into intervening in Khalkha affairs, but the Qing's decisive military victory gave it the authority to settle these disputes permanently according to Manchu rules.

Kangxi established a clear order of precedence among the Khans before the meeting, placing the Jebzongdanba Khutukhtu, the Tüsiyetü Khan, the Jasaktu Khan's younger brother Tsewang Jabu, and the Chechen Khan in the first rank, and ordering the other nobility in seven declining ranks. Over 550 members of the Mongolian nobility were assigned to specific ranks. Each of the Khans performed specified rituals, including three kneelings and nine prostrations, and each was assigned a seat at the great banquet.

The meeting was held from May 29 to June 3, 1691, at Dolon Nor, a small settlement on the edge of the steppe 250 kilometers north of Beijing. The emperor received the Khalkha Khans at a great banquet, followed by military parades to impress them with the empire's might. The firing of cannon and the display of firearms caused them to "tremble with fear and admiration."[4] A total of sixty-four small cannon, eight large cannon, and eight mortars were placed in the visiting Mongol camps. The emperor himself, armed, on horseback, led the demonstration of seventy pieces of artillery. He asked Gerbillon if European kings also made great voyages, and complained that the Manchus were receiving inferior guns from Jesuit sources.[5]

At the meeting, the emperor openly declared that the Tüsiyetü Khan and

Khutukhtu had committed crimes. Galdan's invasion had been brought on by the Tüsiyetü Khan himself, leading to destruction of his state and the loss of his family. Out of his own benevolence, the emperor had rescued the Khan's people. He pardoned them, as they begged his forgiveness. The Jasaktu Khan, by contrast, deserved pity, as he had been harmed for no reason. Both the Tüsiyetü Khan and the Jebzongdanba Khutukhtu were given fiefs and Manchu noble titles, and all swore to maintain peace. Refugees would be returned to their homes.

In the emperor's view, the Khalkhas were a "disorderly" people in need of "discipline" *(fadu)*. Enrolling them in banners kept their territories distinctly separated, avoiding pastureland conflicts. Each Khan kept his title; the younger brother of the murdered Jasaktu Khan succeeded to his position, with a title approved by the Qing. Qing officials took over the final authority for granting titles of leadership among the Khalkhas.[6]

The Khalkhas gained materially from their submission, as the Qing provided them with food and animals to relieve their suffering. They also gained new titles, confirming their authority. But in return, they gave up their right to move at will. Enrolling in banner organizations meant that Manchu officials strictly supervised their movements between pasturelands. Not all Khalkha leaders accepted the terms of this arrangement. Batur Erke Jinong, though he had joined the Qing at Dolon Nor, rejected such controls, insisting on his right to change pastures.

The Dolon Nor assembly also provided the Qing with greater authority over the Mongols in its rivalry with the Dalai Lama. An envoy was sent to Tibet to inform the Dalai Lama of the emperor's success in bringing peace to the Khalkhas.[7] At the same time, he warned that Galdan, whose followers were starving, might turn to the Dalai Lama for aid. The emperor vowed to exterminate *(jiaomie)* Galdan if he violated his oath not to attack the Khalkhas. Isolating Galdan from Tibetan support, however, required both threats and material incentives. Trade restrictions had been imposed at the border town of Dajianlu (T. Dar-rTse-mDo), now in Sichuan, which divided Qing and Tibetan realms, during the time of conflict. These were lifted now that peace was restored.

Although both armies faced severe shortages, Galdan's forces, meanwhile, were in a state of much greater exhaustion, and, unlike the Manchus, Galdan had no secure refuge. First he fled north, intending to replenish his dying herds by capturing animals from Khalkha tribes. When these efforts failed, he had to continue on foot.[8] Galdan then headed west toward the Ordos region. Qing troops were not able to block his movements beyond the Yellow River because they too lacked supplies, but they could establish defensive positions to keep him out of the Ordos. Galdan retreated to Khobdo, far away in Mongolia beyond the reach of Qing troops. Proposals for a major expedition there against Galdan had to be rejected because of his inaccessibility.[9] His forces could threaten Hami, an important supply point with a sympathetic Muslim population, which was too far out the Gansu corridor for Qing forces to garrison it in strength, but as long as the Qing kept troops in Ganzhou, Galdan did not dare to attack.

The Qing's greatest fear was that Galdan would be able to rebuild his strength from the resources of the pasturelands of Mongolia combined with grain production of the Central Asian oasis populations. After his loss in battle, with nearly all his cattle and sheep gone, his men were forced to cultivate fields and even catch fish to survive, but if the Zunghars could establish independent sources of grain, they could revive their formidable strength. Qing officials therefore proposed confiscating grain stores from the Muslims in Hami and holding them at the military garrison in Jiayuguan.

Despite their anxieties, there was little they could do to mount another major campaign immediately. Most of their concerns during this period were about reducing the size of frontier garrisons in order to economize on supplies.[10] Repeatedly, efforts to move small units beyond interior forts ran up against limited supplies of grain and horses. In addition, the new Mongol allies, many of them desperate refugees from the battlefields, required relief grain.[11] Food was a useful weapon in the contest for control of the Mongols, but even the huge Chinese agrarian economy could deliver only limited amounts to the frontiers.

The Qing made further efforts to isolate and encircle Galdan by contacting his kinsman and enemy Tsewang Rabdan, whose rebellion in 1690 had almost forced Galdan to give up his intervention in Khalkha Mongolia. Qing envoys, hoping to exploit the division between them, sent gifts to Tsewang Rabdan in 1691. Telling Galdan, "Your animals are all gone, you have nothing to eat. Men are dying in extreme want," the emperor offered to make peace between him and Tsewang Rabdan if he would submit. This strategy aimed to reproduce the success of the Qing as peacemaker among the Khalkhas, but Galdan rejected it. In Hami, one of Galdan's subordinates killed the Qing envoy Madi, sent to Tsewang Rabdan.[12] Although Galdan denied responsibility, the emperor blamed him directly, combining threats and incentives to induce his surrender. Tsewang Rabdan had sent a secret memorial to the emperor, along with tribute gifts, and maintained contact after Madi's death. The Qing policy had apparently succeeded in detaching the Khalkhas, gaining the Dalai Lama's and Russian neutrality, and splitting the Zunghar homeland. Yet Qing officials had to give up the idea of an all-out advance to Khobdo in search of Madi's killers. Galdan was still out of reach.

Galdan himself, aiming to win over allies wherever he could find them, approached the Russians, and tried to enroll the Khorchin prince Biliketu on his side.[13] But the Qing captured Galdan's letter to the prince, only lifting the cloud of suspicion from him after an investigation, and won him back to Qing submission. He presented gifts to the emperor on his birthday.[14] The Russians, as noted earlier, rejected Galdan's feelers in order to preserve the terms of the Treaty of Nerchinsk.

Relations with Tibet became the most critical contest. Until the battle of Ulan Butong, the emperor had treated the Dalai Lama and his envoys with great respect, constantly stressing their shared interest in peace among the Khalkhas. After the submission of the Khalkhas at Dolon Nor, the edicts from Beijing sounded the same tone but added a note of menace: the Dalai Lama must not respond to Galdan's appeals for material aid, or else the Qing would cut off trade relations with Tibet. The emperor's suspicions of collaboration between Galdan and Tibet increased; in November 1691, after receiving an appeal for peace from the Dalai Lama, he responded forcefully: "You lie when you claim to be advising peace. You are now plotting with Jilong Khutukhtu, who is part of Galdan's camp. He is not advising peace. Galdan is now sneaking into our borders, plundering the Uzhumuqin area. You lamas are not passing on my edicts. You are greedy for profit, deceitful, and are concealing Galdan's activities." Kangxi assumed collusion between Galdan and the Jilong Khutukhtu, the envoy of the Dalai Lama whose proposal for negotiations after the battle had given Galdan time to escape.[15]

By 1692 Galdan had reduced his demands. Instead of three requests, he had only one, supported by the Dalai Lama: the return of the seven Khalkhas to their original lands. This, of course, would have meant releasing them from the bonds of the banner system and making them vulnerable to Galdan's pressure. The emperor had to reject this request, but he also strongly warned the Dalai Lama not to persist with any further support of Galdan's independence. He had not revealed to the Tibetan lamas his goal of exterminating Galdan, and he continued to stress their common interest in benevolence, as demonstrated by his feeding of the starving Khalkhas. But the message to isolate Galdan became sterner.

In December 1693 the *sDe-pa* revealed that he, and not the Dalai Lama, had been managing affairs in Tibet. He agreed with Kangxi's refusal of Galdan's three requests, and at the same time asked for an official seal from the Qing, which was granted. At the same time, he asked the emperor not to deprive Galdan and Tsewang Rabdan of their titles as Khan. This request was refused, with the response that an "outer barbarian" *(waifan)* had no right to determine decisions of the Chinese emperor.[16]

Cannon cast in 1690, with Manchu and Chinese inscriptions, for use in the Galdan campaigns. The cannon was named "General who exerts power over long distances." Because of its small size (about 1 meter long) and wheeled carriage, it could be transported on long campaigns.

Strengthened by these successful rebuffs of the Dalai Lama's mediation, the emperor insisted on Galdan's surrender. Galdan tenaciously offered to apologize for his rude language but asked for an imperial grant of 50,000 to 60,000 taels. The emperor insisted that only a personal audience would make it possible for Galdan to submit and receive imperial favor. He had no expectations that Galdan would accept such an audience, but this was part of his strategy to lure Galdan closer to Beijing so that he could do battle with him.

At the same time, the emperor grew increasingly suspicious that Galdan was gaining allies among the Muslims of Xinjiang. Because Galdan used Muslim messengers whenever he sent envoys to the Qing, the emperor accused Galdan of sending Muslim spies into China. Of course, the Muslim oasis inhabitants of Hami and Turfan, long familiar with both nomadic and Chinese trade, made natural intermediaries, but the Kangxi emperor wanted to remove middlemen between the Qing and Mongols. By 1695 he had even apparently become convinced that Galdan himself had converted to Islam.[17] Perhaps his curious delusion is explicable only by the conviction of the Qing emperor that he had coopted all the other peoples in Central Asia, winning them over to submission or at least non-intervention. If Galdan appeared to reject the Dalai Lama, the Mongols, and the Qing, he must belong to the only group as yet beyond Qing control: the Muslims of Central Eurasia.

Reports that Galdan was moving east out of Khobdo stimulated a new Qing mobilization. One hundred camels with special food supplies were bought to carry heavy cannon.[18] The emperor expected Galdan to attempt to move south to Tibet via Kokonor. To block this move he ordered preparations for a scorched earth campaign to burn all the grasslands along the Ejina River, north of Kokonor.[19] But the campaign to destroy Galdan once and for all depended on drawing him into another battle in Mongolia.

In September 1695 the emperor outlined a definitive plan to entice Galdan into battle. The Khorchin prince Biliketu, formerly suspected of colluding with Galdan, had captured some of Galdan's abandoned documents, including an invitation to a meeting. He would send an envoy to Galdan, telling him that ten Khorchin banners wanted to submit to him and inviting him to advance east. Kangxi vowed to "personally lead a large army thundering after him, so that he cannot escape. We will definitely exterminate him."[20] He knew by now that Galdan was not preparing any new attacks on the empire, but he had determined to eliminate his tenacious rival. He prepared to set out on his second personal expedition on April 1, 1696.

The Battle of Jao Modo

Discussions of strategy for the second campaign focused first on determining Galdan's intentions. The crucial issue was logistics: supplies of horses, cannon, and grain. Unless Galdan could be lured in closer, they all had to be hauled thousands of miles from northern and northwest China to Mongolia. The emperor's greatest fear was that Galdan would once again escape, as he had at the battle of Ulan Butong.

In August 1695 Galdan seemed to be moving out of Khobdo toward the Qing frontier, but by the next month it became clear that Galdan would not march closer. He remained in the Kerulen–Tula River area to wait out the winter snows. Efforts to entice him nearer would not succeed.[21] Spies reported large concentrations of troops along the Kerulen River, where "the ground was all trampled," estimating Galdan's force at five thousand to six thousand troops.[22] Although he had few sheep, he now had abundant horses and camels. Even though Galdan's lack of aggressive intent would make it harder for the Qing to reach him, it allowed time for the Qing to supply a huge army.

Galdan himself, in his memorials to the emperor, indicated no awareness of the plans to exterminate him. He still offered to resolve outstanding disputes, with a view to establishing a clear boundary line between the two empires.[23]

Cautious, "cowardly" officials in the court, however, were not enthusiastic about a plan to march long distances through the desert. Many advised waiting for Galdan to approach more closely. Heading all the way out to the Kerulen River immediately, and marching through the winter, as the emperor wanted, risked arriving before the spring grasses had sprouted. They knew well that the lack of grass for horses would be a major limit on the mobility of the army.[24] But the emperor's intense resentment of Galdan's escape at Ulan Butong led him to insist on immediate preparations. Even after mobilization began, there was continual opposition to the emperor's personal participation in the campaign. Councilors urged the emperor not to risk the health of his "jade body" but instead to rely on the valiant efforts of his troops. They were, of course, concerned about the great costs of the campaign and the risk of instability at home while the emperor was away. At this early point, the emperor did not yet become angry at his Han officials' "reluctance to tire themselves with military affairs." He only noted that because he had been too ill to be present at the battle of Ulan Butong, the crafty Galdan had escaped, so he insisted that his personal presence was required. His eldest son could handle affairs at home.[25]

Fiyanggû, commander of the West Route Army, was the only enthusiastic supporter of the campaign, but even he persuaded the emperor that it would be best not to march in winter but rather to leave the following spring. The Qing forces would have time to fatten up their horses during the winter, move rapidly, and catch Galdan in early spring, just before his horses could be nourished on new spring grass.[26] Three armies set out: the West Route Army, led by Fiyanggû, with 30,000 men; the East Route Army, led by Sabsu, with 10,000 men; and the Capital (Central) Army, led by the emperor, with 32,970 men. (See Map 6.) Sabsu's army stopped at the Khalkha River to block movement of the Mongols to the east, so only two armies took part in direct pursuit. Another army, led by Sunsike, with 10,000 men, would set out from Ningxia to join Fiyanggû. Fiyanggû's role was to block Galdan's escape route, so he had to arrive at the Tula River before the Central Army reached Galdan's camp at the Kerulen River. It was 2,000 *li* (1,160 km) from Guihua, where the West Army set out, to Galdan's camp at Bayan Ulan, and an additional 1,000 *li* (580 km) from the capital to Guihua. The West Route Army would leave around March 22, carrying eighty days' supplies, with fifty days' supplies sent to follow.[27] Zhili, Shandong, and Henan would together provide 1,333 carts, each carrying 6 *shi* of grain. Governors of each province would provide carters

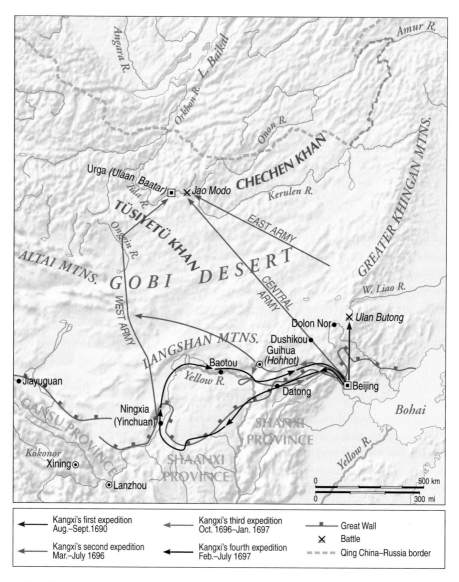

Map 6. The Kangxi emperor's Zunghar campaigns, 1690–1697.

and escort troops. All of North China's provinces bore the burden of the campaign, but the man chiefly responsible for grain supplies was Yu Chenglong, Governor-General of Zhili. He had six thousand carts built to carry supplies to the frontier. Extra allocations from the center were given to each provincial governor to spare some of the burden on the local people.[28]

Grain purchases were vital to the campaign's success. Men who worked in grain supply would receive equal military honors with soldiers who fought in battle.[29] But the poor northwestern provinces would have great difficulty supporting the army's needs. They grew only one crop per year, and they suffered frequent droughts. Distributing rations to troops and officials in the capital before they left would relieve the strain on local grain markets, but it was too much of a burden on the men to carry all their supplies with them. The Shaanxi army needed 22,400 *shi* for five months, much more than it could carry. Substituting cattle for one month's rations, and having soldiers themselves carry 0.05 *shi* with them, reduced the total somewhat, but they would still need to carry silver to buy supplies in Gansu markets. Every man was allotted silver taels, ranging from 20 taels per month for generals to 2 taels for soldiers.[30] On the march, merchants followed along behind the army, trading in separate encampments. Since many of the troops, who came from the northwest, knew local markets well, General Yin Huaxing gave them money to buy their own grain.[31]

Horses, the second vital element, could not be obtained from the interior. For them, the Qing depended almost entirely on its Mongol allies. As early as August 1695, officials went to the Khalkhas to purchase horses. They bought one thousand at the major horse markets in Guihua and two thousand from each of the six Ordos and ten Khorchin banners; other tribes supplied smaller numbers. Even feeding the horses in the capital over the winter proved to be difficult. Fengtian prefecture, north of Beijing, made its contribution to the campaign by providing 300,000 bundles of grass for eight thousand horses.[32]

But the Mongols made for unreliable allies. Severe discipline had to be enforced against both Mongols and Chinese troops who sold horses to them. The Khalkhas were "expert at stealing horses." Two Khalkhas discovered trying to steal horses were sentenced to have their arms and legs broken and their ears and neck cut.[33] Yet Mongol troops were essential to the campaign, especially crack troops for rapid pursuit. Each chief had to supply troops, but they had to be the strongest, most experienced men, particularly from the prosperous elite families.[34] It was equally important to avoid unrest among the Mongols, especially those who might fear that the army passing through their territory intended to punish them as well as Galdan. Here Tsewang Rabdan, the Zunghar leader who had split with Galdan, became a useful Qing ally. He could reassure other Mongols that Galdan was the only target, and thereby undercut Galdan's efforts to rally all of the Mongols against the Manchus and Chinese.[35] Tsewang Rabdan was allowed to increase the size of his tribute missions from two hundred to three hundred people, thus increasing his profits from trade, along with gifts of brocades, silver, tea, and furs; and the emperor promised to send to him any Muslim merchants captured in Galdan's territory during the campaign.[36]

Gunpowder weaponry was the third crucial element. Addressing his troops, the emperor allocated cannon to each banner to ensure total Qing victory, saying, "Nothing is fiercer [*meng*] than [gunpowder weapons], they are vital weapons for the army. Gunpowder is the key to exterminating Galdan."[37] Except in the Three Feudatories rebellion, where the enemy used gunpowder but did not prevail, imperial armies had won nearly all their battles without using cannon. This time, by contrast, the army would be well provided. At the great meeting at Dolon Nor, where "the firing of cannon thundered through the mountains and valleys," cannon fire had impressed the Mongols extremely. The army carried at least 235 large cannon weighing from 8,000 to 10,000 *jin* (5,000 kg), and 104 lighter cannon weighing 100 to 800 *jin*. There were many varieties, including "Western [Xiyang] bronze cannon" and "Taiwan light cannon." In a military review, when all the banners' cannon fired in succession, deserters from Galdan's army viewing the display were "greatly astonished" and predicted that "Galdan would be destroyed in a day."[38] Beyond Guihua, the cannon would have to be transported on camelback. The cannon taken to Ulan Butong were too heavy, so lighter cannon were used, but transporting this artillery over such long distances considerably slowed down the army. It nearly caused Fiyanggû to miss his scheduled rendezvous to prevent Galdan's flight.

The emperor set the departure date of the Central Army from Beijing at March 26, 1696, between 3 and 5 AM. The West Army left from Guihua on March 20 between 9 and 11 AM. Sun Sike gathered his ten thousand troops at Ningxia and left from there on March 24.[39] The Central Army could march in four stages to Dushikou 150 kilometers northwest of Beijing without extra horses; beyond Dushikou, they could average up to 60 *li* per stage, a total of approximately sixty stages. For each stage, a relay station provided forty relief horses.

Along the march, strict discipline was imposed. Troops had to rise between 3 and 5 AM; they were not allowed to light fires to cook breakfast in order that they might break camp early. Negligent officers who failed to get the soldiers moving early were punished. Water, grain, grass, and horses were the primary considerations. This early in the spring, most ponds and springs were frozen over. Wells had to be dug by chopping through ice at each stage of the march. At one spot soldiers dug seventy-five wells and created forty-five ponds. It was seen as a very good omen when water suddenly bubbled up from a frozen spring.[40] Horses could easily die from overexertion. Sweating heavily on the march and suddenly stopping for rest could exhaust them; then they had to be galloped to warm them up. They could not be given water until their sweat had dried. The troops had to be careful to avoid poisoned wells and grasses.[41]

Thirteen hundred carts followed behind the army, the supply carts bunched close together to prevent attacks. The emperor, his generals, and troops, who marched ahead of the grain carts, were very relieved when the supplies arrived. Yu Chenglong had continual problems with his supply train and soon fell behind schedule. Rain and mud slowed progress, and many cattle died. Soldiers had to build roads out of willow sticks and mud in order to cross giant sand dunes. As the carts moved out into the desert, they left behind part of their supplies at magazine posts to provide for the return journey.[42]

Meanwhile, the emperor urged his army on. Accompanied by the Jesuits Gerbillon and Pereira, he took regular sightings of the polestar to determine his latitude.[43] He prayed to the spirits of wind and rain to provide a smooth journey. Six of Kangxi's sons accompanied him on the campaign, but his eldest son, Prince Yinreng, remained in the capital to take charge of affairs in the emperor's absence. Kangxi's letters to his son describe the landscape, the progress of the campaign, and his personal health. These Manchu letters give fascinating insights into Kangxi's character. They form one of the most remarkable travel documents in Chinese literature, providing an almost daily record of the emperor's changing moods. As new information or supplies arrive, or fail to arrive, the emperor's confidence waxes and wanes. He also describes in detail the terrain through which the troops pass, paying attention to different types of grasses, the abundance of marmot burrows, water sources, and the different kinds of deserts. He sends back plants for the prince to grow. When stuck in a place with "nothing but sand and rocks," he still collects colored stones in a chest to be sent as a gift to his family in Beijing.[44] These letters, which vividly depict the hardships and delights of the campaign, are analyzed further in a later chapter.

A severe snowstorm struck the expedition soon after it set out, but for the most part the emperor found the environment he passed through quite favorable. As the weather warmed, supplies of grass and water became more easily available, and his horses stayed healthy. At one point, however, when no water or grass was found within a radius of 40 to 50 *li*, the emperor wondered if Heaven had abandoned him. Then, late at night, a spring was found on the top of a mountain, just enough for a one-night stopover.[45] On May 14 he passed a stone marker left by the Yongle emperor during his expeditions in the early fifteenth century.[46] Kangxi worried about constant rain and snow; but the Mongols rejoiced. They praised him for bringing good grass in the fourth month, the early spring, when sheep and horses were critically weak after the long winter.[47]

Not everyone shared Kangxi's confidence. When it was reported that Galdan had sixty thousand Russian troops supporting him, councilors Songgotu, Yisanga, and Tong Guowei urged the emperor to return to the capital.[48] This time it was not civilian Han officials but two of the highest-ranking Manchu officers, his close advisers, who foresaw calamity. Furious, the emperor said: "I have made careful plans, and made offerings to Heaven, Earth, and the ancestors . . . Among the soldiers there is no one, even down to the stable boy, who does not want to exterminate Galdan. But you high officials are base womanly cowards who fear putting out effort . . . I will certainly kill anyone who hesitates, or withdraws from this campaign." After a dramatic confrontation, they knelt before him, begged his forgiveness, and agreed on the correctness of his plan. Galdan's clever disinformation had nearly halted the expedition. As the officials later learned, Galdan had in fact sought Russian aid and discussed with twenty Russian envoys obtaining at least one thousand troops and cannon, but the Russians had made no definite commitment.[49]

The Manchu advisers' primary concern, however, was not the Central Army but Fiyanggû's West Army. Galdan did not yet know that the Qing were leading a huge army against him, but he was expected to flee west as soon as he learned of it. If Fiyanggû could not reach his designated battle station before then, Galdan would have escaped again, and the campaign would fail. Early reports from Fiyanggû were encouraging. He reached the Qing frontier posts on April 14, and expected to reach Wengjin (Onggin) on May 3, Tula on May 24, and Bayan Ulan, Galdan's camp, on May 27. To keep up his speed, he did not wait for his supply carts to catch up.[50] But then, after a month with no word, Fiyanggû reported that snow and mud had bogged him down. Unable to move his cannon, he had left most of them behind at the frontier, although he had been able to carry fifty-nine cannon farther on by camel. He could bring only fifteen days' worth of rations to Wengjin, and twenty days' to Tula; but by advancing quickly, he would meet with Sunsike on May 30. He now hoped to reach Tula on June 2 and Bayan Ulan on June 6.[51]

Hearing this, the Central Army faced a great dilemma: to advance or to wait? Waiting would use up precious rations; advancing too quickly would drive Galdan into flight before Fiyanggû could block him. A military council discussed the options.[52] Those who felt that Galdan would stand and fight urged a quick advance, but many feared that he would escape. It would still take nine days to reach Galdan's camp, giving him plenty of time to move far away. The army waited for several days, until May 23, risking the chance that Galdan would soon hear of the army's presence. Then the grain carts arrived, 300 camels and 173 wagons, with 1,000 *shi* of grain (300 tons): supplies were "heaped up like mountains," astonishing the Khalkha troops with their abundance. But the army had already consumed sixty days' worth of its total rations and needed to send for more. Yu Chenglong still could not bring up all his carts. The troops were now camped in an area with "nothing but sand and rocks."[53]

Reports, which later appeared to have been exaggerated, claimed that Galdan had ten thousand soldiers, ten thousand armed servants, and seven thousand vassals, with plenty of provisions and animals.[54] Fiyanggû was advancing toward the Kerulen with ten thousand men, but the exhaustion of his horses forced him to leave many men behind. The army of Sunsike was reduced to two thousand Chinese troops, most too exhausted to march. General Yin reported: "We rushed here without time to nourish our horses, so many died crossing the Gobi. Our water is all gone, and we constantly faced strong winds and rain for days at a time. The troops were cold all night, and starving men and horses collapsed."[55] By the time they arrived at Onggin, they had lost nearly all their horses in the cold and had supplies for only one month. Sending back all but the strongest men in order to conserve supplies, Sunsike marched on with Fiyanggû.

On May 26 the emperor decided to follow a third plan: to send envoys to Galdan offering negotiations. The envoys took with them several Zunghar captives, who would be released to join Galdan's forces. By stalling Galdan for a while with communications, the Qing army would gain time for Fiyanggû to block his retreat.[56] Once again the emperor used disingenuous language, asserting that his sole interest was peace on the border, that he had no intention of exterminating Galdan. He had saved from starvation the Khalkhas who had fled Galdan's attacks; now he wanted to meet Galdan personally to form an alliance. "Let us meet and determine our boundaries [*dijie*] and resume our former tributary relations . . . I am not trying to entice you into destruction."[57]

Imperial envoys told Galdan's nephew Danjila that the emperor was coming in person to negotiate with Galdan. When they informed him (falsely) that Fiyanggû had reached the Tula River and that escape was impossible, Danjila gave a "cry of anguish." The next day, all the imperial troops were drawn up in ranks, "filling the hills and fields without end," their "weapons glistening in the sunlight."[58] The emperor was certain that the sight of this massive force would break Galdan's spirit. By now, he expected Fiyanggû to have arrived at the Tula River, so he did not fear Galdan's escape, even though he hoped for a direct confrontation. On June 7 he reached the Kerulen.[59] The river, flowing through steep hills, had very little water. Zunghar patrols watched the troops advance but did not resist. There was no sign of Galdan's troops, although traces of his encampment were found. Clearly, he had left only a short time before. Denouncing Galdan as a coward, the emperor vowed to continue his pursuit. Leaving behind all but sixteen cannon, he sent envoys ahead to urge Galdan to surrender. Captured soldiers reported that Galdan had fled into the forests at Bayan Ulan. Had Fiyanggû got there before him?

At the Kerulen, the Qing troops found exhausted horses, abandoned by Galdan, and severe drought conditions. The grass had not sprouted. Old people left behind described the Zunghar flight as a "panic." Parts of Galdan's army were attacking one another; women and children were committing suicide. And word came that Fiyanggû had reached the Tula River as planned on June 6. These were auspicious signs, but the Qing troops now faced a severe grain and fodder shortage. They had used up the rations they had brought with them, and Yu Chenglong's reserve supplies had not yet arrived. The emperor himself was eating nothing but mutton. Reluctantly, he realized that he would have to turn back with the main army to find his grain carts. Sending Maska ahead with a small detachment of cavalry and light artillery to continue pursuit, he began his "victory march" home on June 12. Although he expected success, he knew that the West Route Army also lacked grain supplies. He revealed his depressed mood in a letter to the prince, describing a landscape "with no good places for thousands of miles," asking for clothes to be sent from home, and expressing his longing for his son.[60]

Fiyanggû's long-awaited report arrived the next day. Fiyanggû had known that Galdan was at the Kerulen, but his troops were too weak to advance rapidly. Their rations would run out between June 3 and June 10. Yu Chenglong could drag his carts over the sandy hills at a rate of only 20 to 30 *li* per day, and they could not move against a strong wind. On May 31 Galdan was ten days ahead of them, and he had burned all the grass for miles around. Galdan had gone to the Kerulen expecting to find Russian musketeers and large cannon. By June 2 Fiyanggû was able to block Galdan's escape route with fourteen thousand men. On June 12 the two armies met in battle at a "terrible place" in the midst of the desert, called Jao Modo, from the Mongolian "Jaghun Modu," meaning "one hundred trees." It was a small valley with a river at the bottom, surrounded by hills.[61] Fiyanggû's men, unable to carry provisions, had marched for eleven days, living off horseflesh and camel meat just like nomads. Galdan had only five thousand men armed with two thousand fowling pieces. General Yin argued strongly for occupying the hills, even though the sun was setting. To climb the hills, his men had to fight fiercely against Mongol sharpshooters. When the army finally camped above Galdan on the hill, they had gained the strategic advantage. The Manchu troops fired their great cannon and advanced behind a wooden barricade, protecting their bodies with padded cotton armor. When they were ten steps away from the enemy, "arrows fell like rain." Even the news that the emperor was approaching had frightened many Mongol soldiers into abandoning their weapons and fleeing. Galdan was unable to control his troops, who broke ranks and fled. His kinsman Arabdan attempted to resist, but then the Manchu cavalry attacked, killing thousands of men and capturing over twenty thousand cattle and forty thousand sheep. Galdan and Danjila escaped with only forty to fifty men.[62]

The emperor received Fiyanggû's victory report before he crossed the Great Wall on July 3. He entered Beijing four days later. Kangxi had gained a great victory, justifying his iron determination to advance into the steppe. In an expedition of ninety-eight days, traveling over two thousand kilometers to the Kerulen and back, he had "extinguished" Galdan's flame. He returned to hold a great victory celebration. Even though the emperor, and possibly Galdan himself, viewed the victory as ordained by Heaven, it had been a close call. The emperor's thanks to Heaven reflected tremendous relief at a miraculous victory.

The surrender of Galdan's greatest general, Qasiqa, revealed Galdan's strategic plan, one which fit perfectly with classic nomadic strategy.[63] Galdan had thought he could attain his "Great Enterprise" *(amba baita)*, the unification of the Mongols, by staying in the area of the Kerulen and Tula. He regretted his penetration to Ulan Butong. He had planned to retreat if a large Manchu army advanced until the troops exhausted their grain and silver supplies. But on hearing that the emperor was with the army, the Mongols lost their courage. Galdan wanted to fight the Manchus in the forest but could not stop his troops from fleeing. He was prepared to fight the West Route Army alone, but the military feat of sending three armies to the Kerulen had terrified his troops so much that they were beyond his control.

Both sides were at the extreme limit of their supply lines, but the Qing troops depended crucially on grain from the interior, while the Mongols still had plentiful sheep and cattle. Without grass, they could not last much longer in one place, but they were free to move. If Fiyanggû had not been in exactly the right place to block them, Galdan could have escaped. Fiyanggû had had to travel very far west to find water, and the journey had exhausted nearly all of his animals. He had abandoned many supplies because he lacked animals to carry them. When he arrived at Tula, his men were "à la dernière extremité," in Gerbillon's words. They would have died of hunger if Galdan had not come to meet them in battle. Capturing Galdan's abundant provisions saved their lives.[64] Ironically, Galdan could have retreated back to the Kerulen, saved himself, and left Fiyanggû's army to starve; but he overestimated his own strength in facing the weakened Chinese. The Manchus and Chinese fought desperately, knowing that they had nowhere to go and nothing to lose.

Galdan was also betrayed by his fellow Zunghars. When he sent a message to his kinsman Arabdan at Bayan Ulan, telling him that Kangxi was coming, Arabdan replied, "You have land with no women, children, or cattle, I have land with women, children, and cattle. Didn't you know what the Manchus are like? I will not fight with the Manchus."[65] Arabdan abandoned Galdan, although he later appeared at the battle of Jao Modo.

Choruses of praise for Kangxi's stunning victory came from Chinese officials, Manchu chiefs, and Mongolian Khans and Jasaks. They expressed their gratitude to the emperor for relieving them of Galdan's plundering attacks. The Mongols viewed the emperor as a Khan with magical powers, who could bring water and fresh grass to the areas through which he passed (though, in fact, all the digging and searching for wells was done by the Mongols themselves). The emperor responded by incorporating a wider circle of Mongols within the Qing kinship realm: "I formerly saw all within the passes as one family; now all within the Kerulen–Tula are one family." One Mongol prince reported (erroneously) that Galdan had killed his wife and children when he heard that the great army was coming.[66]

The Emperor Rewrites History

Historical reinterpretation was already under way. The emperor and his ministers quickly placed the victory within a long historical context. They compared the campaign to those of Yin Gaozong and Zhou Xuanwang, ancient rulers whose campaigns took three years and traveled thousands of *li*,

> but our emperor went much farther into the steppe, over three thousand li, and only took eighty days . . . [T]he Mongols collect like birds and disperse like animals, lacking any fixed abode. That is why it is extremely difficult to exterminate them. This time we surrounded them with a pincer movement of troops, thus we completely eliminated them [*jian*]. This was done by Heaven; no human force could have done it. Now the deserts are permanently cleared, and the border is secure. This is an achievement rarely seen in history books. The Han could not do this to the Xiongnu, Tang could not do this to the Turks.[67]

The Qing victory had already been inscribed in the history books as one surpassing the achievements of the greatest emperors, despite the fact that Galdan still remained alive and the frontier threat had not ceased. A consciousness of the Qing as completing and transcending the achievements of its predecessors had nevertheless begun to form, placing the dynasty in a progression of increasingly expansive territorial conquests. The editors of the military chronicle *Record of the Emperor's Personal Expeditions to Pacify the Northern Frontiers (Qinzheng Pingding Shuomo Fanglue)* noted that "since ancient times expeditions against Mongolia have been a vain waste of food and exhaustion of men and horses."[68] This time, however, Heaven had decreed the total extermination of the Mongolian menace. By attributing favorable outcomes to Heaven, the Manchu rulers incorporated the fortuitous accidents of history into a broader historical perspective. Opponents of the campaigns had failed to recognize the auspicious signs. Many Manchu and Han officials had urged the emperor to abandon a personal expedition, or to delay its start, and to give up pursuing Galdan after he had fled. But the emperor had rejected their advice, and as a result "the borders are firm, the inner and outer realms are peaceful." Such retrospective historiography attributed superior insight into Heavenly forces to the emperor, who incorporated sagely wisdom and Heavenly will in his strategic thinking. Not only did the emperor follow the ritual prescriptions of his predecessors, as when he performed the same sacrifices to Heaven and Earth that the Yongle emperor had performed after his frontier expeditions, but also he went beyond them by turning the "propensities" *(shi)* of Heaven to more effective use.[69] His "sacred military might" *(shengwu)* allowed him to "defeat the fierce enemy like breaking a rotten branch." In 1842 Wei Yuan's famous book *A Record of Sacred Military Campaigns (Shengwuji)* would synthesize the concepts of unity of Heaven, military victory, and sage rulership that originated with these conquests.[70]

Inclusion and exclusion were the twin mythistorical strategies deployed after the victory.[71] As the newly subordinate Mongols were welcomed into the Qing family, Galdan and his followers were forced out. Many other peoples with undetermined allegiances, however, remained on the frontiers. It was still necessary to drive a wedge between them and Galdan. The emperor printed hundreds of leaflets for the Mongolian princes of Kokonor urging them to capture all remaining members of Galdan's family. He stressed that Galdan had violated the ways of the Dalai Lama by invading the Qing frontiers and had claimed support from the princes of Kokonor, the Russians, and "China's Muslims" (Zhongguo Huizi) in order to plot to conquer China and set up a Muslim as its ruler.[72] Kangxi once believed that Galdan had converted to Islam, and he feared Galdan's use of Muslim spies in the Hami and Turfan oases. He also realized that it would be difficult to use Muslim troops against Turkic peoples in Kokonor. Clearly, the Muslim peoples of the region were not reliable, even though the chieftain of Hami had offered his services in capturing Galdan. The emperor's primary strategy at this point was to win over Mongols by convincing them that Galdan had violated his oaths to the Dalai Lama, thus excluding himself from the Way of the Buddha, Tsongkhaba. Turning his attention to the princes of Kokonor meant deeper involvement in the links between the Dalai Lama in Tibet and Mongolians.

Tibet, however, remained another ambiguous subject, of which the Qing rulers had little knowledge. Kangxi's greatest shock came after the victory at Jao Modo, when Zunghars who surrendered told him that the Dalai Lama had died nine years earlier. In fact, the fifth Dalai Lama had died in 1682, and the *sDe-pa*, or regent, had assumed power. Kangxi only learned the true date of the Dalai Lama's death later from Tsewang Rabdan. Events in Tibet were certainly murky. Kangxi presumed that the *sDe-pa* had usurped power and concealed the Dalai Lama's death in order to forge a stronger anti-Qing alliance with the Zunghars. Zahiruddin Ahmad argues, using Tibetan sources, that the Qing misunderstood the nature of power relations in Tibet, and later deliberately propagated the story of usurpation and concealment in order to highlight the treachery of Galdan and the *sDe-pa*.[73] Contrary to the Qing view, the *sDe-pa* was no "minor official" who illegitimately usurped power after the Dalai Lama's death; he was a senior adviser to the Dalai Lama, entrusted with secular duties in 1679. Soon after, the Dalai Lama withdrew into meditation. It was not uncommon to postpone notices of a lama's death for astrological reasons. Ahmad argues that there was no deliberate attempt by the *sDe-pa* to deceive the emperor, and that the Chinese could not understand the Tibetan view of reincarnation. The *sDe-pa* may have believed that the fifth Dalai Lama had left his body to go into meditation, and would return later in his sixth reincarnation.

Nevertheless, a clear shift in Tibetan policy was apparent after the fifth Dalai Lama's death. The *sDe-pa* had actively promoted a more sympathetic view of Galdan by trying to mediate between Kangxi and the Khan, and by trying to ward off military action. Now, in the emperor's eyes, the *sDe-pa* stood exposed as an active confederate of Galdan, and the Kokonor Mongols' obedience to Tibetan lamas threatened to draw them away from the Qing. The Kokonor princes themselves proclaimed dual and equal allegiance, saying, "In the East is the emperor, in the West is the Dalai Lama."[74] At the risk of alienating them, the emperor moved strongly against the *sDe-pa*. Earlier emissaries from the Dalai Lama were kept in separate residences outside the city, but the latest emissary from the *sDe-pa* was to be arrested for collaboration with Galdan.[75]

Two months later, as the fruitless pursuit of Galdan continued, the emperor severely rebuked the *sDe-pa* for instigating Galdan's revolt: "You were originally the Dalai Lama's subordinate, and I granted you the title of king of Tibet. Now I know that you publicly revered Tsongkhaba, but secretly allied with Galdan, and deceived the Dalai Lama. You pretended that the long-dead Dalai Lama was still alive. You sent Jilong Khutukhtu to Galdan's camp to recite scriptures, prolong negotiations, and allow Galdan to escape. You promoted the marriage of the Kokonor princess Boshokhtu Jinong with Galdan. Galdan believed your inciting words."[76]

According to a captive's report, Galdan had told his followers after the defeat: "It was not me who wanted to penetrate deeply into China; it was the Dalai Lama's order. He said that a southern expedition would be auspicious. The Dalai Lama has killed me, and I have killed you people." From this report, the emperor concluded that the *sDe-pa* bore the ultimate responsibility. Clearly the Dalai Lama would not have approved a military invasion if he had been alive. The emperor vowed to send another large army "to Yunnan, Sichuan, or Shaanxi. Following the precedent of Galdan, I will personally lead an army to punish you."[77]

Meanwhile, Galdan's whereabouts remained unknown. One report had it that Danjila and Arabdan, Galdan's top lieutenants, had met at the Bortala River, then separated to look for Galdan. No one knew where he had gone. He could not go to Hami, held by his enemy Tsewang Rabdan.[78] Ayuki Khan of the Torghuts was too far away, and not friendly to Galdan in any event. The Russians were interested only in trading relations, not in sheltering a defeated Khan. So the sympathetic *sDe-pa* in Tibet seemed to be Galdan's only option, although he might instead try to attack Tsewang Rabdan at Hami, or head for the Altai Mountains. The goal of the Qing was to prevent Galdan from crossing through Kokonor, picking up Muslim followers, and reaching the protection of the *sDe-pa* in Lhasa. Kangxi's third expedition against Galdan aimed to wipe out this "lone wolf" once and for all.[79]

The Final Campaigns and the Fate of Galdan

Conditions were unpropitious for a third expedition in 1696. The West Army still desperately lacked food. Its horses were exhausted, its carts were all broken, and relief grain from the Central Army had not yet arrived.[80] Galdan had gathered a total of over five thousand troops, although he had very few animals. He had headed first for Wengjin, from which he would either attack Hami or head for Tibet. Fiyanggû was ordered to head in person for the border to block Galdan, to burn all surplus grain supplies so that they could not be captured, and to send his cannon back to the capital. Time was of the essence.

Once again the Qing profited from divisions among their enemies. Galdan met with Danjila and Arabdan, but the three could not agree on strategy. Galdan wanted to seize grain at Wengjin and march on Hami.[81] Danjila favored heading for the Altai. Arabdan wanted to loot the Russian area. Because the majority disagreed with Galdan, no decision was taken. Arabdan broke with Galdan, leaving with two thousand men. Galdan and Danjila at most one thousand troops, no tents, no clothes, and no food. His men were "only following him to death, searching for a place with land [you guotu zhi di]."[82] They headed for Tamir, plundered the region, then moved farther into the desert. By now Galdan had just one or two horses and no cattle or sheep. His followers abandoned him, surrendering to Tsewang Rabdan or the emperor rather than face starvation.

As Galdan's followers dwindled, the emperor gained new servants, including the "Huihui king Abdulishite" of Yarkand, who visited the capital. Galdan had seized his father at Ili in 1682, and only now was he able to return. The king vowed to use his twenty thousand troops at Yarkand to seize Galdan, or to send troops from Turfan to capture Arabdan. Tsewang Rabdan was praised for his loyalty and ordered to capture and execute Galdan if he came to Hami: "We cannot let Galdan remain in the human world. If he wanders into your territory, or flees to Hami, if you capture him, execute him and send his head to us. This will display your obedience."[83]

Further instructions to the Dalai Lama aimed to win him over and separate him from the sDe-pa's pro-Galdan policy. The emperor claimed that sDe-pa had facilitated Galdan's escape at the battle of Ulan Butong. Clearly the Dalai Lama would not do this; it was the sDe-pa, he believed, assuming the Dalai Lama's name.[84] The sDe-pa was ordered to hand over Jilong Khutukhtu to the emperor, to let the Panchen Lama rule the Tibetan faith, and also to send him to China along with Galdan's daughter.[85] All correspondence in Tibetan or Mongolian between the Dalai Lama, the sDe-pa, and Galdan was to be intercepted or confiscated. Qing officials luckily did intercept envoys from Galdan to Tibet passing through Xining, obtaining letters that revealed Galdan's hopes for Tibetan support.[86] In these letters Galdan reported on his loss in battle and asked for aid from the Dalai Lama. He hoped that recitation of sutras in temples in Tibet would help him out of his plight.

By October the emperor was ready. Fiyanggû's resistance to active pursuit of Galdan was making him impatient. He rebuked Fiyanggû for having failed to arrive at the rendezvous point in the previous expedition, allowing Galdan to escape, and he believed that they still could have pursued and crushed Galdan at the time. Now that Galdan was starving, this was a "great opportunity sent from Heaven" which they could not pass up. Yu Chenglong returned to the capital, having transported 27,000 *shi* of grain, distributing 18,000 *shi* and storing the remainder in granaries. Supplies seemed sufficient. The emperor announced that he would set out on October 14, 1696, from the capital on a "hunting expedition" to the Ordos.[87]

This expedition could not capture Galdan, whose whereabouts were unknown. Its goal was to demonstrate Qing wealth to the Mongols of the region, with the hope of enticing all of Galdan's supporters to surrender. Unlike in the previous expedition, the emperor now had substantial numbers of Western Mongol allies. Hosted by leading lamas in the region, he traveled at a leisurely pace. One hundred thousand sheep traveled with him. Passing through Guihua, he reached the shores of the Yellow River on November 22, the site of a large warehouse for rice, containing 70,000 *shi*. Twenty days' supplies were distributed. On the next day the emperor measured the breadth of the river with his Jesuit surveying instruments, reporting that the grass there was "so high you can't see the horses." A week later he crossed the frozen Yellow River with his supply train and entered the Ordos region.[88]

Meanwhile, Fiyanggû reported a serious defeat of an effort by Danjila to raid the grain stores at Wengjin (on the Onggin River).[89] The Qing troops had already burned most of the grain stores in the region, leaving them little to live on. In writing to his son, the emperor said that Danjila's original intention had not been to steal grain at Onggin, but his followers claimed that it was better to attack than starve to death.

With the failure of this raid, Galdan's only way to get food was to attack Hami, but this could offer an opportunity for the Qing armies to crush him again. Or he could hope to survive the winter in his camp, in the Jasaktu Khan's territory, forty days' march from the Qing frontier. The emperor wavered. Why waste men and horses trying to crush Galdan now, especially since it would be impossible to reach his camp during the winter? He told Fiyanggû to turn back. They could fatten up their horses, wait until spring, and then pursue Galdan. Meanwhile, they would attract more Zunghar followers to surrender and disperse them to scattered grazing lands.[90]

The Ordos was a rich region with fine grass for the horses and excellent prospects for hunting. In his letters home the emperor praised the invigo-

rating fresh air, the wonderful taste of the mutton, and the fine workman-
ship of the Mongolian saddles.[91] The Mongols in turn were extremely impressed with the huge herds of cattle that the Manchus had brought with
them. Observing herds of sixteen thousand cattle and seventy thousand
sheep for one banner, they said, "Since our ancestors' times, we have considered one to two thousand head as making a man rich. We have never
heard of ten thousand head."[92]

When Fiyanggû arrived with his exhausted West Route troops, the emperor praised their endurance and held a great celebratory banquet.
Fiyanggû now had sufficient supplies, but his troops needed rest. The sim-
plest strategy would have been to wait comfortably in the Ordos while
Galdan died of starvation in his isolated camp. Surrounded on all sides by
enemies, losing supporters daily, he was like an animal in a cage.[93] Still, the
emperor was anxious to march to Hami. Fiyanggû objected that the distance was too great and his troops were famished. Jiayuguan was a thousand kilometers away, and it was twenty days' march from Jiayuguan, at
the end of the Great Wall, to Hami, a distance of five hundred kilometers.
Sunsike could not go beyond Suzhou, near Jiayuguan, because he lacked rations. The emperor was still anxious to proceed at least as far as Ningxia.
But on December 19 he met the famished troops returning from the distant
steppes and discovered how truly exhausted his army was. Fiyanggû then
reported the arrival of Galdan's envoy, Geleiguying, to discuss surrender
terms.[94]

It could have been a trick. Fiyanggû recommended seizing Geleiguying
and not sending him back. But Geleiguying kowtowed to the emperor
and vowed that the Zunghars sincerely recognized their crimes and wished
to surrender: "We Zunghars were ignorant. We coveted the wealth and
women of the Khalkhas and did not realize that Heaven's will is without
partiality. This was our crime. Now many Zunghars want to submit. Our
lord cannot be ranked with the Khalkhas." The emperor smiled and said,
"These words are just. Even though you are foreigners [waiguo zhi ren],
you understand reason [li]. Galdan is ignorant; he has failed to accept my
benevolence. He has chosen his own death."[95] He offered generous terms.
Zunghar nobles would be given official rank; others would be assigned
to banner service. Captured women and families would be returned. He
claimed that unlike previous rulers, who loved military victory, he prided
himself on putting peace foremost. The traditional Chinese conception of
"coerced followers" (xiecong) also provided grounds for pardoning even
the most treacherous rebels. Offers of wealth and honors were expected to
bring around even the stubborn Galdan.

Galdan's letter to Kangxi, brought by Geleiguying, clearly affirmed his Buddhist beliefs and the justice of his campaigns:

Buddha teaches that humans cannot clearly foretell events, but all great Khans who unify the world worship the three treasures of the Dalai Lama, as we have. That is why since Altan Khan the seven banners of the Khalkhas have been the patrons of the Dalai Lama. Since Gush Nomun Khan, we four Ölöd have also been patrons of the Dalai Lama. We have each lived peacefully and separately in our lands. We have not waged war against the Jebzongdanba Khutukhtu or Jasaktu Khan. They failed to respect the Dalai Lama's representative, causing the great turmoil. My cause was just, but I will submit to the emperor's grace.[96]

Galdan faced great pressure from his ministers and followers to submit to the emperor. Even though his own letter scarcely admits any guilt, Geleiguying's report to the emperor reveals considerable distress in the Zunghar camp. Most likely, from Galdan's perspective, the surrender talks were only a tactic to win time, pacify his people, and give them the strength to last the winter. He still hoped for rescue from the Dalai Lama and the Khans of Kokonor.

On December 21 the emperor decided to accept Galdan's surrender. He sent Geleiguying back to Galdan, setting a time limit of seventy days for a return report. He would remain in the Ordos hunting to await a reply. If no reply came, he would advance his troops.

Just at this time the bondservant Dadaduhu memorialized that the army had nearly used up its supplies and had to turn back. The furious emperor, accusing Dadaduhu of stirring up doubts among the people, ordered his execution. Once again he vowed, "If grain supplies are exhausted, we will go to riverbanks and marshes to get grain. I will eat snow to pursue Galdan; we absolutely cannot turn back."[97] Dadaduhu's crime was to reveal the logistical weaknesses of the army in front of Galdan's envoy. The Qing generals had Geleiguying followed until he was far from the camp. Only then did Kangxi announce that the army would return to the capital. All the troops were delighted.

Both Galdan and the emperor were in extreme situations, although Galdan was much worse off. Both faced increasing dissension from their high generals and troops, but neither would give in. Weary fighters slugging out the last rounds, they had to call a temporary truce to rebuild their strength and regain support. Although the Ordos was rich, it would not support a large army over the winter. The weather was turning cold, the emperor missed his sons, and he would get no reply from Galdan anyway for the next seventy days. So, despite his vows to Geleiguying, he turned back and arrived at the capital on January 12, 1697. This third expedition had lasted ninety-one days. Several thousand Zunghars had surrendered, even though there had been no decisive battle. It had succeeded as a demonstration of Qing wealth and power to the already subordinated Mongols; it had blocked Galdan from escaping to Kokonor or Tibet; but it had not yet eliminated Kangxi's indomitable foe.

Kangxi had little expectation that Galdan would surrender. Yet he also knew that another expedition would require even more time and planning. Once again, opposition surfaced. Censor Zhou Zihuang objected to another personal expedition, arguing that subordinate officers could easily subdue such a petty bandit, but the emperor replied that he must pursue Galdan to the end. He invoked the great consequences of Wu Sangui's uprising twenty years earlier, which had spread unrest even to the northwest frontier.[98] Still, he wavered for some time until the *beg* of Hami reported the capture of Galdan's fourteen-year-old son Sebteng Baljur.[99] This was "Heaven's gift" to the Qing. It left Galdan abandoned and alone, without any heirs. This was a strong incentive to advance once again to the northwest and confront the isolated Galdan. He had only five hundred to six hundred men left, many of whom would desert him when faced with a strong military presence.[100]

Galdan was now camped in the Altai Mountains, over 1,600 kilometers northwest of Ningxia and twenty-nine days' march north from Jiayuguan. Because Galdan's forces were so weak, the Qing armies could travel light and fast. Two forces of three thousand troops each would set out, one from Ningxia and one from Jiayuguan. The start of the expedition was set for February 27, 1697. Because of their previous experience, the supply officers developed much more careful and cautious plans than in the earlier campaigns. Only Mongol allies with many horses could join the army. Less was more. The route to Ningxia was well known, and the emperor was anxious to go. He collected information from the Khalkha Mongols about the route. On the previous expedition he had crossed the wall and headed straight for Köke Khota, but on this trip, the emperor went along the inside of the Great Wall to Yulin, taking the opportunity to inspect the Shaanxi landscape. His small force of four hundred men struggled over rocky mountains, ravines, and deep sand. The Ming Chengde emperor (r. 1506–1521) had visited here during his northwest expedition, but Kangxi wrote to his son that his travels would equal or surpass that hapless emperor's. Although Kangxi did not resemble the abusive Ming ruler, a poor warrior interested mainly in military pomp, this tour had more symbolic than military significance. Historical precedents echoed in the emperor's mind.[101]

On March 26, at Shenmu, between the Yellow River and the Great Wall in Shaanxi, the emperor interviewed Sebteng Baljur, Galdan's son, trying to find out if his father would surrender. The terrified boy could not give a definite answer, but hoped that his father would give in to the imperial might. Kangxi regarded the boy as a "small, inferior person" lacking his father's courage. Gerbillon, however, found him to be well built, "triste et étonné," and thought he held up well under questioning. The boy was sent on to Beijing.[102] Kangxi planned to have the boy executed in the capital along with his father.

The Hami *beg* who had arrested and delivered Sebteng feared that Tsewang Rabdan would take revenge on them, and, as expected, Tsewang Rabdan indeed soon demanded custody of the boy, his greatest weapon against Galdan. When Hami asked for Qing protection, it came under formal Qing authority. The first Turkic oasis now joined the Qing sphere.[103] Soon after, the Princes of Kokonor submitted. Except during the Yuan dynasty, Kokonor had never been under imperial control. This was an unprecedented submission to imperial rule of "outer barbarians," as described in former histories.[104] In a letter to his son, the emperor expressed his "great joy" at gaining the submission of these powerful local rulers without a battle. Stretching the truth a good deal, he even claimed Tsewang Rabdan as his subject. In reality, Tsewang Rabdan was only an ally of convenience, willing to cooperate in the defeat of Galdan, but not a permanent subject.[105]

Tibet remained the one major inaccessible region beyond Qing control. But Galdan's losses and the defection of other allies had shaken the regent's resolve.[106] The "terrified" *sDe-pa* now denied that he had ever supported the "rebel" Galdan; he identified the emperor with Manjusri Buddha, and vowed great gratitude to the emperor for granting him the title "King of Tibet." He did try to prevent the Panchen Lama and Galdan's daughter, now in Tibet, from being summoned to the capital, but the emperor refused his request. The regent confirmed, at last, that the fifth Dalai Lama's death had occurred in 1682. His story was that the Dalai Lama before his death had assured the lamas that he would be reincarnated the next year, but he told them to keep his death secret until his successor was sixteen years old.[107] The *sDe-pa* promised that the present Dalai Lama, now fifteen, would be revealed *(chuding)* by the end of the year. He asked the emperor to conceal this fact until the tenth month, but it turned out that the new Dalai Lama had already been revealed to Tsewang Rabdan. Refusing to cooperate in this deception, the outraged emperor proclaimed it to all the Inner Mongolian banners.[108] The revelation of the new Dalai Lama was actually advantageous to Kangxi, because all along Galdan had claimed to be acting on the legitimate orders of the Dalai Lama; but now he stood exposed as relying only on the usurping regent.[109] The regent, likewise, expecting Galdan's defeat, withdrew his support in order to curry favor with the rising Qing power.

Now on the brink of victory, the emperor was magnanimous. He would pardon the regent's crimes and seek peace among all the Mongols:

> I note that Mongols beyond the borders have always resisted China. From the Han, Tang, Song and Ming dynasties they have harmed us . . . No dynasty until ours has exerted authority over Mongolia, and made them submit in their hearts [guixin]. Using troops is cruel; the ruler does it only if necessary. It is like using needles on a person with illness; we do not inflict pain for no reason on the skin. Ruling is like this: in times of disorder [luan] we need force, in times of peace and order we use pacification [fusui]. Since ancient times those who loved distant expeditions caused losses to the country's spirit. So I value most not creating trouble.[110]

Having ensured the temporary subordination of Tibet, Kokonor, and Tsewang Rabdan, the emperor continued his pursuit of Galdan. From Yulin to Ningxia, the route led outside the wall and along it through the southern Ordos desert. Unlike the previous short venture into the rich fields near the Yellow River, this crossing of the Ordos led through deep salt and sandy wastes with very little water. During the Ming dynasty this region, where the Great Wall lay within the Yellow River bend, was the chief headache of strategic planners, and a major subject of debate.[111] Mongol tribes constantly attacked the wall and raided within it, while Ming officials disagreed hopelessly over launching expensive, useless campaigns or hunkering down for humiliating defensive tactics. Kangxi agreed that it was a wise policy to extend the wall through the Ordos because it was not defensible otherwise. He enjoyed having his aides debate different calculations of the distance to Ningxia. He now realized that the route outside the wall to Köke Khota offered much more water and grass than this more direct desert crossing.

Local peasants had dug breaks through the wall in order reach their cultivated fields outside. It was made only of tamped-down earth and piled-up rocks, fifteen feet high and six to seven feet wide at the top. Towers spaced along it accommodated three to four guards each, and men to light watchfires. Defenses here clearly could not stop a serious cavalry attack, but Galdan and other Mongols, unlike in the Ming, were in no shape to mount any challenge.[112] The emperor declared that he would give up the "trivial" hunt for animals in order to focus on human prey. The weaker the Mongol enemies became, the closer they came to the animal order in Manchu eyes.[113]

On April 17 the Qing troops arrived at Ningxia, 1,400 kilometers from Beijing, after fifty-one days on the march.[114] The Ningxia region was a beautiful, rich landscape with cheap food supplies and abundant irrigation. The emperor's main concern was to prevent excessive extractions from the area's population. Summoning the local elite, he encouraged them to aid the army without burdening the peasantry. Yu Chenglong planned grain shipments to reach the Altai Mountains. He could carry 3,000 *shi* of grain up the Yellow River to its northwestern bend in boats, then transfer supplies to camel and baggage carts. It would take many days to reach Godoli Balaghasun, a staging point 1,200 *li* away in the Southern Altai Mountains, but by June, Yu had transported huge quantities of grain there—forty-five days' supply for each man. His troops built walls six feet high and pits nine feet deep to guard the enormous stores. Yu's efforts made the critical difference in the victory over Galdan. According to Wei Yuan, after Galdan's death a Qing general told Danjila, Galdan's chief general, "'The man who destroyed your state is the Grain Transport Commissioner Yu Chenglong.' Danjila hung his head in shame."[115]

The emperor spent nineteen days in Ningxia making preparations for this great logistical operation. His transition from frontline commander to supply sergeant proved very frustrating. He complained to his son about his constant preoccupation with arranging silver and grain supplies for the troops.[116] By May 19 he had completed all his preparations and boarded a boat to travel downstream to Baita on the bend of the river. The townspeople of Ningxia surrounded the troops, begging them to stay; local merchants had made great profits from supplying the army.[117] Before leaving, he sent out further calls for Galdan's surrender, encouraged Tsewang Rabdan to help in crushing his Zunghar rival, and set a date for troops to start for Galdan's camp.[118] Then he watched the troops set out from Baita.

Abandoning his earlier vows to march for twenty days across the desert in pursuit of Galdan, the emperor continued downstream from Baita and returned to the capital, this time taking the shorter route across the steppe. Despite the merchants' delight, the poor region of the northwest had been heavily burdened by the imperial presence, and he had been away from the capital for over seventy days. One letter indicates growing distrust of his son's "coldness," foreshadowing the later severe loss of confidence in his heir that would lead to the great succession crisis of the end of his reign.[119] The emperor returned home on July 4, 1697, after a 129-day journey, his longest yet. Most of his time, however, was spent not in the steppe but in the towns within the wall or on the Yellow River.

Kangxi could not know that all of his frenetic preparations had been rendered moot by Galdan's death even before he arrived at Ningxia. Reports from the envoys sent to discuss surrender terms arrived in Ningxia shortly after the emperor got there. They indicated severe dissension within Galdan's camp. Drinking with Galdan in his tent, Danjila and another Zunghar leader, Urjanjab, denounced Galdan for bringing about the destruction of their state and failing to defend the "Way of Buddha": "We have followed you until the end . . . but now we cannot bear it anymore," they said. "The road divides in two," either surrender or death. Others reproached Urjanjab for praising the Khan in times of prosperity and deserting him in adversity. Galdan had only three hundred men left, many of whom had only one skinny horse. Others were starving to death. But Galdan refused to surrender. Danjila invited the envoy to his tent, offering to surrender to the emperor himself if he would be beneficent. Another noble follower of Galdan, Noyan Gelong, praised the emperor as a living Buddha.[120] The emperor's order pointed out that Galdan was surrounded on all sides by enemies; if he relied on the emperor, he would live, he would keep his title of Khan, and he and his followers would become wealthy. Thus Galdan's men learned that Kangxi was camped in the Ordos with abundant grain and cattle supplies. Danjila was clearly impressed enough to want to surrender, but he could not move Galdan, so the envoys left. Geleiguying, Galdan's own envoy, himself deserted the camp and joined them.

Soon after, refugees reported hearing cannon fire near Galdan's camp. They learned that Galdan was moving farther northwest, into the Altai Mountains. He had split with Danjila and moved off with only one hundred men. Then, on April 4, 1697, at Aca Amtatai, between Kara Usu Lake and Khobdo, Galdan suddenly died under mysterious circumstances. The emperor did not hear of Galdan's death until the night of June 2, fifty-nine days later, while resting at Baotou on his return journey. Fiyanggû met envoys from Danjila who reported that Galdan had caught an illness one morning and died that same evening. They did not know what the illness was. When asked why they had not reported this earlier, they claimed that Danjila's men and horses were so weak they could not move. Immediately before his death Galdan had said, "I believed that the Zunghars were a good people; I did not expect them to be so faithless."[121]

The emperor's first reaction was to suspect poison. He told his son that either Galdan had committed suicide or he had been poisoned by one of his followers. The truth would not be known until they had interrogated Cembu Sangbu, Galdan's trusted doctor, who had prevented even Danjila from offering meat to Galdan.[122] But in his meeting with Fiyanggû the next day, and in all subsequent pronouncements, he settled on the suicide story. The emperor and his ministers had often predicted that Heaven's great rewards to the Qing and Galdan's despair would lead him to kill himself. Once again, these predictions had come true.

In fact, no evidence indicates that the astonishingly stubborn Galdan had any intention of committing suicide, and his Buddhist commandments forbade him, a living Buddha and reincarnation of a high monk, to do so. It is possible, as some scholars believe, that Galdan died of a sudden natural illness (such as a brain seizure).[123] His illness could certainly have not been a slow degenerative one like smallpox, the most common and most feared cause of death among Mongols exposed to outside influences. Yet he died very shortly after the stormy meeting with Danjila and other top aides reported by Kangxi's envoy. Given the severe disagreements over surrender within Galdan's camp and his evident distrust of even his most loyal aides, I think the emperor's first suspicions were correct: Galdan was poisoned by one of his followers, most likely Danjila, who gained credit with the Qing for delivering Galdan's body and saved himself from complete ruin.

But this outcome did not fit imperial mythistory. Compilers soon altered the story to make it accord more neatly with the thesis that the Qing emperor embodied Heaven's will. The date of Galdan's death was moved later in time by a month, to the lunar month 3*/13 (May 3) instead of 3/13 (April 4), so that the entire expedition would not be revealed as useless.[124] In subsequent letters to his son and in proclamations to the army, the emperor insisted that his interrogation of Danjila's messenger confirmed the suicide story. Later commentators noted that "the emperor predicted that Galdan would kill himself [zijin], and he has done so. The emperor is so farsighted that he understands the enemy like a god."[125]

The Chinese edition of the Qingshilu (but not the Manchu one) endorsed Kangxi's claim, and so have nearly all subsequent historians. Yet the reports contained in the Qinzheng Pingding Shuomo Fanglue, and Kangxi's original letters to his son, preserve the recalcitrant facts that contradict the imperial mythmakers.

On July 4 a great military review celebrated the emperor's return to Beijing. Bannermen, merchants, elders, and women lined the streets of the capital, holding incense and prostrating themselves before the procession. The Grand Councilors listed the emperor's great feats—defeating the rebellion of the Chahar Mongols, suppressing the Three Feudatories, conquering Taiwan and "entering it on the registers" (ru bantu) as an overseas territory (haiwai), collecting tribute from Russia, which never before had had contact with China—now crowned with the "final elimination" of the

Mongol menace. They boasted, "No emperor from the past can compare with this." At the Taihedian a great ceremony celebrated Galdan's extermination. Officials reported the victory to the Temples of Heaven and Earth, the Taimiao and other shrines, and the ancestors at the imperial tombs.[126]

Qing officials paid tribute to Galdan's great military skill, reckoning that he had subdued 1,200 towns in the western regions, including the Muslim oases, Bukhara, Turfan, and the Kazakhs, and defeated several hundred thousand men in the Khalkha banners. This tribute to Galdan undermined the notion of him as a mere "rebel," but building him up as a great military leader was necessary to justify the costly personal expeditions against him.

Rewards and punishments followed the celebrations. Nearly all officials and criminals under death sentences (except those convicted of the "ten great evils") received pardons. Several thousand troops received bonuses of 5 to 6 taels annually for three years. Ilagukesan, the high lama adviser to Galdan, who recited sutras for him before battle, was condemned to death by slicing, but over two hundred other lamas in contact with him were pardoned. Even the Jilong Khutukhtu, the peacemaker sent by the Dalai Lama who urged the Zunghars into battle, was pardoned, after pleas for his life from the Panchen Lama. Surrendered Zunghar troops were incorporated into the Chahar Mongol banners.[127] Muslims who had joined with Galdan were also spared execution. Chinese officials, like Yu Chenglong, scheduled to be punished for delays in grain transport, were now pardoned and rewarded with promotions. Fiyanggû became first-rank prince. General Maska, who had failed to capture Ilagukesan and been stripped of his position, was now restored to a lower rank. The "probationary ethic" in action had kept these officials in suspense until the victory, but now it was time for leniency.[128]

It was still necessary to display military might before the Mongol Khans. At a great banquet for the Khans of Kokonor, troops passed by and thunderous cannon roared, "shaking the mountains and valleys." These Khans, a crucial link between the Zunghars and Tibet, now presented tribute and seemed to submit to the overpowering might and "godlike mystery" of the emperor. Gunpowder in the imperial presence had a powerful symbolic effect. Soon, as the Yongzheng emperor discovered, these Khans would be much less obedient.[129]

Leniency did not apply, however, to the body of Galdan himself. It was not enough for the Qing to remove Galdan from the human world. Even his corpse had to be eliminated. The goal was to treat him the same as Wu Sangui: to burn the body, display it at the execution ground in the capital, then pulverize the bones and scatter them through the streets. The head would be hung on the city wall, displayed to the people, and later sent around to all the Khalkha Forty-nine Banners who had surrendered to the Qing. Thus the polluting presence of Galdan's spirit could be eradicated. His son would suffer the same treatment.[130]

But the Mongols had other ideas. Danjila had already burned the body but kept the head and ashes. Danjila was determined to take Galdan's remains to Tibet to present them to the Dalai Lama, but he was captured by Tsewang Rabdan, who took custody of Galdan's remains. The emperor's envoys demanded that he return them to Beijing. They also demanded that he hand over Galdan's wife, son, and daughter in his possession. After the arrival of the ashes, they would be executed along with Galdan's son Sebteng Baljur, already in Qing custody. Tsewang Rabdan replied, however, that by Mongol custom "we do not take revenge on useless people," and that he harbored no enmity toward Galdan's family. Galdan's children and his ashes were not objects of revenge. It was also taboo to entrust a corpse to other people.[131] He would throw the ashes in the water or scatter them in the fields. He did, however, hand over for execution the lama Ilagukesan.

As the Qing envoys made clear, however, by Chinese custom "all the family of rebels are to be wiped out, corpses captured, all must be entirely swept away [qiongjiu saochu]."[132] In the Qing view, if Tsewang Rabdan refused to deliver the remains, his tributary relationship with the Qing, and his earlier vow to help eliminate Galdan, would be exposed as a lie, and the Qing would cut off all access to their territory for Tsewang Rabdan's traders. Tsewang Rabdan agreed with the Qing that Galdan had been a threat to both of them, and he rejected the usurpation of power in Tibet by the sDe-pa, but he was already staking out an independent position on Galdan's legacy. After a severe imperial rebuke, he agreed to deliver the remains but asked for mercy to be shown to Galdan's family. He also asked to keep Galdan's remaining followers, because he needed their strength to launch attacks on the Kazakhs to his west. The Lifanyuan insisted that these men, and Galdan's family, could not be allowed to stay in Mongolia, but the emperor relented partially. He allowed Galdan's men to remain, but insisted on the return of his wife and children.

Finally, in the fall of 1698, Manchus, Mongols, and Chinese assembled on the military training ground in Beijing to watch Galdan's bones be crushed and scattered to the winds. Sebteng Baljur was pardoned and given a wife and first rank in the Imperial Bodyguard. In 1701 Galdan's daughter arrived in Beijing to live with her brother.[133]

What does this ritual dispute reveal about the Qing–Mongol conflict? As Evelyn Rawski has shown, Qing legitimation relied heavily on the constant performance of prescribed rituals.[134] These rituals were both public and private, and they combined Confucian, shamanistic, and Tibetan Buddhist practices. The court frequently visited temples in the city to ensure auspicious harvests and moral order. But there is one ritual she does not discuss: executions. These, too, were highly conspicuous performances by which the dynasty displayed its power and authority. As Lu Xun's Ah Q noticed, proper behavior by both the victim and the executioner was expected.

Capital punishment of common criminals followed a hierarchy defined by the penal code ranging from hanging to execution by slicing. Major rebels, however, because of the sheer scale of their crimes, went well beyond ordinary violations of law. In fact, if Galdan were treated as a rival power, his actions would not amount to a crime at all, since he would have been playing by different rules. The Qing would have to recognize his interest in the security and autonomy of his state instead of merely seeing a compulsion to destroy social order. Although such a geopolitical vision suited the diplomatic interests of Qing officials before victory, it would not fit the imperial ideology of the Qing after its defeat of the Mongol armies. So Galdan had to be reduced to a common criminal but treated to a punishment even more extreme than for a common rebel. Although death by slicing was intended to ensure that the victim's soul would not survive, crushing bones to powder and scattering them over a parade ground went even further. It was a degree of obliteration not found in the penal code: it represented the ultimate in imperial erasure of an enemy from both the human and cosmic realms. The determination to eradicate totally Galdan's alien presence explains the emperor's tenacious insistence on recovering his body. In the mid-eighteenth century the Qianlong emperor would attempt the same against Amursana, the final representative of Zunghar resistance.

Tsewang Rabdan, for his part, also asserted cultural values recognizable to the Qing: we do not make enemies of our kinsmen. To him, Galdan was family. If Galdan persisted, even symbolically, the Zunghar state could rise again. The emperor had to cast Galdan out of the familial role and place him in the criminal pigeonhole. Only after his bones were retrieved, crushed, and ritually expelled from the human and even physical realm could his specter be eliminated permanently.

But the family principle won out for the rest of Galdan's followers. The principle of "coerced followers" *(xiecong)* allowed for leniency for nearly all except the top leader. Regarded as innocent dupes of a clever manipulator, followers of peasant rebels and nomadic raiders usually received pardons. Even Galdan's top lieutenants were pardoned, and some were given official positions. His wife and children were also pardoned. Their actions were partitioned from the evil of Galdan himself. Incorporation and extreme exclusion each required the other. Once the body and soul of Galdan himself was physically annihilated, removing any potential pollution, all

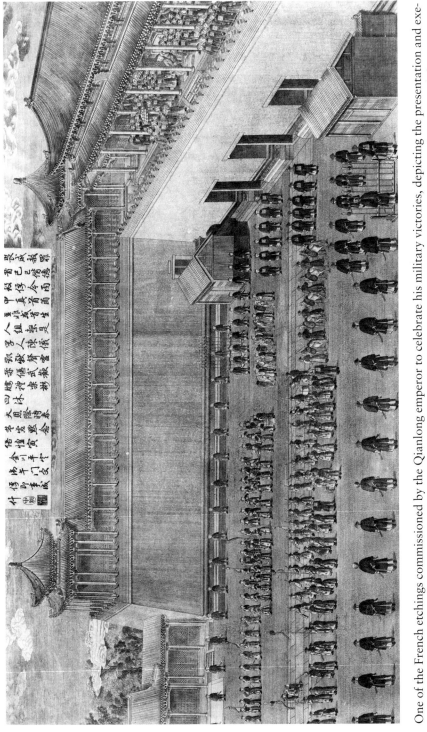

One of the French etchings commissioned by the Qianlong emperor to celebrate his military victories, depicting the presentation and execution at Beijing's Meridian Gate of captives taken in the Jinchuan campaigns. The group of men kneeling on the extreme left are presenting the head of Khoja Jihân to the emperor, who sits on the high dais on the right.

others personally connected with him were purified and could be reincorporated into the human realm.

With the successful conclusion of the great Galdan campaigns began the Qing project to establish a definitive demarcation of the dynasty's position in imperial space and time. Until Galdan's defeat, the character and even prolonged survival of the dynasty remained uncertain. Would it last for centuries as one of China's great eras, or would it be a relatively short-lived conquest regime, overthrown by another more powerful Mongolian regime, like the Jurchen Jin (r. 1115–1234 CE)? And would the extent of Qing rule include permanent dominion over the vast areas beyond the wall, or would it end up like the Ming, confined to defensive positions after brief forays into the steppe? The elimination of the Zunghar leader seemed to indicate relative stabilization and permanent control. So the emperor began a great project to map the entire extent of imperial domains shortly after his victory. In a later chapter I discuss the significance of this vast effort to inscribe legibility onto Qing domains, known as the *Chart of the Comprehensive Gaze over Imperial Domains (Huangyu Quanlan Tu)*, or "Jesuit Atlas." It was published in several editions from 1717 to 1721, but the use of Jesuits in surveys closely connected to strategic concerns began in 1700. By the end of the seventeenth century, with their greatest adversary apparently eliminated, Qing rulers could put down definitive boundaries of their territorial claims.

Similarly, the emperor laid the basis for placing his conquests in historical time by commissioning an official history of his campaigns, *Outline History of the Personal Expeditions to Pacify the Northwest Frontier (Qinzheng Pingding Shuomo Fanglue)*. Begun in 1699 under the supervision of top officials and Hanlin compilers, it was published in 1708. Later I will analyze in detail this complementary effort of the Qing to fix its narrative alongside its mapping of imperial terrain. In both cases, the emperor and the scholar-officials he patronized moved quickly to set in print a selective, limited spatial and temporal perspective, excluding alternative versions and designed to last for all time.

The late-seventeenth-century conquests, however, did not conclude the northwest story. Kangxi's later years, and the curious reign of his son, the Yongzheng emperor, indicated that serious challenges to his authority persisted, and major underlying constraints on Qing mobilization had not yet been overcome. As Chapters 6 and 7 demonstrate, the Zunghar resistance to undisputed control of the northwest lasted for more than a half-century beyond the Kangxi emperor's victories. His successors built on his achievements, but in retrospect they were only temporary successes.

6

Imperial Overreach and Zunghar Survival, 1700–1731

T HE death of Galdan by no means ended the power of the Zunghar state. Under Galdan's nephew and successor Tsewang Rabdan (r. 1697–1727), the Zunghars reached the peak of their power. Galdan Tseren (r. 1727–1745), Tsewang Rabdan's son, not only held the state together but also ambushed a large Qing army and drove it back in humiliation. Yet within fifteen years after Galdan Tseren died, the Zunghar state and people had vanished. When internecine struggles for leadership destroyed the unity of the Zunghars, the young Qianlong emperor seized his chance to eliminate them. Although Qianlong's victory was sudden, it was not foreordained. For the first half of the eighteenth century, the three empires maintained an uneasy coexistence, interacting more through trade than through war.

From 1700 to the death of the Kangxi emperor in 1722, the frontier remained relatively stable in Turkestan, but Qing intervention in Tibet opened a new arena of competition. The 1720s were a period of transition for all three states, marked by the death of Kangxi in 1722, the death of Peter in 1725, and the death of Tsewang Rabdan in 1727. New rulers aimed to carry on the policies of their predecessors, but with considerably less vigor. Of the three successors, it was Galdan Tseren who ruled the longest and gained the most success. The Yongzheng emperor, at first cautious and austere, launched a reckless attack in Mongolia that ended in a resounding defeat. He reluctantly settled for a truce, and put economic pressure on the Central Eurasians. The Russians gained their long-awaited access to the China market, opening the frontier town of Kiakhta in 1727, but the trade with China proved to be a disappointment. Galdan Tseren held his state to-gether, gathered commercial resources, and maintained his position be-tween the two giant empires.

Modern Chinese historians reveal ironic ambiguities in their discussion of this period. Although they must portray the Zunghars as "splittists" who undermined the unity of the peoples of China, they also praise Tse-wang Rabdan for resisting Russian "aggression" against "our people," the Mongols included. Russian historians, conversely, view Tsewang Rabdan as holding off Manchu expansionism. In fact, it is difficult to convict any of the regimes of unilateral expansionism. Nationalistic focus on unity and the zero-sum binary game obscure the multiple interactions among the con-tending peoples. This period is full of surprises.

The Rise of Tsewang Rabdan

Tsewang Rabdan was the son of Sengge, the brother whose assassination brought Galdan rushing back from Tibet. Already in his twenties, he had hostile relations with his uncle, who kidnapped the princess to whom he was betrothed and sent assassins to kill him. Tsewang Rabdan fled to the Bortala valley to escape Galdan's pursuit, and held him off in a pitched bat-tle.[1] When Galdan moved east in 1690 to intervene in the Khalkhas' inter-necine struggles, Tsewang Rabdan took advantage of his uncle's absence to expand his strength into Khobdo in Galdan's rear. After the battle of Ulan Butong, which severely damaged Galdan's strength, Tsewang Rabdan grew even stronger, but his proposal to partition the Zunghar empire was re-jected.[2] As Galdan prepared for his next battle with the Qing in 1696, Tsewang Rabdan opened secret contacts with the Qing, promising to cap-ture and deliver Galdan to them. In return, he asked the Qing to send back to him any Muslim merchants who fled from Galdan into the Qing interior. He was allowed to send tribute embassies of up to three hundred men to Beijing, which would provide him with valuable trade goods.

With the death of Galdan in 1697, Tsewang Rabdan formally took un-disputed control of his state. Because he lacked a Chinggisid lineage, he could not call himself legitimately "Khan" of the Zunghars. He had ob-tained from the Dalai Lama the title of Erdeni Zoriqtu Hongtaiji in 1694. The Russians referred to him as "Kontaisha."[3] Instead of trying to confront the powerful Manchus, he focused on the Kazakhs to his west. In 1698–99 he launched a series of attacks on the Kazakhs on the Irtysh and lower Xier rivers.[4] Although he used the pretext that the Kazakhs had blocked a Zunghar trade embassy, the causes lay deeper. Galdan's losses had deprived the Zunghars of a great expanse of pastureland, which Kangxi refused to return. Meanwhile, the Kazakhs blocked their access to the west, and Russian settlements moving up the Siberian rivers threatened to confine them even further.[5]

Tsewang Rabdan, more than his uncle, had to focus much of his attention on preserving access to territory and trade routes instead of winning over the allegiance of other Mongol tribes. He began to behave more like a territorial sovereign hemmed in by other states and less like a free-ranging nomadic conqueror. Greater stability in the definition of Zunghar borders aided the growth of settlement. He developed agriculture, crafts, and industrial production with the use of captives from Turkestan, Russia, and even Sweden. He maintained control of Turkestan by granting lands to the Muslim lords in return for payments in kind for his state. He also developed closer ties with the faraway Torghuts (Kalmyks) on the Volga River. The Qing themselves sent Tulisen on his great expedition to gain support from their Khan, Ayuki, for an alliance against Tsewang Rabdan. When Sanjib, the son of Ayuki, left the Volga for Tsewang Rabdan's territory with ten thousand to fifteen thousand households, Tsewang Rabdan gained a powerful contingent of men and cattle. Sanjib had broken away from his father and returned to Mongolia with the original intention of seizing Tsewang Rabdan's throne. Tsewang Rabdan defeated him, however, and sent Sanjib back home, but kept his fighting men for himself.[6]

Up to 1715 the Zunghars clashed most severely with Russia, not the Qing. Russians began moving south of Krasnoyarsk in the early eighteenth century, provoking attacks by Zunghar troops. Both sides competed for the exaction of fur tribute (iasak) from native Siberian tribes. In 1710 the Zunghars destroyed the Russian fortress of Bakan between the Biya and Katun rivers, attacked Baraba and Kuznetsk, and exacted tribute from the inhabitants of Barabinsk.[7] Peter I in 1713 ordered Matvei Gagarin, governor of Siberia, to negotiate an end to these conflicts. Tsewang Rabdan, however, consistently refused to recognize the Russians' rights to this territory, and ordered them to destroy their fortresses at Krasnoyarsk, Kuznetsk, and Tomsk. Dual payments of iasak continued to be an issue between the Russians and Zunghars until the end of the Zunghar state. The Russians could never exact unquestioned and exclusive revenue collection rights in Siberia until their Mongol neighbor had been eliminated by the Qing.

But tensions were greatly heightened when reports came to the Tsar in 1713 of the discovery of gold in Zungharia.[8] Governor Gagarin had purchased samples from "Bukharans," or Turkic traders, who told of huge deposits in "Eskel" on the Amu Darya River. (These reports probably referred to Yarkand, which is not on the Amu Darya.) Tsar Peter, whose motto was "Gold is the heart of the state," was desperate to fund his Great Northern War with Sweden. He ordered an expedition to travel up the Irtysh River and to build fortresses along it and at lakes Balkash, Yamysh, and Zaisang, in the heart of Zunghar territory. The expedition would then attempt to capture Yarkand and investigate the sources of gold in the region. Led by Lieutenant Colonel Ivan Buchholz, a former Captain of the Guard, the army of two thousand men departed Tobolsk in July 1715, arriving in October at Lake Yamysh, where they built their first fortress. They took with them a contingent of Swedish artillery and mining engineers, including Lieutenant J. G. Renat, who would contribute substantially to the Zunghar economy after his capture.[9] Gagarin assured Tsewang Rabdan that the Russians had only friendly intentions, and that they would support Tsewang Rabdan if he did not interfere. But Tsewang Rabdan's brother and best general, Tsering Dondub (Ch. Celing Dunduobu), besieged the Russians with ten thousand men; they stormed and destroyed the fortress on February 9, 1716. Weakened by starvation and pestilence, the hapless Russians had to withdraw up the Irtysh River, where they built the more defensible fortress of Omsk.

Another Russian envoy had meanwhile returned to St. Petersburg with samples of gold collected around the great "Blue Lake" (Kokonor), further exciting Russian greed. The Russians persisted in exploration and fortress construction, rebuilding the fortress at Yamysh and building Semipalatinsk in 1718. Although Tsewang Rabdan objected, the Russians knew that he was concerned with fending off attacks by the Kirghiz–Kazakhs and holding the oases of Hami and Turfan against Chinese pressure, so they paid him little attention. In 1719 Major Ivan Mikhailovich Likharev again penetrated Zunghar lands, building a fortress on Lake Zaisang. At first the Zunghar army feared a Russian–Chinese alliance and refused to attack, but when they learned that there was no alliance, the Zunghars attacked in force with twenty thousand men. Using heavy cannon, Likharev held them off with his small force until a truce was agreed upon. Tsewang Rabdan's losses at Hami and Turfan, and his debacle in Tibet, meant that he could not risk war with Russia. Fearing a Qing invasion, he had to allow the construction of the fortress at Ust-Kamenogorsk in return for Russian withdrawal and promises of aid against the Manchus.[10] The gold expeditions ended without any success: the lure of El Dorado in Turkestan proved to be a will-o'-the-wisp (until the oil discoveries of the twentieth century). But the haunting possibility of gold discoveries gave the Zunghars one more chance to win the Russians to their side.

Tsewang Rabdan had accommodated Russian fortifications in the hopes of gaining an ally against the Qing, but he had no obvious mineral wealth to offer that could compare with the Beijing fur trade. The Manchu envoy Tulisen had succeeded in persuading the Russians not to support Tsewang Rabdan; and Tsewang Rabdan would not submit as a vassal either to China or to Russia. He stubbornly and successfully maintained his people's autonomy throughout his reign.

Three Central Eurasian Travelers

With most military action suspended, diplomatic activity flourished. Qing resources had been exhausted by the difficult military campaigns against Galdan, and the emperors were not inclined to launch new ones immediately. Tsewang Rabdan aimed to shore up his defenses during this lull by investigating opportunities for military aid from Russia in return for gold exploration. After Russia stabilized its border in 1689, the fur caravans sent from Siberia to Beijing in the next two decades were extremely profitable for the Russian state. Russia expected even more lucrative prospects from the Kiakhta treaty of 1727.[11] All sides engaged in mutual spying, testing, and exploration.

Three travelers, each of different nationalities, left fascinating accounts that illuminate this period of cross-cultural engagement. Best known to Chinese historians is the Manchu envoy Tulisen (1667–1741), who was sent on a mission to Ayuki Khan of the Torghuts from 1712 to 1715. He wrote his report on the mission in Manchu, and a somewhat different Chinese version appeared later. Shortly thereafter, the Scotsman John Bell crossed Central Eurasia in the opposite direction on a mission from the Tsar; and the Russian Ivan Unkovskii undertook a mission to Tsewang Rabdan's headquarters from 1722 to 1724. These accounts, in addition to providing valuable geographical information, show how three Central Eurasians—a Russian, a Mongol, and a foreign servant of the Tsar—viewed the Qing state.

Each of the travelers acted in both a personal and an official capacity. Bell traveled as a member of a Russian embassy led by Leon Vasilievich Izmailov, whose main purpose was to obtain information about China's military capabilities and prospects for commercial exchange. Tulisen's ostensible mission was to facilitate the return of Ayuki's nephew Arabjur from the Chinese frontier to the new Torghut homeland on the Volga River. He expected Ayuki Khan to propose a joint expedition against the Zunghar state, but he was instructed to decline any such alliance. Ayuki, dissatisfied with the burdens of Russian servitude, told Tulisen that he felt closer to the

Manchu rulers than to the Russians, and asked for Qing intervention to improve relations with Russia and the Mongols. Tulisen also took the opportunity while he journeyed through Russian territory to check out the empire's commercial and strategic resources, and to prepare for a possible invitation to meet the Tsar. Tulisen and John Bell crossed paths at Selenginsk, and Tulisen later escorted Bell from the frontier to Beijing. Coming from opposite ends of the continent, the two envoys had much in common. Each was a representative of a people on the edge of a great new empire in formation, and each made a successful career out of serving the empire's interests.[12]

By contrast, Unkovskii represented an effort by the Russians to explore opportunities for alliance with the Zunghar Mongols against the Qing empire. Tsewang Rabdan considered becoming a vassal of the Tsar like Ayuki, and he offered the Russians access to suspected gold sands in the deserts of Turkestan in return for their support in the form of a twenty thousand–man army and weapons to defend him against Qing attacks.

Each of the three texts represents a particular combination of state interest and individual responses to the growing Qing power in Central Eurasia. Each report mixes the genres of travel, espionage, and diplomatic literature. They combine exploration, geographical surveys, intelligence gathering, diplomatic interviews, and personal reactions to the landscape. In four different languages (Manchu, Chinese, Russian, and English), they provide four different perspectives on the nature of China's expansion on its northwestern frontier. Tulisen's and Unkovskii's writings were in the guise of official reports to be presented to their sovereigns, but the texts themselves have the character of personal journals. Bell's *Travels* was a private account, not published until nearly fifty years after his return.

During the early seventeenth century the Torghuts had migrated thousands of miles across the steppe to the lower Volga, where they were accepted into the service of the Russian Tsar.[13] They maintained kinship ties with the Zunghars but never consented to be put under their dominion. Their relations with the Russians were also burdensome. The Tsars exempted them from taxes but compelled them to join in military campaigns. Of all the Mongols, they had migrated the longest distances to find open living space, but even they could not escape the reach of the agrarian empires surrounding them. They also maintained contacts with Tibet, preserving their Buddhist faith. Known as the Kalmyks, they remain today as an autonomous republic in the Russian federation. They represent the westernmost extension of Buddhism in Eurasia.

The pretext for Tulisen's mission was closely tied to the growing links between the Qing, the Zunghars, Russia, and Tibet.[14] Arabjur, the nephew of Ayuki, Khan of the Torghuts on the Volga (r. 1673–1724), had traveled to Tibet on a pilgrimage sometime between 1698 and 1703, but found himself unable to return to the Volga because of wars between Ayuki and Tsewang Rabdan. The Kangxi emperor gave him refuge, allowing him pastures in the northwest. Finally, in 1712, Ayuki demanded the return of Arabjur just at the time when a Russian caravan was setting out from Beijing. This was an ideal opportunity for the Qing emperor to use his Russian connections to establish a link with the distant Torghuts, so he asked the Russians to escort five imperial envoys with a message to Ayuki to discuss Arabjur's return. Tulisen was not the head of the mission, but he was the only one to write an account of it. As one of the most extended pieces of Manchu writing about Central Eurasia, it reveals critical aspects of Qing policy toward the region. Arabjur, however, did not join the embassy, and ultimately he was never sent back. Qing objectives were grander than the return of one Mongol to his tribe.

The imperial instructions to Tulisen are a masterpiece of Qing ideological dissimulation. Kangxi directed a special edict to Ayuki, responding to his sincere presentation of tribute, expressing the emperor's wish to have Arabjur reunited with his uncle. Knowing that Ayuki and Tsewang Rabdan were on bad terms, however, he expected Ayuki to propose a joint alliance against Tsewang Rabdan. He gave Tulisen specific instructions on how to respond:

> If Ayuki says, "Let us, having joined together, strive to attack Tsewang Rabdan in a pincer movement from both sides," you should definitely not say anything. Say only, "Tsewang Rabdan is [on very] good [terms with] the Great Khan [Kangxi]. He has been sending countless emissaries to ask after the Khan's health. The Great Khan likewise has been moved to bestow grace in the same manner. Although one might think that his strength is weak, that he is in need, or that he is exhausted, there are certainly no circumstances under which our Sage Lord will attack him. But this matter is great. If we envoys entertain this suggestion it would not be right. Although you have requested us to speak to our Sage Lord, we realize that our Lord says, 'May all living beings under Heaven live in peace and well-being.' We can strongly affirm that the emperor has no intention of disturbing Tsewang Rabdan."[15]

In other words, the envoys were to assert that the emperor had no intention of destroying Tsewang Rabdan, and to reject an explicit alliance against him. Even though Kangxi had repeatedly called for the extermination of Galdan and his Zunghar state, he now claimed to have renounced ambitious efforts to intervene in the distant steppes. The Torghuts themselves saw this embassy quite differently.

At the same time, the envoys were instructed to respond positively to any invitations to meet with the Russian Tsar. They were also told to be very flexible in adapting to Russian customs:

> [If the Tsar sends you an envoy] it is all right to meet him following the laws of his country. Say to the man that he sends, "Previously when Nikolai of your country came to our country, he behaved badly. We are not like that" . . . After you have met the Tsar, if he should ask, "What does your country esteem?" answer only: "Our way of life takes loyalty, filial piety, benevolence, righteousness, and faith as its chief principles. We follow them seriously, both in ruling the country and in our personal conduct. In matters pertaining to life and death, we have nothing to fear. We simply say, 'If we die we die' . . . Because our country puts first such principles as loyalty, [etc.], we have no wars and no heavy punishments. For many years, we have lived in well-being and peace."[16]

This embassy provided the emperor with an opportunity to spread an idealized version of his rule to new peoples with whom the expanding empire had come in contact. For external consumption, imperial rule represented peace, loyalty, and benevolence. The emperor did not boast of military conquests to the Russians, as he did to his own subjects, nor did he speak openly of diplomatic alliances or trade. But invoking his desire for peace also included a promise to respond to threats: "If Russia dispatched troops to its borders, we might become suspicious and send our troops there. Our two countries have lived in harmony for a long time. We intend to preserve this relationship. Yet 'once troops have been sent to the frontier for use, they will be used. Do not have any doubts.'" His emissaries, however, should stress the difficulty of any major armed confrontation:

> I believe the Russians will certainly ask about what types of cannon we have. If they do ask, say: "The distance is very far; it would be very difficult to bring them to the border. Along the way, there are very many mountains, cliffs, woods, dense forests, precipices, and narrow passes. There is certainly no way for us to bring them there. We do not perceive a need for it, and to achieve it would be very difficult. Thus, by our country's laws, these kinds of things absolutely could not occur at

the frontier. Our prohibitions are very strict. And even if our Sage Lord ordered it, he certainly could not attain it."[17]

The envoys were also told that Russian customs were degenerate and corrupt, and that they should avoid any excessive drinking or disorderly behavior. Most of the imperial instructions were intended to present a peaceful, disciplined image to these unsophisticated people. At the same time, the emissaries were to gather extensive information about the country through which they traveled. Tulisen, on his return, prepared a detailed map of Siberia for the emperor which was at least equal if not superior to the maps prepared by Russian and Western surveyors.[18]

Tulisen provided his own intriguing insights into Russian attitudes. In his account, Siberian Governor Gagarin praises Kangxi's benevolence and draws invidious comparisons with his own Tsar:

[Gagarin] then said—"Your emperor of China is indeed a most excellent and most divine personage; while he is thus occupied in promoting the prosperity and riches of his empire, and in preserving on all sides the blessings of peace, your Excellencies may no doubt happily and uninterruptedly follow your respective pursuits . . . In this empire also, while the late Chahan Khan [Peter I] lived, we were free from labor and care. In his reign, all men, whether of high or low estate, rested in peace . . . But latterly, for these twenty years past, our empire has been engaged in incessant wars; and to this day, we are still fighting and contending without any respite . . . China is at present the only empire which enjoys any peace or tranquility. Our present Chahan Khan, even when he was yet a child, was always fighting and contending with the children who were his playmates. Those children are now become generals in his armies. We should have still been at rest at this time, as heretofore, if he had only followed the steps of his father."[19]

Gagarin is made to say that Peter the Great, who did indeed practice military drills as a child, compares unfavorably with Kangxi, whose farsighted benevolence achieves peace without aggressive military action. Is this the genuine view of a Siberian governor far from Moscow, or is Tulisen putting words in his mouth? Gagarin may well have viewed Peter's engagement in European wars as a distraction from his task of defending Siberia and negotiating favorable terms with China. China, after all, produced considerably more wealth for Russia's treasury by its purchases of Siberian furs than did the nations of Europe. It is not impossible that the views of Tulisen and the Siberian governor converged, even though Tulisen expresses Gagarin's views in purely orthodox Qing rhetorical style. But it seems unlikely that Gagarin would criticize his Tsar openly in Tulisen's presence. In any event, Tulisen, like John Bell, draws on Russian testimony to support the image of the kindly, peaceful Qing emperor.

After Tulisen returned to Selenginsk, he dispatched a letter to Gagarin with a very different message. Tsewang Rabdan had by then begun his attacks on Hami. The letter explained that Tsewang Rabdan used to be a loyal tributary, who was treated "with great kindness and compassion," but "the disposition of Tsewang Rabdan is by nature deceitful and false [Ma. *banitai koimali holo*]. His essence being thus, he definitely cannot change. Inquiring into Tsewang Rabdan's crimes, we have sent [an army] to make war against him."[20] Tulisen urged the Russians to seize Tsewang Rabdan and his followers if they crossed the border in an attempt to gain refuge from the Qing army.[21]

Thus in the Qing view, Tsewang Rabdan, by rejecting imperial benevolence, had removed himself from any reach of pardon and deserved to be eliminated. The Chinese text referring to Qing action uses the term *zhengjiao* (a righteous campaign of extermination), whereas the Manchu text uses only *dailambi* (to make war on).[22] "Extermination" was the term repeatedly used by Qing rulers facing Zunghar leaders who insisted on their autonomy. Kangxi used metaphors of "root and branch" elimination against Galdan, and Qianlong incessantly harped on the need to exterminate the last vestiges of the Zunghar state. The carefully constructed image of Chinese benevolence was used to persuade the Russians to refuse shelter to refugee Mongols.

Tulisen was also prepared to answer questions from Ayuki Khan. The Khan asked many questions about the Qing, especially the Manchu rulers and their activities. He knew that the emperor often went hunting north of the capital, and that he had a separate residence in Rehe, as well as an administrative center in Mukden. He also knew that the Manchu script was derived from the Mongol script. Concluding that Manchus and Mongols were so similar that they must have had a "common origin" (Ma. *emu adali*; Ch. *tongyuan*), he wondered how they had come to separate from each other. Tulisen promised to obtain more information from the emperor on his return. In Tulisen's report Ayuki stated that although the Torghuts were a "people of an outer state" (Ma. *tulergi gurun-i niyalma*; Ch. *waidi*), in form and clothing they were extremely similar to the people of the Central Kingdom (Ma. *dulimba-i gurun*; Ch. *zhongguo*) yet completely different from the Russians.[23] Ayuki clearly had in mind the Manchus, not the Han Chinese, when he stressed the similarities between the two peoples. The Qing rulers also could offer Ayuki closer ties with Tibet, because they had frequent envoys from the Dalai Lama. Ayuki was especially interested in obtaining medicines from Tibet, access to which was now blocked by the Russians. Thus Tulisen could effectively use the multicultural reach of the Qing state, embracing Tibetans, Manchus, and Mongols, to draw another Mongol Khan over to his side.

Tulisen's report, originally written in Manchu, with the title *Lakcaha Jecende takûraha ejehe bithe* (Jottings on the places where one sent me in the cut-off frontiers [outside the empire]), was published in Chinese in 1723 as *Yiyulu* (Record of strange regions). It was so fascinating that Europeans soon translated it into several languages. A French translation appeared in 1726, a German and two Russian translations in the late eighteenth century, and a (rather inaccurate) English translation by Sir George Staunton in 1821. European observers, then and now, describe Tulisen's mission as an extraordinary event, for China, in their view, almost never sent its official representatives out of the empire. Their parochial focus blinded them to the empire's many foreign contacts preceding the European encounter. Seen in a Central Eurasian context, Tulisen's embassy was only one in a long lineage of exploratory expeditions, including Han Wudi's expeditions to obtain the blood-sweating horses of Ferghana, Zhang Qian's mission to the nomads in the second century BCE, or the Tang emperors' dispatches of monks to India. Obtaining information about the peoples of Central Eurasia, especially new tribes who appeared on the borders, had always been a significant goal of those empires which, like the Han and Tang, looked outward to the northwest. The Qing embassy set out at a time when other world empires, such as the British and the Russians, were also sending their envoys, merchants, and travelers on missions of exploration. Like their contemporaries, the Qing emissaries combined strategic, geographical, and commercial objectives.

The exact objective of the embassy is still unclear. Did the emperor hope to conclude a military alliance with Ayuki against Tsewang Rabdan? Since the Qing had previously allied with Tsewang Rabdan against Galdan, it is certainly plausible that they would once again try to play off one barbarian against another. Even though imperial instructions directed Tulisen to reject initially any such proposal by Ayuki, this was only the opening negotiating position. If Ayuki really had military strength to offer, the emperor could have changed his point of view. The alliance with Tsewang Rabdan itself was kept very well concealed. The Torghuts themselves saw a Qing alliance as the purpose of the mission, and Tulisen's envoy to Beijing may in fact have proposed such an alliance when he requested the return of Arabjur.[24] The view of the Russian envoy Glazunov in 1730 was that Kangxi's goal was to induce the Torghuts to return to Qing territory. In

1712, however, Tsewang Rabdan had not yet attacked Qing territory, and Kangxi had no intention of launching an army against him. The Torghuts did come back to the Qing frontiers in the 1770s, but no such promises were made at the time of Tulisen's visit; and, as we shall see, whether or not to receive the long-departed Mongolians was a contentious issue in Qianlong's reign.

More important than establishing an immediate alliance was the gathering of information. Within Tulisen's report, Russia and eastern Mongolia feature more prominently than Ayuki Khan himself. The court was willing to make many concessions to Russian customs in order to obtain a meeting with the Tsar. Tulisen provided the Qing court with much valuable information about Siberia. His report, one of the great pieces of travel literature of the time, offers astute observations on geography, natural environment, and social customs. It is both an imperial ethnography and an intelligence document, serving to guide foreign policy and to inform the Qing rulers about their international environment. Strategic concerns about Russian and Zunghar intentions motivated this distant expedition, and the report itself broadened the horizons of the Manchu elite. John Bell performed a similar task for his Russian masters with his travels eastward across Central Eurasia from 1716 to 1720.

John Bell (1691–1780) left home in 1714 to serve the Russian Tsar, like so many of his fellow Scots. In 1719 he set out from St. Petersburg for Beijing, passing through Siberia and the territory of the Buriat and Khalkha Mongols. Many years later, in 1763, he published his *Travels from St. Petersburg in Russia to Diverse Parts of Asia,* described by a reviewer in 1817 as "the best model perhaps for travel-writing in the English language."[25] One part of Bell's *Travels,* the "Journey from St. Petersburg to Pekin," begins with his departure from the Russian capital and ends with his arrival at the Qing court. Along the way he describes in great detail the topography, flora and fauna, and peoples across Central Eurasia, mingling a personal diary with discussions of politics and natural history.

In addition to his curiosity about the customs and local histories of the places through which he passed, Bell had very perceptive insights into the crucial role of logistics for mastery of the steppe. His primary sources of information were Russian. He learned most about steppe peoples "from an ingenious and penetrating gentleman, who fills a public office in this place [Tobolsk], and was employed in several messages to him from the late governor of Siberia."[26] His comments about relations between the Qing and the Mongols, however, also closely reflect the Qing official point of view.

After his arrival at Selenginsk on May 29, 1720, Bell noted:

The Mongalls are a numerous people, and occupy a large extent of country, from this place to the Kallgan, which signifies the Everlasting Wall, or the great Wall of China . . . One may easily imagine, from the vast track of land which the Mongalls occupy, that they must be very numerous; especially, when it is considered, that they live in a healthy climate, and have been engaged in no wars, since they were conquered, partly by the Russians on the west, and partly by the Chinese on the east; to whom all these people are now tributaries. In former times the Mongalls were troublesome neighbors to the Chinese, against whose incursions the great wall was built.

Kamhi [Kangxi], the present emperor of China, was the first who subdued these hardy Tartars; which he effected more by kind usage and humanity than by his sword; for these people are great lovers of liberty. The same gentle treatment hath been observed by the Russians, towards those of them who are their subjects. And they themselves confess, that, under the protection of these two mighty Emperors, they enjoy more liberty, and live more at ease, than they formerly did under their own princes.[27]

Bell's "Mongalls" are the Khalkhas, or Eastern Mongols, particularly those under the leadership of the Tüsiyetü Khan. The gratitude of the Khalkhas toward Kangxi stemmed from his intervention in the dispute between the Jasaktu Khan and Tüsiyetü Khan, which had provoked Galdan's invasion. Kangxi's "kind usage" at first meant sheltering refugees from the internecine Mongolian battles within Chinese borders and offering famine relief to starving Mongols. In return, however, the Khalkhas were enrolled into banners, their pasturelands were carefully delimited, the succession to the Khanship and other ranks was put under Qing supervision, and they had to provide levies of horses to support Qing campaigns. Russia's rule of its subject Mongols was arguably less systematic but more onerous. Tribute exactions by Siberian governors and Cossacks were more capricious, but Mongol "liberties" were not so circumscribed. The new "liberty" of the Mongols really meant freedom from the dangers of war, while they lost their customary freedoms to migrate and pasture where they pleased. The border treaty between Russia and China prevented them from fleeing across the vaguely demarcated frontier to escape excess exactions by one side or the other. Some, like Gantimur and the Torghuts, escaped these constraints, but most were bound by them.

Bell's comment reflects a view of Mongol–Chinese and Mongol–Russian relations that suited both the settled empires and certain elements of the

Mongol elite, but it tells less than the full story. In 1719–20, when he wrote his account, the Kangxi emperor in his last years had indeed seemed to achieve his goals of settling Mongolian disputes through "kind usage." The memory of his effort to eliminate the Zunghar state was now twenty years old. Bell had absorbed both the Russian desire for peaceful commercial relations and the self-image of the Qing as a benevolent, impartial arbiter interested in peace among peoples.

Bell also commented on the Qing wars with Tsewang Rabdan. After noting his arrival at Tobolsk, on December 16, 1719, Bell wrote:

> The Emperor of China was some time ago engaged in a war with the Kontaysha about some frontier towns, of which the latter took possession, and maintained his claim with a strong army. The Emperor sent against him an army of three hundred thousand men, under the command of his fourteenth son, who is reckoned the best general of all his children. Notwithstanding their superiority in numbers, the Kontaysha defeated the Chinese in several actions. The Emperor thought it best to accommodate the difference, and a peace was concluded to the satisfaction of both parties.[28]

This passage refers to Tsewang Rabdan's attempted invasion of Hami in 1715.[29] Yinti, the Kangxi's emperor's fourteenth son, was designated Fuyuan Jiangjun and sent with a large force (but not 300,000 men) to Gansu and Mongolia to deter Tsewang Rabdan. There were no major battles, but the Qing did recover Hami and Turfan, and a truce was later negotiated. The source of Bell's version is rather unclear, but "Kontaysha," derived from "Hongtaiji," is the regular Russian title for the Zunghar rulers. Presumably, this was an account given to Bell by Russian officials in Tobolsk, and reflects their best understanding of the relations between the Qing and Zunghars. As texts discussed later also indicate, the Russians tended to look on the Qing military forces as being of poor quality, but they also gave the Qing emperor credit for being farsighted and benevolent. This emerging image of a rather weak but benevolent regime in Beijing suited the Russian aims of establishing diplomatic relations based primarily on trade.

Bell further notes:

> It must be observed, that the Chinese, being obliged to undertake a long and difficult march, through a desert and barren country, lying westward of the long wall; being also encumbered with artillery, and heavy carriages containing provisions for the whole army during their

march; had their force greatly diminished before they reached the enemy. The Kontaysha, on the other hand, having intelligence of the great army coming against him, waited patiently on his own frontiers, till the enemy was within a few days march of his camp, when he sent out detachments of light horse to set fire to the grass, and lay waste the country. He also distracted them, day and night, with repeated alarms, which together with want of provisions, obliged them to retire with considerable loss.[30]

This comment must refer to the battle of the Manchu commanders Seleng and Elunte with Tsewang Rabdan's forces at the Kara-Usu River on October 5, 1718, in which the Qing forces, consisting of two thousand Green Standard troops, ten thousand local "chieftain troops" *(tusi),* and a small number of Manchu troops, were surrounded and crushed.[31] It was only after this stunning defeat that Kangxi designated his fourteenth son to lead the army. It is a very perceptive observation about the nature of warfare between the Qing and its nomadic rivals, or in fact about warfare between settled agrarian regimes and nomads in general. Similar withdrawal and scorched earth tactics were used by the Crimean Tartars against the Russian empire's expansion to the south, and by the Parthians against the Roman empire. Bell comments: "This method of carrying on war, by wasting the country, is very ancient among the Tartars, and practiced by all of them from the Danube eastward. This circumstance renders them a dreadful enemy to regular troops, who must thereby be deprived of all subsistence, while the Tartars, having always many spare horses to kill and eat, are at no loss for provisions."[32] As the discussion of Kangxi's Galdan campaigns has indicated, Russians and Chinese both had to solve this fundamental logistical problem of the steppe. Russian armies in the Crimea created *tabory,* or "moving fortresses," grain wagons that were surrounded by defensive troops, which trundled forward as the Tartars retreated.[33] Only by the mid-eighteenth century were the Chinese, over a much vaster terrain, able to create a chain of magazine posts stretching from the Gansu border out into Xinjiang. Bell perceived both the general problem of logistics in the steppe and the way nomads deployed logistical attacks in battle.

Artillery Captain Ivan Unkovskii's mission to Zungharia in 1722–1724 was the last futile Russian attempt to induce the Zunghar Khan into submission. Despite the failure of the Buchholz and Likharev expeditions, Tsar Peter maintained his drive to find gold in Zungharia. Tsewang Rabdan had driven off two Russian armies, but he still expressed interest in an alliance with Russia against China. Unkovskii was sent to continue negotiations. He left Moscow in February 1722 but only arrived at Tsewang Rabdan's camp in November, just after the death of the Kangxi emperor. Tsewang Rabdan now took a harder position against Russia, launching further attacks against the Kazakhs and reiterating demands for the destruction of Russian fortresses. Unkovskii left in September 1723 with his mission unfulfilled. He did, however, collect a great deal of valuable information about Zungharia. His journal entries are extremely revealing; they provide an almost unique account of personal dialogue with a Central Eurasian ruler.[34]

On December 11, 1722, a high-ranking noble came from Tsewang Rabdan's camp to meet Unkovskii with a list of questions from the Khan. The journal lists the questions submitted by Tsewang Rabdan's ministers *(zaisang)* side by side with Unkovskii's replies. This exchange offers interesting indications of the different perspectives of both sides about China:

Zaisang: Cheredov told [the Khan] that fortress towns [*gorody*] were built by Russia along the Irtysh in case the Tsar wanted to make war on China.

Unkovskii: Cheredov was not authorized to say that; the towns were built not for war but to search for ore . . .

Zaisang: Cheredov spoke of a search for golden ore.

Unkovskii: And I was ordered to ask permission of the Kontaisha [for this search]. And if the search for gold and silver succeeded, the gains for you would be large, as I explained in detail to the Kontaisha [Tsewang Rabdan].

Zaisang: The Kontaisha asks that the Mongols submit themselves to the beneficent protection of your Imperial Highness, as Ayuki Khan submitted; and we would rejoice at this, and request an army of twenty thousand men [to be used] against the Chinese Khan, and nothing else.

Unkovskii: On this subject I explained to the Kontaisha in detail that when he committed himself to written negotiations, as were done with Ayuki Khan, then His Imperial Highness would defend you, as his subjects, against your enemies; but he would first attempt to persuade the Chinese Khan by his orders to commit no injuries against you, and if the Chinese Khan did not listen, then he would find ways of bringing support to you.[35]

This dialogue has a refreshing directness seldom found in the official diplomatic exchanges. Clearly the Zunghars expected Russian military aid against China in return for their submission to the Tsar. They even asked for the Russians to help them subdue the Khalkha Mongols, just as the Russians had helped Ayuki gain dominance over his neighbors. By invoking the oral discussions with the previous envoy, Ivan Cheredov, they tried to tie down the Russians to definite commitments of aid. Unkovskii, however, avoided promising direct support, deferring the question to negotiations. Tsewang Rabdan did not know of Ayuki's dissatisfaction with Russian subjection, which he had revealed to Tulisen, nor did he know of Ayuki's proposal to ally with the Qing. Ultimately, Tsewang Rabdan refused to become a Russian subject when he learned of the death of the Kangxi emperor, and when he realized that it would weaken his position to accept Russian troops on Zunghar soil. He told Unkovskii that he had received envoys from the Yongzheng emperor offering peaceful relations, and he had also received emissaries from the Khalkha Mongols and the Khoshots. He felt that China was now in a weakened position. Perhaps Tsewang's victory over Qing armies in 1718 and the truce settlement in 1722 had led him to overestimate his strength and misunderstand the degree of his isolation.[36]

Tsewang Rabdan, however, displayed curiosity about geopolitical relations across the Eurasian continent. He asked Unkovskii repeatedly about Peter the Great's fleet, his wars with the Turks and Swedes, the nature of Russian religious beliefs, and whether the Russians drank tea. In a second private dialogue with Unkovksii, he tried to learn about the power of China:

Kontaisha: The Chinese boast that no one is stronger and braver than them, and all peoples bring them tribute [*dan'*].

Unkovskii: I hope you will not take it amiss if I say this, but His Imperial Highness ordered me to bring various things for you: What do you consider them to be: tribute or something else? He replied that the Tsar sent gifts in gratitude for his [Tsewang Rabdan's] beneficence, not as tribute. I said it is just the same with the Chinese Khan, people send gifts [*podarki*], not tribute [*dan'*].

Kontaisha: Whom do you consider to be stronger, the Turkish sultan or the Chinese Khan?

Unkovskii: We consider the Turks to be braver than the Chinese, and the Chinese behave poorly in military actions. After that I told him that among all peoples there are bad characters [who bring unreliable reports that one should not believe].[37]

This discussion of the nature of gifts presented by one sovereign to another is reminiscent of the issue faced by George Macartney at the end of the century. Should goods offered to a sovereign be regarded as "tribute," indicating the willing subjection of the presenter to the recipient, or as "gifts," simply indicating an expression of friendship? It is a particularly complex question in this Central Eurasian example because of the three-way ties among Russians, Mongols, and Chinese. Izmailov's embassy to Beijing, of which John Bell was a part, did perform the *ketou* according to Qing ritual, and did not openly contest the Qing description of Sino-Russian trade as "tribute." Even though the Russians had signed a treaty with China providing for exchanges of goods under the guise of tribute, they did not want to indicate to the Zunghar Mongols that they regarded themselves in any way as subordinate to the Chinese. Too close a relationship with China would endanger their access to the golden sands they hoped to find in Zungharia. So they portrayed their relationship, and that of all other countries, with China under the guise of an amicable exchange of "gifts" and not the hierarchical relationship of tribute.

The Russian envoy took care to denigrate Chinese military power as well. Since Tsewang Rabdan clearly knew of Chinese military might from Galdan's experience, and he probably also knew of China's destruction of the Russian fortress at Albazin, the Russians did not want to arouse suspicions that they lacked either the capacity or the willingness to confront China if necessary. On the one hand, Tsewang Rabdan may have been gratified to hear that Russia did not consider China to be very strong. On the other hand, he may have been misled into overconfidence about his own chances of survival if he faced China on his own. He had recently won victories against Qing armies, and the death of the Kangxi emperor might lead to a less aggressive Qing policy. As a result, he refused to become a Russian subject, and this decision effectively ended any prospects for Russian military aid. But the Russians made the right economic choice in the end. The fur trade with Beijing proved more profitable than the illusory golden sands of Turkestan.

During his ten-month residence in Zungharia, Unkovskii enjoyed frequent access to the Khan and his ministers, and he was invited to observe religious and ritual processions and horse-riding competitions. Despite the conflicting interests of the Tsar and the Zunghar Khan, the envoy could meet Tsewang Rabdan in a "middle ground," in Richard White's term, a "world of common contact and common meaning," where mutual curiosity and geopolitical interest inspired the two cultures to learn more about each other.[38] Like Tulisen and Bell, Unkovskii reported factual information to his sovereign that served state interests, but he gave detailed personal accounts in his journal that go well beyond the restrictions of diplomatic protocol. For this brief period, Russia faced east as much as it faced west, while the Qing relaxed its efforts to dominate the entire middle ground. By promoting the exchange of information across these vast spaces, these three envoys helped to construct images of a common Eurasian world.

The Penetration of Turkestan and Tibet

During the late years of Kangxi's reign, the Qing extended their control farther west with major military campaigns against both the Zunghars and Tibet. This expansion culminated in the expedition of 1720 to Lhasa. Qing intervention in Tibet is often treated as a separate campaign, connected with the internal politics of Tibet, but it was intimately linked to the goal of exterminating the Zunghar state. It grew out of an unsuccessful effort by Kangxi to eliminate the power of Tsewang Rabdan, Galdan's successor. Kangxi failed because Tsewang Rabdan was too far away, but he succeeded in Tibet because of internal rivalries and because the Qing could gain access to Tibet via Kokonor.

Tsewang Rabdan avoided open conflict with the Qing until a schism occurred in Tibet, instigated by Lazang Khan (1656?–1717) of the Khoshot Mongols of Kokonor (Ch. Qinghai). Lazang (T. Lha bzang), the grandson of Gush Khan, the great sponsor of the Tibetan lamas, killed his elder brother and seized the Khanship in 1700. Supported by the Chinese, he aimed to restore Khoshot supremacy over Tibet after Galdan's failure. Tibet became a vast ground of contention between these rival Mongol leaders, but ultimately the rivalry played into the hands of the Qing.[39]

Power in the Tibetan state had long been divided among different sects of monastic Buddhists, each of whom depended heavily on support from Mongol patrons. At the top of the state there was a three-way division of power among the Dalai Lama, his Mongol patrons, and the temporal administrator (T. *sDe-pa*, Ch. *diba*), who also served as regent when the Dalai Lamas were in their infancy. In the mid-seventeenth century, Gusri Khan of the Khoshot Mongols had installed the sect he patronized, the Gelupa (T. dGe-lugs-pa), or "Yellow Hats," in Lhasa, winning a victory over the rival Karmapa, or Red Hat, sect.[40] Gusri Khan supported the Dalai Lama, suppressing rebellions against his power, allowing him to enforce discipline in the monasteries and carry out a census of the tax-paying population. After Gusri Khan's death, the fifth Dalai Lama, Nag-dban-blo-bzan, became stronger, as Gusri Khan's successors constituted only weak rivals. The Dalai Lama retired from secular authority, yielding power to his natural son, the regent Sanggya Gyatso (T. Sangs-rgyas-rgya-mts'o).

As discussed earlier, the *sDe-pa* concealed the death of the Dalai Lama in 1682 from the Qing and ruled by himself until the defeat of Galdan. He aimed to establish a "really absolute government" that would centralize Tibet and open it to the outside world. Many foreign visitors, including Indians, Chinese, Mongols, and Muslims, brought in gold, silver, cloth, and other trade goods, stimulating economic growth. He used this revenue to build roads and bridges and to support scholarship.[41] As the regent turned outward, Kangxi denounced him for his alliance with Galdan and his defiance of the Dalai Lama's instructions. In 1697 the *sDe-pa* was forced to conciliate the furious Chinese emperor by officially subordinating himself to the sixth Dalai Lama, Tshangs-dbyangs-rgya-mtsho.[42] In fact, the regent kept his power while allowing the young lama, described by the Jesuit Ippolito Desideri as a "dissolute youth, addicted to every vice, thoroughly depraved," to indulge in wine, women, and the writing of love poetry.[43] The *sDe-pa* also resisted efforts to control Lhasa by the Khoshot and Khalkha Mongols, who were Galdan's principal rivals.

In 1705, however, Lazang Khan, with the support of Kangxi, invaded Lhasa, killed the regent, and established himself as the primary ruler of central Tibet, while uniting several kingdoms under the central power in Lhasa. Under Lazang Khan, Tibet seemed to be regaining its unity and autonomy. Lazang Khan, like the Kangxi emperor, welcomed foreign missionaries to his court, intimating that he might convert to Christianity, and enormously impressing the Jesuit Desideri with his sophistication, generosity, and curiosity.[44] Kangxi, equally impressed, granted Lazang the title of Yifa Gongshun Khan, "The Law-Abiding Obedient Khan." Blaming all the disorder in Tibet on the usurping *sDe-pa,* the emperor feared that the sixth Dalai Lama would succeed in reaching Tsewang Rabdan and inspiring a renewal of the Zunghar–Tibetan alliance.

Supporting Lazang's efforts to overthrow Zunghar influence by expelling the sixth Dalai Lama, Kangxi told Lazang to seize the "false" (sixth) Dalai Lama and present him to the court, but while under escort passing through Kokonor, the Dalai Lama died. Although he may have died of illness, persistent strong rumors suggested that he was murdered by Lazang's men.[45] Lazang Khan placed his own candidate for Dalai Lama on the throne, but the Tibetans were strongly loyal to their former spiritual ruler, who had predicted that he would be reborn in Kokonor after his death. Soon reports arrived that a young child had indeed been born, in Litang, on the eastern border of Kham, in 1706, and that he was a Khubilghan, a living Buddha incarnating the spirit of the former Dalai Lama. Lazang and his deputy monks, denying that the child showed signs of being a true reincarnation, forbade him to come to Lhasa, and the Chinese cooperated by keeping the boy under arrest "for his own protection" in a fortress in Xining. (Note the uncanny parallels to the conflict between rival Panchen Lamas in Tibet today.)

Meanwhile Tsewang Rabdan had begun to take an interest in Tibetan affairs, responding to the new level of Chinese support for Lazang Khan and to appeals from the Yellow Hat lamas, who hated Lazang Khan's rule. His attack on Hami in 1715 was intended to put pressure on the Chinese and the Khoshot Mongols to keep them out of Tibet, but it also alerted Kangxi to the encroaching dangers on China's northwestern borders. As the Qing began to prepare a large army to repel Tsewang Rabdan, in a surprising victory his army of two thousand men was driven away from Hami by the Muslim *beg* and some two hundred Qing troops. The *beg* was rewarded with 15,000 taels from the Qing treasury. Qing rule now began to extend to the oasis Muslims as well as the Eastern Mongols.[46] The emperor immediately began to prepare a military expedition to "exterminate" *(jiaomie)* Tsewang Rabdan just like Galdan, to "wipe out the evil so as to have eternal peace."[47] Expenses this time were estimated at about 3 to 4 million taels to support three armies of ten thousand men each that would march to Tsewang Rabdan's headquarters in far western Mongolia. Tsewang Rabdan was estimated to have an army of forty thousand, plus the ten thousand Torghuts he had captured from Ayuki Khan's son. The Qing, for their part, drew on fifteen thousand troops from their Khalkha Mongol allies, in addition to the Manchu, Mongol, and Chinese banners.

These expeditions attempted to repeat the pattern of the Galdan campaigns, but conditions had changed substantially. The emperor was now too old and ill to participate personally. Ever since he deposed his son Yinreng for immoral behavior, in 1708 and again in 1712 he had suffered repeated attacks of mortal illness; his hands shook too hard to allow him to write, and he suffered fainting spells that impeded his decision making. Unable to decide on a successor, he repeatedly instructed his sons not to intrigue against one another, to no avail. At the same time, the quality of civil and military administration declined. Corrupt superior officials extorted funds from lower officials, who pressed on the people, inciting armed resistance. During these military campaigns, Finance Ministry Vice President Seertu, in charge of providing rations for the troops, embezzled official funds, shortchanging Manchu, Mongol, and Han soldiers alike.[48]

As before, Kangxi tried to lure Tsewang Rabdan closer to Beijing with peace offers but threatened punishment if he withdrew. Now over sixty years old, the emperor constantly recalled the bold decisions and great successes of his prime twenty years earlier.[49] This time, however, the distances and supply problems were much greater than during the Galdan campaigns. Hami lay far out the Silk Road, nearly 1,200 kilometers west of Ulan Butong and over 500 kilometers northwest of Suzhou, the closest major military supply base, and the garrison at Jiayuguan at the end of the Great Wall. And Hami, ruled by a *beg* loyal to the Qing, was only the eastern border of Tsewang Rabdan's realm. The real target, in the most grandiose plans, was Ürümchi, 500 kilometers further west, or even Ili and the Irtysh River, far away in the Altai Mountains. The expansive ambitions of the Qing generals, urged on by the emperor, led them to plan for stupendous logistical and military feats. As it happened, they fell far short of their dreams, but they did substantially strengthen supply routes, commerce, and access to the region. These campaigns initiated the Qing penetration of the great Turko-Mongolian region which would later come to be known as Xinjiang (New Frontiers).

Their first effort was to build a supply base at Barköl (Ch. Balikun), 100 kilometers north of Hami, to serve as a base for advances farther west. First 20,000 *shi* of grain were to be transported by horse cart, using three thousand carts to carry supplies in twelve stages from Jiayuguan to Hami. But by March 1716 it was clear that these supplies could not support the garrison, and five thousand troops had to return to Gansu. General Xizhu was fired for failing to pay sufficient attention to supplies, even though he protested that "I only lead the troops; I have nothing to do with military supplies."[50]

Previous campaigns had divided responsibilities ethnically—Han generals took charge of logistical support, and Manchu and Mongol generals led troops—but now the roles blurred. Manchu generals had to learn mundane details of grain transport, and several Han Chinese demonstrated significant military talents. Nian Gengyao, in particular, of the Chinese Bordered Yellow Banner, did an excellent job as Governor of Sichuan in supervising supplies, leading him to be promoted to Governor-General in charge of military affairs at Chengdu. Funingga (Ch. Funing'an), the Manchu general in charge of the Xinjiang campaigns, profited from his experience in his previous post as granary superintendent.[51] At the same time, Qing troops as they advanced burned the grasslands to deprive Tsewang Rabdan's horsemen of their supplies. As John Bell had noted, this ruthless tactic had been employed by nomadic warriors from Mongolia to the Crimea, and both the Qing and the Russians now learned how to respond in kind.[52] In a few years, the Vice President of the Ministry of War, Li Xianfu, could boast that his men were thoroughly familiar with grain transport to the far-flung garrisons. Oases formerly isolated in the desert could now be reached regularly by troops; the road from Hami to Barköl had become a "highway."[53] Li was praised as a "Hanren" who had learned not to be afraid of the difficulties of supplying troops on the frontiers. In this case, military cooperation promoted the unity of Han and Manchu.

Other officials continued to criticize the expense and risks of these campaigns, but the emperor would allow no objections. Liu Yinqu repeatedly warned against the suffering that transport to the frontier inflicted on both men and horses. He claimed that three to four feet of snow blocked the route from Ganzhou to Barköl, but he was fired for incompetence, and the emperor claimed that he had lied about the difficulties.[54] After being rebuked by the emperor several more times and condemned to death, he was eventually pardoned and ordered to spend his time cultivating fields on the frontier under military supervision. Shi Yide, the Gansu provincial Commander-in-Chief *(tidu)*, also faced execution, until he was pardoned, for declaring that it was a waste of money to spend 250,000 taels on supplying these garrisons. The emperor replied, "He doesn't understand that I will spend several million taels if necessary."[55]

Despite all the planning, the limitations of the harsh environment required repeated postponements of a major effort. The campaign for 1715 was called off as the generals focused on building up supplies at Barköl. Fearing renewed attacks by Tsewang Rabdan on Hami, they strengthened their defenses. The next year they again put off any advances, as many objected to the difficulties of transport.[56] Even the increasingly frustrated emperor had to admit that logistical obstacles could not yet be overcome.

The Qing's conception of its natural borders kept expanding as the armies marched west. Hami was now regarded as "no different from the interior" since it had repelled Tsewang Rabdan's attacks and been fortified. By April 1717, 8,500 troops at Barköl were prepared to advance to capture Turfan. Then this vital oasis on the eastern edge of Turkestan would once and for all be "entered on the country's registers" *(ru guojia bantu)*. Even so, success was uncertain, and there were disturbing reports of "narrow-minded people [*xiaoren*] who spread rumors and undermine morale."[57] A more modest objective, considered as a fallback, was not to attempt to hold Turfan, but to advance so as to alarm Tsewang Rabdan's supporters with the army's might in the hope of inducing the surrender of his Mongol allies. A second army would head for Ürümchi with a similar objective. This plan echoed Kangxi's expedition to the Ordos, which achieved no direct military objectives but greatly impressed the local Mongols. Turfan and Ürümchi, however, unlike the Ordos, were oases in the desert 350 to 500 kilometers west of Hami, and there were no pastoralists nearby to be impressed.[58]

Both armies did advance far enough to run into Zunghar patrols, which they defeated in two battles just east of the oases of Mulei and Pizhan. The delighted emperor at first urged Funingga to proceed farther and track down all the Zunghars he could find. Commander Furdan even planned for a full-scale advance to Tsewang Rabdan's headquarters as far as Ili or the Irtysh River. But east of Turfan, three hundred Zunghars fought back, firing their fowling pieces and killing an important Mongol prince before they

fled. At this point, word came that Tsewang Rabdan was preparing to invade Tibet, so the Xinjiang expedition was called off. As with Galdan, it
was more important to defeat the Mongol leader personally than to capture
several remote oases.[59]

Although the generals drew up plans to continue the "righteous extermination" the next year, the central strategic concerns shifted to Kokonor
and Tibet, making it difficult to carry them out. Finally, two years later,
Funingga defeated the Zunghars in two skirmishes, occupied Pizhan, and
marched his army to Turfan, where the Muslim *beg* surrendered. Further
campaigns deeper into Xinjiang were called off. Qing armies had now extended the empire's reach into the Turkic Muslim areas beyond the Great
Wall. For the first time in one thousand years, armies from northeast and
North China had conquered one of the major oasis cities of Turkestan.
Outside Turfan, the abandoned Han and Tang garrison cities of Gaochang
and Jiaohe still stood, as they do today, to remind them of their predecessors' achievements.[60]

Aggressive plans for frontier settlement evolved out of the demands of
supplying the campaigns. Military agrarian colonies *(tuntian)* had been a
time-honored practice since the Han dynasty.[61] Troops who tilled the soil
could make their garrisons self-sufficient while also establishing a permanent presence on the frontier. Plans were made shortly after the capture of
Hami to develop settlements at Suzhou, Barköl, and Hami under military
supervision. Exiled criminals and soldiers were to be the first settlers from
the interior.[62] Top officials received rewards for promoting land clearance.
In 1717 General Furdan reported that he had sown seed and dug canals,
and all the new crops were flourishing. After Qianlong's conquests of Turkestan in the eighteenth century, this program of land clearance and settlement would be developed on a much larger scale.

Qing generals also planned to build walled fortresses in the steppe at
Khobdo, Ulan Gumu, and other places in Khalkha territory. Here, too, exiled criminals were set to work clearing land. Postal relay stations linked
these military settlements to the interior.[63] Permanent settlements in Mongolia had begun with the conversion of the Mongols to Tibetan Buddhism
in the sixteenth century. The first towns grew up around the monastic establishment. These included Hohhot (Ch. Huhehaote), whose major construction began in 1555, and Urga (modern Ulaan Baatar), the headquarters of the leading Buddhist cleric of Mongolia since the early seventeenth
century.[64] Qing military garrisons, containing from two hundred to one

thousand troops, now became the second locus of settlement in pastoral lands. The commanders searched for strategic sites in broad plains near ample supplies of water, grass, and wood. The settlements guarded the routes to the Altai and Outer Mongolia, and they served as base camps for grain and weapon storage. These were large wooden enclosures, containing spaces equivalent to two thousand rooms *(jian)*. Construction workers sent from the interior stayed for at least one year to build them. Gradually these camps evolved from military and penal colonies into sites of civilian settlement.

In Kokonor as well, Qing troops began to construct walled fortresses near Mongol pastoralists. After selecting a site to clear land, they left the remaining pastures for the Mongol tribes. They "drew a sharp border that may not be crossed" to separate the settlers from the indigenous pastoralists.[65] The Kokonor Mongols, loyal to the Qing emperor, did not begrudge small amounts of land to the new settlers, but an inexorable process of penetration had begun.

The construction of Qing fortresses in the steppe mirrored the earlier Russian advance into Siberia, but the process of penetration differed greatly. In both cases, garrisons built small fortified units dispersed across alien territories, and military occupation paved the way for larger waves of civilian agrarian and mercantile settlement. The Russians, however, had spread first across the forest zone, avoiding the grasslands and desert, and did not encounter substantial resistance until they ran into Manchu territory. They extracted fur tribute from the tribal peoples without much armed conflict. The Qing, by contrast, first had to confront the Mongols in the grasslands with large military forces before they could secure the region with a network of forts and settlers. When they began to settle, the surrounding populations seemed to be both subdued and loyal. But the subsequent history of rebellion and conflict indicates that Qing penetration of the pasturelands was still fragile.

The influence of the Qing rulers in Tibet now depended on their protégé, Lazang Khan, who had installed his own Dalai Lama in Lhasa. The Qing also kept in reserve the new Khubilghan in Xining but held back from imposing a solution to the divided spiritual authority, awaiting Tsewang Rabdan's actions. In 1716, having repelled Tsewang Rabdan from Hami, the Qing rulers began shifting troops to Xining.[66] Although Tsewang Rabdan was soon expected to enter Tibet, it remained unclear whether he would act as Lazang Khan's ally or his enemy. Lazang's son had married Tsewang Rabdan's daughter, and Tsewang Rabdan promised to support Lazang militarily in exchange for gold to help him defend the Zunghar state against the Russians and Kazakhs.[67] But Lazang Khan had also accepted titles and

support from the Qing. Would he join with Tsewang Rabdan to attack
Kokonor or defend it on behalf of the Qing? Kangxi warned Lazang Khan
about Tsewang Rabdan's treachery, but in either case Qing troops were
much too far from Lhasa to offer support. Many ministers advised a wait-
and-see attitude.

In the summer of 1717, Tsewang Rabdan sent his best general, Tsering
Dondub, with ten thousand men against Lazang Khan. Tsering Dondub led
his troops into Lhasa on an extremely difficult march over "the highest
route in the world" through "absolutely barren regions," forcing Lazang
Khan to barricade himself in the Potala Palace.[68] The Jesuit Ippolito
Desideri, who was in Lhasa at the time of the invasion, described Tsering
Dondub as "passionate, expert, and proud, daring, intrepid and warlike,"
even going so far as to compare him to Alexander the Great.[69] Shi Yide
noted that Tsewang Rabdan's general had led three thousand men from
Yarkand and Kashgar into Tibet, crossing "three great snowy mountains
... marching 10,000 *li* for a year. The men ate dogs' flesh, and they had no
support troops or provisions. With only one horse each they marched into
west Tibet and attacked Lazang Khan." The Zunghar army's feat intimi-
dated Shi Yide, who reported the dedication of the soldiers with "won-
derment" (Ma. *ferguweme giyangname*). The emperor refused to back
down. The ultimate goal of exterminating Tsewang Rabdan justified any
expense.[70]

Yet the nearly 100,000 Qing troops in Sichuan and Xining did not move.
They expected that Tsering Dondub's men, exhausted by the heavy snows,
would have little strength when they arrived in Lhasa, even though they
could inflict a good deal of damage on the way.[71] Only Lazang Khan's desperate appeals for imperial support instigated Qing mobilization. Lazang
claimed that if he lost Lhasa, the entire Yellow Teaching would be eliminated. Kangxi ordered the Manchu general Erentei (Ch. Elunte) to march
on Lhasa with seven thousand men, mainly Chinese and Muslims, via the
northern route from Xining through the desert, and Namujar would march
with ten thousand Tangut troops by the longer but more secure route
via Dajianlu in western Sichuan. But before they set out, word arrived of
dreadful looting and massacres perpetrated by the Zunghar army. On November 30, 1717, Tsering Dondub had ordered the city to be sacked and
the monasteries stripped of their treasures. Tsering Dondub, formerly a
monk from the rival Shigatze monastery, could now take revenge on the
privileged lamas of Lhasa, backed by a ferocious army. Three days later, he
attacked the Potala, killed Lazang Khan, and seized the Dalai Lama and
Panchen Lama.

The northern relief army advanced to Kela Usu, on the banks of the

Salween River over 1,000 kilometers from Xining. There the Zunghars surrounded them, killed Erentei, and besieged them with their food supplies running out. They destroyed the entire force in September 1718. Funingga himself received no reports about this crushing defeat; he had to ask, in vain, an envoy from Tsewang Rabdan to provide him with information.[72] Kangxi then designated his fourteenth son, Yinti, the Fuyuan Dajiangjun, to lead three armies into Tibet from the northwest.[73] With this appointment, the aging emperor hinted that Yinti could be the new heir if he distinguished himself in battle.

As Yinti assembled his massive army of 300,000 troops in Xining, Sichuan Governor Nian Gengyao, well aware of the difficult terrain, argued that Tsering Dondub might in fact surrender to the Qing. According to Qing intelligence, Tsering Dondub was not on good terms with his co-general, and he feared retaliation by the jealous Tsewang Rabdan. Nian's proposal to begin secret negotiations with Tsering Dondub was, however, rejected.[74] The new living Buddha, or his agents, also were concerned about the disruption Qing troops would create in his country, even though he relied on the army to escort him back to Lhasa. The Mongol princes of Kokonor still feared Tsewang Rabdan's retaliation and were concerned about even further dependence on the Qing. The majority of the top ministers, Manchus and Han alike, argued for merely guarding the Sichuan and Kokonor borders. But the emperor brushed off all such concerns. Disturbances in Tibet would clearly affect the border peoples in Sichuan, who were "of the same kind" (yilei). He insisted on a comprehensive campaign that would simultaneously strike at Tsewang Rabdan in Turkestan and at his generals in Tibet. The Khubilghan, under the new title "Sixth Dalai Lama, Diffuser of the Teaching, Awakener of Sentient Beings," would be escorted by the army and placed on the throne in Lhasa, with the support of the Kokonor princes. Once again, as at Ulan Butong, timidity and indecisiveness threatened to undermine his bold strokes. In his view, in times of crisis, only autocratic decision making (duduan) could achieve success.[75]

Yanxin, the emperor's nephew, and Galbi (Ch. Garbi) led the army out of Xining in February 1720, while Yinti stayed in Xining to rally Khoshot support and guard the Dalai Lama. The Dalai Lama followed in May. On September 24, 1720, the army took Lhasa, as the Zunghars had already fled. Five chief lamas who supported the Zunghar intervention were executed, and the Dalai Lama was placed on his seat in the Potala. Tibetans surrounded the soldiers, playing music and prostrating themselves, declaring, "Since the Zunghars plundered and raped us we thought we would never see the sun shine again."[76] Eventually the classic lama–patron relationship between Tibetan clergy and Central Eurasian rulers would be transformed, for the Qing had become "the dominant military power in the region."[77]

But Qing troops could not stay long. Nian Gengyao led the victory march home, by the shortest possible route, as supplies were nearly gone and the horses exhausted. The close association of Nian Gengyao and Yinti established during this Tibetan campaign would play an important role in the shadowy politics of succession after the Kangxi emperor's death and earn them both undying suspicion from the Yongzheng emperor. Yinti was recalled to the capital upon Yongzheng's accession and put under house arrest, from which he was not released until the death of Yongzheng in 1735.[78]

The official sources give a picture of a uniform, cooperative alliance of the Khoshot Mongols and the Qing army, who entered Tibet with overwhelming force, driving out the destructive, barbarian Zunghars, to the delight of the Tibetan people, who welcomed their liberation by external intervention. Other sources, such as Yinti's suppressed memorials, give a different picture. First, they show that the Khoshot Mongols, who had had good relations with the Zunghars in the past, joined the expedition only reluctantly. For several years the Khoshots failed to follow Qing orders to cooperate with the army. Nian Gengyao reported divisions among the Khoshots, which were denounced by the Kangxi emperor. When, on July 1, 1719, the emperor asked the Khoshots for ten thousand men, Lobzang Danjin, though eager to support the Qing, was ashamed to confess that his brothers would not send troops.[79]

Yinti's memorials also reveal the active role of Tibetan guerrilla warriors mobilized by Sonam Gyapo, chief of Khangchen, known as Kancennas (Ch. Kangjinai). Kancennas aroused bands of thousands of fighters, who ambushed Zunghar patrols and succeeded in blocking the routes of retreat to Zungharia. At a banquet Kancennas killed sixty-five Zunghar envoys, and was praised for this by the emperor.

Again, contrary to the impression given by the *Fanglue*, the Zunghar army had already begun its retreat from Lhasa before the Qing army arrived. Kancennas's activities help to explain why. The troops had already suffered damaging guerrilla attacks, indicating the hostility of the local population. Many suffered as well from disease (possibly altitude sickness). Once they heard that a Qing–Khoshot army of anywhere from 100,000 to 1 million men was coming, bringing the Dalai Lama from Kokonor, and that the road home was blocked, the troops found themselves in a desperate situation. "A Zunghar soldier was drinking wine and crying in the house of the Tibetan Danjin. Danjin asked him, 'Are you crying because you are homesick?' and he replied: 'You should be able to understand my misery. Now Kancennas at Gari [and others] with three thousand troops have blocked our way home. We cannot retreat. Furthermore, the great general, Kangxi's son, has brought several hundred thousand troops, and the Qinghai troops are bringing the Dalai Lama back to his throne. How can our few troops defend against such a force?'"[80] Only one-quarter of the Zunghar army ever returned home.

Thus the success of the Qing Tibetan campaigns was the outcome of complex motives of multiple actors, including the divided Tibetans, the quarrelsome Khoshots, the desperate Zunghars, and the disciplined Manchu, Mongol, and Han troops led by the emperor's son.

The stele set up in Lhasa the next year to commemorate the conquest told a simpler story. It described the history of events in Lhasa since the death of the fifth Dalai Lama, including the usurpation of power by the regent and his failure to report the Dalai Lama's death to the Qing for sixteen years. Lazang Khan, with the support of the Khoshots, then eliminated the regent, "revived the Teaching [of Buddha; *xingfa*]." Tsewang Rabdan merely plundered and destroyed temples and massacred lamas. Although Tsewang Rabdan also claimed to "revive the Teaching," he actually destroyed it. (All of the rival contenders for power over Tibet justified their military activities as designed to "revive the Teachings" of Buddha.) The emperor then sent thousands of Manchu, Mongol, and Han troops, who braved malarial jungles to reach Tibet, where they killed the enemy, "pacified" [*pingding*] Tibet, and (truly) revived the Teaching *(zhenxing fajiao)*. According to the inscription, these unprecedented *(conggu wei you)* achievements exceeded those of all previous generations, and all Mongols and Tibetans praised the boldness of the emperor and his divine might *(shenwu)*.[81]

Tsewang Rabdan himself, in letters written to the Qing emperor, claimed to share many of the same ideals. He too favored peace in Tibet, and he had intervened in order to prevent heretical and immoral activities by the monks who were rivals to the Yellow Sect and to stop the oppressive actions of Lazang Khan. He had "destroyed the Red Sect, which deviated from the Way," and seized Lazang Khan's wife and children.[82] Tsewang Rabdan offered to cooperate with the Qing emperor, just as he had done when Galdan was alive, if the emperor would refrain from active intervention in Mongolia or Tibet. But now the emperor had grander designs.

The stele concisely summarized the essential elements of the imperial message to the newly conquered regions, stressing that it was Qing power that had restored the Buddhist order revered by Tibetans, testifying to the emperor's divinely inspired mission. Kangxi had taken a step beyond his predecessors, embracing the Tibetan religious hierarchy in addition to the Mongols, Manchus, and Han. Prince Yinti's skill in coordinating the diverse members of the alliance got little credit; now it was solely the emperor's own boldness that deserved recognition. Each imperial victory quickly subsumed the conflicts and contingencies of conquest under the all-encompassing gaze of the universal sovereign.

The success in Tibet inspired even more ambitious plans. Funingga proposed to advance immediately with seventeen thousand men from Barköl on a three-month campaign to eliminate the Zungharian base permanently, at a cost of over 350,000 taels. Yinti and the top generals Furdan and Funingga gathered in the capital to plan the great extermination of the Zunghar state. Yinti enthusiastically supported an immediate invasion. At first the emperor gave his approval, but then he postponed the assault for a year, concluding that it would be impossible to capture Tsewang Rabdan in far-off Ili.[83] Rumors arrived of Tsewang Rabdan's death, or of serious dissension in Zungharia. A captured Zunghar soldier reported under interrogation that Tsewang Rabdan had imprisoned his son-in-law Galdan Danjin. The Zunghars had suffered losses from attacks by the Burut and Kazakhs to their west, and many of their cattle had died of disease. They were saying, "Surely the Chinese have put a curse on them." He confessed that his people "great and small, sadly said to one another: 'Certainly the Han have sent envoys to the Russians, Kazakhs, and Burut, and now they will make an alliance to attack us simultaneously. If they do this, how can we survive? What will happen to our pastures?'"[84]

The emperor decided to send the Jebzongdanba Khutukhtu, the leading Buddhist cleric of Mongolia, to Tsewang Rabdan to invite him to submit to the Qing. He would have to yield up Lazang Khan, whom he was sheltering, and promise never to disturb the Qing borders again. If Tsewang Rabdan rejected negotiations, the military campaign would be launched.

This time the generals were confident that they could defeat the enemy because the Zunghars had limited supplies of gunpowder and cannon and lacked discipline. Qing generals were gaining increasing confidence in the decisive power of gunpowder weaponry. They also felt that they could overcome the nomadic military advantage by sending several cavalry divisions in a pincer attack.[85] Yet they had serious concerns about providing supplies for the army based in Barköl. The grain harvests in this oasis region, centered in Turfan, were seriously limited. Building up military settlements in Turkestan became a more important focus the longer the army remained there. The troops and support staff at Barköl and Turfan, numbering over 33,000, needed 6,690 *shi* of grain monthly, and the 25,000 troops in the Altai needed 5,000 *shi* monthly, for a total of 140,280 *shi* per year. Barköl had produced a harvest of only 20,000 *shi,* and Turfan was even less successful.[86] The tight supply situation meant that the troops must either advance quickly or else put their efforts into substantial restocking of provisions before a campaign. So no definite decision had been made to advance as Yinti headed back to the frontier.

On December 21, 1722, Yinti was suddenly called back to the capital with the news that his father had died and his brother Yinzhen had assumed the throne as the Yongzheng emperor (r. 1723–1735). The absence of Yinti from the capital during the crucial last days of Kangxi's life allowed Yinzhen, with the support of the General Commandant of Gendarmerie of Beijing, Lungkodo, to engineer his own succession. Lungkodo produced a testament, claimed to be in Kangxi's hand, declaring Yinzhen the heir to the throne, but historians have debated the legitimacy of his succession ever since.[87]

The Kangxi emperor had twice deposed his second son, Yinreng, who had committed many improper acts, but he had never been able to designate an heir. As many of his sons formed factions to plot for the succession, frontier campaigns played a vital role in determining whom the aging emperor would favor, for Kangxi regarded military merit as a key element of fitness to rule. Yinreng himself, even after his second deposition in 1712, tried to get himself appointed Generalissimo of the armies on the northwest frontier in order to restore himself to favor.[88] Yinshi, the eldest son, who had accompanied his father on three campaigns, gained great favor until he was accused of engaging a sorceress to place a curse on Yinreng. Yinsi, the emperor's eighth son, also rose in stature because he had accompanied his father on the Galdan campaign of 1696. When Yinsi was stripped of his rank for engaging in intrigue, Yinti, as commander in chief of the armies of the northwest campaigns, "was regarded by many as the Emperor's real choice for the throne."[89]

Yinti's brother Yinzhen, however, had never led an army to battle but only drilled troops in Beijing. The emperor also regarded ritual deportment as another skill of a successful ruler, and Yinzhen had demonstrated his abilities best in conducting imperial rituals on Kangxi's behalf. He participated in twenty-two rituals, more than any other son, and also joined actively in policy debates in the capital. Feng Erkang argues that Yinzhen was not a low-ranking usurper but just as plausible a candidate as Yinti.[90] Yinzhen, in fact, was a prince of the first rank (*qinwang*), while Yinti was at first only a *beizi*, and later a prince of the second degree (*junwang*). Xu Zengzhong, however, stresses that since military merit had always been the primary qualification for rule since the Manchu conquest, Yinti's successes in his campaigns clearly made him the favorite choice as the next emperor. In the final political battle for the succession, an active military man who was often away on campaign lost to a civilian ritual and policy expert who had never left the capital.[91]

Some have suggested that Yinti was deliberately sent away from the capital as part of the succession plot. Others argue that the emperor recalled Yinti to the capital in order to prevent him from achieving success on the frontier that would bolster his claim to the throne. Despite the contradictory rumors of the contending candidates, I believe that Yinti had legitimate tasks to perform on the frontier to help the aging Kangxi emperor plan once again his culminating extermination campaign against the Zunghars. Only by chance was he absent at the emperor's death. Yongzheng later claimed that Yinti was incompetent and had little military experience, and, as noted earlier, tried to suppress evidence of his achievements in the Tibetan campaign. Exactly whom the emperor named as heir in his last days, or if he named anyone, will probably remain, in Huang Pei's words, an "insolvable puzzle," but clearly, frontier expansion changed the succession to the throne and the writing of Qing history at the same time.[92]

The New Emperor Changes Tack

The Yongzheng emperor's succession inaugurated a new phase in Qing expansion, one with mixed and contradictory goals. In Turkestan, Yongzheng continued the gestures his father had begun toward Tsewang Rabdan to encourage him to stabilize the border and send tribute missions to Beijing. As the paramount leader of the Yellow Teaching in Mongolia, the Jebzongdanba Khutukhtu, who died in 1723 at the age of ninety, had been a loyal supporter of the Qing, who led the Khalkha tribes to submit to the Qing when Galdan rebelled. He had also been a valuable link between the Qing and the Western Mongols. After his death the emperor dealt directly with Tsewang Rabdan's envoys, promising them that the Qing had "no intention of destroying your state." All he required was the return of the rebel Lazang Khan; but, they were told, "it depends on you whether we follow the emperor's mercy [ren'en] or military might [wulie]."[93]

Although Yongzheng continued to threaten retribution if his generous offers were refused, he indicated that he was much more interested in cutting back on military adventures. He began a sustained program of troop withdrawals from the distant frontiers. At first he declared that no troops at all were needed in Kokonor; he planned to concentrate them instead in Barköl. The outbreak of Lobzang Danjin's rebellion in 1723 negated this goal, but the program of consolidating troops in fewer posts closer to the interior continued. Several considerations favored this program. The troops were exhausted from staying for long periods of time at their posts; therefore, there should be regular rotations to the interior. Local populations, too, were excessively burdened with supply demands for the garrisons. Underlying this retrenchment was Yongzheng's program of domestic austerity and institutional reform.[94] He pulled troops out of Tibet in April 1723, concentrating them in Xining and western Sichuan. Only after Nian Gengyao protested did he agree to build small guarded fortresses on the roads west of Dajianlu.[95]

Funingga, who had led the most aggressive campaigns against the Zunghars in the last years of Kangxi's reign, was clearly frustrated when the new emperor decided to negotiate for peace. The blunt general, first praised for his outstanding military capabilities, must have offended Yongzheng on his return to the capital, because he was soon sent to a demeaning post in Shaanxi and stripped of his noble ranks, for unclear causes, in 1728.[96]

Meanwhile, in Turkestan, Nian Gengyao began to implement the new defensive strategy, relying on static defenses, reduced forces, and the promotion of military colonies *(tuntian)*. Only 2,000 men remained at Barköl, 1,500 at Turfan, and 2,000 at Hami. At Bulongjir (500 *li* from Jiayuguan) he built a new fortress with 5,000 troops. This large outpost was established as Anxi *zhen* in 1725.[97] In Tibet, likewise, after the suppression of Lobzang Danjin's rebellion, the emperor rejected Nian Gengyao's request for 6,000 additional troops west of Dajianlu. Control in Tibet relied on only a very small garrison in Lhasa and support from the leading Tibetan aristocrats.

The Muslims of Turfan became the objects of a tug-of-war between the two rival states, as Tsewang Rabdan tried to move them north while Yongzheng tried to move them south. Turfan was more of a strategic burden than an asset: its grain supplies were too meager to support both a large garrison and the local population. Barköl, an entirely military town, was more suitable. When Zunghar raids began again in 1731, General Yue Zhongqi demanded troop reinforcements, but the emperor rebuked him for failing to organize his resources and told him to focus his defenses on Gansu. The Turfan question was a troublesome thorn in the side of the emperor, who wanted to pull his military forces back and reduce costs. He preferred moving people in to sending troops out.[98]

New internal conflict quickly drew the emperor, despite his intentions, into condoning a second substantial military intervention in Tibet. In 1720 the Qing invasion force had initially installed a military government in Lhasa, which was welcomed by Tibetans happy to see the brutal Zunghar forces driven out. The great Potala Palace of the Dalai lama, looted by the

Zunghars, was restored and even improved with imperial support. The office of regent was abolished, while the new seventh Dalai Lama, a twelve-year-old boy, served as the figurehead for rule by leading Tibetan nobles. The two most powerful were Sonam Stöbgyal, the chief of Polha in western Tibet, known as Polhanas (Ch. Polonai), and Kancennas.[99] Both had organized popular resistance to the Zunghars.[100] Three Manchu officials, the Asahan Amba, supervised the administration with a garrison of three thousand men. But the local government remained unstable in the hands of regional rulers who could not create a functioning central council.

The Chinese occupation army was a heavy burden for the Tibetans. The price of grain was rising on local markets, even as the Qing was spending a large amount to transport grain thousands of kilometers from the interior. Generals Nian Gengyao and Yanxin had agreed with Kangxi that troops in Lhasa should be reduced as soon as possible.[101] But Yongzheng ordered a rapid and complete withdrawal to support his retrenchment drive, based on maintaining peace with the Zunghars and relieving burdens on the civilian population. Kancennas urged the emperor to reconsider as the troops marched away.

The Khoshot princes had been accustomed since the days of Gusri Khan to exerting substantial influence in Tibet, but the Qing intervention followed by sudden withdrawal left them no role. The Tibetans themselves were to govern Tibet, without a regent or a Khoshot Mongol protector. The old tripartite balance of Mongols as military protectors, the Dalai Lama as spiritual authority, and the regent as temporal administrator had lost two of its props. Instability and confusion resulted. A number of the Khoshots resolved to invite Tsewang Rabdan to intervene in order to restore their influence.[102] They believed that the Qing had betrayed a promise from Kangxi that allowed them to appoint a Khan of Tibet from among themselves.

Prince Lobzang Danjin (T. Blo-bzan-bstan-dsin) was a grandson of Gusri Khan, a powerful Kokonor chief who had supported the Chinese intervention in Lhasa.[103] Chaghan Danjin, another grandson of Gush Khan from a different lineage, was his major rival. Chaghan, backed by Yongzheng, appeared to be expanding his territory at Lobzang's expense. In July 1723 Lobzang attacked three Khoshot princes, also grandsons of Gusri Khan, including Erdeni Erke Toghtonai, who fled in defeat, asking for Qing protec-

The Yongzheng emperor (r. 1723–1735) in court dress.

The Yongzheng emperor in daily life.

tion. Nian Gengyao advised non-intervention, saying, "If the [Kokonor princes] should now forget their great indebtedness to our country and kill their own flesh and blood, it is of no concern to us." He knew well that, as so often in nomadic warfare, an advance by Qing troops "would only waste the strength of our own forces while the Mongols fled far off into the distance on their well-fed horses."[104] But the new emperor overruled Nian

Gengyao, ordering him to protect Erdeni Erke if he fled to Qing lands. Qing support of refugees from a rising Mongolian power paralleled the course that had drawn Kangxi into internecine disputes among the Khalkhas and Zunghars. Lobzang Danjin would be offered the opportunity to repent and submit to the Qing, but if he refused, a righteous army of extermination (zhengjiao) would be sent against him. Lobzang, as expected, rejected Qing offers to mediate a peace agreement. Changshou, the Qing envoy, reported that Lobzang intended to defeat Chaghan Danjin and assemble all the princes of Kokonor to proclaim him Khan. Rumors spread that the Zunghars would soon enter Kokonor.[105]

Nian and the emperor then agreed on a secret plan to "secure" (ding) Kokonor.[106] What they feared most was a potential alliance of the discontented princes against Qing rule and a positive response to their appeals to Tsewang Rabdan. They granted Chaghan Danjin the title of qinwang, equivalent to Lobzang's rank, so as to encourage him to split from Lobzang. As expected, the Qing shift of support induced Lobzang to attack Chaghan Danjin on September 16, 1723. Lobzang assumed to himself the title of Dalai Hongtaiji, aiming to unite all the Khoshot Mongols as they had been under Gusri Khan. This provided the pretext for Qing military intervention. Nian was again cautious, believing that Chaghan Danjin could hold out against Lobzang, but the emperor ordered him to advance immediately. On November 16, 1723, the Qing army battled with Lobzang outside the Taersi, or Kumbum monastery (20 kilometers from modern Xining), driving him back. Lobzang besieged the Xingcheng fortress on November 27 and attacked the garrisons in Ganzhou and Liangzhou along the Gansu corridor, but he lost quickly, and in less than a month the war was over.

Zunghar support for Lobzang never arrived because Tsewang Rabdan was busy holding off the Russians and Kazakhs. He had had no intention of supporting the princes in Kokonor, but he did shelter Lobzang Khan when he fled there for refuge.

Before the conquest, the emperor urged the troops not to mistreat the local population. They should not rape women, violate graves, loot the property of those who surrendered, or destroy houses, temples, and monasteries.[107] After the conquest, however, the Qing troops took revenge on the lamas and villagers who had supported the princes' resistance. Their ultimate goal was to destroy Lobzang Danjin and all his followers. They killed hundreds of noncombatants, burned down 150 villages, and launched a terrifying assault on the Gonlun monastery (Ch. Kuolongsi), headquarters of the lCang-skya Khutukhtu (Ch. Zhangjia Hutukhtu), an ally of Lobzang, killing its six thousand monks and burning it to the ground.[108]

The Kumbum monastery in Kokonor. Photo taken by Frederick Wulsin, 1923.

Rituals in the capital celebrated this campaign as equivalent to the repression of the Three Feudatories and the destruction of Galdan.[109] Officials formally reported the victory to eleven temples around the city, including the temples of Heaven and Earth, the altars of Grain and the Imperial Lineage, and the tombs of the imperial ancestors. A stele inscribed in the Imperial Academy depicted Lobzang Danjin as an evil rebel with a "wolf's heart and owl's nature," and praised Nian Gengyao for killing his "crazed" followers and obtaining the surrender of hundreds of thousands of others in such a short time.[110] Even though this campaign was much shorter and easier than the Galdan campaigns or the repression of the Three Feudatories revolt, Yongzheng could rightly claim to have brought another vast territory under permanent Qing control. No longer could the princes of Kokonor act with real autonomy from the Qing.

After the repression, officials imposed strictly the banner and *jasak* administration on Kokonor that had been enacted in Mongolia. Nian Gengyao oversaw detailed plans for incorporation and reconstruction of the territory. The princes *(taiji)* now became *jasaks*, or banner commanders, under the supervision of Qing military personnel. They were allowed three tribute missions per year. Khalkha Mongols in Kokonor were organized into separate banners, which freed them from subordination to the Khoshots and provided the Qing with a balance against Khoshot independence. As Nian recommended, the entire territory now became part of the "interior" *(neidi)*. Local Tibetans (Fan) would be governed by *tusi* (tribal headmen) watched over by Qing garrisons. Their ties to the Dalai Lama would be cut. He could no longer collect taxes from Tibetans in Kokonor; instead, he would be granted 5,000 *jin* of tea annually as compensation. The temples, which Nian described as "filthy hovels," had been autonomous governing entities, collecting tribute from their followers and used for weapon and food storage as well as religious activities. Now they would be limited in size to two hundred rooms *(jian)*, with a maximum of three hundred lamas, and inspected twice a year.[111]

The causes of the war with Lobzang Danjin have been much debated, but the simple assumption of the emperor and his generals that it was a "rebellion" against Qing rule is problematic. The term "rebellion" *(panluan)*, used by both Qing and modern Chinese historians, implies a previously "loyal" population who then rejected imperial grace and directly challenged the emperor's authority.[112] Until 1723, however, the Khoshot Mongols had been quite autonomous of Qing authority, although they had engaged in temporary alliances with the empire. Many of them had joined in the expedition to Lhasa, though some with great reluctance. Katō Naoto argues that there were pro-Qing and anti-Qing factions among the Kokonor princes, and that Lobzang Danjin's attack on Chaghan Khan represented a struggle between these two factions; but Ishihama Yumiko argues more convincingly that there were no clear lines between the feuding princes, and at one point there was a serious potential for an alliance of the princes against the Qing, with Zunghar support.[113] The Yongzheng emperor, seeing the division among the princes, took advantage of their weakness to launch a military campaign with the intention of bringing all of Kokonor under Qing control. The suppression of Lobzang's power eliminated permanently the autonomy of the Kokonor princes and excluded them from any influence over Tibet. The Qing acted primarily out of fear that these princes and their followers could forge an alliance with the Zunghars or move to Zunghar territory. Lobzang himself never intended to draw in a major Qing army, and his rival, Chaghan Danjin, who had supported the Zunghar invasion of Tibet, was also no friend of the Qing. But because of their internal strife, the Yongzheng emperor could seize the opportunity to gain a quick victory relatively close to the Qing military base at Xining.

Yongzheng in this case pushed his aggressive policy against the resistance of the cautious generals Nian Gengyao and Yue Zhongqi. Once entrusted with the campaign, however, Nian and Yue acted with great decisiveness, brutality, and success. The emperor at first praised Nian highly in his rescripts. Any expansive military policy would have to depend heavily on this vigorous Chinese-martial general. But Nian fell out of favor very quickly. In 1726 he was condemned to execution for ninety-two crimes of maladministration, corruption, and treasonous intrigue, and was allowed to commit suicide. Yue Zhongqi helped provide evidence of his "crimes." Nian's rapid downfall was closely connected to his intimate knowledge of the shadowy circumstances of Yongzheng's succession; his great military success made him both indispensable and dangerous. Without Nian, the emperor would find himself unable to expand further, and he would overreach his grasp, suffering an embarrassing defeat.[114]

Control of Kokonor still remained precarious. Disturbances in Tibet in 1727 threatened to spread to the Kokonor Mongols, but no open resistance broke out. Lobzang, however, remained alive in Ili and could still exert an attractive power from there. As Galdan Tseren, Tsewang Rabdan's successor, continued to refuse to send him back, the court feared that some of the Kokonor Mongols would abandon their responsibilities to the Qing and try to move to Zungharia. The Kokonor banners now owed horses to the Qing armies; these were supposed to be purchased at market prices, but local officials could exact extra burdens. When the Khoshot Prince Rajab (Ch. Lachabu) attempted to move away from his pastures to avoid the burdensome horse levies, he was commanded to return, while the emperor ordered an investigation by local officials. In 1731 Prince Norbu, who had been sent to guard against Zunghar invasions of Kokonor, rebelled against the burdens of serving the Qing, but after ten days of plundering, he fled west and was soon captured.[115] Most of the Kokonor princes actively supported the Qing in putting down the rebellion. Still, the concerns about the loyalty of the Kokonor princes led the emperor to deliver them a long edict, reminding them that they were descendants of Gusri Khan, who had received many favors from the Qing, and that the Qing had supported the Yellow Teaching, while the Zunghars were violators of the faith and came only to stir up trouble. He told them that if they tried to flee to join Lobzang, "it is too far, and your herds will die; how can you support yourselves? . . . Also the Zunghars are surrounded by enemies and are always fighting. In every battle they will put you on the front lines. Isn't it better for you to stay in your ancestors' pastures and enjoy eternal peace?"[116] Even though the Khoshot princes had originally moved to Kokonor from Zungharia, the emperor encouraged them to regard Kokonor as their ancestral home. He offered them peace and stability under Qing rule, provided they gave up the freedom to move.

The program of troop withdrawals resumed after the end of the rebellion. Contributions for degrees, allowed as a temporary measure to raise funds for the campaign, were now eliminated.[117] Tibet soon became an arena of conflict again, however, because of increasing divisions among the Tibetan nobles.[118] The capable Kancennas, the anti-Zunghar governor on whom the Qing relied, had aroused increasing hostility among other ministers, which culminated in his murder on August 5, 1727.[119] The Manchu brigadier general Oci requested immediate reinforcements to put down resistance. Meanwhile, Polhanas quickly mobilized his troops to wipe out his rival Napodpa (Ch. Arbuba). Jalangga, President of the Censorate, and Governor-General Mailu organized fifteen thousand troops from Shaanxi, Sichuan, and Yunnan to enter Tibet, leaving Xining on June 13, 1728. On July 3 Polhanas seized Lhasa before the Qing troops arrived and arrested Napodpa and the leaders of the opposing forces.[120] He had kept the Qing emperor informed of his activities, quickly winning support for his side in the civil war. The Qing armies marched quickly through Kokonor, taking care of logistical demands by having the soldiers carry two months' grain with them, plus 4 taels each to purchase more.[121] When Jalangga arrived in Lhasa in September 1728, he and Polhanas put Napodpa and the others on trial for the murder of Kancennas. Tibetan sources report that the rebel ministers defended themselves by accusing Kancennas of contacts with the Zunghars.[122] But the Manchu judges, unimpressed, decided in favor of Polhanas and condemned the ministers to death by slicing. Polhanas was appointed governor of both eastern and western Tibet and richly rewarded by the emperor. Jalangga, when he withdrew his forces, removed the ineffective Dalai Lama from Lhasa. He left two high Manchu officials (amban) in Lhasa with a garrison of only two thousand men, as the emperor realized that a large force would severely burden the supplies of the poor Tibetans.

Both of the contesting sides in Tibet tried to link the civil war to the Zunghars. The Qing official account, reflected in Wei Yuan's *Shengwuji*, accuses the Zunghars of colluding with the Tibetan rebels.[123] But as Luciano Petech concludes, confirmed by contemporary documents in the *Fanglue*, the revolt was an internal Tibetan affair, not a rejection of the Qing protectorate; charges of Zunghar involvement came after the fact to justify Qing intervention. Only in 1729, when the Yongzheng emperor launched a more aggressive anti-Zunghar policy, did he try to suggest any Zunghar involvement in the Tibetan war. After his second successful military intervention, Yongzheng congratulated himself on "finding a policy to settle Tibetan affairs once and for all" *(yongyuan zhi dao)*.[124] When it came to Mongolia, however, he would not be so lucky.

When Tsewang Rabdan died in 1727, his son Galdan Tseren took power.

Relatively peaceful relations with the Qing lasted for only a year, as both sides tried to feel their way to a new relationship. The Qing secured the border with Russia with the Kiakhta treaty of 1727, finally resolving the disputed questions addressed in the Nerchinsk treaty of 1689. The Russians, induced by trading concessions, could be relied on not to support the Zunghars, and they would exert control over the mobile peoples of Siberia and Manchuria, fixing them in place. The negotiations determined the border between Siberia and the Khalkha Mongols, who were now under Qing control, over a distance of 2,600 miles. No refugees or criminals would be sheltered by either side, and boundary stones would mark the frontier. Sava Vladislavich, the Russian envoy, called the border an "everlasting demarcation line between the two empires."[125]

Galdan Tseren, likewise, was offered regular tribute trading missions if he would agree to determine borders with the Qing. A Zunghar embassy visited the capital in 1728. But two strict conditions limited the prospects for peace: Qing determination to cut off the Zunghars from any formal relations with Tibet, and the surrender of Lobzang Danjin to Qing custody. When Galdan Tseren requested permission to send men to conduct ceremonial tea offerings for the monks in Lhasa, called *man-ja* (Ch. *jiancha* or *aocha)*, in order to aid the propagation of the Buddhist faith, the emperor contemptuously refused: "The Zunghars are a small tribe in the northwestern corner; what relations can there be between the propagation of Buddhism and your offering of a *man-ja?*"[126] These ceremonial missions, with their accompanying trade caravans and lamas, were an important spiritual and commercial link to Tibet for all the Mongols. Earlier, during Tsewang Rabdan's reign, the Qing stripped the rank from a Mongolian *jasak* who had allowed Tsewang Rabdan's envoys to cross his territory on a tea mission to Tibet.[127] Qing policy now aimed at stabilizing but also isolating the Zunghar state from both its closest cultural neighbors, Mongolians and Tibetans, and from potential aid from Russia. The surrender of Lobzang Danjin would complete this process by removing all concerns about divided loyalties of the Kokonor Mongols. For this reason, Galdan Tseren could not cut his fragile links to Kokonor and Tibet.

In 1729 the emperor abandoned his peace policy and called for an aggressive campaign to exterminate the Zunghar state. He engaged in a lengthy justification of his decision, reviewing all the outrages committed by the Zunghars since the days of Galdan. All the other Mongols had now submitted to the Qing; only the Zunghars stubbornly refused to surrender. According to Yongzheng, after his victories over Galdan, the Kangxi emperor should have proceeded to eliminate the Zunghars, but he feared criticism for "exhausting the army with excessive campaigns" *(qiongbing duwu)*, and so he did not. Later, Kangxi vowed to exterminate Tsewang Rabdan, after first offering him a pardon. Yongzheng had also offered to pardon Tsewang Rabdan, but the latter's raids on Hami and intervention in Tibet indicated his hostile intent. Galdan Tseren now said he wanted peace with the Qing, but the emperor accused him of following his father's path and introduced the new charge of colluding with rebels in Tibet. Even though sagely emperors tried to avoid *qiongbing duwu*, using troops only as a last resort, Yongzheng vowed to finish the task begun by Kangxi. There would be no military glory to be gained by wiping out these remote tribes, but if they were allowed to survive, they would seriously endanger the nation *(guojia)*.[128]

Yongzheng cited many of the same causes as Kangxi to justify his campaign, but he struck a more defensive tone, one of exasperation rather than confidence. From the imperial point of view, merciful acts intended to arouse gratitude and promote prosperity among these obstreperous Mongols had been repaid only with violence. A repeated pattern of Zunghar broken promises justified reluctant endorsement of extreme acts of violence. The Qing, by contrast with the Ming, viewed the Mongols as human actors who could take responsibility for their decisions. Ming rulers could see them only as equivalent to beasts, constantly driven by greed and violence, over which the empire could exert no control. Paradoxically, alienation from the Mongols and belief in their inhumanity had led the Ming to practice a more defensive policy. The rulers made no grand efforts to eradicate these nomads: since they were more like a natural force than a human society, it would be as futile as trying to eliminate wolves or floods. By contrast, the Qing goal of universal peace among humans led the Qing to endorse elimination of those humans who obstinately refused to knuckle under to the imperial view. Humans who chose to resist the Qing terms remained human, but they had to pay the costs of their choice: "righteous extermination" *(zhengjiao)*, designed to return the world to a rational order.[129]

Concepts of universal peace and benevolence, however, fit awkwardly with endorsement of violent repression. These tensions are more prominent in Yongzheng than in Kangxi. His repeated references to the classical phrase *qiongbing duwu* indicate that he knew that the proper role of a wise ruler, in Confucian terms, was to exert moral suasion, not material force. Kangxi, by contrast, was closer to a Central Eurasian tradition that valued individual valor on the battlefield along with efficient administration and moral authority. The three values were more coherently united during his reign, as the expansion of his rule brought with it increasing peace and active support of the Manchu regime. Yongzheng faced greater tensions in an

empire now straining at the limit of its administrative and logistical resources. His most common response was retrenchment, careful husbanding
of resources, and lengthy, cautious preparation. His primary goal had been
withdrawal and consolidation of troops, sparing burdens on the treasury
and on the local people. The intervention in Kokonor against Lobzang
Danjin was exceptional, brief, and apparently successful. But the persistence of the Zunghar state ate away at the imperial sense of unity like an
open sore. As long as one group recognizably part of the traditional Central
Eurasian world of Mongols, Tibetans, Muslims, and Manchus insisted on
rejecting the universal sovereign, he could not be content. Yongzheng's attitudes toward the Zunghars exhibit glaring contradictions between expressing contempt for them as a "small, remote tribe in the northwest corner"
and viewing them as a major threat to the security of the entire national
community. The new aggression of 1729 was not based on strategic logic.
The emperor's overweening ambition was generated by the burgeoning
ideology of the empire, which had to enforce universal peace over all its
component parts. The Qing, of course, was not the only empire that has elevated minor powers into major security threats.[130] Yet Yongzheng vacillated over launching a new campaign, since he lacked a legitimate cause,
except for the demand for the return of Lobzang Danjin.[131]

In April 1729 Furdan was made Generalissimo for Suppressing Rebels
(Jingni Dajiangjun), in charge of the North Route Army, while Yue
Zhongqi, with 324 officers and 26,500 troops, was appointed Generalis-
simo for Pacifying the Distant Frontier (Ningyuan Dajiangjun) of the West
Route Army. Both would set out in June and July, converging on Galdan
Tseren's base in Ili.[132] A great review of the troops was held in Beijing in
June 1729. Suddenly, the emperor and his brother both fell ill with influ-
enza, and his brother passed away on June 18, 1730. With the death of
his brother, Yongzheng lost a key adviser.[133] Then an envoy arrived from
Galdan Tseren, promising to hand over Lobzang Danjin.[134] Seizing this opportunity to negotiate peace, the emperor recalled the generals to the capital and delayed the army's advance for a year. Furdan and Yue Zhongqi returned to the capital in January 1731.

Just as they arrived, Zunghar detachments began raiding frontier posts in
Kokonor and Barköl, taking away large numbers of horses. Driven off
from Turfan, they besieged the strategic pass of Gas in Kokonor. Yongzheng took no aggressive action, even though Yue Zhongqi insisted on
strengthening the frontier garrisons with at least five thousand more
troops. The emperor insisted on keeping major forces in the Gansu corridor
and at Xining, and not sending large forces out beyond the pass. He regretfully turned down Yue's sixteen proposals for bolstering the frontier garrisons, admitting that he respected Yue's passion to wipe out the enemy

who had stolen so many horses, but confessing that "now is not the right time." He found Yue's efforts to support Turfan, however, to be "nonsense" and "every proposal ill considered."[135] Luckily, the garrison at Turfan succeeded in driving off the Zunghars and recovering the stolen horses, while the Mongolian *jasaks* successfully defended Kokonor. Here was a complete contrast to Kangxi's relationship with his commanders: now it was the cautious emperor who held back an aggressive frontier general. Yongzheng said, "I really cannot make up my mind . . . [A]t this moment according to Heaven's will and the general state of the situation we can do nothing but wait quietly."[136]

The approach of spring renewed the confidence of the emperor and his generals. By March 1731 all the ice had melted on the rivers and roads, making transportation more convenient. Hearing reports of Galdan Tseren moving to attack Halashar, a small Muslim settlement 200 kilometers southwest of Turfan, Yue Zhongqi again asked for authority to launch an attack, but the emperor told him to stay put and prepare his defenses in Barköl.[137]

At the same time, he grew very sensitive to criticism that army provisioning policies were driving up local market prices in Shaanxi. Revealing his paranoid fantasies, he blamed these complaints on his old enemies, Yinti, Nian Gengyao, and Yanxin, who had "spread underground rumors to incite people." Announcing openly that "in the future, our demands for military supplies will be greater, and prices will inevitably rise," he denounced the "ignorant people with selfish goals" who failed to understand the larger benefits that the campaign would bring. Once again, Yongzheng's elaborate self-justification and fear of criticism contrasted notably with Kangxi's ferocious repression of dissent. He did not cashier any dissenters, but sent officials to Shaanxi to "persuade" the people *(huadao)* into accepting the burden of supplying the army, while at the same time warning that he would punish any extortion by local officials from the people.[138]

Faced with continuing harassment from Zunghar raids at Turfan, the emperor finally agreed to allow Yue to advance against Ürümchi, 170 kilometers northwest of Turfan, where he could build a fortress and wipe out the enemy "nests."[139] Seizing Ürümchi, a much larger oasis, might also resolve the severe supply problems at Turfan, which could not support a large force. The emperor now deferred to Yue's knowledge of the local situation, stating, "I am thousands of *li* away; you must decide on the spot." Unlike Kangxi, he expressed no interest in personally leading an expedition. He also indicated skepticism of Yue's abilities to resolve the difficulties of both attacking Ürümchi and defending Turfan, saying, "I am beginning to lose faith in you."[140]

Meanwhile, Furdan with his northern army had advanced to Khobdo and begun to build a fortress there. This was farther west than any Qing forces had ever penetrated into Mongolia. Galdan Tseren was said to have 10,000 troops guarding his border with the Kazakhs, while two loyal generals, the elder and younger Tsering Dondub (Ch. Celing Dunduobu), had set out with 30,000 men to attack the Qing army. Another general, Lobzang Tsering, had split with Galdan Tseren and led his 3,000 households south, heading for the border with Kokonor. Furdan thought that this division of forces offered the Qing a good opportunity to attack. Ten thousand men in three divisions advanced to meet the Zunghars, leaving 7,300 behind to guard Khobdo. According to reports, the younger Tsering was three days' march away with only a small force. On July 20, 1731, he found 2,000 of the enemy and attacked them with 3,000 troops, forcing them to flee.

Furdan was actually marching into a trap. Small Zunghar forces lured him forward with harassing raids while the main force stayed hidden in the mountains. On July 23 the Zunghars poured out of the mountains and surrounded the Qing army with a full force of 20,000 at Hoton Nor, a small lake 210 kilometers west of Khobdo.[141] After fierce fighting, on July 27 Furdan was able to break the siege and retreat with his men back to Khobdo. The first reports coming to the capital indicated that Furdan had lost his entire army; later it appeared that he had sustained heavy damage. Only 2,000 men made it back to Khobdo.[142] Eighty percent of the Qing army was lost, and nearly all of his Mongolian allies were wiped out.

Furdan, confessing that he had advanced too rashly, desperately pleaded with the emperor to sentence him to execution. The emperor rebuked but pardoned Furdan, praised him for leading a successful retreat, and insisted that he focus his efforts on the defense of Khobdo. Furdan launched into an active construction campaign to fortify the walls at Khobdo, planning for a large fortress, 7 kilometers in circumference with walls nearly 5 meters high, and a garrison of 16,000 troops. This garrison would be 1,500 *li* (870 km) west of the nearest Qing base at Chahan Sor (near Uliyasutai), very difficult to supply, and too far away for immediate support. The Grand Council decided to abandon the fortress and withdraw troops back to the more easily defensible line at Chahan Sor.[143]

Yongzheng could take some small consolation from Yue Zhongqi's successful raid on Ürümchi. When reports of Furdan's encounter with a large Zunghar force first came in, Yue immediately set out for Ürümchi, hoping that this gesture would force the Zunghars to divert their forces there. But Furdan was routed too quickly for this feint to have any effect. Yue Zhongqi could not hold Ürümchi; he soon withdrew to Barköl.

The military reverses of 1731 drove the emperor to despair. In an extraordinary rescript to Yue Zhongqi, he poured out his anguish in one of the most emotional and revealing documents produced by any ruler of the Qing. Nothing had worked as expected. Because his armies had violated basic rules of military strategy, they had met disaster. Ultimately, he had to take the blame. As he said, "Painfully I reflect on my responsibility, and I find that we, ruler and minister, have brought all the blame on ourselves." (See Appendix B.) The supreme Lord of Heaven found himself baffled by inscrutable foes and abandoned by cruel Heaven. The world seemed out of joint. For now, only Yue and the emperor knew the full scope of the disaster, but they needed to make long-range plans. The emperor considered abandoning the Zunghar campaigns entirely, but that would mean giving up the great enterprise begun by his grandfather: to end once and for all the nomadic menace. He resolved to press on, but much more cautiously, waiting until more propitious times arrived. Turfan could be abandoned after putting up a fight; endorsing body-count logic, the emperor had no other strategy than to kill as many Zunghars as possible.

Galdan Tseren, encouraged by his victory, sent his armies to plunder the region southeast of Khobdo, hoping to weaken Qing and Khalkha resistance. He also appealed to the Khalkhas to join with him, as common descendants of Chinggis Khan, against the Manchus. His letter to the Khalkhas declared, "You are descendants of Chinggis Khan, who are subordinate to no one. Why not move your pastures to the Altai, and live together with us in peace? We can unite to resist any military threat."[144] But the Khalkhas refused and instead joined battle with the Zunghars near Erdeni Zhao (or Erdeni Zu), the seat of the highest-ranking living Buddha of Mongolia. The Khalkha leader was Tsereng, a descendant of Chinggis Khan who had been appointed head of a new Khanate, the Sayin Noyan, in 1725 as a reward for his services to the Qing. In the battle, over ten thousand Zunghars were killed, but a remnant escaped west of the Altai.[145] The grateful emperor appointed Tsereng military governor of Uliayusatai, built him a city with a palace, and on his death made him the first of only two Mongols who had memorial tablets installed in the Imperial Ancestral Temple. Yongzheng could claim no credit for this victory, since his Khalkha allies had done the fighting, but now both sides, exhausted by war, were ready to negotiate.

Yongzheng's aggressive ambitions had led to a military disaster, the first major defeat of a Qing army by the Zunghars. Driven by the goal of surpassing his father's glories, Yongzheng violated his own instincts for cautious retrenchment. Once again, tried-and-true nomadic tactics had lured an army from China beyond its supply lines and destroyed it. Retrenchment and stabilization of the border became the main watchwords of Qing policy for the next twenty years.

7

The Final Blows,

1734–1771

TEMPORARY peace set in for over a decade, as new leaders took power. Qing tactics shifted to trade and tribute, using the classic "five baits" of the days of the Han and Xiongnu to transform the Zunghars, or to soften them up for conquest. The new emperor never gave up the goal of eliminating the rival state, but he waited for more propitious times. Meanwhile, the Zunghar leaders desperately searched for allies and resources, from Beijing, Lhasa, Central Eurasian traders, and Russia, to hold their fragile state together. But when a succession crisis broke out in 1745, one faction invited Qing forces into Zungharia, leading to the extermination of the Zunghar state and people. Fatal individualism was indeed fatal.

Transforming the Barbarians through Trade

In September 1734 Yongzheng sent his top ministers to Zungharia to negotiate a peace that would divide the Khalkha and Zunghar domains. The negotiations did not produce a settlement because Galdan Tseren preferred a boundary at the Khanggai Mountains, while the Qing envoys argued for a line running along the Altai Mountains and Irtysh River.[1] Yongzheng ordered maps to be made of the border, but no peace treaty was signed. Yongzheng immediately began reducing the numbers of forces stationed on the frontier. Galdan Tseren sent his first tribute embassy to Beijing in 1735, but then the Yongzheng emperor died. Yongzheng's successor, Hongli, the Qianlong emperor (r. 1736–1795), rejected the first tribute mission, but he

Trading post, or caravanserai, in Inner Mongolia. Photo taken by Frederick Wulsin, 1923.

ultimately decided to continue the truce policy. Under Yongzheng, the empire had spent over 50 to 60 million taels fighting wars with the Zunghars, but it had failed to eliminate them.[2] War had damaged the northwest economy severely; two-thirds of the Zunghars owned no animals.[3] Peace, stabilization of the border, and trading relations offered considerable attractions to both sides. Commercial exchange, however, could never be sharply separated from security interests.

In the seventeenth century, Galdan had also pushed for closer trading relations. He sent his first trading mission in 1671, and trade volume rose with successive missions up to 1688.[4] But the growing conflict with the Khalkhas led the emperor to restrict most trade to the border, and after Galdan's invasion of Khalkha territory, all trade was cut off. Tsewang Rabdan likewise requested commercial access to Beijing, but his invasion of Tibet ended these efforts.

Qianlong used the strong desire of the Zunghars for trade as a lever to obtain a final delimitation of the boundary. In 1739 a truce was agreed on and regular trade relations were established.[5] For the next fifteen years, the Qing and Zunghars closely joined their economies together. This officially regulated "tribute" trade, from the Qing perspective, allowed three types of missions: embassies to the capital, border trade at Suzhou in western

Equestrian portrait of the Qianlong emperor (r. 1736–1795), by the Italian court painter Lang Shining (Giuseppe Castiglione), ca. 1790.

Table 7.1 The Qing-Zunghar trade: Tribute trade at Beijing and Hami

Year	No. of traders	Goods	Silver (taels)
1735	22	Various hides	14,197
1735–36	26	Sheep (344); horses (237); camels (113)	N/A
1737–38	24	Animals; grapes; sal ammoniac; antelope horns	17,111
1738–39	42	Horses (428); camels (145)	40,000+
1739–40	65	Sheep (3,000); horses (701); camels (388); grapes (1,700 *jin*); sal ammoniac (10,000+ *jin*); antelope horns (5,000+)	53,000+
1742/2–7 months	42	Sheep (5,000+); horses (484); camels (715); grapes (174 packs); sal ammoniac (86 packs); antelope horns; hides	N/A
1742/9	26	Sheep (5,629); horses (146); camels (114)	N/A
1743–44		Sheep (545); horses (84); camels (42)	N/A
1744–45	38	Cattle (378); sheep (7,669); horses (543); camels (191); hides; grapes; antelope horns	N/A
1745–46	28	Cattle (28); sheep (945); horses (290); camels (95)	N/A
1746–47	46	Cattle (690); sheep (13,700+); horses (913); camels (217); hides	N/A
1748	28	Sheep (1,267); horses (407); camels (87); hides	N/A
1749–50	47	Cattle (129); sheep (2,585); horses (678); camels (181)	10,200+
1750–51	52	Cattle (156); sheep (3,600–3,700); horses (957); camels (346)	10,500+
1751–52			9,000+
1754	33	Animals; hides	8,175

Source: Zhungar Shilue Bianxiezu, *Zhungar Shilue* (Beijing: Renmin Chubanshe, 1985), pp. 134–137.

Gansu, and "presentation of boiled tea" *(aocha)* to lamas in Tibet, following a route through Xining. Substantial archival sources allow us to investigate these trade routes in detail. Although it lasted less than two decades, this trade reveals a great deal about the nature of Qing trading relations with all "barbarians" on the frontiers, northwest and elsewhere.[6]

As Governor-General Qingfu put it, the goal of trade was to "transform" *(xianghua)* the barbarian peoples by offering them goods from the interior in exchange for peaceful relations.[7] The Zunghars were allowed to send missions to the capital every four years, in 1738, 1742, 1746, 1750, and so on, and to trade at the border in 1740, 1744, 1748, 1752, and so on. The basic regulations followed the same principles as the Russian caravan

Table 7.2 Trade at Hami and Suzhou

Year	No. of traders	Goods	Hami (taels)	Suzhou (taels)	Total (taels)
1743–44	122	Cattle (260) Sheep (26,800) Horses (545) Camels (726)	9,790	41,000	50,790
1746	213	Cattle (2,642) Sheep (40,615) Horses (1,628) Camels (726)	13,130	95,923	109,053
1748	136	Cattle (402) Sheep (71,505) Horses (984) Camels (585)	12,744	74,000	86,744
1750	301	Cattle (2,200) Sheep (156,900) Horses (1,900+) Camels (1,000+)	7,868	186,200	194,067
1752	200	Cattle (1,200) Sheep (77,000) Horses (1,279+) Camels (588)	N/A	N/A	N/A

Source: Zhungar Shilue Bianxiezu, *Zhungar Shilue*, pp. 134–137.

trade, but the missions to the capital avoided arriving during the same year as the Russians. The main goods offered for sale by the Zunghars were animals (horses, sheep, cattle, and camels), furs, certain medicinal products (sal ammoniac and antelope horn), and dried grapes from Turkestan. (See Table 7.1.) In exchange, the Qing provided brocades, tea, rhubarb, and, if necessary, silver. The size of embassies was limited to one hundred men for border trade and two hundred to three hundred men for trade at the capital; traders could stay at the border no more than eighty days to conclude business, and the numbers and quantities of goods were specified in advance. Exports of gunpowder, metals, and weaponry were prohibited.[8]

Following the emperor's orders, officials made great efforts to ensure that trade proceeded smoothly and that the embassies were well treated. They offered medical care to Mongols who became ill while in the capital— an important service, as nomads were known to be vulnerable to smallpox and other urban diseases.[9] Even though the two societies had just concluded nearly fifty years of warfare, there was no wrangling over the *ketou* and ritual precedent. Mongols and Manchus understood each other, and

Table 7.3 Boiled tea *(aocha)* missions to Tibet

Year	No. of traders	Goods	Silver (taels)
1741	300	Cattle (400) Sheep (7,392) Horses (1,716) Camels (2,080) Sal ammoniac (19,000+ *jin*) Antelope horns (82,700) Grapes; hides	105,476
1743	312	Sheep (2,800+) Horses (2,300+) Camels (1,700+) Hides; grapes; antelope horns	78,000
1747	300	Sheep (3,000) Horses (3,000+) Camels (2,000+) Hides	164,350

Source: Zhungar Shilue Bianxiezu, *Zhungar Shilue*, pp. 134–137.

the emperor viewed the Zunghars as part of his realm, deserving his protection and generosity *(fusui)*.

The Suzhou trade, however, quickly grew well beyond expectations, straining at official limits. (See Table 7.2.) From a value of 10,000 taels in 1738, it leapt to 105,000 taels in 1741. Furthermore, these figures omit a substantial amount of private trade carried on alongside the officially reported trade. The Zunghar traders constantly pressed for relaxation of trade restrictions, asking for annual missions, and that missions heading for the capital be allowed to sell non-tribute goods at the border. Border officials were caught by surprise when huge herds of animals and large numbers of men turned up at their posts, straining available local pastures. Rather than be held responsible for keeping these people at the border, they agreed to allow trade even in off years. As the tables show, despite the official restrictions, trade occurred every year, with one exception, from 1738 to 1754, and sometimes traders arrived twice in one year. Volumes were higher in official years, and highest during capital mission years, but significant trade occurred every year. When Zunghars asked that trade be permitted at Hami, 875 kilometers northwest of Suzhou, to relieve the pressure, officials reluctantly agreed.[10] The traders asked very high prices for their animals, causing officials to engage in weeks of haggling, and they extended their time at the border waiting for more goods to arrive.[11]

The second tribute mission to Beijing illustrates vividly the pressures that the traders put on frontier officials.[12] Chuinamuke, a relative of Galdan Tseren, headed the caravan of forty-two men, 634 pack loads, and five thousand sheep which arrived at the border early in 1742. Chuinamuke immediately asked for permission to sell the animals at Hami or Suzhou, in violation of the tribute regulations. Yong Chang, the military commander at Anxi, decided to be lenient, following the emperor's policy of "cherishing men from afar" *(huairou yuanren)*. Most of the men, animals, and over five hundred packs stayed in Suzhou, lodged at the Qing's expense, while a small group of fifteen men presented the tribute in Beijing. Yong Chang supplied them with grain, tea, and tobacco and sent them on their way on March 3. The emperor agreed to recompense the traders for any animals that died en route.

A month later, however, Governor-General Yinjishan took a much harder line. He regarded the traders as "crafty and greedy" barbarians who "traded useless products for the goods of the Central Kingdom" and plotted to spy out conditions in the interior. In 1739 Shaanxi and Gansu local officials had bought 17,000 *jin* of dried grapes, for which there was no demand, but eventually unloaded them at one-third the original purchase price, a loss of 10,000 taels to the treasury. Yinjishan agreed that officials should be "flexible in accordance with circumstances" *(quanheng zhongqing)* but also firm, so as to control the traders' "insatiable desires" *(wuyan zhi qiu)*. The previous year, on the pretext of presenting boiled tea to Tibet, the traders had brought large piles of goods to Xining, then turned around and gone home without ever entering Tibet. Clearly they had "inconstant natures" and could not be trusted. When the delegation returned from Beijing, however, after further haggling, the Governor-General ultimately agreed to buy up the unsold goods, calling in merchants to negotiate sales at reduced prices. Obviously relieved when the traders returned to their "nests," he once more vented his exasperation: "They have hundreds of tricks," he complained; the only way to treat them was with "a principled balance between generosity and restraint."[13]

The arrival of the 1748 caravan at the border led to more amusing negotiations between exasperated officials and disingenuous traders, reported in vernacular Chinese in the documents. (See Appendix C.) Once again, the wily caravan men brought along extra people, described as "doctors, cooks, and accountants," attempted to unload excess goods at outrageous prices, pleaded for help in disposing of sick animals, and expressed fulsome appreciation of the emperor's benevolent grace. Grumpy officials eventually gave in to most requests, and the traders promised not to commit offenses again.[14]

One other incident of this year indicates that trade relations did have

wider effects in the Zunghar territory.[15] Ajibardi and Niyasi, two young
Turkestani men from Turfan, galloped up to the frontier on stolen horses to
plead for refuge. Captured by the Zunghars at a young age, they had been
forced to perform slave labor for the masters, and had been beaten severely.
They vowed that it would be "better to die in Chinese territory than under
the Zunghars." Ajibardi, whose parents were discovered to be alive in
Guazhou, was handed over to Emin Khoja, the *beg* of Turfan, while Niyasi
was sent to the capital. A few months later a thirty-year-old Zunghar escaped from servitude, having heard that he could "live a better life" under
Qing rule. Though rather suspicious of the motives of these deserters, the
officials found them to be useful sources of information, and giving them
refuge helped reinforce the emperor's reputation for generosity. Peaceful
trade relations did appear to be softening up the Zunghar empire's support.
Soldiers and merchants were engaging in private trading on the border, despite official prohibitions.[16] Border trade, though exasperating, promised
larger political gains if the wealth of the Chinese interior lured away the
Zunghars' subject peoples.

The border trade not only altered Zunghar internal relations but also began to change relations with the frontier merchants. Border officials, realizing that merchants knew prices better than the government, decided to cooperate with them. They created a system of "merchant management under
overall official supervision" *(shangban er guan wei zongshe zhaokan).*[17]
Nineteenth-century advocates of self-strengthening programs would later
call this arrangement "official supervision and merchant management"
(guandu shangban). The quantities of goods which the Zunghars brought
to the border exceeded what local markets could bear. Dried grapes and
rare medicinal products like sal ammoniac and antelope horn, obtained
from mines in Turkestan and pastures in Mongolia, piled up in warehouses
when no one could arrange distribution. Cattle and sheep served local
interests better because they could be used to support military garrisons,
but even these herds exceeded local demand. Furthermore, Zunghars constantly insisted on being paid in silver, thus threatening to cause a substantial bullion outflow. Border officials did not have much tea and cloth on
hand, and they would exhaust their treasuries if they bought everything
in silver. The Qianlong emperor resolved to contain silver within the empire so as to maintain the stability of the currency. Turning to merchants
would solve the problems of limited demand, bullion outflow, and insistent
traders.

In fact, the "Zunghar" missions were dominated by experienced Central
Asian merchants who moved bulk goods and currency along the tracks of
the ancient Silk Roads. In 1748, for example, of a total of 136 men, 46

were Mongols and 90 were Turkic Muslims (Chantou Hui). Three of the four headmen of the caravan were Turkic.[18] The caravans mixed together diplomatic envoys, Zunghar officials, herders, merchants, and certainly, as the Qing suspected, spies. They pursued joint goals of generating revenue for the Zunghar state, reviving the devastated pastoral economy, and gathering information about their huge neighbor. Qing policy aimed to reduce intercultural contact as much as possible, especially to prevent the Zunghars from confronting any Khalkha Mongols, by limiting their stay and keeping them constantly under close military escort. But the growing size of the trade forced officials to bring in other participants who had private interests separate from those of the state.

Very few merchants in the northwest, however, had sufficient capital to handle the large quantities of goods. A merchant needed at least 100,000 taels to engage in this trade, but demobilization of the military had undercut the primary support of Suzhou's economy. In Gansu there were almost no wealthy merchants, and in Shaanxi most merchants ran small pawnshops scattered all over the province. In 1744, however, Li Yongxiang arrived from Xi'an to take responsibility for the border trade. The Governor-General loaned him 28,741 taels to supplement his capital, expecting repayment the next year. Thereafter, the government had to continue giving inducements to draw traders from the interior. It paid many of their transport costs and supplied them with carts formerly used for military supplies. When the merchants complained that the amount of goods to be brought by the Zunghars was unpredictable, officials agreed to loan them funds to make up the difference.[19] When the "useless" high-value medicinal goods could only be disposed of at low prices, causing merchants to lose money, the officials made up their losses.

Gansu Governor Huang Tinggui argued that it was vital to expand market demand, because this trade was a "national security" affair *(guojia gongshi)* in which all parts of the empire were involved. He allotted responsibility for disposing of goods primarily to the northwest provinces—30 percent to Gansu and 70 percent to Shaanxi—but he urged Zhili, Henan, Shandong, and Shanxi to mobilize their markets as well. These provinces had dense populations and abundant merchant capital, unlike the northwestern regions "at the back of beyond" *(tianmo zhi qiongbian).*[20] It was their responsibility to relieve the northwest of its glut of unsold goods. Whatever could not be sold in the North China region should be sold at Chongwenmen, the main gate of the imperial capital.

Over time, the trade evolved more systematically to suit the needs of the Zunghar traders. When they specified the types of cloth and tea they needed, border officials would recruit merchants and loan them capital *(ziben)* to proceed to Jiangnan to obtain the necessary goods.[21] These interest-free loans ensured that Zunghars would dispose of their goods quickly, while merchants had sufficient capital to pay them. Often, however, the treasury lost funds after the trading season ended.

Concern about the outflow of silver drove the state itself to engage in substantial commercial transactions. Silver constituted only 6 percent of total exports in 1738, but its share rose over time. In 1743 Zunghar traders accepted half of their payment for furs in silver, but Governor Huang Tinggui thought this excessive. The Zunghars were supposed to "supply what they lack, not increase what they own" *(ji qi suo wu, bing fei li qi suo you)*, that is, trade sheep for daily use goods, not grapes for silver.[22] In 1746 the Zunghars demanded 40 percent payment in silver, but after much haggling accepted 20 percent.[23] Huang Tinggui and other provincial governors tried as much as possible to make the trade a barter trade. In short, by advancing money to merchants the Qing state injected silver into its interior economy so as to shore up a barter trade on its frontiers, a version of mercantilism, or bullionism, that many European statesmen would have endorsed.

In 1750 the Zunghars brought goods worth 186,000 taels, the largest amount ever, which they exchanged for 167,300 taels' worth of cloth and tea, with the balance in silver. Governor-General Yinjishan, concerned about the loss of wealth, again urged strict limits to the trade. The Qianlong emperor, reversing his earlier views, now regarded the loss of silver as of slight consequence compared to the political benefits derived from the trade.[24] Still, the court resolved to cut it back to the level of 1748, or 80,000 taels, but internal upheaval among the Zunghars after the death of Galdan Tseren in 1745 had already begun to hurt commerce. The high volume of trade in 1750, after the assassination of Galdan Tseren's successor, may indicate strong efforts to accumulate revenue by rival contenders for leadership of the Zunghar state. Traders at the border told officials that Tsewang Dorji Namjal was "crazy," and his elder brother Lama Darja had been put in charge until he got better.[25] When Dawaci made his bid for power, the Qing shut down all trade in 1753 to induce his submission. They viewed his requests for trade missions as motivated by intelligence gathering. Seventeen fifty-four was the last trading year. By the next year the Qing army had occupied Ili, ending the unified Zunghar state.

The "boiled tea" (Ch. *aocha* or *jiancha*, T. *manja*) trade with Tibet (see Table 7.3) was even more sensitive than the border trade, for it allowed direct access by the Zunghars to Tibetan monasteries.[26] Broadly speaking, *manja* meant a pilgrimage carrying religious donations from Mongols to Tibetan lamas, accompanied by trade along the route.[27] During the truce period, the Qing allowed three major missions to Tibet to pass through their territory, but each produced angry disputes since the Zunghar and Qing goals differed. For the Zunghars, trade with Tibet was an opportunity to reestablish alliances with Buddhist clerics and with the Khoshot Mongols of Kokonor, as well as to make commercial profits. For the Qing, this trade in the guise of ritual presentation could unify Mongols under the Tibetan Buddhist church, which in turn was subjected to Qing patronage. This trade clearly illustrates how Buddhist patronage and commerce were strongly influenced by security concerns.

The *manja* trade route via Xining was established as early as 1642–43, when the Khoshot Mongols invaded Lhasa to support the Dalai Lama's Yellow Teaching sect, giving Mongols much more convenient access to Tibet than the dangerous route over the Kunlun Mountains.[28] Once the Qing established control of the Khoshot Mongols in Kokonor in the 1720s, all trade missions had to pass through their jurisdiction. Soon after Galdan Tseren took power in Zungharia, in 1728, he requested permission from the Yongzheng emperor to send boiled tea missions to Tibet to express his support for the Dalai Lama, but as noted earlier, the emperor contemptuously refused him because Lobzang Danjin was still in Zunghar hands. Lhasa was in the midst of civil war, and the emperor suspected that the anti-Qing faction had Zunghar support.

Under Qianlong, shortly after the truce negotiations were completed in 1739, Galdan Tseren once again requested permission to send missions to Tibet, and this time the emperor agreed, under certain conditions. Missions would be limited to three hundred men. (At first the emperor tried to limit their size to one hundred men but relented when the Zunghars claimed this number was insufficient.) They first had to pass through Hami and Suzhou before reaching Dongkeer temple, outside Xining, where they would be allowed to exchange goods. They would be under strict military escort, and they would avoid all contact with the Khoshot Mongols, who would be moved away from the route through which the traders passed.[29] Five hundred troops, provided with 30,000 taels for transport and food costs, would accompany the mission. Claiming that his men, who were not immunized against smallpox, would be infected in the garrison towns, Galdan Tseren tried to send the mission directly to Xining, avoiding Hami and Suzhou, but the emperor angrily refused. Finally, in 1741, the mission arrived at Dongkeer, bringing animals, furs, and dried grapes. There the traders sold their goods for a total value of 105,476 taels, of which 80,000 taels were in silver.[30] They were, however, denied permission to present offerings at the nearby Labrang and Taersi (Kumbum) monasteries. These monasteries were key assembly points for the Khoshots, and the Taersi monastery had been a stronghold of Lobzang Danjin's rebellion. The Kokonor Mongols were still restive under Qing control, as Norbu's rebellion of 1731 indicated, so the Qing wanted no Zunghar involvement in the region.

By August 1741, having finished its business, the Zunghar mission asked to go home without traveling to Tibet, claiming that the climate in Tibet was too hot, or too cold. When the mission arrived at the border in 1742, General Yong Chang berated the merchants for betraying the emperor's trust. He strongly suspected that the *aocha* mission had turned back only because they expected no profits from trading in Tibet. Furious, the emperor denounced them for violating imperial orders, swearing that he would never allow any future missions.[31] But if the goal of their mission was to establish contact with lamaseries and the Khoshot tribes in Kokonor, they realized that severe Qing restrictions were designed to prevent this. They achieved their commercial goals, but saw no future in their diplomatic endeavor.

Nevertheless, in 1743, under strict escort, a second mission traded up to 100,000 taels' worth of goods.[32] The caravan sent in 1743 did arrive in Lhasa, and presented rich gifts to the Dalai Lama. Polhanas, the pro-Qing Tibetan ruler, had no love for the Zunghars, who had killed Lazang Khan, but he accepted the mission, while surrounding the capital with troops.[33] The Qing's greatest windfall from this mission was the capture of the elusive Lobzang Danjin. He had grasped the opportunity to accompany the mission to return home from Zungharia, but he was seized and sent to Beijing.

The third mission was sent in 1747, after the death of Galdan Tseren, by his successor Tsewang Dorji Namgyal, to offer prayers on behalf of the deceased leader. Its merchants traded goods worth 164,350 taels, while the Qing officials allotted 160,000 taels for the costs of the escort.[34] In early 1748 they celebrated a great feast in Lhasa and presented a large lump of gold to the Dalai Lama. The officials were concerned that the Zunghars, whom they suspected of spying, might establish a connection between Tibet and the Jinchuan rebels in western Sichuan, and the Tibetans complained of the high cost of these missions. The emperor declared that he would allow no further contacts between the Zunghars and Tibet. Chaos in both Tibet and Zungharia in the 1750s put an end to these connections.

Despite their mutual suspicions, both sides still found reasons to continue the trade. If Galdan Tseren called back his first mission because of the tight restrictions, he clearly had more than commercial goals in mind. Reg-

ular contact with the lamaseries in Kokonor and Lhasa was clearly a crucial support for his state. He may also have feared that Qing troops were
moving back into the region of Khobdo, so he needed to consolidate his
forces.[35] Galdan Tseren astutely did not count on peaceful relations lasting
forever. He would take advantage of the trading loophole to extend his
links to the Tibetans, while the Qing made strong efforts to limit contacts
with unreliable subjects. The Qing relied on the hostility to the Zunghars of
Polhanas, their ally in Tibet, plus the large military escort to prevent any
trouble. If the Zunghars used the missions to spy out conditions in Tibet,
the Qing escorts, too, could demonstrate their support of the Tibetan rulers
while encouraging economic links with the interior under strict control. Ma
Lin has argued that the *aocha* missions "contributed to developing the
unity of our multinational nation," but they were too limited to have much
of an economic effect.[36] They did, however, serve Qing strategic goals by tying Tibet and Kokonor together under the aegis of the Tibetan Buddhist
church, demonstrating the power of patronage of the universal emperor.

Aocha missions continued through the eighteenth and nineteenth centuries on a smaller scale after the destruction of the Zunghar state.[37] Small
groups of fewer than ten people did not require licenses, but the central
government still approved larger expeditions by Khoshot and Torghut
Mongols who went regularly to Tibet to pay homage to the lamas. Most of
these expeditions were organized by lamas, not by secular nobles. Trade
and religious pilgrimage were still linked, but in dispersed fashion, as no rival centralized state could use them for its purposes. Increasing communication with Tibet did begin to tie the frontier regions of the empire together,
while the emperors strengthened their control by supporting the ecclesiasti-
cal nobility to balance against the secular lords. The principle of divide and
rule operated effectively to fragment any potential opposition.

Peace with the Zunghars did not genuinely soften Qing attitudes. The
Qing regarded these barbarians as greedy, violent, and untrustworthy. The
Qing believed, however, that the emperor's grace would soften them so that
they would accommodate to imperial dominion. Barbarians by nature had
"insatiable desires" *(wu yan zhi qing)* and "shameless greed" *(tanli wuchi)*,
but by controlling their actions and "cherishing" *(huairou)* them, the Qing
could tame them.[38] Tying the Zunghar elites to the interior with trading
links would make them less inclined to attack the frontier.[39] This type of
"loose reign" *(jimi)* policy was a well-established method of dealing with
northwestern nomads. Frontier trade was thus a "national security" affair,
to which all parts of the empire should contribute, even if the economic
gains were slight. Commercial concerns, however, were not irrelevant:
frontier officials were supposed to limit the outflow of silver and cooperate

with interior merchants to produce goods that the Zunghars would buy, as well as ensure distribution of Zunghar goods in interior markets.

Officials constantly described this trade as "tribute" *(gong)*, but this term covered a great variety of meanings.[40] Using the term "tributary system" in the sense employed by John K. Fairbank to characterize all of Qing trading relationships is in one sense trivially true but in another misleading. As James Millward and others have pointed out, the word "tribute" encompassed many different kinds of trading and power relationships, in the Ming as well as the Qing.[41]

The Zunghars occupied an ambiguous, borderline role in this relationship. On the one hand, they were clearly not alien, new peoples, like the Europeans or Russians. The Manchu rulers knew well the habits of Mongolian nomads, and part of the ruling coalition included them. Nor were they like the loyal tributary states of Japan and Vietnam, which participated in trading relations as part of a broad East Asian network.[42] Unlike in the Ming, when the rulers in Beijing had no control over the steppe, the Manchus had already won over a substantial portion of the Mongolian tribes. They were not making large protection payments to nomadic invaders to stave off damaging raids; the treasury lost some money on the trade, plus the expense of escorting missions, but the net economic cost was low.

On the other hand, the Zunghars could not be considered loyal Mongolian subjects, even though they were referred to as being part of the "interior" *(neidi)*. The frontier trade was a kind of experiment designed to test whether or not the Zunghars deserved imperial protection and whether they could coexist with the great Manchu empire. As Thomas Barfield has argued, large nomadic confederations frequently rose in tandem with centralized imperial regimes, using them as sources of revenue through either raiding or trading.[43] Rulers in Beijing had an interest in keeping nomadic confederations united, because it was easier to channel goods through a single ruler, so long as his power did not become too great. Nicola Di Cosmo has argued that Xiongnu raids on the Han dynasty were a result of the inability of the Xiongnu chieftain to control his nobility.[44] Ming rulers likewise suffered economic damage on the northwest frontier both because of the disunity of the Mongolian tribes and because their defensive bulwarks could not protect the frontier against raids. The Qing solution, to draw a sharp boundary line through the steppe and induce quiescence through trade, seemed to stabilize relations for a short period. The Zunghars might have become a dependent but partially autonomous state, linked to the Qing and other Mongols through trade and Buddhist ritual patronage. But at the first sign of division among the Zunghars, the rulers

The Manchu general Machang, famous for victories in the Turkestan campaigns.
Portrait by the court painter Castiglione.

were ready to embrace the military option and return to their primary goal
of eliminating the state and its people.

The Death Knell of the Zunghar State

The death of Galdan Tseren in 1745 stimulated the internal divisions that
brought about the Zunghar state's destruction. Within five years of his
death, internecine conflict had torn apart the state, and defeated members
were seeking Qing support. Galdan Tseren had three sons and one daughter. His second son, Tsewang Dorji Namjal, succeeded him in 1746, taking
the title of Hongtaiji. He was a violent, perverse, paranoid man, said to be
interested only in drinking and killing dogs.[45] When his sister, Ulan Bayar,
tried to restrain him, he had her locked up, fearing that others were trying
to take power from him. In this case he was correct. His more popular elder
brother Lama Darja (or Lama Dorji) plotted with Sayin Bolek, the husband
of Ulan Bayar, to kill Tsewang Dorji Namjal in 1750 while he was on a
hunting trip. When he discovered the plot, Tsewang Dorji Namjal marched
against the conspirators, but he was defeated. His eyes were put out and he

The Mongol prince Dawaci, supporter of the Qing campaign against Amursana. His portrait was one of a series commissioned by the emperor to honor military allies of the Qing.

was imprisoned in Aksu along with his other brother, Dashi Dawa. Followers of Dashi Dawa then surrendered and were settled in Chahar.

Qing officials watched developments in Zungharia closely. With misgivings, they allowed Tsewang Dorji Namjal to send envoys to Tibet to hold ceremonies in memory of his father. The death of Polhanas in Tibet in 1747 threatened to send Tibet into turmoil again, but fortunately for the Zunghar envoys, they were able to return without difficulty. But Tibet then broke out in rebellion, and General Bandi had to lead his army to Lhasa to install a reliable successor. Lama Darja was refused permission to contact Tibet. Zungharia was thus cut off from its spiritual roots.

Meanwhile, Lama Darja fell into conflict with two leading warriors: Dawaci, a Zunghar noble, the grandson of the elder Tsering Dondub, the most famous of the Zunghar generals, and Amursana, a prince of the Khoit tribe, the grandson of Lazang Khan and a descendant of Tsewang Rabdan. Dawaci, centered in Tarbaghatai, refused Lama Darja's orders to pursue Dashi Dawa's men into Qing territory. Instead, he attempted to submit. When Lama Darja tried to arrest him, Dawaci fled to Kazakh territory along with Amursana, then returned to confront Lama Darja in Tarbaghatai. In December 1752, when Lama Darja's own troops revolted and killed him, Dawaci was made "Great Chieftain" (Da Taiji) of the Zunghars and killed all of Darja's men. But Dawaci, once in power, became a drunkard and a wild man, who developed a hatred for Amursana. Amursana did not belong to the Zunghar nobility, so he depended on Dawaci's position to maintain his influence among the Zunghars. Yet after he gradually gained influence among the Khoshots, Derbets, and Khoits through marriage alliances and negotiations, he proposed to Dawaci to divide the Zunghar lands between them. Dawaci refused and attacked Amursana, forcing him to flee to the east. In September or October, Amursana reached Khobdo and made the fateful Faustian bargain. With his five thousand men, he would submit to Qing authority if the Qing would place him at the head of the Zunghar state.

Other Zunghar leaders had also been fleeing the internecine struggle to find refuge with the Qing. They received lavish welcomes, including princely titles and many banquets at the emperor's summer residence in Chengde. But all previous Mongol refugees had been settled within existing Qing territory, under close control. Amursana was the first to return to Zungharia with the backing of Qing armies. The emperor grasped this opportunity, at the invitation of one of the leading contenders for power, to intervene directly in Zunghar affairs beyond the borders. By the end of 1754, Qianlong had decided to send two armies of 25,000 men each against Dawaci: one by the northern route through Uliyasutai, and one by the western route leaving from Barköl.[46] Bandi would lead the northern army, with Amursana as his second in command; Yong Chang and Salar led the western army. In March 1755 the troops set out, with two months' rations per man, planning to meet in Bortala. (See Map 7.)

Qianlong gave elaborate justifications for his campaign, invoking Kangxi's campaigns against Galdan, but praising Galdan Tseren's observance of the boundary and his presentation of tribute. Dawaci, he claimed, was only a usurper, whose violence had caused many Zunghars to flee his

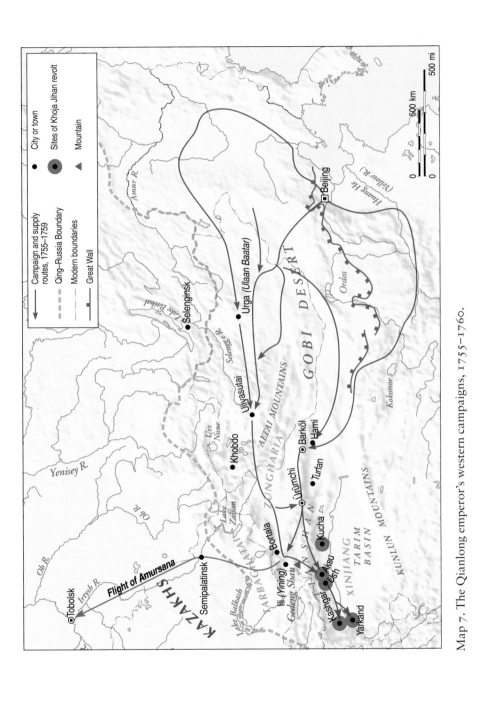

Map 7. The Qianlong emperor's western campaigns, 1755–1760.

lands, forcing the Qing to provide for them. He also betrayed concern that the long period of peace had undermined Manchu commitment to war: "Our old Manchu customs respect righteousness and revere justice. Young and old, none are ashamed to fight for them. But after enjoying such a long period of peace, inevitably, people want to avoid putting on armor and joining the ranks of war."[47] But now the Qing had to seize this opportunity to protect the Khalkhas under its embrace and establish security on the borders. Qianlong saw this campaign as a means of solidifying control over the Mongolian frontier and keeping up the fighting morale of the increasingly sedentarized, pacific banners.

All the players in this final act of the eighteenth-century Great Game now mobilized their supporters. The Qing put pressure on its Khalkha allies to provide support for the coming campaign, while the Zunghars looked to Russia for aid. The Kazakhs, new entrants on the scene, received appeals from both Qing and Zunghar envoys. The Russians knew that with only a few soldiers scattered among distant fortresses, they were in a weak position to face major Qing forces. They refused to accept Zunghar refugees and tried to make peace among the Zunghars. They accepted dual payments of *iasak* to both Russian and Zunghar collectors but refused requests by Lama Darja to destroy fortresses on the Irtysh and Ob rivers.[48]

Ablai, leader of the Middle Horde of the Kazakhs, had sheltered Dawaci and Amursana against attacks from Lama Darja. When Amursana split from Dawaci, however, he, like the Qing, seized the opportunity to capture herds and territory from the fractured Zunghar state.

The campaign itself was short. Deprived of allies, and under attack from both east and west, Dawaci had no effective response. His men were divided into small, uncoordinated groups, while he spent most of his time drunk.[49] By the middle of 1755, many of his *zaisang* had surrendered. The west army passed through Ürümchi, joined with Amursana and the northern army, and reached Bortala in June 1755. Hearing of the Qing approach, Dawaci fled to Gedengshan, 180 *li* southwest of Ili, where he made his last stand with ten thousand men. A night attack on July 2, 1755, by a small patrol scattered Dawaci's men, forcing him to flee south across the Tianshan, where he was captured by the Hakim Beg Hojis of Ush. Sent in captivity to Beijing, he was made a prince *(qinwang)* and married into the imperial clan.

The Qing success was rapid, but the armies could not be supported for long. The generals quickly withdrew their troops, leaving only five hundred men in Ili. Qianlong claimed to have been reluctant to use force at first, but now he boasted of achieving a permanent settlement of the nomadic security threat, implying that he had succeeded where Kangxi and Yongzheng had failed. He praised Fu Heng for his support, in contrast to the timid opponents of the plan. He stressed the need for a long-term settlement of the Zunghar problem, but also noted the low expenses of this campaign compared to the costs of the previous ones.

Yet once again the elimination of one Zunghar leader only created another problem. Amursana congratulated the emperor on his victory. As a Qing supporter (though he had actually done no fighting), he had been given the title *jiangjun* (general), but now he expected to receive the only title that really counted among the Zunghars: that of Khan. Amursana had raised this demand before the expedition was finished, but Qianlong had deferred an answer, for his real intention was to divide and rule. He would make Amursana Khan only of the Khoit, one among four equal Khans. Amursana rejected this offer, arguing that the Zunghars needed one single ruler. He refused to use the official seal or clothes given him by the Qing. Instead, he used the seal of Galdan Tseren, the last officially recognized leader of all the Zunghars. Once again the specter of a unified Mongolian state loomed over the steppe.[50]

As Amursana continued to gather more troops while delaying his formal submission, other disturbing rumors spread. Some said, falsely, that he had gathered the support of fifty thousand Kazakhs; but it was true that Amursana had offered money to the Tibetan lamas to support his claim to lead all the Zunghars. Reports arrived of his efforts to knit alliances with the Buruts, Yarkand, and Kashgar. Despite growing suspicions, Qianlong hesitated to take action. He invited Amursana to visit him at Chengde to be invested with his title, along with the three other Khans, but Amursana declined. Perhaps fearing excessive reliance on his allies, Qianlong at first declined the proposal of the Khalkha Mongol Erinchindorj to arrest Amursana and bring him forcibly to the emperor, but then agreed to have Erinchindorj escort Amursana to Chengde. On August 20, 1755, he ordered Bandi to capture Amursana, but Amursana had anticipated him. He escaped Erinchindorj's custody and fled to the Irtysh River before Bandi could arrive.

The scattered armies in Ili were unprepared for a major revolt. Bandi, besieged in Ili after trying to capture the city, committed suicide. Yong Chang quickly retreated from Ili and asked for reinforcements. Failing to hold Ürümchi, he retreated to Barköl. Qianlong fired Yong Chang, replacing him with Tseleng. Declaring that he would capture and wipe out Amursana's forces, the emperor offered rewards to Mongol chieftains who aided the pursuit, and insisted that Ablai of the Kazakhs capture Amursana if he fled there. He announced a scorched earth policy of devastating the pasturelands of all nomads who rebelled.

In the middle of Amursana's rebellion, the Khalkha prince Chingünjav (Ch. Qinggunzhabu), ruler of the Khotogoits in far northwest Mongolia and an important ally, rejected his orders and deserted his posts.[51] From the summer of 1756 through January 1757, Chingünjav mounted what would be the most serious rebellion by Khalkha Mongols against Qing rule until the end of the dynasty. Chingünjav's revolt exposed the tensions created by the vise-like grip of the Manchus and demonstrated the cost inflicted on the Outer Mongols by Qing demands to support the Zunghar campaigns. Before they could finish off Amursana, Qing generals had to divert most of their forces to ensure stability in Khalkha, where their control was fragile and many Mongols suffered poverty and official oppression. At the same time, the revolt showed that, like their Zunghar brethren, the Khalkha Mongols could not unite effectively against the Qing juggernaut.

After submitting to the Qing at the Dolon Nor assembly of 1691, the Khalkha Mongols had been incorporated into a "banner" system, designed to maximize administrative control while reinforcing their military organization, and to fragment their power while emphasizing their loyalty to the dynasty. These banners, however, performed quite a different function than the Mongol, Manchu, and Han banners that had created the Qing conquest elite.[52] Each basic banner unit, or *khoshun* (Mo. *khushuu*, Ch. *qi*), had at its head a prince, or *jasak*, whose position required confirmation by the emperor. The three traditional Khalkha *aimaq*, or clan confederations claiming a common ancestor, under the Sechen, Tüshiyetü, and Jasaktu Khans, were now divided into multiple *khoshun* instead of individual clans. At first there were seven *khoshun*, but the number of *jasaks* soon expanded rapidly. By 1755 the four Khalkha *aimaq* contained over eighty *jasaks*. (The Qing had created the new Sayin Noyan *aimaq* in 1725.) These new *jasaks* owed their power to Qing rule, and they undermined the hereditary claims of the Khans of each *aimaq*. The *aimaq* had become territorial units, not confederations personally subordinate to the Khan. With stipends, seals, ceremonial duties, and required attendance at court, much as in the Japanese *sankin kōtai* system, the court kept these nominally independent rulers under close watch while confirming their authority over their clans. No longer could Mongols move freely from one tribal unit to another; they were confined to fixed territories, carefully policed and mapped.

A local bureaucracy in Urga increased the burdens on the Mongols, obliging them to provide corvée duties at guard posts and postal relay stations and to sell their livestock to officials for military campaign use. Local officials often paid below market price for animals, forcing the Mongols to go into debt to Chinese moneylenders to support themselves. As they had done earlier in Inner Mongolia, Chinese merchants penetrated the Khalkha

The valiant warrior Ayuxi, a Zunghar who fought for the Qing. Condemned to death after being captured, Ayuxi pleaded for his life, swearing loyalty to the Qing. He displayed excellent riding skills and was unsurpassed in the use of the spear, so he was put in command of 24 Turkestanis, who routed a force of 6,500 Zunghars. The emperor had Castiglione commemorate him with this portrait.

territory, taking advantage of the Mongols' needs for cloth, tea, and other goods to bind them with debt contracts. The fixing of boundaries, corvée obligations, and other requirements, such as pasturing imperial horses, along with the rise of static monastic establishments, increased pressure on the grasslands while reducing the manpower available to raise herds.

The wars with the Zunghars in the late Kangxi and through the Yong-zheng reigns further devastated the economy. By one estimate, the Qing requisitioned 4 million animals from the Khalkhas from 1715 to 1735, paying as little as 7 silver cash per sheep.[53] The cost of supporting Zunghar refugees further stressed the carrying capacity of the grasslands. In 1751 Qianlong prohibited trade between Khalkhas and Zunghars on the border. In order to clear their debts, the Khalkhas had to go further into debt to the Chinese merchants, and to repay Chinese debts, they had to sell their animals at low prices to get silver. Thus, over the first half of the eighteenth century, the formerly mobile Khalkha nomads had seen their economy forcibly monetized with Chinese capital, stressed by increasing demands for livestock for Qing military campaigns, and confined within rigid adminis-trative boundaries under close bureaucratic control.

Chingünjav fit very poorly with this new ideal of the obedient, settled nomad. A legitimate descendant of Chinggis Khan, he inherited control of the Khotogoit tribe from his father, with Qing confirmation. Although he rose to high posts in the local administration, he repeatedly clashed with officials, who accused him of neglecting his duties. Impeached for "laziness" as *Jasak beile* of the Jasaktu Khan's *aimaq*, he was later attacked by the emperor and demoted for defying the prohibition on border trade with the Zunghars. Chingünjav's obstreperousness exasperated his Manchu superiors, but it makes sense as the behavior of a Mongol official who envied the freedom of the "true nomad," in Owen Lattimore's term.[54] Coming from the remotest region of the Khalkhas, he prized his independence more than bureaucratic regulation.

Chingünjav grudgingly bore his burdens and joined Amursana to march against Dawaci, but severe frost in the winter of 1755 left his Khalkhas with little support to provide. The final straw was the execution of Erinchindorj, elder brother of the Jebzongdanba Khutukhtu, and the escort of Amursana, who had suspiciously allowed him to escape Qing custody. At first, Chingünjav himself came under suspicion. He was stripped of his rank and arrested three times but ultimately cleared. The Qing needed his loyalty, but it also needed a scapegoat. The court then fastened on Erinchindorj. According to some accounts, Chingünjav and the Jebzongdanba Khutukhtu were forced to witness Erinchindorj's public execution in the capital in May 1756. (Later accounts claim that Erinchindorj was allowed to commit suicide.)

In July 1756 Chingünjav rejected Qing orders to pursue Amursana and returned to his pastures. Soon after, Khalkhas all along the border fled their guard posts, and the court declared Chingünjav a rebel while urging the Khalkha nobility to remain loyal. Chingünjav spelled out his grievances in detail: the Qing had oppressed the Khalkhas by seizing their horses and cattle, and had executed Erinchindorj, a descendant of Chinggis Khan, the ancestor of all the Khalkhas.[55] Qianlong, in his response, denied that his campaigns had oppressed the Khalkhas: his men had paid for animals with silver; and he insisted that no one, however noble his lineage, was immune from punishment. But he knew that Chingünjav's resistance threatened to draw in all the disgruntled Khalkha nobility. The emperor, after some hesitation, decided on severe repression of the Khalkhas before finishing with Amursana. Diverting military forces from the pursuit of Amursana, he made the Khalkha Mongol Tsengünjav (Ch. Chenggunzhabu) responsible for putting down unrest. Meanwhile, Mongol mobs looted Chinese shops at guard posts and relay stations, while Manchu local officials and *jasaks* pleaded for the court to restore order.

Chingünjav, however, failed to take advantage of the discontent. Even though he appealed to the Mongols as descendants of Chinggis Khan to throw off Qing rule, very few of the nobility joined him. He also failed to coordinate activities with Amursana. Although he approached the Russian governor at Selenginsk for aid, the Russians took a cautious wait-and-see attitude. They found it more beneficial to obey the terms of the 1727 treaty with the Qing than to back a hopeless uprising. The decisive actor in the revolt was the Jebzongdanba Khutukhtu, the leading Buddhist cleric of Mongolia, who, more than anyone else, enjoyed popular support from all the Mongols. At first he vacillated between calling on Russian aid and acting as intermediary between Chingünjav and the Qing court, but in the end he was overawed by Qing power. Telling the Khalkha leaders, "In my opinion, the Emperor took pity upon and succored us Khalkhas when we were cast into confusion by Galdan Boshukhtu, and has from age to age conferred various weighty favors," he urged them to return to their guard posts.[56] During the critical months of the winter of 1756, Chingünjav failed to garner more than two thousand men to support him. In January 1757 a ferocious assault by Qing troops crushed his army, captured Chingünjav, and executed the ringleaders and their families. In a key concession, at the same time the emperor announced that no Khalkha troops would be used in the suppression of Amursana. Combining small carrots with heavy sticks, the Qing withstood this "ragged affair," which in practice had become an uncoordinated series of desertions and looting rather than any coherent resistance.[57]

The most important long-term outcome of the revolt was the Qing declaration that further incarnations of the Jebzongdanba Khutukhtu must be discovered in Tibet, not in Mongolia. As he would later do with Tibet, the emperor took control of the Buddhist hierarchy by removing local lamas from participating in the selection of their chief cleric.

Modern Mongolian historians have held up Chingünjav's revolt as a heroic national resistance movement of the Mongolian people against Qing oppression, while Chinese historians, by contrast, hardly mention it, or else view it as nothing more than an outbreak of banditry. Western and Japanese evaluations fall somewhere in the middle of the spectrum, finding evidence of general resentment of Qing rule created by economic and administrative abuse, but seeing the Mongols as once again compromised by their "fatal individualism," with their loyalties focused far more on tribal units and personalities than on national unity.[58] As we shall see, the contrasting interpretations of this revolt dictated by the anachronistic requirements of modern nationalism mirror the later distortions of the historiography of the entire Zunghar campaign, just as the fragmentation of the Mongols which sabotaged their resistance and opened their society to foreign penetration by Chinese merchants ironically foreshadows China's own fate in the nineteenth century.

During the pursuit of Amursana, Qianlong was repeatedly disappointed with his field commanders. One by one they let him down. Either they failed to attack vigorously, letting their elusive enemies escape, or they sought excuses to avoid dangerous encounters, or they failed to cooperate with one another, allowing the enemy to slip through their uncoordinated forces. Qianlong the desk general, confined to his palace in Beijing, showed little understanding of or compassion for the constraints that faced his field generals. Amursana's successful flight from Ili brought down heavy recriminations and severe punishment from Beijing.

The first victim was Yubao, who was blamed for permitting Amursana to escape.[59] Yubao claimed that his two thousand troops were too few. He had also judged that with only four to five days' rations left in the garrison, and few horses, he lacked the resources for rapid pursuit, so he returned to Ili. Suspicious of a cover-up, the emperor dismissed Yubao from his post but allowed him to remain in the army to prove himself, demonstrating the "ethic of conditionality" in action. Yubao was pardoned the next month and demoted. One month later, however, he was arrested and sent to the capital for punishment.

The emperor's wrath, however, soon turned on Yubao's colleague Tseleng, who was General in Charge of Pacifying the West (Dingxi Jiang-jun) when Amursana escaped from Ili. Tseleng resisted orders to advance rapidly against the fleeing Amursana, claiming that his troops lacked supplies, but the emperor blamed him personally: "Leaders of troops should suffer the same hardships as the troops, not indulge in extravagance and waste." Dardanga, by contrast, was promoted for his enthusiasm. Dardanga had advanced deep into Kazakh territory, while Tseleng sat at his camp expecting new supplies. The emperor, however, had all fresh supplies sent to the more vigorous Dardanga. He rebuked Tseleng for requesting more troops, when he knew that Amursana had fled with very few men. Tseleng wanted to leave five hundred men in Ili before advancing and to withdraw detachments he had already sent out. Tseleng may have rightly been cautious in the face of genuine supply problems, but the emperor found his "stick in the mud" behavior outrageous. When Tseleng then told Dardanga to withdraw his troops, after pulling back Yubao's men to pasture their horses, he drew an impeachment for military negligence. "The way to use troops is to advance and not retreat," lectured the emperor. "The pursuit of the rebels is in the hands of timid, ignorant men." How could Tseleng claim that lack of rations prevented his advance, or worse, required the withdrawal of already advanced troops? Would it not use more rations to send horses and men forward and back?[60] Tseleng had arrived at his camp by the western route twenty days earlier than Dardanga, yet Dardanga had the surplus, while Tseleng was exhausted. Tseleng had also paused to buy animals from nearby Mongolian tribes instead of merely using the animals sent to him from Barköl. Tseleng and Yubao were arrested and sent to the capital for punishment. The two unfortunate generals were attacked by Zunghars while under escort back to Beijing.

Dardanga, by contrast, earned great credit for defying his fellow general's orders and engaging in aggressive, perhaps reckless, initiatives. The emperor supported both his insubordination and his aggressive behavior, rewarding him with the top general's post, formerly held by Tseleng. Although Dardanga won praise for killing and capturing many Kazakhs, soon he too would fall victim to the emperor's unrealistic expectations about steppe warfare when he failed to capture Amursana. The approach of winter forced the emperor to agree reluctantly to withdraw troops. Ablai, the Kazakh chief, while denying that he knew Amursana's location, also suspiciously refused to provide evidence about him. With thunderous threats, the emperor told Ablai that if he did not turn over Amursana, the Great Army would return the next spring and completely exterminate his tribe. Dardanga nevertheless had no choice but to withdraw without success.

Dardanga was showing signs of negligence in the emperor's eyes. He had sent an envoy to negotiate with Ablai, keeping two Kazakhs behind as hostages, but the Kazakhs escaped because they were not guarded. In November 1756 Dardanga and commander Hadaha gathered their armies together for the winter but failed to coordinate their responsibilities. They lost their double-eye peacock feathers for this error. The emperor had shrewdly assessed another motive for Tseleng's failure to advance: if he was unable to pursue Amursana, he was more likely to be pardoned than if he vigorously pursued him and failed to capture him. This was exactly Dardanga's fate.

Blaming the cowardice of Yubao and Tseleng for Amursana's escape allowed the court to avoid confronting the constraints of the steppe. In the court's view, sheer human will could overcome the most difficult conditions, if only the right man were in charge. Failure was due to "barriers in the mind," not material constraints.[61] Even the yearly winter withdrawal of troops, demanded by the severe weather, was accepted with great reluctance. Each year the emperor, hoping to finish off the enemy, was tempted to extend the campaign dangerously far into winter.

In the end, Dardanga and Hadaha proved no more successful than their predecessors. Both failed to capture Amursana, and they let the treacherous Ablai escape. The enemy, the emperor charged, had "made fools of them." Dardanga's army, it turned out, had been only one or two *li* away from Amursana, a "cart ride away," but unaware of Amursana's location, Dardanga had instead waited for the Kazakh Ablai to bring Amursana forward. Hadaha had in fact met Ablai but failed to arrest him for his treachery. Amursana's nephew, now captured and under interrogation, revealed that the two generals had narrowly missed an opportunity to capture Amursana himself. But Amursana, knowing of the planned withdrawal of the armies for the winter, had simply followed them on their retreat back to his old haunts. He, in fact, was able to move much more quickly about the steppe than the heavily armed Qing troops. Ablai had submitted when faced with a force of only thirty men. With a little effort he could have been caught a year before. And, like their predecessors, the two commanders had failed to coordinate their actions. Dardanga, denounced as "hopelessly incompetent" *(hutu wuneng),* and Hadaha, who was criticized for avoiding all decisions, were ordered to face a military court-martial and blasted as the "shame of the Manchus." They were sent to Rehe to "wear armor" and redeem themselves.[62]

For the next year's campaign, the emperor was determined to advance troops much more deeply into more "remote, precipitous" parts of Kazakh territory than Tseleng had been willing to enter.[63] The failure of Tseleng and Yubao to take responsibility must not be repeated by the new commanders, Jaohûi (Ch. Zhao Hui) and Fude. They must cooperate with each other.

The year 1756 had opened with two concurrent rebellions against Qing authority by two of the most influential Mongol leaders: Amursana and Chingünjav. Both threatened to mobilize more supporters. Amursana at first claimed that he only wanted to return to the peace established under Galdan Tseren, denying any intention to rebel. His disingenuous appeal to precedent aimed to win over more Mongol allies. A smallpox epidemic in Bortala, Amursana's headquarters, forced him to flee to Kazakh territory and seek allies there. Qianlong ordered a full-scale search, while inflicting a scorched earth policy on Amursana's abandoned pastures. His greatest concern was the potential alliance of Amursana with the Kazakhs, the most remote of the nomadic tribes known to the emperor, and the most difficult to intimidate. The Qing ruler preferred to win them over as allies, but he offered them both the carrot and the stick. If the Kazakhs captured and returned Amursana, he would give them large rewards, but if they did not, he would send a great army to wipe them out.

By the winter of 1756–57 the emperor was a frustrated man. His armies, backed by a huge supply train reaching from the plains of North China to the steppes of Xinjiang, had harried Amursana's men into the mountains of the Kazakh steppe, broken them up into small bands, and captured or accepted the surrender of thousands of his followers, yet the defiant man who would be Khan still survived. Faced with two rebellions in critical regions, and furious at Amursana's betrayal, Qianlong rejected all leniency. He now ordered the massacre of all Zungharian captives: "Show no mercy at all to these rebels. Only the old and weak should be saved. Our previous military campaigns were too lenient. If we act as before, our troops will withdraw, and further trouble will occur." In another edict he declared: "If a rebel is captured and his followers wish to surrender, he must personally come to the garrison, prostrate himself before the commander, and request surrender. If he only sends someone to request submission, it is undoubtedly a trick. Tell Tsengünjav to massacre these crafty Zunghars. Do not believe what they say."[64]

He clearly had to overcome resistance from local military commanders, since he repeated his order several times, using the term *jiao* (extermination) over and over again. General Jaohûi was praised and awarded high rank for reporting massacres, as was Tangkelu, who captured the Khoit Chebudeng Dorji and "exterminated his followers." Tangkelu was allowed to incorporate his enemy's families and cattle into his own tribe. Other commanders, like Hadaha and Agui, however, were punished for merely occupying Zunghar pastures while allowing the people to escape. The remnants of Amursana's shattered bands were to be tracked down even into Russian territory and eliminated.[65]

The emperor deliberately targeted young and able men in order to destroy the Zunghars as a people. When Chebudengzhabu captured a group of Khoits, whom he was going to award to the loyal Khalkhas, the emperor instructed him to "take the young and strong and massacre them," and award only the women as booty.[66] Even some Zunghar youths who surrendered after the defeat of their elders could not be spared, since "their ancestors had been chieftains." They had to be executed or made bondservants of the conquering soldiers.[67] In 1756 the court had recommended the use of food relief to win over the Zunghar people by giving them grain, tea, and animals if they surrendered. Now the emperor implicitly recommended the use of starvation tactics, commenting that it would be "easy to exterminate rebels because they had run out of provisions."[68] Old men, children, and women were to be spared and sent as bondservants to other Mongol tribes and Manchu bannermen, but they would lose their tribal identity; they could not preserve their tribal *(otoq)* names or their titles, such as *zaisang* (minister or clan leader). Reliable Mongols designated to supervise these remnants took instead the Chinese official titles *zongguan* and *fuzongguan*.[69]

After these edicts were issued, reports came in of Qing detachments pursuing rebel bands and slaughtering them by the thousands. Imperial orders insisted that the captives must not be treated according to the usual rules for dealing with bandits: "These are not ordinary cattle rustlers. They must all be captured and executed. Why should we have to distinguish leader and follower? These tribes have many bandits; if we do not completely exterminate them [*jiaomie jingjin*], it will be no good for the Mongols and merchants." The goal was not merely to put down a rebellion but to "cut off the roots" of the Zunghar resistance.[70] Russian governors in Siberia heard that Manchu troops had massacred men, women, and children, sparing no one.[71]

Some signs of a more lenient policy appeared after mid-1757. By this time, Amursana's effort to unify the Zunghars had clearly failed, and no longer posed a major threat. The imminent rebellion by the Khojas of Turkestan meant that the Qing had to avoid driving other Zunghars over to the side of the Turkestanis.[72] Large numbers of Zunghars were submitting to the Qing, who regarded them with great suspicion. Those who appeared "completely trustworthy" were allowed to move to interior pastures after September 1757, but the slightest indication of disloyalty justified their extermination. The emperor clarified that he "did not formerly have the intention [of eliminating the Zunghars]. It was only because they repeatedly submitted and then rebelled that we had to wipe them out."[73] Nevertheless, Generals Jaohûi and Shuhede in the same month received criticism for failing to show sufficient zeal in exterminating the rebels. They had apparently shrunk back from wholesale slaughter, despite continual prodding.

By contrast to his policy toward the Zunghars, the emperor hesitated to eliminate completely the Tibetan lamas of the Yellow Teaching. He was angry with the lamas, whom he regarded as inciting the Mongols to resistance, and he had ordered Tsengünjav to exterminate those he found upon his arrival at Ili. But by July 1757, four Zunghar *otoq* had surrendered, and the court feared that a massacre of the lamas would unnecessarily alarm the Zunghars. The rebel Nima tried to stir up the rest of the Mongols by saying that the Qing "was wiping out the Yellow Teaching." Soon, declared the emperor, all lamas connected with his revolt could be killed, but for the time being it was better to temporize.[74] Such tactical retreats from all-out massacre in the interests of winning over possible Mongolian support did not fundamentally alter the Qing's basic aim, which was to eliminate all prospects for autonomous Mongolian resistance.

This deliberate use of massacre has been almost completely ignored by modern scholars.[75] The massacre policy was a clear break from previous Qing methods of managing relations with the Mongols. Until this time, the

Qing rulers had primarily adopted the time-honored diplomacy of "using barbarians to fight barbarians" by alternately supporting different factions of nomads against one another, or else they executed individual ringleaders of rebellions. But they had never attempted ethnic genocide before.[76] With this policy, the Qing succeeded in imposing a "final solution" to China's northwest frontier problems, which lasted for about a century. The Zunghars disappeared as a state and as a people, and the Zungharian steppe was almost completely depopulated. In his history of the Qing military campaigns, the *Shengwuji*, Wei Yuan, who estimated the total population of the Zunghars at 600,000 people, stated, "Of several hundred thousand households, 40 percent died of smallpox, 20 percent fled to the Russians and Kazakhs, and 30 percent were killed by the Great Army. [The remaining] women and children were given as [servants] to others . . . For several thousand *li* there was not one single Zungharian tent."[77] Zungharia was left as a blank social space, to be refilled by a state-sponsored settlement movement of millions of Han Chinese peasants, Manchu bannermen, Turkestani oasis settlers, Hui, and others.

The use of massacre for ethnic extermination was also atypical of Qing policy either before or after this time. The term "extermination" *(jiao)* had been used before to describe the appropriate action toward non-Han barbarians. Manchus, of course, did use terror tactics against Chinese cities in the lower Yangzi "pour encourager les autres." The ten-day massacre at Yangzhou in 1645 is the most notorious example.[78] Later suppressions of domestic rebellions produced many capital sentences, but only after interrogation and judicial proceedings. The theory of distinguishing between ringleaders and "coerced followers" aimed to minimize the number of executions. Many were pardoned after their sentences were reviewed at the autumn assizes.

Wholesale massacre of an enemy tribe was more typical of Central Eurasian practice. Even so, most of the killing was directed only at the young male warriors who fought back. If a tribe surrendered, its men were usually incorporated into the victor's tribe, because nomadic conquerors needed warriors. Many served as slaves or bondservants, but they might keep their tribal identity or intermarry with the victors. Seldom did one tribe aim to exterminate all the productive labor of its enemy. In the sparsely populated steppe, fighting men were scarce—and valuable. Women, children, and older men were not eliminated after conquest.

The Zunghars, however, could not be treated like other domestic rebels (especially Han rebels). The Qing army did not need more Central Asian warriors; it already contained Manchus and docile Khalkha Mongols. The Zunghars were no longer out of reach, protected by logistical limits.

Kangxi had treated Zunghar recalcitrance as the product of his personal struggle with the Zunghar leader, Galdan, and focused all his efforts on eliminating him. He personally relished the idea of man-to-man combat (at a distance) in the steppe. Qianlong, by contrast, stayed in the capital directing his field generals from afar. And he came up with a classically neat bureaucratic solution to the unruly steppe: eliminate everything that moved, and create a blank slate.

The Zunghars were the one Central Eurasian people who, unlike the Eastern Mongols, had ferociously insisted on preserving their autonomy from Chinese rule. The Eastern Mongols had given the Qing the right to allocate their pasturelands, distribute relief grain, settle their disputes, and levy troops and animals from them for its wars. They paid the cost of allowing penetration of their territory by Chinese settlers, corruption of the aristocracy by Han merchants and decimation by smallpox and other diseases introduced by Han settlers, but they survived as a people to become an independent state in the twentieth century. The Zunghars, by contrast, completely disappeared. Only folk memory kept their struggle alive.

In the final massacre, Qianlong bared his teeth. He had called himself a ruler who showed equal favor to all, aiming to encompass a variety of different peoples under one harmonious realm. But those who resisted the imperial embrace faced extermination. The emperor's edicts from this period expose the tension within the mid-Qing between the ideal of benevolence and the reality of repression. Taking a remarkably defensive tone, he defended himself against unnamed critics who regarded the campaigns as wasteful and cruel. Asserting that "the constant nature of the Zunghars is greed, cruelty, craftiness, and the love of disorder," he nevertheless insisted that "the Zunghar masses are not basically strong willed," and that it would take only a few days to quell them:

> Yet ignorant outside observers have raised irresponsible criticism. They say this campaign should not have been begun, since, once it started, it only caused more turmoil; wouldn't it have been better not to start at all? They really don't realize that the Zunghars have caused trouble on the northwestern border for over four hundred years. My grandfather and father solidified the frontier against Galdan and Galdan Tseren. Their repeated military expeditions made a long-lasting peace on the frontier, and I have inherited this project from Heaven. Now these barbarian tribes have become disaffected and their minds have gone astray, offering an opportunity for revolt. How can I sit back and let them be lost? Would I not be laughed at by later generations? How could I face my grandfather and father in the afterlife?

> This is why we made careful plans and toiled to do the unavoidable; it
> was not out of a temporary love of glory, but to prevent border unrest
> and diligently make long-term plans.[79]

The emperor showed concern about his personal dignity and later reputation, trying to ensure that others would give him credit for long-term
strategic planning and not merely a love of glory. He also defended his policy of extermination as a defense of "our Khalkha tribes" against violent
attack, arguing that he had intended to use only the classic "loose reign"
(jimi) policy that allowed border tribes a great deal of autonomy, but the
"ignorant" followers of Amursana had brought extermination on themselves by refusing to accept peace, contrary to Qianlong's "basic sentiments" of generosity *(benhuai)*. Finally, he argued that the great victories
on the frontier could not be thrown away by retreating and allowing the
nomad threat to revive. In addition, he noted, the total cost had been only
17 million taels, much less than the 50 to 60 million taels spent by Yongzheng. He concluded by proclaiming that he had dedicated himself to the
campaign "not because I abandon ease and love toil, but because the situation demands it," because "the superior man daily concerns himself with
the people's happiness and sufferings."[80] In this extended defense of his military project, the emperor pleaded for sympathy from those who saw no
use in expensive campaigns on remote frontiers. By placing himself in the
lineage of conquerors since Kangxi, and emphasizing their ever-expanding
achievements, he promised to bring an end to a security issue that had
lasted for centuries. And he justified the complete elimination of those who
stood in the way.

By October 1756 Qing troops had fought and defeated the Kazakh supporters of Amursana and captured one of his *zaisang*. Amursana fled farther west, still protected by the Kazakh Ablai. By November, winter cold
forced the troops to withdraw and wait until the next year. The Kazakh attitude toward Amursana had been ambiguous. On the one hand, Ablai offered tribute and promised to capture Amursana, but, on the other, captured *zaisang* of Amursana reported that Ablai was giving support to the
rebels.[81] Ablai sheltered Amursana briefly in the summer of 1756, and offered him a small number of men to resist the Qing, but soon expelled him
from Kazakh territory, realizing that he had little hope of victory. When
Ablai submitted to Jaohûi, he claimed that he had tried to capture Amursana, but Amursana had stolen his horses and escaped. He expressed gratitude for Qing aid and promised the submission of all the Kazakhs. Less
than a week later, the Kazakh Nima was captured, and other Kazakhs surrendered once they heard about Ablai's submission.

Deprived of all allies, Amursana now offered to submit to Russia if the Tsar would build a fortress for him between the Irtysh River and Lake Zaisang to serve as a base for attacks on the Qing. The Tsar refused to take any action that might lead to war and offered to protect Amursana only if he agreed to resettle on the Volga along with the other Kalmyks.

In early 1757 Jaohûi reported that Amursana had turned back from the Russian border. Not knowing of Chingünjav's fate, he turned east in a desperate effort to join forces. The emperor thought that now was the perfect opportunity to capture Amursana, despite the winter cold, and that both armies should make every effort to arrest him. He assumed that Amursana could not escape to Russia because of the treaty agreements. The Qing armies divided into four units to track Amursana down. In July, Amursana turned up at the Russian fortress of Semipalatinsk and surrendered to the Russian commander. Discovering that he was fatally ill with smallpox, the Russians quickly sent him to Tobolsk, where he was kept quarantined outside the city. He died there on September 21, 1757, at the age of thirty-five.

The Russians concealed the facts of Amursana's flight and death, hoping to derive leverage from possession of his body. They told Qing envoys that Amursana had drowned while crossing the Irtysh River.[82] Qing officials dredged the river for a month but found nothing. Their suspicions grew. By October 1757 Jaohûi was certain that Amursana had fled to Russian territory and that the Russians had lied about his death. They had, in fact, already buried him in Selenginsk. Repeated insistence by the Chinese on Amursana's return brought no results until February 1758, when the Russian representative admitted that Amursana had died of smallpox and invited the Chinese to view the body at the Selenginsk fortress or at the Kiakhta border.

Even though Amursana's body might have rotted by this time and become unidentifiable, and the Russians made no mention of other followers of Amursana captured with him, Qianlong decided to send two representatives to the border not just to view the body but to reclaim it. He was confident enough to announce Amursana's death two days after receiving the Russian report. But the Russians refused to return the body. The emperor, however, insisted on obtaining Amursana's corpse, saying: "The state only needs to capture Amursana. When he has died, and his body is retrieved, the entire Zunghar affair can be called a success."[83]

Wrangling with the Russians over the return of Amursana's body caused a major diplomatic conflict for many years. The Qing repeatedly sent letters to St. Petersburg demanding the corpse, while the Russians replied that there was no need to disturb their friendly relations over the issue of a few rotten bones. The Qing put pressure on the Russians by placing their

Orthodox monks in Beijing under house arrest, forbidding them to have any contact with Han people, and threatening to cut off trade. The Qing claimed that under the terms of the Kiakhta treaty of 1727, Russia was obliged to return any refugees who fled across the border; but from the Russian point of view, since the border with Zungharia had not been determined by 1727, Amursana and his followers did not qualify as "refugees." Russian intransigence also derived from a concern to protect the imperial image in the eyes of other Central Asian peoples, who would be watching carefully the relative balance of power between the two empires. Apparently, the emperor never got Amursana's body back.[84] Unlike his grandfather, Kangxi, who could triumphantly display Galdan's head and crush his ashes on the military parade ground in Beijing, Qianlong had to settle for an inconclusive victory.

Chinese historians now claim that the Russians aimed to use Amursana, dead or alive, to expand their control over Zungharia. They blame the Amursana rebellion mainly on the Russians, who had tried to split apart the "naturally united" Chinese Mongolian nationality. In their view, as a divisive influence on the Mongolians, Amursana deserves a "totally negative historical significance." Russian historians, by contrast, view Amursana's actions as a valiant effort of the Mongolian people to resist the aggressive expansionism of the Qing in Central Asia.[85] Once again, the two nationalisms mirror each other. Each ascribes essential unity to the Mongolian people and blames conflict on intrigue by outsiders. Chinese charges of Russian aggression are countered by Russian charges of Qing expansionism. Just as the fate of the last Zunghar opponent of the Qing remained unclear even after his death, so do historical interpretations of the last days of his struggle continue without resolution.

The Conquest of Turkestan

Qing wars did not end with the destruction of the Zunghar state. One more set of campaigns penetrated even further into Central Eurasia, to the oases south of the Tianshan range. I can describe these campaigns only briefly, but they put the capstone on the empire's relentless expansion, bringing a large proportion of the Turkic oasis-dwelling population under Qing control.[86]

The oases of southern Turkestan had been under the leadership of the Makhdūmzāda Khojas, saintly families claiming descent from famous *shaykhs* of a Sufi brotherhood of the fifteenth and sixteenth centuries. The Zunghar rulers confirmed their power over Turkestan and relied on them heavily for food supplies but kept them closely watched. Tsewang Rabdan had declared Khoja Mahmut the leader of all Turkestan, but Galdan Tseren kept him imprisoned in Ili. After Mahmut's death and the first invasion of Ili in 1755, Qing troops released his sons, Burhān ad-Dīn (Ch. Bulanidun) and Khoja Jihān (Ch. Huojizhan), sending Burhān ad-Dīn, known as the Elder Khoja, back to Yarkand but keeping the Younger Khoja, Jihān, in Ili. Khoja Jihān then joined Amursana's revolt, but fled from the Qing army to Yarkand, where he urged his elder brother to rebel, warning:

> If we follow the court's orders to submit, we will be imprisoned in Beijing, just like the Zunghars. My ancestors for generations were under others' control. Now, by chance, the powerful [Zunghar] state has collapsed, and no one is pressing on us. If we do not seize this opportunity to create an independent state, we will be slaves forever. That would be disaster. The Central Kingdom has now taken Zungharia, but has not yet decided its policy [toward Turkestan]. Its troops cannot come here, and if they do come, we will resist them until their supplies are exhausted. We can break them without fighting.[87]

Khoja Jihān evoked the same drive for autonomy and reliance on remoteness and difficulty of obtaining supplies as did the Zunghar state builders. His strategic calculations were almost correct. His brother agreed and began a revolt by local *begs* and *ahunds* (Islamic notables), who collected a large army and fortified themselves in Kucha, the key town giving access to the region from the east. Qianlong appointed Yarhashan General in Chief of Repressing Rebellion (Jingni Jiangjun), giving him ten thousand men to besiege Kucha. Expecting an easy victory, Yarhashan made no preparations against a counterattack, preferring to spend his time playing chess. The Turki army then burst out of Kucha on the evening of July 28, 1758, and fled west. The emperor had Yarhashan called back and executed.

The Khojas, however, found no support in Aksu, where the local *beg* had already helped the Qing to capture Dawaci, so they moved farther west, occupying Yarkand and Kashgar. Building walls and clearing the fields, they devastated the surrounding land, driving the local population into the city, so as to leave nothing for an advancing army. Now Qianlong sent his best frontier general, Jaohûi, who had completed the suppression of the Zunghars, south to the edges of east Turkestan to besiege the rebels. But at the battle of Blackwater Camp, just outside Yarkand, the Younger Khoja's army, outnumbering Jaohûi's forces by four to one, surrounded the Qing forces and placed them under a desperate siege that lasted for three months. Luckily for the Qing troops, they could dig for water, and they discovered underground grain storage pits, so they were able to endure steady attacks until a relief column arrived from Ürümchi.

Meanwhile, the Kirghiz attacked Kashgar, the stronghold of the Elder Khoja. Khwush Kipäk, the former *hakim beg* of Kashgar, advised Jaohûi on the best invasion routes.[88] Both Khojas fled to Badakhshan, where they were captured and killed. Once again, the Qing generals wrangled long and hard with Sultan Shah (Ch. Suoledansha), the ruler of Badakhshan, to retrieve the two rebels' corpses.[89] After further threats, they finally obtained the head of Khoja Jihān and the corpse of Burhān ad-Dīn for transport back to Beijing. On December 13, 1759, the Qianlong emperor proclaimed the completion of the Zunghar campaigns, notifying "all subjects of the Center and Peripheries" that with the "entry onto the registers" *(ru bantu)* of Zungharia and the retrieval of the heads of the rebel Khojas, he had achieved "eternal peace and security on the borders."[90]

The campaigns in Turkestan mimicked in brief the century-long Zungharian adventure. The Khojas had sought to create an autonomous, united state, protected from Qing power by its remoteness, but they were undone by division between the oasis communities and the astounding logistical achievements of the Qing quartermasters. Once again, contrary to modern nationalists, there was no unified "Uighur" nationality either fighting against the Qing state or yearning to be incorporated within it. Despite the Qing's rapid success, some generals, like Yarhashan, demonstrated extreme incompetence; Jaohûi's travails, however, resulted from bad luck rather than bad leadership. The armies' composition was truly multiethnic, including Mongol and Manchu generals, Han supply commanders, and even some surrendered Zunghar troops. Although Qing forces now had long experience with distant frontier campaigns, the emperor again displayed his "anxiousness to declare victory and retreat."[91] He still tried to minimize costs on the frontier, even at the risk of allowing small forces to be nearly wiped out. Perhaps the easy victory over Amursana allowed the emperor and his commanders to think that they would have just as easy a time in the very different conditions of the region south of the Tianshan.

One final uprising indicated that the Central Eurasian borders were still not entirely secure, and foreshadowed the greater troubles to come in the nineteenth century.[92] In 1765 the town of Ush, a city of nearly 1 million people in the Southern March of Altishahr, rebelled. The previous *beg* had captured Dawaci and refused aid to the two Khojas, but the emperor, still suspicious of his loyalty, had replaced his administration with carpetbaggers from Hami. The new *beg* extorted grain and violated the wives of the former *beg,* while the drunken military commander did nothing to stop him. Two hundred and forty Turkestani porters began a revolt to reject oppressive corvée duties. They gathered local support. Two to three thousand rebels did battle with local forces, defeating reinforcements sent from Aksu, 100 kilometers to the east. Fearing that the *beg* of Kokand might intervene, the emperor ordered larger detachments from Ili and Kashgar. Exiled convicts were drafted to scale the walls of the besieged city. The Ili and Kashgar commanders failed to cooperate with each other, dragging out the siege and allowing many rebels to escape, but the city finally surrendered in September 1765. The Qing commanders killed over three hundred rebels and deported tens of thousands to Ili. They then rebuilt the city from scratch, imposing strict controls on abuses by *hakim begs* and attempting to enforce tight segregation of the Han and Muslim populations.

The Ush rebels, like Chingünjav's Mongols, resented both the Qing labor levies and the presence of abusive Han officials and exploiting merchants. Both attempted to garner wider support, but neighboring towns or tribes generally refused to cooperate. Harsh repression brought tighter controls in both Mongolia and Xinjiang, but unrest simmered in the latter. Drunken criminal exiles touched off a riot in Changji in 1768, and in the early nineteenth century, Jahangir brought in a new rebel army from the west. Opium smuggling from Kokand gave local officials the same problems with suppression campaigns that plagued their fellow officials on the south coast.[93] Turkestan joined the empire as a by-product of the Zunghar campaigns, but the elimination of the Zunghars did not by itself ensure firm control of the region.

The Return of the Torghuts

In the early nineteenth century Thomas De Quincey observed:

> There is no great event in modern history, or perhaps it may be said more broadly, none in all history, from its earliest records, less generally known, or more striking to the imagination, than the flight eastwards of a principal Tartar nation across the boundless steppes of Asia in the latter half of the last century . . . In the abruptness of its commencement, and the fierce velocity of its execution, we read the wild barbaric character of those who conducted the movement. In the unity of purpose connecting this myriad of wills, and in the blind but unerring aim at a mark so remote, there is something which recalls to the mind those almighty instincts that propel the migrations of the swallow and the leeming [*sic*], or the life-withering marches of the locust.[94]

Out of the epic Long March of the Torghut Mongols from the banks of the Volga back to their Mongolian homeland, De Quincey created a minor classic of English literature. As historical fiction, his account rivals the works of Sir Walter Scott in dramatic scenes, vivid characters, and melodramatic conflict. In fact, not all of De Quincey's account is made from whole cloth; the text he relied on, Benjamin Bergmann's *Nomadische Streifereien unter den Kalmuken,* relied in turn on oral Russian and Mongolian sources which are not found in the official documents. The complete history of the Torghuts, based on full use of Mongolian, Manchu, Russian, Chinese, and Western documents, has not yet been told, nor is there room to tell it here.[95] I can only highlight its significance for the evolving Qing imperial vision and the end of the last autonomous Mongolian tribe in Eurasia.

Modern Chinese historians describe the Torghut migration as the inevitable "return" of one of the empire's lost peoples to the benevolent embrace of the emperor, driven by Russian oppression. It is true that the Torghuts on the Volga suffered from Russian military demands and from encroachment by other settlers, but their incorporation into the Qing after their harrowing journey was by no means inevitable. In fact, some of the Torghuts, known as "Kalmyks," stayed behind in the area where they still live today, in an autonomous republic of Russia. And those who arrived on the Qing border in 1771 did not get a uniformly enthusiastic welcome. Michael Khodarkovsky has described in detail the experience of the Torghuts under Russian dominion. Here I will recount only the debates about their admission to the empire that took place when they first arrived on the Qing frontier. These debates reveal the initial uncertainty about the status of these migrant nomads, and the legacy of Qing, Russian, and Zunghar interactions in determining the decision to absorb these remnants of the "last known exodus of a nomadic people in the history of Asia."[96]

Kho Urlük (?–1644) had led his people out of western Mongolia in order to escape the turmoil of the early-seventeenth-century steppe and to find pastures where they could live freely. Although Tsar Ivan had conquered Astrakhan and Kazan', the Russian state had not yet established a strong grip on the lower Volga. Like the Don Cossacks, the Torghuts—or Kalmyks, as the Russians knew them—formed nearly autonomous communities under their own chiefs. Although they swore oaths of allegiance to the Tsar, they had more of the status of independent allies than of vassals. Under Ayuki Khan (1669–1724), their greatest leader, they expanded their control over a huge swath of territory of 300,000 to 400,000 square miles in the steppes north of the Caspian Sea.

They maintained contact with Mongolia and the Qing during this period. They sent tribute missions and were allowed to join "boiled tea" missions to Kokonor. In 1698 Arabjur, the son of Ayuki Khan (1669–1724), took five thousand men to Lhasa with Qing permission. Tulisen's embassy to Ayuki in 1712, ostensibly designed to facilitate the return of Arabjur, appeared to the Torghuts as a Qing effort to recruit support against Tsewang Rabdan, but the Torghuts refused to commit to an alliance. From time to time they explored the possibility of returning to their homeland, but as long as the Zunghars remained powerful, and at war with the Qing and the Kazakhs, conditions in the steppe were too unsettled to allow them to move. Over the seventeenth and eighteenth centuries, Russian administration gradually encroached on Torghut autonomy, with increasing demands for military service coupled with efforts to intervene in local administration. Russian penetration of the steppe was similar to the Qing move into Mongolia: in each case, Mongolian chiefs found themselves under growing constraints while Russian or Han Chinese settlers moved into their territory. The Russians did not have the rigidly bounded banner units of the Qing, leaving the Torghuts freer to move about, but they exacted substantial military service from their vassals. In this respect, the Torghuts were no different from the Cossacks and other mobile peoples settled on this steppe frontier.

The decision to leave the Volga in 1770 resulted from pressures building up on the community and a fortuitous opportunity. Khodarkovsky finds that "Russia's growing control of Kalmyk administrative affairs, its excessive demands for Kalmyk cavalry, the loss of prime pasture lands to expanding military and agricultural colonies, and fear of coercive settlement and coercion were among the critical factors contributing to the Kalmyks' decision to depart for Jungaria."[97] In 1762 Empress Catherine declared that the Khan could not freely select his advisory council but had to obtain the Tsar's approval. New demands for Kalmyk cavalry to serve in another war with the Ottomans in 1768 were the final straw. Catherine II arrogantly demanded 20,000 horsemen from the Kalmyk population of 41,523 tents, ignoring the Kalmyks' need to defend themselves from raids by neighboring Kazakhs and Kuban.[98] Only 10,000 Kalmyks joined the campaign in 1769, and they returned home in September, defying Russian commands, in order to tend their herds over the winter.

Internal rivalries for power also played a role. Tsebek Dorji Tayishi, the leading Kalmyk noble, thought he deserved the Khanate, but under Russian pressure the Kalmyks had chosen the young and irresolute Ubashi. To take revenge on the hated Russians, and in the hope of establishing his own power outside Russian territory, Tsebek Dorji planned the audacious escape, drawing Ubashi along with him. Tsebek Dorji addressed a crucial meeting of Kalmyk nobles, declaring:

In all respects, your rights are limited by the Russians. Not only do
their officials mistreat the Kalmyks, but also the government itself
seems to have the intention of turning these independent steppe people
into settled peasants. The banks of the Yaik are covered with Cossack
fortresses; the northern borders are settled by immigrant Germans,
and soon you will be torn away from the Don and Terek, the Kuma
and Volga, by other settlements; your nomadic life will be limited to
waterless regions, and your herds destroyed. You have no other choice
in the future except to bend your neck under the yoke of slavery, or to
quickly leave the Russian empire to escape your destruction. The decision you make will determine your fate.[99]

Ubashi Khan planned the mass exodus for early 1771, taking advantage
of the fact that not all the Russian soldiers had returned yet from the Ottoman campaign. He wanted to wait for the Volga to freeze so that the
Kalmyks on the west bank could join the main body, but was forced to
leave early when the Russian governor discovered his plan. On January
5, 1771, over 30,000 tents, or 150,000 to 170,000 people, set out for
Zungharia. Ubashi brought about three-quarters of the nomadic population with him. Although Ubashi told the Qing officials that the failure
of the river to freeze had forced him to leave 13,000 tents behind, those
who stayed back were mainly Derbet or Khoit tribesmen who disapproved
of the mass migration.[100] By June 1771 the emigrants had reached Lake
Balkash, eluding Russian pursuit but suffering great losses from winter
frosts, hunger, disease, and Kazakh raids. When they stopped there to re-
group, the Kazakhs surrounded them and inflicted devastating injuries on
their exhausted warriors and herds. By the time he contacted officials in Ili,
Ubashi had only 15,000 tents, or 70,000 people, left.[101]

In this epic Long March, Ubashi had lost at least 100,000 people, and his
dreams of free pastures had been crushed. As C. D. Barkman notes, "It is
quite clear that the Torghuts had not intended to surrender to the Chinese,
but had hoped to lead an independent existence in Dzungaria."[102] Only after their arrival in the old Ölöd pastures around Lake Balkash did they realize that the steppes had no room for them. Qing armies had eliminated the
Zunghar state and induced the Kazakhs to pay tribute, while Russian fortresses marked the border across Siberia. "The Kalmyks had escaped Russian tentacles only to be ensnared in Chinese ones."[103]

Yet the frontier commanders were most reluctant to allow these long-lost
nomads to cross the border. Manchu documents in the special archive discussing the Torghuts reveal considerable suspicion and resistance.[104] Iletu,
the Manchu commander at Khobdo, first recorded receiving a Russian re-

port of Torghut movements on June 14, 1771, indicating that the Kazakhs were blocking the Torghuts' efforts to reach the border. The Russians had demanded that the Qing not accept these "rogues and traitors," Russian subjects who had deserted military service.[105] Under the Kiakhta treaty, refugees, deserters, or criminals who crossed the border were to be returned. Iletu was in a quandary. The Torghuts could not be forcibly returned to Russia without causing a new war, but he saw no way to settle them near Ili. He proposed to send them much farther east, into Chahar territory. The emperor quickly denounced Iletu for his ignorance of frontier conditions: he found no problem in mixing the Torghuts with other Ölöd tribes in western Mongolia. He dispatched Shuhede, who had been suppressing the rebellion in Ush, to Ili to take charge, limiting Iletu's role to managing local defense.[106]

The Kazakhs, in the midst of war with the Torghuts, also called for aid. They exaggerated Torghut strength, putting it at eighty to ninety thousand tents, and as tributaries of the Qing, they expected military support, since the Torghuts had plundered tens of thousands of their animals. Cleverly invoking the recent war with the Khojas, Ablai urged quick military action so that the rebels could not flee into the distant steppe, where a large force would be needed to track them down.[107]

A further issue was the presence of Prince Shereng (Ch. Sheleng) among the Torghut migrants. Shereng had joined Amursana's revolt then fled into exile. Now he was returning as one of the leaders of the Torghut *ulus* alongside Ubashi Khan. He claimed to want to submit, but could he be trusted? Iletu was skeptical; he thought that Shereng was refusing to admit to his crimes. Qianlong brushed aside such fears, concluding that Shereng's surrender was sincere.

The emperor had concluded remarkably quickly that the Torghuts, as the final remnant of the Zunghars, who were now included as "our Mongols," deserved refuge within the empire. He rejected Russian demands on the grounds that the Russians had refused to return Shereng and other supporters of Amursana.[108] The Torghuts were not refugees but subjects of the Qing, even though they had left over a century earlier. Qianlong projected the militarily established boundaries of the Qing backward, retrospectively including within their embrace all the Mongols of times past. He was aware that "if Ili were an empty land, the Torghuts might want to recover their old pastures," but now that it was filled with troops and walled cities, they knew they had no choice but to settle in districts determined by the Qing.[109] He rejected Kazakh requests for aid, advising Ablai not to "fish for profit" in turbulent waters. Although he regarded 90 percent of the Torghuts as loyal, he admitted the need to guard against disruption by the disloyal 10 percent. When Commander Batu Jirgelang wanted to levy twenty thousand troops to guard the borders, however, the emperor rejected this request as excessive. He thought that fewer than ten thousand would be needed. Remembering Chingünjav's rebellion, the frontier commanders were especially worried about demanding fighters from the Khalkhas, so the emperor stopped all levies of troops from them.[110]

By July 29, 1771, Qianlong had overridden the objections and determined to settle the Torghuts within the empire. He ordered officials to schedule an audience for Ubashi at Chengde, and to search for lands to settle them. He had 200,000 taels of silver sent out from Anxi, Barköl, and Ürümchi for relief supplies and travel costs. Further arguments in the Torghuts' favor derived from their feeling of alienation in Orthodox Christian Russia, where, the emperor claimed, they had not been allowed to send missions to Tibet. By contrast, the Qing would permit the Torghuts to send *aocha* missions to Tibet whenever they chose, after notifying the Lifanyuan. When the Zunghars had had an independent state, control of *aocha* missions had been a key tool for limiting their access to Lhasa; now, it served to lure the Torghuts closer to the interior and away from the uncertain border. Now that Tibet had "entered the registers" *(ru bantu)*, in the Qing view, the Yellow Teaching could bind the Mongols closer to the empire instead of alienating them from it.[111]

Although the frontier officials followed the emperor's orders, not all of them were convinced. Qishiyi's account of frontier affairs, written in 1777, displays a deeply skeptical view of the loyalty of the Torghuts. His perspective preserved a potent alternative to the benevolent imperial gaze, one based more firmly on local experience of the turbulent frontier than on the soothing banalities uttered in the capital. I shall discuss his views later.

At least three commemorative stelae celebrated the return of the Torghuts: one in Ili and two at the entrance to the miniature Potala Palace in Chengde, the court's summer villa north of Beijing.[112] The two at Potala were written in four languages—Manchu, Chinese, Tibetan, and Mongolian—although Manchu appears to have been the primary language of the text. In the sycophantic but accurate words of Yu Minzhong, Hanlin scholar and intimate adviser of the emperor and editor of his poems, "His Majesty has discovered the difficult art of including many facts in very few words, and of giving to these few words an extremely broad and deep meaning."[113] The inscription, titled "Record of the Return to Obedience of the Entire Torghut Tribe" (Turhute Quanbu Guishunji), indeed summarizes concisely the story of the arrival of the Torghuts on the border and their acceptance by the emperor in the face of opposition. According to Yu, the emperor wrote the text in little more than fifteen minutes, but he brilliantly captured the essence of the event. The inscription frankly discusses the suspicions about the rebel Shereng, the frontier commanders' demands for more troops, and the emperor's confidence that the Torghuts could do no harm if they were given supplies and carefully watched. The text justifies the unexpected and completely voluntary "return of the Torghuts to submission" (Ch. *guishun*, Ma. *jihe bahaha*) as a clear sign of Heaven's will favoring the benevolent emperor. Later I discuss in detail what these and other stelae reveal about the empire's sense of its historical position. They put the public seal of completion on the entire great project that had begun with Kangxi's Galdan wars. Kangxi's grandson could now claim convincingly that the "Western Regions have been fixed and will flourish." He expected perpetual peace on the frontiers, because "of all the Mongolian tribes there are none who are not the Great Qing's subjects."[114]

The return of the Torghuts was, as the Russians would put it, the final "gathering of peoples" under the all-encompassing Qing embrace. It was a second ending to the millennial struggle of the settled empire with the steppe. One people had been eliminated; another had been resuscitated and returned to the fold. After extermination came revival, a satisfying conclusion for the imperial project. Nationalists in the future would constantly invoke the trope of "return" *(gui)* as the metaphor describing the unification of peoples under the new nation-state. The concept of history projected as a cycle of exodus and return underpinned the imperial and nationalist states' claims to legitimate rule over the multiple peoples under their domination.

Unlike the imperial image, the Torghuts themselves did not prosper in the long run. Ubashi enjoyed a sumptuous banquet at his audience at Chengde, received many gifts from the emperor, and kept his title of Khan, but he was no longer in charge of his people. They were split up into ten banners in four leagues dispersed across hundreds of kilometers in northern Xinjiang, in order to make sure that these Mongols would never unite to challenge the empire.[115] Two banners under Shereng were settled near Khobdo, and four others south of Karashahr. Qing officials forced many of them to take up farming so as to prevent them from increasing their numbers. Qishiyi in 1777 found that many of the men had turned to banditry and the women to prostitution.

In hindsight, which group made the best choice: those who left the Volga, or those who stayed behind? Did the Torghuts really gain greater "freedom to lead their nomadic life, to preserve their customs, and to practice the Buddhist religion than their brethren on the Volga?"[116] By 1947 the resettled Torghuts in China numbered about 57,000, but under the People's Republic they disappeared as an ethnic group into the general Mongol nationality.[117] By contrast, the 13,000 Kalmyks who remained now have their own autonomous republic within Russia, with a population of 300,000 in 2004.[118] We could debate the wisdom of their choice, but it is clear that when these last free nomads came under domination from the great agrarian empires that surrounded them, the steppe ended, and a great chapter in world history closed.

PART THREE

The Economic Basis of Empire

8

Cannons on Camelback:
Ecological Structures and
Economic Conjunctures

As we have seen, logistical limits repeatedly tied the hands of the Qing generals. At Ulan Butong, for example, if Fiyanggû had not fortuitously run into Galdan's retreating army, his men would certainly have starved. The vast distances, barren deserts, and low-yielding lands of the frontier protected the nomads while blocking Chinese dynasties from projecting power into the region.[1]

Yet nomads also faced supply constraints. Although they, unlike Chinese armies, could support themselves on the grasslands, their herds died when severe winter storms covered the grasses with snow. The grasslands also limited the size and mobility of large nomad armies, which depended on quick forays and retreats, avoiding lengthy, static defense. As Galdan learned at Ulan Butong, battles near the Qing capital brought disaster, but he could still escape westward. Kangxi showed in his later campaigns, however, that he could lead troops all the way to the Selengge and Tula rivers, near the heartland of Mongol power. The nomads were no longer protected by distance. The millennia-long structural limits on Chinese power had begun to break down.

Strategic considerations drove both sides to alter the natural environment. Just as the Qing began to penetrate the northwest, the Zunghars, too, began to exploit their own territory. Most accounts of the development of Xinjiang ignore this crucial shift from a pastoral to a settled economy, but like so many of their predecessors, the Zunghars built their state by combining pastoral, agrarian, commercial, and mineral resources.

Batur Hongtaiji had founded a capital near Kibaksarai (Kobuk Saur), surrounded by cultivated fields.[2] In 1644 he built three brick cities, including monasteries, and asked the Tsar for chickens, pigs, hogs, carpenters, stonemasons, and merchants. Cut off from China and eastern Mongolia, he depended on Turkestan and Russia for grain and labor. "Bukharans" (war captives from Turkestan) served as agricultural laborers and as the key Central Asian trading links.[3] Caravans heading for Moscow profited from trade until the Russians stopped them in 1647. In the 1670s Sengge expanded the use of Russians for trade and of captive Turkestanis to cultivate fields. Zunghar troops forced the Russians to trade with them before allowing them access to salt lakes.[4] Galdan added trading missions to Beijing after restoring diplomatic ties in 1677. Twice a year he sent tribute missions to exchange furs and horses for silk, cotton textiles, and money. In 1683 the Qing cut them back in size from thousands of men to only two hundred, forcing the rest to trade at the border. Beijing's limitation of trading missions was one of the grievances that incited Galdan to attack the Khalkhas in 1688. Galdan believed, with reason, that Beijing aimed to win over the Khalkhas by favoring them with closer commercial ties.

Galdan the State Builder

The Ming loyalist statecraft scholar Liang Fen investigated Galdan's early efforts to build his economic base.[5] Based on nearly a decade of travel in the northwest, his book, *Qinbian Jilue* (An account of the northwest frontier), written about 1687, describes how Galdan obtained minerals and gunpowder for his army: "[Galdan's] wealth and population dominated the Western Regions . . . [He] extracted oil from sand, baked earth to make sulfur, and used sulfuric acid to make saltpeter, white as snow. Copper, lead, and fine steel came from the ground. Rocks by the water's edge produced gold and pearls: [there were so many that] they put them aside and did not use them. No one could surpass them in swift horses and numbers of barbarian riders." (As this passage indicates, he seems to have learned the technology of Persian steel refining from his contacts with east Turkestan.)

Liang Fen also notes:

[Galdan] did not obtain military supplies from distant places, because he was very clever at making high-quality weapons himself. He made armor with small links of chain mail, as light as cloth. If an arrow could pierce it, he had the armourer killed. He also sent emissaries to the Huihui [including Russians and Turkestanis], to teach him the use

Cannons carried on camelback. Although cannon were difficult to carry and of limited value in battle, both the Qing and the Zunghar armies highly valued these weapons and employed foreign experts to cast them.

of gunpowder weaponry and battle tactics, using first fowling pieces, then archery and swordsmanship. He ordered his soldiers to carry fowling pieces, short swords, bows and arrows, and knives around their waists. He loaded his cannon on camels. People who heard their thunderous roar near and far submitted.[6]

The cannons on camelback show that Galdan had transcended raiding, supplying his army with heavy weaponry designed for permanent conquest. He conquered Turkestan and Russian territories by adding overpowering military might to the mobility of a nomadic army. According to Liang Fen, Galdan also established a rudimentary taxation system by delegating a traveling inspector to exact payments of horses, oxen, and sheep from frontier tribes, and to keep careful track of income and expenses. This man, who "represented Galdan's eyes and ears . . . gathered up people and goods in his net."[7]

To ensure regular income, Galdan demanded corvée labor from one-

Table 8.1   Trade between Zungharia and Siberia (via Yamysh and Semipalatinsk to Tobolsk) (rubles)

Year	Exports from Zungharia	Imports to Zungharia
1724	3,633	4,446
1725	3,621	3,691
1726	16,203	4,837
1727	11,679	4,041
1728	12,233	18,413
Total	47,371	35,430

Source: I. Ia. Zlatkin, *Istoriia Dzhungarskogo Khanstvo, 1635–1758* (Moscow: Nauka, 1964), p. 381.

third of the settled population each year in rotation and restricted the mobility of the Mongolian tribes subordinate to him. In southern Turkestan he collected tribute from the autonomous Khoja chieftains but prohibited the sale of slaves, which would deprive him of manpower.[8]

Tsewang Rabdan carried on Galdan's projects of strengthening the state, enhancing the productive resources of the local economy, and furthering trade, but his dependence on the Qing increased. As noted in a previous chapter, he returned Galdan's ashes to Beijing only after the Kangxi emperor threatened to cut off the caravan trade. Although disputes continued to break out with Russia over levies of tribute, refugees, and Russian military expansion southward, Zunghar caravans traveled frequently to Semipalatinsk, Tobolsk, and Yamyshev and became a significant presence in Siberian markets.[9] (See Table 8.1.)

Tsewang Rabdan and Galdan Tseren also developed agricultural production at Ili, the Irtysh River, and Ürümchi by bringing in Turkic oasis dwellers, called Taranchi, who knew the special skills of high-yielding irrigated agriculture. A Qing soldier captured by Tsewang in 1731 reported seeing wide fields and gardens, and even some Zunghars themselves began to take up agriculture, in the form of military colonies, imitating Qing practice.[10]

Finally, no discussion of the Zunghars' construction of their economic and technological base can ignore the extraordinary odyssey of the artillery officer Lieutenant J. G. Renat and his fellow Swedes.[11] By 1711 some eight hundred Swedes captured by the Russians at the battle of Poltava two years earlier had scattered across Siberia. They provided the Tsar with useful information and were especially skilled in mapmaking.[12] Renat then joined Buchholz's gold-hunting expedition to Lake Yamysh, where he and other

Swedes were captured by the Zunghars in 1716. He did not return to Sweden until seventeen years later.

The Zungharian captives represented many nationalities. They comprised Russians, Swedes, Manchus, and Chinese, possibly including some surveyors sent out by the Jesuits at Kangxi's behest.[13] Tsewang Rabdan had them build factories to produce velvet, cloth, and paper; Renat was set to work at military production. Supervising local corvée laborers, he produced at least fifteen cannon and twenty mortars during his stay. He also taught the Mongols how to smelt iron for bullets and mine gold and silver, as well as how to print books.

Renat also aided the Zunghar force of five thousand men that attacked Lukchun, near Turfan, and he fought against Qing troops in the Altai, helping the Zunghars in their victory over Furdan. Major L. Ugrimov, a Russian emissary who visited Galdan Tseren, mentioned that Renat had planted his own garden on the model of the Taranchi Turkis, containing fruit trees surrounded by a brick wall.[14]

Even more crucially, Renat helped Galdan Tseren to produce the first maps of Zungharia. (Galdan Tseren was no primitive nomadic chieftain; he was said to carry with him a hundred camel loads of books.)[15] On his return to Sweden, he took with him two maps, with Mongolian place-names, which are now held in the Uppsala University library.[16] One of them appears to be an original Mongolian map, drawn by Galdan Tseren himself. The second one is a copy of a map captured from the Chinese at Barköl or Turfan. These were the first Mongolian maps of Central Eurasia, and they surpass in accuracy and detail anything done by the Russians or Chinese during the eighteenth century. Although scholars debate the degree of Chinese and Russian influence on them, they were unique hybrid cultural objects combining Swedish cartographic techniques, Chinese forms, and Mongolian local knowledge. They demonstrate the importance of cartography to the military planners and the extremely accurate information they could obtain from interrogating local people.[17]

In sum, competition with the Qing state drove the Zunghars to undertake significant steps toward "self-strengthening." Like many earlier nomadic empires, they established cities, developed agriculture, fostered trade, and generated tax revenues, but the primary motivation was not "assimilation" to settled societies' customs but mobilization of resources for defense. Internal upheaval after the death of Galdan Tseren in 1745, however, curtailed these investments. By 1748 the metal factories had been abandoned as unprofitable, as the Zunghars reverted to roving raids and internecine strife.[18] Within a decade Qing troops had taken advantage of this internal disorder to eradicate the Zunghar state.

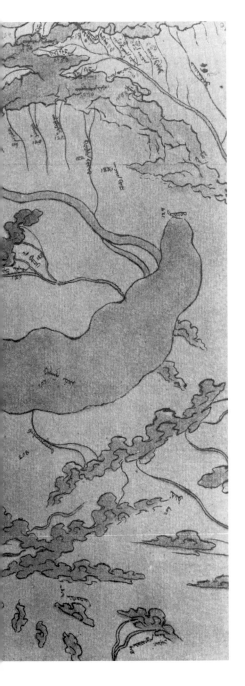

Map of Zungharia drawn by the Swedish ar-
tillery officer Johan Gustaf Renat or by the
Zunghar ruler Galdan Tseren (r. 1727–1745).
Note the extensive labeling of rivers in Mon-
golian. South is at the top, following Chinese
tradition. Lake Balkash appears at the right.
(Numbers added by John Baddeley, a later
British commentator.)

Nian Gengyao and the Incorporation of Qinghai

While the Zunghar leaders were reaching in all directions to gather resources for their fragile state, their Qing rivals were also strengthening their
grip over newly acquired territory. After Mongolia, Kokonor (Ch. Qinghai)
became next on the list of incorporated regions. Unlike the piecemeal incorporation of Mongolia, the systematic planning for Kokonor exposes the essential Qing methods for bringing the frontier into the empire.

As described earlier, when the Khoshot Mongols of Kokonor threatened
to unite themselves under Lobzang Danjin and restore their control over
Tibet, the Yongzheng emperor designated Nian Gengyao as Fuyuan
Dajiangjun (Generalissimo in Charge of Pacification of Remote Regions) to
suppress this "rebellion." After brutally defeating Lobzang Danjin's army
in 1724, Nian outlined a plan for the reconstruction and incorporation
of Kokonor into the empire. Its provisions for military security, economic
development, and administrative reform were designed to ensure that
Kokonor, formerly an autonomous territory ruled by Mongolian tribes,
would become a permanent part of the Qing realm.[19] Nian's proposals epitomize the process of Qing imperial formation so well that they are worth
discussing in some detail. He first emphasized all the benefits that the
Khoshots had received from the Qing emperors, claiming all of Lobzang's
tribesmen *(tonglei)* as subjects of the Qing. The initial task was to determine rewards and punishments. Lobzang Danjin himself had escaped.
Three princes who aided the Qing suppression received titles. "Coerced followers" *(xiecong)* could be pardoned, but it was decided that the active
leaders of the rebellion deserved execution. Nian explained the Qing decision carefully to an assembly of the Khoshot princes, outlining in detail the
crimes of eight men who could not be pardoned. Then he had the men
dragged before the assembly and had their heads cut off, in order to "rec-
tify the laws of the nation [*guojia*]."[20]

Next, he fixed the territories of the Mongolian tribes. In his view, because
the Ming did not control the region, the hereditary lineages of Mongols and
Tibetans had maintained their autonomy, leading to continual plundering
and conflict. Now that the rebels had been rooted out, the Mongols would
be organized into banner companies, modeled on those introduced into Inner Mongolia. The pasturelands' boundaries would be fixed, and the Mongol leaders would be named *jasaks*: banner commanders subject to confirmation by the Qing court. Each tribe would be allocated to a separate
grazing ground, and no tribe could interfere with another tribe's pasturelands. Following tradition, every year an assembly leader *(mengchang)* supervised the annual meeting of the Khoshots. Lobzang had used his status

as hereditary *mengchang* to consolidate his support, but Nian was determined to prevent the emergence of another powerful unifier. Now the *mengchang* would be selected by Qing officials.

Classification was the third effective control technique. Nian exploited divisions among the Mongols to serve imperial unification. Some of the Khalkha Mongols, instead of submitting to the Qing at the great assembly of 1690, had fled south and sought protection from the Khoshots of Kokonor. Now that the Qing had taken over this region, these Khalkhas had the opportunity to free themselves from Khoshot domination by accepting Qing rule. Their chiefs would become *jasaks,* and they could take over territory confiscated from Lobzang Danjin's rebels. Nian explicitly stated, "Thus we will divide the strength of the Kokonor princes, and the Khalkha princes will no longer suffer the shame of being slaves; they will become their own tribes."[21] These Khalkhas were explicitly defined as a new tribe *(buluo)* and settled separately from the Khoshots in Kokonor. Thus, internally, the Qing constructed new ethnic communities in order to divide and rule, just as its foreign policy of *yiyi zhiyi* played off one "barbarian" against another.

Similar distinctions were applied to the Tibetans (Xifan) in Kokonor, whom Nian regarded as the original inhabitants of the region. They had joined Lobzang "in swarms," saying "they only knew of the existence of Mongols, and knew nothing of Chinese civil administration or garrisons." But now, Nian proclaimed, they were "our common people [*baixing*] . . . their lands are our lands; how can they serve the Kokonor princes?"[22] These native Tibetans had to cut their ties to lamaseries and Mongolian lords in order to become loyal subjects owing duties directly to the imperial administration. They became another defined population within the territory. Nian thus aimed to sort out multiple populations who owed obligations to different superiors into defined groups subordinate to only one superior authority.

Enforcing control over the local Tibetans also meant challenging the Dalai Lama's suzerainty by splitting up the territorial boundaries of Tibet. Once again, Nian justified this division historically. Of the four tribes of the Tangut, two, Zang and Wei in western Tibet, belonged under the Dalai Lama's jurisdiction, but Kokonor and Kham in eastern Tibet, because they were dominated by Gusri Khan, deserved a separate classification.[23] After Lobzang's defeat, the Kham region was to be attached to the neighboring interior provinces of Sichuan and Yunnan. Nian did not regard this reorganization as taking territory away from the Dalai Lama; his "lands of incense and fire [*xianghuo*]" in the west remained under his control, but the Qing would "save several hundred thousand Tibetans from water and fire" by detaching them from the Dalai Lama's jurisdiction.[24] In return for the loss of revenue, the Qing would make annual payments to the Dalai Lama and allow him to conduct trade at Dajianlu on the Sichuan border. This division of the Tibetan cultural region by the Qing corresponds closely to its current administrative boundaries under the PRC.

Further discipline of Kokonor required severe limitations on the power of the lamaseries. These were some of the largest establishments in the entire Tibetan region, containing up to three thousand monks and many interconnected buildings.[25] They were significant centers of power, supported by dues from local Tibetans. From Nian's point of view, the lamaseries could not be authentic religious institutions, because they gave refuge to "criminals," stored weapons, and supported the rebellion. It was perfectly proper to burn them down and massacre their residents. Afterwards, the lamaseries would be limited in size to three hundred monks, all of whom had to register with local officials and undergo twice-yearly investigations. Rent payments could not go directly to the lamaseries but had to be submitted to the government for distribution to them.

In sum, after eliminating a minority of "rebels," the Qing administrators organized the remaining "coerced followers" into fixed "tribes," defined as territorially and administratively circumscribed units, with leaders appointed by the state. They intermingled different groups so as to balance them against one another, distinguished "natives" from later arrivals, and replaced multiple allegiances with one direct line of authority.

On these frontiers, the Qing rulers faced the same challenges as other Eurasian empires, and used the same tools. The Russian and Ottoman empires also defined stable borders and sharpened their categorizations of peoples in the eighteenth century, and the British did the same in India in the nineteenth century.[26] All of them conducted ethnographic surveys of the new regions, fixing identities in place for fiscal convenience and preservation of local order.[27] They replaced the fluctuating alliances of the autonomous nomadic society with fixed, hierarchically determined posts of authority. This drive toward clarifying the state's vision of its peoples, however, did not erase all difference. The bureaucratic structure had to adapt to the frontier; it did not replicate the uniformity of the interior. *Jasaks* were not merely district magistrates in Mongol clothing, nor were they Manchu bannermen. (Later on I discuss further examples of Qing administrative diversity in Xinjiang.)

At the same time, Nian promoted immigration in order to forge links to the interior and create a more peaceful, settled society. He proposed to send ten thousand Manchu and Han settler households into Kokonor to "dilute" the strength of the Mongols and turn them toward stable cultivation.

These policies partially contradicted the state's urge to simplify. With one hand local officials untangled tribal affiliations by creating separate territorial and kinship entities under an orderly administrative structure, while with the other they introduced more diversity into the region by adding new peoples who could clash with the indigenous inhabitants. Nian's policies contained in the microcosm of Kokonor the tensions that strained the entire empire after its great push outward.

Nian likewise fostered trade to bind the frontier to the center. Before the conquest, in Nian's view, the Mongols had traded as they pleased, exchanging "useless hides and furs for our useful tea and cloth." Han traders in search of profit headed for the territory, creating a "spirit of wickedness" (jianxin).[28] Free trade relations also had allowed Lobzang to spy out conditions in the interior before he rebelled. Now trade at the frontiers would be regulated. Mongolians would be divided into three groups; each group could come to the capital on a licensed trade mission once every three years, in rotation. Over nine years, all would have a chance to trade. Regular trade at border markets was allowed twice a year. Troops would patrol the markets to ensure that no one crossed the border without permission.

These Central Eurasian precedents set the pattern for other treaties. Nian's proposals of 1724 anticipated the similar trade regulations that the Qing negotiated with the Russians in 1727, in which border trade was confined to the town of Kiakhta, and tribute missions to the capital were allowed only with official permission. The Canton trade system of handling Western merchants at the end of the eighteenth century embodied the same principles. As Joseph Fletcher has shown, China's first "unequal treaty" settlement was negotiated with the Khan of Kokand in 1835. Its provisions for extraterritoriality, merchant autonomy, and permanent resident political representatives were applied equally to the British after the Opium War in 1842.[29] Nian's proposals demonstrate that the same was true for an earlier period: regulated trading arrangements in Kokonor set the framework for the Russian and British treaty arrangements.

Finally, Nian proposed to construct a huge fortified border along Kokonor's northern frontier. He envisioned a connected series of fortresses that would in effect extend the Great Wall line of defense far out the Gansu corridor to Ganzhou and Anxi, cutting off Kokonor from contact with the Zunghars to the north. He would clear out all Mongols from this area and bring in large numbers of settlers to populate the garrison towns. As Nian noted, and as the Qing found later in Xinjiang, criminals sentenced to military exile would make ideal cultivators of the soil.

Nian did not realize all of his grand vision. The unnecessary fortress line was never built, and migration to Kokonor was slow. Yet his proposals uncannily forecast the primary measures of frontier control of the Qing, Nationalist, and PRC governments. Repression, settlement, state simplification, migration, and commercial integration sum up the policies of all three regimes. Yet the empire was less thorough, and thus more benign. The Qing repression of revolt in Kokonor was brutal but not wanton. The large lamaseries were dismantled and reestablished on a limited scale, with reduced influence, but they were not eliminated. Unlike its Nationalist and Communist successors, imperial ideology was not hostile to Tibetan Buddhism per se; it was concerned only with the potential for the institution to create centers of resistance. Under appropriate restraints, the monks could facilitate imperial control, so long as the emperor put himself at the top of their hierarchy.

We may note some surprising parallels between Kokonor's situation and current events in Tibet.[30] Both feature the appearance of rival incarnate lamas, one backed by the orthodox hierarchy, one by the Chinese; the use of forcible intervention to impose a solution on Lhasa; and the concern to prevent foci of resistance to state control. But the Qing never conducted all-out ideological campaigns against Tibet's religion; Mao's notorious (apocryphal?) statement to the Dalai Lama that "religion is poison" would never have been uttered by a Qing emperor. During the Cultural Revolution, thousands of monastic establishments were destroyed by Red Guards, and many monks were humiliated and killed. The Manchus inflicted only a nasty, sharp military shock on the resisting lamas, after which they allowed the institution to continue. Except when they had their own militarily dominant empire in the seventh to ninth centuries CE, Tibetans have always been in the unfortunate position of choosing between unsatisfactory, violent, or indifferent protectors. Mongolian patronage did help the Dalai Lama centralize his state from the sixteenth to the seventeenth century; but the eighteenth-century Zungharian intervention in internal conflicts left the Tibetans with the choice of only one patron: the Qing emperor in Beijing. Yet after the 1720s, Tibet, Mongolia, and Kokonor remained at peace under loose Qing suzerainty. Not until the twentieth century did nationalist upheaval bring new threats to Tibetans and Mongolians under Qing administration.

Administering the Frontier

By eliminating the rival Mongolian state, the Qing rulers added a huge territory to the northwest region. It took an entire century to digest the new lands and peoples. Many of these lands were added on to the existing provincial administration of Gansu province. Within the northwest macroregion, defined by G. William Skinner as including Gansu, Shaanxi, western Shanxi, and a piece of Sichuan, Gansu was the most peripheral part. It formed the hinge between the regular administrative structure of the core and the new requirements of the frontier regions. Imperial policies on grain provisioning, taxation, and military support had to be adapted to the special circumstances of this frontier, and they were stretched further when the even more alien regions of the far northwest were added on. But the practices established as variations within a bureaucratic norm in Gansu served as models for greater experiments in Xinjiang. In this section I examine the position of the northwest region, Gansu especially, within the empire as a whole, and the processes of administrative expansion and economic change that drew Xinjiang closer to the interior.[31]

As the empire expanded, officials created new administrative units and reshuffled old ones to adapt to new needs. They redirected bureaucratic resources not only through material flows but also through alterations in the structure of field administration. G. William Skinner and Gilbert Rozman have analyzed the institutional structure of the Qing empire by showing the distribution of administrative levels in relation to the urban hierarchy.[32] Skinner, in particular, has demonstrated that many aspects of the formal designation of bureaucratic posts were allocated in accordance with the two crucial functions of revenue collection and military defense. Skinner's model, however, is a static analysis, reflecting generally the structure of the empire in 1893, though some of his data are estimated for 1843. We also need to examine how bureaucratic posts changed in response to the increase in territory and economic activity.

At the top of the administrative hierarchy of China proper stood the Governor-General (zongdu), which first became a regular position under the Qing.[33] He usually supervised two or more provinces and served concurrently as governor of one of them. From the founding of the dynasty until 1760, the numbers and jurisdictions of the Governors-General shifted constantly, until settling down to a total of nine (eight in China proper and one in Manchuria). As Figure 8.1 shows, the northwestern regions were particularly unsettled. In the early Qing, Gansu and Shaanxi were grouped together as the Shaanxi Sanbian, while the Sichuan Governor-Generalship included Huguang. In 1653 Sichuan was added to Shaanxi and Gansu and separated from Huguang, but in 1661 it was split off again under its own Governor-General. Shanxi was added to Shaanxi and Gansu for a short time, and Huguang was again joined with Sichuan, but by 1674 Shanxi had no Governor-General, Shaanxi and Gansu were joined, and Sichuan was separate from Huguang. This would ultimately be the stable configura-

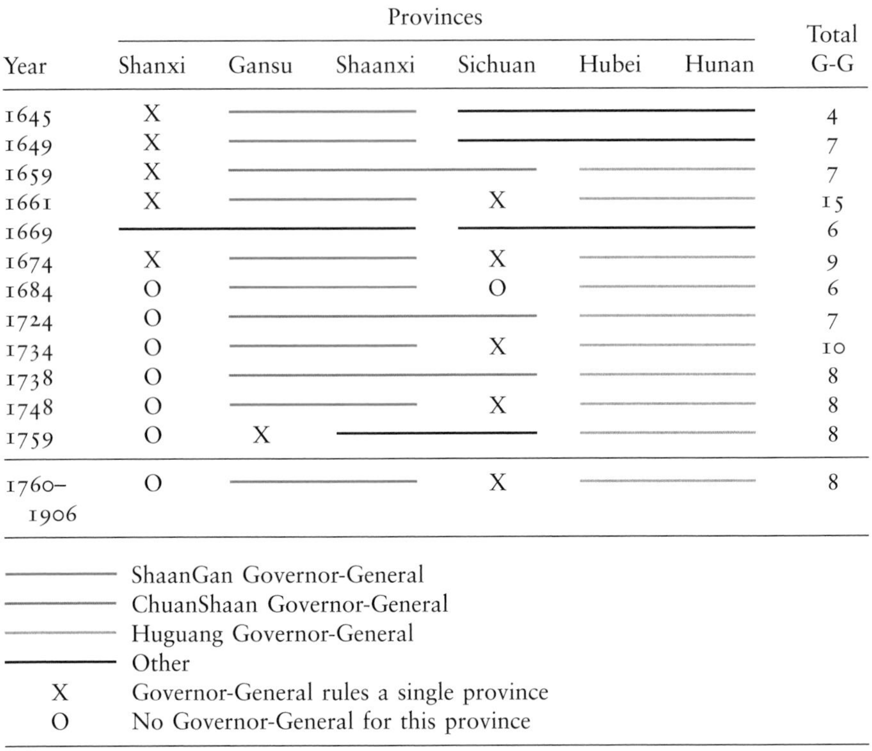

Year	Shanxi	Gansu	Shaanxi	Sichuan	Hubei	Hunan	Total G-G
1645	X						4
1649	X						7
1659	X						7
1661	X			X			15
1669							6
1674	X			X			9
1684	O			O			6
1724	O						7
1734	O			X			10
1738	O						8
1748	O			X			8
1759	O	X					8
1760–1906	O			X			8

——————— ShaanGan Governor-General
——————— ChuanShaan Governor-General
——————— Huguang Governor-General
——————— Other
X   Governor-General rules a single province
O   No Governor-General for this province

Figure 8.1   Qing northwest and central Governor-Generalships (major changes only). Only six of the eighteen provinces of Qing China are shown. *Total* indicates total Governor-Generalships for all provinces. *Source:* Qian Shifu, ed., *Qingdai Zhiguan Nianbiao*, 4 vols. (Beijing: Zhonghua Shuju, 1980), 2:1510–11.

tion, but the jurisdictions shifted back and forth for the next eighty-six years, with Sichuan sometimes joined with Shaanxi and Gansu, and sometimes separate. Gansu briefly gained its own Governor-General during the final years of the conquest of Xinjiang, but in 1760 the partition of responsibilities was finally resolved with three separate Governors-General for Shaanxi–Gansu, Sichuan, and Huguang. This highly volatile division of the northwest indicates the changing responsibilities of the Governors-General of the region.

The Governors-General here, because of their military responsibilities, dominated over much weaker provincial governors. For the same reason, only Manchus could serve as provincial governors of Shanxi, Shaanxi, and Gansu until the mid-eighteenth century.[34] The shifting boundaries clearly reflected changes in the military demands on the northwest, such as the war against the Jinchuan rebels in Sichuan in 1749 and the invasions of

Table 8.2 Governor-Generalships after 1760 and macroregion overlap

Governor-Generalship	Macroregion	Degree of overlap
YunGui	YunGui	High
Liangguang	Lingnan	High
Minzhe	Southeast coast	Moderate
Huguang	Middle Yangzi	High
Sichuan	Upper Yangzi	High
ShaanGan	Northwest	High
Liangjiang	Lower Yangzi	Low
Zhili	North China	Low

Source: G. William Skinner, ed., *The City in Late Imperial China* (Stanford: Stanford University Press, 1977), pp. 214–215; G. William Skinner, "Presidential Address: The Structure of Chinese History," *Journal of Asian Studies* 44, no. 2 (1985): 271–292.

Xinjiang in the 1750s. After this period, Gansu had no provincial governor. The Governor-General moved to Lanzhou and took charge of the main military and economic functions: funneling supplies along the Gansu corridor to the Central Eurasian frontier. After a century of turmoil, the mid-eighteenth-century decisions fixed the definition of most boundaries of administration.

The distribution of the Governor-Generalships indicates that Qing administration at the highest level responded to physiographic constraints. After 1760 the boundaries of most of the eight Governor-Generalships of China proper (excluding Manchuria) corresponded quite closely to the eight physiographic macroregions described by Skinner. (See Table 8.2.)[35] To be sure, as Skinner insists, administrative boundaries never fit exactly with physiographic regions at any level of the marketing hierarchy. The two with the worst fit were the Governor-Generalships of Zhili and Liangjiang. The Zhili Governor-General did not encompass the entire North China plain, since Shanxi, Henan, and Shandong had no Governor-General at all. The Liangjiang Governor-Generalship included Jiangsu, Anhui, and Jiangxi, even though the northern parts of Jiangsu and Anhui belonged to the North China plain, and Jiangxi belonged to the middle Yangzi macroregion (or was a separate macroregion). Broadly speaking, however, the other Governor-Generalships after 1760 accommodated themselves to the existing physiographic regions, and those which fit best were on the edges of the empire. Since the primary functions of the Governor-General were those of military and logistical coordination, these men were especially valuable in allocating resources efficiently for imperial expansion on the frontiers.

In the early Qing, however, when the constant shifting of positions indicated the fluctuating pressures generated by territorial expansion, these units did not fit closely with physiographic macroregions. It took over a century of boundary juggling to bring economic structure and administrative hierarchy into rough correspondence. From 1661 to 1760, the number of Governor-Generalships grew as large as fifteen and as small as six. (See Figure 8.1.) It is noteworthy that each emperor in the early years of his reign experimented with different configurations: Kangxi briefly increased the number of Governors-General to fifteen, and Yongzheng decreased them to nine. Qianlong kept the total at eight, but shifted Sichuan back and forth, and for a short time split Yunnan and Guizhou.

A debate over the northwestern Governor-Generalship indicates the conflicting logics determining its boundaries. In 1759 ShaanGan Governor-General Yang Yingju memorialized to request an adjustment of military responsibilities in the northwest.[36] He argued that the conquest of the western regions had made his responsibilities too great, so he proposed to make himself the Governor-General of Gansu alone, and put Shaanxi under the Sichuan Governor-General, changing the jurisdictions of many of the military units. Yang wanted to ensure closer coordination and greater centralization of control over interprovincial transfers. He insisted that communications between provinces should go through the Governor-General, eliminating all lateral communications from one governor to another, and all military financing must be approved by the Governor-General in Shaanxi.[37]

The Deliberative Council rejected his proposal; military campaigns were still continuing, and the councilors did not want to cause disruptions. Guyuan military commander Zhang Jietian proposed to station the new Gansu Governor-General in Suzhou, in the far west of the province, so as to ensure closer supervision of the western regions. But the emperor called this a "muddled" idea, and argued in favor of keeping the official headquarters in a more populated region in the east: "Liangzhou is better because merchants can flock there, and it is convenient. Suzhou is far away, and it has been neglected. These military people don't understand this. For controlling the newly subjected tribes, Suzhou is closer. But we should not decide according to private interests."[38] In effect, the emperor rejected arguments based on military security alone in favor of greater revenue collection from the more densely populated regions in the east. He and the top officials knew that revenue and security were the prime determinants of administrative boundaries, but their imperatives often conflicted. At the highest and lowest levels of the hierarchy, the Qing constantly tinkered with bureaucratic boundaries and posts in response to these two demands.

Turning to provincial administration, I examine changes in Gansu to il-

Table 8.3 Incorporation of military units into civil administration in Gansu

Reign	Number of military units abolished
Shunzhi (1644–1661)	12
Kangxi (1662–1722)	4
Yongzheng (1723–1735)	32
Qianlong (1736–1795)	1
Total	49

Source: Niu Pinghan, *Qingdai Zhengqu Yange Zongbiao* (Beijing: Zhongquo Ditu Chubanshe, 1990), pp. 473–477.

Note: An additional six *weisuo* were created from 1718 to 1724 and abolished in 1759.

lustrate how the Qing created a frontier provincial structure during the eighteenth century, and how its experience provided a model for the much larger task of incorporating Xinjiang at the end of the century. Gansu province was created when Shaanxi province, inherited from the Ming, was split into two Provincial Administration Commissions, Left and Right; the Right Commission became Gansu province in 1667.[39] It contained four prefectures and inherited the Ming structure of military units *(weisuo)*, which were autonomous garrison commands stretched along the northwestern frontier. The Qing gradually incorporated these units into the civil administration. There were forty-nine *weisuo* within the western section of Ming Shaanxi. Twelve of these had been abolished in the Shunzhi reign and four more during the early Kangxi period. But it was the Yongzheng reign which carried out the most drastic reduction, abolishing thirty-one *weisuo* and putting them under the civil administration. (See Table 8.3.) The reduction of *weisuo* was in accord with Yongzheng's policy of reducing military costs by putting more territory under civilian control.[40]

Two key elements of the Qing field administration were the "span of control" and strategic designation of posts. Span of control refers to the number of subordinate units under a higher-level one. Skinner uses this term to refer only to the number of county-level units under a prefecture, but it can be applied at any level.[41] In the Qing, the span of control at the center (the number of Governor-Generalships, or the number of provinces) varied from nine to fifteen for Governor-Generalships, and from fifteen to twenty-two for provinces. At each level of the hierarchy there were several different kinds of offices, each of which had a particular function. (See Figure 8.2.) Creating new units at any level increased the span of control of the higher units, but also added additional officials to the bureaucracy and reduced the span of control at the next lower level. Thus, creating a new province

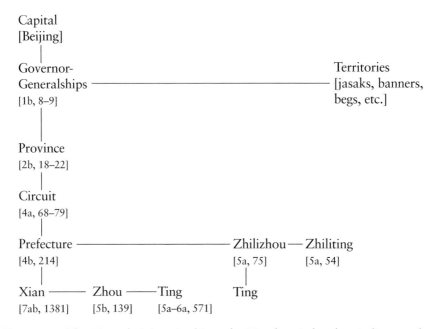

Figure 8.2   The Qing administrative hierarchy. Numbers in brackets indicate rank in the bureaucratic hierarchy, followed by the total number of units, which varied over the course of the dynasty. The figure follows Brunnert, which reflects the situation around 1907; Hucker and Skinner give slightly different numbers. For *xian*, the common English term is "district" or "county." *Zhou* and *ting* are often called "independent subprefectures." *Sources:* I. S. Brunnert and V. V. Hagelstrom, *Present Day Political Organization of China* (Taibei: Book World Co., 1911), pp. 395–438; Charles O. Hucker, *A Dictionary of Official Titles in Imperial China* (Stanford: Stanford University Press, 1985); G. William Skinner, ed., *The City in Late Imperial China* (Stanford: Stanford University Press, 1977), pp. 301–307.

(such as Xinjiang in 1884, or Taiwan in 1885) increased the span of control of the capital by adding new provincial governors, but reduced the span of control of provinces over prefectures. Creating new prefectures would increase the provincial span of control but reduce the number of county-level units per prefecture. Increasing the number of salaried officials was something that Chinese dynasties were reluctant to do, because it added to their fiscal burdens, but reducing the span of control increased security by making each official responsible for fewer subordinate units. Once again, fiscal and security considerations stood in an uneasy balance against each other.

   The administrative units of the imperial bureaucracy were remarkably stable at the lowest level but quite variable at higher levels. The number of county-level units has changed little: the Qin empire of the third century BCE had about 1,000 *xian*, and China today, with a much larger territory and population, has 2,143 county-level units, many with nearly the same boundaries.[42] An expanding dynasty like the Qing, however, did have to include more territory under its civil administration, so it converted military-ruled regions into new civil administrative units. The culmination of this process at the highest level was the designation of Xinjiang and Taiwan as provinces in 1884 and 1885, but analogous changes had been made at lower levels since the eighteenth century.

Shifting units between levels was a more common, and more attractive, administrative change than creating new units because it did not increase the number of officials, although it could change their ranks and salaries. Often the motivation was to increase supervision over strategically important areas. When counties *(xian)* became *zhilizhou* or *zhiliting,* they were placed directly under the provincial governor instead of having a prefect in between. The governor appointed especially experienced men to fill these posts.

According to Skinner, the designation of posts and the span of control varied by region in relation to the two prime concerns of the empire: revenue collection and defense. The span of control was to be high in regional cores and low in the peripheries so as to maximize the tax collection from the most prosperous areas and maximize supervision of authorities in strategically important peripheries. *Zhilizhou* and *ting* were to be concentrated in the peripheries because of their special status as units directly administered by the provincial governor.

Gansu, however, when it was created in 1667 out of Shaanxi province, did not fit this pattern at all. (See Table 8.4.) It was the most peripheral province of the empire, but with four prefectures and thirty-seven counties, its span of control, at 9.25, was very high.[43] It contained no *zhou* or *ting* at all. In effect, the administration was split into two parallel hierarchies: the *weisuo* military units and the civilian structure. Skinner's generalizations apply better to the "normalized" empire of the late nineteenth century, after it had digested its new territorial gains, thanks to the early Qing. In the seventeenth century, new provinces like Gansu were quite anomalous, but over time the administrative units were adjusted to bring them closer to the normal structure. These shifts were especially common in northwest China.

The short Yongzheng reign probably marked the most intensive reordering of administrative units in the Qing dynasty until its very last years. In Gansu, Yongzheng created four new prefectures out of the garrisons and raised four subordinate *zhou* to *zhilizhou.* In Shaanxi also, Yongzheng raised nine *zhou* to *zhilizhou* and created two new prefectures.[44]

As with the lower levels of the hierarchy, creating new prefectural level units could have one of two motivations: security or revenue collection.

Table 8.4 Gansu field administration (after 1777)

Prefectural unit	Creation	Location	No. of *zhou*/*ting*	No. of *xian*
Lanzhou Fu	1667	East	2/1	4
Pingliang Fu	1667	East	2	3
Qingyang Fu	1667	East	1	4
Gongchang Fu	1667	East	1/1	7
Jingzhou Zhilizhou	1777, from Pingliang	East	1	3
Qinzhou Zhilizhou	1729, from Gongchang	East	1	5
Jiezhou Zhilizhou	1729, from Gongchang	East	1	2
Ningxia Fu	1724	East	1/0	4
Xining Fu	1724	West	0/1	3
Liangzhou Fu	1724	West	0/1	5
Ganzhou Fu	1724	West	0/1	2
Suzhou Zhilizhou	1729	West	1/0	1
Anxi Zhilizhou	1773	West	1/0	2
Total			12/5	45

Source: Niu Pinghan, *Qingdai Zhengqu Yange Zongbiao* (Beijing: Zhongquo Ditu Chubanshe, 1990), pp. 462–477.

Gansu's new units fell into both categories. Even though Gansu as a whole was only a periphery of the northwest macroregion, the province itself was stratified into zones of different marketing density.

The three eastern *zhilizhou*—Jingzhou, Qinzhou, and Jiezhou—were clearly located in more productive regions. Jiezhou, in fact, the most productive prefecture with the best rainfall and the farthest south, belonged not to the northwest macroregion at all but to the upper Yangzi. Creating these three units increased the span of control of the provincial governor, thus increasing his access to revenue from these productive regions. They controlled an average of 4.3 county-level units.

The five western prefectures, however, were formed out of military units for strategic purposes. They controlled an average of 3.6 county-level units, and they contained three of the province's five *ting*. Ningxia prefecture, including four county-level units, fell in between, combining both functions. The branching of the Yellow River here created considerable irrigation water for the fields, but the prefecture ran directly along the Great Wall, bordering Mongolia. It constantly provided grain supplies for other counties, but it also supported substantial military forces.

In the early to mid-eighteenth century, then, even before the final elimination of the Zunghar state, the Qing administrative structure, like a boa constrictor, had begun to digest its new territorial acquisitions. Most of the new territory remained outside the regular civil administration, but parts had begun to move from military districts into county-level units, and new prefectures balanced the revenue and security demands of the new northwest province. Many other administrative and social changes ensued on the local level, such as the building of walls, the growth of cities, and the proliferation of official and sub-official posts. The experience with Gansu in the early period of Qing expansion in the northwest set the stage for the huge task of swallowing Xinjiang at the end of the century.

9

Land Settlement and Military Colonies

Nian Gengyao's proposal to introduce military and civilian settlers into Kokonor carried on a long-standing imperial tradition. In principle, military colonies *(tuntian)* combined several advantages. Economically self-sufficient military units spared costs when soldiers practiced cultivation and defense in rotation. Once they brought their families to join them, the soldier-settlers formed the nucleus of permanent settlements. Merchants followed, linking the garrisons with interior trading networks. Then peasants arrived, relieving population pressure in poor interior provinces, diminishing the prospects of famine or revolt, and mixing non-Han people with more loyal settlers from the interior. In Chinese terms, military colonies were a policy of *yiju liangde* (killing two birds with one stone).

In fact, permanent military colonies faced great difficulties. The Han dynasty, in the second century BCE, had set up military colonies beyond the Great Wall, as did the Tang and others, but these colonies were expensive to maintain. During the great Debates on Salt and Iron, in 81 BCE, literati attacked the policy of establishing salt and iron monopolies in order to pay the expenses of military colonies on the Han northwestern frontier.[1]

The abandoned garrison towns of Jiaohe and Gaochang in the Turfan oasis testify to the haunting presence of these ephemeral imperial efforts at colonization.[2] Jiaohe reached a peak population of five thousand under the Tang dynasty. Its ruins now stretch for 1,700 meters north-south and 300 meters east-west on top of high cliffs west of Turfan. Gaochang, even larger, also began as a Han garrison town and expanded by the seventh century to become a large Buddhist community and the center of the Uighur kingdom of KaraKhoja in the ninth century. The Mongol invasion destroyed both cities in the fourteenth century. Rediscovered by German archaeologists Albert Grünwedel and Albert von Le Coq in the early twentieth century, Gaochang yielded large numbers of manuscripts, mosaics, frescoes, and statuary to these modern-day adventurers and plunderers. The fate of the famous cave paintings of Bezeklik nearby, taken to Berlin by von le Coq and partly destroyed by American bombs during World War II, epitomizes the vulnerability of these lost Central Eurasian cities.

Ming emperors and officials made valiant efforts to develop military colonies on a large scale. They quickly failed.[3] Zhu Yuanzhang, the first Ming emperor, expanded them on an unprecedented scale, especially on the northwest frontier and in Liaodong. By the end of his reign, 33,500 soldiers had opened over 16,000 *qing* (400 square miles) of land in Gansu province. Zhu boasted of his ability to support over 1 million men in an army without using any civilian grain production at all. Two-thirds of the soldiers in Shaanxi were ordered to cultivate fields, while the rest stood watch. But the troops made poor peasants. By 1392 two-thirds of them had run away. The low yields of frontier lands, hardships of agricultural labor, and embezzlement of funds by officers made soldiering very unattractive, and rendered it impossible to produce enough grain to feed the troops. In the fifteenth and sixteenth centuries, reformers repeatedly proposed changes to restore production and reduce corruption, to no avail. As Arthur Waldron notes, "Military farming simply did not work."[4]

The failure of military colonies to support themselves required innovative commercial policies. Merchant-supported colonies brought civilian settlers and flows of silver to the frontier to pay the troops to buy grain. Despite their founder's intentions, Ming officials created an expensive mercenary standing army, not a self-sufficient low-budget force of hardy yeomen. They withdrew garrisons from advanced positions in the steppe, built the Long Walls to shelter the colonists, and supported them with commercial supply lines from the interior. This was just the opposite of the Han and Tang system of far-flung isolated garrisons. Zhang Juzheng, the great reformist Prime Minister, tried to revive the *tuntian* in the mid-sixteenth century. By 1582 he had increased their nominal area to 600,000 *qing*, or 15,000 square miles.[5] Yet the system completely fell apart by the early seventeenth century, after nomad raids drove off cultivators, much government land and water conservancy was diverted to private uses, and unequal tax and corvée burdens forced soldiers to flee. Private cultivators prospered more than soldier-settlers, especially when the commanders themselves leased out their garrison plots to land speculators. Ming defense strategy, eroded from within by profit incentives and harassed from without by con-

The ancient abandoned garrison town of Jiaohe, near Turfan.

stant raiding, never found a genuine solution in the precedents of the imperial tradition.

Qing efforts, however, were much more extensive and permanent. As early as 1692 the Kangxi emperor had insisted that troops beyond the Great Wall cultivate land to support themselves, so as not to burden the local people.[6] He first discussed military colonies in 1715, after the Qing had subdued the Khalkha Mongols. With the approval of the Khalkha Khans, Qing troops investigated the most suitable places in eastern Mongolia for agricultural cultivation. These colonies, he declared, would "not only save on transport costs, and allow one to exhaust the earth's resources [*jin dili*], but they will also make the enemy barbarians disperse to poor areas, while our generals enjoy a peaceful sleep on their pillows and mats." Once again the settlements combined the goals of economic development and security. They could even provide grain to Mongol allies in times of need. In places like Ulan Gumu and Khobdo, small garrisons of a thousand troops would be initially supplied with large grain shipments from the interior until they could support themselves from their fields.[7]

Criminals sentenced to military exile, of both high and low status, made excellent subjects for involuntary migration to the frontier.[8] Guizhou governor Liu Yinqu, for example, who had opposed the emperor's military expeditions into Turkestan, was spared execution but sent to Mongolia as an exile to cultivate the fields.[9]

By the 1720s General Furdan could report steady progress in digging irrigation canals, clearing fields, and planting crops. The land was very fertile, yielding up to twenty times the initial seed, but he urgently needed iron plows to clear the land.[10] At the best locations, like Ulan Gumu, Chahan Sor, and the area just south of Khobdo, where there were ample supplies of water and wood, the Qing generals could pursue a large-scale program of building fortresses across Mongolia. These fortresses held thousands of troops, who cultivated the fields and stood guard.[11]

As noted earlier, the Qing fortress-building project resembled in some respects the Russian penetration of Siberia: by linking the garrisons together with sentry posts, the military forces could dominate a large area with relatively few men; and by cultivating the land, they could relieve the burden of sending supplies from the interior. The Russians, however, faced easier economic conditions and a less powerful native population. They profited from exacting tribute from the native Siberian tribes in furs, which they could sell in the markets in Beijing. The Qing presence in Mongolia gained no economic profits; the Khalkhas were at least temporarily subordinate allies, but a sense of insecurity always persisted, and the resources of the

Mongolian grasslands and scattered forests and fields were much less abundant than those of the Siberian forests.

Under Yongzheng, the other principal region targeted for settlement became the oases stretching along the Gansu corridor into eastern Turkestan, from Jiayuguan as far as Hami (Qomul), Turfan, and Barköl. Here the promotion of military colonies supported the larger shift in imperial security policy toward defensive concentrations of troops at key points, fortress building, consolidation of forces, and reduction of expenses. These were highly vulnerable outposts constantly raided by the forces of Tsewang Rabdan, and they had insufficient supplies to support major troop concentration. At the main Qing military base at Barköl, 300 kilometers east of Turfan, there were sufficient supplies and prospects for good yields from newly cleared land, but troops could not necessarily reach Turfan in time to hold off damaging attacks.[12] One proposed solution was to build up Turfan's agricultural resources through extensive land clearance.

Within the Gansu corridor, at Suzhou, Shazhou, Guazhou, Dunhuang, and Anxi, it was easier to find cultivable land; the main task was to promote settlement. Three to four thousand troops were sent to each of these towns (five thousand in Anxi) from 1722 to 1724 to revive the abandoned military settlements. Peasant settlers from the northwest provinces of Gansu and Shaanxi were preferred, however, because they had experience with dry field farming, and they came voluntarily.[13]

For the most part, these early colonization efforts did not attract private traders, so the state maintained strict control over the grain markets. But there were already signs of commercial interest. General Jalangga feared that at Anxi "wicked people from the interior would seek profit" by buying up surplus grain supplies, so he ordered *tuntian* cultivators to sell only to state officials. The emperor approved the policy, but urged officials to buy only at market prices and to store surplus grain in granaries. Even this distant oasis had a grain market, which attracted traders from the interior who responded to price signals.[14]

Deportation from Turfan

The effort to create a defense line in east Turkestan based on military settlements ran into great difficulties. The debate over Turfan, the largest oasis, illustrates Turkestan's severe constraints on military supply and defense.[15] As noted in Chapter 6, Tsewang Rabdan's attacks on Hami and Turfan in 1715 had initiated a new period of conflict. Qing conquest of the oases

An elderly Muslim gentleman from Turfan, in traditional garb.

in 1720 represented the first expansion of Chinese imperial control into Turkestan since the Tang dynasty. But holding these territories proved difficult. Yongzheng's troop withdrawals left Turfan especially vulnerable to raids should Tsewang Rabdan turn hostile. The emperor's policy relied on the assumption that the Zunghars would remain cooperative if they were offered the opportunity to send trade and tribute missions through Khalkha lands. But Zunghar raids on Turfan continued, as it became clear that Turfan could not produce enough grain to support both the local population and a substantial garrison. In 1722 the troops needed to borrow supplies from the natives when their own grain supplies ran out.

Tsewang Rabdan, meanwhile, was attempting to carry off Turfanis to Halashar, because these agriculturalists could be valuable producers of grain for his state.[16] Many Turfanis instead fled to the east, appealing for protection from the Qing. When Tsewang Rabdan retreated the next year, after some discussion the Qing generals decided not to put a large garrison in Turfan. Instead they would maintain the garrison at Barköl, six to seven days' march away. But supplies were tight at Barköl also, and these troops could not arrive in time to protect the Turfanis from raids on their herds.[17]

These considerations led to proposals to induce the Muslims of Turfan to move closer to the Chinese borders. Four to five thousand people, or half the population, were offered lands to settle around Anxi and Suzhou; Anxi was still 225 kilometers beyond the end of the Great Wall but 665 kilometers closer to the border. Kangxi had embraced them as "our people" *(womin)* and vowed to protect them against Zunghar raids, but the new emperor would not expend large military resources in the distant oasis.[18] In fact, very few Turfanis accepted the offer. Only 650 people departed the oasis for a new home, even though Qing troop withdrawals left them more vulnerable. Those who did settle in Suzhou suffered from poor harvests and mistreatment by local officials, which drove them into debt. In 1731, however, when Zunghar raids resumed, there was further unrest in Turfan. The garrison now numbered three thousand, but it could not support itself, and officials had to distribute relief to the local people as well.[19]

Yue Zhongqi outlined an extremely ambitious sixteen-point proposal for a massive military occupation of east Turkestan.[20] First he urged an all-out attack on Ürümchi with a large army, leaving only a small garrison in Turfan. If he succeeded, he could move the defense frontier 175 kilometers westward, relieve supply burdens in Turfan, and destroy the Zunghar army. The emperor, however, was skeptical that he could succeed. In the end, Yongzheng delegated the decision to Yue Zhongqi.

Yue then asked for substantial increases in troop strength, expansion of military colonies, and shipments from the interior. The thirty thousand troops in Barköl prepared for the military expedition would move to Turfan and be replaced by eighteen thousand more men from Ningxia and the Ordos; twenty thousand men would attack Ürümchi from Turfan, and ten thousand would advance from Barköl. In case of victory, eighteen thousand would be stationed in Ürümchi to hold the town. Yue made detailed estimates of the supply demands for such a large force. He expected that lands cleared around Turfan city could support ten thousand troops, and smaller towns in the region could support at least five thousand more. The total current harvest at Turfan, Barköl, and Tarnaqin combined was 50,000 *shi* of barley, to be ground into grain for making noodles, but barley was hard for the troops to digest. Additional supplies of 30,000 *shi* of millet shipped annually from Suzhou to be mixed with the barley would be necessary. The expanded army also needed a total of 60,000 horses, including cavalry mounts and pack animals. Forty thousand were available at Barköl, 8,000 could be purchased in Zhili, Henan, and Shanxi, and the allied Mongols would be asked to provide the rest. The attacking army also needed 34,000 camels to carry over 60,000 *shi* of grain, and 200,000 sheep, while each soldier himself carried two months' rations on his back.[21]

Yue's careful estimates indicated the vast scale of preparations necessary to launch a truly decisive campaign. He realized that a serious military effort would take at least three to four years, and would have to root out the Mongols from their faraway nests, at the same time leaving enough troops in the oases to defend against raids. The emperor regretfully refused Yue's requests. He understood how shameful it was for Yue's garrisons to stay in defensive positions holding off nomad raids, but now was not the right time for a decisive campaign.[22] Yue did launch a sally against Ürümchi, but he could not hold the town.

At this juncture, Imin Kwaja (Emin Khoja), the chieftain of Turfan, besieged by the Zunghars and desperate for Qing support, began to organize a mass emigration from Turfan. After repelling the Zunghar army, in 1733–34 he led nearly ten thousand people on a long march inland across 700 kilometers of desert, settling them in Xin Guazhou, just west of the Anxi garrison. For his efforts he was granted the title of *jasak fuguogong*, and his people were organized into a banner, with Imin as the banner chief, the first Turki to receive this honor. For two decades the Turfanis lived there in poverty, as in a refugee camp, while their homelands were devastated by warfare. They were allowed to return in 1754, as the Qing prepared its final blows against the fragmented Zunghar state. As they moved back to Turfan, they left behind 20,000 *mou* of cultivated land and 4,800 small houses which they had built. On their return, further conflict broke out, as Mangalik Bek, another Qing banner *jasak*, who had remained behind and supported the Zunghars until their defeat, resisted Qing imposition of Imin Kwaja as an equal power in the oasis. When Mangalik Bek's resistance was suppressed, Imin Khwaja became the undisputed ruler of Turfan as a banner *jasak* prince. Turfan retained this peculiar structure, the only Turkestani oasis organized as a banner, because of its close involvement with the Zunghar wars.

The Turfani migration toward the border was "voluntary" in the sense that Imin's people chose to protect themselves from Zunghar attacks by abandoning their home. But an important factor in their decision was the Qing refusal to guarantee the oasis against attack. The limitations on supplies for large garrisons in the oases of Turkestan meant that armies could not stay in one place very long; they had to attack vigorously or retreat. The long-term solution was to build up the productive resources of Turkestan so as to support both an expanded population and a military apparatus. This development came after the mid-eighteenth century, when the Qing began the aggressive promotion of the settlement of Xinjiang.[23] Most studies of the Qing settlement of Xinjiang only begin with this later period, but the earlier experience with Turfan is revealing. It shows, once again, how precarious were the natural resources of the region, how many constraints they placed on active expansion, and what difficulties these created for security and economic livelihood there.

This semi-voluntary population movement was only one of many migration projects promoted by the Qing. Through coercive and material incentives, the Qing rulers shifted not just military forces but thousands of agrarian settlers around their empire as they incorporated progressively larger territories into the state. From its origins as a "booty state" in early-seventeenth-century Manchuria, the Qing had used deportations and mass kidnappings to build a human resource base. As Hong Taiji commented in 1643, "One is not happy enough when merely taking goods, one is only satisfied when one takes people."[24] Now the Qing induced migration toward the empire's borders in order to incorporate more peoples into the expanding state. These early eighteenth-century negotiations set the stage for the aggressive penetration of Turkestan thereafter.

Settlement of Xinjiang

After eliminating the Zunghar state, the Qing began to promote much more actively the colonization of Turkestan.[25] This colonization program has been studied extensively by Chinese scholars, and several shorter accounts in English have appeared, especially the excellent study by James Millward. Here I focus on how the Qing colonization program contributed to the cultural diversity of the empire and changed the ecology of the region.[26]

Modern studies of the settlement of Xinjiang carry on a tradition that extends from Wei Yuan's *Shengwuji* to other nineteenth-century works. By stressing the contribution of Qing policies to the integration of the empire and the positive effects on economic development of the region, they assert that the formation of modern China's identity as a "multinationality na-

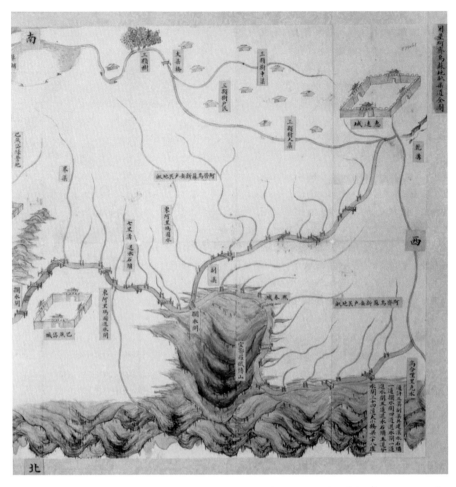

Map of settlements in Xinjiang. These settlements lie just north of the Ili river. South
is at the top. The map features canals and, in red, dams built along the rivers. On the
upper right is the fortified town of Huiyuan, on the lower left is Bayandai. The rivers
flow at the base of the large mountain range on the bottom (north) of the map.

tion-state" *(duo minzu guojia)* grew smoothly out of these projects of "unification." Scholars of the Nationalist period and in the People's Republic
take very similar approaches. Chen Tsu-yuen opened his Ph.D. dissertation,
written in France in 1932, by noting that Sun Yatsen envisaged sending 10
million soldiers and civilian colonists to Xinjiang and Mongolia: "This is
why the land clearance of this province under the Qing is of great interest:
it can provide useful information to the Chinese government for future
exploitation."[27] He discusses the organization of local government, the
sources of labor for land settlement, the location and number of settle-

ments, the development of communication and transport routes, taxation, and the economic and political consequences of the incorporation of Xinjiang as a province. Many subsequent studies follow the same model.

Chinese historians of this project view it much as Frederick Jackson Turner viewed the settlement of the American West, as the "opening of the frontiers" to settlement *(bianjiang kaifa)*. The Han immigrants, and the state subsidies they brought with them, raised the productivity of lands which had been vacant or used only for low-yielding activities such as grazing. Like the North American settlers of the New World, the modern historians and their Qing ancestors viewed the replacement of grazing with intensive agriculture as an advance in social and economic development.[28] Fixed settlements, dense populations, and high agricultural yields attracted merchants. Denser trade routes tied the newly colonized regions more closely to the interior. From the Chinese nationalist perspective, colonization contributed to the integration of China's minority peoples into the nation.

These historians describe much of the process of settlement accurately, but the assumptions behind their accounts are problematic. They take for granted that Xinjiang "naturally" belonged under the rule of the Chinese state, and that its recovery from the "rebel" Zunghars fulfilled a preexisting definition of national territory. For them, imperial expansion completed the construction of modern Xinjiang as a "multi-nationality" autonomous region with clearly defined borders. They portray the Qing as a developmental state dedicated to improving the economic livelihood of all its subjects and uniting them under the leadership of the Han nationality.

Our post-nationalist, postcolonialist age brings new perspectives to this fascinating subject, introducing themes of ethnic and political diversity, ecological constraints, and the social tensions of colonialism. The Qing was only one of several expanding, colonizing empires in eighteenth-century Eurasia.[29] Furthermore, because the Xinjiang frontier was only one of many frontiers on which the Qing expanded, we need a holistic view of frontier policy. The emperor, the Grand Council, and a specialized group of officials who spent most of their careers in the peripheries defined its underlying objectives. The lives of each of these men, such as Agui, Nayancheng, Chen Hongmou, Nian Gengyao, and Song Yun, would repay closer analysis.[30] Since their common interests and talents set them off from those officials who served in the interior, they provided unity for imperial planning. Although no single policy was applied all over the empire, the issues were the same everywhere. This special Qing vision of a unified empire needs careful examination.

Unlike modern historians, the Qing ruling elite did not conceive of a unified people *(minzu)* defined by nationalist ideology, nor did they claim that Xinjiang had always belonged to China. They knew well that these conquests were unprecedented, and that colonization required new policies. The real Qing motivations were simpler: security and self-sufficiency. The main goal was to make the region pay its own way, including support for permanent large military garrisons. Some scholars claim that yields from the newly cleared lands were enough, but as James Millward has shown, grain supplies alone came nowhere near meeting total military costs. Large shipments of silver from the interior paid for salaries, equipment, clothing, and construction costs. Despite the development of gold and jade mines, Xinjiang never justified itself economically, and economic development was never the primary goal.

Because Xinjiang depended so heavily on substantial support from the interior, its security costs were always controversial. Jiangnan literati who criticized spending on the new territories always met with stern imperial rebukes. More surprising than the emperor's hostility is the fact that the critics gained such an open and influential voice, indicating that they had substantial support. The debate over the value of Xinjiang was in fact a discussion of the proper boundaries and identity of empire. For the Qing disputants, the conquest was not an obvious outcome of a continuous expansion to fixed boundaries. The boundaries had to be constructed in the process of conquest and constantly justified.

History provided one means of legitimizing the conquest. Then as today, historians drew a picture of a continuous Chinese presence in the oases from the Han and Tang garrison towns to the present. Modern maps, like Tan Qixiang's historical atlas, perpetuate the myth by drawing clear lines of imperial territorial control. The historical atlas, another key component of nation formation, supports the convenient fiction of the nation-state as a geographically fixed entity with clear, continuous, long-lasting boundaries. By painting one space in one color, these maps conceal the limited state control over frontier territories, the varied types of administration, and the shifts of empires and trade routes that caused cities to flourish and then collapse into ruins.[31] Precarious, disconnected settlement was normal in this vast region, as Sven Hedin and others discovered, and the Qing establishment of a permanent military and civilian presence, which lasts to this day, was in fact unprecedented, not a linear outgrowth of earlier expansions.

Instead of placing Xinjiang's colonization in a smooth sequence from the Han to the modern nation, let us ask what allowed the Qing to break through the limits that frustrated earlier imperial efforts. Military, institutional, diplomatic, and cultural changes allowed this breakthrough, but the eighteenth-century economy was the base of imperial control.

For the interior, the terms of the early Qing fiscal settlement had made it impossible for the state to know clearly local agrarian conditions. In the early seventeenth century, in order to win over the Han elite, the Manchu conquerors had agreed to leave most of the Ming fiscal system in place, abolishing its most burdensome surcharges, and they had given up their initial project of conducting a new empire-wide land survey.[32] The state collected a fixed sum of revenue in silver, based on land quotas set in the late sixteenth century. Newly cleared land was supposed to be reported for taxation, but elites in collusion with local officials successfully concealed nearly all of it. China's registered land area hardly increased at all from 1753 to 1910, even though cultivated land area grew by an estimated 33 percent.[33] Despite repeated denunciations, top-level officials rarely learned of concealed land clearance. Only in flagrant cases, where, for example, a sandbar threatened to flood a major city, could Beijing take notice.[34] This fiscal arrangement, so frustrating for economic historians, was convenient for imperial rule. Guaranteed large, stable revenue, enough to support a small salaried bureaucracy, a large standing army, and a luxurious imperial household, the rulers could rely on the cooperation of the much larger local elites to enforce local order.

But the frontier was different. Here, on the one hand, there were no entrenched literati to block state consolidation. On the other hand, the established elites had little sympathy for imperial administrators, and they were often culturally alien. No longer held in check by embedded social formations, military and civilian administrators had the freedom to try out new methods of control. Zungharia after the conquest was a tabula rasa for pioneering frontier officials.[35] Its experience indicates the aspirations of the bureaucracy once it was freed from social constraints. We can look at the colonization program in a new light, then, not just as economic support for soldiers, or as the culmination of a nation-building project, but as the implementation of colonialists' dreams on an open frontier. In short, it paralleled the projects of empire builders around the globe. Scholars have begun to examine the "tensions of empire" in Asia and Africa in comparative perspective, focusing on the British, French, and Indonesian experience. The Qing empire should be added to their list.[36]

As its name indicates, Xinjiang, or "New Frontier," was the product of an imperial vision. Xinjiang, however, was only one of many new regions that came under Qing control in the eighteenth century. From 1683 to 1760, Xinjiang, Taiwan, the southwest provinces, Mongolia, Kokonor, and Tibet all became permanent territorial acquisitions. This short, explosive period of expansion generated new thinking about the character of the empire. We cannot consider any one region in isolation from the others, since issues of frontier rule were part of a single discourse.

What ideals did the Qing rulers have for their new territories? Some scholars have described the Qing project as a "civilizing mission," by anal-ogy with French imperial aims.[37] In this view, imperial officials followed traditional Confucian imperatives of transforming barbarian peoples into civilized humans in order to create a uniform, orderly hierarchy. But Qing goals were by no means so simple. Such "transformation" *(hua)* was only one aim, and it was offset by equally strong imperatives to preserve primi-tive peoples from corrupting contact with civilization.[38] Furthermore, the ideals generated from the center, or from high-ranking officials, always ran up against barriers to implementation from highly varied local situations. A second major tension of the empire was the gap between these inconsistent ideals and their implementation in local administrative practice.

Difference was inherent in the imperial project, both because the vision did not endorse uniformity and because localities resisted rationalization. At the same time, the imperatives of bureaucratic efficiency pushed for standardization of administrative practice. The special position of the Manchus, as themselves minority rulers of a Han-dominated empire, made them especially sensitive to the eradication of difference. A completely ra-tionalized, civilized empire that treated all its subjects the same would have removed all marks of Manchu identity. Scholars who endorse the "siniciza-tion thesis" about the Qing make just this claim: that the Manchus became completely assimilated to Han culture and rested their legitimacy solely on claims to create order, following the Mandate of Heaven.[39] But this thesis ignores prominent aspects of Qing rule. It neglects the continual concern of the Manchu elite to maintain its separateness from the Han mass, ex-pressed in its marriage policies, separate residence, and religious rituals, and especially in the banner institutions that were its basis of control.[40] In addition, the sinicization thesis, like the civilizing mission thesis, ignores how the Qing continually reinscribed difference alongside uniformity in its subject populations. The tension between difference and uniformity applies as much to the Han as to the non-Han populations, but it was on the fron-tiers that it became most evident. Here cultural diversity was not just inher-ited but constructed.

The Qing set up all of Xinjiang as a military camp in 1760 under the au-thority of the commander (Ili Jiangjun) in Ningyuan (later moved to Hui-yuan) and his deputies in Pizhan-Turfan, Kur Kara Usu (Qingsui cheng), Tarbaghatai (Suijing cheng), Ush, and Kashgar.[41] This fact alone set it apart from the rest of the empire. As the one region which had been gained in its entirety through a rapid military conquest, it stood out as the one where the army dominated. Mongolia had joined the empire in a gradual process of negotiated surrender and military campaigns extending from the early rise of the Manchu state until 1760. In Tibet and Kokonor, Qing armies had made brief forays and left small garrisons behind but relied on local Tibetan and Mongolian elites. In Taiwan and the southwest, substantial Han immigration in the Ming had preceded the arrival of Qing troops. In Xinjiang, except for Hami and the failed colony at Turfan, very few Han settlers entered the region until after 1760. The garrisons of 10,000 to 23,000 men stationed around Xinjiang introduced considerable diversity themselves. They included Manchu, Chinese, and Mongolian bannermen, Chahars, surviving Zunghars, Torghuts returned from the Volga, tribal Manchus such as the Xibo and Daghurs, and Green Standard Chinese troops from Gansu and Shaanxi.

Besides the military commander, there were multiple civilian administrative structures, frequently reshuffled from 1759 to 1773. In 1759 Anxi prefecture in Gansu governed the new *zhiliting* of Hami and Barköl, and included Pizhan (Turfan) and Qitai in 1771–72. Ürümchi and Zhenxi became *zhiliting* in 1759–60, followed by Ili in 1764. They were all formally under the authority of the Gansu provincial treasurer until 1773, when Barköl was elevated to become Zhenxi prefecture, governing Hami, Pizhan, and Qitai, and Anxi was demoted to a *zhilizhou*. Dihua *zhilizhou* was created to govern Ürümchi and the new counties of Changji, Fukang, and Suilai. Until 1882 the regular civil administration included only one prefecture and one *zhilizhou* in eastern Xinjiang and the *zhiliting* of Ili. Most of the vast territory lay beyond it.

Even in eastern Xinjiang there were multiple jurisdictions. The Muslims of Hami and Turfan were organized, unusually, as banners, with their chieftains designated as *jasaks*, who had autonomous control over their people. Other Mongolian tribes in the region were also ruled by *jasaks*. In addition, the military colonists followed their banner or Green Standard commanders, while the civilian colonists (Han and Taranchi) and criminal exiles supported the garrisons and were governed by their respective civilian authorities.

In Altishahr, the oasis towns ringing the Tarim basin, *begs* governed independently, under supervision by military residents. Here the Qing kept their forces separate from the native population in small cantonments and rotated the forces frequently to prevent permanent settlement. They also kept out civilian colonists and, as much as possible, Han merchants. Local administration was run by Turkestanis, and justice followed Islamic law. Qing influence, however, was still apparent. The *begs* themselves were no longer hereditary nobles; subject to the Qing rule of avoidance, they wore the queue and Han clothing. They could abuse their power much like district magistrates through bribery, manipulation of prices, and ties of indebtedness, but alongside them the religious establishment flourished, and the Qing did not intervene. It is hard to imagine a greater contrast with the situation in Kokonor, for example, where the lamaseries were deliberately destroyed.

In summary, there was a gradient of administrative structures across the region from east to west, becoming progressively less similar to the interior civil administration and more dominated by Central Eurasian customs as the Han presence faded out. There were three distinct civil administrative structures—*junxian, jasaks,* and *begs*—each deriving from a different cultural tradition (Chinese, Mongolian, and Turkic). On top of this civil structure was the military presence, which was concentrated in Ili in the north, where nearly 100,000 personnel and their dependents resided, significant in Hami–Turfan–Barköl, and minimal in the south, where there were no permanent forces. The military structures were divided into banners and Green Standards, and the banners themselves accommodated a dizzying variety of ethnic groups. The differing structures of native, civilian, and military administration balanced one another as the Qing rulers deployed their limited forces across this huge space. This did not reflect a single civilizing project or nationalist incorporation but rather multiple negotiations between bureaucratic, coercive, and local environments.[42]

Tax obligations and property rights also reflected the diversity of the region. Han military colonists carefully surveyed their lands, estimated harvest yields, and handed over their crops to the state in return for stipends. Bannermen, by contrast, acted like self-cultivating peasants. Their banner units owned the land collectively in principle, but this changed to private ownership in the nineteenth century. They supposedly supported themselves from their own production, although in fact they often contracted out cultivation rights to immigrant Han peasants or merchants in exchange for fixed rents. The exile colonies had no rights to their land; all their settlements were attached to the military colonies they served. They received less land than the soldiers, generally of poorer yield, and officials took the entire crop. Han civilians *(hutun)* received an average of 30 *mou* (5 acres) per household, and were organized under the same *lijia* tax collection system as in the interior. They were supposed to repay the loans of seed, tools, and animals which got them started, but even though they paid no taxes for the first six years, the low prices of grain put them in arrears quickly. Eventually the state reduced or forgave much of their loan obligations. Usually their tax rates were the same as in Gansu, where most of them originated. The Muslim colonists, by contrast, reckoned their harvest not by yields per land area but by the ratio of crop to seed planted. This method of reckoning harvests was characteristic of traditional Muslim agriculture, adapted to a low-yield, extensive cultivation region.[43]

Officials discussing these tax systems persistently paid attention to incentives for improving agricultural output. Many local officials tried to devise tax policies appropriate to each group that would ensure incentives for the cultivator to increase production as well as increasing the surplus paid to the state. Originally, on Muslim lands, the Qing state took 40 percent of the crop in kind, considering these lands as state land. Imperial Commissioner Agui argued for switching taxes to fixed rents in order to make collection easier and improve incentives. On Han military colony land *(bingtun)*, the entire surplus went to the state, and settlers were bound to the land. Harvest yields were carefully measured, and rewards and salaries were given to officers and soldiers for improving yields. Agui argued in 1766 for increasing rewards for soldiers who could improve yields above the average.

Bannermen, by contrast, owned their land collectively as part of their garrison. But in the early 1800s the Qing implemented a land reform program which granted banner soldiers hereditary land rights. As Song Yun noted in his report of 1804, collective ownership of property led to "laziness," so he recommended dividing up the land and expecting each man to provide for himself. He believed that this would create incentives for each cultivator to grow a surplus beyond his family needs, and that granaries to feed the poor could be provided from this surplus. In fact, Manchu bannermen, never interested in agricultural cultivation in the first place, soon leased out their holdings to Chinese and Taranchi tenants. Private, commercialized land relations developed, including loans at interest and mortgages.

Han and Taranchi settlers also owed labor dues for construction work in cities and on road building. The Turkestani settlers were state peasants, owing rents and labor dues to the state, with no freedom to leave the land. The Han settlers, by contrast, ranged from criminal exiles, who had no freedom, to completely independent landowners, and even merchant landowners. In Zungharia the Qing created no single unified system of land rights. The diverse character of settlement was reflected in separate arrangements for each group.

In east Turkestan and southern Xinjiang a well-established land system had already been in place long before the conquest. Local *begs* were large hereditary landowners. Those who rebelled against the Qing lost their lands, but the loyalists were given increased holdings, including attached peasants, from confiscated property. *Begs* were incorporated into the administrative system. Like other Qing officials, they collected "nourishing virtue" salary supplements, but in the form of land and people, not in cash. Peasants here were in a nearly slave-like condition. The new rulers inserted themselves at the top of an old hierarchy, confirmed most of the local rulers, and left agrarian relations as they were.

Colonization and Land Clearance

We now turn to the material details of agrarian production. The Qing promoted military colonization on a much more extended scale than their predecessors. The decision to encourage colonization grew directly out of officials' awareness of the difficulties of supplying armies in the field. The colonization of Central Eurasia in fact began half a century earlier than the final conquest of the region, in the early eighteenth century. The two primary impulses were to increase grain production in the oasis settlements so as to provide reliable supplies for the troops, and to relieve population pressure in the poorest regions of China's northwest so as to give relief to drought-stricken peasants and ward off social unrest. A third motive, often not so openly expressed, was to ensure permanent imperial control of the region by constructing a new settler society there, composed of a mixture of peoples immigrating from the interior.

Colonization began under purely military auspices, and settled soldiers were the first new agriculturalists to clear land, but civilians soon followed them. Over time, the civilian population expanded, and soldiers began to lease their land illegally to civilian investors, creating a de facto trend toward civilianization and privatization. Qing officials encouraged this move, believing that giving peasants land rights would encourage more intensive cultivation. But the ultimate result of the decline of military control was to undermine imperial authority over the region. Social tensions created by the settlement push in the eighteenth century had been held in check when the military administration dominated, but in the nineteenth century, with the decline of military forces, many of the new structures established in the previous century broke apart, making Xinjiang a constant source of upheaval.

The Qing also embraced many diverse types of frontier settlement, military and civilian. It brought to Xinjiang different kinds of military units, for different purposes, and later sent criminal exiles there under military supervision. The civilian settlers, mostly Han peasants from the northwest, worked under different forms of agrarian institutions, spanning the range from near serfdom to complete independent ownership. Furthermore, Turkic settlers moved from southern Xinjiang to the north brought with them their own distinctive structures and local leadership. Thus the Qing constructed a new society in northern Xinjiang, much more diverse than ever before. The evolving colonization project overlaid new peoples and structures on earlier ones, creating a palimpsest composed of multiple layers of institutions and social groups.

The high cost of grain transport during the Galdan campaigns stimulated the Kangxi emperor's interest in the history of military settlement. In 1700 he told his subordinates to look into the experience of the Han general Zhao Chongguo, who had first implemented *tuntian* on the frontier.[44] After 1715 he began active efforts to establish colonies at Turfan, Hami, Anxi, and Barköl in the east, and at Khobdo and other places near the Irtysh, Orkhon, and Tula rivers in the north. The northern colonies aimed to protect the Qing's Khalkha allies against retaliation by Tsewang Rabdan. In the east, each of the attempts to use soldiers to clear fields lasted only a short time. Barköl, the main concentration point for troops campaigning against Tsewang Rabdan, established a small colony of five hundred men in 1716, but it was abandoned in 1726. After reestablishing it in 1729, Yue Zhongqi then proposed to clear up to 100,000 *mou* using five thousand men, but the emperor rejected his proposal, and most of the troops were withdrawn by 1734. Qing armies occupied Turfan in 1715 and sent five thousand colonists there in 1722, but in 1725 all but one thousand men were pulled back to Barköl. They returned briefly in 1729, but Qing forces could not hold the oasis securely. Instead, as we have seen, the Turfanis as a people moved into the interior. Hami and Anxi, which were closer to the border, lasted somewhat longer, but by 1742 they too were abandoned because of poor harvests, even though Nian Gengyao had recommended investing in larger settlements.

In this early period, soldiers cleared land only temporarily to support the main garrisons while they prepared for a campaign. During the Zunghar wars, the military's primary aim was to use the maximum possible force in battle. Diverting soldiers to agricultural work came second. Despite the economic gains of production in the region, which would cut transport costs substantially, both the Kangxi and Yongzheng emperors chose not to make the necessary long-term investments. Immediate strategic considerations outweighed the farsighted views of Yue Zhongqi and Nian Gengyao.

Beginning in 1758, Qing officials launched a serious, continuous campaign to promote extensive agricultural settlement. Each form of settlement had particular fiscal and agrarian features.

Five different types of settlers entered Xinjiang during and after the conquest. First on the scene were two kinds of military colonists, both Manchu bannermen and Han Green Standard troops. The first major military colonies were established in Ürümchi; they expanded westward to reach a total of 13,400 cultivator-soldiers.[45] Farther west, in Ili, rebellions forced the Qing to give up on early efforts, but from 1761 to 1772 it established increasing numbers of colonies. Again, military colonization is by no means unique to China, or to the Qing dynasty. The notoriously brutal colonial schemes of Tsar Alexander I and his general Alexis Arakcheev in early-nineteenth-century Russia are the most conspicuous European example.[46] Still, the Qing colonies in Xinjiang were more successful than those of previous Chinese dynasties and other imperial states: they lasted longer, fewer soldiers deserted, and they grew into permanent settlements. Although they were never self-sufficient, they did not bankrupt the treasury.

Third came exiled criminals. After 1758 the Qing began sending convicts regularly to the newly conquered region. Ordinary criminals became bond-servants of Chinese garrisons. Cashiered officials were exempt from penal labor and lived separately from commoners, but they often served in local administrative posts during the period of their temporary exile. Joanna Waley-Cohen has described the legal, political, and symbolic functions of the exile system.[47] Exile colonies had only slight direct impact on land settlement because their numbers were small. Nevertheless, they did mix together people of very different social strata from all over China. Tax resisters, secret society members, military deserters, corrupt administrators, and talented officials who were victims of political intrigue all shared the rigors of the frontier, at least temporarily. Among the literati it was a common enough experience to forge bonds of loyalty that may have influenced literati activity after their return. In this way, exile created networks spanning regional, cultural, and class boundaries.

Fourth, Han civilian settlement began after 1761. The main focus of this state-sponsored program was the poor peasantry of Gansu. This province suffered frequent drought; it had the lowest agricultural yields in interior China; its tax base was very low; and its peasants constantly faced threats of starvation.[48] The settlement program was designed to offer a safety valve for this region by encouraging the poorest peasants to migrate to Ürümchi. By 1781 nearly twenty thousand households had emigrated. They obtained full official support for transport costs, animals, agricultural tools, seed, and housing. Organized official settlement ceased after 1781, but other Han peasants continued to head for the frontier on their own.

Fifth were Muslim settlers from southern Xinjiang. Realizing that the difficult agrarian conditions of the region required special expertise, Qing administrators recruited Muslim Turkic-speaking dwellers of the oasis cities of southern Xinjiang (Altishahr) to move to the north to clear new land. Their expertise with irrigation of arid lands was particularly valuable.

These Taranchis, as they were called, set up separate Muslim colonies, especially in Ili. They brought with them not only their agricultural skills but their local political system as well. Their hereditary Muslim leaders *(begs)* were recognized by the Qing as official community representatives with bureaucratic ranks. Although they came from southern Xinjiang, they too were immigrants, just like the Manchu military and Han civilians. The only "natives," the Zunghars, had been nearly exterminated. The Muslims' religion and language, local leaders, tax obligations, and property rights set them off sharply from the Han and Manchu settlers.

Such administrative and cultural diversity posed severe challenges to imperial governance. The Qing's problems were those of empires everywhere: how to persuade extremely variegated groups of people to remain under a single authority. It was imperial expansion that had created the problem in the first place. Military force and competent civil administrators could contain tensions, but they also needed other techniques.

Clearance by military colonies *(bingtun)* began in 1757 with the restoration of lands in Gansu, Hami, and Barköl, followed by new clearances in Ürümchi and the Ili valley through the 1770s.[49] The soldiers came from the Green Standard forces of Han troops, mostly from garrisons in the northwest.

The *tun* was the basic settlement unit, marked by a walled-earth fort, holding from 15 to 250 men. The fort included room for soldiers and their families, agricultural tools, granaries, and local offices. It was not merely a defense post but a complete administrative and production "unit," like the modern *danwei*. Every *tuntian* area was governed by a major official *(tuntian dachen)* who reported to the military governor in Ürümchi. On average, each soldier received 20 *mou* of land, plus animals, tools, and seed. He did not have ownership rights in the land, nor could he choose his crops. The state granted the colonists usage rights only, and prescribed which crops would be grown. The predominant crop was wheat, with smaller amounts of barley, millet, and sesame. The surplus was distributed in two ways. In Anxi only, the crop was split evenly between the colonists and the state. In the other colonies, cultivators paid a fixed quota to the state and kept the rest for their families. The latter system generally provided greater incentives to increase yields. In Ürümchi, the standard quota was 12 *shi,* but rewards were given to cultivators and officials if they gave 15 *shi* or more to the state. In 1784 Fukangan rejected a proposal to raise the required quota in Ürümchi. He argued that the labor supply was limited, and requiring more grain would divert men from their military duties; it would also cause them to expand military landholdings, interfering with private production. He thought that the existing land provided sufficient grain for the garrison. The troops needed 30,000 *shi;* the previous year's harvest had been 90,000 *shi,* and there were 800,000 *shi* stored in the granaries. At this point it appeared that the colonies were working successfully.[50]

The cities of Ürümchi and Ili also had special granaries designated for military use. As the *Sanzhou Jilue* noted, "The interior granaries are for relieving the people, but Xinjiang's granaries are mainly for military supplies."[51] The only nonmilitary use was the allocation of seed to new *tuntian* settlers. Surplus grain could be sold on the market to raise revenue; but unlike the civilian granaries of the interior, these granaries were not intended to level prices or provide famine relief.[52] We have abundant information about the functioning of the civilian granary system, but the scale and uses of the military granaries still remain obscure. Study of Ürümchi's military granaries would help to illuminate this parallel system.

During the nineteenth century, the effectiveness of the military colonies and their granaries declined. Troops were withdrawn from the region in the 1820s to meet pressing military needs in the interior, and much of the military land was converted to civilian use.[53] Although granary stores were plentiful in the 1780s, much of the grain rotted in the succeeding decades. As the scale of cultivation declined, troops depended more on market sales of grain, but the influx of civilian settlers had driven down market prices. By the early nineteenth century, 200,000 civilians in Ili had cleared 1.8 million *mou* of land.[54] Wu Dashan had calculated in 1766 that a garrison of six hundred men, without their families, rotated every five years for other troops, could support themselves and store a surplus, but his estimate relied on selling surplus grain at the high price of 1.6 taels per *shi.* This was the market price in 1762, but by 1770 it had dropped to 0.5–0.7 tael per *shi* of wheat. At these prices, individual troops could not support themselves. The shift to family farming by civilians, or resettled soldiers, was driven by awareness of this deficit. The "decline" of the military colonies was, in another sense, testimony to the success of the Qing in promoting economic development of the region as it moved from a military garrison zone toward a more civilianized economy dominated by private farmers.

Other soldiers came to Xinjiang for different reasons. Banner colonies, or *qitun,* were established to restore the morale and military strength of the banner troops. Composed predominantly of Manchus and Mongols, they had been the core of the conquest army.[55] After the conquest, banner forces in the northwest neglected military drill and seemed to become more "corrupted" by the civilian life around them. They also became more impoverished, as their stipends could not support them, and they were forbidden to engage in commerce or agriculture. This general phenomenon had concerned the court throughout the eighteenth century, but now it extended even to those closest to the northwestern frontier. Xinjiang was seen as a relatively unspoiled region that could restore their morale. Some 11,500 troops were sent there between 1764 and 1774. At first they did not till the soil; they were supported with stipends in kind. The revenue came from state-run money-changing shops established in Ürümchi. The Qing officials thus used the resources of the flourishing commercial economy to shore up the archaic virtues of the pure, if impoverished, bannermen. By the Jiaqing reign, however, rising costs of living made these revenues insufficient, and the bannermen were ordered to support themselves on the land. They had cleared up to 120,000 *mou* by the end of the century in Huiyuan and Huining. Turkic cultivators provided them with seed, and the state invested heavily in digging irrigation canals to make these lands productive.

Unlike the *bingtun,* the bannermen themselves never cultivated the land. This was to be done by "surplus men" *(yuding),* the sons of banner families who had not inherited their father's post. Rights to the produce also differed. At first, the lands were worked collectively. All the grain was to be given to the state and then shared out among the banner commands. On some of the lands near the main garrison, cultivators worked vigorously, seeing themselves as sharing in the garrison's welfare; but on other lands farther away, they neglected the fields, seeing them merely as state land. In 1804 Governor Song Yun turned collective holdings of 80,000 *mou* in Huiyuan and 40,000 *mou* in Huining into private property, eliminating the soldier-cultivators' stipends while establishing special state granaries to buy up their surplus production. He argued that making landholding a private property right would increase incentives to work: "At first, the land was state property, cultivated collectively so as to instruct the men in cultivation. But this led to laziness, so the land was divided. Now each is not paid allowances from the treasury but provides for himself. Formerly they feared that if they worked hard on the land, their salaries would be cut; now that this [new system] has been explained, they work hard."[56]

With this anti-collectivist agrarian reform, reminiscent of China after 1979, frontier officials shifted away from the original goal of maintaining a collective banner identity toward ensuring that each soldier supported himself as a private landowner. In fact, the banner cultivators themselves began calling in tenants, illegally, to till the soil for them, and by 1830 prohibitions on renting out land were ended.[57] By the mid-nineteenth century the Qing had in effect created a new landed elite in the region, a Manchu and Mongol stratum relying on tenant labor by immigrant Han peasants.

Another distinct group of soldier-cultivators entered the region: elements of the Suolun, Chahar, Xibo, and Oirat garrisons from Zhangjiakou and Manchuria. Like the Manchu and Mongol banner colonists, they received stipends, though at a somewhat lower level, and some of them progressively established themselves as independent landowners. The Xibo garrison members were the most successful. They progressively gained economic power, expanded their landholdings, and maintained their distinct prosperous colonies through the end of the Qing dynasty. They remain the only native Manchu-speaking minority in China today.[58]

Exiled criminals formed another class of involuntary settlers. Earlier dynasties again provided precedents, but the Qing had much larger territories available. Exiles came to Xinjiang from all over the empire, and from many social classes. Wang Xilong gives sixty-six examples of criminals who faced exile, including counterfeiters of copper coins, armed robbers, parents who killed their children for having illicit sexual relations, drug peddlers, feuding lineages, kidnappers, arsonists, those who brought false charges at court, and deserters from military service, to name only a few.[59] Many convicted of crimes deserving capital punishment had their sentences commuted to exile at the autumn assizes. Impeached and convicted officials were another distinct group. Exiles generally first served as bondservants to the garrisons, not as agricultural laborers, but beginning in 1716 they could till the land if they chose. Labor scarcity provided strong motivations to use the exiles productively. By one estimate, about 160,000 exiles went to Xinjiang from 1758 to 1911.[60] Like the soldiers and civilian colonists, they received agricultural implements, seed, and up to 30 *mou* of land to establish themselves, but since they had little chance to own their lands, their yields were notably lower.[61]

From the beginning the exiles fought back: they staged the first major revolt in Xinjiang in 1768. A *tuntian* official held a celebratory banquet for some of his exile friends; he provided large quantities of liquor and gathered men and women together. When the drunken official forced the women to sing, their outraged husbands went on a violent rampage, killing the official, raiding the military warehouses for weapons, and occupying the city. With a force of one thousand, they marched out of the city to confront a relief force of only 150 men sent from Ürümchi, but the exiles' untrained horses fled when the two sides exchanged gunfire. All of the rebels were massacred.[62]

Exiled criminals sometimes bribed soldiers to let them escape. After the riot had revealed lax administration, officials tightened up controls. Tattooing on the face the name of the crime and the place of exile made detec-

tion easy, and those who fled faced immediate execution.[63] After five years
of field labor, however, followed by eight to ten years of mining labor, criminals could join the civilian population. Few managed to achieve this arduous goal, but the state did provide funds for exiles' families to join them so
as to encourage them to settle down. Some were able to join the army and,
if they achieved extraordinary merit during a campaign, gain their release
to return home. Nearly all the exiles, however, remained in the region for
their entire lives.

A second kind of exile had not committed such egregious crimes but
ended up in Xinjiang for being implicated in local disturbances. Officials
deported one hundred members of a powerful lineage in Hubei that had
abused its local influence and a group of one thousand miners on the southwest frontier who had attempted to flee to Vietnam.[64] These settlers arrived
in groups, which were dispersed around the region; they worked under civil
instead of military jurisdiction and acted like civilian settlers. They were yet
another of the many disparate groups that cleared the land.

Many disgraced officials were also exiled to Xinjiang, but they did not
cultivate the land. Over fifty officials implicated in a corruption scandal in
Gansu in 1781 went to Xinjiang, returning thirteen years later.[65] Hong
Liangji, the famous scholar who narrowly escaped decapitation after he directly criticized the emperor in 1799, was first sent to Ili but was pardoned
three months later. Failure to prevent deficits, the inability to manage foreigners, or the commission of crimes by subordinates could all get officials
in trouble. More than 10 percent of the Governors-General serving from
1758 to 1820 suffered banishment to Xinjiang.[66] Civil and military officials
of all ranks from the lowest to the highest could end up in the region.
Xinjiang thus collected a microcosmic sample of Chinese society from the
interior, added to the native Turkestanis, military administrators, and nomads already there.

Civilian settlers *(mintun)* became the majority of new migrants to Xinjiang. Before taking Xinjiang, officials had begun to encourage settlement
in western Gansu. Here, too, the Qing experimented with several different
types of land allocation before settling on one that provided the maximum
private incentive to increase production. In western Gansu, for a time, officials established a sharecropping system, which divided the crop 50–50 or
40–60 between the new settlers and the state.[67] In the Yongzheng reign,
the Gansu settlers supplied much grain to the armies still in the field in
Xinjiang. By 1736, however, because of disappointing harvests, the sharecropping system ended, and the settlers' holdings became private land on
which they paid fixed taxes. In western Gansu, now securely part of the in-

terior, the new peasants assimilated to the resident population. State farms worked with hired labor—a second experiment—cleared about 50,000 *mou* in Anxi, but were terminated after four years.

The most successful projects relied on a form of indentured servitude much like the kind used to settle the New World. Settlers received travel funds, clothes, food, seeds, tools, animals, start-up loans, and 30 *mou* of land. For five years they had to work the land, but they paid no taxes. After five years, once they began paying taxes, they became independent land-owners. In Ili, after three years, they paid taxes of 0.1 tael per *mou* until their debts were repaid, and 0.05 taels per *mou* thereafter.[68] This system es-pecially attracted the poor peasantry of the northwest, who lacked the cap-ital to clear their own land. In 1726 Yue Zhongqi claimed to have settled 3,300 poor households in Shazhou, Gansu. From the 1760s, significant numbers began to move into Xinjiang out of western Gansu.[69] The first set-tlers were single men or landless laborers, but soon most migrants brought their families along, especially after officials broadcast reports to encourage emigration. By 1803 over 155,000 civilians had cleared 1,014,879 *mou* in Barköl and Ürümchi. By 1820, the total land cleared, including Ili, equaled more than 1,080,000 *mou*.[70]

This state-supported settlement program attracted many others from the interior, who rushed to the new frontier eager to improve their lives. ShaanGan Governor-General Wen Shou, touring the region in 1773, enthu-siastically recounted the sight of shops clustered "as closely as the teeth of a comb" along market streets, peddlers thronging the roads, and peasants busily working on fertile lands. In his view, Xinjiang was a "paradise" *(letu)* that offered great opportunities to all newcomers, and he urged the state to promote further clearance.[71] Hired laborers who came to the region enjoyed high wages—up to 1 to 2 taels per month—and paid low food prices, so they could save their money and before long buy land.

Merchants who brought large sums of capital could invest in land imme-diately and hire laborers to clear it, with official support. These "merchant colonists" *(shanghu)* formed another important group of civilian migrants. Some controlled very large estates, like the thirty-two merchants in Ili who owned a total of 39,600 *mou*. In Ürümchi in 1778, 1,136 merchant house-holds obtained land and seed loans on the same basis as the peasant set-tlers, even though they did not work the land themselves. Lazar Duman ar-gues that the presence of these merchant capitalists made Xinjiang a highly stratified society, dominated by a landlord-official elite, but most of the merchant land clearances were not as large as those in Ili; 50 *mou* per per-son appears to have been an average amount.[72] Governor-General Wen Shou did not fear the influx of merchants from the interior; instead, he offered them investment opportunities so that they would become a settled, property-owning class.

Except for the merchants, who paid in silver, nearly all settlers paid taxes in kind. Wen Shou set a rate of 0.08 *shi* per *mou*, or 2.4 *shi* for an average plot. Given five years to establish themselves, this was a reasonable amount for most cultivators. Once they became taxpayers, they enjoyed the full property rights of all the settled peasantry.

Turkic agriculturalists were the last important group of contributors to support the Qing conquest.[73] They were the only cultivators who had extensive experience with the special form of irrigated oasis agriculture practiced in Xinjiang. They were known as "Taranchi," originally a Turkish word, which the Qing took from the Mongolian *tariyaci* (or Oirat *tarän*) for "farmer."[74] As noted earlier, the Zunghars, when they occupied the Ili valley, brought many Taranchi up from the southern oases to promote their land clearance program. The Taranchi made up a substantial proportion of the twenty to thirty thousand people whom the Zunghars brought to northern Xinjiang.[75] When they captured Yarkand in 1680, they deported much of the local population to the north as bondservants producing for the Zunghar state.

At the same time, other Taranchi helped the Qing. The *beg* of Hami promoted land clearance after Qing troops drove off Zunghar raiders in 1718. Qing officials helped him to dig irrigation canals. In 1719 he sent 608 *shi* to the garrison in Barköl. In 1730 he reported harvests of 3,000 to 4,000 *shi* from four to five hundred new settlers, and between 1730 and 1736 he sent a total of 27,500 *shi* to the Qing garrison. The Qing paid him 1 tael of silver for each *shi* provided to the military. A second settlement was begun in 1739 at Caibash Lake, but the Qing stopped making payments in 1742, and the lands were converted into civilian colonies, paying 40 percent of their product in kind to the state. By 1753, because of poor harvests and the silting of irrigation canals, both colonies were abolished.

In Turfan, Qing officials and the local *beg* attempted to establish agricultural colonies on the Hami model until the entire population moved to the interior in 1731. Over eight thousand Turfanis arrived at Guazhou, Gansu, in 1733. Qing officials built five forts for them and gave them 8,000 *shi* of seed to plant 40,000 *mou*, as well as exemptions from tax and corvée. Poor harvests left them unable to repay their loans, from which they were finally exempted in 1738. In 1755 they returned to Turfan, and the Qing called in other peasants to take over these cleared lands.

Ili became the major site of Turkic agricultural settlement under Qing sponsorship after the conquest. In Ili the Taranchi were the largest group of cultivators. (See Table 9.1.) War had nearly depopulated the region, but

Table 9.1 Types of cultivators in Ili

	Taranchi	Military	Civilian	Banner	Criminal	Total
Population (indiv.)	30,415	2,500	1,085	5,073	117	39,190
Land *(mou)*	180,000ª	50,000	66,211	40,584	1,611	338,406

Source: Wang Xilong, *Qingdai Xibei Tuntian Yanjiu* (Lanzhou: Lanzhou Daxue Chubanshe, 1990), p. 214; Wu Yuanfeng, "Qing Qianlong nianjian Yili tuntian shulue," *Minzu Yanjiu* (1987): 96.
Note: Figures for Civilian and Criminal may be for households, not individuals.
   a. Wu gives 90,000; this figure is taken from Wang.

General Jaohûi established the first Taranchi settlement of one thousand households there to support his initial garrison of four to five thousand men. Immigrants arrived from Aksu, Kashgar, Ush, Shayar, Yarkand, Khotan, and Sailimu in the south, and from Turfan and Hami to the east. By 1768, 6,383 Taranchi households provided a substantial amount of the resident Qing garrison's grain. Qing officials recognized the need to give the cultivators incentives to exploit the fertile land exhaustively. Agui, for example, proposed to change from share rents to fixed rents, stating:

> [Under share rents] during a good harvest, [the settlers] will not gain benefits, and will neglect the land; we will need to supervise them, but the people are too many, and we cannot supervise them all. We fear that during planting time they will embezzle seed and store grain illicitly for themselves after the harvest. If we set a fixed amount to be supplied each year, and let them keep the surplus, not only will there be no disturbances, but they will know that diligent effort will improve their livelihood.[76]

Because fixed rent collection risked creating deficits in poor harvest years, the *hakim beg* established charitable granaries to loan grain to cultivators in times of need. A loan taken in the early spring, before the crops had begun to sprout, could be repaid from the fall harvest with an interest payment of 10 percent.

Officials also supported experimental plots where they tried to improve yields with different planting methods. In Ili, General Ming Rui brought in special high-quality seed from Pizhan for testing. He found that more extensive sowing gave higher yields: 0.025 *shi* per *mou* sown on 43 *mou* yielded a harvest of 55.3 *shi*, but 0.015 *shi* per *mou* sown on 66 *mou* gave a harvest of 101 *shi*. Recognizing that agrarian conditions in Xinjiang were quite different from those in the interior, he recommended that these planting methods be extended to other fields.[77]

Ili's production was more than enough to meet demand. Each Ili cultivator received 30 *mou* of land and 1.5 *shi* of seed, in millet and wheat, and was expected to deliver 16 *shi* to the garrison.[78] In a good year, 1.5 *shi* of seed yielded 40 *shi* of grain, so the settlers were giving 43 percent of their crop to the military—slightly more than the 40 percent paid in Hami. Twenty thousand troops and officials in Huiyuan and Huining needed a total of 166,600 *shi*, of which the Taranchi provided 103,000 *shi*, or 62 percent of the total grain supply. The Chahar, Eleut, Suolun, and Xibo garrisons supplied their own grain, and the Green Standard troops supplied half of their grain, but the Manchu troops relied entirely on the *huitun* settlements. By 1782 the granaries held 500,000 *shi*, but their holdings declined to 282,000 in the Jiaqing reign (1796–1820).

Although the Taranchi were not permitted to leave, and some were punished for fleeing, many other tenants from the south flocked to Ili to till its fertile lands. They preferred the Qing fixed rent system to the repeated exactions of smaller but more arbitrary amounts by the *begs* ruling in the south. The Ush rebellion of 1765, discussed earlier, resulted from abuses by the local *beg*, who could not be restrained by Qing officials.

In Ili, Qing officials reinforced the local social hierarchy to ensure stability and production, leaving in place the existing system of rule by local *begs*. Unlike in Turfan, the *begs* in Ili were not guaranteed hereditary posts; each succession had to be approved by the ranking Qing official. The *hakim beg* at the top of the hierarchy supervised thirteen other ranks of subordinates, a total of eighty-seven officials. Each *beg*, like the civil officials of the interior, received a "nourishing virtue stipend," beginning with 500 taels for the *hakim beg* and proportionately less for lower ranks. The *hakim beg* and his subordinates also received large land grants: 200 *patman* of land with one hundred men to till the land.[79]

Indirectly, Qing policies to fill up Xinjiang also developed Central Eurasia beyond the empire's borders. By the mid-nineteenth century, control over the settlements had declined. The *hakim begs* and their subordinates demanded more rents from their people; they extended their lands to encroach on state and Han settlers' land; and they neglected irrigation works. Many settlers fled. The uprising in Ili during the Taiping rebellion caused further instability. Russians occupied the Ili valley in 1871, remained for a decade, and took 100,000 Taranchis and Chinese Muslims with them when they withdrew. Chinese historians claim that the Russians forcibly deported them, but in fact they were fleeing the savage repression inflicted by Zuo Zongtang's armies. Under the name of "Dongans," 70,000 of these Chinese-speaking Muslims now contribute to the ethnic mix in Kazakhstan and Kyrgyzstan.[80]

Economic Development

Transcending the narrow goals of military support, the conquerors of Xinjiang soon promoted a full-scale program of economic development. Alongside the military colonies, civilians expanded their settlements with state support. The increased agricultural population in turn attracted merchants, who stimulated the growth of towns and commercial links with the interior. Other state programs beyond land clearance supported these developments. Horse markets, mines, and towns completed the picture.

Armies may march on their bellies, but their supplies move on horseback. During military campaigns, all generals had to concern themselves first and foremost with the supply of horses. Because of limits on pastureland within China proper, every dynasty needed to trade with nomads for horses. When it came to judging horseflesh, nomads always had great advantages over the typical Chinese civil official. Dynasties with stronger Central Eurasian connections, like the Tang, could get better deals, and larger supplies of horses, than those, like the Ming, who had sealed themselves off from the steppe. But horse supplies were always crucial to the survival of an empire and accounted for a very significant part of the budget. The Ming rulers established the most systematic method of trading tea and cloth for horses at fixed frontier markets. But their defensive policy was very expensive and left them highly dependent on the Mongols.

The Manchus had established an Imperial Stud (Taipusi) to supply animals for court use, and they had other pasturelands available in Manchuria. But when the military campaigns of Kangxi penetrated Mongolia, the cost of providing horses at these distances became prohibitive. Shaanxi and Gansu could not supply enough to meet the demand, and sending horses from Guihua was very expensive. Mongols and Tibetans in Kokonor provided mares for 8 taels each and stallions at 12 taels each, an extremely high price.[81] As the foregoing narrative indicates, the high death rate of horses on campaigns meant that replacements on a large scale were needed, and the campaigns could last only a limited time before supplies ran out.

In 1736 the first horse farms were established in Ganzhou, Liangzhou, Xining, and Suzhou in Gansu, with a total of 1,200 stud horses. By the early nineteenth century these had increased to 20,000. But the wars of the 1750s called for far larger supplies. A fifty-thousand-man army, at three horses per soldier, required a minimum of 150,000 horses at the outset, and more than 200,000 to provide for replacements over a four-year campaign. Qing generals now had Mongolian allies from whom they could levy animals, but as we have seen, excessive exactions could drive the Mongols into revolt. Only in 1760 were large stud farms opened in Xinjiang at Ili, Barköl, Tarbaghatai, and Ürümchi. Ili, the largest center, had to meet a quota of 9,524 horses every three years. By 1826 it had 50,000 breeding horses. Subsequently, Qing officials established additional farms for sheep, cattle, and camels. By 1826 Ili had 10,000 cows, several thousand camels, and about 42,000 sheep.[82]

In addition to purchases from Mongols, Xinjiang officials could now draw on a new source: the large pastures controlled by the Kazakhs, who had become tributaries of the Qing. At Ürümchi, Chinese offered brocades, cloth, tea, metal utensils, medicine, and porcelain—the typical trade goods of the Silk Road—in exchange for cattle and horses. Ili soon surpassed Ürümchi, and the Kazakh pastures drove prices down considerably, to 2.47 taels per stallion, mare, or gelding, and 1.5 taels per head of cattle. As one official noted, the value of animals on the frontier was quite different from in the interior: at these Kazakh prices, one cow in the interior was worth four frontier horses, and one donkey was worth two horses.[83] Kazakhs also paid a tax of 1 percent of their herds when they crossed the border, and Kazakh tribute missions presented special gift horses to the emperor.

The stud farms were under tight military control, with a top official in charge supervising soldiers, each of whom tended twenty-four or more animals. Careful inspections counted and culled the herds: the Ili farms had to breed a new stock of horses equivalent to one-third of their total herd every three years, and cattle 80 percent of their herd every four years. The heavy demands on the farms were a result of the multiple needs for horses on the frontier. The most intensive demand came from the military colonies and guard posts, where 30 percent of the horses and 15 percent of the cattle needed replacement every year. Routine military service was not as intensive for livestock as field labor, as only 17 percent were worn out annually. Horses were also needed in the mines, and they were given as relief supplies to nomads struck by disaster. A major military campaign, especially the campaign against Jahangir in 1826, could mean a sudden demand for fifty thousand horses from the northwest pastures. For the most part, the stud farms could meet routine demands, and sometimes there was a surplus, as in 1782, when excess horses were sold at 3.3 taels each.

Until the 1850s the stud farms seem to have solved one of the most persistent supply problems that constrained all imperial armies. After 1850, however, the stud farms shared in the general disorder of the region. Like all the other new institutions there, they quickly degenerated when official oversight slackened. Without the triennial inspections, herds rapidly declined. By 1853, 40,000 of the 100,000 horses in Ili had died of disease.

Table 9.2 Iron production in Ürümchi

Year	Production *(jin)*	Surplus above quota
1765	61,440	8,660
1766	76,000	31,178
1767	61,440	3,016
1768	56,480	11,540
1769	56,800	11,200
1770	61,280	12,000
1771	56,800	22,500

Source: *Ulumuqi Zhenglue, tiechang;* cited in Wang Xilong, *Qingdai Xibei Tuntian Yanjiu* (Lanzhou: Lanzhou Daxue Chubanshe, 1990), p. 251.

Pasturelands were turned into cultivated fields as soon as troops withdrew. Efforts to restore the farms at the end of the century had only limited success; by the 1890s there were only 10,000 horses in Barköl and Ili combined.[84]

The intensive agriculture introduced by the Qing generated new demands for agricultural implements, so officials invested in iron mines to produce both tools and weaponry. Original stocks imported from the interior quickly wore out. As with horses, it proved cheaper to produce replacements locally. Beginning in 1773, Ili officials developed iron mines, while other mines produced lead and copper for currency, bullets, and weapons. The military ran them all.

For the most part, Turkic cultivators used only wooden tools, but Han settlers, who dug the soil deeper and cultivated it more intensively, needed iron plows, hoes, sickles, and reapers. Their demands were constant, as 30 percent of the tools wore out each year. Green Standard soldiers did the first hard digging. Metal artisans brought from the interior received a generous wage of 0.2 *taels* per day plus 1 *jin* of food for their scarce skills. After 1773, exiled criminals became the predominant labor force. New regulations provided that after five years criminals could become ordinary civilians, and after eight years in the mines they could return home. The minimum time period was later extended to ten to twelve years, indicating that their labor was badly needed. Agricultural development in Xinjiang, although it relied on independent farmers to till the fields, also required a bonded labor force of convicts under military supervision who provided the basic tools of production. (See Table 9.2.)

By incorporating and developing Xinjiang, the Qing empire brought on itself opportunities and dangers. It secured the region from control by other powers and from a disturbing autonomy, and it drew fixed borders with Russia that, for a time, prevented incursions from the Tsarist empire. Colonization and integration policies intensified the exploitation of natural resources and encouraged substantial immigration from the interior. To some extent, emigration from the northwest eased pressures on resources there. By compensation, the officials had to invest heavily in irrigation works, tools, seed, and animals in Xinjiang to keep its agricultural settlements viable. They raised the productivity of the soil, expanded the land area at the expense of pasture, and generated important commercial links with the interior. Xinjiang become closely bound to the Han core in a way it had never been before.

Yet development generated tensions that could be contained only by force. The first wave of settlers, the soldiers, cleared fields as part of their mission but later became civilian landowners. They were the most reliable population. The exiled criminals came unwillingly, and could easily riot or flee when control became lax. Civilian settlers arrived in droves, provided they received heavy subsidies from the state. As these groups mixed with the local Turkic population, however, and as Chinese Muslims and other traders joined the ethnic macédoine, tensions rose. The vast expanses and variegated populations could not be encompassed by one administrative regime; therefore the Qing employed many systems to embrace its multitudes.

Since the region never paid for itself, continual subsidies from the interior were required simply to hold the existing ecological and social balance in place. During the nineteenth century, however, as resources were diverted toward the interior, Xinjiang began to unravel. The repeated rebellions, culminating in wholesale occupation for twenty years by Yakub Beg in the mid-nineteenth century, were an unintended consequence of the high Qing's developmental policy.[85]

10

Harvests and Relief

MANAGING the frontier economy required a vastly expanded information-gathering apparatus. The Qianlong emperor implemented a system of empire-wide reporting on prices, harvests, and rainfall which provided voluminous data on agrarian conditions. The purpose of these reports was to allow officials to intervene as needed with relief measures. Officials who ran the "evernormal" granaries established in every county relied on market reports for the timing of their interventions to stabilize prices. They could sell when supplies were short and restock when they were abundant.

The collection of standardized statistical data from localities is considered to be the hallmark of a modern state. The creation of the concept of "society" as an entity has been ascribed to the normalization disciplines enacted by nineteenth-century European states, among which statistics was foremost.[1] In this sense, Qing practices of the eighteenth century look precociously "modern."

The most detailed harvest reports in the entire empire came from Xinjiang. No other lands in the empire were watched so closely. Only where all the cleared land was under military control could officials measure precisely the yields in relation to the seed. Regular reports on agricultural yields indicated that garrison supplies were being carefully monitored so that troops could be allocated accordingly.

How successful was the imperial program to settle peasants, clear land, and raise agrarian productivity in the most arid region of the empire? Were the rural producers able to provide sufficient grain for both themselves and the troops? How variable were yields and prices in relation to climate fluctuations? What were the effects of grain markets and official granaries in leveling prices and linking regions together? To what extent did agriculture depend on extensive investment in production by the state? The Qing information-collection apparatus on the frontier provided the data to judge the sustainability of agriculture there.

Harvests and Yields

Collecting data on *tuntian* yields formed part of a larger systematic program of information gathering on the rural economy carried out throughout the empire in the eighteenth century. After the emperor ordered provincial governors to build up storage in granaries to be used for leveling price fluctuations, he also called for monthly reports on grain prices and regular reports on climate, grain storage, and harvests. This comprehensive effort at imperial mapping of the terrain made visible to state officials the local details of agricultural production.[2] Two essential elements of this program were accurate measurement and standardization. For harvest reports, local officials established a target figure that represented the ideal harvest under perfect conditions. They measured actual harvest as a percentage of this figure, on a scale from 1 to 10 (or in some cases 1 to 100).[3] The harvest figures themselves represent not a uniform level of output per land area but a comparison to the best possible yield. They are a valuable source of data for measuring the variability of harvests by region and over time, but they do not in general indicate the absolute output.

The *Collected Statutes of the Qing Dynasty* specified that harvests of 8 and above were "plentiful" *(feng)*; 6 and above were "average" *(ping)*; and 5 and below were "deficient" *(que)*. In practice, however, any harvest report of 7 or less was accompanied by considerable evidence of drought, poor yields, and threats of famine in some local areas. This was just as true in the paddy fields of Guangdong as in the arid northwest. Officials avoided reporting harvest ratings as low as 5 because that would have required them to give relief to the entire population. Instead, they indicated the presence of poor harvests with reports of 6 or 7, which allowed them to distribute relief to selected districts and populations. In practice, then, a figure of 8 or more indicated an abundant harvest, 7 or less indicated a poor harvest, and 6 indicated the presence of severe disaster conditions which qualified the region for extensive relief operations. The emperor carefully scrutinized low harvest reports. In 1772, for example, he insisted that the Gansu governor check the method by which he averaged local county reports to make sure that the figure for the provincial harvest was genuinely 6.5 and not 7.[4]

The *tuntian* lands, however, did report absolute yields per *mou,* or yields in relation to the seed planted. Thus they show us not only how harvests varied but also whether there were increases over time. Because military officials depended on these lands for their soldiers' rations, they paid careful attention to the yields delivered by the peasants under their control. On civilian lands beyond military control, civil officials, who collected only a small fixed tax, were much less concerned with absolute amounts collected than with whether the peasants dropped below a minimum level of subsistence. Both of these harvest measures can be used to gauge the sustainability of agriculture in the Qing northwest. We can examine these questions for selected years and regions, concentrating primarily on Gansu province and eastern Xinjiang.

In an earlier essay I discussed the important role of granaries run by civil officials in ensuring constant food supplies in Gansu.[5] Here I concentrate on the equally important role of the military colonies in Gansu. The military colonies represent the productive possibilities for agriculture under the best possible conditions. On them, officials carefully supervised the cultivators and provided all the needed supplies of grain, tools, and irrigation. Comparing the *tuntian* yields with the harvests on Gansu's civilian lands reveals the gap between the best practice attainable with state subsidies and the normal situation faced by the peasant farmer. Since it was mainly Gansu and other northwestern peasants who brought their cultivation methods to Xinjiang, an examination of Gansu indicates the kinds of practices that developed in the more distant frontier.

Gansu's crops were predominantly millet and wheat, as they are today.[6] Some fields were planted with winter wheat, to be harvested in the summer, and other fields with spring crops, to be harvested in the fall. The main summer crops were wheat, beans, and barley; the main fall crops were millet, buckwheat, and oats. Along the Yellow River, especially around Ningxia, a relatively high percentage of the land could be cultivated, but farther away from water sources, much of the land could be used only for grazing. On the Gansu corridor extending westward to Xinjiang, in Ganzhou, Liangzhou, and Suzhou, intensive cultivation was possible only in oasis towns. As one memorialist put it: "[These regions] are near the Tianshan Mountains, and people rely on melted snow from the mountains for water; areas without melted snow from the mountains are *gobi* [hard desert]."[7]

Gansu's climate was more similar to that of Xinjiang than to that of the North China plain. Both regions experienced hot, dry summers, very cold, dry winters, and low summer rainfall: the extremes of continental climates. Traveling officials noted a definite shift in the climate as they proceeded west from Shaanxi to Gansu, and a further shift as they crossed the Yellow River. The farther west they went, the colder and dryer the climate became, and the later the crops sprouted in the fields. Annual precipitation of 25 to 50 centimeters was just barely adequate, but, as in North China, much of it fell in the winter months. The absorbent loess soil, however, soaked up the melting snow and retained it in the ground for crops sprouting in the spring. Officials and farmers kept very close track of the vital snowfall in the early spring and reported it annually to Beijing.[8]

Gansu was the third-largest province in area in the empire, next to Yunnan and Sichuan, but the most sparsely populated. (In the Qing, Gansu included the modern Ningxia autonomous region and parts of Qinghai province.) Because its cultivated land area was also so low, however, less than 3 percent of the total, its ratio of cultivated land to population was near average.[9] In its cultivable regions Gansu supported a dense rural population, nearly equal in density to that of much of the North China plain or the uplands of Shaanxi. Its population totaled nearly 15 million in 1787.

The tables in Appendix D list the harvest reports for selected years in the eighteenth century. With an average of 7.6, most of the time Gansu's harvests were sufficient to support its population, but harvests were highly variable. During at least nine out of thirty harvest seasons for which we have data, the figure for the average provincial harvest was below 7, indicating that significant regions faced disaster. Even in the most abundant years, certain counties always needed relief supplies.

The correlation of harvests between successive years is low, an average of 0.31, where 1.00 indicates perfect correlation. Even between summer and fall harvests of the same year the correlation is only about 0.60. The high variability of harvests made it difficult for officials to plan for relief. They could not even expect the same districts to be hit by disaster every year. Disaster could come in the form of drought, sudden floods, or hailstorms, and could strike almost anywhere. Officials had to be prepared to shift grain supplies quickly to meet harvest shortfalls.

As noted earlier, on military farms in the northwest, the state tracked agrarian yields very closely. Each year the officials loaned the cultivators sufficient grain from the granaries for their subsistence and for planting their fields. The cultivators themselves contributed small amounts of seed capital *(ziben)* in the spring. After the fall harvest the officials first deducted the original seed loans, then took half (or, in Anxi, 40 percent) of the harvest to store in the granaries to support the troops. Nearly every year the government recovered its loans. From the available archival reports, we can calculate the total yield on the three *tuntian* lands in Liangzhou, Anxi, and Suzhou in Gansu, Muslim colonies in Hami and Anxi, and both military and Han civilian farms in Ürümchi. These reports provide some of the most accurate and systematic data on farm yields anywhere in the empire. (See Appendix D.)

Average yields were quite high and stable. The average yield per *mou* in Gansu was 2.35 *shi* per *mou*, compared to 1.5 to 3.0 *shi* per *mou* on rice paddies in the lower Yangzi and 2.0 to 3.0 *shi* per *mou* on wheat fields in Jiangnan in especially good years.[10] Wheat yields in the lower Yangzi generally averaged only 1.0 to 1.5 *shi* per *mou;* Philip Huang estimates wheat and millet yields in several North China villages in the 1930s ranging from 0.5 to 1.6 *shi* per *mou*, and the PRC government set a target of 2.5 *shi* per *mou* (400 *jin*, or 200 kg) for lands north of the Yellow River in 1957.[11] Since annual rainfall in most of the northwest was less than the average for North China, this makes the Qing achievement even more extraordinary. The correlation between seed yields on military farms and the provincial harvest was also quite low, only 0.39, indicating that harvests on these lands were relatively protected from the droughts that hit the rest of the province.

The Muslim cultivators in Guazhou and Anxi planted seed over a wider area than the Gansu peasants. They had extraordinarily high seed yields, averaging 6.12, and higher yields per acre than in Gansu. In Hami, also, where yields were measured in proportion to seed planted, seed yields were quite high, ranging from 9 to over 15. In Barköl, the central military base, however, where the weather was quite cold and only barley could be grown, yields were much lower, averaging only 0.84 *shi* per *mou*. All of its millet was imported from Hami. Its granaries frequently suffered deficits, which were also filled from Hami.[12]

As these data indicate, Gansu as a whole suffered from frequent drought and uncertain harvests, but the heavy investment in military colonies by the Qing officials succeeded in maintaining very high, stable yields for the privileged settlers under their direct control. The Qing also, however, mobilized its state grain holdings to serve the civilian population in times of famine through an impressive system of granaries.

Granary Reserves

By the mid-eighteenth century, Gansu had an extensive network of "ever-normal" granaries *(changpingcang),* which could sell grain on the market to reduce price fluctuations. A collective study of the operations of this imperial civilian granary system found that Shaanxi and Gansu had the highest per capita reserves in the empire, along with Guangxi and Guizhou in the southwest. In both of these landlocked frontier regions, with a heavy military presence, imperial policy required high levels of official storage because "they must keep military provisions in readiness."[13]

These reserves grew over the course of the eighteenth century from 1.0 million to a peak of 4.8 million *shi*.[14] From 1741 to 1792, when the level of reserves empire-wide increased by 54 percent, Gansu more than tripled its holdings. Its strategic location, its relative lack of merchant wealth, and its distance from networks of water transportation made Gansu a prime target of the officially run granary relief system.

To be sure that grain reserves were used effectively for relief, we need to know not only the per capita level but also the rate of distribution. Unlike in some provinces, officials in Gansu did not report the actual turnover rates of the granaries. The normal expectation was that 30 percent of the stores would be sold each year, so that nearly the entire stock would be turned over in three years. Since there was usually some harvest shortfall somewhere in the province in any given year, and since officials constantly discussed where and how to distribute grain, it seems that most of the civilian grain supplies were actively employed in relief distribution and price-leveling sales. Gansu's problem was not too little use of its reserves but too much. The actual holdings in the granaries often fell far short of the official targets because so much had been disbursed for relief supplies and loans to farmers. In 1763, for example, its true reserves were only 1.832 million *shi,* far below the target of 3.2 million.[15] Gansu officials had great trouble in restocking their granaries.

The collective study focused almost exclusively on the civilian granary system, but the huge military granaries operated alongside it. (See Table 10.1.) Although imperial administrators tried to keep military and civilian granaries distinct, in practice they interacted with each other constantly. During major campaigns, especially, the abundant memorials on military grain supply reveal that all the granaries faced pressures to divert their holdings from civilian relief to military rations.

Earlier efforts at empire-wide civilian granary systems, like that of the Tang dynasty, had failed because they could not meet military needs.[16] The great rebellions of the late eighteenth century caused "decisive aggravation of granary problems" because endemic structural weaknesses made it impossible for the granaries to meet the combined demands of civilians and soldiers. By the mid-nineteenth century, rampant diversion of civilian supplies completely undermined the system.[17] Gansu was one of the first provinces to face these pressures. By 1762, 250,000 *shi* had already been allotted to the military, reducing total reserves to less than 900,000 *shi*.[18]

In addition to direct diversion of supplies, market operations also linked

Table 10.1 Military granary reserves in Gansu

Place	Year	Amount (*shi*)	Source	Comment
Hexi	1754	1,653,200	GZDQL 8.836	
Hexi	1756	780,000	GZDQL 14.235	
Anxi	1753	80,000–100,000	GZDQL 7.188	
Anxi	1754	68,000	GZDQL 9.842	Annual purchases of 5,000–6,000 *shi*
Suzhou	1756	170,000	GZDQL 13.447	

Source: GZDQL–Guoli Gugong Bowuyuan, ed., *Gongzhongdang Qianlongchao Zouzhe* (Materials from the Gongzhong Archives, Qianlong Reign).

the civilian and military granaries. Prices on local markets soared when military purchases coincided with harvest failure and the local population's need for relief. By loaning grain to soldiers in advance of the harvest, officials could spread out the impact over the year, but they could not reduce the aggregate demand.[19]

The frontier provinces of Yunnan and Guizhou had the greatest military presence and also very high per capita granary reserves. James Lee estimates that military grain allocations amounted to 500,000 *shi* of unhusked grain per year, roughly the same as that for the civilian population.[20] Together, these could support 5 to 15 percent of the registered population for a year. The southwestern provinces also were hit with heavy military demands during the wars with Burma from 1765 to 1770, and later during the invasion of Vietnam in 1788. Military demands during wartime rose to as much as one-third to one-half of the civilian granary stocks.[21]

The southwest had, however, very different problems with its grain stocks from those affecting Gansu. During the rapid buildup of reserves in the mid-eighteenth century, grain stores might grow faster than the needs of the local population, and the older reserves would rot. In the arid northwest, spoilage was generally not a problem: only about 1 percent of the grain was lost annually. In the damp southwest, by contrast, much of the grain was lost if it was not sold: Guizhou lost 70 percent of its holdings by 1776 because officials had been unable to turn them over quickly enough. During the late eighteenth century, officials had less trouble keeping grain from rotting since wars and harvest failures generated increased demand. They seem to have been relatively successful at keeping prices stable.[22]

Gansu, by contrast, seldom had problems with civilian oversupply. There was no lack of peasants and soldiers needing relief. To be sure, in certain districts, like those bordering Sichuan, moisture was a definite threat. Governor Wu Dashan, when he arrived from Sichuan in 1755, noticed that military grain stores had increased to 62,000 *shi* in Jiezhou prefecture, much more than the troops there needed, and he feared that the grain would soon rot. Earlier requests to shift to collection in cash had been refused, because the Ministry of Finance felt that it was vital to maintain large grain stores in the remote peripheries of the empire. Governor Wu now thought that the commercial economy had developed enough so that grain could be purchased on the market, so he asked that levies from the peasants producing for the military be made in cash instead of in kind. This was further evidence of the penetration of the commercial economy into the province.[23]

The Contribution Scandal

In a number of ways, the eighteenth-century experience of Gansu as a frontier province forecast problems that would face the entire empire in the nineteenth century. Deficits in its holdings, the constant pressure of military support, and annual harvest failures challenged the capabilities of its officials to the utmost. Again, foreshadowing later developments, they quickly realized the need to turn to the private grain market, and especially to promoting relief in cash. The shift to distribution in cash instead of grain meant not a "failure" of the imperial effort to store grain for relief but a change in the methods by which the government would relieve harvest failures. Instead of relying primarily on distributions in kind and sales to lower prices, the officials worked through the market by giving money directly to the stricken farmers. Gansu, like Shaanxi, even though it was on the periphery, pioneered these methods.[24]

Yet Gansu had to support a very large military population until the end of the Zunghar wars, and this made its situation quite distinct from that of other provinces. The military colonies could support the established garrisons, but the troops marching through the province on the way to Xinjiang also drove up grain prices and strained local supplies. After the conquest of Xinjiang, Gansu still had to provide substantial support for the new garrisons stationed there, which numbered at least 125,000 people, including dependents. Gansu's tax accounts, as well as its granaries, were almost always in arrears because of these multiple demands. Periodic exemption from annual tax collection was one of the most significant ways of providing relief for the local population.

There were, then, a number of good reasons to shift from distribution in kind to distribution of money: the official granaries would put less pressure on local markets because they would not have to purchase so much to restock; granaries could meet more realistic targets; less grain would spoil;

and grain traders would be attracted to remote regions. Officials, however, constantly debated the relative advantages of cash and grain relief, and many were skeptical.[25] Cash was harder to track within the bureaucracy because it could easily be shifted between accounts. This practice, called *nuoyi* (illegal diversion), was forbidden but extremely common. Peculation, or diversion of public stores to private supplies, was also easier with cash than with grain. Giving money to needy people required them to go to the markets themselves, and this was not easy for the elderly, children, or the sick. When taxes were collected in money, as they had been since the Ming Single Whip reforms, the government made great efforts to ensure that tax-payers paid individually in person. It still could not stop the practice of "proxy remittance" *(baolan)*, by which small farmers entrusted payments to landlords or brokers. The same thing in reverse could happen with relief payments: "proxy recipients" could collect the payments and deliver only small amounts to the truly needy. But the Qing was moving in the direction of contracting out many of its basic functions to non-official groups. This was inevitable so long as the formal bureaucracy remained small while the population and its social activities increased. "Pettifoggers," or legal specialists, took over plaintiffs' cases before the magistrate for a fee; merchants in large cities, like Hankow, assumed substantial local government functions.[26]

In the early eighteenth century, Gansu also suffered from "bumper crop famines" *(shuhuang)*, characteristic of a region that was inadequately monetized, where grain yields fluctuated widely, and the population was too poor to store its own grain.[27] When farmers had a good harvest, they rushed to the market to sell all their grain, thus driving prices to unprofitably low levels. If a poor harvest struck the next year, they could be wiped out, since they had neither cash nor grain on hand. Officials had a strong interest in making sure that grain producers had sufficient cash to pay their taxes. Here the state's most important role was to prop up prices during the harvest season by purchasing grain with official funds and storing it in government granaries. Later, as more merchants came to trade in the northwest, the bumper crop famines would become less common. Injecting money into the frontier economy both kept up prices in the short term and fostered commercialization in the long run.

The increased pressure to provide grain induced officials to devise new ways to encourage building up granary stores. In an ingenious but ultimately fatal innovation, they turned to the merchants. Shaanxi–Gansu Governor-General Yong Chang and Gansu Governor Eleshun, reporting on the military colonies in Anxi in 1754, noted that its local granaries, holding 147,000 *shi*, used to be sufficient to support the garrisons and the small civilian population.[28] But now more people had immigrated from the interior, and merchants had arrived to meet their needs. Furthermore, 80 to 90 percent of the soldiers now had brought their families with them, and the garrison had increased to ten thousand men. Finally, Hami, the oasis farther west, depended on Anxi for grain shipments up to 100,000 *shi* in bad years, an amount that exceeded the local supply and was expensive to transport. The officials proposed to take advantage of the presence of wealthy merchants by encouraging them to contribute grain in return for examination degrees *(juanjian)*. By registering in Anxi and arranging to deliver grain to the granaries, their sons would get *jiansheng* degrees. Each contributor would have to provide 80 *shi* of unhusked or 40 *shi* of husked rice, or the equivalent in wheat, plus "labor costs" of 4 taels and "granary fees" of 3.2 taels per degree. Costs of transport to the garrisons ran 1.0 to 1.5 taels per *shi* in Suzhou, and higher in Anxi. This meant that the cost of a *jiansheng* degree could be as high as 300 taels per person, although the average was 130 to 200 taels. This was much higher than the standard rate of 108 taels set in 1736.[29] When rising prices threatened to discourage merchant contributions, the amounts required were lowered by up to 30 percent, depending on the local market price.

These proposals had strong precedents, since Ming officials had also sold degrees as a result of a military crisis.[30] The court initiated the sale of *jiansheng* studentships for grain or horses after the emperor was captured by the Mongols in 1449. Between 1678 and 1682 the Manchus briefly sold degrees on a large scale during the repression of the Three Feudatories rebellion.

Northwestern governors had promoted contributions *(juanna)* many times before for brief periods, in order to increase grain stores, in 1691, 1703, 1714, 1715, 1717, 1720, 1724, and 1734, but these contributions were mostly collected from serving officials and those who already held degrees.[31] In 1691, for example, as the first Galdan campaigns began, a contribution of 1,000 *shi* would buy a recommendation for promotion from district magistrate to prefect.[32] The southwestern provinces also sporadically used contributions to raise grain supplies. Yunnan collected over 100,000 *shi* in this way by 1681 and 428,638 *shi* in 1732, until the practice was stopped in 1768.[33]

The intense competition for degrees in interior China was getting tighter as the rising population competed for a fixed quota. Gansu itself produced very few natives who could get examination degrees. Governor Chang Jun revealed in 1763 that 70 to 80 percent of those taking exams in Gansu came from the lower Yangzi and Zhejiang.[34] Immigrants had flocked to the province to take advantage of its more lenient quotas, but as the number of immigrants increased, purchasing degrees became a more attractive way to use their wealth, and one appealing to local officials eager to fill the granaries.

The prospects of getting degrees at higher levels made the purchase of a *jiansheng* even more attractive. The northwest had very favorable quotas at the two highest levels, the *juren* and *jinshi* degrees. Gansu had failed to produce a single degree holder between 1644 and 1702, but then a reform of the provincial quota system favored it so much that there were 255 *jinshi* degree holders from Gansu by the end of the century. The *jiansheng* was the first step on the ladder of success, but it made higher rungs possible.[35]

Governor-General Yong Chang set a target of 150,000 *shi* of unhusked grain from these contributions, equivalent to 1,875 contributors. Expecting higher grain stores to result from contributions, he asked that the provincial quota be raised from 3.43 million to 3.6 million *shi*. Even at such high prices, he expected merchants to transport grain to the frontier "enthusiastically", and he was right.[36] From 1741 to 1745, Governor Huang Tinggui had reported collecting 1 million *shi* of contributed grain, or an average of 200,000 *shi* per year, so this figure may have seemed reasonable. By 1761 newly constructed granaries held 700,000 *shi* of contributed grain.[37]

Shaanxi governor Lu Zhuo also had great problems with stocking his granaries. He likewise proposed to allow merchants from outside the province to contribute grain in exchange for degrees in seven counties which bordered the Ordos desert, but his proposal had been rejected. When he tried again in 1756, the Board of Revenue agreed to allow a one-year experiment.[38] The court, however, dismissed Lu Zhuo for inadequate supervision of military grain supplies and replaced him with Chen Hongmou, from Gansu. Chen discovered that Lu indeed faced a problem, since the granaries in these strategic border counties were nearly all empty. Merchants, however, traveled beyond the Great Wall to purchase grain (the Ordos was one of the few northwest regions where cultivable acreage lay outside the wall). Since their grain purchases did not have a harmful effect on local markets within the passes, Chen recommended that merchants be allowed to contribute this grain in exchange for degrees to fill the border granaries. One of the main considerations, then, in discussions of this question was to ensure that merchants purchased grain beyond the local markets. If they purchased only locally, they would simply drive up prices, bringing no benefit to the people, but if they could be induced to transport grain from outside, the local people would benefit from increased trade. The contribution program, then, not only provided social mobility for the merchant classes but also fostered increased trading linkages.

By 1758 all but two counties in western Gansu were collecting contributions. Prospects for increasing grain stores looked quite favorable. Ten counties had collected over 8,000 *shi* from 114 people in only three or four months, and the governor expected "merchants and people near and far" to "rush to contribute" to the granaries. During 1758, 463 people contributed 6,967 *shi*.[39]

In 1766, however, all collection of contributions in Gansu and elsewhere was stopped.[40] The argument given was that too much was being collected in money and not enough in grain. The emperor feared that large purchases on the market would drive up prices, or that coercive purchases *(lepai)* from the people would deprive them of their own reserves. Instead, he allotted 3 million taels to the province, to be used to accumulate grain reserves slowly, purchasing only when market prices were low. In this way officials could prevent the impact of bumper crop famines but at the same time inject money into the economy when needed. But in 1774 the emperor once again allowed Gansu and Shaanxi to continue collecting grain contributions in return for degrees.

Gansu was a high-priced early experiment in which the Qing state offered social advancement to mobilize merchant capital to serve strategic needs and to relieve the local civilian population. In some respects it followed the Ming dynasty's use of merchants to supply the frontier garrisons in return for monopoly salt licenses, but with characteristic Qing differences. These frontier merchants obtained no monopoly privileges, and degrees were available to anyone with the money to pay for them. As the commercial economy expanded on the frontier, the Qing sought to tap the new flow of resources for the benefit of local stability. Shifting away from their primary dependence on the land tax, officials looked for new sources of support from trade.

But relying on mercantile wealth had dangerous implications. Unlike soldiers or settled peasants, the merchants were mobile and not under official supervision. They could just as easily use their wealth to bribe poorly paid local officials, and they could leave the province as quickly as they had arrived. An investigation in 1810 exposed a major corruption scandal that revealed how deeply involved Gansu had become with mercantile interests, and how these connections had unsettled the local administration. In 1781 a provincial treasurer and his cronies in the magistrate's offices of Gansu had taken advantage of the new famine relief policy to line their own pockets.[41] The provincial officials involved in this scheme diverted the silver contribution funds into their own pockets and took huge amounts of wealth with them when they left the province for other posts. They were discovered only by accident, when the outbreak of a rebellion in Gansu forced the new governor to investigate the provincial accounts closely. In this case a policy designed to have positive developmental effects by directing mercantile capital to a poor frontier region only ended up recycling the silver back into the hands of greedy southern officials.

In addition to indicating the limits to official control over grain collection, the 1781 scandal also showed how monetized Gansu's economy had become. Only the wide availability of cash, and of merchants willing to pay, could have made this scheme possible in the first place. Besides providing subsistence, a second key element of the Qing incorporation of the frontier was integrating the border economy with that of the interior. This meant both standardizing coinage and promoting closer coordination of prices. Strategic concerns drove these policies of commercial integration as well. Qing policies had caused considerable integration of markets within Gansu by the end of the eighteenth century. The same policies were promoted to draw Xinjiang closer to the interior, but on an even larger scale.

The Relief Campaign of 1756

We can learn more about the impact of military logistics on northwest agriculture by looking closely at the effects of Qianlong's armies on grain prices in Gansu in the 1750s. Because his ambitious campaigns coincided closely with critical pressures on the local food supply, officials had to wrestle simultaneously with supporting the armies on the march and relieving the local peasant population.

Grain harvests in Gansu were fairly abundant in 1754, but they began diminishing in successive years. (See Appendix D.) The harvests of 1775 ranged from 7.5 to 8.0, and 1756 harvests averaged 7.5, but 1757 and 1758 harvests dropped to the critical level of 6.5. In 1759, the worst year, the average of 5.5 indicates nearly total drought conditions over the entire province. (See map, page 371, and Appendix E.) Fortunately, harvests rebounded for the next three years, but 1763 was another time of dearth. By then, however, military operations had been concluded. Droughts struck in later years, but they did not have the same impact. Prices rocketed to peak levels during 1759 and 1760. By my calculations, the average effect of drought and military pressure in 1759 and 1760 was to increase high grain prices by 2.10 taels and low grain prices by 1.19 taels over their average level of 1.09 taels.[42]

Although we do not have complete documentary information, we can trace the outlines of the large-scale relief campaign conducted by the imperial officials in the northwest during these years. They drew on all the means at their disposal to ensure that peasants received relief and the troops received their rations.

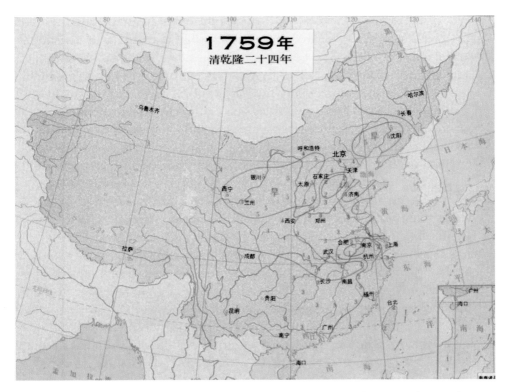

1759年
清乾隆二十四年

The northwestern drought of 1759. The blue circles enclosing the numeral "5" indicate the most severely struck regions.

The year 1756 was a busy time for northwestern officials. The emperor had sent a great army after the Mongol prince Amursana, but in order to pursue him, the generals had to build up stocks of horses, grain, and soldiers at the central headquarters in Barköl, and nearly all of these supplies had to come through Gansu. Fortunately, this year Gansu harvests were on the whole abundant, although certain counties had been struck by disaster. In the middle of the year, when it seemed that the rebels had nearly been captured, troop withdrawals were ordered, but Amursana escaped, to the great shame of the generals.[43] With Amursana out of reach for the winter, the laborious process of accumulating supplies for the next year had to begin all over again. By the end of the year, Huang Tinggui could report that sufficient supplies were stored at Barköl, and there was no need for further transport from Gansu.[44] Grain stocks then amounted to 26,000 *shi* at Barköl and 81,000 *shi* at Hami.

At the same time, twenty-six counties received disaster relief in Gansu and thirteen in Shaanxi, even though the overall harvest figures averaged 7.5. Recognizing the heavy military demands on the province, the emperor exempted Ganzhou, Suzhou, and Liangzhou from current taxes and canceled their back taxes. Shaanxi was able to refill its granaries after the harvest at a cost of 100,000 taels, and Gansu also had an abundant harvest.

In 1757 Amursana was still at large. It was feared at first that he would flee to the Kazakhs, but Ablai of the Kazakhs then submitted to the Qing and promised to aid in Amursana's capture. Even though the Kazakhs would later become an important source of military horses, the campaigns still had to rely primarily on accumulating supplies from China's interior. In preparation for the next year's campaign, Gansu received 2 million taels for military expenses and further tax exemptions.[45] Governor-General Huang Tinggui's request for an extra allocation of 4 to 5 million *shi* of grain for military rations had been rejected, but the capital officials realized that Gansu could not support a large number of troops. Their strategy for 1757 was to assemble a fairly small force in Barköl that could move quickly to secure a victory before its supply demands were too great. By keeping troop numbers down, the emperor recognized, he could avoid complaints from the interior provinces.[46] Grain supplies for these four to five thousand troops would be met by adding stores from Shaanxi to Gansu's holdings.

The year 1757, however, was worse for harvests than 1756, and in 1758 harvests remained just as bad. (See table in Appendix D.) Rising prices for grain, especially in Gansu's western prefectures, not only threatened the livelihood of the local population but also raised the cost of supplying the garrisons in Barköl and Ili. These supplies included many other materials besides grain. The army required thirty thousand horses, to be collected at Barköl, but Gansu could provide very few of them.[47] Most of the horses came from Shaanxi, and were sent through Gansu to Xinjiang. The official price of 8 taels per horse was too low to meet market rates and had to be raised to 10 taels.[48] Oxen were even more critical to peasants, so that raising official prices from 4.4 to 6.0 taels was still not sufficient. Officials had to pay 8 taels per animal, but they were ordered not to purchase too many so as to avoid burdening the local population.

Transport costs also rose when harvests were poor. The normal price for military transport of grain in Hexi was 0.2 taels per *shi* per 100 *li,* but in this year the cost rose by 50 percent to 0.3 taels per *shi* per 100 *li.*[49] In eastern Gansu, over the steep mountain routes from Jingzhou to Lanzhou, costs were lower than in the west, at 0.16 taels per *shi* per 100 *li,* but still higher than normal.[50] Transport costs from Sichuan ranged from 0.11 to 0.16 taels per *shi* per 100 *li.*[51]

The increasing harvest disaster affected both the soldiers and the civilians.[52] Garrisons at Anxi were usually given cash to purchase grain in Suzhou, but this year, because of high prices, they had to loan four months' grain rations to the troops, a total of 1.6 *shi* per soldier, in advance, for the winter months, to be repurchased in the spring. (Average yearly grain rations for soldiers were about 5 *shi* per year.)[53] The military rationing system was operating like the "evernormal" civilian granaries, holding off demands on the market in times of scarcity in the hope of restocking after better harvests arrived.

Faced with increasingly serious signs of famine in 1758 and 1759, provincial officials launched a full-scale relief campaign in Gansu, exempting all current taxes, accumulated arrears, and unpaid loans in the most heavily hit areas.[54] These exemptions included *diding* (land tax), *haoxian* and *yanglian* (nourishing virtue salary supplements), grain and hay supplies, and loans of seed for planting. The *haoxian* surtaxes were normally not exempted, but Gansu was so severely hit that they were included, amounting to a total of 33,400 taels and 158,640 *shi* of grain. The western districts, Ganzhou, Liangzhou, and Suzhou, which faced the heaviest military demand, received the greatest exemptions.

Tax exemptions, of course, only had an impact on the future; they did not provide immediate relief. Direct relief distribution had begun in late 1757 for twenty-two *zhou* and *xian* that were struck by frost and hail and flooding from mountain torrents, but disastrous drought conditions *(hanzai)* appeared to be confined to parts of Anxi, including 113,900 *mou* of military land.[55] In 1758 extensive distribution of relief began throughout the province. At first it was still possible to purchase grain in low-price areas, like Ningxia and Gongchang, for transport to other areas that lacked irrigated fields. Governor Wu Dashan estimated relief needs in mid-1758 at 500,000 *shi* of grain and 300,000 taels of silver. He also noted that Gansu could not provide its share of military supplies that year.[56] Transport costs, however, were so high even within the province that it might be preferable to buy locally even at higher prices. It cost 4 taels per *shi* to ship grain from Gongchang to Suzhou, for example.

The normal practice in Gansu was to give relief half in kind and half in money. The usual official conversion rate was set at 1 tael of silver per *shi*, but now, because of high grain prices, rates were raised to 1.2 taels per *shi* in eastern Gansu and 1.3 taels in the west. Because of the additional burden of military supply, however, the emperor raised each rate an additional 0.10 tael to 1.3 and 1.4 taels, respectively. These rates indicate that the empire expected military purchases to raise grain prices in the province by less than 10 percent.[57]

In 1758, however, Governor-General Huang Tinggui pushed to have all relief distributed in money for areas where grain was still available. He expected further grain shipments from neighboring provinces to make up for deficits. In fact, it was not possible to give out all relief in cash, but Huang's proposal indicates a move toward further monetization of the relief distribution system and an effort to apply inherited rules flexibly.[58] During 1759 he gave cash loans for planting seed in the spring in areas where the soil was too dry to be planted immediately.[59]

By mid-1758 loans and relief were being distributed to twenty-three or twenty-four of Gansu's sixty-three county-level units.[60] This was clearly inadequate, and officials feared unrest. The emperor warned his officials to be lenient: "Whenever there is a disaster, crowds form to plunder goods . . . [and] local officials use crowd violence as a pretext not to give relief. Later they punish the people as thieves. If crowds are truly famine-stricken people who plunder for food, and if they do not have weapons and their numbers are small, governors should be lenient according to the situation."[61] The emperor was more concerned that local officials would deny relief than he was about mass unrest. As far as we can tell, there were no major uprisings in Gansu during these famine years, but the potential remained. In 1749, for example, crowds of over one thousand people had gathered at some county offices to demand tax remissions and granary distributions. They were led by "evil gentry" (liesheng), probably lower-degree holders from the local population. The crowds dispersed quickly, but troops were put on alert to prevent major conflict.[62]

As the spring of 1759 approached, peasants faced the critical period when crops planted the previous winter had not yet sprouted and fields had to be prepared for summer planting. They called it the "time when the brown and green do not meet" (qinghuang bujie); French peasants knew it as the soudure. Every year at this time, grain stores reached bottom and prices soared. The four-month relief campaign that carried the population through the winter now had to be extended by three more months, as there was little sign of rain. At the same time, government granaries sold their stores to reduce prices: millet at 2.4 taels and wheat for 2.2 taels per shi.[63]

Just at this crucial moment, the emperor's long-trusted northwest Governor-General, Huang Tinggui, died. Because he had managed the logistics of the campaigns so superbly, his death was a great blow. Governor Wu Dashan, now promoted to Governor-General, was ordered to follow Huang's precedents strictly.[64] Prices, however, continued to rise ominously in Lanzhou. To avoid straining local markets, military quartermasters were told to stop buying supplies on local markets and instead distribute supplies in kind.[65]

As prices peaked at over 4 taels per shi, officials desperately attempted to induce merchants to bring supplies into the province.[66] Sichuan was the most productive neighboring province, and grain could be moved by water routes into southern Gansu, but the cost of land porterage to the rest of the province was extremely high. From Lueyang in Shaanxi, on the upper Jialing River near the border, to Gansu by land, a distance of 1,200 to 1,700 *li*, would cost 2 taels per *shi* in transport costs alone, in addition to the water transport costs to reach Lueyang. Since Shaanxi held 1.2 million *shi* in granaries on the border with Gansu, it seemed more logical to obtain the bulk of grain supplies from Shaanxi and to use Sichuan's surplus to relieve the strain on Shaanxi. Shaanxi was facing its own harvest crisis, for which it received tax exemptions, but it could ship up to 400,000 *shi* of grain to Gansu. Ultimately, over 200,000 *shi* of Shaanxi's grain were allocated to granaries in Gansu.[67]

This complex interprovincial transfer scheme relied not only on government movements but also on expectations of the responses of merchants and consumers to grain markets. As one official noted: "Even if transport costs [to Gansu] are high, as prices rise, small peddlers and porters will not sit still. Households who hold grain will hear of the [high prices] and offer it for sale, thus helping the public by leveling prices."[68] Shaanxi's shipments could serve as a pump-priming mechanism, creating expectations that prices would drop, thus inciting households with grain to unload their hoards. At the same time, Sichuan's supplies would dampen resentment in Shaanxi at losing its own vital grain stores. The fear that "foolish people will resent" having grain shipped out of their locality, and would create grain blockages, was on the minds of officials and the emperor. Throughout the crisis, concern surfaced that "people of the interior would resent" the diversion of their local supplies.[69] In many other parts of the empire, grain blockages occurred frequently in response to the arrival of outside merchants at local markets.[70] By announcing in advance that Sichuan grain supplies were arriving, the officials could manipulate expectations in Shaanxi and hope to keep grain prices low.[71]

At the same time, officials insisted that the shortage must be relieved by "all possible means" *(duofang)*. Other, more favored provinces were urged to economize on their consumption for the sake of the stricken region. Textile producers were urged to reduce consumption and send their surplus to Gansu so that its people could spend their money on grain.[72]

When material supplies were not enough, officials turned to other means, including public works and ritual activities. They hired famine-struck peasants to rebuild city walls, enacting the principle of "using labor to provide relief" *(yigong daizhen)*.[73] Recalling the great North China grain crisis of 1744, in which the government had relieved over 1.6 million people in Zhili and Shandong, the emperor fasted, conducted prayers for rain, and ordered the release of those imprisoned for petty crimes, so as to "gain the grace of Heaven."[74] As rain began to fall in the fourth to seventh months of 1759, relieved officials and farmers prepared to plant summer crops, looking forward to a plentiful fall harvest.[75] But they were disappointed. The rains came too late, and the fall of 1759 continued at disaster levels. Many of the fields replanted in the summer turned out to be barren.

Much of the rest of the empire was suffering, too. Zhili and Shanxi faced insufficient rainfall for most of 1759, but the rains finally arrived, and they produced adequate harvests, although swarms of locusts moved into Shanxi from Henan and Zhili. Shandong required relief in sixteen counties. Shaanxi, in addition to supporting Gansu, had to divert supplies from its civilian evernormal granaries to support military units.[76] Zhejiang also had shortfalls, but purchasing relief grain in Jiangsu and Guangdong threatened to drive up prices there, so 150,000 *shi* were shipped down the river from Hunan. Without the great grain production boom of Hunan, fed by the clearance of lake and river borders by enthusiastic settlers from downstream, much of the lower Yangzi would have suffered severe shortages.[77]

The overriding goal of the authorities during this crisis was that "military supplies and agriculture should both not be obstructed [*junxu yu nongye liang wu yiwu*]." Part of the evernormal granary stores, usually intended only for civilian use, had to be diverted to the military. By the fifth month of 1759, Gansu had already used half of the 2 million *shi* in its granary for both military and civilian relief.[78]

Military grain requirements were much higher per capita than for relieving civilian famine. Daily rations for soldiers were 8.3 *he* (weighing 8 to 10 *jin*) of raw millet (boiled into gruel) or 1 *jin* of noodles and bread per day.[79] Relief for civilians was at most 5 *he* per day. The average monthly military grain ration was 0.4 *shi* per month, or 4.8 *shi* per year, while adult civilians received 1.8 *shi* per year.[80] Usually, 80 percent of military rations was given in cash and 20 percent in kind, but since purchases on local markets drove up prices, soldiers were given advances in grain to last them through the winter months. Officials also sold grain to level prices for the benefit of the military. In Jingyuan garrison, for example, they released 1,000 *shi* onto local markets from county granaries so that troops could buy grain. Wheat and millet prices had soared to 4 to 5 taels per *shi;* sales were made at 2.2 to 2.4 taels per *shi.*[81] In 1757 the government met military demands from within the province by shipping 50,000 *shi* from eastern to western Gansu, but in 1759 extra supplies had to be brought in from Shaanxi.[82]

Gansu officials staved off famine only by nearly totally depleting the province's granaries. Reserves of 2.35 million *shi* had dropped to 1.2 million *shi* by the first month of 1759.[83] A later report, from 1763, revealed how low the granaries' holdings had fallen. After the two bad years of 1758 and 1759, total grain stores in Gansu dropped to 490,000 *shi*. By 1763 they had still not recovered to their 1756 level of 3.3 million *shi*. Even the nominal holdings of 2.9 million *shi* included unrecovered loans of 1.2 million *shi* and grain sold but not yet repurchased of 527,000 *shi*, so the actual holdings were only 1.169 million *shi*. This report reveals the dual character of Gansu's granaries: on the one hand, they were never able to meet their target figure of 4.5 million *shi*, but on the other, their reserves were very actively used to relieve harvest failures. In good years, reserves could be built back up to more than 3 million *shi*, giving Gansu province one of the highest per capita holdings in the empire.

In sum, out of severely limited resources, northwestern officials fashioned a highly interventionist famine relief regime that just barely managed to save the local population. Military mobilization and drought strained the empire's food supply to extreme limits in its poorest, most vulnerable interior region. Relief officials used every trick in the book to move grain there: granaries, merchant inducements, interprovincial shipments, rain prayers, public works, tax relief, loans, and gruel stations. Pulling out all the stops worked in this case because the underlying concern for security drove military and civilian officials to work together to relieve peasants and soldiers together. In the future, such smooth cooperation would be rare.

11

Currency and Commerce

QING markets, like all others, were made, not born. The system did not work perfectly, and it did not grow naturally. Like the nationalist teleology, the myth of laissez-faire views markets as growing organically and sequentially. This myth likewise ignores the contingent character of market systems and their dependence on the institutional context. The imperial state fostered their growth with specific measures, which have been studied in detail.[1] What needs emphasis here is the link between these market-fostering initiatives and the security needs of the state.

From the sixteenth century, the flood of New World silver to China helped the integration of local and regional markets. Studies of the correlations of grain prices between regions in the eighteenth century indicate how closely attuned peasants and merchants were to market conditions at a distance, and how grain flows directed by price differentials compensated for harvest shortfalls.[2] My analysis of Gansu found that these integrative trends extended even to the northwest. The Yongzheng emperor, much more concerned with the internal economy than with frontier supply, insisted on the need to allow resources to "flow without obstruction" *(tong)*. He maintained that provincial officials should not have a "border consciousness" *(ci jiang ci bian)* when it came to grain and silver trade. Qianlong could build on the structure of the early eighteenth century, so that when his officers purchased grain for military needs, markets responded, and local shortages were compensated by imports.

Since markets required money, Chinese officials had long experience in discussing the relationship between currency supplies and commerce.

Rulers could not simply command money to flow; they had to devise incentives to induce traders to direct currency toward border regions. Currency policy and security aims, inextricable from each other, shaped the frontier discourse on war and money. Here, I will examine three aspects: (1) the military motives of monetary policy; (2) the coexistence of highly localized markets and interregional trade displayed in currency circulation; and (3) the impact of state policies on monetary integration of the frontier.

Money on the Frontier, from Song through Ming

Classical writers and dynastic rulers recognized that control of the currency supply was vital to the maintenance of social and economic order.[3] Since the Han dynasty, the chief form of money under state control was the "cash" *(qian)*, a round coin with a square hole in the middle, made from an alloy of copper and other metals (tin, zinc, or lead). Strings of cash of up to a thousand coins served as the primary medium for all daily transactions. By increasing the output of the mints, or changing the metallic composition of the coin, officials could adjust the number and quality of coins in circulation. The state had two goals in regulating the currency supply: obtaining revenue, and stabilizing markets so as to ensure the welfare of the people. It could obtain revenue directly from seigniorage charges, the difference between the costs of production at the mint and the value of the coins in circulation. Indirectly, when taxes were collected in money, the treasury gained from the extension of commerce through the country. Greater access to markets for their crops made it easier for peasant farmers to pay taxes.

No dynasty, however, could completely dictate the use of money. Merchants, consumers, and farmers used only monetary media which they trusted. State backing was not always enough to ensure that a coin would be used. The paradoxical effects of Gresham's law, in which bad money drives out good, meant that a coin of high value would be hoarded, while counterfeit and debased coins circulated. Coins with high copper content could be melted down when the value of the metal itself exceeded that of the coin. Mints in search of profit were tempted to produce debased coins with low copper content; in the long run, however, they drove up prices when they were produced in excess quantities, and inflation wiped out the state's short-term fiscal gains. Writers about monetary policy constantly debated the proper methods of achieving a balance among the government's fiscal needs, the stability of market exchange, and the uncontrollable fluctuations of the demand for monetary media. Often they blamed "hoarders, speculators, and counterfeiters" for manipulating the currency. Like the notorious "gnomes of Zurich" today, these generic stereotypes served as useful scapegoats for officials who could not understand or control monetary dynamics. Autonomous markets constantly balanced the effects of official policy.

From circa 1000 to 1700 CE, as Richard von Glahn shows, the state steadily lost control of its currency supply to market forces. The most "fundamental reorientation of monetary policy" occurred in the early seventeenth century, marking the "final surrender of the state's sovereign authority over monetary matters to the market."[4] The rise of uncoined silver as an alternative monetary medium to the bronze coin, defying strenuous official resistance, represented the victory of market exchange over state policy. Most officials and monetary analysts opposed the use of silver, because it was costly to mine, its production was beyond state control, and they feared that shortages of silver would damage the commercial economy.

During the sixteenth century, however, silver flooded into China from the New World in response to increasing demands for money from its rapidly commercializing economy. Since the value of silver in relation to gold was much higher in China than in the rest of the world, European and Japanese traders were delighted to bring silver to China. During the last century of the Ming dynasty, at least 7,300 metric tons of silver flowed into the country. The total output of the Spanish American mines from the mid-sixteenth to the end of the eighteenth century was at least 3 billion pesos, or 75,000 tons of silver, most of which eventually ended up in China. In addition, over 10,000 tons of silver entered China from Japan.[5]

The Ming state became an active proponent of the silver economy when it converted nearly all tax collection to silver over the course of the fifteenth and sixteenth centuries in the famous Single Whip reforms. Many scholars lamented the growing influence of money on social values, marked by crazes for commodity consumption and growing bribery and corruption. The disgruntled literatus Zhang Han (1511–1593) lamented that "people pursue what is profitable to them, and with profit in mind they will go up against disaster. They gallop in pursuit of it day and night, never satisfied with what they have, though it wears down their spirits and exhausts them physically."[6] Still, they could not deny that the influx of precious metals fueled a remarkable social transformation, tying China irrevocably to the world economy with silver threads.

Recently, scholars analyzing the impact of New World silver on the world economy have begun to recognize China's dominant role as the world silver sink. Andre Gunder Frank even sees silver flows as the single factor determining cycles of political and economic events around the world.[7] But nearly all of these writers treat China as a single black hole. We know that huge amounts of silver flowed into China through the southeast coast, but we still know very little about how it was distributed within the empire. Significant parts of the empire remained outside the silver zones where commercial exchange dominated. Even though Ming officials mandated the Single Whip reforms for the whole empire, they had an uneven regional impact. In addition, large parts of Central Eurasia, which were not under Ming control, belonged to entirely different currency regimes, inherited from the Mongol empire. In the long run, however, frontier security required monetary integration.

I shall first briefly survey attempts to join security and currency before the Qing. Since the Song dynasty, state policies toward the currency supply were strongly marked by the need to shore up frontier defenses. Wang Anshi's policies promoting commercialization of agriculture in the 1060s aimed to ensure higher revenues, so that the dynasty could pay its armies to fight on the northern frontier. Although much of his rhetoric stressed the "welfare of the people," the primary goal of Wang Anshi's reforms was to build up military power by promoting commercial exchange. Miyazawa Tomoyuki argues that the primary mechanism driving the monetization of the Song economy was the state demand for cash to pay its armies on the frontiers. Salt and tea monopolies and commercial taxes all mobilized merchants to serve security goals through the market.[8]

Security goals also drove the invention of state-backed paper money, China's greatest contribution to world monetary innovation. Originally, mercantile houses circulated paper notes in order to adjust their ledgers without carrying heavy coins from place to place. The Song rulers, recognizing its convenience, established the world's first state-backed paper currency. These notes appeared to solve the problem of exerting state control over markets, as they both increased monetary circulation and raised revenue. It was all too tempting, however, to overissue notes that were not backed by silver or coin. This would temporarily increase revenues but ultimately devalue the notes until they became worthless and touched off raging inflation. Both the Song and Yuan dynasties achieved considerable success with paper issues at the beginning, but ultimately they succumbed to the lure of overissuing, thus making their notes worthless and causing the economy to collapse. The Yuan introduced substantial use of silver to China, and after an early failed experiment the Ming rulers swore off paper entirely.

The late Ming rulers faced growing security challenges on the northwest frontier from Mongol raids and on the northeast frontier from the growing Manchu state. They attempted to meet their fiscal needs by two means: enacting very high tax surcharges, in silver, to support troops on the northwestern frontier, and stepping up the production of bronze coin. The goal of the increased coin output was to make profits from mint production, but the profits were few, and much of the revenue was embezzled by local people at the mints, while increasingly debased coins were minted. The surcharges became a major issue for factional disputes at the court and for protests from taxpayers around the empire. Since the revolts that brought down the Ming originated with troops on the northwest frontier who had not been paid, the tax surcharges clearly failed to achieve their goal.

In sum, none of the government policies designed to make money off currency manipulation worked very well. Paper issues and coin debasements were attempts to resist or deceive market participants by using the authority of the state to decree the value of monetary media. "Theoretical cartalism," one of the currents of classical monetary thinking, as von Glahn describes it, held that the state could fix the value of money independent of market forces. Such efforts at fiat money could work only if the state already possessed sufficient authority in the market; they could not rescue a state that had lost its credibility. And one of the key elements of credibility was military victory on the frontiers. Well-paid and well-disciplined troops who won battles added to any dynasty's legitimacy, making its fiscal efforts more likely to succeed; losing or defensive armies undermined faith in the state's long-term stability, generating furious debates over which desperate fiscal and monetary expedients to pursue. In this sense, military concerns drove currency policy, and not, as officials hoped, the other way around. Military security and tax collection could create either self-reinforcing virtuous or vicious cycles. Currency and fiscal reform could not rescue a state that had already lost control of its frontiers.

The frontier figured in currency policy in a second way—not just as an arena of military conflict but as a relatively unmonetized region. Even when they were under military control, these regions remained relatively autonomous from the interior core. Frontier officials constantly tried to create tighter linkages with the interior by encouraging the flow of goods, merchants, and money to the periphery. Unification of currency standards, however, turned out to be a frustrating task. The Song never united its currencies. Different regions used different coins throughout its reign: Sichuan was quite separate, and Yunnan's use of cowrie shells connected it more closely to Burma and South Asia than to China. The Ming made sporadic efforts to open mints to produce more coin, but the high cost of mining copper, mainly in the southwest, and transporting it to mints in the core led it to give up these attempts after a short while. Copper scarcity continued to plague the Ming. Yunnan, ironically, continued on a cowrie shell local currency even after it opened copper mines. The northwest remained outside the sphere of coin circulation during the fifteenth century. Ming writers noted that local people in Shaanxi used cloth, grain, and silver, not coin, for local exchange. The great debasement program of the Wanli era also failed to have much impact. A mint was opened in Shaanxi in 1576, but it closed in 1582.[9]

The other major Ming initiative to integrate the frontier was the tea–horse trade exchange at the frontier, followed by the officially licensed merchant colonies. As discussed in Chapter 2, efforts to mobilize merchant capital from the lower Yangzi to supply grain, salt, and cloth to troops on the frontier did bring investment in land clearance, but they do not seem to have monetized the frontier economy, since most of the merchant exchange was a barter trade.

We should not, therefore, exaggerate the impact of silver imports on China's economy during the sixteenth century. Only portions of its vast land mass had the flourishing commerce that demanded silver; other regions remained autarkic and unmonetized. Even the huge presence of military garrisons along the Great Wall did not generate a regional commercial economy, as long as the troops' needs were generally supplied in kind. Ming officials accepted the dominance of the silver economy grudgingly, at the same time complaining about its damaging social effects and expressing frustration over the concomitant loss of state control. The Qing would embrace the commercial economy much more wholeheartedly and push the impact of money out to its farthest frontiers.

Integration and Stabilization

The seventeenth century represents an interesting interlude during which one dynasty succeeded another and monetary policy remained in flux. Three major issues surfaced: radical proposals to ban gold and silver entirely by dissident supporters of the fallen Ming; the question of "bumper crop famines," where money shortages appeared to cause poverty even though harvests were good; and the long-lasting "Kangxi depression" from 1660 to 1690. All three were connected with the incomplete integration of the regions of the empire into a single currency zone.

Huang Zongxi, Ming loyalist and famous critic of imperial autocracy, wrote his treatise "Waiting for an Enlightened Prince" *(Mingyi Daifang Lu)* in 1662. In it he provided a historical survey of money in each dynasty, and made the radical proposal to ban gold and silver from the economy. According to Huang, gold and silver had not been the standards for exchange before the Yuan dynasty, but when the Yuan abandoned the copper cash, gold and silver became the reserve store of value, while paper notes were the circulating medium. The early Ming prohibited the use of gold and silver but allowed people to exchange their bullion for paper. "This amounted to swindling the people and taking away their wealth." Now that silver alone was used for taxes and market transactions, "it has become the greatest evil in the land." The scarcity of silver was the fundamental cause of poverty, in Huang's view, because bullion was sent to Beijing "like a flood of water." In peacetime, about 20 to 30 percent of it came back to the people, "but since the great crisis arose, all the gold and silver of the capital has been drained out to the regions beyond our borders."[10] Land values and prices had fallen to less than 10 percent of their previous values because there was no currency in the markets.

Huang's solution was to abolish the use of gold and silver and produce much more bronze coin to alleviate shortages of means of exchange. Without gold or silver, there would be no large gap between the rich and the poor, and no hoarding by wealthy households. Because bronze coin was so hard to carry, people would not leave their hometowns. Society, in Huang's ideal, would return to local self-sufficiency and equality.

Those who praise Huang as a critic of autocracy also need to remember his anti-commercial, anti-monetary bias. Unlike modern liberals, Huang did not view limitation of centralized power as compatible with the growth of a market economy. On currency policy, Huang was the most radical of the Ming loyalist critics of the Qing; Gu Yanwu shared some of his views but still allowed a place for bullion. Huang's discussion indicates strong resistance to dependency on a wider world. He correctly recognized that silver, a foreign good, could flow out of the country just as easily as it could flow in, and its supply could not be controlled by the government. Other writers attempted to balance the money supply while preserving an exchange economy, but Huang was willing to abandon interregional exchange entirely in the interests of equality and stability.

In fact, the ideal economy he envisioned did exist in China in the far northwest, as imperial investigators would discover in the early eighteenth century. There, officials found very few wealthy households, little hoarding of wealth, and limited local trade. Huang was one of a line of commentators who implicitly endorsed the simpler, uncommercialized life of the periphery as a solution to troubled times. In the twentieth century, Gu Jiegang would also praise the rugged, pure northwest as the source of virtues that could redeem China from foreign invasion and domestic turmoil.[11]

Huang's views were nearly unknown during his lifetime. Imperial officials and statecraft writers shared his diagnosis but not his solution. They agreed that the shortage of currency caused the deflation of prices in the late seventeenth century, but many of them blamed deflation on the obstruction of trade, not its growth. Again, security concerns intervened in economic policy when the Kangxi emperor decreed a blockade of the southeast coast, and the deportation of its population inland, in order to prevent commercial resources from going to the regime of Zheng Chenggong, which ruled Taiwan from 1661 to 1683. Many writers argued that this trade embargo damaged the entire economy, not just the southeast region, by shutting off the flow of silver into the country. In fact, the cutoff of silver exports by the Tokugawa shogun in 1668 may have had a greater impact, and Richard von Glahn argues that the fundamental cause of the depression was not currency shortage but subsistence crisis.[12] But official perceptions were different. In this case, officials argued against damaging the prosperity of the country in the interests of military expansion. While the Ming literati and officials, suspicious of the impact of silver, had endorsed the closing of the southeast to trade, Qing writers, in opposition to imperial policy, strenuously argued for opening it. Jiangnan literati, who found their commercial interests hurt by the imperial trade policies, succeeded in getting the trade ban lifted in 1684.

Trade was a common tool of warfare and diplomacy, and denying supplies to the enemy an effective method of weakening his powers. But henceforth, Qing military commanders and officials had to take care that their economic policies did not damage the welfare of local populations. Whatever its real causes, the Kangxi depression experience alerted officials to the need to protect commercial interests when they incorporated new regions into the empire.

A second issue of the seventeenth century, the *shuhuang,* or "bumper crop famine," also had implications for frontier policy. We have already seen this baffling phenomenon in eighteenth-century Gansu; in the seventeenth century it was more general. Since everyone believed that prosperity depended on a good harvest, rising poverty in the midst of plenty seemed inexplicable. The *shuhuang* occurred when abundant harvests drove prices so low that a significant fraction of the local population could not earn enough to make a living. Farmers without grain reserves, who depended on selling their crop, suffered when prices plunged rapidly, and hired laborers without land lost employment when farmers lost income. Refugees flocked to gruel distribution centers, even though grain prices were low. In Amartya Sen's terms, this was a form of "entitlement failure," when poverty persisted in the midst of abundance, because poor people lacked the resources to purchase grain or obtain it by labor.[13] In the Kangxi period, many blamed the *shuhuang* on the shortage of currency, and the remedy was to inject more money into the local economy. Hiring laborers for public works was one of the most effective means of generating employment, reviving monetary circulation, and relieving the poor. From our perspective, Qing relief policies seem surprisingly precocious, anticipating by centuries those of modern welfare states.[14]

When Gansu suffered just such a failure in 1736, currency shortage was linked to market integration.[15] Relief officials realized that the famine occurred because of Gansu's isolation from the rest of the empire. The local people had no grain stores, merchants did not buy their grain, and access to the region was difficult. If the northwest were integrated with the rest of the empire, merchants would flock to the region to buy grain, introducing money into the economy and regenerating exchange. These officials rejected Huang Zongxi's ideal of an isolated village; they knew that such idyllic places were all too vulnerable to disaster, even when harvests were good.

Qing response to the *shuhuang* famine demonstrates a growing awareness of the complex relationships among grain harvests, grain prices, currency, and popular welfare. Unlike the ambivalent writers of the Ming, Qing writers consistently promoted merchants' penetration of distant regions so as to draw them into wider circles of commercial exchange.[16] In one sense, the state surrendered many of its prerogatives to market forces; in another way, it increased its control by ensuring that wider circles of territory were attached by an invisible hand to the interior. This favoritism toward the market, however, did not mean complete "laissez-faire." Officials and statecraft writers had to monitor the currency supply carefully in the interests of preventing popular suffering. Unlike modern states, however, they had very limited monetary tools at their disposal.

The primary motivation of Qing monetary policy was to maintain a stable value for the bronze coin, at an ideal value of 1,000 coins to 1 tael of silver.[17] Unlike many Ming officials, Qing writers did not reject the silver economy, and they ruled out the revival of paper money. Silver flows were beyond official control, though vital for the interregional transfers of tax payments between local treasuries and for long-distance mercantile activities. The government controlled the issuing of bronze coin, but it faced several difficulties, including the scarcity of raw copper and the proliferation of counterfeit coin. The value of the bronze coin fluctuated widely depending on the relative supplies of copper and silver and the demand for the currency in the marketplace.

Until the early eighteenth century, the main problem was that coin was too cheap. In Jiangnan it took over 2,000 standard coins to obtain 1 silver tael in the mid-seventeenth century.[18] The low value of cash was blamed on the proliferation of debased counterfeit coin. The solution ordered by the Yongzheng emperor was to buy up counterfeit coin with silver from government offices and remint it into high-quality, standardized official coins. This policy ran into difficulties everywhere, but the frontier posed special problems. Gansu Provincial Treasurer Zhang was told to use 20,000 taels of silver to purchase counterfeit coin, but he noted that there was very little silver in Gansu, and very little use for it. Copper coin was used for paying taxes as well as for daily needs, and people mixed together official and counterfeit coin indiscriminately. He was not able to use more than 5,000 taels of his allowance. Zhang recommended expanding local mint production after the military campaigns were over.[19] Zhang had discovered two essential features of Gansu's economy: the very limited impact of the silver inflow and the great demand for cash. As long as counterfeit coin met an important need for small-scale exchange media, it could not be driven out of circulation.

Governor Shi Wenchuo found that local government offices in much of the province functioned mainly with a copper cash, or even grain, economy in the early eighteenth century.[20] Tax collectors were faced with three different currency zones: the southeastern region collected taxes in silver, the central region collected them in bronze coin, and the western regions collected them in grain. Cash was cheap in central Gansu, with a market rate of 1,070 to 1,100 per tael, but it could not be exchanged for silver at county offices; those who needed silver had to pay extra transport costs to obtain silver from distant moneychangers.

During the eighteenth century, Qing officials made strenuous efforts to establish a uniform, high-quality bronze coin as the standard unit for exchange throughout the empire. By persuading the market to accept high-quality coins, they hoped to facilitate integrated exchange over broad areas, ensure stable government revenues, and eliminate the vices of counterfeiting and hoarding. They succeeded almost too well. By the beginning of the eighteenth century, bronze coin had become scarce. Increasing commercialization feeding a growing market demand for small change clearly was one factor, as was the inability of government mints to produce enough coin. As counterfeit coins with varying mixtures of lead and tin proliferated, intense discussion raged at court over the problem of "expensive coin" *(qiangui)*.[21]

The value of bronze coin in terms of silver began to rise in the eighteenth century, reaching values of 600 to 800 cash per tael.[22] In the official view, expensive coin damaged popular welfare by making coin less available for daily use. It also, of course, reduced the tax burden, since taxes were paid in silver, but apparently officials thought the costs outweighed the benefits. Expensive coin coincided with the onset of the eighteenth-century inflation, as silver imports again began to rise, so it was difficult to untangle the causes. Officials tended to blame the usual suspects: wealthy hoarders who were holding coin supplies off the market. Just as they treated grain shortages with policies designed to discourage hoarding, they aimed to force the wealthy to release their stocks. The mints increased their output of coin, but the emperor, in an edict of 1752, feared that increased hoarding would still decrease circulation. His goal was to "widely circulate the wealth of the country" *(guobao guang wei shutong)* by inducing the wealthy to surrender their hoards.[23] He ordered investigations in each province to determine the incidence and causes of expensive cash.

Reports from the northwest once again illuminated the special features of the frontier. Shaanxi and Gansu had very few wealthy households, and very little hoarded coin. Local people sold their grain for cash, using silver only to pay taxes. When they bought land, they used both cash and silver for prices under 10 taels and silver for large purchases greater than 10 taels. Merchants carried from several tens to several hundred strings of cash, but they kept them in constant circulation. The exchange rate ranged from 780 to 900 cash per tael, not a very high rate. Since officials believed that the "vice of hoarding" was found only among the rich, they decided that it was best in this area to leave people alone. The state would punish only those with large hoards of coins, over a hundred strings.

Taxes, too, had to adjust to a non-monetized local economy. In 1753 only Gansu and the southwestern provinces of Yunnan and Guizhou had land tax *(diding)* quotas in grain higher than quotas in silver, and of these, Gansu had the highest ratio: 508 to 299, or 1.7 to one. Sixty-three percent of Gansu's taxes were collected in kind.[24] In 1908 Gansu still collected 370 million *shi* of taxes in grain, compared to 532 million taels in cash. Grain collections were 1.3 times larger by market value than the value of taxes collected in money.[25] In 1908 Xinjiang collected nearly all of its taxes in grain or in straw. There was no *diding* tax, and only 90,000 taels of commuted taxes. By market value, 90 percent of Xinjiang's land taxes were still collected in kind. Since both provinces collected so much of their land taxes in kind, commercial taxes and contributions made a proportionately greater addition to the money supply there than in other places.

These reports confirm Kuroda Akinobu's description of a dual economic structure in which coins circulated in local markets for daily needs while silver was used only for interregional trade and tax remittances.[26] As the coin famine spread over the country during the Qianlong reign, the value of coin rose. It took 1,100 coins to buy one tael in 1696, but under 700 in 1701. The Qing responded by ordering the largest-scale production of coin from the mints since the Song dynasty. But its efforts were hampered by the scarcity of copper, the high costs of mint production, and an inability to prevent the proliferation of counterfeit coin.[27] The government issued high-quality coins to soldiers and official employees, but the coins did not return to the government offices. They remained in circulation only in local areas, and did not create a unified currency standard. Counterfeit coins, varying widely in composition of copper, lead, or tin, circulated along with official coins, and the official coins themselves were debased with lead and other metals because of the copper shortage.

Despite the Qing efforts to create an integrated empire-wide system of currency that would meet the growing demands of commerce, monetary circulation remained divided into two spheres. Unminted silver served as the store of value that allowed interprovincial exchange of taxes and merchant remittances, while bronze coin remained confined to highly localized, unconnected markets for daily consumer products.

Kuroda's analysis helps to resolve a paradox in the study of Chinese market integration, one that is particularly conspicuous in the northwest. On the one hand, evidence from price correlations indicates highly integrated markets between prefectures and provinces across the empire.[28] On the other hand, local studies often find significant obstructions to the flow of labor and capital.[29] Two maps of grain prices in Gansu display this contradiction. The first gives the picture of price correlations for the period 1739 to 1864. (See Map 8a.) As I have described elsewhere, these connections lead to the conclusion that goods and money flowed quite freely between districts within the province, creating an interconnected trading network. If, however, we exclude the two famine years 1759 and 1760, price correlations indicate very little connection between markets. (See Map 8b.) Which is the correct picture?

Both are correct, but for different reasons. The common movement of prices in the first map is not simply a result of common harvest conditions across the province, since, as I argued earlier, harvest and weather varied substantially across the province. Furthermore, if prices responded only to a common harvest failure, all prefectures' prices would be highly correlated with all others, and this is not the case. The price correlations do indicate a systematic, articulated pattern of trading relationships between prefectures, but these flows were most active in crisis conditions. During famine years, officials intervened both to level prices with granary sales and to encourage

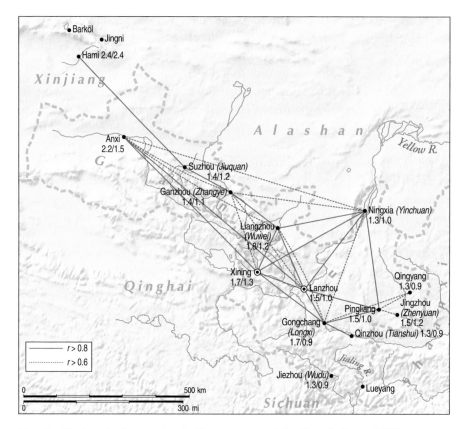

Map 8a. Grain price integration in Gansu, 1739–1864: Correlations of differences of annual average millet prices. For data source for maps 8a, 8b, and 9, see p. 709.

merchants to move grain to areas of need. The large-scale interprefectural movements of grain were financed with silver. The visible hand of the state is apparent in these correlations, but it worked in tandem with private trade. In non-crisis years, however, most trade in daily goods remained confined to local markets, and the copper currency sphere ruled. Then price integration fell apart.

Price correlations in silver taels at the prefectural level demonstrate one important feature of the Qing economy, but they do not reveal the circumstances of markets at lower levels. Economic integration was stretched like a thin net over the vast expanses of the empire, supported by official and private movements of grain and money; but its action was sporadic, especially in peripheral regions. There was no irreversible linear trend toward increasing integration of the empire; in the nineteenth century, many of the integrative trends were reversed. R. Bin Wong and I have suggested that the

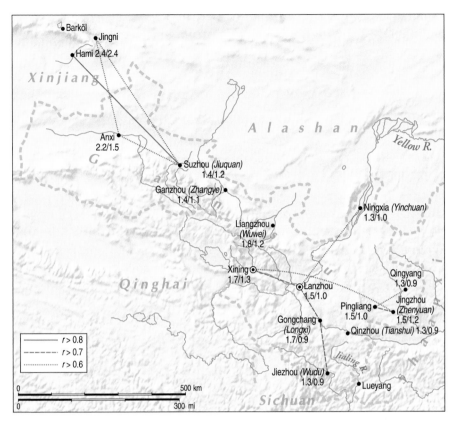

Map 8b. Grain price integration in Gansu with famine years omitted, 1739–1864: Correlations of differences of annual average millet prices.

ties linking the middle Yangzi to Jiangnan through the rice export trade declined in the nineteenth century. Kenneth Pomeranz has argued that in South China, regions outside the lower Yangzi became increasingly self-sufficient, as people and resources migrated there and ties to Jiangnan loosened.[30] With the decline of the imperial infrastructure of water conservancy, many regions of North China also lost their connections to the core. By the early twentieth century, Shandong was divided into several distinct currency zones, just as Gansu was in the eighteenth. It had, in effect, reverted to frontier conditions.[31]

The northwest was always more loosely tied to the center than was South China, and more heavily dependent on the state. The problems with currency circulation in the region, and the partial integration of its grain markets, indicate significant limits to imperial economic unity—limits that would become increasingly conspicuous in the nineteenth and twentieth centuries. This overview of frontier currency policy highlights the importance of regional differences in market integration for drawing conclusions about the empire as a whole.

The foregoing discussion of Gansu sets the stage for the next one: the incorporation of Xinjiang. James Millward has brilliantly described policies undertaken by the Qing to promote the integration of Xinjiang after the conquest. Noting the special impact of frontier conditions on administrative reforms, Millward argues that the emperor encouraged a "political culture of innovation" that urged officials to break free of precedent. Such flexibility was, in his words, "a product of fiscal and political necessity."[32] Innovations in Xinjiang included unusually heavy reliance on income from trade, greater dependence on merchants to support tax collection, and targeted policies to reform local currencies so as to link local markets with the interior.

I agree that frontiers stimulated new ideas, but I would stress that Xinjiang's new policies did not spring *de novo* out of the post-conquest period. They had their roots in measures taken in the northwest before Xinjiang joined the empire. Xinjiang's administrators, who all had ties to Gansu, drew on their experience to design methods of attaching Xinjiang to the interior.

Merchant contributions were key elements in the support of both Gansu and Xinjiang. From the first years of conquest, when lower Yangzi merchants paid 1.5 million taels to celebrate the emperor's victory, through the nineteenth century, merchant funds for degrees and offices were critical to relieving Xinjiang's chronic deficits.[33] As we have seen, Gansu's relief funds relied heavily on merchant contributions in exchange for degrees. Revenue sharing *(xiexiang)* between wealthy, surplus provinces and poor, peripheral ones directed large amounts of funds from North China, middle Yangzi, and lower Yangzi provinces especially toward the northwest and southwest frontiers. *Xiexiang* funds directed to Xinjiang through Gansu ranged from 845,000 to over 900,000 taels per year in the late eighteenth and early nineteenth centuries, rising to over 4 million taels annually by the 1840s. As Millward notes, however, these funds were inadequate to meet the expenses of local *begs,* who relied on exactions in grain and *pul,* the local currency, from their Turkestani subjects. Somewhat like Gansu's currency system, Xinjiang's fiscal and monetary flows were divided between the large interprovincial transfers approved by the center and the localized, "supplementary" illegal exactions for local offices.[34]

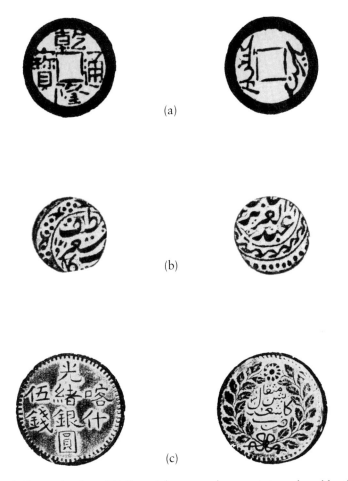

Copper and silver coins from Xinjiang (obverse and reverse), introduced by the Qing: (a) copper cash introduced in Yarkand in the Qianlong reign, with Chinese, Manchu, and Arabic script; (b) silver coin with Arabic script; (c) silver coin from late-nineteenth-century Kashgar with Chinese and Arabic script.

The central monetary task for Qing officials in Xinjiang was to reorient the region away from its Central Eurasian connections and toward the empire. Xinjiang had even more diverse currency zones than the northwest, and they faced in different directions. Chinese cash circulated in the eastern oases of Hami and Turfan, and silver moved through towns north of the Tarim basin, but in southern Turkestan a distinctive copper coin, the *pul*, circulated. The Zunghars had begun the process of drawing the region's currency together by trying to collect all *pul* in circulation, melting it down, and replacing it with new coin. The Qing followed Zunghar practice in 1759, starting up the mint in Yarkand and creating a new coin, marked

"Qianlong currency" on one side and "Yarkand" in Manchu and Arabic on the other. Other mints produced additional coins through the eighteenth century. As in the northwest, at a slight lag, the growing commercial economy in Ili created a severe shortage of coin, inducing the Qing to mint the genuine Chinese bronze coin there in 1775. Unlike Gansu, however, Xinjiang did not have to rely on distant copper shipments; it obtained its copper from local mines.[35]

The exchange rate between silver and copper remained a constant concern in Xinjiang as well as in the interior. The *tänggä* (clearly derived from Mongolian *tängge* for "money") was the east Turkestani term for the 50-*pul* unit. The Qing officially set the *tänggä* as equivalent to the silver tael, but the Grand Council agreed to adjust the officially designated exchange rate to accord with the market rate. Millward calls this "a great departure from the policy in China proper" of keeping a fixed rate of 1,000 cash to 1 tael, but in fact we have seen similar flexibility operating in the northwest.[36]

The wide variation in *pul*–tael exchange rates in Altishahr, ranging at times from 100 to 220 in the same year, indicates that local markets were not closely integrated.[37] At the same time, local officials profited from diverging exchange rates to pay many of their administrative costs. Thus Kuroda's argument about the separation of local currency zones reinforced by local government autonomy is supported even more strongly by this evidence from Xinjiang. Qing currency policy succeeded only to a limited extent in creating an integrated zone in Xinjiang. It pulled the region away from its Central Eurasian linkages, but left local markets intact, and did not connect them closely to the interior.

Price correlations reveal the same structure for grain markets. (See Map 9.) The eight towns in Xinjiang for which we have price data, plus Anxi in Gansu, are all oases surrounded by large deserts. (See Figure 11.1.) The grain price curves in the three towns clustered in the oasis which is now modern Ürümchi (Changji, Fukang, and Dihua) are naturally very close to one another. Qitai, Pizhan, and Turfan, which are about 200 kilometers away across the desert, however, also have close ties to the Ürümchi region. Clearly, these six towns were all part of a common marketing network. Most striking, however, is the fact that Yihe (Barköl), which lies nearly 500 kilometers away from Ürümchi and 350 kilometers from Turfan, still follows their price curves very closely ($\rho \geq 0.80$). Military demand created this link. Barköl was the central concentration point for Qing garrisons during the eighteenth-century campaigns, and Turfan was an important secondary concentration point. There was considerable military traffic between the two oases, requiring extensive shipments of supplies from Barköl to Turfan. Ürümchi was a much larger oasis, more self-sufficient, but Tur-

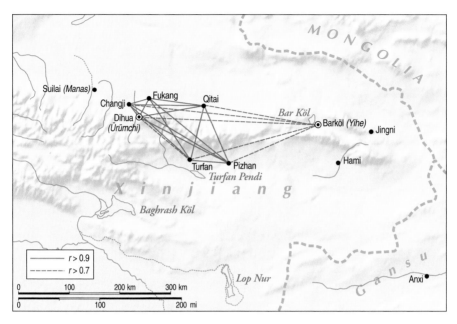

Map 9. Grain price integration in Xinjiang, 1777–1860: Correlations of differences of annual average wheat prices.

fan had trouble supporting its own local population and a substantial military garrison. Supplies from Barköl allowed Turfan to feed itself and to engage in trade with Ürümchi to the west. The military supplies from Barköl underpinned the marketing network of the seven towns.

Hami and Anxi, the oases farther down the Gansu corridor, had no connection to the other towns. There is very little connection of the wheat prices in these two oases either to Ürümchi or to the interior via the Gansu corridor to the southeast. Although military supplies came out to Barköl along the corridor, once they filled the warehouses, they did not create continuous commercial flows back to Gansu. Only the heavily subsidized military supply routes could overcome these high costs of transport. Merchants did follow the armies, but civilian trade was not regular enough to make Xinjiang a truly integral part of the empire.

Even more than in Gansu, then, the economic integration of Xinjiang depended on extensive state intervention, but the state's primary goal was to make Xinjiang self-supporting, not dependent on the interior. The marketing network of the eastern oases, backed by military shipments, was not tightly attached to the interior.

In sum, Xinjiang received substantial subsidies from the center, but it also developed its own innovative fiscal policies. With a series of experimental measures, Qing officials tried to bind the new frontier to the inte-

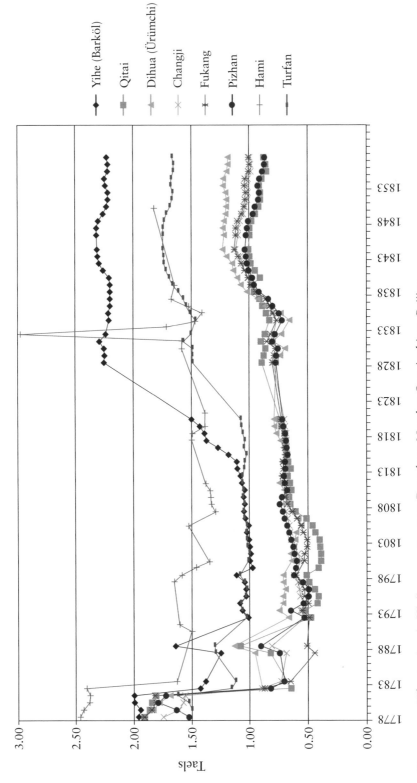

Figure 11.1. Wheat prices in Xinjiang, 1778–1856. Data from Number One Archives, Beijing.

rior. They only partially succeeded. Xinjiang was the first place in the Qing to tax commerce for provincial revenue. Later, this policy became well known in the rest of the empire as the *lijin* levy. Xinjiang never became self-sufficient, so it was a drain on the treasury, but it also never became truly integrated with the interior by private trade. Local trade flourished within the province, but it was not profitable to ship grain there from the interior. This partial integration accounts for the difficulty the Qing had in holding on to the region during the nineteenth and twentieth centuries.

Commerce as a Weapon of War

Commerce was an important resource for the Qing, and the rulers used merchant capital and merchant skills flexibly and creatively. They relied heavily on merchants to transport military supplies. Merchants set up markets at the major military camps, providing important supplements to basic rations. Manipulating the direction of trade flows was also a critical part of Qing frontier policy. When Mongolian tribes surrendered to the Manchus, the first task was to fix them in place by defining the boundaries of their pasturelands and limiting their movement. The second step was to promote trading links with the interior. Mongols had to provide mounts for military purposes, but they also provided animals and furs in exchange for grain and other daily goods. Han merchants began to penetrate the Mongolian territories soon after they submitted to the Qing.[38] The Mongol nobility and clergy established close ties with merchants through debt relationships that made them dependent on capital flows from the interior. Some scholars argue that class differentiation within the tribes began at this time, because the nobility prospered while the common herders suffered.[39] Evidence is scanty, but it is clear that participation in markets spread beyond the elite alone. The Mongols who submitted to the Qing gave up both their economic autonomy and geographical mobility in exchange for peace, material goods, and the mixed blessings of "civilization," in Chinese terms.

The Zunghars likewise increasingly focused their economic sights on Chinese markets. Although they continued to explore multiple sources of trade through the early eighteenth century, looking to Russia, Central Asia, and Tibet, China's irresistible wealth drew them in. During the time of truce, from 1734 to 1755, Zunghars who flocked to frontier markets put considerable pressure on Chinese merchants and officials to meet their demands. The Qing treated the Zunghars as tribute payers who would be "transformed" *(xianghua)* into civilized humans by offering gifts to the benevolent emperor. Trade with the Zunghars was not like the Ming frontier

Tribute horses presented
by Kazakhs to the
Qianlong emperor.
Portrait by the court
painter Castiglione,
1757.

trade, which was an unequal exchange highly beneficial to the Mongols. Qing garrisons and settlers benefited greatly from the sheep and cattle that the Zunghars brought to Suzhou, in Gansu. The Zunghars, for their part, profited heavily from the trade as well, whether they received silver or Jiangnan brocades for their goods. Using the frontier trade, the Qing officials could reduce the pressure to support their settlers from the interior, at the same time encouraging greater participation of interior merchants in frontier economic networks. Officials made great efforts to ease risks for merchants by loaning them funds, paying transport costs, and facilitating communication between the Zunghars and their suppliers.

Still, in the end, Qing goals were more strategic than economic. The rulers were willing to meet the constantly increasing Zunghar demands in the Qianlong period, but they always had the option of cutting off trade to keep the barbarians in line. As with the Russians, they enforced policies by turning the tap on and off. Frontier peoples were regarded as fundamentally insatiable, but it was preferable to turn their avarice toward material profit instead of war. Yet even as they reduced troop concentrations, the frontier officials carefully escorted the foreign traders, suspicious that they were engaging in espionage as much as commerce.

The shift to maritime trade routes, then, did not have a major impact on the Central Asian frontier, nor was it the primary cause of Mongol decline. Trade continued to flourish and even increase on the frontier from the seventeenth through eighteenth centuries, as the Qing rulers carefully used their control of continental trade to extract submission from the nomads. The old Silk Routes shifted to the official border towns, but the same goods and the same merchants moved along them. Maritime revenue would not become important to the Qing until the late eighteenth century, when the British arrived in Guangdong. By that time, the Manchus already had extensive experience in using trade to manipulate boisterous barbarians, and they applied to the south coast the lessons they had learned in the northwest.

In 1757 Ablai, chief of the left branch of the Kazakhs, sent a mission offering to establish trading relations with the Qing. The emperor, in the midst of his western campaigns, was delighted to receive the grateful "return" to submission *(guishun)*, as he saw it, of a nomadic people which had never had any contact with a Chinese empire. The Kazakhs also promised to provide a valuable resource, horses, at reasonable prices, in exchange for tea and cloth from the interior. The next year, officials established a regular

Table 11.1   The silk trade from Jiangnan to Xinjiang

Decade	Total (bolts shipped)	Annual average	North (Ili, Tarbaghatai)	Percentage north	South	Percentage south
1760s	107,605	10,760	38,020	35.3	2,280	2.1
1770s	70,800	7,080	64,400	90.9	5,930	8.4
1780s (4 years only)	28,050	7,012	9,500	33.9	2,300	8.2
1790s (7 years)	19,939	2,848	9,200	46.1	9,489	47.6

Source: From Lü Xiaoxian and Li Shouju, "Qianlongchao neidi yu Xinjiang sichou maoyi gaishu," in *Qingdai Quyu Shehui Jingji Yanjiu*, ed. Ye Xian'en (Beijing: Zhonghua, 1992), pp. 742–755. But Wang Xi and Lin Yongkuang, *Qingdai Xibei Minzu Maoyishi* (Beijing: Zhongyang Minzu Xueyuan Chubanshe, 1991), p. 445, gives much more complete data.
Note: Breakdown of north versus south not given for every year.

trading relationship with the Kazakhs that would continue uninterrupted for ninety years.

This trade has been discussed in detail by James Millward and several excellent Chinese scholars.[40] It became a systematic form of cooperative official and private exchange that linked the lower Yangzi imperial silk factories with the northwestern border towns. (See Table 11.1.) The main trade took place first at Ürümchi, and later at Ili, in the north, but silks were also sent to the towns in the south. The northern trade bartered cloth for animals, especially horses and sheep. The Kazakhs provided horses at much cheaper prices than in the interior, and the garrisons badly needed these mounts. Long cattle drives from the northwest across blazing desert sands had exhausted the horses and killed off many sheep. Between 27,000 and 28,000 sheep died on the way from Barköl to military camps farther west.

In the south traders exchanged cloth for coins (*pul* cash and silver), which were used to purchase grain and meat from the Kirghiz and local Turkestanis. The southern trade was driven by the extremely high cost of delivering grain from the interior: purchasing grain in Shaanxi or Gansu cost 1 to 2 taels, but transporting it to Altishahr cost an additional 20 taels.[41] The highest volumes were reached during the first three decades, averaging 6,760 bolts of cloth per year through 1796, with the peak year in 1780. As trade in the north declined steadily to a fairly constant level of around 2,000 bolts per year through the nineteenth century, the southern trade came to dominate. Kazakhs placed orders for the special types of cloth they liked, mostly cheaper satins and silks in bold colors, which were delivered "on spec" by Jiangnan officials in the silk factories. In Soochow,

200,000 workers at 30,000 looms produced silk under official supervision.[42] Silk did not necessarily come directly from the factories. It could be
produced on putting-out contracts by local households or purchased directly on private markets.[43] Then it was shipped in sealed boxes, under official escort, to the frontier. It took nearly two years from placing an order
to receiving delivery, but officials carefully shepherded the shipments on
their way.

In both trades, officials were instructed to trade at market prices so that
both sides got a "fair deal" *(liang de qi ping)*.[44] Petty traders were welcome
to participate. The vital needs of military provisioning drove military commanders, local officials, and merchants of all stripes to cooperate. At the
same time, the Qing linked the economy of Xinjiang to the interior and extended its commercial influence even farther west into Central Eurasia. The
Kazakhs reoriented themselves away from other Central Asian suppliers as
they grew increasingly dependent on Chinese goods. As demand spread beyond the nomadic elite to the common herders, they ordered larger supplies
of coarser, cheaper silks. They were also able to sell part of their product to
the Russians when Russian access to Chinese goods at Kiakhta was cut off.

Up until the end of the eighteenth century, the Kazakhs, like their
Zunghar predecessors, had some room to maneuver, but in the nineteenth
century they succumbed to Russian expansion. The Qing did not attempt
to resist Russian incorporation of the Kazakhs, keeping its trade at a constant low level. Neither trade fully supported the costs of imperial dominion in Xinjiang; it always remained a deficit region. But the trading networks defined linkages to the interior at the same time as they drew a
boundary in the west.

Tribute and Frontier Trade

This discussion of frontier trade implies new ways of approaching China's
relations with the world beyond its borders. In the simple Fairbank model
of China's foreign relations, all trade with foreigners was conducted under
the rubric of "tribute" *(gong)*, a Sinocentric concept stressing the superior
position of the emperor and his benevolent grace in allowing outsiders to
present him with gifts.[45] James Millward and others have convincingly
demonstrated the inadequacy of this concept for grasping the complex interactions of the Qing empire with its peoples.

Tribute had different meanings for different people. For example, *begs*
from Xinjiang oasis towns, who were Qing officials, presented "tribute" to
the emperor, but Kazakh horse traders did not. Even though Kazakh "trib-

ute" horses appear in a famous painting by Baldassare Castiglione, the Qianlong emperor explicitly declared that Kazakh traders were not to be treated like tribute emissaries. Because they were only merchants, Qing officials would not cover their costs of travel and lodging. Tribute missions, then, were not just for "foreigners," and not all trade was tribute.[46] Each Qing trading relationship was negotiated in particular contexts of economic need, cultural definition, and security goals.

Nicola Di Cosmo has argued that we must examine tributary forms of behavior not only at the imperial center but also as they are implemented at frontier points of contact. He has developed the concept of tribute as an "environment" that surrounded all of the Qing's relations on its frontiers, comprising commercial, security, and ritual relationships.[47] I would rather call it a kind of intercultural language, serving multiple purposes for its participants.[48] Like "pidgins," or trading languages in all multicultural contact zones, tribute discourse permitted extensive commercial exchange, masking the different self-conceptions of its participants with formal expressions but allowing each, in different degrees, a measure of autonomy.

Since Millward and Di Cosmo confine themselves to the post-conquest period, after 1755, they do not discuss how these varied diplomatic and commercial arrangements grew out of the earlier process of Qing expansion. The Zunghar relationship with the Qing strongly conditioned treatment of the peoples of Xinjiang after it was brought under Qing control.

The Zunghar trade also helps to clarify the "puzzle" of what Chinese merchants brought back with them from the frontier. The answer is: much less than they took out there. As the northwest markets were limited, and the Zunghars frequently brought "useless" products for which there was little demand, merchants had difficulty making profits. Gansu did have products that were wanted in the interior, like its famous spiced tobacco, sold in Jiangsu, Sichuan, and Guangdong.[49] After the 1770s, jade became an important item of eastward trade, and a lucrative source of illegal profits.[50] But before this time, Qing official intervention resolved these problems, at a cost to the treasury. Advances to merchants were usually not repaid in full, and debts were forgiven, because the officials needed to attract merchant capital. Sometimes the Zunghars took the losses, as when they had to unload goods at bargain basement prices. When they sent all their healthy animals to the garrisons, however, officials recompensed them for sick and dead beasts. Silver continued to flow across the border, despite efforts to limit the traffic. This subsidized trade was a direct loss for the state treasury, but an indirect gain when the costs of financing military occupation are included. By inducing interior merchants to cooperate with frontier officials in trading with the nomads, the state reduced the costs of bringing supplies from the interior, thus cutting the costs of supporting its far-flung garrisons. The Kazakh silk–horse trade grew out of these early experiences to become a systematic, sustained trading system across the western border.

Chinese dynasties had repeatedly, and usually unsuccessfully, aimed to exchange products of the interior for one of the two crucial commodities the empire could not produce on its own: horses. (The other was silver, obtained first from Japan and later from the New World.) The late Tang rulers spent huge amounts of silver to buy horses from the Uighurs (see Chapter 1). The Song and Ming tea–horse trades ultimately failed, for a number of reasons, including official efforts to force low prices on the nomads, corruption, and possibly, as Morris Rossabi claims, "Confucian scorn for commerce."[51] In the Song and Ming, it is true, only low-level officials were assigned to these demeaning posts. Millward argues that the Qing trade for horses with the Kazakhs, by contrast, did succeed in establishing long-lasting, equitable trading relations, because high-ranking officials supervised it, trade relations were handled pragmatically, and "the Manchus knew their horseflesh." The underlying reason for such sustained attention to the trade was the crucial need of Qing military forces for sufficient supplies of animals. All these features, however, also characterized Qing relations with the Zunghars.[52]

Two other special circumstances made the Kazakh trade "depoliticized and equitable": the uncertainty of Qing control of Xinjiang during the final military campaigns, and criticism from the interior of the cost of these campaigns.[53] Both factors applied equally to the Zunghar trade during the truce period. Exhausted by the costs of battle, and needing to answer grumbling from the interior, the emperor told his officials to adapt flexibly to the traders' needs. Vigorous bargaining took place: Zunghars asked outrageously high prices, but reduced them when officials resisted. The officials, for their part, could not enforce artificially low prices but had to respond to market demand. Efforts to impose fixed low prices had sabotaged the tea–horse trades of the Song and Ming, as nomads sought private traders who offered better deals. Both the Zunghars and Kazakhs found official prices attractive enough to induce them to keep coming to border markets, increasing their supplies over time. Private traders maintained a presence significant enough to provide competitive pressure.

The Zunghar trade did cause problems in the early years, when rotting, unneeded goods piled up in the warehouses, but in successive years, the traders brought fewer rare products and confined themselves mainly to animals. The Zunghar and Kazakh trades went through a parallel process of mutual accommodation as each side determined the other's needs in advance. Soon, specifications for goods were transmitted from the border traders to the interior merchants, while officials made up for mismatches between supply and demand.

As Fan Jinmin points out, however, the Kazakh trade moved closer to a real commodity trade, in which officials were directly involved.[54] In the Zunghar trade, the main official goal was stability; the actual profit or loss was of less concern. Officials "stood aside" after giving merchants their advances. In the Kazakh trade, both officials and traders responded quickly to market demands so as to ensure a "fair deal" and secure profits for both sides.

A comparison of Qing commerce with the Kazakhs, with the Zunghars, with the Russians, and with the British at Canton illuminates some of the special features of these relationships. These four frontier trades, viewed from the Qing perspective, varied along a continuum from security-driven to profit-driven. The Russian trade had entirely security interests: even the lavish furs that Russian caravans brought to Beijing found few takers among the Manchu nobility. The Zunghars, by comparison, offered horse and cattle products with real value in the northwest, yet the predominant Qing goal was to tame these nomads with trade. The Kazakh trade lay between the extremes of the Zunghar and Canton trades. It was more commercially than politically oriented, and officials had a greater stake in the profits, but it was still driven primarily by the need for horses. The Canton trade delivered significant profits directly to the imperial household, did not provide strategic goods, and generated even closer official and foreign merchant partnerships. (The Xinjiang jade trade, which delivered its profits directly to the imperial household, also anticipated the Canton trade.)[55] The Zunghars and Russians had been clear military threats to the border; they needed both a sharp application of coercion and the softer methods of material gain to induce them to act properly. Officials used condescending terms for the Kazakhs, too, but did not regard them as a major military concern. In the early years of the Canton trade, before opium became prominent, the British traders were not seen as dangerous, only greedy. There was a progressive diminution of consciousness of danger as the northwest expansion reached its successful conclusion.

The Kazakhs were regarded as new peoples who had never before been in contact with the empire, but the Zunghars were well known. Kazakh trade, as the emperor specified, was to be regarded not as a "loose reign" policy designed to rein in obstreperous nomads, but as a form of trading relationship with peoples beyond the empire's limits. Some modern historians, however, have gone so far as to include the Kazakhs within the Qing empire. Immanuel Hsu, for example, in his textbook on modern China, included the Kazakh territory as part of the "area of Chinese sphere of influence" in 1775. The Qing did confirm Kazakh tribal leadership but had clearly drawn the line on its own expansion by the 1750s: Mongolia and Turkestan east of the Pamirs were within its orbit, Russians and Kazakhs were not.[56]

Yet the Zunghars were not mere traders beyond the empire's limits. They were the Manchus' greatest enemies. Did the Qing intend the truce to be permanent? How plausible is it to imagine a stable frontier at the Altai, with a persistently independent Mongolian state? I find this scenario unlikely, especially given the swift action by the Qianlong emperor to take advantage of Zunghar divisions to eliminate the state. Even though the Zunghars were no longer threatening, and trading relations flourished, the Qing could not tolerate a rival *Mongolian* Central Eurasian state. In this sense, Qing definitions of geopolitical strategy were cultural and even ethnic. All Mongolians had to be encompassed by the universal empire; but other peoples need not be. By the mid-eighteenth century, each major Central Eurasian group had attained a defined status in relation to the empire: Mongols were incorporated, or exterminated; Russians were divided off by a fixed, mapped border; Kazakhs traded across an ill-defined region but were not objects of conquest; Turkestanis were split between the domains east and west of the Pamirs. The return of the Torghut Mongols represented the final gathering of the Central Asian peoples under the embrace of the tricultural Qing elite. Trade, security, and ethnic definitions together determined who was within the empire and who was beyond the border.

PART FOUR

Fixing Frontiers

12

Moving through the Land

I N this chapter I examine the spatial techniques employed by the Qing rulers to define territorial boundaries and limit mobility. Charles Maier has periodized modern world history with the concept of "territoriality," by which he "means simply the properties, including power, provided by the control of bordered political space, which until recently at least created the framework for national and often ethnic identity." He notes that in the seventeenth century, around the world, new dynasties or "more cohesively organized territorial states" fortified their frontiers and redefined sovereignty to give themselves unrestricted authority within their own domains.[1] European historians commonly connect this transition with the signing of the Peace of Westphalia that ended the Thirty Years' War in 1648, but the European states defined their territories culturally as well as diplomatically.[2]

For Maier, "the seventeenth and eighteenth centuries comprise the great epoch of enclosure: enclosure of common lands within the villages of Britain and western Europe, enclosure of state borders."[3] Thus the securing of borders against external violation went in parallel with the securing of social and territorial boundaries within each state. Maier rightly notes that this process was not limited to western Europe. Russia, China, and the Ottoman empire in this period likewise developed controls over population movements, clearer definitions of the space under the ruler's command, and treaties establishing state boundaries. Russia defined its borders in the east by signing a treaty with China as it tightened controls over peasant mobility within its domains. China eliminated the autonomy of pastoral populations within its borders after it had eliminated the Zunghar regime.

"To pacify and settle" in Chinese *(pingding)* and Manchu *(necihiyeme toktobumbi).*

We may summarize the goals of imperial ideology toward the frontier regions with two Chinese and Manchu terms which appear in the titles of the
campaign histories and recur frequently in official documents: *ping* (Ma.
necihiyembi): "to level, smooth out, console, subjugate, pacify," and *ding*
(Ma. *toktobumbi*): "to fix, make sure, pacify, bring under control."[4] *Ping*
not only means "to make peace" *(heping)* but also implies flattening out,
creating a plain *(pingyuan),* removing obstacles that block an unobstructed
view. In their mapping, information-gathering, and history-writing projects, Qing rulers and scholars aimed to expose local information to the
comprehensive gaze of the authorities. They also tried to standardize the
administrative landscape so that bureaucrats could handle multiple local
peculiarities with uniform, simplified rules.

China shared this drive for simplification with other Eurasian states.
Many eighteenth-century European regimes tried to create uniform mappings of natural and human landscapes. Scientific forestry, for example, reshaped forests to produce a uniform, reliable yield. The designers of the
gardens of Versailles used military designs for manipulating earthworks to
model an ordered, highly visible, uniform landscape.[5] In China this impetus
toward rationalization of cultural space can be found in the expanded examination system, with its thousands of cells, "cultural prisons" in which

candidates were locked up to produce essays; in the abolition of the *tusi,* or native headmen, in southwest China, who were replaced with the regular county administration; and in the formal emancipation of "mean" people who had anomalous social status.[6] On the frontier the extension of civil bureaucratic forms from the interior to newly conquered regions expressed the same drive. Historical narrative, documentary compilations, and stone inscriptions (stelae) also set in place visible, approved, smoothed-out versions of public memory.

Ding/toktobumbi means to make things permanent and fix them in place. It implies not just repression of rebels with military force, but replacing mobile populations with settled populations who can be counted, assessed, and subjected to corvée. The *baojia* registration system tagged all villagers with their place of residence in an attempt to make them collectively responsible for one another's crimes and tax payments. The Qing assigned nomadic tribes to pasture areas which were carefully patrolled by banner troops. Later, maps indicated specifically the locations of each tribe and the borders of its terrain. Officials carefully counted the populations assigned to military colonies and bannermen and measured their land yields annually. The registers of the state farm populations, which tracked between 5 and 15 million people, now provide extraordinarily accurate information for demographic historians.[7]

Still, none of these imperial projects entirely succeeded. James Scott's depiction of the all-seeing state describes failed visions, not realities. In Immanuel Kant's words, "From the crooked timber of humanity can no straight thing be made."[8] Many pressures undercut the efforts of imperial officials to create a perfectly ordered, perfectly visible society. The huge, growing, and increasingly mobile population strained against local control. The expansion of the empire to unprecedented limits, and the concomitant development of markets, offered new opportunities for people to move around. The marking of space and people faced technical limits and genuine resistance. As James Scott has argued in another context, we should not confuse hegemonic projects with social reality. Beneath the surface, multiple particular identifications survived despite the best efforts of rulers to smooth them out.[9] When submerged alternative visions emerge into the light, revolutions often result. Even if it is difficult to discern the hidden resistances in historical sources which come overwhelmingly from bureaucracies, we can detect their traces by careful linguistic analysis.[10]

This chapter surveys the techniques used by the Qing to stabilize territorial and temporal control, proceeding from the most to the least solid in material terms. It discusses travel, inscriptions, and maps. Traveling placed the rulers' bodies in the landscape with a privileged vantage point, and travel accounts collected and commemorated the personal experience for posterity. Yet different kinds of travelers and different kinds of accounts created alternate perspectives on the new imperial landscape. Inscriptions planted words instead of bodies on the ground, replacing the physical presence with an abstracted one. The multiple languages on stelae addressed different audiences. Maps put down in print a selective overview of the empire under a comprehensive gaze, with the aid of new cartographic techniques introduced from western Europe. The duality of secrecy and publicity in their use reflected the cross-purposes of mapping for all states: defining public space and collecting strategic information. Each of these techniques of exhibiting authority expressed multiple meanings that often overflowed the containers designed by the central state. Chapter 13 explores similar contradictions expressed in the rewriting of history under imperial sponsorship and alternative conceptions of time in accounts of the conquest.

As Richard Strassberg's large anthology demonstrates, travel writing has been a long-established part of the classical Chinese literary and historical tradition. Emperors, officials, and private individuals wrote accounts of their visits to both familiar and exotic locales.[11] Their travels left impressions on themselves and on the places they visited. They altered the experience of those they encountered and even changed the sites themselves. Modern tourists were not the first people to alter indelibly or even destroy historic and natural settings. Chinese visitors engraved texts in the rocks of places that inspired them, most conspicuously at sacred mountains and the dramatic karst hills of Guilin. By inscribing his text in stone, the "traveler sought to participate enduringly in the totality of the scene. He perpetuated his momentary experience and hoped to gain literary immortality based on a deeply held conviction that through such inscriptions, future readers would come to know and appreciate the writer's authentic self. At the same time, the text altered the scene by shaping the perceptions of later travelers and guiding those who sought to follow in the footsteps of earlier talents."[12] The rocks at Guilin today bear inscriptions by famous persons from imperial officials and poets to Zhu De, commander of the Red Army.

Although some protested marring landscapes with excessive inscription, most Chinese viewed writing on a site as civilizing it, leaving it marked with evidence of *wen*. "By applying the patterns of the classical language, writers symbolically claimed unknown or marginal places, transforming their otherness and bringing them within the Chinese world order."[13]

Those who left written accounts also transmitted to their readers a fixed version of their personal experience. Paradoxically, the travel writer knows that he passes through a place for only a brief period of time, but he cannot resist generalizing about essential, eternal qualities of the land and peoples he meets. Travelers project their own personalities and social environment into the landscapes they cross; like fiction writers, they create "autoethnography" as much as objective description.[14] As with the other cultural markers described here, travel and geographical accounts give us the self-conceptions of those engaged in the imperial enterprise side by side with "scientific" details.[15] They are not neutral sources of data, but they illuminate the interactions between the new arrivals and the peoples they attempted to understand and control.

Travel and Authority

The early Qing emperors spent a considerable amount of time moving from place to place. As in early modern Europe, the personal presence of the king was a vital element of Central Eurasian rule. On military campaigns, by sharing the same space with his troops, joining them in suffering and heroism, the leader transmitted his charisma to them while also carefully supervising their actions. Imperial tours in peacetime marked certain places as especially significant, either as sites of summer palaces away from the capital (as in Rehe, Manchuria, or in Versailles, France), or as sacred landscapes that embodied ideals of the empire. But emperors were not the only travelers who marked out imperial space. Envoys, scholars, and literary figures also created resonances wherever they went. The fascination of the new territories created audiences for adventurers, pilgrims, merchants, and writers. From the top to the bottom of the social hierarchy, the people moving through Qing territories established new boundaries for their collective imaginations.

Subjects of other empires also produced accounts of Central Eurasia, passing through the same spaces as Qing representatives. British and Russians who negotiated with the Qing and Zunghars described the region, combining ethnographic, geographic, and political information. Comparing these accounts with Qing texts casts more light on the Qing imperial project. These multiple narratives from inside and outside the empire do not add up to a single coherent vision, but they display diverse concepts of space and human environment across the continent.

During his three last campaigns against Galdan, from 1696 to 1697, the Kangxi emperor sent over one hundred letters from his camp in the northwest back to his son, Prince Yinreng, in Beijing. Not only are these letters an invaluable source for evaluating the accuracy of the Chinese published and archival record, but they also offer remarkable insights into the character of the emperor himself.[16] Chapter 5 relies on these documents extensively to reconstruct the emperor's campaigns. Here I consider how they inform our view of the emperor when seen as a traveler's tale.

Kangxi himself, of course, did not describe his letters as a "travel account" *(youji)*. But what if we view them as part of the tradition of classical travel literature? Even though they were written in Manchu during a military campaign, they display similarities to the classical Chinese accounts in both the historiographical and the lyrical tradition. Historical writers, including poets and travelers, presented themselves as "processor[s] of information" and collectors of documents, who recorded their observations of natural features for the guidance of those who came after them.[17] Confucius himself had told his students to study the *Book of Odes* not only to "bring you near to being useful to your parents and sovereign" but also to "help you remember the names of many birds, animals, plants, and trees."[18] Since knowledge about peoples and lands on the frontier informed strategic planning, rulers relied on this form of public history. Data collection always aided imperial interests, especially when the ruler gathered it himself.

In his letters, Kangxi repeatedly describes the location of water sources, the abundance of grass, and heights and distances measured with the trigonometric skills he learned from the Jesuits, not just for immediate practical use but so that later conquerors would profit from his information. He knew that before him the Yongle emperor in the early fifteenth century had followed almost the same route. Kangxi paid close attention to details such as the different names for grasses and the effect of gerbil holes on the safety of horses. He shipped back home a box of colored stones which he had collected and an herb that he thought would be a useful anti-malarial drug. He described the cave dwellings of Shaanxi, and he calculated the distance from Beijing to Ningxia. At the same time, he constantly asked for information from the capital—on the timing of a solar eclipse, the blooming of flowers, the arrival of birds in spring. As an indefatigable empirical investigator, the emperor could demonstrate his geometric skills, play amateur natural historian, indulge his curiosity about new places, and request reports from the capital all at once.

Kangxi's activities echo the earliest inspection tours described in the *Book of Documents*, and especially the description of the Zhou emperor in the *Mu Tianzi Zhuan*, in which the ruler "demonstrates his control by journeying to distant locations by horseback and chariot, engaging in political and religious rituals, hunting, banqueting, accumulating and distributing tribute, judging his subjects, and receiving benefits in encounters with spiritual beings."[19] Kangxi's campaign accounts relate precisely the places where he rested, the banquets for allied Mongolian tribes, and extensive hunting, all of which testify that both nature and humans welcome his presence. Miraculous events, like the unprecedented abundance of water and grass, or the marvelous ability of the emperor to cross the Yellow River in a small boat (echoed by Mao swimming the Yangzi?), showed that Heaven supported the imperial will.

In both the ancient and Qing accounts, however, the rulers had to respond to undercurrents of unease. The Confucian *Zuo Commentary to the Spring and Autumn Annals* criticized Emperor Mu for "indulging himself" (*si qi xin*) by traveling around his realm, and the emperor himself, as portrayed in the *Mu Tianzi Zhuan*, wondered whether leaving the capital was a sign of his moral weakness: "The Heavenly decree changes not / A son of Heaven I am made / But the will of Heaven I follow not, / Leaving my people in distress. Tears suddenly fill my eyes / When the parting music is sounding, And my heart is filled with sadness / As I think of my millions hoping for my return."[20]

Kangxi likewise faced constant grumbling by his top advisers that political stability would be endangered if he stayed away too long from the capital. There were both moral and practical reasons for their anxiety. The "politics of centrality" rested on the view that "power emanated from a fixed center."[21] To leave the capital only for personal indulgence threatened serious consequences. The constant seasonal round of rituals at the Temple of Heaven and elsewhere would be disrupted if the imperial body were not present to keep the cosmos on its regular course.[22] Kangxi's third campaign caused especially severe anxiety back home, since it did not look at all like a military expedition. As we shall see, the editors of the campaign history *(Fanglue)* deliberately ignored the abundant documentation of Kangxi's hunts in the Ordos in order to make his activity look more serious. Qianlong justified his southern tours as efforts to improve water conservancy: he was not just having fun.[23]

Officials left behind knew well the disadvantages of the ruler's being away from the capital. They phrased their entreaties for his return in terms of concern for his health, but they also knew that the people could grow increasingly alienated during the emperor's absence. In 1691 troops heavily in debt tried to force their way into the Forbidden City while the top leaders were away on campaign.[24] The tension between the ruler's personal will and the imperatives of bureaucratic routine showed both in military policy making and in the determination of Kangxi's successor. The emperor's urge to travel exacerbated both issues.

Opposing forces of personal attraction and bureaucratic systematization

strained at early Qing administration.[25] Although order in the capital required the ruler to be in the symbolic center of the empire, authority on the
frontier in the early Qing also depended heavily on his personal presence.
Kangxi's four personal expeditions to the northwest indicated his active
participation in the military campaigns that expanded the empire. He could
claim personal credit for the victory, and he inspired the soldiers with his
bodily presence. Chinese infantry and officials providing support behind
the lines might obey written orders, but his Manchu troops and Mongol allies responded enthusiastically to the model set by their leader.

Kangxi's letters show that he thoroughly enjoyed his time in the steppe,
out of sight of carping literati. He found the austere life in tents invigorating, and regarded battle as a necessary toughening experience for all
who exercised leadership. He encouraged his sons to lead campaigns, and
judged their character by their success. The letters place as much stress on
personal character and moral example as on practical details or objective
observation. Kangxi's letters certainly do not fit the mold of the Daoist-in-
spired travelers who wrote lyrical poetry about blending into the landscape, but they are much more personal than the dry lists of places and peoples in the geographical accounts. In their mix of the personal and the
descriptive, the letters reflect the hybrid character of their author, a ruler
restless with the imperial bonds that he himself had reconstructed. The letters from the northwest also indicate Kangxi's close personal attachment to
his son: he frequently tells him that he longs to be home, as he instructs
Yinreng to pay attention to state affairs even when he is looking at plants
and animals: "The Crown Prince is a very filial boy. He probably, while
viewing flowers, birds, fish, or beasts, takes pity on his poor parent, who is
suffering in these extremely remote salty sands. But do not worry about
me! You should devote yourself completely, day and night, only to the affairs of the country and our household [Ma. *gurun boo-i baita*, Ch. *guojia*],
and in your free time relax by consulting the classics and histories about the
successes and failures of former generations."[26]

While constantly expressing concern for his son's health, Kangxi also
bombarded him with requests for information, from the trivial to the most
vital. A solar eclipse in the capital caused particular concern. The emperor
wanted to know the exact time of the eclipse; when he heard that clothing
prices had risen on the day of the eclipse, he insisted that an order be given
to prohibit people from "forming groups" *(jiedang)* to discuss the ominous
event.[27]

One curious incident indicates the great pressure on the prince to satisfy
his father's every whim. In the margin of a letter from his son, Kangxi
wrote, "It should be about the season for the arrival of the songbirds in the

capital; please let me know if you have seen them." After receiving this comment, the prince wrote back immediately to say that he had seen two birds himself, but then he was confined to the palace the next day for business. He sent men out to the Summer Palace to look for the birds, but they saw very few. But, the prince says, he "broke out in a sweat all over his body" on seeing the emperor's comment, and "felt he had nowhere to hide." He begged his father not to put such minutiae in his correspondence, but Kangxi replied that he always asked about small things in his letters to everyone, though usually not, he admitted, in orders to his ministers.[28] Clearly, even the favored Crown Prince stood in fear of his awe-inspiring father, and felt compelled to please him.

The emperor's letters to his son are particularly poignant in light of the prince's later fate. Kangxi had named Yinreng, his second son, heir apparent in 1676, and appointed him to act as regent during the campaigns of 1696 and 1697. While he was on campaign, the emperor heard reports of immoral behavior by his son, and on his return ordered the execution of several officials associated with him.[29] But the emperor did not turn against his feckless son until 1708, when he placed him in confinement, accusing him of plotting to take over the throne. Yinreng was pardoned and released in 1709 but confined again in 1712. After this time the emperor refused to designate an heir apparent, despite official requests.

In the letters, Kangxi does not express direct suspicions, but he mingles expressions of close personal attachment with moral instruction and demands for righteous behavior and accurate reporting from home: Yinreng was being tested for competence with every communication from his father. After the revelations of the prince's misconduct, the emperor's anxiety and rage were particularly severe because he had relied on his son so heavily during his time away from the capital.

Kangxi's combination of paternal sternness and intimacy with his sons models in microcosm the idealized relationship of an emperor to all of his subjects. Confucian texts like the *Classic of Filial Piety* promulgated filial relations as the basis of all stable rule. In fractal fashion, father-son relationships especially characterized authority relations at all levels, from emperor to minister, high official to low official, and local magistrate to his people, and within lineages and families.[30] But none of these idealized hierarchical relationships could eliminate tension, mistrust, and resentment. Kangxi's letters reveal openly both the common concerns of any father about his sons and the particular salience of filiality as a principle of imperial rule.

The dark side of filial obedience was betrayal. Favorite sons who disappointed a father's expectations could suffer extreme punishment. The note

of betrayal of a benevolent father/ruler is echoed both in Kangxi's treatment of his sons and in his policies toward the Mongols. In each case he
sought to evoke loyalty by enacting benevolent policies toward his subjects,
as toward his sons, expecting them to respond with warmth and obedience.
Yet since this was an unequal power relationship in both cases, even the
most generous father/ruler could not suppress suspicions of resentment or
immoral behavior, just as his subordinates struggled to carve out small
spaces of autonomy from his unrelenting gaze. The prince tried to deflect
requests for information on trivial matters; the Zunghars aimed to secure
an autonomous state; but both tried to push back against relentless pressure for control from the energetic ruler. Ultimately, both were disgraced in
imperial eyes. But the need to use force in itself compromised the claim to
rule only by soft bestowal of favors. Emperors liked to think of themselves
as bringing only a gentle rainfall, but far too often they had to deliver thun-
derbolts. Having to legitimize the use of force was a constant strain for the
rulers themselves and for their loyal ministers, eulogists, and historians.

The personal and political were closely intertwined, as the emperor's
mood rose and fell depending on the progress of the military campaign and
his faith in those at home. At his lowest point in the spring of 1696, he betrays great anxiety over the upcoming battle and longs for his son: "When I
was leading the troops forward I had no time to think about you; now that
Galdan has fled and I have seen with my own eyes his exhausted condition,
I have appointed the appropriate troops to pursue him. Send me four coats
of cotton gauze and four linen jackets, old ones which you have already
worn, so that your father can wear them when he misses you." After telling
the prince to prepare food for his return, he continues:

> Examining Galdan's situation, I see that he has nowhere to stand.
> However, we have had no news from Fiyanggû. If Fiyanggû reaches
> Galdan, Galdan is certainly finished: even if he escaped ten thousand
> times, he could not prosper. Whatever happens, he is done for. I have
> scouted from the Tono mountains to Bayan Ulan, and found no secure
> place to camp. Under Heaven, on this earth, there is no place like the
> Khalkha land. Except for grass, there is nothing of value here out of
> the millions of things in this world.[31]

In this letter, the emperor expresses his anxiety, longing, and frustration
at being far away from home in the midst of an inconclusive campaign. He
had decided to turn back because his troops were running out of food.
Galdan had fled, with smaller detachments in pursuit, but imperial success
depended crucially on Fiyanggû's ability to intercept the Mongol army.

Whether Fiyanggû could prevent the Mongols from escaping to the west was by no means guaranteed. Although he put on a brave face, expressing confidence in ultimate victory, the emperor faced the prospect of wasting his efforts in another futile, expensive march. His impressions of the landscape as a wasteland revealed his depression: at other, more confident times, he exalted the abundance of the grasslands. But here he turned to his son for consolation, revealing deep longings for personal intimacy— so deep that he wanted to wear his son's clothes. This extraordinary document merges the highly personal character of Kangxi's rule, his fluctuating moods, and his dedication to both family and military valor. In the guise of a description of his travels, the writer uses the landscape to reveal his most intimate feelings.

Historians of East Asia and Europe have recently begun to look closely at how rulers use ritual to display their ideals of authority.[32] In these rituals, as orchestrated movement of bodies through defined spaces, rulers and subjects performed in symbolic, indirect forms the political relations that defined their hierarchies. Ritual was not simply a cynical covering for naked coercion but an active force constructing power relationships. In the broad sense, rituals included all routinized movements through space where participants interacted in defined ways, but the scale of movement could be very large or very small. The travels of the emperors around their empire were both practical inspection tours and ritualized expressions of their bodily presence. In the gardens of Versailles, nobles and kings staged their relations in more controlled spaces than on the battlefield, but in both places they exerted power in public forms.

Russian Tsars similarly needed to stage ritual displays to justify their rule. Russian coronation ceremonies featured large processions entering Moscow with great displays of armed might and luxurious clothing. Until the eighteenth century, the Tsars flaunted their foreign ancestry and their distance from their subjects, reinforced by religious ceremonies that endowed them with superhuman powers. During succession struggles in the eighteenth century, however, critics used accusations of foreignness to discredit their rivals. Catherine the Great was the first Russian ruler to make a tour of her realm, indicating concern for all her subjects.[33] Qing rulers had begun this symbolic indigenization through touring earlier. Despite their non-Han origins, the Qing emperors traveled to exhibit their intimacy with their subjects and their concern for the people's welfare. They did not abandon their Manchu identity, but they immersed themselves in the Han popu-

The Kangxi emperor departs for an inspection tour of the South. Handscroll by Wang Hui and others.

lation symbolically while putting on display their Central Eurasian connections in the form of tributary envoys or captives.

Chinese emperors shared common objectives with their European counterparts, as seventeenth-century observers knew. Voltaire had already noticed the parallels between the Kangxi emperor and Louis XIV (r. 1643–1715), and so did the Jesuit Joachim Bouvet, who described Louis's greatness to Kangxi when in his service.[34] European monarchs also traveled extensively through their domains. Dorinda Outram, for example, mentions several types of royal travel in early modern Europe: fact-finding missions, ritual observances, domestic excursions for pleasure or for security, and foreign diplomacy.[35] Travel could also help monarchs escape from social and political entanglements at their courts while exhibiting the determination of the king to mark the expanses of his territory with his personal presence. This list does not exhaust the motivations for royal travel, and these motives are not mutually incompatible. Often a single royal tour combined many goals. In both Europe and China, royal travel exhibited authority and expressed the ruler's personal taste.

Kangxi's expeditions to the northwest were certainly fact-finding missions as well as military campaigns, but they did not fit comfortably with orthodox notions of ritual progress. Ritual observances were supposed to be contained within the predictable, orderly confines of the capital city: the Temples of Heaven and Earth and the ancestral shrines. Wide-ranging travels through the trackless steppes horrified the cloistered minds of the ritualists who prescribed imperial obligations. Ming emperors, like the Wanli emperor (r. 1573–1620), had chafed unsuccessfully against the tight bonds of ritual obligations.[36] The Kangxi emperor was able to break through these bonds because of his personal dynamism. He was the Central Eurasian mobile warrior who could reject ritual bonds before they were firmly set. The Qianlong emperor fit more comfortably into his elegant prison, but even he needed to break out. He never went to war personally, but he frequently left the capital. In his bodily movements Kangxi restlessly pushed at the limits of restrictions urged on him by his advisers. Although Qianlong accepted the elaborate controls that regularized his actions, he too used ritual processions as a means of escape.

Kangxi's travels also blurred the boundaries between "domestic" and "foreign" travel. In western European states, where, by the seventeenth century, boundaries had become more definitely established, domestic and foreign goals could be sharply separated. Within their realms, rulers traveled to secure social order, to check up on local officials, to experience the pleasure of examining their domains, and to visit their family homes on country estates. Beyond their boundaries, they traveled for diplomatic negotiations with other monarchs, or to create marriage alliances as part of foreign policy. Kangxi, however, mixed domestic and "foreign" purposes just as he mingled business and pleasure. He genuinely enjoyed the rugged life on the steppe: Mongolia was not a homeland of the Manchus, but it evoked the rigors of the hunt and the battle which were the common cultural features of both peoples. Since Nurhaci, Manchu rulers had often invoked their common lineage with the Mongols for diplomatic purposes; as they had borrowed the Mongol script, they also borrowed Mongol traditions of horseback riding and shamanism.

The Mongols were "part of the family" of peoples of the empire. The Manchu term *gurun boo-i baita* (affairs of the country and our household) is linguistically equivalent to the Chinese term *guojia,* but arguably places a greater stress on familial loyalty, and separates more distinctly matters of family and state.[37] By tying the Mongols to him through kinship linkages, and by physically imposing himself on them in their own territory, the Kangxi emperor demonstrated the unity of the Central Eurasian peoples who composed his empire.

Logistical and political constraints, however, prevented him from reaching western Mongolia, the home of the Zunghars. The Eastern Mongols were within reach of a determined, vigorous ruler, but the Western Mongols were not. The greater alienation of the Western Mongols from the Qing reflected not only physical distance and lack of control but also the lack of an imperial presence, and the lack of personal ties. Physical distance alone did not determine allegiance: Zunghars traveled regularly to even more distant Tibet, and lamas came from Tibet to both eastern and western Mongolia. Cultural choices influenced, but not determined, by physical and political constraints sent the two halves of Mongolia in separate directions.

The emperors revealed different strategies of cultural assertion through their attitude toward imperial mobility. The Kangxi and Qianlong emperors both traveled extensively through their domains, but in very different directions and for different purposes. The Yongzheng emperor, by contrast, seldom traveled far. In addition to heading northwest on military campaigns, the Kangxi emperor also went south. Michael Chang calculates that the Kangxi emperor went on a total of 128 imperial tours from 1681 to 1722. He demonstrates that the famous southern tours of Kangxi, like his travels in other directions, were closely connected to considerations of military security and cultural domination. Kangxi's visit to Mount Wutai in northern Shanxi in 1683, for example, a site closely linked to Tibetan Buddhism in the Yuan, served to promote the cult of Manjusri in the eyes of Mongol observers.[38] The tours closely resembled military campaigns in the structuring of their camps, the detailed organization of logistics, and demonstrations of archery and horsemanship. As with the military campaigns, the emperors faced criticism for leaving the capital for too long, and they had to defend themselves against charges of indulging in pleasure trips. Chang argues that imperial touring, in whatever direction, found its justification not in the Han literati classical tradition but in Central Eurasian precedents of rule by personal presence of the man who marked his domains on horseback.

Qianlong, the desk general, never went to the northwest, and never engaged personally in battle, but he considered control of the region vital to his reign. He substituted the written word for his personal presence by marking up the terrain with numerous stelae in many languages. Emblems of imperial presence in the northwest thus shifted from personal to virtual, as the written word stood in for the emperor's body. Qianlong toured the lower Yangzi (Jiangnan) six times, in 1751, 1757, 1762, 1765, 1780, and 1784.[39] These were lavish processions, with none of the hardships of the steppe, but they replayed the cultural conditions of the early conquest years. Although they were billed as "inspection tours" so that the emperor could learn about local conditions, their primary purpose was, in Chang's words, a "constant reenactment of a narrative of Manchu conquest and military superiority."[40] Qianlong brought Central Eurasian tributary representatives with him to Jiangnan so as to show the Han literati the scope of the empire, and to show the tributaries its wealth. He constantly invoked the theme of military discipline while on tour, insisting that bannermen ride on horseback and not on sedan chairs, and conducting hunting, riding, and shooting exercises to test their skills. He wrote poems about the northwest frontier while riding through the rice paddies of the south. Qianlong went on about 150 trips, including the six major southern tours, and was on the road an average of three to four months per year.[41] Chang argues that Qianlong's tours were neither the wasteful extravagance criticized by nationalist Chinese writers nor the purely administrative inspections of southern water conservancy as justified by the emperor. They were expressions of "ethno-dynastic" ideology which staged the linking of the multiple peoples and spaces of the empire under the emperor's personal gaze.

The three rulers' methods of movement indicated a shift in the relationship of imperial authority to the wider society. Kangxi took a hands-on approach, engaging personally in battlefield planning, civil administration, and personnel decisions while being constantly on the move. Yongzheng began the shift toward confinement, restricting his movements but still exerting personal force over a select number of high officials. Qianlong's ritualized movements fit better with the much larger and busier empire of the eighteenth century. His personal interventions in administration were sporadic, just as his tours still put him at a distance from local realities. The "Soulstealers" sorcery scare of 1768 indicates that the emperor could intervene in bureaucratic routine when he chose to; but even in this case the bureaucrats deflected his most insistent demands, as they did on the northwest frontier.[42] Unable to confront the local situation directly, the emperor could exert control only through officials and documents; his scope for personal, unpredictable judgment was radically reduced.

Private and public personas also distinguished the rulers. In Kangxi's letters, behind the façade of the confident, boastful conqueror we can easily see the man besieged by loneliness and doubt. Yongzheng revealed his anguish to a few trusted men, like Yue Zhongqi, but he lost faith in them just as he opened himself up to them. Qianlong almost never let the mask slip. When he left the capital, he produced no personal documents directed to close family at home. Even his poems consist of public reflections on the empire and conventional phrases about the responsible ruler, not individualized expressions of joy or despair.

Emperors were not the only travelers, and emperors by themselves did not create the "flourishing age" of the high Qing; others added details to the picture. In Chapter 6 I discussed the less easily controlled, more individual perspectives of three travelers from three different countries who crossed Central Eurasia on diplomatic missions. Their information sources, filtered through cultural screens, generated variegated views on the Qing–Zunghar conflict. Bell stressed the benevolent intentions of the Kangxi emperor in promoting peace between the contending Mongols. Unkovskii's interview with Tsewang Rabdan, by contrast, demonstrated a keen awareness of military competition. In blunt language, the Zunghar Khan asked the Russians to supply him with a large army to attack the Qing in exchange for allowing them to search for gold and silver in his domains. Neither side gained what it wanted from this deal. But the encounter also illustrates how Russians and Zunghars attempted to position themselves against the Qing in Eurasia. Tulisen's mission, like the travels of the emperor he served, gathered valuable information about the Mongols and Russians while exploring the possibilities of alliances against Zunghar power.

These traveler-envoys provide diverse views of the Qing, Mongols, and Russians which both echo and conflict with those of the emperors. No single perspective captures the entire situation. Each writes from a particular cultural position and political interest, and each writes in order to persuade, not merely record. We can capture the full story only by attending to the multicultural symphony produced by the writers' different locations.

George Staunton, the first English translator of Tulisen, adds a fourth line of counterpoint to this intertextual polyphony. He regards the writings of Bell, the Scot, as the most objective source, in contrast to the "vain boasting and courtly style which the Chinese historian falls into on every occasion, in which his sovereign or his country are in any way directly or indirectly concerned." Staunton quotes excerpts from Bell's journal in apposition to Tulisen's account so as to set off "truth" against the "falsehood of these arrogant pretensions of the Chinese."[43] Staunton reflects the disabused attitude of the British in the early nineteenth century, who were frustrated by the failure of the Macartney mission and exasperated by China's resistance to their imperial vision. But Bell is not a neutral reporter either. He shows considerable admiration for the abilities of the Zunghar Mongols as well as the Chinese. Could this not reflect his own cultural location as a peripheral person from the edge of the British empire, serving another emperor outside his homeland?

Tulisen, by contrast, cannot approve of any Mongols except those who submit to the emperor. Obedience to tribute relations is for him the touchstone for deciding who deserves incorporation and who deserves elimination. Unkovskii, who wanted to avoid committing Russia to military support of the Zunghars, depicts the Qing as peaceful and militarily unthreatening. Tsewang Rabdan knew better. He had the most reason to see the Qing as militarily powerful and expansive. But with hopes of a new Qing policy after the death of Kangxi in 1722, he chose not to put himself under Russian subjection, which was the price he would have to pay to get Russian support. He, too, had reasons to minimize the long-term Qing threat to his autonomy.

So all the players in a way constructed the image of a benevolent, peaceful, prosperous Qing China for their own purposes. The image of a ritualized imperial structure, relying primarily on moral suasion and not military force, would become increasingly prominent in both Western and Chinese eyes through the nineteenth century. This picture replaced the image of a powerful, militarized, expansionist regime held by most of the Central Eurasian actors who encountered the Qing in its prime.

Travel narratives of the Qing frontiers reflected the process that brought the territory under imperial control. A brief comparison with Taiwan illustrates the special characteristics of the northwest. Accounts by fascinated literati about Taiwan, one of the first new territories to join the Qing, span the period from the late Ming to the end of the Qing dynasty. Emma Jinhua Teng describes the variety of tropes used to depict the island.[44] Taiwan's peoples and landscape, unknown before the seventeenth century, inspired wonder, bafflement, and criticism. The native inhabitants seemed to Chinese writers to be a primitive people, innocent of history, writing, or civilization. Some writers treated them as remnants of an unspoiled paradise, the blessed isles placed by mythology off the eastern coast; others saw them as threats to core Chinese values because their sexual and familial practices violated orthodox codes. During the eighteenth century, officials like Lan Dingyuan viewed the Taiwanese as prime objects of colonization; he was the most extreme proponent of a "civilizing mission" that included aggressive promotion of settlement by Han peasants from the mainland, education, and compulsory assimilation to mainland values. Other officials, however, tried to protect the aboriginal inhabitants from Han encroachment, both to preserve social order and to minimize the costs of administration.[45]

Qing views of Taiwan thus exhibited the same tensions between localism and uniformity that characterized frontier policy elsewhere. Should the native inhabitants be left alone to preserve their distinctive cultural features, or should the officials promote rapid assimilation? Contrary to Stevan Harrell's argument, the Qing did not have a single coherent "civilizing mission" toward their frontiers.[46] Policy and perceptions of Taiwan alternated depending on the author and context. Some writers, like Yu Yonghe, viewed their travels as a journey of personal self-fashioning; others, like Huang Shujing in 1736, dedicated themselves primarily to gathering and classifying new information. Taiwan could be a "living museum," an implicit critique of corrupt morals on the mainland by a surviving natural community, a source of information to verify accounts of the marvelous, or an enticing but disturbing example of sexual freedom, a place where women had unnatural powers. There was no simple trend toward greater "empiricism" over the course of the Qing, but Qing writers did come more and more to stress common understandings between the natives and themselves. Taiwan, like the other frontiers, served as a useful screen for projecting anxieties about how to contain multiple identities within a single imperial vision.

Teng's analysis of travel writing on Taiwan helps to put in context the similar writings about the northwest. Xinjiang, in particular, generated a very different kind of writing from Taiwan because it was, for literati, first and foremost a place of exile.[47] For those convicted of crimes, Xinjiang was literally a penal colony; even for officials posted there in the normal round of their duties, traveling "beyond the pass" *(guanwai)* appeared to be leaving the civilized world. Both Taiwan and Xinjiang presented officials with puzzling questions of engagement with alien terrain, but these contradictions were more sharply highlighted in the northwest. On the one hand, Central Eurasian peoples, unlike the Taiwan natives, had a long recorded history of their own, which Chinese officials could not deny; on the other hand, they were seen as irrepressibly violent and savage, the most constant enemies of the Han Chinese state. Xinjiang also contained marvelous landscapes and abundant new resources awaiting exploration, but its harsh climate threatened all who ventured there with death from drought, heat, or starvation. Officials engaged in similar projects of ethnographic classification and compilation of gazetteers, as elsewhere, but the significance of their efforts was strongly influenced by military and strategic goals.

One individual, from the highest rank of the literati class, left a vivid portrait of his brief sojourn in Xinjiang that expresses a personal perspective on the northwest frontier. Ji Yun (1724–1805), a native of Zhili, obtained his *jinshi* degree at the young age of thirty and soon gained the prestigious post of Hanlin compiler. He then spent two years in exile from 1769 to 1770 in Ürümchi because of his involvement in a bribery case. After his return with an imperial pardon, he regained his prominence, becoming one of the chief editors of the great imperial encyclopedia, the *Siku Quanshu*. On the way home between Barköl and Hami, traveling frosty roads and stopping in lonely hostels, he wrote 160 poems about his experience on the frontier, later published as *Miscellaneous Poems of Ürümchi (Wulumuqi Zashi)*.[48]

Ji Yun's poems express the personal reactions of one member of the cultured Qing elite to the raw but invigorating new territories that had joined the empire. He did not regret his experience or complain about his sufferings. He enjoyed the bustling life of the city, with its tightly packed shops, its crowds of shoppers, its brothels, and flute music in the evenings. He could also boast about the natural wonders of Xinjiang, describing the marvelous mountain torrents that burst out so fast they flowed uphill over the dams built to control them, or the powerful winds that "blew men and horses around like whirling leaves."[49] He toured ancient ruins and mused on their origins, and he discussed local legends with the remaining Mongols. Ji Yun fully embraced the developmental ethic of Qing officials and tried to make himself useful by constructing a reservoir. Local people put him off with objections until he had to go home.[50]

In Ji Yun's poetry we sense the exhilaration of mastery, represented by the new conquests that indicated new powers over man and nature. He claimed that the weather had changed since the conquest: Ürümchi used to be cold and barren, but now with the home fires burning from thousands of new settlers, the entire region had become warmer.[51] He showed no nostalgia for the lost primitive cultures of the Mongols or Hui, and he praised the abundant yields from the military colonies. Ji Yun's writings expressed in personal form the official policies of integration and development for the northwest. They broadcast exotic information about and enthusiasm for the new possessions of the empire to the literati audience back home. The long tradition of "border poetry" usually depicted this frontier as a place of forlorn exile, but Ji Yun, at least temporarily, had made it his home. The domesticated frontier now became another resource to be added to the Qing literary tradition.

Marking Space in Stone

The Kangxi and Qianlong emperors erected large stone tablets, or stelae, to celebrate their military victories, and placed them on mountaintops and in temples in Beijing. They followed a long tradition: ever since the Qin dynasty, stone tablets had conspicuously displayed public evidence of Heaven's will. In the third century BCE Qin Shihuangdi climbed the sacred Mount Tai, erected a stone tablet, and performed the *fengshan* rituals to give thanks to Heaven for designating the victorious emperor as a recipient of its grace.[52] The permanent, public presence of a huge stone monument proclaimed to all the inevitable victory of the Son of Heaven. In the second century BCE Han Wudi likewise celebrated the completion of his military exploits by offering sacrifices at Mount Tai and engraving his reign title in stone. The large stone tablet became known in folk belief as the "mouth-piece of Heaven." In Chapter 70 of the vernacular novel *Men of the Marshes (Shuihuzhuan)*, a large tablet descends from Heaven, revealing that the 108 bandits who had previously wreaked havoc had now received Heaven's mandate to carry out heroic acts on behalf of the ruling dynasty.[53]

Stelae thus united the powers of Heaven and Earth, and their symbolism penetrated both imperial and common understandings of legitimate authority. They proclaimed in the most permanent form, protected from the ravages of weather, the achievements of the empire. They fixed in stone an orthodox version of history, free of the doubts that might afflict skeptical scholars. A single large stone block, by its massive presence, excluded the possibility of alternative interpretations.

Our modern versions, in the form of memorials, likewise attempt to establish in public spaces a historical view that will unify the population around symbols of heroism. Since modern democracies constantly contest memorial designs, stone alone clearly does not eliminate the multiplication of meanings.[54] Debate still rages over highly charged events, especially wars like the war in Vietnam, even after the memorials are built. Likewise in Qing China, whether the debates were visible or not, the imperial version carved in stone did not deliver the final answer for everyone. Yet the turn to memorialization indicated a decisive shift in social consciousness, an effort to create closure out of the inescapable flux of events.

Although all stelae used a stereotyped public language, their style of pre-

(a)

Stele instructing visiting officials to dismount from their horses, with inscriptions in six languages. From left to right: (a) Chinese, Manchu, and Mongolian; (b) Tibetan, West Mongolian, East Turkish.

sentation varied significantly. Most notably, Qing multilingual inscriptions revived a practice of the conquest dynasties which had been abandoned by the Ming.[55] Kublai Khan had issued his commands in six languages: Mongolian, Uighur, Arabic, Persian, Tangut, and Chinese. The prominent inscription on the Yuntai ceremonial arch, near the Juyongguan gate in the Great Wall, also written in six languages, still testifies to the Yuan impulse to address multiple audiences.[56] Likewise, the stone at the southern en-

(b)

trance to the Qing Imperial Palace instructed visiting officials to dismount from their horses in six languages.[57] The Qing used four languages—Chinese, Manchu, Mongolian, and Tibetan—for the large number of stelae placed during the eighteenth century in the temples around Beijing and the great lama Buddhist monasteries in Chengde, Manchuria.[58] These inscriptions bore clear political messages addressed to the major constituencies of the empire, and they linked the Qing rulers particularly closely to the sponsorship of Buddhism. Let us examine three inscriptions related to the conquest, focusing on the messages they broadcast and the concerns they addressed.

In 1697 the emperor wrote inscriptions for five stelae celebrating his victory over Galdan. One was placed at the critical battle site of Jao Modo, three on surrounding mountains where the emperor viewed the battle, and one in the Imperial Academy in Beijing.[59] These inscriptions collectively embrace the combination of military force and divine sanction that ensured victory. Each emphasizes a different theme. The stele erected on Chahan Qiluo peak stresses that "those whom Heaven covers [*fu*] are all our children." The emperor has brought peace to his people and ensured their prosperity. The stele at Tuonuo peak focuses on the "thunderous military might" *(zhenlei tingwei)* of the six armies personally directed by the emperor. With this awesome power, he exterminated the demons threatening the land and brought security to distant wilderness. The tablet at the Imperial Academy, strategically placed for the instruction of degree holders, elaborates in great detail, based on extensive classical citations, the thesis of the "unity of the civil and military way" espoused by the great rulers of the past. The sagely ruler strives to avoid the use of military force: "All that Heaven covers [*fu*], all within and beyond the seas . . . was granted to one man, who from past times to now, day and night concerns himself with nourishing all that live . . . [H]oping for peace on the borders, he desists from using troops, in order to give the people rest [*yanbing ximin*]."

But Galdan, who "poisoned the region beyond the passes," threatened the security of the interior and so required extermination. "To repress bandits is the way to give rest to the people. To sweep away barbarians is the way to bring stability to the interior." Stressing his personal participation in the campaigns, sharing the suffering of his soldiers, the emperor insists that he "could not avoid using troops to ensure the people's security" *(bu de yi yongbing yi an min)*. Even though he wanted to use civil means *(wende)* to transform the world, his ministers and subjects urged him to launch the campaigns to protect the realm. Ritual texts supported the unity of civil and military actions: the sage kings prayed to temple spirits before they left on campaigns and after their return victory. For the ancients, "military and civil were one" *(wenshi wushi wei yi);* rituals conducted at the banqueting table for diplomatic envoys could impress them so much that military force would be rendered unnecessary *(zunzu zhechong).*[60] This emperor, likewise, once he determined *(ding)* his will, displayed overpowering might that awed the petty barbarians into submission. The Mongols are compared to noxious insects who damage farmers' crops, and to animals that scattered and fled to their nests at the approach of the Great Army, whose "ten thousand chariots," like the course of the dragon, dominated everything in its path. Thus the army united irresistible human and natural forces.

These inscriptions epitomize the established view of the conquest, omitting the inconvenient details. Many ministers, as we have seen, urged the emperor not to go personally on campaign, and the "barbarians" of the frontier did not simply submit; they fought back fiercely. Nor did they simply succumb to the superior virtue of Qing rule; until the Qing showed its superior military and economic strength, they asserted their autonomous culture. But in the publicly constructed myth, the way of the swordsman and the way of the penman were united effortlessly. The emperor was the pillar uniting the Heavens above and the Earth below, and he took on the task not for personal glory but out of duty to larger forces. The inscription in the Imperial Academy states: "If the border bandits are not eliminated, our people will not be secure. Gods and humans all are aroused to do this. The necessary punishment from Heaven, how can one man begrudge the labor of it? How can he not desire to give peace to the world?" Now the image of the reluctant agent of superhuman powers masks the traces of personal ambition or revenge revealed in the course of the contest. The public narrative sets in place a determined ruler, inevitable natural forces, and a predetermined glorious outcome.

Kangxi's inscriptions repeatedly focus on the emperor's personal presence at the site as an inseparable part of his authority. He stresses that he climbed the mountain on which the stele is placed, and he describes the panoramic view of the battlefield from the top: "I climbed Langjuxu Mountain, viewed the distant source of the rivers, and broadcast afar my mighty virtue [*dewei*] so as to pacify the peoples of the wild." For Kangxi, placing himself in a high position allowed him to view the vast expanses of his land and transmit his charismatic influence at a distance. Qianlong, by contrast, visited the sacred mountain at Wutai six times during his reign, but he never went to battlefields.[61] His presence at these sites was only virtual. Instead of testifying to the emperor's physical presence, Qianlong's stelae transmitted his *de* through the power of inscribed words alone.

In 1755 and 1758 the Qianlong emperor commissioned two quadrilingual inscriptions, written in Oirat Mongolian, Manchu, Tibetan, and Chinese, celebrating his victory over the Zunghars. He had these stelae erected in the Imperial Academy in Beijing, and in areas in Ili through which the Great Army had passed.[62] The 1755 tablet was set up shortly after the defeat of Dawaci and the entrance of Qing armies into Ili. It begins much like the Kangxi stelae, describing how Heaven covers the entire world and the emperor responds obediently to Heaven's commands. Then it relates the history of the Qing state from its origins, and Qianlong proclaims his mission to be the "cultural unification of the world" *(sihai tongfeng)*. After this proclamation of his ideals, he turns to a direct denunciation of the Zunghars: "Alas, you poor Zunghars! You are the same people as the Mongols [Ch. *tonglei*, Ma. *emu adali*]: Why do you split from them? For generations you have stubbornly refused to transform yourselves [Ch. *genghua,* Ma. *Wen ci cashûlaha:* lit. turned your back on civilization] and made enemies by constant raiding." He thus turns against the Zunghars the very claim made by Galdan. Galdan had appealed to Mongol unity against the Qing, but now that all the Mongols had been conquered, the victorious emperor uses the claim of Mongol unity to incorporate all of the Mongols under his rule. He contrasts his diligent efforts at creating unity with the "pitiful" division of the Zunghars. They have "turned their back on civilization" and continually plundered and murdered one another. He denounces Dawaci as a drunkard, comparing him to a "snake," and a "worm" eating the fruit of the Mongol people. The emperor, having compassion for the people's suffering, sent the Great Army to relieve them, and it conquered the enemy easily, with no obstruction. Again the rebels, like animals, scattered and fled. Dawaci was "trapped like a rat or a bird; he had nowhere to hide." Now all the Oirats belonged to the emperor's land.

The inscription summarizes pithily the new constraints on the nomads: they were free to roam as they pleased with their flocks, but they had to adhere to the territorial divisions marked out for them and avoid quarrels. They are directed to resist incursions by the Burut and Kazakhs beyond the border. If they do this, they are guaranteed all they can eat and drink, as well as permanent peace and prosperity.

The 1758 inscription commemorates the defeat of Amursana. Once again, it asserts Heavenly support for the Qing victories: "Those whom Heaven nourishes can never be killed, even if they are defeated; those whom Heaven overthrows [*fu*] cannot be set upright, even if others support them." The Chinese text plays on the multiple meanings of the character *fu* (to cover, overthrow, reverse) to express Heaven's will. In the 1697 and 1755 inscriptions, Heaven covers *(fu)* all things, so it has all-embracing scope; in the 1758 text, Heaven overthrows *(fu)* those who resist its might; later in the 1758 text, the Zunghars' defeat is ascribed to their inconstancy *(fanfu wu chang),* in opposition to the unwavering imperial will. Yet they are also stubborn in their defiance of Qing control, "unwilling to change their ways." The emperor also invokes Buddhist precepts against the Zunghars, saying, "You claim to revere the Yellow Teaching, but you are really demons who eat human flesh." The emperor portrays himself as a reluctant warrior, someone who does not favor warfare but was nonetheless drawn into the campaign to save the suffering people: "I do not approve of war, or see it as a virtue, but it was unavoidable." Clearly "Heaven supported the emperor; [victory] was not [a result of] human effort." The inscription ends with an interesting discussion of future plans for Ili's reconstruction. The court had not yet decided whether to promote military colonies in the region: "As for creating military colonies so far away, we are still uncertain that it will succeed. We will consider this secretly, and Heaven will decide its success. I can only weigh circumstances, and cannot plan definitely yet." Even in this public declaration of fixed Heavenly will, the emperor revealed the uncertainty of his plans for settlement in the region.

Like Kangxi's inscriptions, these tablets directed messages at the subordinated peoples to justify the imperial victory, but Qianlong's inscriptions also spelled out specific moral lessons and duties for the conquered peoples. The four languages directed their messages to different quarters, so the texts varied substantially in style. The Manchu version expressed its position differently from the Chinese, and the Mongolian and Tibetan texts were translated from the Manchu. While the Chinese text drew on the rich resources of the classical tradition, making allusions to the *Book of Odes*, the philosopher Zhuangzi, and the essays of the poet Han Yu, for example, the non-Chinese inscriptions used more immediately comprehensible language. In the Chinese version, for instance, the survey of the expansion of the Qing described the emperors spreading their fame from their "palace" *(zhaizhong)*, but the Manchu, Mongolian, and Tibetan texts specify it as "founding the throne in Mukden."

The Manchu and Mongolian texts also substitute more clear-cut expressions of domination for the lofty Chinese abstractions. Where the Chinese states abstractly, "All have masters and all are servants" *(xi zhu xi chen)*, the Manchu and Mongolian texts state more concretely that "all became subjects of the great Manchu nation" (Ma. *ayan manju gurun uheri be jusen obuha*, Mo. *ayan manju ulus-in albatu bolghobai*). Line 16 describes how the army "put them [the Mongols] in order" (Ch. *du zhi*), which in Manchu is *dahabuha*, "subjugated." The Chinese describes how the Mongolian ministers and chiefs "hurried to submit" *(yingxiang konghou)*, or "became subjects" *(chen)*, but the Manchu and Mongolian state that they "performed the kowtow" (Ma. *hengkilenjihe*, Mo. *mürgüke irebei)*. The Altaic texts spell out pointedly that the Mongols are subjects of a Manchu state dominated by military power backed by Heaven.

Manchu also serves as the bridge language between Chinese and Mongolian, as it incorporates vocabulary familiar to both audiences. The Manchu text combines Chinese administrative terminology like "entering the charts and registers" *(nirugan dangsede dosimbumbi*, equivalent to Chinese *ru bantu*, or *ru dangzi)*, with Mongolian words like *adulambi* (Mo. *adughul-)*, "to herd," or *nukteme*, "nomadize" (from Mongolian *nutuq*, "camp," "pastureland"). By sending multiple, overlapping ideological messages to their variegated audiences, the inscriptions demonstrate the key role of the

Manchu language as the hinge between the settled Chinese literary tradition and the mobile culture of the steppe.

The Oirat Mongolian inscriptions, written in an alliterative style, translate Qing concepts of border definition, subjecthood, and order into a language familiar to the Mongols. The Oirat text attacks the Zunghar people as "thieves" (Mo. *khulaghaici*), people with evil thoughts who rejected the teachings of Yellow Sect Buddhism, bringing on themselves poverty and destruction. The 1755 inscription describes Dawaci as "contemptible," forced to "creep into a burrow" like a rat. But it also betrays concern about the loyalties of the conquered Zunghars, instructing them to "oppose external forces all together . . . Be on guard against letting the Burut commoners approach you . . . Stop trying to heed the words of the Kazakhs." Here the emperor draws a clear line between the subordinated Zunghars and the "external" (Mo. *ghadanakiyigi*) Kirghiz and Kazakhs, and warns the former not to make contact with these outsiders. The inscription both marked the territory of Qing control, by claiming to "enter on the map" the Ili region, and drew the line between those within and those beyond the border.

At the same time, these inscriptions exposed the ambiguities in Qing definitions of imperial space. In the abstract moral conception expressed by the Chinese text, Heaven's rule was universal, the emperor enacted Heaven's will, and all peoples irresistibly submitted to him. In the practical world of politics, which is more evident in the non-Chinese texts, the empire is bounded. Heaven does not influence everybody, enemies lie across the border, and the realm needs to be defended. Certain regions have "entered the map," but others lie beyond it. The first, Chinese concept appeals to all peoples to join in the "cultural unity" proclaimed by the emperor; the second designates the surrendered Mongols as border guards, holding off the Kirghiz, Kazakhs, and Russians, who lie beyond the cultural realm. In this alternative ideology, a specific entity, the "Manchu nation," dominates over other peoples, primarily because of its military power, and secondarily because of the moral authority derived from that force. Moral righteousness alone does not bring about voluntary submission.

Qing proclamations constantly evoked multiple moral traditions: the emperor's status as "Khan" among Central Eurasians, his protection of the Yellow Buddhist faith, and his Confucian obedience to Heaven all supported his claims; later, he also embraced Islam. But they could never entirely suppress latent contradictions between the generalized invocation of moral norms and the realities of sovereignty on the ground. As the discussion of maps which follows demonstrates, this tension between universal moral claims and bounded territorial sovereignty is characteristic of all imperial spatial claims, British or Chinese. The inscriptions reveal this tension in the variations between the multiple languages in which the empire pronounced its legitimacy.

The Yonghegong lamasery is located in the northeast corner of Beijing, close to the Imperial Academy. For thirty years it was the residence of the prince who became the Yongzheng emperor, and it took its name "Yong" (harmony) from his title. The emperor changed the name on his accession from "Yongdi" (imperial residence) to "Yonghegong" (meaning imperial palace or temple). In 1744 the Qianlong emperor renovated and rededicated the temple to his late father and erected two huge tablets bearing an inscription in four languages—Chinese, Manchu, Mongolian, and Tibetan—in two octagonal pavilions in the first courtyard of the temple.[63] Nearly fifty years later, in 1792, the emperor had a second large stele and pavilion placed farther within the temple complex, containing his "Proclamation on the Lama Teaching." Both inscriptions directly address the frontier peoples whose allegiance to Tibetan Buddhism was critical to Qing control.

The original Chinese text was written by the emperor himself, while the Manchu, Mongolian, and Tibetan were derived from it by translation bureaus in the court. Later legends held that Qianlong himself had written the Manchu, that the Mongolian leader Efu Celing wrote the Mongolian, and that the Qing's ally in Tibet, Polhanas, wrote the Tibetan versions. The spread of these legends indicates the successful assimilation of this product of the imperial administration into the local cultures of the frontier regions.

In the 1744 inscriptions the emperor justifies his conversion of his father's residence into a Tibetan Buddhist temple, arguing from historical precedent and from his responsibility to protect all the faiths of the empire. The Tang and Song emperors, and the Yongzheng emperor himself, had converted their predecessors' residences into Buddhist temples in order to preserve worship of their divine spirits. Qianlong thus claims to unite past and present time *(houxian yikui, jinxi tongfu)*. He compares the deceased emperor to Sakyamuni, who, by realizing Nirvana, had "extended blessing to all sentient beings." The eulogy to Yongzheng, carved in stone, extols the power of his spirit, which surpasses that of the Tang and Song temples. This temple is like the Hall of Swans, where Buddha's disciples gathered, or the deer park where his pupils meditated. The "thousand-fold universes, numberless like the sands of the Ganges, share the flavor of your pure essence, which, surpassing thought, permeates our marrow, penetrates our skin."[64] With this dedication, the emperor assimilates himself and his forefathers to

Stele at the Tibetan Buddhist monastery Yonghegong, Beijing, with the Qianlong emperor's 1792 proclamation on the Lama Buddhist establishment.

the irresistible power of Buddhist spirits to span eons of time and space. The filial duty of the emperor to his father matches perfectly with the transmission of spiritual and temporal power. The language stresses the vastness and magnificence of the imperial spirit, which brings unity to all its subjects. The Qing had inherited and surpassed its predecessors because of this universal appeal.

The non-Chinese languages, however, use different styles and terminology from the elaborate classical allusions of the Chinese text. While the Manchu text puts the allusions in simpler form, the Mongolian text generally features only the Buddhist connotations. As Ferdinand Lessing comments on the Tibetan text, "When the eulogy assumes a hymnic tone, Buddhist imagery spreads out its dazzling riches." Despite the variations, there is no hint of tension between Buddhist and other traditions, and not even a mention of the fact that this temple, unlike all previous imperially conse-crated temples, contains only Tibetan monks.[65]

The 1792 inscription strikes a very different tone. It, too, is written in four languages, and it directs its message specifically at the Mongols and Ti-betans, but it lacks poetry or elevated spiritual language. Instead, the em-peror portrays himself as the historian and policy maker who understands how to use a distasteful faith in the interests of imperial control. Lessing calls it a "self-justification and philippic against Lamaism." In 1744 it is the "filial son, friend of priests," who speaks; in 1792 "an old man, full of acri-mony and acerbity . . . gives us glimpses into that world of ruse and intrigue which, as he supposed, menaced his temporal sway."[66]

In the style of a philosophical classic, all four languages of the inscription contain commentary on the principal message in smaller characters.[67] In the commentary, the emperor cites historical precedents to bolster his argu-ment, which is a tirade against the abuses of tradition perpetrated by the Ti-betan Buddhist monks, and openly declares that the empire supports the Lama Yellow Teaching in order to keep the Mongols pacified.

He traces the origins of the relationship between the Yellow Teaching and imperial power to the Yuan dynasty, when many monks were given the title "Teacher of the Emperor" (Dishi), a tradition that was continued by the Ming. The Qing gave this title to only one monk, Lcangs-skya (the Zhangjia Khutukhtu, under Kangxi), but it followed Yuan and Ming prece-dents in granting the titles of Dalai Lama and Panchen Lama to the leading clerics of the church. They were also given official seals to allow them to "control" (tongling) the members of the order both within and without the empire. Qianlong derives the word "lama" from the Tibetan bla for "above" and ma for "man."[68] He can thus assimilate the Tibetan monks to the Chinese shangren, or sage.

Qianlong justifies protection of the Yellow Teaching as a means of keep-ing order among the Mongols. He never claims to be a Buddhist believer himself. Instead, the emperor has to justify himself against critics who claim that he has been too favorable to the Yellow Teaching. He notes that unlike the Yuan dynasty, the Qing rulers never "distorted principles [of jus-tice] in order to fawn on the monks." According to the emperor, monks under the Yuan dynasty had so much illegitimate authority that they could issue commands equal to those of the emperor, extort money from mer-chants, and beat and rob ordinary people with impunity. The Qing, by con-trast, kept the monastic order under strict control, and used it to "soften" (huairou) the violent Mongols so as to make them obedient.

This inscription was set up after Qing armies had entered Lhasa to repel invasions by the Gurkhas of Nepal. The effective Manchu general Fukang'an had achieved a spectacular military victory, "one of the most astounding campaigns in Chinese history," marching thousands of miles across Tibet in 1792 and forcing the powerful Gurkhas to sue for peace and send tribute to Beijing.[69] Qianlong later counted these victories as two of his ten great military campaigns. But in the inscription he blames the Gurkha invasion on abuses by the Tibetan Buddhist monastic establishment. Succession to the rank of Dalai Lama, Panchen Lama, or the other Khutukhtu (living Buddhas) of Mongolia was by tradition to be determined by selecting a *khubilghan* (reincarnated spirit) of the deceased lama from among the most talented young male children in Tibet. Qianlong noted, however, that increasingly, succession to the lama ranks occurred hereditarily, within certain powerful noble families. When the Jebzongdanba Khutukhtu died, a consort of the Tüsiyetü Khan was expected to provide the new Huktukhu, but she gave birth to a daughter, causing a scandal. A lama of the rival Red Hat sect took advantage of the confused succession to claim the position, and he invited the Gurkhas to invade to support him.

By blaming the lamas' intrigue for the Gurkha invasion, Qianlong justifies his proposal to reform the means by which lamas were selected. He ordered that a golden urn be sent from Beijing to Lhasa, in which would be placed the names of proposed candidates for the next reincarnation of the Dalai Lama and Panchen Lama. The lamas and the Qing resident *amban* would supervise the selection of the next Grand Lama by drawing lots from the urn. In this way, Qianlong proposed to remedy the abuses created by hereditary succession, and to establish a recognized, regular process of selecting the next Panchen or Dalai Lama. A similar process, carried out at the Yonghegong in Beijing, would be used to choose the Khutukhtus of Mongolia.

Qianlong's inscription is a tendentious interpretation of imperial relations with the Tibetan Buddhist church, designed to support increasing control over its procedures. The emperor's greatest fear, clearly, is the increasing autonomy of the clerical hierarchy and its closer relationship to the Mongolian nobility, displayed in the de facto hereditary succession of lamas within Mongolian noble families. The Golden Urn procedure was designed to break this grip by establishing the Tibetan Buddhist hierarchy as a separate, parallel one under Qing official control. It was, in effect, another version of the time-honored imperial practice of "setting barbarians against barbarians," an attempt to split the Tibetan Buddhist clerics from the Mongolian Khans. Even though Qianlong regarded the belief in *khubilghan* reincarnations as illogical and contrary to the principles of Buddhism, he found it a useful instrument for imposing control over the

Mongols and Tibetans. But he claims greater "fairness" *(gong)* for his procedure compared to choosing the successor from a noble clan, which he prohibits as "egotistical" *(si)*. Qianlong defends his intensive study of Tibetan scriptures as giving him the cultural understanding necessary to institute this reform. Thus he portrays himself to the Tibetans as such a learned ruler that he has outdone the Tibetan clerics themselves in his insight into their traditions, and to the Confucians, who criticized him for his immersion in heterodox texts, as a practical statesman, using these barbarian traditions to enforce the virtues of justice *(gong)* on all the peoples of the empire: "If I had not studied Tibetan scriptures, I could not make these claims. When I started to learn the scriptures, I was criticized [Manchu text: by some Chinese] for being biased toward the Yellow Teaching, but if I had merely nourished the vain ambition of clinging to old patterns, how could I have succeeded in inspiring awe and preserving peace among the Old and New Mongol for several decades, or in punishing with execution the lamas who stirred up trouble in Tibet?"[70] Superior knowledge, a sense of universal justice, and the will to deploy ruthless force are all expressed in this statement. It enacts a narrative of history and defines the cultural scope of the universal ruler as directed from the imperial center.

The Tibetans themselves may not have viewed their history the same way at all. Alternative Tibetan texts depict the lamas as indeed Teachers of the Emperor, grateful for imperial recognition of Buddhist wisdom, but in no way subordinate in authority to him.[71] The titles of Dalai Lama and Panchen Lama were bestowed by Mongolian Khans on the lamas, and only later confirmed by Chinese dynasties. A separate Tibetan Buddhist hierarchy maintained itself, closely allied with Mongolian protection, until the eighteenth century, when the elimination of the Zunghars and the Khoshots of Qinghai undercut the political props to Tibetan Buddhist autonomy.

Qianlong's stratagem has contemporary resonances. The Golden Urn method devised by Qianlong figured prominently in the debate between the PRC and the Dalai Lama in 1995 over the choice of successor to the Panchen Lama. Beijing argued that the Golden Urn lottery was the method sanctioned by precedent, and that the Dalai Lama was breaking with Tibetan Buddhist tradition by appointing his own candidate from exile.[72] The Tibetans replied that the Golden Urn lottery was imposed by the emperor after his military victory, that it was seldom used in practice thereafter, and that the Dalai Lama was entitled to choose successors to the Panchen Lama however he pleased. There were as a result two contending candidates for Panchen Lama, one installed in Beijing, the other held under arrest, probably in Xining. When a communist revolutionary government espoused the sanctity of a tradition established over two hundred years ago by an emperor of what that government used to call a stagnant "feudal" regime, the historical mythmaking of the Qing continued to exert power over the contemporary relations of China and Tibet.

The public, stereotyped, orthodox language of these inscriptions conceals multiple interpretations and dialogues with unseen adversaries. Although each stele pretends to be an eternal statement, each comes from a particular historical context. Each asserts completion and control, yet implicitly recognizes the fragility of its authority. Even the most frozen ideological poses, when examined closely, reveal ambiguity, diversity, and change.

Maps and Power

Joanna Waley-Cohen describes the Qianlong emperor as "obsessed with war." He called himself the "Old Man of Ten Victories" (Shiquan Laoren), invoking his ten famous military campaigns. He wrote poems, commissioned paintings, conducted rituals, and filled the countryside with memorials to his battle victories. In the emperor's eyes, military victories legitimated Manchu rule and served to "stiffen the sinews" of flaccid Chinese subjects who objected to the costs of war.[73]

Although the emperor himself never engaged in battle, he flooded the country with memorials of war and honored his generals for their exploits. Besides the voluminous writings celebrating his campaigns, including 1,500 of his own poems and the imperially commissioned campaign histories, Qianlong stamped the landscape with visual reminders of war. In 1760, at the Wumen, or meridian gate, of the capital, he held a ritual execution of prisoners *(qianshou)* taken on the Xinjiang campaign, and had the event commemorated in a painting by Xu Yang. The court painter Baldassare Castiglione produced sixteen battle paintings referring to the Zunghar wars. Chinese painters produced several scrolls illustrating the campaigns.[74] The Ziguangge pavilion in Zhongnanhai contained one hundred portraits of officials, most of them Manchu or Mongolian, who had displayed outstanding military merit. The stelae and war memorials placed next to the Confucian academy in northeastern Beijing reinforced the message of the combined power of *wen* (civil culture) and *wu* (military might). North of the capital, in the Xiangshan hills, military monuments and temples dotted the landscape, and farther away, at Mukden, Chengde, and the hunting grounds of Mulan, the Qing court displayed its Central Eurasian traditions even more openly. Even in the heart of literati culture in the south, Qianlong's southern tours reinforced the message that the conquerors had mastered both martial and aesthetic traditions. By bringing Central Eurasian tributaries with him to Jiangnan, he deliberately mingled the two cultures.

Qianlong also commissioned a series of sixteen prints by top-quality French engravers.[75] These engravings, like the maps of the "Jesuit Atlas," mixed Western and Chinese graphic traditions under imperial sponsorship in order to broadcast images of imperial might. They show scenes from the campaigns in Ili in the 1750s, including the emperor's reception of Amursana as his ally, the rebellion of Amursana and siege of Barköl, Jaohûi's defeat and pursuit of Amursana, and his battles with the Khojas of Turkestan. They also portray the emperor receiving the homage of the Central Eurasian peoples who had joined his empire, including Ölöd, Kazakhs, Torghuts, Muslims, and others. The dramatic, crowded scenes of hundreds of men and horses trampling the landscape contrast with the orderly, carefully rationalized scenes of reception of tributaries and captives. Captions on each engraving explain in detail the scenes and their participants. Although the emperor had ordered production of a limited number of copies for internal circulation only, the engravers made copies in Europe which were later published in France. Like the "Jesuit Atlas," the engravings distributed the vision of imperial might around the world, despite the emperor's wishes.

These processions and memorials were the public face of the Qing military enterprise, which glorified its unprecedented achievements in territorial expansion while enshrining them in literary works, on paper, and in stone. Many other Qing construction projects not explicitly linked to military campaigns still promulgated the achievements of the expanding empire. Boundary markers, like the willow palisade across Manchuria and the stones delimiting the Russian border, showed the extent of imperial rule. Frontier cities, with more orthodox geographical orientations and more regular wall shapes than the cities of the interior, displayed the power of the state to rebuild the open spaces of the frontier in accord with its own design.[76] The great cartographic projects of the Qing likewise graphically imposed order on the landscape in order to serve their grand strategic vision.

The Kangxi emperor launched, and the Qianlong emperor continued, a project of creating large-scale, comprehensive maps of the empire. Since I have discussed the significance of the Kangxi emperor's mapping projects elsewhere, I only summarize here my argument placing Kangxi's project in comparative perspective.[77] Maps, as instruments of military, fiscal, and

Engraving of Qianlong's military campaigns in Turkestan, 1755–1760, depicting the first effort by General Jaohūi to relieve the siege of Yarkand in 1758.

Engraving of Qianlong's military campaigns in Turkestan, 1755–1760, depicting a victory in 1759 by General Fude, who with only 600 men put to flight a Muslim force of over 5,000.

commercial power, define strategic locations and efficient routes of march for armies, measure the landholder's obligations by fixing him in place, and point out trade routes. All early modern states and empires used maps to control their realms, and they all used new cartographic techniques.

Chinese empires had developed a long tradition of comprehensive mapping, which expressed their visions of control and their images of the empire's place in reference to other peoples.[78] The Qing rulers built on this tradition, but added to it the new technology introduced by the Jesuits in the seventeenth century. Their cartographic ambitions surpassed their predecessors' in detail and scale. At the same time, their maps revealed the unavoidable tensions inherent in the effort to subsume so many divergent cultures and places under a single uniform gaze. Furthermore, their neighbors, the Russians and Mongols, produced their own geographic visions, which interacted with those of the Qing but reflected different orientations toward the Eurasian continent they shared.

Joseph Needham argued that China led the world in cartography for centuries because of its long experience with the grid and its focus on exact measurement. The "Jesuit Atlas," for him, was the culmination of Chinese contributions to "scientific" cartography. Many scholars now reject this sharp distinction between cultural and scientific representation. The history of cartography has broadened its own vision in recent years. Earlier studies told a story of progressively more accurate depictions of space through the development of scientific surveying techniques. Most historians drew a sharp distinction between "religious" maps, primarily concerned with the depiction of sacred cosmologies, and "scientific" cartography, focused on accurate representation of the natural world. The leading forces in this increasing precision were the early modern European explorers and geodesists, driven by an interest in expanding knowledge. Other countries—Russia, for example—were described as lagging behind Europe but aiming for the same results.[79] Until recently, most discussions of map production evaluated the accuracy of early modern maps by comparing them with modern topographical knowledge. Recent studies of cartography, however, have found that geographic knowledge is inextricable from the political environment, and there is no sharp distinction between cultural and scientific styles of representation.[80] Cartography did not develop in linear fashion toward exactness but responded to shifting cultural conditions.

The states that sponsored the surveyors had their own strategic imperatives which demanded certain kinds of topographic knowledge and suppressed others. All maps construct space according to political interests. Exact measurement does not obliterate cultural content. Cartography does not simply become more exact; it also shifts its forms of representation in response to cultural needs. Each change of representation conceals as much as it reveals. Mapmakers produce silences and erasures as well as detailed new content. This new perspective on cartography complements well recent studies in the history of science in general, which likewise criticize a simple story of increasing exactitude in the measurement of nature by showing the close connection of early modern science to its cultural context.[81]

This recent work, however, has still left the impression that only western Europeans pursued cartography as part of their imperial projects. In fact, other agrarian empires of Eurasia, especially Russia and China, also promoted surveying on a large scale. Several scholars have examined in detail the consequences of the Qing's development of geographical knowledge for modern China's territorial identity.[82] Here I focus on the connections between European and Chinese cartography related to frontier expansion.

When rulers asked for maps of their realm, they usually wanted the large-scale view, based on centralized, standardized measurement. As James Scott has argued, the baffling variety of local customs, local measures, and local ecologies formed a valuable barrier for subject peoples against the increasingly intrusive claims of the state. States aimed to measure landholdings, population, and productive capacity uniformly, obscuring local detail, in order to extract resources more efficiently. Mapping subject peoples complemented the effort to fix them in place.[83]

From the sixteenth century, French kings systematically applied mapping to military operations and began the comprehensive use of maps for civil government. Louis XIV and Colbert in 1661 set four major goals of cartography: military, juridical, fiscal, and religious. Each defined boundaries so as to clarify lines of authority.[84] The Jesuit order supported these projects by teaching the newest surveying techniques. By the late seventeenth century, the French state surpassed England and the Netherlands in scientific cartography. Jean Dominique Cassini (1625–1712) began a complete national survey of France, completed by his son and grandson in 1744.

From this base, the Jesuits developed skills which appealed to rulers around the world. They used their technical expertise to induce rulers to allow them to proselytize for Christianity while they served imperial needs. The Russians, Chinese, and Mongols also produced significant large-scale maps as they contended for power in the seventeenth and eighteenth centuries. Their cartographic enterprises included boundary definition, controls over mobile populations, abstract depictions of territory, and cultural definitions of people and places. Much of the activity in this Central Eurasian conflict paralleled the projects of the early modern European states.

Although earlier Chinese dynasts had long recognized the political value

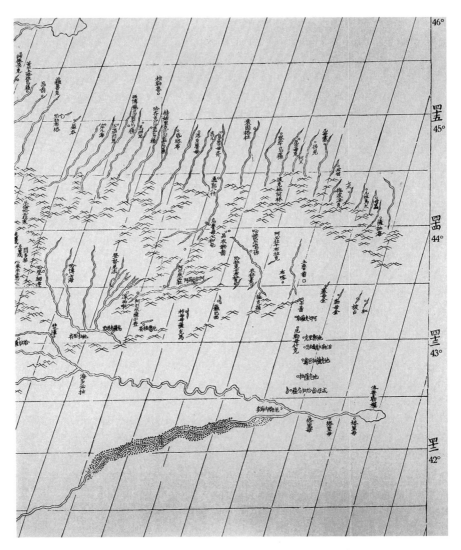

Plate showing Zungharia–Tianshan–Kashgar from the "Jesuit Atlas" *(Huangyu Quanlan Tu)*.

of maps, the Kangxi emperor, like his European contemporary Louis XIV, promoted the mapping of empire on an unprecedented scale.[85] He delighted in the measurement technology that he learned from the Jesuits. They accompanied him on his northern campaigns against Galdan, where Kangxi employed what he had learned from his weekly lessons in geometry to determine latitude by measuring the position of the pole star, and to measure the height of cliffs. Afterwards, he commissioned the Jesuits to produce for him an atlas of the entire empire, the famous "Jesuit Atlas" *(Huangyu Quanlan Tu)*, published in three versions from 1717 to 1721.[86] The emperor could now claim to have mastered his entire realm under his "comprehensive gaze" *(quanlan)* simply by leafing through the printed sheets. Until the compilation of the atlas, he had viewed his realm by placing his body in the terrain, either on military campaigns or on imperial tours; now he could see all of it from the privacy of his palace. From 1715 to his death in 1722, the ailing emperor traveled only to the Eastern Tombs and Rehe; he never again ventured south or beyond the Great Wall.[87]

The compilation of the atlas was one component of a broader project to systematize and rationalize the ruler's knowledge of space and time. An edict of 1713, for example, ordered the synchronization of the calendar, regulating times of sunrise and sunset and the twenty-four hours of the day in the Khorchin region of Mongolia, based on the Jesuits' new measurement techniques.[88]

The stages of production of the atlas indicate its close connection with strategic concerns.[89] The Jesuits in 1700 first produced a survey of the capital to help protect against periodic flooding. The emperor personally checked the accuracy of their techniques. In 1708 he called on them to map a portion of the Great Wall. The success of this project inspired Kangxi to call for a map of the entire empire. The surveyors began with the homeland of the Manchus around Mukden, Chengde, and the Ussuri and Amur rivers. From there they proceeded to survey the province that included the capital. In 1710 further surveys of sparsely settled territory on the Amur helped to establish the strategic bases along the border negotiated with the Russians. Finally they proceeded to the other provinces, fixing a total of 641 points of latitude and longitude by astronomical and geographical measurements. The court issued five woodblock editions and one copper edition of the atlas between 1717 and 1726, and even, some say, a version engraved in jade. Clearly the rulers wanted the atlas to be, as the Qianlong emperor said, "handed down for all eternally."[90]

The Manchus drew on many sources for expanding their knowledge of these little-known frontiers. The project depended crucially on local officials and native assistants. The Jesuits mapped Tibet, which they did not visit, by relying entirely on Chinese and Manchu sources. Russians helped the Chinese to map the border. Nikolai Spafarii had presented to the court in Beijing a hand-drawn map of the entire Russian empire, and the Jesuits had gathered more information from Spafarii's embassy which they passed on to Beijing.[91] Other maps with Manchurian and Mongolian inscriptions portray areas not surveyed by the Jesuits.

Nearly all studies of the "Jesuit Atlas" stress its role as an initiator of in-

Detail from the map of Central
Asia by Philipp Johann von
Strahlenberg, 1736.

tellectual progress. In this view, the Jesuits' new cartographic techniques brought "scientific cartography" to China.[92] But as J. B. Harley has argued, it is an illusion to distinguish sharply between purely "scientific" and purely "rhetorical" maps. No maps are completely objective representations, independent of the circumstances of their production. The "Jesuit Atlas," too, contains embedded cultural assumptions revealed by comparison with Russian and Mongolian maps of the same region. The scope of the atlas is sharply bounded. Regions beyond China's administrative or cultural influence are marked merely with empty space. The only manmade structures noted in the atlas are the Great Wall, the symbolic marker of the division between China proper and the non-Han territories to the northwest, and the Willow Palisade, the symbolic barrier protecting the Manchus' homeland in the northeast.

The new survey techniques, as implemented in the atlas, both expanded and constrained the imperial gaze. Areas that could not be surveyed in detail, or for which accurate information was unavailable, had to be left blank. This included much of Mongolia and Manchuria, including territory up to the Nerchinsk boundary, which the Qing claimed to control.

A comparison of the maps of the Swede Philipp Johann von Strahlenberg and of Kangxi's Jesuits indicates the different concerns directing their investigations. Strahlenberg's map gives equal attention to all of Central Eurasia, but Kangxi's atlas provides information only on the regions directly of concern to the Qing state. Strahlenberg puts in almost equally large type "Imperium Russicum," "Tattaria Magna," "Sina," and "Magni Mogolis Imperii Pars." Recognizing the coexistence of several empires in Eurasian space, he does not sharply divide them from one another. The borders between Russia and China are not marked distinctly, even though the treaty had been negotiated and surveyed only thirty years earlier. Although the Siberian regions have greater detail, the map clearly depicts deserts, steppes, mountains, lakes, and rivers of all of Central Eurasia. The latitude-longitude coordinate system is a universal, global one, transcending the administrative boundaries of states. Chinese and Russian provinces are named, but in between the empires are numerous "kingdoms" *(regnum)* of the diverse peoples of Central Asia: "Cosaci Horda" (Kazakhs), "Euloeth Kalmaki" (Zunghars), "Regnum Kaschkar."

The intricate crisscrossing of regional names, topography, large-scale and small-scale divisions, and detailed labels creates a sense of multifarious complexity, for Strahlenberg's map was not produced by a systematic, imperially endorsed survey imposing uniform abstractions on the landscape. Instead it reflected the local knowledge embedded in the experience of the travelers, merchants, and inhabitants of the region. The names and peoples create a buzzing, booming confusion of labels; what ties the space together is the universal latitude-longitude grid. This alternative perspective on Eurasian space highlights the achievements, and the limitations, of the Qing imperial view.[93] The Qing view expressed in the atlas was far more systematic, but it gained its clarity at the cost of excluding local detail and suppressing knowledge of rival powers beyond its borders.

The "Jesuit Atlas," by contrast, is radically simplified. The maps of the northwest frontier show only blank space beyond the Great Wall, except for the map of the Ordos region, where the Yellow River goes beyond the wall. This was, during the Ming, the most troublesome area of conflict between the empire and Mongolian tribes.[94] The map of Zungharia, titled "Zawang Arbutan Tu" (Tsewang Rabdan), contains only a few placenames, sketchy mountains and rivers, and much blank space. The Qing did not control this region in the 1720s, nor were they well informed about it. After the conquest of Xinjiang in 1760, the number of place-names on Qing maps increased dramatically, but the Qing focus on administrative boundaries and place-names excluded cultural and ethnographic information of the kind included by Strahlenberg.[95] The atlas gives no hint that diverse peoples moved through the space it depicts, or that there were contested claims to the area. The Jesuits and their assistants did depict places they did not visit, including Japan, Korea, and Tibet as well as Xinjiang, so they were not devoted exclusively to direct observation. But they included no Russian territory or Russian place-names, while including many Manchu and Mongolian names.

Thus the imperial state contained the threat of the new cartographic technology. The atlas's focus on administrative units, its suppression of evidence beyond the cultural frontiers, and its erasure of the sphericity of the earth and the multiplicity of peoples on it reinforced the monocentric cultural universe of the Qing and confirmed it with more precise measurements. These were techniques of state simplification that increased the purview of the autocratic gaze but did not challenge it. Scientific knowledge served power; the truths it spoke were limited to what the rulers wanted to hear.

In the eighteenth century, world cartographic leadership passed to the British, who planned to survey systematically the Indian subcontinent. Matthew Edney's outstanding study describes the complex process of political, institutional, scientific, and cultural negotiation that finally culminated in the Great Trigonometrical Survey and publication of the *Atlas of India*

from the 1820s forward. His work embeds the history of cartography fully in the politics of empire.[96]

Edney points to the ironic gap between the cartographers' claims to create a perfect, uniform grid and the actual practice of surveying, dependent on flawed instruments and unruly assistants, and bogged down in bureaucratic infighting.[97] Despite these limitations, the Great Trigonometrical Survey "held the promise of a perfect geographical panopticon."[98]

Edney's description of British imperial aims shows striking parallels to those of the Qing empire. Like their Chinese counterparts, the British "surveyors and bureaucrats extolled a map's virtue for bringing an 'entire country' into a 'single view.'" The message of cartography was that "this is an imperial space to be governed by us."[99] Edney correctly notes that "the rational, uniform space of the British maps of India was not a neutral, value-free space. Rather, it was a space imbued with power relations," but he is wrong to claim that "cartographic representations of India established the essential character of the subcontinent according to a *European* conception of space."[100] Both the Manchu and the British conquerors shared the drive to create a comprehensive, abstracted vision of an imperial realm. Qing bureaucrats imposed a uniform grid on their territory that fit closely with the administrative configuration of the empire even though it did not reflect features of the local terrain. The Jesuits brought the new technology of triangulation to China, but their aims harmonized with the goals of their employers. Abstracted space was not a unique European invention but a common product of the imperial drive of both empires.

Edney also points to tensions between publicity and secrecy in imperial cartography. In the eighteenth century, the East India Company tried to restrict knowledge of its Indian surveys so as to prevent its information from leaking to the rival French.[101] The three presidencies of Bombay, Madras, and Bengal were unable even to obtain maps from one another, a situation that created much duplication and waste. Even though the growing need for shared standardized information led to the appointment of a Surveyor-General for all of India, the bureaucratic hierarchies ruling India kept their surveying knowledge as long as possible sealed off from one another. Military men, who directed local surveys, regarded them as strategic intelligence, not to be disseminated widely. Only the *Atlas of India*, published in the 1820s in London, not in India itself, finally defined the public, uniform British image of India.[102]

Politics obstructed the dissemination of cartographic knowledge in Russia just as in India and China. Few people in Russia knew of Strahlenberg's map, even though it was one of the most important sources of information about Siberia of its time.[103] The Qing cartographic program also exhibited

Map of Shaanxi and Gansu provinces from the imperial encyclopedia *Gujin Tushu Jicheng*. This widely distributed version omits the modern latitude and longitude lines shown on the "Jesuit Atlas," which had restricted circulation.

this conflict of secrecy and publication.[104] Woodblock editions distributed the atlas beyond the circle of the court and high officials. The distribution to wider audiences in the empire, however, omitted the most radically innovative element of the atlas: its use of globally universal lines of latitude and longitude. Even though the Jesuits had adapted their grid to Chinese sensitivities by putting Beijing at zero degrees longitude, their grid, unlike the traditional Chinese one, made imperial space only one portion of the globe instead of a cosmic and geographical center of civilization. Versions of the atlas printed in 1726 in the imperial encyclopedia *Gujin Tushu Jicheng* had much less detail and omitted the latitude and longitude coordinate lines.[105] The Jesuit atlas was, in effect, published in China in two versions: a precise, "internal circulation" version that included the longitude and latitude markings, and a public version that lacked them. The first version, for strategic use by the court, was not widely distributed within China.

The atlas itself did not create a revolution in Chinese cartography. Although Joseph Needham claimed that the Jesuits' scientific cartography built on a long-standing tradition of native Chinese achievements, more recently other scholars have noted the slight effect of the Jesuit cartographic techniques in the long run on Chinese map production.[106] The traditional grid continued in use through the end of the nineteenth century, unaffected by the latitude-longitude system. Several hybrid maps tried to combine new and old techniques, but these remained within the context of the tributary-system view of the world. They did not disrupt imperial China's complacency about its centrality in the world or its condescension toward foreign peoples.

The "secret" court version, however, was printed and disseminated widely over Europe by the French mapmaker Jean Baptiste Bourguignon d'Anville, who published the large-scale map in Jean Baptiste du Halde's *Description de la Chine*. Europeans placed China within a global context informed by their knowledge of other imperial spaces. For them, Qing imperial space was not a cosmic center but a section of the Eurasian continent, a new terrain for the expansion of knowledge.[107] The contrasts in the distribution of the atlas in Europe and in the Qing empire demonstrate how social and political environments shaped technical knowledge. The same maps had different implications in different contexts of imperial expansion.

The Zunghars created their own maps of this contested space, relying on their Swedish prisoner Johan Gustaf Renat. Renat took with him on his return to Sweden two maps of Zungharia. According to Renat, Galdan Tseren drew one of these maps himself, and the other was copied from a Chinese original. (See map, pages 308–309.)

Renat's maps were the first indigenously produced Mongolian maps of the steppe since the Yuan dynasty.[108] Galdan Tseren, like the other state builders, needed a comprehensive view of his realm. The maps do not have a grid, but they are roughly drawn to scale, and the relative positions of terrain features are accurate. Both of them contain a large number of Mongolian labels of river tributaries, towns, stations along roads and rivers, and fortresses. Despite John Baddeley's claim that the "Mongolian" tradition of mapmaking is to give only place-names and no terrain features, these maps prominently feature mountain ranges, rivers, lakes, and empty spaces.[109] Yet they also do not follow the model of the Chinese and Russian maps. They lack defined boundaries, latitude and longitude lines, and a clear frame. Most striking is the very disproportionate scale of Lake Balkash and the Irtysh River: the lake is portrayed as much larger than its natural size. Clearly the lake and river occupied a central position in the Zunghars' conceptions of their territory.

These maps, along with the evidence of development of agricultural, military, and industrial production given in Chapter 8, indicate that Galdan Tseren was engaged in a genuine state-building effort similar to those of his giant neighbors. By labeling his realm, he showed that he realized the importance of naming fixed locations. He did not, however, gain nearly as comprehensive a view of his territory as his rivals. The boundaries of his realm remained ambiguous, while the Russians and Chinese were rapidly clarifying the limits of their domains. Their conception of space left no room for an autonomous Mongolian state.

Expanding the Imperial Gaze

As the Qing empire expanded in the eighteenth century, it continued to add territories and place-names to its maps.[110] The mapping of Xinjiang reshaped spatial conceptions but also created tensions. When the Qing viewed itself as an Inner Asian empire, it included Turkic and Mongolian place-names in their original scripts and spellings. But to the extent that the emperor justified his place in a succession of Chinese rulers from the Han to the Tang, he assimilated the names of Central Eurasian places to those found in classical sources. The early nineteenth century showed greater shifts toward Sinification. Travel diaries and scholarly research linked local places to classical antecedents. Maps worked together with historical study to weave these new regions inextricably into the imperial fabric, giving it new colors and shapes while at the same time officials pretended that Xinjiang had always been part of the imperial dominion. The empire's expanding spatial imagination laid the groundwork for the unquestioned truths that would undergird modern definitions of the nation.

Nineteenth-century maps of the Mongol banners displayed graphically

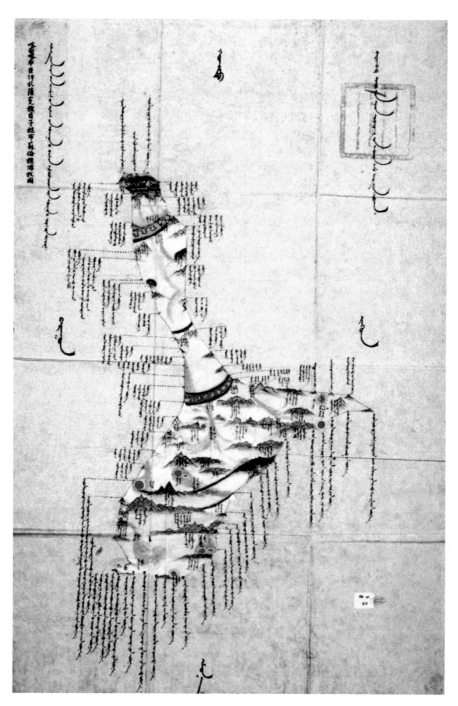

Map of Mongolian banner: Setsen Khan, 1907. This map clearly delimits the Khan's territory, with sixty-nine border markers labeled in Mongol, and it includes significant mountains, walls, and lakes.

the full incorporation of the once mobile nomads into the bounded empire. These beautiful maps, produced in the hundreds, defined the territory of each Mongol tribe with precise borders, labels, guardhouses, and terrain features. Like the ethnographic atlases of the southwest, and the lists of tributary peoples in the *Zhigongtu*, they put the Mongols into discrete categories, fixed them in place, and classified them under a systematic gaze of an ordered regime. The Manchu labels attached to the maps showed that the surrendered Mongols had submitted themselves to their superior Central Eurasian kin.

Mark Elliott's study of the creation of "Manchuria" in the Qing and modern nationalist imagination also highlights the role of frontier cartography in generating China's "geobody."[111] In his account, "Manchuria" emerged during the Qing as an increasingly distinct place within the empire from the seventeenth through the early nineteenth centuries. Surveying and labeling supported travel, poetry, ritual, and political decisions to clarify the extent of imperial control. Under the Qing, the vaguely defined "western regions" (Xiyu), home of shifting ethnonyms, turned into more strictly determined administrative jurisdictions, designated, as in the "Jesuit Atlas," with names of prefectures and district capitals. Manchuria, as the homeland of the Manchus, gained special prominence during the eighteenth century as it was reconstituted into an idealized reservoir of Manchu culture, protected from the corrupting influence of Han civilization. The ritual cult of Changbaishan and the Qianlong emperor's "Ode to Mukden" singled out the wonders of Manchuria's landscape in order to provide the Manchu rulers with a more coherent sense of their own identity. Thus the transition from "space" to "place," from undifferentiated frontier to demarcated region, began under the Manchus in the seventeenth century, not under nationalists in the late nineteenth.

Qing ideals ran up against contradictory social practice, here as elsewhere: most Manchus refused to return to Manchuria, while Han settlers defied prohibitions on immigration to open fields beyond the Willow Palisade. Still, the vision of a protected space with distinctly local characteristics reveals the Qing consciousness of ruling over a collection of regions with separate identities. The conception of Manchuria as a distinct geographical unit was exhibited in Qing maps, and Europeans picked up the concept from the "Jesuit Atlas." From the Europeans, the concept of "Manzhou" traveled the globe, returning to China with the Japanese imperialist efforts to define "Manchukuo" as a historically separate region. As Chinese nationalists furiously denied that Manchuria had ever been separate from China, they suppressed the ideas of cultural distinctiveness inherent in the Qing definitions of the region. Nevertheless, as with all frontier territories, the Qing rulers had to manage contradictory impulses: claims to imperial unity deriving from Heaven's will conflicted with the recognition of distinctive characteristics of each region. The ironic gap between the surveyors' claims to universal, standardized abstract space and the local particularities of place reappears time and again in studies of cartography under imperial sponsorship, from Britain to Qing China.

All ruling dynasties gained their power by conquest, but some proclaimed this fact more openly than others. In their public spectacles, Russian Tsars openly claimed their foreignness as a badge of legitimacy. Outsiders had created the Russian ruling elite ever since the local princes had invited the Varangian Rus' to bring order to their chaotic land. Peter the Great inflicted radically new customs derived from the West on his boyars, determined to drag them by force into the modern world. Catherine II, in milder form, civilized her people by introducing secular, sentimental themes from the France of her time.[112] Other royal lineages, such as the Bourbons of Louis XIV or the traditional Japanese emperors, might claim to be the "natural" choice of Heaven. Playing down their external origins, they minimized the contingencies that had brought them to power. The Meiji emperor, however, claimed to unite in his person and actions both the traditions deriving from the Sun Goddess and the new technologies coming from the West.[113] Russian ideology lay at the extreme end of the spectrum ranging from the alien new to the nativist old ways; Meiji Japan lay closer to the middle.

Where did the Qing public persona fall on this scale? In between, but uncomfortably. The Manchus themselves were indeed foreign conquerors, a fact they could not hide, but they conducted their public ceremonies so as to mingle the new and the old before the eyes of the Han Chinese and the Central Eurasian elites. The imperial tours demonstrate the characteristic Qing aim to have it all, to express several cultural meanings with a single event.[114] By displaying Manchus, Mongols, and foreign tributaries to the Jiangnan elite, they deliberately mixed cultures together. The inscriptions on stone had to address their messages in different languages, but the visual displays delivered their multiple meanings all at the same time: another exemplar of *yi ju liang de* (two birds with one stone). The imperially commissioned maps likewise mixed inner and outer, old and new, adopting the global coordinates introduced by the Jesuits but centering the longitude lines on Beijing. In the popular versions, the numbered latitude lines disappeared, assimilating them closer to traditional practice. These mixed spatial representations appealed to multiple audiences under a façade of harmony, but it took active cultural work to hold the disparate pieces together.

Marking space also marked time by constructing public boundaries between the present and past. The emperors claimed unprecedented achievements, rooted in military conquest and traditions alien to the Han majority, but they also linked their actions to classically derived precedents: place-names in Chinese, not Turkish, stelae evoking ancient emperors, emperors who rode on horseback and wrote thousands of poems. But mastering the flow of time also required engaging it directly, through the active production of history.

13

Marking Time: Writing
Imperial History

In the mid-seventeenth century, Paul Pellisson-Fontanier proposed to write a history of King Louis XIV's reign, and outlined these principles for his project: "The King must be praised everywhere but, so to speak, without praise, by a narrative of all that he has been seen to do, say, and think. It must appear disinterested but be lively, piquant, and sustained, avoiding in its expressions all that veers toward the panegyric. In order to be better believed, it should not give him the magnificent epithets and eulogies he deserves; they must be torn from the mouth of the reader by the things themselves."[1] Louis Marin, in discussing Pellisson's proposal, argues that historian and ruler write each other into existence. Just as the ruler commissions an official account to make the writer a royal mouthpiece, so the historian creates the royal persona through his narrative, reproducing the ruler's power and transmitting it beyond the temporal limits of his reign. Official historiography in both France and China reveals the interaction of narrative and authority, as each actor self-consciously turns his special skills to the mutual advantage of both.

In this chapter I examine the Qing project to encompass its historical terrain as it encompassed its territory, by producing an authoritative account of the frontier conquests. This project paralleled the Qing efforts at economic and political-military integration described earlier in this book. As before, I recognize the empire's impressive feat of embracing multiple lands and peoples under a uniform narrative, but also note that integration was incomplete. Beneath the surface, diversity and contradictions strained at the imperial effort to hold things together. Just as local administrations varied widely, and market exchange tied upper-level markets together only sporadically, so the historical narratives could not resolve all discrepancies or exclude alternatives.

Kangxi's Campaign History

The Kangxi emperor, conscious of his place in history as he conducted his military campaigns, revised the historical record as he created it. As I have shown, Qing officials and the emperor constructed the myths that Heaven's will had doomed Galdan to defeat, that the emperor had foreseen his enemy's death, and that Galdan had committed suicide out of despair. They suppressed the inconvenient facts of the great logistical limitations on Qing military action, the unpredictability of the outcome, and substantial well-grounded resistance to the campaigns. By redating Galdan's death, they fixed in the historical record the myth of only three successful expeditions, omitting the fourth, useless one. As we know, Kangxi's two battle victories did not, in fact, eliminate the Zunghar state. The Zunghars inflicted a humiliating defeat on the Yongzheng emperor, and the state survived for another sixty years. The official history had to smooth out these uncomfortable anomalies.[2]

In August 1696, shortly after returning to the capital, the Kangxi emperor ordered three Grand Secretaries and the Hanlin Academy to compile a detailed history of his campaigns against Galdan, titled in Manchu *Beye dailame wargi amargi babe necihiyeme toktobuha bodogon-i bithe* (Records of the *personal* military expedition to pacify and fix [determine control of] the northwest regions) (BWNB), and in Chinese *Qinzheng Pingding Shuomo Fanglue* (QPSF).[3] Manchu and Chinese versions were published, each in fifty-one *juan*, around 1710, with a preface by the emperor dated 1708; the Chinese version was a selective and altered translation of the Manchu. A new Chinese edition of 1778 was included in the great imperial encyclopedia, the *Siku Quanshu*.

The Bodogon-i bithe-i kuren, or Fanglueguan, the office for compilation of these histories, was first established in 1682 to write, in Chinese only, the history of the suppression of the Three Feudatories from 1673 to 1681, titled *Pingding Sanni Fanglue*.[4] The second campaign history, written in Manchu and unpublished, described the victories over the dissident Mongols Ligdan Khan in 1634 and Burni Wang in 1676. The BWNB/QPSF were the first bilingual campaign histories; they were followed by a series of others, especially the *Daicing gurun-i fukjin doro neihe bodogon-i bithe* (Records of the campaigns for opening the way and originating the Great Qing

State), or *Huangqing Kaiguo Fanglue,* covering the founding of the dynasty from 1583 to 1644 (commissioned in 1774 and published in 1789), and the *Jungar-i ba-be necihiyeme toktobuha bodogon-i bithe,* or *Pingding Zhungar Fanglue* (Records of the expedition to pacify and fix the Zunghar regions) (commissioned in 1755 and printed in 1772, in 172 *juan*). The Qing published over ten of these vast compilations by the end of the dynasty, but only the BWNB/QPSF designate in the title the emperor's personal participation in the campaigns.[5] The participation of three Grand Secretaries indicates its extraordinary significance. Several of the compilers had participated in the editing of the official Ming history; many were products of the special examination of 1679 that admitted Ming loyalists to the official degree system.

The *Fanglue,* or military campaign history, was a new Qing genre. Although they had some Ming precedents, the Qing official campaign histories vastly exceeded in scale those of previous dynasties. Their purpose was to inscribe the dynasty's military achievements into the literary tradition that was its ultimate judge.

The BWNB/QPSF cover the years 1677 to 1698, in Chinese, Manchu, and Mongol versions.[6] They present in chronological order imperial edicts, memorials from the major officials on the campaign, and communications from Galdan, the *sDe-pa* in Tibet, and other participants. They also include many of the emperor's letters to his son, written in Manchu from 1696 to 1697 during his second, third, and fourth campaigns. They do not include all the documentary evidence: the *Qingshilu* contains some additional information, but the *Fanglue* is much more comprehensive. In addition, comments by the compilers provide summaries and retrospective views about the significance of key events.

Lionel Gossman, in his commentary on Edward Gibbon's *Decline and Fall of the Roman Empire,* notes that "the now familiar division of the historical or narrative text into *discours* (the dialogue of the narrator with the reader) and *histoire* (the actual narrative of events) provides in itself the essential condition for what is commonly called dramatic irony: The narrator and the reader share knowledge that the characters themselves do not possess—in this case because they stand outside the time of the actors or characters and know the end of the story that the latter are living."[7] The compilers of the *Fanglue* demonstrate their awareness of this dramatic irony, but they exempt from it one character: the emperor himself. Every other actor—the generals who opposed the expeditions, Galdan and his followers who failed to understand the will of Heaven, the other Mongols who submitted without understanding their destiny—had only a limited view of the process they engaged in. But they granted the Son of Heaven retrospectively the power to foresee everything.

The goal of the compilation was to create a permanent record memorializing the achievements of the Qing armies. Its immediacy makes it an extremely valuable primary source. As noted earlier, contradictory details that were removed in later retellings are retained in this vast compilation, so that alternative stories can be constructed out of it. But the *Fanglue* is not an unbiased collection. All communications from Galdan are mediated by translation and transmission through the Chinese memorialists and envoys. Nevertheless, lacking the original documents, we can at least partially reconstruct Galdan and his supporters' own perspective on the campaigns. The *Fanglue* is an intermediary stage of historical reconstruction, neither merely archival compilation nor fully smoothed-out narrative. The Qing compilers and their official sponsors constructed it as a textual memorial ensuring the permanence of the conquests in the literary tradition. Modern historians can use it for a different purpose, because it makes possible multiple readings of the events.

Since ancient times, Chinese historians had closely linked writing and authority.[8] In the fifteenth century, the Yongle emperor had inscribed his exploits on both stone and paper: stelae survived in the steppe which the Kangxi emperor noted as he passed by. Similarly, the Qing rulers put down in permanent form their hard-won victories so as to insert the expansion of the state into a textual tradition.

Many scholars, including myself, have relied heavily on these compilations as source material. Until the publication of substantial quantities of documents from the Qing archives, the *Fanglue* were often the only available source for the innermost decision making of the emperor and his high ministers on military affairs. The Fanglueguan, often called the Office of Military Archives, had access to highly sensitive original documents, and part of its task was to compile these materials related to specific campaigns. Since its primary task, however, was to publish an officially approved history of the campaigns after they were completed, the office was not a neutral transmitter of archival documents but an active interpreter of the events, remolding them to fit the orthodox dynastic perspective. It was really a historiographical office, on the front lines of turning the infinite flux of events into a consistent narrative.[9]

Scholars have only just begun to compare the *Fanglue* with the original documents that are their basis, but they have discovered remarkable and revealing discrepancies between the archival record and the published texts. The portrait of the early Manchu state given in the *Kaiguo Fanglue* differs substantially from that found in the earliest Manchu documents.[10] Likewise, Borjigidai Oyunbilig has published a devastating and meticulous analysis of the BWNB/QPSF texts showing, first, that the Manchu original draws in a highly selective manner from the archival documents, and that the Chinese translation adds further deviations from the Manchu texts.[11] These alterations generally reinforce the authority of the emperor by removing embarrassing or contradictory details, elevating his personal role in the campaigns, and denigrating the capacity of his enemies. The editors had a common goal: to glorify the achievements of the emperors, demonstrating that their farsighted plans were supported by the will of Heaven.

For example, Oyunbilig examines the *Fanglue*'s use of sixty-one Manchu archival documents published by the Palace Museum on Taiwan related to Kangxi's expedition from October 14, 1696, to January 1697. He finds that 60 percent of these documents were not used at all, 28 percent were partially cited, and 11 percent used the emperor's rescripts but not the accompanying memorials. Worse still, the compilers selected the documents for a preconceived purpose. The documents revealed an unheroic view of this campaign, since it ultimately led to no significant victories, and the emperor himself actually spent very little time in military preparations. Most of his activities, reported enthusiastically to his son in Beijing, consisted of traveling, hunting, and hosting banquets with Mongol allies. Although these activities, I have argued, did have positive diplomatic results, especially because they impressed the Mongols of the Ordos region with the empire's wealth and generosity, they did not fit well with the prescribed categories of a "military campaign." Therefore, the compilers omitted and manipulated documentary evidence so as to give the impression that the emperor was engaged in active strategic military planning. As Oyunbilig puts it: "To fulfill their preconceived idea, the compilers either ignored the original edicts, or abridged, altered, or placed them in a new order. In this manner, the letters from the palace originally reporting on the hunts and travels of the emperor were manipulated into 'testimony' of an imperial 'military campaign.'"[12]

The compilers also falsified and distorted documentary evidence about significant decisions made by the emperor during his campaign. Galdan had sent his envoy Gelei Guyeng to Kangxi with an offer of peace in December 1696. Galdan pretended to be willing to surrender to the Qing, but he was really only trying to buy time in order to stave off a Qing attack before the winter set in. He could then recover his strength in the spring and hope to escape the Qing's reach. Oyunbilig argues that Kangxi took Galdan's offer seriously, estimating that Galdan was indeed utterly exhausted and without hope. In addition, Kangxi's own troops were suffering from severe food shortages, and he was anxious about the situation in the capital. This was the expedition in which the enraged emperor vowed to eat snow rather than give up his campaign, but was overcome by the resistance of his troops. Kangxi thus decided to turn back, giving Galdan seventy days to fulfill his promise to submit. As it happened, Galdan did not surrender, and within sixty-eight days the emperor would launch his final expedition. The *Fanglue* compilers altered the reasoning and dates of Kangxi's discussion with Gelei Guyeng so as to make it appear that Kangxi had seen through Galdan's deceptive offer from the start and really waited the full seventy days he had set as a deadline.[13] The original Manchu documents transcribed and translated by Oyunbilig reveal clearly the uncertainties and constraints that limited the Son of Heaven's vision.

When they prepared the Chinese edition of the BWNB, the compilers transformed the text in further revealing ways. The Manchu edition was a carefully constructed account designed to exalt the autocratic ruler and transmit his glory to future generations. The Chinese edition, addressed to a much larger audience—the Han literati—not only created a uniform evaluation of the emperor's achievements but placed them within the classical Chinese literary tradition as well. Subtle alterations of wording expose the gap between the Manchu and Chinese expressions of cultural difference, spatial organization, and historical understanding.

The Chinese text was published in 1710 along with the Manchu one, and follows the same organization.[14] The new edition of 1778 may have introduced further distortions. In a number of places the editors continued the Manchu practice of minimizing the emperor's errors by cutting out his statements that "Galdan is easy to defeat" when the course of the campaign indicated its difficulty, and by correcting the emperor's faulty estimates of times and travel distances.[15] They removed more evidence of the embarrassing hunting expeditions that distracted Kangxi from single-minded military planning. More interesting are the terminological changes that show the transformation from the Manchu to the Chinese perspective. Chinese terminology added moral and spatially centered perspectives to neutral Manchu vocabulary. Where the Manchu text describes envoys and tribes as "coming here" *(jidere)*, the Chinese has them "coming to the interior" *(xiang nei er lai)*. Armies that "moved against Galdan" *(Galdan-i baru ibehe)* become "punishment expeditions" *(jin tao)*. Often Manchu verbs meaning simply "to come" are translated by the Chinese term "to return" *(gui*, not *lai,* "to come"). *Gui,* a term with rich moral and political resonances, implies returning to the proper Way by peoples who have lived either in ignorance or in rebellion against the true ruler. The term appears frequently in place-names on the frontier, as in the Qing renaming of the Mongolian town Köke Khota (Blue City) as Guihua cheng (City of Return and Transformation).[16]

Other spatial terminology reveals efforts to stabilize and clarify the borders of the empire. Where the Manchu refers to travelers passing by guard posts *(karun)*, the Chinese text has them crossing "within the borders" *(jingnei)*. As the discussion of mapping in Chapter 12 argues, the Qing rulers were demarcating their frontier territories more clearly through the eighteenth century. Most interesting of all are the increasing signs of fixing ethnic identities among the Mongols. Where the Manchu text refers to "all Mongols" *(uheri Monggoso)*, the Chinese text uses "the multiple Frontier-Subject Mongols" *(Zhufan Menggu)*.[17] The crucial term *fan*, not found in the Manchu, originally meant "hedge" or "protecting wall," and was extended to cover all the peoples on the edges of the empire who professed allegiance to the Qing regime. The Lifanyuan (Court for Management of the Outer Dependencies), established in 1638, incorporated these groups as a separate unit of the Qing administration. The Lifanyuan designated a single group, with its own name, "Mongols," as one of those with a particular dependent relationship to the central state.[18]

Chinese terminology also fixed distinctions within the Mongols. The Western Mongols, or Ölöd, consisted of a number of separate tribal groups, whose leadership and composition fluctuated substantially over the sixteenth to eighteenth centuries. Different scholars still give divergent evaluations of which tribes were part of the Ölöd confederation before the rise of Galdan.[19] Mongolian chronicles of the seventeenth century described them as the "Four Oirats" (Dörben Oyirad), a term which may have reflected the parallel designation of the Eastern Mongols as descended from the "Forty Myriad Mongols" (Döcin Tümen Monggol) of the fifteenth century. This was a general designation for the Western Mongols, not a specific division into tribes. The Chinese text, and nearly all subsequent Chinese references to the Zunghars, used the term "Four *Tribes* of the Ölöd" (Elute Sibu), implying four fixed, genealogically defined tribal lineages. Similarly, the Manchu and Mongolian term *jasak*, meaning "commander," originally derived from the Turkish *yasak*, for "order," "command," "law," was turned into the term *buzhang*, or "tribal chieftain." The Qing rulers, as they expanded their domains, proceeded to classify and incorporate into increasingly static categories the undifferentiated groups which they controlled.[20]

The Chinese text also denigrates the Mongol enemy more vividly than the Manchu text. Its animal imagery places the Zunghars beyond human civilization. Galdan, when he retreats, "hides in his nest" and "runs head over heels" like a rat. Pamela Crossley has argued that these racial and genealogical elements of imperial identity emerged only in the Qianlong reign, but the terminology used by Kangxi's editors already invokes them.[21]

Military men often dehumanize their enemies, of course, and accuse those who retreat of cowardice. The Manchus commonly drew analogies between hunting and warfare, seeing the great annual hunts in Manchuria as rehearsals for military campaigns. Chinese vocabulary, however, added further demeaning overtones to this contempt, for mobility itself was suspect. Just as the pastoralist's constant movements with his flocks marked him as alien to the settled agriculturalist, the commanders of lumbering Qing forces stigmatized nomadic armies' greatest tactical asset—their ability to move rapidly—as nothing more than a coward's flight.

The changes in the text reveal in specific details, then, the cultural changes that marked the expansion of the Qing. As it embraced more territories and peoples, the empire also embraced the story of the conquest itself in an encompassing narrative. Later writers drew on the manufactured documentary record laid down by Kangxi's editors to create ever more stereotyped depictions of the complex process of imperial expansion.

As these critiques reveal, the documentary record left by the Qing themselves offers an extremely partial vision of the conquest. A long filtering process has extracted from the abundant source materials one remarkably consistent account that has lasted for many generations. Does this constant tampering with historical materials taint every account with hopeless bias, including this one? Much of my narrative in the earlier chapters draws heavily on the *Fanglue* compilations, but wherever possible I have tried to check them against original materials. Still, the archives in Beijing and Taiwan contain treasure troves of relevant material that I have not been able to use. We can only hope that successive researchers incorporate wider ranges of materials and interpretive perspectives, so as to correct the limitations of earlier scholarship. Our histories will always be only imperfect efforts to capture the ungraspable realities of the past.

Furthermore, despite considerable editorial manipulation, the *Fanglue* documents do not tell a completely unified story. Within them we may discover inconsistent elements that support a different interpretation. Despite the best efforts of the editors to present a supremely confident, consistent imperial will, the *Fanglue*, by virtue of its very abundance, contains contradictory information. As I have done in the previous chapters, we can reconstruct the campaigns as a continual nick-of-time overcoming of near-fatal obstacles, not a smooth path to victory. In addition, the available published archival materials and selected unpublished documents support a more complex account than Kangxi's officials wanted to portray. Contradictions resided both within the official record itself and outside the published orthodox account.

Nevertheless, powerful forces supported the continuation of the orthodox Qing narrative. Kangxi's successors generated an even larger corpus of officially massaged documentary "evidence," and Chinese nationalists have carried on the tradition into the twentieth and twenty-first centuries. Today, the Number One Archives in Beijing also curiously continue this Qing practice. The archives' Manchu section has now published the complete collection of *Zhupi Zouzhe* memorials of the Kangxi and Yongzheng emperors, but only in Chinese translation and not in facsimile reproduction, unlike the Taiwan archive. They have translated the Manchu documents into classical bureaucratic Chinese, a language which no one uses today, instead of creating a scholarly edition of the Manchu materials, with a translation into contemporary written Chinese. Even though the translations are fairly accurate, they still of necessity introduce Chinese terminology which only imperfectly reflects the Manchu originals. Oyunbilig draws the extreme conclusion that these publications are "of very little use" for scholarship, except as indexes to the contents of the original Manchu documents. In the heart of the archives of the People's Republic, Qing traditions of translation and compilation endure, quite alien to modern standards of textual research and archival publication.[22]

Yongzheng and the *Dayi Juemilu*

The Yongzheng emperor, characteristically, did not order the compilation of any *Fanglue*. As a reluctant promoter of frontier expansion who never went on a personal campaign, he could not glorify himself as a military conqueror. And he did not wish to commemorate the military successes in Tibet and Kokonor of his political rivals, his brother Yinti and his father's favorite general, Nian Gengyao. He in fact suppressed a great deal of documentation about his brother's expedition to Lhasa.[23] In 1731 his own effort to attack the Zunghars had ended in embarrassing failure.

Yet the emperor was still concerned about his place in history. He altered or suppressed the Veritable Records *(Shilu)* of the Kangxi reign in order to remove suspicions about his succession to the throne. But Yongzheng made his most lasting contribution to the construction of the empire's historical identity in his extraordinary text the *Dayi Juemilu,* "Great Righteousness Resolving Confusion," or "Record of How Great Righteousness Awakens the Misguided," published in 1730 to justify the Qing conquest after the exposure of anti-Manchu sentiments in the Zeng Jing case.[24]

The failed Hunanese licentiate Zeng Jing, an impoverished rural schoolteacher, had been so excited to discover the writings of the late Ming anti-Manchu writer Lü Liuliang (1629–1683) that he launched a foolhardy effort to overthrow the Qing dynasty. Putting together Lü's strong ideological attack on the Manchus with rumors that the Yongzheng emperor had killed his father and brothers and seized the throne, Zeng sent his disciple Zhang Xi with a letter to Yongzheng's trusted general Yue Zhongqi to argue that as a descendant of the famous Song loyalist Yue Fei, he should throw off the oppressive rule of the Manchus, who had seized Chinese territory. Yue immediately exposed the plot to the emperor and, after extensive interrogation, obtained confessions from Zeng and his disciples. The actual conspiracy involved only a few disgruntled scholars in one remote rural county who never took any open action. Yongzheng, however, concerned about the persistent rumors questioning his legitimacy, decided to use Zeng to promulgate his undisputed right to rule. He pardoned Zeng and Zhang and published their interrogations, along with imperial edicts, in a large text, over ten thousand characters in four *juan*, titled *Dayi Juemilu*. The emperor required the text to be distributed to every county school, and ordered punishments for education directors if their students had not read it.

Zeng Jing was a nobody, but Lü Liuliang had been a well-known, if not particularly original, scholar from Zhejiang, who had written works on Neo-Confucian classical philosophy.[25] Lü refused to take up office after the Manchu conquest but never advocated open resistance. Lü's anti-Manchu ideas were conventional wisdom among Ming loyalist scholars who declined service under the Qing. Anti-Manchu themes were not the center of Lü's thought, but the suspicious emperor singled him out as a vehicle for exposing the latent anti-Manchu sentiment that he thought was especially prevalent in Zhejiang. His vicious treatment of Lü's family and works— desecration of his grave, burning of all his books—contrasted sharply with the lenient treatment of Zeng and Zhang Xi, who were pardoned after they confessed their crimes. In this way the emperor could pose as both the stern judge, who punished the lèse-majesté of insults to his father by Lü, and the benevolent ruler rewarding those who repented under his reign.

Many scholars have studied the political circumstances surrounding the Zeng Jing case, but relatively few have examined in detail the ideology of the *Dayi Juemilu* itself.[26] The *Dayi Juemilu* is a daring effort by the emperor to confront and assimilate the entire Chinese literary tradition, drawing on its classical texts to show that his dynasty brings to its peak the steadily widening circle of civilization. Yongzheng is primarily concerned with setting the Qing firmly within the line of legitimate dynasties in military, political, and cultural terms. But Yongzheng's text is not merely an abstract ideological statement. It is closely tied to the specific military, political, and institutional achievements of his reign and those of his predecessors.

This text explicitly lays out the contrast between the racialist and culturalist ideologies of rule.[27] Zeng and the Ming loyalists, citing classical texts, argued that the relationship between Hua (Han Chinese) and Di (northern barbarians) was like that of humans and animals, not ruler and subject. Because the Chinese were born in the central lands, they were civilized; but the barbarians came from the periphery, so they had a totally different and incompatible character. Since Hua and Di could not coexist, it was proper for the Hua to drive the barbarians out. According to Zeng, Confucius believed that the purpose of establishing a state in China was to protect civilization against destruction.

The emperor argued just the opposite: that the difference between peoples is defined by their culture, not by their territory or lineage. Those from outside the Central Plain can be civilized because the key relationship that preserves social order is that of ruler and subject. The Ming dynasty had fallen apart because the Chinese rebelled against their ruler; the Manchus had actually saved the Chinese from disorder, inheriting the Mandate of Heaven. So they took power legitimately, just as the Mongols and other conquest dynasties had done in the past.

The emperor's text not only refutes Zeng's and Lü's attacks on Manchu legitimacy but also outlines a broad justification of the right of all peoples to rule China, regardless of their origin. Did not Mencius say that the sage emperor Shun came from the "eastern barbarians" and King Wen from the "western barbarians"? Civilization had spread out from the heartland to incorporate progressively wider circles: in the past, Hunan and Hubei had been beyond central control, but they had long since become part of the civilized world. The Qing had simply extended this expansion to its ultimate limits by finally bringing the Mongols under imperial rule.

The basic Heavenly principle invoked by the emperor was that only those with *de* (virtuous power) could rule the world, but *de* was accessible to anyone who practiced benevolence and righteousness. The Great Unity *(dayitong)* attained under Manchu rule arose because the state's humane rulers gained the allegiance of peoples both "inner and outer" *(neiwai)*. Qing rule rested on a broad spatial vision, which presumed a terrain of moral consciousness that continued to expand over ever larger regions. Yongzheng attacked his critics as people with "narrow, parochial, selfish views" *(xiangqu jiangyu zhi sizhong qianjian),* who sought only their private interest and rejected the welfare of the many.[28]

Yongzheng's greatest concern was to overcome the consciousness of territorial borders *(cijiang bijie)* that threatened the unity of the empire. Just as he attacked local officials who obstructed the free flow of grain across provincial boundaries, he attacked the thesis of the sharp division of the barbarian from the civilized *(huadi zhi fen).* In the emperor's eyes, the capacious, expanding boundaries of the new empire secured the indissoluble unity of its member peoples. He tied civilization's power closely to military and administrative incorporation.[29] Not even the greatest dynasties, the Han or Tang, had succeeded in eliminating the threat of attack on the northwestern frontier. Only the Qing had finally been able to eradicate the basis for ethnic division because it included all peoples under its control. Ideologically speaking (though not yet in fact), all the Mongols were now part of the human, civilized realm, since they had joined the banners and allied themselves with the Qing, thus "returning to the maps and registers" (*gui bantu*).

Yongzheng finished his edicts in the *Dayi Juemilu* in 1729. He had not yet suffered his humiliating defeat in Mongolia; he could still claim plausibly that the empire continued to expand. The interventions in Kokonor and Tibet had brought vast new regions into the empire, and in 1729–30 it appeared that the Zunghars, the last remaining Mongol holdouts, would soon submit. The trade treaty with Russia had stabilized the border and created regular caravan trade under the guise of tribute missions. Yongzheng's historical view seemed justified by the recent course of events.

Yongzheng's sense of expansion also relied heavily on Kangxi's achievements, and he sought to place his own reign in close continuity with that of his father. Like his father, he claimed, he distributed famine relief, granted tax remissions, constructed waterworks, and worked to root out corruption. Even though Yongzheng enacted some of the most drastic institutional domestic reforms since Wang Anshi in the eleventh century, his ideological statements played down substantive change in favor of continuity.

Virtue, however, did not erase all differences among humans. The Manchus remained Manchus, and distinctions between inner and outer endured. Yongzheng angrily rejected the Zunghar view of the Manchus as "Manzi," or "southern barbarians," the term used by Mongols ruling the Yuan dynasty for southern Chinese: "When these rebels use 'barbarian' as a term of rebuke, they are like beasts who are drunk in life and dreaming in death." Manchus could take pride in their status as a separate people whose home was in the Changbai Mountains. Yongzheng was not trying to obliterate all distinctions with a universal cultural template. He continued the project, which had been begun by Kangxi, of fixing frontier peoples in distinct places, with distinct identities. Qianlong continued this process more systematically, but he did not create a sharp break.[30]

Zeng argued that the first eighty years of the Qing exhibited disorder equal to that of the early Yuan dynasty, and that the Qing was doomed to fall soon, just like the barbarian Yuan. Yongzheng strongly defended the record of the Mongol Yuan.[31] The Yuan, founded by "outer" peoples like the Manchus, deserved to be enrolled in the continuous line of legitimate dynasties, but the Qing would surpass its achievements by virtue of its longevity and prosperity. In mastering time and space, the Qing followed but went beyond its ancestors, and both conquest dynasties and Han-ruled dynasties belonged to the same tradition.

Zeng had accused the Manchus of "stealing" power from the Ming, but Yongzheng replied that, on the contrary, the Manchus, by taking revenge on behalf of the Ming against the rebel armies of Li Zicheng, had "wiped away its shame [*xuechi*]." The emperor claimed (falsely) that all Ming officials and soldiers gladly supported the Manchu entry into the Central Plains and (more plausibly) that all the people benefited from the new conquerors' rule. Thus, where Zeng and the Ming loyalists stressed the sharp temporal division between Ming and Qing, Yongzheng strove to override the sense of catastrophic change by invoking images of cultural continuity and restoration. The restoration of order was the essential process that trumped identification by language or race.

But not all human beings deserved to join the community of humanity. Righteousness, above all, determined the difference between men and beasts, and righteous behavior was defined above all by political stability.[32] Among the five basic social relationships, that of ruler and subject was primary:

> What makes humans different from animals are the principles of morality. The Five Relationships are the basis of human morality: if you defy one of them, you are not human. The primary relationship of these is that of ruler and subject. How can we call people human if they have no rulers! Those who want to get rid of rulers are just like animals. Those who fulfill the Five Relationships are human, those who destroy Heavenly principle are animals; you cannot divide human from animal on the basis of "civilized" [Hua] and "barbarian" [Di]. Those who are given rulers by Heaven's mandate, but try to defy Heaven, cannot avoid being exterminated by Heaven.[33]

Because Yongzheng's highly authoritarian, politicized version of these common Confucian principles focused on the need for obedience, he turned one of Confucius' most controversial statements about non-Han peoples to his own use. In the *Analects*, Confucius refers to the contrast between barbarian kingdoms and those of the Central Plain, stating, "Di di zhi you jun, buru zhu Xia zhi wang ye." This passage has two diametrically opposed meanings. Arthur Waley translates it, "The barbarians of the East and North have retained their princes. *They are not in such a state of decay* as we in China." Bruce Brooks and Taeko Brooks translate it as, "The Yi and Di with rulers are *not the equal* of the several Xia states without them."[34] The latter is the more traditional translation, asserting the inferiority of for-

eign peoples *even if* their states are well ordered. The key difference in interpretation depends on whether the word *buru* is translated as "not equal to"
or simply "unlike." But Yongzheng interprets this passage to justify the supreme importance of good government: outer peoples who retain good rulers are blessed with wisdom, while "the Han people with bad rulers have
turned into animals." Moral government has nothing to do with location in
the interior or exterior.[35]

Yongzheng's ideology allowed all people moral freedom but punished
them severely if they violated his version of proper behavior. The Ming officials had regarded all Mongols as no different from natural forces, beyond
their control, but Qing rulers offered them the opportunity to become "human" by joining in the Great Enterprise. For Yongzheng, the enrolling of
the Khalkha Mongols in the forty-eight banners proved that Qing values
were open to all. "Transformation" *(xianghua)* of one's political identity
meant recognizing the true representatives of the will of Heaven, as the
Ming officials who agreed to serve the Qing had done.

Rebels who rejected Qing rule, however, did not deserve the name of
humanity. They were nothing more than animals, who brought destruction
on themselves. Yongzheng repeatedly uses animal imagery to describe Zeng
Jing and his supporters, calling them "ants," "bees," "dogs," "frogs,"
"wolves." In the emperor's view, Heaven will inevitably eliminate them
from the world. Like Kangxi, with his concepts of incorporation and extermination, Yongzheng divides his world into those who deserve to exist and
those who do not, depending on their subordination to the imperial will.

Yongzheng's ideology exhibits a glaring contradiction. Like Calvinists
and Marxist-Leninists, he combined visions of an inexorable transhuman
process with an intense focus on individual responsibility. If punishment
of wrong is inevitable, why was such aggressive action needed to root it
out? Why mount an enormous campaign against a few poor, obscure rural
schoolteachers? Here Yongzheng revealed his great respect for the power
of language. He knew that "our dynasty did not win by military force
alone."[36] The astounding rise of the Manchus from a small tribal band to a
vast army came not from strategy but solely from virtue *(daode)*. Here
Yongzheng clearly deviates from his father's experience. Kangxi would
never have minimized the importance of careful planning and the close engagement of the ruler in military affairs. Yongzheng, however, distanced
himself from such details, and he distanced the force of *daode* from particular landscapes and battles. It became a general underlying "propensity"
(shi) that revealed itself in broader trends. The language of the ruler, transmitted through his edicts, was the force that overrode the limitations of logistics, weather, terrain, and the fog of war.[37]

But if words were the ultimate weapon, others could mobilize them too.

Yongzheng cited Confucius' attack on "glib" *(ning)* speech to emphasize the danger of smooth talkers who could mislead ignorant people. Zeng and Lü were cunning wordsmiths who could "master people with their mouths" *(yu ren yi kou ji).*[38] Others could easily fall into their traps. Yongzheng knew about the rumors that he had poisoned his father, abused his mother, and massacred his brothers to secure his power; these underground attacks were more threatening to him than the open resistance of the remnant Mongol state. Anonymous placards attacked Zeng as a "running dog" for surrendering to the Qing.[39] Zeng's and Lü's arguments could be taken up by the supporters of Yongzheng's brothers, whom he had imprisoned or exiled. Looking backward, claimed the emperor, we know that the Three Feudatories, the Chahar Khan, Galdan, the Kokonor chiefs, and the Tibetans "flared up briefly but turned into ashes" because of Heaven's will.[40] But looking ahead, the emperor saw many enemies, uncertain authority, and the need for stern, arbitrary imposition of his language of rule.

Qianlong's Account of the Zunghar Mongols

In 1763 the Qianlong emperor ordered the compilation of a general history of the Zunghar Mongols. He told officials to collect all available Mongolian genealogies along with Chinese official documents so that the full story could be put on record. Immediately after the elimination of the Zunghars as a people, the Qing's inscription apparatus would establish their definitive history, just as each Chinese dynasty wrote the official history of its predecessor and then destroyed all its records. None of the Mongolian genealogies collected by the emperor's orders appears to have survived. Once again, the victorious dynastic rulers nearly succeeded in erasing alternative views from the record.

The history of the Zunghars was the first of a series of imperially commissioned compilations of information about the newly conquered territories, including the *Qinding Xiyu Tongwenzhi,* published in 1766, a multilingual compilation of place-names and Mongolian genealogies; the *Qinding Huangyu Xiyu Tuzhi,* a gazetteer of Turkestan compiled from 1756 to 1782; the *Iledkel Shastir,* the trilingual biographical compilation on the nobility of Mongolia and Turkestan, compiled from 1779 to 1795; and the *Zhigongtu,* containing over three hundred color pictures of "tributary peoples," with Manchu and Chinese captions, compiled from 1790 to 1805.[41] All these works served as important sources of information for nineteenth-century officials and scholars. Zuo Zongtang, for example, the Governor-General of Shaanxi and Gansu who put down the Muslim rebel-

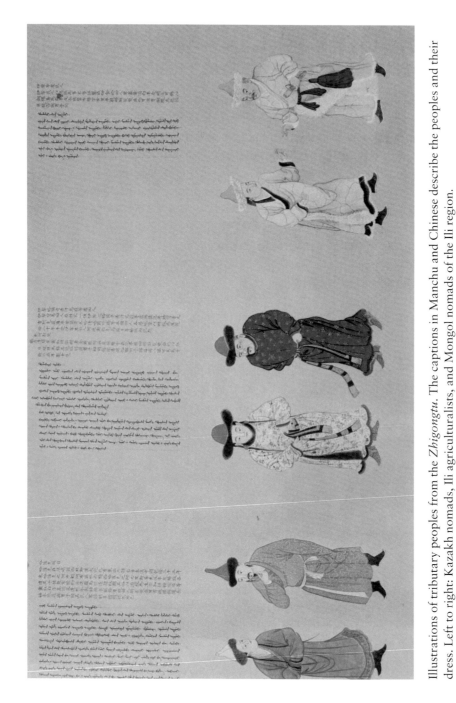

Illustrations of tributary peoples from the *Zhigongtu*. The captions in Manchu and Chinese describe the peoples and their dress. Left to right: Kazakh nomads, Ili agriculturalists, and Mongol nomads of the Ili region.

lions of 1862–1877, consulted the *Qinding Huangyu Xiyu Tuzhi* in his youth.[42]

In his commissioned history, the *Zhungar Quanbu Jilue* (Complete record of the Zunghar tribes), published in 1763, the emperor claims the right to create the historical memory of the Zunghars:

> Since ancient times, many have written about the Outer Barbarians, but truth has been scarce and contradictions abundant. Isn't it because of their remoteness and the lack of knowledge of their language? Only one out of ten, or ten out of a thousand, have got it right. Add to this the textual errors, and there is very little one can rely on. Now that we have subordinated the Zunghar tribes, we have granted a noble rank to only one person, the son of Dawaci, whom we have settled in the capital. And we have built a fortified town in Ili for the residence of the General, who keeps peace, and ensures the prosperity of agriculture and herding. Considering that [the Zunghars] were originally a great tribe [*buluo*], they should not lack a recorded history. So I have personally looked into the facts of the matter and written them down to facilitate the compilation of the campaign history [*fanglue*].[43]

He traces the generations of Zunghar chiefs from the Oirats of the Ming dynasty down to Galdan and his successors. In this text, the emperor who had seized the Mongolian genealogies had available much clearer information about the intricate kinship connections between the Zunghar chieftains than he had during the wars. Instead of pure "bandits" with no social connections, the Zunghars could now be seen as a people with a specific identity, defined by their lineage. They also had a fixed administrative structure. Qianlong carefully divides the tribe into twenty-four *otok* (clans directly dependent on the Khan), twenty-one *anggi* (clans dependent on a chieftain), and nine *jisai* (clans that supported the lamas). Each clan is carefully listed with its number of households and its *zaisang* (ministers), forming a total of 200,000 households (i.e., tents), or 600,000 people united in one "nation." The emperor also describes the fiscal structure of the empire, stating that the Zunghar Khan levied taxes on the twenty-four *otok*, the Mongols of Uriangkhai, and the four Muslim towns of Yarkand, Kashgar, Aksu, and Khotan. Qianlong concludes by subsuming the history of the Zunghars under the universal pattern of dynastic decline, referring to the Han writer Jia Yi's description of the fall of the Qin dynasty: "It is said that it takes only one man to destroy what ten men have built. In examining the history of the Zunghars, I have found that this is indeed perfectly true. Jia Yi stated: 'If one does not practice benevolence and justice, the state's security is endangered.' Even barbarian rulers are not exempt from this rule."[44]

This text uses classical Chinese categories of lineage and administrative hierarchy to fit the turbulent history of the Zunghar state into a static model, giving a consistent structure to what was in fact a shifting set of alliances. Native Mongolian clan divisions, transmuted through the Chinese classifying lens, become fixed relations of subordination and kinship connections. To classify the tribes is to claim hegemony over their definition, something that is possible only after their defeat. Mongolian chronicles, by contrast, do not give populations for each clan, and do not order them in a consistent hierarchy. As discussed earlier, scholars today still dispute the exact terminology and affiliation of the Mongolian clans. Yet even though the Zunghars had disappeared, the Qing historians needed to embrace them as peoples who followed the universal laws of history.

The *Pingding Zhungar Fanglue,* edited by Fu Heng, commissioned in 1755 and completed in 1770 in 172 *juan,* became the largest official campaign history compiled in the Qing. It covers the period from 1700 to 1765 exhaustively, providing a wealth of documentation on the smallest diplomatic incidents and the most minute logistical details. It is one of the series of monumental scholarly products of the Qianlong reign, which culminated in the 36,000 *juan* of the *Siku Quanshu* (Complete record of the Four Treasuries) in 1783. Many of the leading empirical research scholars, like Zhu Yun, worked on the compilation of both works.[45] As part of the *Siku Quanshu,* along with ancient classics and historical works, the *Pingding Zhungar Fanglue* joined the succession of orthodox histories legitimating the imperial conquests from ancient times.

The first chapter of the *Fanglue* establishes a legitimate succession to the title of Khan, which in Qing eyes meant recognition of the right to pay tribute. According to it, the Zunghars originated under the Yuan as the Alutai tribe, later called "Elute" in Chinese, derived from the Mongolian name "Ölöd." As part of the Oirats (Weilate), or Western Mongols, they paid tribute to the Ming dynasty, and were invested with titles by the Shunzhi emperor. In the early Qing, their chief was Gush Khan of Kokonor. Then the "crafty and arrogant" Galdan arose as their chieftain. He invaded the land of the dependent Khalkhas, causing suffering and disorder, until he was defeated by Kangxi at the battle of Jao Modo, after which he took poison and killed himself. Galdan's nephew Tsewang Rabdan enjoyed the emperor's benevolence after his submission, but because of his "wild wolf's ambition" *(langzi yexin),* he attacked Hami and Tibet, killed Lazang Khan, and allowed the rebel Lobzang Danjin to escape punishment. His son Galdan Tseren continued his evil practices until the Yongzheng emperor crushed him at Erdeni Zu. (Yongzheng's defeat in 1731 is not mentioned.) The Zunghar chiefs, terrified into submission, allowed the emperor to fix the border and withdraw his troops. Galdan Tseren sent tribute and allowed trade at the delimited border. But Tsewang Dorji Namjal, who succeeded Galdan Tseren, was even more violent, causing the "usurper" Lama Darja to rebel and Dawaci to continue the old aggressive Mongolian strategy. The Zunghars suffered frequent "internal disorder" *(neiluan)* until Amursana surrendered in 1754. Amursana later rebelled, and the account describes the military expedition against him and Amursana's flight and death in Russia. Honoring its treaty to return fugitives, Russia sent back Amursana's bones and finally established peace on the border, so "the Eastern and Western Burut [Kirghiz], the Left and Right Kazakhs, Tashkent, and the Turkestanis all became civilized [*xianghua*]" after the repression of the rebellions of Burhān ad-Dīn and Khoja Jihān. "In less than five years, territory was enormously expanded, wastelands were cultivated . . . [F]rom the Big Dipper to the Ximeng, all are rulers and subjects [*xizhu xichen*]. Our land has never before been so flourishing or so vast."[46]

This introduction summarizes the Qing expansion concisely from the emperor's vantage point. It presumes an inexorable process of submission by the Mongol tribes which brings peace and prosperity to all peoples. Only the violent, aggressive, ambitious leaders of the Zunghars block the expansion of this peaceful realm. The official account blames them for creating disorder and depicts Qing military campaigns as reluctant responses to the turmoil of the frontier. It erases evidence of Qing instigation of conflict and Qing military defeats. Explicitly designed as a sequel to the Kangxi emperor's personal campaign history, this account links the Qianlong emperor's successes to those of his grandfather, while at the same time it insists that he has surpassed the achievements of all his predecessors.

Qianlong's *Fanglue* is still an essential source. Much more detailed than the *Qingshilu,* it includes information not found in published archival documents. Yet we can be sure that it is highly selective and biased, like its Kangxi predecessor. Qianlong knew that he had completed the project begun by his grandfather, the final elimination of an autonomous Mongolian presence in the steppe and the establishment of stable borders in Central Eurasia. Now that the story was over, he could set its official framework in place. Kangxi's compilation, ending with the death of Galdan, supported the emperor's image as a warrior and peacemaker, but it remained open-ended because the Zunghars as a people survived. Now, under Qianlong, as the title proclaimed, the entire Zunghar "nation" had been pacified, fixed in historical memory as a "great people" whose time under Heaven had run out. Like failed dynasties, the Zunghars deserved to be included in the historical record, but on the victors' terms. They became the tools by which the Qianlong emperor claimed the right to rule the vast territories of Central Eurasia. Just as he had fixed in time and place his own Manchus, who had a clear identity and site of origin in the Changbai Mountains of Manchuria, he placed the Zunghars in a territory and defined their temporal span. With the Zunghars gone, the other peoples of Central Eurasia transformed themselves *(xianghua)* to join the civilized realm, either as part of the imperial administration or as regular tributaries. With the genealogical account of Zunghar origins, and the campaign history that recounted their disappearance, the Qing official historians, in the emperor's name, encompassed another people under a comprehensive temporal gaze, just as they had comprehensively mapped the empire's space. Qianlong's historians laid the foundations for all subsequent historical constructions that portrayed the Mongols as inevitably, essentially, and eternally part of the Chinese imperial and national realms.

We can, however, read the *Fanglue* differently from its compilers. As an emperor-centered compilation, it contains huge numbers of communications back and forth between the emperor and his field officials. They viewed the Zunghars as rebels to be exterminated *(jiaomie)*, a term that is used with increasing frequency near the end of the campaigns. Despite its preconceived framework, it gives an excellent sense of the day-to-day uncertainty, showing that the outcome was by no means predetermined. Qianlong repeatedly attacks his generals for cowardice, for not advancing fast enough to wipe out all the rebels. He takes no account of the logistical constraints operating on them and allows no excuses. But there is plenty of information in the *Fanglue* to permit us to calculate the tremendous supply effort that went into making the campaigns succeed. For all their distortions, by their very bulk these voluminous compilations cannot avoid providing material for diverse accounts of the conquest. It would require an extensive search of the archives to determine exactly what this *Fanglue* omits and how it altered its original sources. But the very systematic, large-scale nature of the compilation process, led by scholars of high quality, ensures that it contains materials that do not accord with the uniform official view. The Four Treasuries project suppressed "off-sequence" texts that gave a different account of the Manchu state's origins, but even its approved texts did not speak with a single voice.[47]

A View from the Frontier

The Manchu official Qishiyi, in his *Record of Things Seen and Heard in the Western Regions (Xiyu Wenjianlu)* of 1777, offers a frontiersman's view of the conquest quite different from that of the imperial center. Qishiyi, who earned his *jinshi* degree in 1754, served as a low-ranking official in charge of grain supply in Turkestan. He narrates vividly the struggle for succession to the Zunghar Khanate after Galdan Tseren's death, describes the states bordering the Qing in Central Eurasia, and recounts the wars against Amursana, Khoja Jihān, and Burhān ad-Dīn, and the return of the Torghuts. Under the pen name "Chun Yuan," he takes on the persona of a commentator who reflects on the general principles exemplified by his account.[48]

Qishiyi's geographical information was very garbled but extensive. He discusses in detail the major cities of Central Eurasia and the customs of many of its peoples, including the Kazakhs, Kirghiz, Andijanis, Hindustanis, Kashmiris, and Ottomans. His discussions include an extraordinary amount of detail about these peoples, clearly gathered from diverse sources, mostly travelers and envoys. This text contains more information about Central Eurasia than any of the other geographical works produced in his time. Wei Yuan's *Haiguo Tuzhi*, published in 1844, is renowned as China's first extensive description of European lands across the sea, but Qishiyi's account reflects an equally significant earlier Qing effort to gather information about western lands on the continental frontier. Wei Yuan, He Qiutao, and other scholars of northwestern geography studied Qishiyi's work carefully, correcting its errors while using its information. He Qiutao regarded Qishiyi's knowledge of Xinjiang, based on his own personal experience, as quite accurate, but his accounts of Russia, the Kazakhs, Kirghiz, Torghuts, and the Ottoman empire as muddled information, based on hearsay and street rumors. Wei Yuan's *Shengwuji* in fact relies heavily on Qishiyi's information for its account of the Qing wars in the northwest. Mixing together misinformation and legend with specific details, Qishiyi reveals the hazy outlines of the wider world of continental Eurasia that the Qing were just beginning to discover. Very different in style from the systematized scholarly compilations sponsored by the state, Qishiyi's text reflects the personal viewpoint of a frontiersman who picked up useful knowledge from daily experience, not from official texts.

He knew, for example, that a woman (Catherine) ruled Russia as a "female Khan," but thought that women had ruled Russia for seven generations, and that some rulers had been killed after being in power for only a few months. When women ruled Russia, he thought, infant boys were killed to prevent them from taking the throne.[49] Qishiyi was not far from the truth, since in fact four empresses had ruled Russia since the death of Peter, and the male Tsars had very short reigns.

His description of Russian wars against the Ottoman empire also mixes fact and fancy. In his understanding, Russia used to be a subject state of the Ottomans, but after 1755 the "White Khan" (Tsar) refused to pay tribute, and the two countries fought a war. Russia suffered a great defeat, losing 200,000 men, and had to provide tribute and 500 boys and girls as hostages to make peace. The Tsar raised more troops, demanding aid from the Torghut Mongols, which induced them to flee Russian territory for China. This description probably reflects the impact of Russian levies from the Torghuts in 1768 for the Ottoman wars.[50] Qishiyi may have confused Muscovy's tributary relationship with the Mongols in the fourteenth century with its relations with the Ottomans. The Ottomans did indeed defeat Russia and Austria in 1737, but they lost a major war with Russia in 1774. The reference to young hostages may reflect a distorted version of the *devshirme,* by which the Ottomans used Christians, mostly captured Slavic children from the Balkans, to serve in their military administration.

Qishiyi knew that the Ottoman empire (which he called "Konggar") was the largest Muslim state in Central Eurasia.[51] He commented: "The Konggar know only Heaven and Earth, sun and moon; they have no doctrines of spirits, sages, worthies, or Buddhas. In the northwest they worship the religion of Lord of Heaven [*Tianzhu*], who makes their state wealthy and their people prosperous. They lack deception and avoid killing. So people admire their rulers, and have no enemies, as Mencius said the benevolent have no enemies. So they are not part of either the Chinese [*huaxia*] or barbarian [*rongdi*] world."[52]

He clearly recognized the distinctive monotheism of Islam, which, like Christianity, recognized only one "Lord of Heaven," and he placed the Ottomans outside the traditional classification of peoples into either sinicized *huaxia* or barbarian *rongdi.* Russia he regarded as militarily weak, but the power and wealth of the Ottomans impressed him greatly. Qishiyi's views fit the seventeenth century better than the eighteenth century, by which time Ottoman power was generally declining while Russia was expanding. But his information had been transmitted through Central Eurasian intermediaries who reflected enduring legends more than immediate historical events. He uses Central Eurasian terminology throughout for political leaders, calling the Russian Tsar and Ottoman Sultan alike "Khans," their Muslim religious leaders "Hakim Begs," and the subjects of the Ottomans *albatu,* equivalent to Chinese "bondservants" *(nupu).* Qishiyi's residence on the frontier had expanded his geographical horizons far beyond the conventional Chinese awareness of those within and those beyond the passes. He knew that the multifarious landscape of Central Eurasia contained realms and peoples whose identities challenged any conventional classification schemes.

Qishiyi was a loyal defender of his state's military conquests. He regarded Amursana, especially, as a "crafty, cruel" leader with a duplicitous "wolf's heart" who had brought deserved catastrophe on the Zunghars. But his interpretation of the causes of Zunghar collapse differed substantially from that presented in the official *Fanglue* and the emperor's edicts. He knew that even after major military expeditions by Kangxi and Yongzheng, "even though [Qing troops] massacred many of them, they could not be exterminated."[53] In contrast to Kangxi's and Qianlong's univocal crowing about the defeat of Galdan, Qishiyi never claims that Galdan committed suicide, and he knows quite well that Zunghar power endured long after Kangxi's campaigns.

Qishiyi's vivid narrative of the last years of the Zunghar focuses on personal rivalries between the successors to Galdan Tseren after his death in 1745. In Qishiyi's account, the Zunghars continued to cause unrest after Amursana's death, angering the Qing emperor, who ordered a wholesale massacre of men, women, and children totaling nearly 1 million people. Qing troops mercilessly tracked down all refugees into the remotest mountain valleys to ensure the extermination of the entire Zunghar race *(zhonglei)*. Placing the wholesale massacre of the Zunghars after Amursana's defeat, unlike the account in the *Qingshilu* and Wei Yuan, and inflating the numbers killed to 1 million instead of Wei Yuan's 600,000, Qishiyi gives us the starkest version of the destruction wrought by the Qing conquest.[54]

As the commentator "Chun Yuan," Qishiyi mimics the role of the editors of the *Fanglue*, who also added personal reflections at the end of the documentary material in their collection. Chun Yuan's view of the causes of historical change differs strikingly from those of the *Fanglue* editors:

> The creation of states, the continuation of families, their rise and fall, life and death, is solely determined by human character [*renxin*]. In respect to mercy and power, men's goals differ; all depends on obtaining men's allegiance. Thus, because of the Zunghars' power, their people became wealthy; because of their courage, their territory expanded; because higher and lower in remote regions were on harmonious terms, they combined forces and expanded to cause trouble in all directions. In their defeat, the Heavenly troops came west like *laxiu* [cutting rotten wood?]; they exterminated 1 million people over ten thousands of *li* of territory in one or two years, and there was almost no one left. How could it be merely that Heaven repressed their race? It was because the usurping rebels followed each other; their wills scattered, they could not unite.[55]

The Zunghars were indeed, in Qishiyi's view, powerful, violent, and threatening, but their destruction was not inevitable. They fell because they had grown disunited, not because Heaven had decreed their end. Oddly anticipating Wei Yuan and nineteenth-century reformers, Qishiyi betrays a certain respect for all militarily powerful, united states, whether or not they belong to the "civilized" Chinese realm. He fears most internal divisions generated by struggles for power and personal ambition, which undermine the state's ability to resist its foes. The Qianlong emperor gets the credit he deserves for his deep strategic understanding, which transcended the narrower, inconstant ambitions of Amursana, but Qishiyi does not indulge in extensive praise of the irresistible will of Heaven. He recognized that personalities drove events in unpredictable ways, and much was subject to the whims of fortune.

Most striking is Qishiyi's open opposition to the return of the Torghuts:

Now the Torghuts today have fled their homes and have no place to live. Russia gave them fertile fields at Ejir, where they could gain a living, and sheltered their people like birds putting eggs under their wings. They enjoyed nearly two hundred years of peace. Ubashi owned millions of livestock which filled the fields. When the Russians met with critical danger they crept forward to save them. Their righteousness cannot be faulted. Then they listened to the treasonous words of Shereng and embraced the path to catastrophe. They wanted to occupy China's borderlands, abandoning their lengthy peaceful livelihood. It was a willful, calamitous scheme. They crossed barren deserts and savage regions of wolves and tigers, until hardly anyone of their tribe survived. Was it merely because they did not keep to their plans, or was it Heaven that oppressed them?[56]

Even though the emperor had decided to welcome the Torghuts back, rejecting the advice of his frontier ministers, Qishiyi suspected their motives, and rightly so. Their documents confirm that initially the Torghuts hoped to reoccupy the Zungharian lands without submitting to the Qing. In Qishiyi's view, by submitting to Russia, the Torghuts owed a loyalty to the Tsar that overrode their ethnicity. Their return to the Qing to escape Russian exactions indicated only that they were "petty men" (*xiaoren*) driven by self-interest. Their appeal for Qing aid seemed to him to be only a pretext for taking over the former homeland of Amursana.

Generals on the frontier, suspicious of any new arrivals on the border, had more immediate security concerns than officials back in Beijing. But Qishiyi also expressed the more traditional sense of loyalty that characterized the earlier years of the dynasty, in opposition to Qianlong's newly fixed identities. Loyalties could be chosen, in Qishiyi's view, and deserved to be honored, regardless of ethnic affiliation. Identities were not assigned at birth, and they were not absolute, but once a man chose his allegiance, he should stick to it. Qianlong, by contrast, welcomed the Torghuts back as lost members of the Mongol nation. He could demonstrate their clear gene-alogical affiliations with the Western Mongols, but Qishiyi thought that moral commitment trumped tribal ascription.

Even in the increasingly formalized labeling of peoples of the late eigh-teenth century, contrasting ideas of moral autonomy, based on different historical senses, divided the frontier officials and the court. In one view, peoples took charge of their destiny and did not simply inherit it; in the other, absolute identities as members of a determined "tribe" or "nation" indicated Heaven's will. Qishiyi, like the emperor, believed in a Heavenly will. His narrative highlighted a short time of freedom for the Torghuts, which allowed them their choice of ruler. After they chose to join Russia, they could not change loyalties again, and Heaven punished them for their betrayal. By comparison with the orthodox policy, however, Qishiyi did not bind the Torghuts to the Qing forever but recognized the role of choice. As a Manchu of the frontier, he was closer to the Central Eurasian world than the emperor closeted in Beijing.

Nomadic Chronicles

The lineage of Chinese and Manchu official historiography culminated in the *Shengwuji*, Wei Yuan's integration of military conquest, Heavenly man-date, and imperial virtue. (See Chapter 14.) Against this intellectual jugger-naut, supported by powerful institutional forces, how could alternative ac-counts prevail? The Mongols themselves maintained a tradition of family chronicles, outside the reach of the Qing history bureaus, which explained historical change very differently than did the Qing official writers. Tibetan biographers also dealt with the Qing conquest from a particular perspec-tive. We can enrich our understandings of the conquest by examining these non-official writings.

Mongolian historiography originates with the *Secret History of the Mon-gols*, a family history of Chinggis's lineage, written circa 1324 CE.[57] After the fall of the Yuan, Mongols continued writing in schools on the border, and the Ming sponsored a four-language translation of Buddhist formulas in 1431, but most of the family chronicles were destroyed in wars between the Eastern and Western Mongols in the fifteenth century. In 1735 the chronicler Lomi lamented, "After we Mongols withdrew beyond the bor-ders of China [in 1368], we lost the existing family registers because we were drawn into the turmoil created by the Oirats."[58] In the mid-sixteenth century, a "Renaissance" of Mongolian historical writing began in the Ordos and spread to the Chahar, Eastern Mongols, and Khalkhas by the seventeenth century. Tibetan Buddhism, reintroduced into Mongolia, added a new strain of church history to the older familial focus. Its influence was first seen in 1579 in a text connecting Altan Khan with the Chinggisid lineage and also calling him the "Incarnation of Chakravarti," the Indian Buddhist wheel-turning king. Ligdan Khan's full-scale patronage of Buddhism, including the translation of 1055 works of the Buddhist canon into Mongolian, established Tibetan Buddhism securely in the Mongolian written corpus. The *White Chronicle (Chaghan Teüke)* of the late sixteenth century is the first historical work which propounds the "mythical connection of Mongolian Princes with Tibetan and Indian Kings."[59] The best-known and most valuable early chronicle, the *Golden Compilation (Altan Tobci)* of 1655, combines Mongolian sources from the thirteenth century onward with Tibetan church history in an integrated account. The *Erdenyi-yin Tobci,* written in 1662 after most of the Eastern Mongols had submitted to the Qing, has been regarded as the "prototypical" Mongolian history. The author describes the descent of Mongol rulers from mythical Indian kings, the spread of Buddhism in Tibet, and the dissemination of Buddhism among the Mongols. Linking Indian, Tibetan, and Mongolian rulership, his leading theme is that of constant rebirth and incarnation. He draws on Mongolian, Tibetan, and some Chinese sources, but the chronicle is still independent of the Qing perspective.

Mongolian historiography changed dramatically after the Qing victory over Galdan and the final incorporation of the Khalkha Mongols into the banners. The Lifanyuan supported pro-Manchu views by disseminating proclamations in Mongolian legitimating Mongolian subordination. Now the turbulent years of conflict between the Khalkhas and Manchus were hardly mentioned; the chroniclers viewed the Manchus as the true preservers of order and the protectors of Buddha. No longer seeing Ligdan Khan as a worthy sponsor of Buddhism, they described him as a wicked rebel. Mongolian chronicles contain no mention of the major social trends affecting the Mongols under Qing rule: the loss of autonomy of the nobility, rising indebtedness, or social breakdown and economic stagnation. These silences, like the dog that did not bark in the night for Sherlock Holmes, reveal much about the perspectives of Mongols who joined the Qing.[60] But even among the pro-Qing Mongols, traces of the alternative tradition survived. Aci Lomi, a banner general, wrote his *History of the Borjigid Clan (Mongghol borjigid obogh-un teüke)* from 1732 to 1735.[61] He wrote it first in Manchu and Chinese versions, which are now lost. Only in 1839 did a

Mongolian translation appear. Lomi drew on an uninterrupted tradition of family chronicles extending from Chinggis Khan to his own day. Lamenting the loss of so many documents during the fifteenth century, he drew extensively on the earlier chronicles, but his is the first Mongolian history to mention the battle of Jao Modo at all, and he says nothing about Tibetan church history. Lomi, an Eastern Mongol noble, was grateful to the Manchus for rescuing the Mongols from internal strife. He wrote:

> Our Mongol people have declined and risen up; we have been torn apart and now are reborn. Truly this is due to the wonderful benevolence [kesig] of His Imperial Majesty. Then Heaven above assisted those within our realm, recompensing our debts to the knowledge and merit of our ancestors. If this had not happened, after the century of chaos that elapsed from Ligdan Khan to Yongzheng, within many tribes the powerful would have oppressed the weak, and kinsmen would have killed one another. We recall with deep [gratitude] that during our unbearable suffering the emperors Hong Taiji and Kangxi with mercy and pity repeatedly granted us abundant aid.[62]

Christopher Atwood notes that "certainly Lomi is untypical of Mongolian historians both in the extremes of his devotion to the imperial grace and in the degree to which Chinggis Khan is ignored as the bestower of grace upon the Mongolian nobility and people." But his chronicle is only the extreme example of other accounts which show that the rhetoric of "repay[ing] the grace of the superior played a large and growing role in Mongolian life, both political and domestic, from the eighteenth century on."[63] The core Chinese concept of *bao* (repaying the favor of parents or other superiors) was translated meaningfully into Mongolian culture through imperial proclamations and unofficial publications, linking the two cultures with a common language.

Contrary to the views of David Farquhar and Pamela Crossley, who both argue that the Manchu rulers used very separate vocabularies of legitimation for each of the peoples they ruled, Atwood shows that cultural concepts from one political tradition can bleed over into another. Qing legitimation practices partially crossed cultural boundaries by linking portions of each tradition with analogous elements of another, with Manchu often serving as the bridge between Chinese and Mongolian ideals. The Manchu translations of the Three Kingdoms tale, for example, and imperial patronage of the cult of Guan Di, who exemplified loyalty in repayment of imperial grace, demonstrated this linkage. In Mongolia, Guan Di became identified with Gesar, the epic hero of Tibetan and Mongolian legend. These linked cultural items created common bonds in both official and popular understandings of the meanings of incorporation into the empire. Atwood concludes that "efforts to separate an Inner Asian language of loyalty, which relied on master-slave relations, and a Chinese one, which relied on modeling the emperor-minister relation on the father-son relation, are artificial."[64]

Yet cultural hegemony was never complete. Historical interpretations by Mongols still differed from the official Qing record. Even the loyal Lomi interpreted Galdan's motivations differently from the Manchus, ascribing Galdan's war on the Khalkhas purely to the personal motive of revenging the death of his brother. Unlike the *Fanglue* and nearly all later Chinese historians, Lomi did not claim that Galdan aimed at hegemony over all of Mongolia, or that he sought to recreate Chinggis Khan's empire. Walther Heissig regards Lomi's interpretation as "the common understanding of his class," the Mongols who supported the Qing.[65] Lomi, despite his allegiance to the Qing, retains the Mongolian focus on personal relations and omits the Chinese overlay of moral ideology.

The Qing official historians, however, set out to penetrate the entire domain of historical writing, in Mongolian as well as Manchu and Chinese. The *Imperially Commissioned Biographies of Central Asian Nobles*, or *Iledkel Shastir* for short, compiled from 1779 to 1795, created a definitive account. As the emperor's decree stated, "To commemorate the aid to our dynasty of the forty-nine banners of Mongolia, and other tribes who have been loyal to us for generations, and done military deeds; we order the Guoshiguan and Lifanyuan to compile biographies of them, to be published in three languages."[66] Qi Yunshi, the compiler, used Manchu, Chinese, and Mongolian archival and private documents, preserving in this compilation much information that has since been lost. The Mongolian version contains more details about the Mongols than the Manchu or Chinese texts: each language had its own purpose and was addressed to a specific audience. The text judges the princes' actions by reference to their loyalty to the Qing but contains the fullest information about their lives available anywhere. It became the most important source for later accounts of the Mongols, showing that the Qing bureaucratic perspective had won the battle to write the imperial history. The *Erdeni-yin erike*, for example, a nineteenth-century Mongolian chronicle long regarded as a valuable primary document of an integrated Mongolian view, in fact copied most of its text directly from the Qing *Fanglue* and the *Iledkel Shastir*.[67] Thus, by the nineteenth-century, the Mongols had lost nearly all access to an autonomous account of their own history that could escape the Qing bureaucratic embrace.

Far to the west, however, one independent chronicler remained. The *Khalimaq Khadiyin tuujiyigi Khuraji . . .* (History of the Kalmyk Khans) (HKK), written after 1819 by an unknown author, describes the history of the Torghuts and their return to Zungharia from a viewpoint beyond the Qing empire's reach.[68] This text offers new insights on Qing relations with the Western Mongols and important alternative interpretations of critical events. Since the Western Mongolian texts have almost never been used by historians, our views remain mostly confined to the Qing framework, but a few examples indicate that other versions of the story need serious consideration. When the author of HKK describes Tulisen's embassy to Ayuki Khan in 1713, he repeats the official Qing justification of the embassy as seeking permission from the Russian Tsar to allow Arabjur, Ayuki's nephew, to return to him, but notes that the Manchus had ulterior motives: "[The embassy came] to view the territory of the Russian people and moreover to try to perceive the nature and condition of the Russian government. If it were possible [they] would cause a quarrel between Ayuki and Tsewang Rabtan. They had come with such an idea in mind." Ayuki, in this account, "was not such a shortsighted man as to abandon his own blood relations in Zungharia and fall in the trap of the foreign Manchus." Thanking the emperor for his consideration, he promised to send a request to the Russian Tsar, but refused to consider an alliance with the Qing. "The emissaries did not attain their own intentions and produced futile results."[69] Even though the emperor's explicit instructions to Tulisen were to reject any alliance with the Torghuts, scholars have suspected that secret oral instructions delivered a different message. The Torghut chronicler offers the most plausible explanation of why the Qing would send an emissary on such a difficult journey; certainly it was not done in order to return one man to his uncle's home.

The HKK chronicler also provides the most convincing explanation of the causes of the return of the Torghuts to Qing territory. He admired greatly the skills of the Torghut Khan Ayuki (r. 1672–1722), who successfully kept his people united and prosperous until his death. His successors, however, tore apart the tribe with internecine quarrels and intrigues, weakening their ability to resist Russian pressure. After 1761, the Russians refused to confirm the succession of Khan Ubashi, the great-grandson of Ayuki, restricting his power. Under increasing Russian pressure, Ubashi conceived of leading his people back to their "ancient homeland" in Zungharia.[70] Ubashi knew that Amursana had been driven out by Qing troops, but regarded the territory as empty. He had no intention of submitting to the Qing when he set out with 33,000 households, or 169,000 people. In the spring of 1771, after a horrifying journey, attacked incessantly by Russians, Kazakhs, and Kirghiz, and starving in trackless deserts, having lost nearly all their animals, the Torghuts arrived at the Qing border with only 70,000 people. Governor-General Shuhede sent an envoy to learn their intentions. The chronicler writes, "As there were no other means of taking Zungharia from the Chinese but warfare, they notified [the Manchus] saying, 'We came in order to become subjects of the Manchu Emperor.'"[71] After some debate, the Qianlong emperor granted them refuge in the Qing empire.

Nearly all Chinese accounts portray the Torghuts as willingly "returning in order to submit" *(guishun)* to Qing domination. Although Qishiyi justifiably suspected them of planning an invasion, he had no definite evidence of their intentions. The HKK chronicler portrays Ubashi's original vision of Zungharia as a "fine country . . . richer than the Volga steppe," where his people would be "dwelling near the most blessed illumined saints and the Tibetan area . . . and [near] our ancient brother Mongols with whom is shared one language and one religion."[72] This view envisaged no domination by other people. Only in their final, exhausted state did the Torghuts come to accept Qing rule. The historical account of HKK stays close to the evolving views of the Torghuts and does not portray them as the inevitable outcome of a Heaven-directed process. But this chronicle remained unknown to the Mongols under the Qing, and was only published in Russia in 1892.

One final refuge remained: oral tradition. When the great Russian Mongolist B. Ia. Vladimirtsov traveled in western Mongolia in the first decade of the twentieth century, he collected a series of legends and anecdotes about the Khoit prince Amursana. The "people's memory," in Vladimirtsov's words, preserved only a selected version of Amursana's activities: they forgave him his vacillation and collaboration and memorialized him as a heroic fighter against Manchu domination.[73] Legends predicted that with the coming of a new era, Amursana would rise again to lead the Western Mongols in a new struggle for independence. According to one legend, when Amursana was pursued by Dawaci, local people concealed him in a cave until he was discovered. He then escaped across the river to Russia and still lives there today, waiting for the time to return and begin the struggle for liberation. Amursana also had magical powers: he could call up a rainbow and hang his gear on it, and he could call down snow and rain to obstruct his enemies. Recalling the power of the Oirat shamans to call down a *jada*, or devastating thunderstorm, Amursana used his powers to crush the army of the Salars that pursued him.

Other anecdotes explained his name as meaning "Amur-sanagha" (Peaceful Thoughts). He was the reincarnation of the fierce Bodhisattva

Mahakala, riding on his horse Maralbashi. After his sworn brother Bandi abandoned him, Amursana swore an oath to return after 120 years to avenge the defeat of the Oirats. He settled in Russia, where the Tsar offered him pastures on a peninsula in the "great sea" to rule his people. Ten years before his return to Mongolia, water would flow in the deserts northeast of Khobdo, and grass and trees would return. Four years before his return, a light gray horse would appear that would ride around the region and lead the Oirat people away.

These tales combined legends, oral history, and prophecy to depict a popular hero who would recreate the united Mongols in a struggle for independence. Rising resentment against Manchu policies generated support for resistance movements. In 1912, when Dambijantsan, a Kalmyk lama from the Volga, claimed to be the reincarnation of Amursana, a new epic poem gave voice to his struggle:

> I am a mendicant monk from the Russian Tsar's kingdom, but I am born of the great Mongols. My herds are on the Volga river, my water source is the Irtysh. There are many hero warriors with me. I have many riches. Now I have come to meet with you beggars, you remnants of the Oirats, in the time when the war for power begins. Will you support the enemy? My homeland is Altai, Irtysh, Khobuk-sari, Emil, Bortala, Ili, and Alatai. This is the Oirat mother country. By descent, I am the great-grandson of Amursana, the reincarnation of Mahakala, owning the horse Maralbashi. I am he whom they call the hero Dambijantsan. I came to move my pastures back to my own land, to collect my subject households and bondservants, to give favor, and to live freely.[74]

Thus the great Qing historiographic juggernaut never entirely eliminated alternative voices. Far away on the Volga, visions of an independent people still survived. With the collapse of the Qing in 1911, Mongolia enjoyed only a brief, turbulent period of autonomy until the arrival of Soviet armies in 1921, but its historical imagination still preserved memories of the battles of the past. Exaggerated and simplified, they nevertheless evoked possibilities for alternative narratives beyond the complete domination of either the Russian or Chinese national inscription projects.

Imperial banquet for Ubashi, Khan of the Torghuts, on his return to Qing territory, held at the Wanfa Guiyi hall in Chengde, ca. 1771.

Led by its victorious emperor, the Qing bureaucracy mobilized its entire panoply of resources to dominate the collective memory of the conquest. Stelae marked the landscape; maps gave a comprehensive view of the territory, and official histories fixed time and interpretations in definite form. The historiographic and inscriptional machinery occupied not only the Chinese textual space but nearly all of the Manchu and Mongolian space as well. One received account of the conquest as foreordained by Heaven and foreseen by sacred rulers drove out doubts, contingencies, and skeptics. The others that survived were fragmented and uncoordinated, scattered among manuscripts in monasteries, oral histories, and remarks by some official dissenters. The Qing mastery of interpretive space seemed to have no rivals.

James Scott reminds us, however, that true "hegemony" never really exists.[75] Despite extravagant claims by ideologues and their latter-day interpreters, smirks of resistance hide behind the public masks of deference. At best we can describe the Qing efforts as a vast project with hegemonic goals, one that appeared to have unusual success by the end of the eighteenth century. The grandiose apparatus of compilation, surveillance, classification, and narrative definitively marked the ideological terrain of the entire empire. But there were cracks in the façade, even within the Chinese textual production system, which were more evident in the linguistic and cultural worlds beyond. Like economic and political integration, cultural integration could never encompass the infinite diversity of the realm under a single uniform gaze. Yet the ambition to embrace multitudes, covering all contradictions under an ideology of Heavenly command, strongly defined the legitimation of rule both by the Qing emperors and by the nation-state that succeeded it. In the next section I discuss the consequences of Qing imperial ambitions for the construction of the modern Chinese nation.

PART FIVE

Legacies and Implications

14

Writing the National History of Conquest

From the seventeenth through the nineteenth centuries, Western and Chinese historians' views of the Qing frontier converged upon a common geopolitical perspective. Although they gave divergent evaluations of the soundness of the dynasty and its policies, they came to agree that China was a powerful entity in eastern Eurasia, one whose autonomy was vital to global security. Imperialists and nationalists were secret sharers, especially in their analysis of the future of the Qing frontiers.

Statecraft Writers and Empire

The statecraft writers Wei Yuan (1794–1856) and Gong Zizhen (1792–1841) built on the achievements of the eighteenth century to support their arguments for strong national defense. Both used history to defend the heavy cost of frontier conquest. They placed Qianlong's campaigns in a lineage reaching back to Han dynasty relations with the Xiongnu, claiming that he had successfully resolved the nearly two-millennia-long issue of securing the northwest frontier. China's borders were now stable, but the empire needed to invest in integrating the frontier regions with the interior. Like the emperor's official historians, they saw Heaven's will manifest in these unprecedented imperial victories, but like Qishiyi, they knew that a wide world existed beyond the frontiers. Carrying on the eighteenth-century project into the nineteenth-century world of international geopolitics, these writers defined the framework within which the Qing in its last century would attempt to maintain control over its conquered peoples.

The scholar and historian Wei Yuan (1794–1856).

Gong Zizhen and Wei Yuan are best known to Western scholars as advocates of resistance to Western maritime incursions, and of extending China's knowledge of European nations.[1] Philip Kuhn has recently pointed out, however, that "ethnocentric" Western scholars tend to exaggerate foreign influence on thinkers like Wei Yuan, ignoring his primary focus on do-

mestic reform.[2] Wei and Gong derived the primary impulse of their reform-
ism from the activist "New Text" school of interpretation, which viewed
classical texts as guides to action, not dusty objects of empirical research.
We should not, however, view Wei and Gong solely as advocates of internal
reform, nor should we stress only their concerns about maritime defense.
As proponents of political activism derived from classical scholarship, Wei
and Gong also closely linked security issues to domestic political reform.
Security for the state meant both defense of its boundaries and maintenance
of internal order. In their thinking, continental and maritime security concerns were closely tied together.

Gong Zizhen was twenty-nine years old when he wrote his prophetic essay arguing that Turkestan should be made into a province.[3] He had obtained his *juren* degree but failed his *jinshi* examination. Unsurprisingly,
the little-known scholar's arguments were ignored when first published in
1820, but they received much wider attention when reprinted in the volume
sponsored by the influential official He Changling and compiled by Wei
Yuan, the *Huangchao Jingshi Wenbian* (Collected imperial essays on Statecraft), in 1827. The Jahangir rebellion of 1826 had drawn attention to
Turkestan's unstable situation, and the costs of maintaining garrisons in the
region drew substantial criticism. Gong not only argued strongly for the
benefits of incorporating the region into the empire but also justified its
conquest as the culmination of a long-standing imperial vision supported
by Heaven.

Unlike the Qianlong emperor, however, Gong located China not in the
center of the civilized realm but at the eastern end of the Eurasian continent. It was a land with fixed borders and a defined territory. It was the
largest country in the world, whose borders stretched to the four "seas,"
for the Qing's continental border represented the ultimate limit of control,
just like the coastlines of the east and south: "Whether by land, or by sea,
large or small mountains, large and small rivers, or plains, our territory is
either registered land or it is like the seas." China's rulers had expanded
first to the east, then to the south coast, but by dominating the Mongols,
the Qing had made the northwest safe and no longer remote or dangerous.
"Was it not Heavenly fate that the empire should reach to the Four Seas?
Even using tens of millions of taels cannot be called wasteful." Gong rejected the "shallow views of ignorant weaklings and vile writers" *(yuru,
pisheng)* who said that supporting the conquest was "wasting the resources
of the interior to support the frontier" *(haozhong shibian).*[4]

Gong also forcefully argued for integrating the region with the interior. All the landless, roaming populations of northwest and North China
should be sent west, supported with twenty-year tax exemptions and fund-

ing for land clearance, while the resident garrisons should give their land to the soldiers as private property. The banners would be eliminated, and civil administrators would take control of all land and tax collection. The region would be systematically divided into prefectures and sub-prefectures, Chinese names would replace the native ones, and the *begs, jasaks,* and other frontier authorities would come under the regular administration.

Gong's radical proposals extended existing trends to their ultimate consequences. Eighteenth-century Qing policies had already promoted immigration into the new territories and created a hybrid civil and military administrative structure, but the Manchu rulers kept Turkestan separate from the rest of the empire and continued to insist that it should pay for its own support. Gong rejected the idea of self-sufficiency, arguing that the new province, like Guizhou and other poor interior regions, could receive substantial subventions from wealthier provinces. Trade, however, would be carefully controlled, so that corrupting "luxuries" could not enter: an official at the Jiayuguan gate would ensure that only grain, cloth, tea, and other essentials could enter the border region, and only melons and hides could be imported from there. In Gong's view, the Han Chinese population could make a new start here, uncontaminated by the social tension and commercial seductions of the interior. Even the exiled criminals in the region and other "wicked people" from the interior could redeem themselves there by working hard on their own lands. Gong's vision of pure virgin soil, the culmination of the extension of culture outward from the imperial center, answered his critics in moral and historical terms.

Wei Yuan supported his colleague in more material terms, stressing what James Millward calls the "forward defense dividend": transferring troops to the frontier relieved the interior provinces of the expense of supporting them at home.[5] In his essay in the *Huangchao Jingshi Wenbian,* Wei likewise praised the empire's extension in all directions, and carefully surveyed all of the people under its control.[6] The Mongols of Inner Mongolia, plus the Tumed and Guihua Mongols, comprised a total of fifty-one banners, each with its own *jasak,* divided into twenty-five tribes. The Outer Mongols formed four tribes and eighty-one banners, collectively known as Khalkha. Farther west were the towns of Zungharia, which had become large settlements after the end of the wars. (Wei did not mention the elimination of the Zunghars.) Beyond them were the "western dependent states," divided into three circuits *(lu),* which included the Kazakhs, Burut (Kirghiz), Andijanis, Afghans, Hindustanis, and others. In Wei's expansive gaze, all these peoples "belonged" *(shu)* to the empire in some sense; only Russia was not a dependent state.

He also had to defend imperial control against the charge of wasting interior resources on barren wastelands. Citing the constant damage caused by nomadic raids in the past, Wei argued that the cost of frontier expansion was fully justified and, furthermore, the region could relieve population pressure in the interior. "Heaven has left us this vast wilderness," he exclaimed, to accommodate the floating population of the "flourishing age."[7]

Because Wei and Gong shared a belief in a cosmic force directing the course of history, Western analysts have often seen them as anticipating the unilinear schemes of historical analysis characteristic of nineteenth-century social theory.[8] They derived their progressivist stance, however, not from Western examples but from what they knew of the Qing's expansion. The eighteenth-century expansion seemed to demonstrate conclusively that China had fulfilled its historical destiny by dominating Central Eurasia. Just like imperialists in the New World and elsewhere, they promoted the filling up of "virgin lands" with immigrants from the core, and the tighter links to the interior, as "manifest destiny" for this large continental state. Material benefits complemented an underlying view of historical change, dependent on assumptions about the natural boundaries of the state derived from the Qing's flourishing age.

Wei Yuan's *Shengwuji* (Record of sacred military campaigns) completed the legitimation of the Qing conquests by synthesizing them into an accessible form. Born in 1794, he grew up during a time of incessant warfare when the empire was desperately fending off internal rebellion and foreign attack. As he noted in the preface, he was born one year before the Miao rebellion of 1795, received his licentiate degree when the White Lotus rebellion was suppressed, attained his first advanced degree after the attack of Lin Qing on the capital in 1814, and gained his *juren* degree during Jahangir's rebellion in Xinjiang of 1822–1828.[9] During the Opium War he served as a clerk in the office of the Liangjiang Governor-General, where he observed China's humiliating loss to the "sea barbarians." In 1842 he used the "sea of documents" available to him, including vast quantities of materials collected in the imperial campaign histories, secret official documents, private writings, and oral information, to create a comprehensive account of the Qing's military achievements that would instruct later generations, the *Shengwuji*. The *Haiguo Tuzhi*, his geography of foreign nations, appeared in 1844. Both works became extremely influential in Japan in the 1850s, just as foreign powers arrived to demand Japan's opening to trade.[10]

Wei Yuan had been anticipated by the Han official Zhao Yi, who as a secretary of the Grand Council wrote many of the communications to the northwest during the Turkestan campaigns, served on the southwest frontier for much of his life, and helped to compile the *Pingding Zhungar Fanglue*. His *Glorious Record of the Imperial Dynasty's Military Accom-*

plishments (Huangchao Wugong Jisheng), published in 1792, bridged the imperial historiographic projects of Qianlong and the private accounts of Wei Yuan and his successors. He discussed seven Qing campaigns, including two, in Burma and Taiwan, in which he had personally participated. Zhao Yi shared Wei Yuan's interest in both military history and the historical evolution of imperial institutions. He also wrote important essays analyzing the rise of the Grand Council and Hanlin Academy. In contrast to Gu Yanwu, for example, who praised the localism of ancient feudalism, Zhao Yi joined the Song tradition of "historical analogists" with the statecraft concerns of the Qing to affirm military expansion and centralized authority. Zhao Yi did not write his history out of anxieties over domestic upheaval and foreign incursions, but he prepared the way for Wei Yuan with historiography that "stressed the role of environment and continuous, cumulative institutional change, instead of looking back to a static and absolute utopian antiquity."[11]

In the preface to the *Shengwuji,* Wei offers a lengthy defense, filled with classical references, of the radical proposition that "fighting war is superior to worshipping at ancestral temples" *(zhan shengyu miaotang).* In other words, defense of secure borders should take precedence over spreading civilized culture throughout the world; ethical universalism must yield to national security. Yet Wei Yuan also stresses the superiority of "human talent" *(rencai)* over material means *(caiyong).* To ensure security, material factors cannot replace psychological factors:

> If material resources [*caiyong*] are insufficient, the state will not be poor, but if human talent [*rencai*] is not dynamic [*jing*], then it will be poor. If commands do not extend beyond the seas, the state is not weak; but if commands do not extend up to the interior borders, the state is weak. So the former kings did not worry about material resources but only about talent. They did not worry that they could not exert their will over the four barbarians, but worried about exerting their will within the four borders. If all officials have ability, the state will be orderly and rich; if all within the borders obey commands, the state will be powerful.[12]

Wei clearly accepted the delimiting of borders achieved by imperial expansion and, like Gong, focused his efforts on strengthening control within them. The state's goal was not to promote culture beyond its borders but to ensure obedience within them. Here we have crossed the blurred boundary separating nationalist ideology from classical norms. For Wei, internal security depends on mobilizing the best men of the empire to compete actively *(jing),* as in battle, to defend it.

Wei derived this proto-militarist ideology primarily from the historical record of Qing conquests, not from his knowledge of Western powers. As Jane Leonard has argued, Wei's interest in foreign countries derived primarily from the classical geographical tradition.[13] Although foreign ideas made some contribution, the classical tradition and its official history contained enough intellectual material to support all three of Wei Yuan's most striking proposals: military defense, global geographic knowledge, and public participation in state affairs.

In its organization the *Shengwuji* follows the expansion of the Qing state. After the opening two *juan* on the founding of the Qing and the suppression of the Three Feudatories, Wei Yuan discusses the Zunghar campaigns as part of his treatment of the pacification of Mongolia. He organizes his account geographically, proceeding from the "Inner Six" Mongolian tribes to the "Outer Four," Kokonor, Helanshan Eleuths, and finally Kangxi's Zunghar campaigns. Successive chapters follow the imperial armies into Zungharia, Turkestan, Tibet, the Gurkha region of Nepal, then Russia, Korea, Burma, and Vietnam. He next discusses the rebellions of the Miao and Jinchuan peoples and the uprisings on Taiwan, followed by an extensive discussion of the White Lotus rebellion. The last four chapters discuss military supplies and other issues. The text sweeps around the borders of the empire to incorporate all of the Qing's major military campaigns.

Wei Yuan's writings linked military conquest, foreign relations, and internal reform within a comprehensive historical vision. Wei put the capstone on the succession of imperial efforts to construct a fixed interpretation of the wars of expansion. His version of the Qing expansion has served as the almost unquestioned basis for subsequent accounts, and even his errors have been perpetuated by later writers. Xiao Yishan's *Qingdai Tongshi* (Comprehensive history of the Qing dynasty) of 1923, for example, incorporates verbatim, without citation, whole passages from the *Shengwuji*. James Millward has pointed out several tendentious claims of Wei Yuan, such as his deliberate underestimate of the number of troops occupying Xinjiang, which have been accepted by modern Chinese historians.[14]

Wei Yuan's treatment of Galdan's relations with Russia indicates how his approach meshed with modern nationalist history.[15] He puts particular stress on Galdan's false claim to have Russian support. Rumors of Russian aid made the Qing generals fearful, but the emperor was convinced of divine support. In Wei's view, the emperor's "extraordinary sacred power" *(shenling qiyi)* resolved all logistical problems by drawing water from the sand, causing grass to grow in the wasteland, and making ice melt on the river. It also induced natural omens that caused the despairing Galdan to commit suicide: "Every night alarming events occurred, everywhere

[Galdan] went he encountered strange omens. Fierce wind and pouring rains followed him. He knew that his followers had rebelled, and he had lost the favor of Heaven [*renpan tianwang*], and that night or day he could be captured, so he took poison and killed himself."[16] Wei Yuan's invocation of natural forces and divine inspiration laid the foundation for all subsequent Chinese accounts of the conquest.

Geopolitics and Emperor Worship

The first Western chroniclers of the Qing conquests were the Jesuits at the court of Beijing. Father Gerbillon accompanied the Kangxi emperor on many of his northwestern campaigns and wrote an eyewitness account of them.[17] From the Jesuit reports, Western readers gained an intimate portrait of the vigorous Manchu rulers—their military prowess, their sponsorship of scholarly research, their interest in science, and, so the Jesuits hoped, their high potential for conversion to Christianity. Jean Baptiste du Halde's *Description géographique, historique, chronologique, politique, et physique de l'empire de la Chine et de la Tartarie chinoise . . .* (1735) encompassed the maximal territories of imperial China, paying special attention to the exploration and conquest of the northwest in the seventeenth century. Frenchmen saw especially close parallels to state formation and competition in Europe. It was Joseph-Anne-Marie de Moyriac de Mailla, in his *Histoire générale de la Chine* of 1708, who first compared the Kangxi emperor to Louis XIV. De Mailla's *Histoire* was one of the first general histories of China, covering the entire imperial period, and based on Chinese sources, or their Manchu translations. The early sections followed the *Zizhi Tongjian Gangmu* (Outline of the comprehensive mirror), the general history begun by Zhu Xi in the thirteenth century and continued in the Ming, but much of the Qing coverage derived from the *Fanglue* campaign histories. De Mailla devoted a large part of Volume 11 to the Galdan campaigns, contrasting the vigor and courage of the young emperor with the "perverse" character of his rival. De Mailla's account reflected closely the emerging Qing imperial view of its own achievements at a time of convergence between Western and European glorification of empire.

In the late eighteenth century, Western views of China shifted from admiration to contempt, just as the major site of contact shifted from Beijing to Canton and commercial relations replaced intellectual debate and technological exchange. England supplanted France as the dominant imperial power, consolidating its supremacy after the Seven Years' War of 1756–1763 and Clive's fortuitous victory at Plassy in India in 1757. The image of

China as a sick man gradually came to replace early impressions of the
vigor of youth.

Although the empire now was much larger, British observers detected
signs of weakness. As Lord Macartney commented after his embassy in
1793: "The empire of China is an old crazy, first rate man-of-war, which a
fortunate succession of able and vigilant officers has contrived to keep
afloat for these hundred and fifty years past, and to overawe their neighbors merely by her bulk and appearance, but whenever an insufficient man
happens to have the command on deck, adieu to the discipline and safety of
the ship. She may, perhaps, not sink outright; she may drift some time as a
wreck, and will then be dashed to pieces on the shores, but she can never be
rebuilt on the old bottom."[18] In nautical verbiage, Macartney repeated the
Confucian principles of government: that disciplined operation of the state
depended on the moral character of the ruler.

One of Macartney's concerns was the effect of a weakened China on the
geopolitical balance in Eurasia. Macartney had spent three years at the
Russian court before coming to China, signed a commercial treaty with the
Russians, and written an account of the Russian empire on his return. In
China he had a close relationship with Songyun, the Mongol official who
had negotiated a new Treaty of Kiakhta with the Russians in 1792.

He foreshadowed the nineteenth-century geopolitical interest in China's
fate when he speculated about Russian actions if the British were to occupy
Macao or Lantao Island: "In such distractions would Russia remain in-
active? Would she neglect the opportunity of recovering Albazin and reestablishing her power upon the Amur? Would the ambition of the great
Catherine, that has stretched beyond Onalaska to the eastward, overlook
the provinces and partitions within grasp at her door?"[19] Macartney, like
Wei Yuan after him, saw that China's fates on the empire's continental and
maritime frontiers were intertwined.

The end of the nineteenth century, the time of high imperialism, revived
interest in the geopolitics of Eurasia. In 1904 the Scot Halford Mackinder
first outlined his strategic vision emphasizing the predominance of great
land powers over the "World Island" of Eurasia. Mackinder wrote fourteen years after the American Admiral A. T. Mahan had stressed the dominance of sea power in history.[20] Whereas Mahan's world geopolitics supported the British navy and rising American claims in the Pacific,
Mackinder focused attention on Russia, Germany, and the continental
powers. Mackinder's influence can be clearly detected in the later theoretical writings of Owen Lattimore and today in the writings of strategists
like Zbigniew Brzezinski.[21] British and Russian competition in the "Great
Game" drew the attention of swashbuckling adventurers, Foreign Office

diplomats, military campaigners, and the novelist of empire, Rudyard Kipling.[22] At the same time, quite a few European historians examined in detail the battles for control of Central Eurasia between the rulers of China and their Mongolian rivals.

The works of John Baddeley, Henry Howorth, Gaston Cahen, and Maurice Courant viewed China as one of several competitive actors in a grand geopolitical competition.[23] The title of Courant's study *L'Asie Centrale aux 17e et 18e siècles: Empire kalmouk ou Empire mantchou?* epitomizes this approach. Central Eurasia is the focus; the name "China" does not appear. The two contenders are "Kalmuks" (Zunghars) and "Manchus," not Chinese, Mongols, Russians, or any other current national definition. Baddeley likewise placed Russia, Mongolia, and China on an equal footing, and Cahen, though his title refers only to Russia and China, in fact includes a great deal of material on the Zunghar state's interactions with both Russia and China. Their imperial perspective spanning national borders saw the expansion of these three empires as a significant world process.

Chinese Historians and the Multicultural State

In the twentieth century, historical minds began to close, as China's nationalists tried to waken the people to respond to imperialist threats. Twentieth-century Chinese nationalists were most concerned with asserting the unity of "nationalities" *(minzu)* in the face of attacks from Japan, Russia, and the western European powers. Since they regarded the Manchus as alien, backward rulers of the Han race, they played down, or almost ignored, the unique features of Qing territorial expansion. For them, Manchu autocracy held back the powers of the united Chinese people, who would generate a strong nation from the bottom up. China's territorial scope dated from the unification of China under the Qin emperor in the third century BCE. Nationalists saw the progressive expansion of imperial control outward into Central Eurasia as a natural consequence of rising Chinese culture and power. They did not give the Manchus credit for expanding the Chinese realm; instead they blamed them for weakening China's position in the world.

Their cursory treatment of the conquests derived from the assumption that Qing expansion was simply a culmination of earlier Chinese dynastic projects, not a breakthrough that redefined the character of the Chinese state. The teleology of nationalist history implied that the Qing had merely fulfilled the mission of its predecessors to encompass all the territory that "naturally" belonged to China. The modern Chinese state then inherited this space and made it the basis of China's imagined community. Modern textbook accounts that stress the continuity of the Qing with earlier dynasties implicitly assume that this remarkable territorial expansion made little difference.

But, as I have argued, Qing expansion was not simply a linear outgrowth of previous dynasties. It represented a sharp break with the strategic aims and military capabilities of the Ming dynasty. The different character of the ruling elite, their success in mobilizing interior China's resources, and the empire's diplomacy in Eurasia made it possible. This expansion in turn had long-lasting effects on the Qing's socioeconomic structures, administrative institutions, and self-concept. The Qing emperors and generals themselves believed that they had achieved something unprecedented, but they linked their achievements to those of earlier dynasties with a successful project of rewriting the history of the conquest. In the interests of creating continuity, they masked the radical implications of their achievements. Nationalists built on the legacy left by Qing official historians to create the version of China's history that predominates today.

In the medium term, the end of the Qing conquests created some of the elements that led to the collapse of the empire in the nineteenth to early twentieth century. From a longer perspective, these conquests, by fundamentally redefining China's territorial and cultural identity, laid the foundation on which the modern nation-state rebuilt itself. We have seen how the rulers developed their self-conception as universal monarchs, embracing multiple peoples with distinct but overlapping cultural traditions in the course of the expansion. There was no single sharp turning point in cultural definition, but rather an evolving consciousness of a Heaven-endowed mission to incorporate many, but not all, of the cultures of Eurasia under a single gaze.

Defining borders and eliminating rivals also meant limiting imperial claims to legitimation. Despite the emperor's boast to encompass "all under Heaven," frontier writers like Qishiyi knew better. Wei Yuan drew on his knowledge of the many rivals to Qing power across the continent. By using foreign consultants to map the extent of the empire's territory, the Qing rulers had also implicitly recognized that they occupied only one part of the earth's surface, a global space measured with universal coordinates of longitude and latitude. From Kangxi's mappings to Wei Yuan's invocation of frontier warfare, the theme of imperial expansion developed continuously as a founding element in the construction of a new national consciousness.

Here I trace briefly the historiography of the conquests in three of the nation-states that now partition the steppe.

Modern Chinese scholars have produced abundant writings on China's northwestern regions. Considering that Tibet, Mongolia, and Xinjiang together account for only 3.6 percent of the PRC's population today, scholarly print per capita must be higher here than for any other region of China. A recent index lists 8,031 articles on the subject published from 1900 to 1988, and another lists over 7,500 books and articles on the Qing dynasty alone.[24] Needless to say, I have only skimmed the surface of this vast literature.

Regardless of the political regime, this historical writing demonstrates remarkable continuity. Ever since 1763, when the Qianlong emperor wrote his "Record of the Entire Zunghar Tribe," Qing, Republican, Taiwanese, and PRC scholars have taken very similar approaches. Han-centered nationalism overrides other methodologies, whether of the *kaozheng*, nationalist, or Marxist-Leninist school. The common narrative thread of pre-destined "unity" links works produced under very different political circumstances. Why is there such uncanny agreement on this basic theme?

"History" in most languages has a dual meaning: the actual lived experience of people in the past and the remembered (written or oral) record of the past. The two meanings are cyclically intertwined. Our lived experience, decisions, intentions, and ideals in the present moment derive from how we interpret our past experience. Likewise, present experience shapes historical interpretation, either as scholarly monograph or as personal memory. In reciprocating motion, present and past influence each other as our pasts and our presents cyclically evolve. Neither totally determines the other, but neither stands alone. The words used in historical production, like all words, are empty vessels, signifiers constantly being refilled with new meanings but never entirely losing the old ones.[25] In interpreting the Qing conquest, historians have continued a cyclical ritual process, perpetuating long-standing myths while renewing them under changed conditions. I discussed earlier how mythmaking began as soon as the conquest was over. Now we begin the hermeneutic circle from its endpoint, looking back from our century to the origins of this perspective. The grand cycle of interpretation is unending; no one has the final word. Whether new perspectives are an improvement over older ones is for the reader to decide.

Russian, Chinese, and modern Mongolian scholars drastically disagree about the meaning of the defeat of the Zunghars. Chinese writers see Qianlong's victory as a natural process of incorporation of "our Mongols" into a Chinese state, and they regard Xinjiang as having always been Chinese territory. They view the Zunghars as mere rebels, deny the existence of widespread anti-Qing sentiments among the Mongols, and ignore the fact that Xinjiang was never permanently controlled by a Chinese dynasty until the Qing. Russian writers call the Qing an aggressive, expanding empire, and they look for signs of class struggle in Mongolian nationalist resistance against the feudal Qing state. One could say that the Russian scholars seem to be more Marxist and the Chinese more nationalist, but Russian writers justify the expansion of their empire, too, without trying to claim that Siberia "always belonged" to Russia. Contemporary Mongolian scholars assert the essential unity of the Mongolian people from earliest times, playing down their real divisiveness.

These nationalist perspectives projected back from modern times contaminate our understanding, for this was not a truly "nationalist" struggle on any side. It was a state-building struggle in which the military and political power of the rulers counted for much more than the nationalities of the people involved. All sides made appeals for mass support at times and invoked symbols of ethnic unity, including Chinggis Khan and Chinese emperors, but the outcome was decided by armies, diplomacy, and economic pressure, not by the modern weapons of newspapers, broadcasting, and mass mobilization.

"Mongol," "Manchu," "Chinese," "Uighur," and "Hui" nationalities in the modern sense did not consistently join the same side of the struggle or express uniform views. They acted to preserve their interests as towns, tribes, families, and individuals during a contest for power among coalitions of elites from disparate backgrounds. To appreciate the true complexity of the Qing's expansive drive is to gain insight into how the multiethnic empire of the Qing differed from the modern Chinese nationalist state.

Wei Yuan, as I have noted, put in place the standard account followed by historians in China ever since.[26] But there are some interesting discrepancies worth comment. From the viewpoint of PRC historians, he committed two grave "errors." They criticize his "class biases" for favoring the repression of popular rebellion, but they find his questioning of the permanence of China's boundaries to be even more serious. He wrote that much of the territory of China defined by the Nerchinsk treaty was "wasteland" newly entered on the registers, and he noted that Taiwan "from ancient times was not part of China." The editors of the 1984 Beijing edition of the *Shengwuji* insist that "these are undoubtedly completely mistaken assertions, which do not accord with historical truth."[27]

Wei Yuan was, of course, correct, but the idea that Qing expansion incorporated new territories violates nationalist myth. Nationalists must claim the Qing boundaries as eternally fixed, endowed by Heaven or by the course of history with natural legitimacy. The Qianlong emperor would smile to realize how successfully he had instilled this myth in the modern Chinese mind.

Dai Yi's *Concise History of the Qing Dynasty* is representative of historical work in the People's Republic of China through the 1980s.[28] The tone of his treatment of the Central Eurasian conquests is indicated in his chapter titles: "Unification of the Minority Peoples of the Border Region and the Strengthening and Development of a Multinational Empire"; "Qing Suppression of the Zunghar Galdan's Divisive Influence and the Unification of the Northwest Region"; "Russian Aggression against Our Northern and Western Borders and Galdan's Mobilizing of the Nationalities in a Divisive [*fenlie:* splittist] Rebellion"; "Tsarist Russia's Aggression against the Zunghar Region and the Zunghar Army and People's Anti-Russian Struggles." His account focuses entirely on the creation of unity, not on the expansion of territory.

Use of the term "unification" *(tongyi)*, never "conquest" *(zhengqu)*, is de rigueur among Chinese historians. We may also note Dai's highly anti-Russian emphasis. In Dai's interpretation, the Zunghar people loved their territory and resisted Russian aggression against it. They rejected Russian efforts to entice them to submit to the Tsar; Dai interprets this as resistance by "our country's Mongols" against Russian aggression. Both Galdan and his enemies, the Khalkhas, resisted Russian attack in the 1670s, but Dai Yi's real hero is the Jebzongdanba Khutukhtu, who induced the Khalkhas to submit to the Kangxi emperor. Dai initially praises Galdan for resisting the Russian invasion, but after Galdan turned against the Qing, Dai stresses the support given by the Russians to Galdan (even though there is little evidence of this). The implicit territory defended by "our country's Mongols" is the maximal extent of Qing power attained only after the 1760s conquests. Dai writes his story as an inevitable progression leading finally toward the borders of the mid-eighteenth century.

Modern Chinese scholarship also makes moral judgments of personalities, reminiscent of the "praise and blame" historiography of the classical period. Ma Ruheng's article on "the [reactionary] life of Amursana" tells the story of the last Mongol prince to challenge Qing rule over the steppe. In Ma's view, Amursana had "totally negative historical significance" because he split the unity of the minority peoples. Chinese historians, says Ma, need to refute Russian and Mongolian historians who praise Amursana for resisting Qing aggression. Ma presumes that nearly all the Zunghars wanted to gain peace by submitting to the Qing. Only Amursana's "wild ambition" *(yexin)* for personal power led him to revolt.[29] As we know, the full story is much more complex. Amursana first called in Qing aid to help him seize power against his rivals, and later rebelled when the

Qing rulers deliberately undercut his efforts to unify the Mongols. The Qing emperor insisted on a military campaign against Amursana, rejecting his cautious advisers' counsel. Qing levies on the Mongol allies for this campaign touched off a rebellion among the Eastern Mongols. Even though Qing troops quickly defeated Amursana, the military struggle itself cannot be reduced simply to his lust for power.

Ma, like Dai, also pursues the anti-Russian theme. In the view of both, Russian aims were unequivocally expansionist, with the purpose of using Amursana to control Zungharia. This interpretation is an obvious allusion to contemporary Sino-Russian conflicts. Ma correctly notes that Siberian governors observed the Zunghar Mongols closely in the 1750s, but he credits the Russians with far too much active agency. They mainly watched and waited, and did not intervene directly in Zungharian affairs.

Ma concludes that "Amursana's revolt was not a military uprising but an effort to split the nationalities backed by the Russians" *(minzu fenlie panluan)*, and quotes Mao Zedong's canonical statement, "Our country is a large and populous nation composed of many different nationalities." He continues:

> The Qing dynasty was a period when our unified nation of many nationalities became increasingly consolidated and developed. Qianlong's suppression of Amursana's revolt continued the tasks of Kangxi and Yongzheng of protecting the unity of the nation and waged a righteous war to resist Russian aggression. This battle not only strengthened and developed the unity of the multinational state but also coincided with the demands for unity of each of the nationalities and their common wish to oppose splittism. Therefore the victory in the war against rebellion was inevitable.[30]

This interpretation exhibits clearly the main traits of nationalist historiography: its belief in a progressive evolution toward unity, its moralistic judgment of historical actors by the standard of popular unity, and its unquestioned assumption that the multiple nationalities composing the modern Chinese nation have always shown undivided loyalty to imperial regimes.

Soviet and Mongolian Attacks on Qing Aggression

Soviet historiography and Mongolian historiography share many of these assumptions, but their evaluation of the Qing is diametrically opposed. I. Ia. Zlatkin's *History of the Zunghar Khanate, 1635–1758* is the most de-

tailed analytical study available in a Western language. Even though he
does not read Chinese, he provides very useful references to Russian archival sources.[31] He rejects Chinese and earlier European interpretations of the
Zunghars as aggressive conquerors of other Mongols. Instead, he tries to
demonstrate the fundamental unity of Western and Eastern Mongols with
the Tibetan Buddhist church against the expansionist Manchu state. He
points out that the Kangxi emperor confirmed Galdan's title of Boshoktu
Khan in 1679, putting them for a while on good terms. But the Qing's main
goal was to prevent the formation of a unified steppe power combining the
Western and Eastern Mongols. Galdan's attack on the Tüsiyetü Khan of
eastern Mongolia led Kangxi to vow destruction of the Zunghars because,
in essence, Galdan was trying to create an independent Mongolian nation,
and the Chinese were determined to destroy it. Zlatkin, like the Chinese,
believes in the natural "unity of peoples" as an underlying force in history,
but he draws the boundaries differently. For him, the united Mongols unsuccessfully asserted their desire for autonomy against the coercive force of
the Manchu state.[32]

Mongolian historians in independent Mongolia put the case even more
strongly. For Mongolian and Soviet historians, the idea of China as a unified multinational state including the Mongolians constitutes the "Maoist
falsification of history," which continues the Sinocentrism of the imperial
period that began two thousand years ago.[33] They trace this Sinocentrism
back to the Mandate of Heaven idea of the Zhou, which puts China at the
center of civilization and regards the non-Han peoples of the northern frontier as no better than beasts. At the same time, Chinese historians argue
that the northern nomadic people were always part of the Chinese cultural
and national realm, so China's wars against them were internal suppressions of rebellions, not wars against an external enemy. By contrast, Mongolian historians insist that the Chinese and Mongols always were completely distinct political, geographical, and cultural units of equal status,
demarcated by the Great Wall. Ironically, modern Chinese nationalist historiography, because it inherits the Qing definition of boundaries, has to
play down the cultural significance of the Great Wall demarcation, while
Mongolian historians overstress its importance in order to protect their autonomy.

For Mongolians and Soviets, the Chinese have been consistently expansionist, using a variety of strategies to penetrate and subjugate the nomads.
They view the uprisings of Amursana and Chingünjav as national liberation movements, not "bandits' revolts." These were "popular movements"
that allegedly involved all the classes and strata of Mongolian society. Vacillating feudal princes joined the Qing, but impoverished herdsmen fought

most consistently. Here we have the classic combination of Marxist-Leninist class analysis with nationalist history, in which the feudal classes become unreliable representatives of the nation while the "masses" become its most passionate defenders. We can recognize parallel arguments in Chinese historians' discussions of nineteenth-century China's relations with the West, with the decadent Manchu ruling elite substituted for the Mongolian nobility.

By contrast, C. R. Bawden points out that the loss of independence was not seen in earlier times as such a tragedy as it is today:

> For the Mongols, the Manchu conquest was to mean, in modern terms, the extinction of their independence, but it is reasonable to ask what sort of independence this was, and whether, in the conditions of the seventeenth century, the loss was a true one. It is only in relatively recent years that national independence for all has come to be considered the political *summum bonum*, and it may well be that we, together with present-day Mongol historians, are . . . applying modern values to a situation to which they are not wholly applicable, by looking on the loss of independence as an evil in itself.

He argues that in the seventeenth century, there was no "cohesive sense of Mongol nationality . . . Loyalties were limited and personal," and the Mongols "had no sense of community."[34] Bawden's view is too extreme, in my opinion, but he indicates how modern interpretations exaggerate the extent of common national feeling among the Mongols before the twentieth century.

Empires, Nations, and Peoples

Clearly the Sino-Soviet split of the 1960s has affected these divergent evaluations of Qing history, but the differences go much deeper. Even in the 1980s, as the reform period began and ideological control loosened up, historians repeated the same themes. The basic assumptions about historical change on both sides are strikingly non-materialist for supposed Marxist-Leninists. They display more a search for a *volkisch* "spirit of a people" than careful attention to basic material factors. Although all three schools invoke class struggle and claim a division between nationalist "masses" and decadent "elites," they provide very little evidence of a real evolution of class consciousness based on changing modes of production. The effort to define stages of development is far less prominent in histories of this topic than the defense of the unity of peoples against foreign aggression. Until the 1980s, the three communist states whose borders met here devoted most of their historiography of the region to defining their national territory against one another. Boundary maintenance won over proletarian solidarity.

We may summarize the characteristic features of this type of historiography with four terms: *teleology, moral evaluation, natural frontiers,* and *essentialized identities.*

1. Teleology reads back causation of events in the past from present outcomes. It is not merely "present-mindedness": all historians are influenced by the concerns of their day. This particular form of present-mindedness takes the current outcome as determined and traces how past processes led up to it. It presupposes an underlying historical process independent of human action that culminates in the nation-state. It is, in effect, a Hegelian assumption about historical change, of which Marxism is only one variant. Its primary flaws are anachronism and excessive determinism. Anachronism means, for example, attributing "class consciousness" to peoples in a society without a capitalist, or even feudal, mode of production. Determinism means the assumption that those who resisted state expansion inevitably had to suffer defeat, which is to ignore the multiple contingent events that shaped the result.

2. We may also note a very strong concern with moral evaluation. Those defined as "rebels" are morally vicious, and historians like to highlight their personal weaknesses. The Chinese historians do not give the Zunghars credit for a positive ideology or a coherent program. There is a noticeable contrast between former Chinese historical treatment of Han peasant rebels, like the Taiping, who used to be seen as anticipating mass peasant revolution, and the treatment of non-Han rebels as "splittists" who endangered the unity of Han and minority peoples.

3. Territorial boundaries are assumed to be natural and predetermined, and very close to contemporary state borders. For the Chinese, "aggression" (by Russians) means the violation of these virtual boundaries even before they have been negotiated. For the Russians and Mongolians, Qing "aggression" means expansion beyond the current borders of the PRC. All national historians have invoked the idea of "natural frontiers" to justify their state's territorial control. Lucien Febvre argued strongly against this concept, showing how all state borders were constructions of a particular period.[35] Nevertheless, some states could make more plausible claims than others, since many of their "natural" boundaries followed clear geographical defining points such as mountains, rivers, and oceans. These claims become much more dubious in Central Asia, where there are no such obvious delimiting factors.

4. Likewise, ethnic identities are naturalized, essentialized, and seen as fixed. Nationalist historians try to establish a continuous genealogy by tracing names, under the assumption that "Oirats" in the Yuan, for example, are the same people as the "Weilate" in the Ming and the "Elute" in the Qing. But many of these ethnonyms referred to confederations of many different peoples, not to a single, fixed entity.

Each of these four features contains a kernel of truth. All historians are present-minded in some sense; moral evaluation is an essential component of historical interpretation; state boundaries did matter in the eighteenth century; and there was some sense of ethnic identity among the Mongols. But using these assumptions uncritically to describe inevitable outcomes of a universal historical process instead of contingent human creations gives us a highly misleading view.

By contrast, first, we need to reintroduce contingency and avoid anachronism. Empathetic identification tries to see events from the viewpoint of the actors themselves, who were not certain of the outcome. Even their goals were not fixed in advance but evolved within a fluid situation. We should be skeptical of the assumption of an underlying impersonal historical process uninfluenced by individual action.

Second, we should take a more objective stance, giving equal weight to all the players, without preconceived judgments. We must try to reconstruct the interests and motivations of the states and actors in their own terms and not interpret them as stages on the way to national states.

Third, we should see boundary consciousness as evolving and constructed, not naturally fixed. The idea of state boundaries was an emerging consciousness in eighteenth-century China, and the narratives of these territorial definitions built the framework for later nationalist historiography, but the boundaries of the Qing empire were not "there" waiting to be discovered. We should not neglect the arbitrariness in the political and social construction of boundaries of the state.

Fourth, ethnic and tribal definitions were likewise historical products of contingent interactions. They were not "primordial." As in modern discussions of the creation of ethnicity or the "invention of tradition," they came from strategies of groups looking for the most beneficial ways to define themselves in a shifting cultural context.

Finally, material factors need close attention. Access to food, water, animals, weaponry, and commercial goods was critical to the survival of these states. All three of them competed to increase their "stateness" in similar ways. They faced constraints of the natural environment, which affected productive use of resources, and of the social and political environment, which affected the willingness of primary producers to yield resources to state builders.

Today, peoples, nations, and civilizations define themselves consistently only in terms of what they are not. Lacking confidence in the stability of our own personal, social, and national identities, we look for, or invent, peoples conceived as radically different from ourselves. If we do not know securely what we have in common, surely we can agree that we have little in common with the barbarian, the primitive, the Oriental, the fundamentalist, the terrorist: in short, the fetishized Other. Michel Foucault pointed out how Western society since the eighteenth century has defined reason primarily by contrasting it with madness. Hayden White has discussed how, likewise, western Europeans examined what it meant to be civilized by creating the image of the Wild Man—an image first of the untamed primitive in the Middle Ages, which was transformed into the "noble savage" in the period of Romanticism. Even in modern social theory this technique persists. Barrington Moore argues that if we cannot agree on what kinds of societies are the best, or the most likely to provide positive values of justice, freedom, and wealth, we can at least agree on the causes of cruelty, poverty, and injustice.[36]

The power of negative thinking can be a genuine effort to examine critically the unexamined assumptions of modern culture. It can be a deconstructive tool, designed to show how Western imperial culture, in particular, has created the fictional Oriental in its own image, for its own imperial interests.[37] But seldom has this form of analysis been applied anywhere outside the modern West. If critics confine themselves to subverting Western values by showing how they depend ultimately on no fixed common core but only on a series of relative, shifting oppositions, they still implicitly find "the West" a privileged site of analysis. Why not look at Asia through the same lens?

Recent discussions of the rise of nationalism share many of the same strengths and limitations. A burgeoning literature now examines the rise of nationalist ideologies in western Europe and the Americas. Different analysts find different times and places of origin for nationalism: Benedict Anderson focuses, for example, on the role of print culture among the creole elites of nineteenth-century Latin America. Liah Greenfeld turns to sixteenth-century England. Erich S. Gruen finds "national identity" even in republican Rome. There, too, Romans sought to define their identity by contrast with the peoples they both admired and distrusted the most: the Greeks. They adopted a legend tracing the origins of Rome to Trojan, not Greek, ancestors in order to "[fit] the Romans within the matrix of Greek legend that stretched back to remote antiquity while marking a differentiation and projecting a separate identity."[38]

Once again, the use of definition by negation proves doubly productive. Nations and their peoples do in fact define themselves by opposition. Scholars of nationalism can undermine spurious claims to essential identities, claims which distort history and can lead to unthinking hostility. But only very recently has this analysis been applied to Asia, and China in particular. Dru Gladney has shown very provocatively how the definition of minorities in contemporary China as eroticized Others serves to discipline the Han majority. Edward Friedman points to the collapse of a secure "Han" identity and the growth of rival regional definitions, centered on new archaeological interpretations and the exaltation of regional cultures.[39]

The present discussion of the place of the northwest frontier in the formation of the Han identity and the role of the Qing dynasty complements these insights. The Qing completion of the northwest conquest reconfigured the identities of "China" and the "Han." The eighteenth century was not the age of nationalism in China, but it set the framework within which the late-nineteenth-century definitions of the Chinese nation had to operate. This framework included the definition of boundaries; the fixed racial and genealogical identities of Han, Manchus, Muslims, and Tibetans; and the imperial project of establishing control over multiple peoples, incorporating the non-Han peoples as subordinate Others.

Qing scholars who analyze imperial ideology should not look at the fully formed ideology of the eighteenth century in isolation. This structure of symbols, texts, inscriptions, and pronouncements defined behavior and thought for the imperial elite, its officials, and at least some of its subjects, but it evolved significantly from the seventeenth century to the eighteenth. During its construction, the Qing rulers competed with rivals who constructed their own ideologies. It was a temporary product of a particular time. By the end of the eighteenth century, the Qing rulers' tone of complacency, wholeness, and completion expressed satisfaction at the successful defeat of their antagonists. Yet without barbarian enemies, they found themselves without a solution for the new challenges of the nineteenth century.

15

State Building in
Europe and Asia

THE Qing conquests decisively changed the history of the Chinese empire, the Russian empire, and the Central Eurasian peoples in between. I have analyzed the Qing–Zunghar conflict as a process of competitive state building, in which both sides had to mobilize economic and military resources, build administrative organizations, and develop ideologies of conquest and rule. The Qing was not an established state facing a disorganized group of "bandits." In the early seventeenth century, the Manchus constructed a state apparatus designed for military conquest. Expansion of their state's territory remained the primary task of the dynasty's rulers until the mid-eighteenth century. At the same time, the Mongols who rejected Manchu domination also created an increasingly "statelike" apparatus of rule in Central Eurasia, one that grew from a loose tribal confederation to approach the structure of a settled regime. Both Manchus and Zunghars built a capital city, promoted agricultural settlement, sponsored trade, and developed bureaucratic procedures as part and parcel of their constant military campaigning. War fed the state as the state supplied the materials for war. The Manchus, once they had conquered the core of China, had far greater economic resources at their disposal than the Zunghars, and they inherited a transportation network that linked the crucial resources of men, grain, and money in dense systems of exchange. The Zunghars had to collect much more fragmented materials over a vast, unintegrated space, and this made their state-building project much more challenging and, ultimately, ephemeral.

Still, the Zunghars were able to hold out for a surprisingly long time against the Qing juggernaut because of two vital factors that protected them: mobility and distance. The high cost of land transport prevented the Manchus from extending their reach beyond the Great Wall unless they had Mongolian allies. Much of the Qing project through the Yongzheng reign was devoted to winning over these allies with economic lures, diplomatic alliances, and military force. Yongzheng's humiliating defeat in 1731 illustrates how the poverty and breadth of Central Eurasia imposed severe limits on the extension of Qing power.

But Yongzheng's domestic reforms laid the groundwork for future expansion by increasing bureaucratic efficiency. The Grand Council and secret palace memorials allowed Qianlong to respond quickly to economic and military needs in the far-flung northwestern domains. The establishment of civil administration in Gansu, followed by the incorporation of Qinghai, paved the way for Qianlong's later incorporation of Xinjiang. After nursing its wounds, the empire was prepared to strike back in the mid-eighteenth century. Despite a severe drought all over the northwest, officials mobilized grain, horses, soldiers, civilians, nomads, grass, uniforms, and weaponry to crush their determined foe once and for all. The steady construction of this logistical network in the midst of battle and diplomacy laid the basis for the unprecedented Qing expansion.

For their part, the Zunghars desperately tried to gather every possible resource to defend their state. They could draw on the Ili valley's fields and the oases of Turkestan. They extracted tribute from Siberian tribes until the Russians drove them out. Central Eurasian trade was a key component of the Zunghar state, as it had been for every nomadic empire. The "Bukharan" caravan traders connected the Zunghars to Russian territories and the great cities of the south. Tibet and Kokonor provided both grain and pastureland and the legitimating ideology of the Tibetan Buddhist church. Other resources lay widely scattered, from the valleys of the Irtysh, Orkhon, and other rivers to the salt and potential golden sands of lakes Yamysh and Balkash. Drawing all of these together would have taxed the greatest of rulers, even if he had not faced the ominous threat of the two huge settled empires closing in on either side.

As luck would have it, both sides did for a time have highly competent, dynamic, aggressive leadership. The Kangxi, Yongzheng, and Qianlong emperors, each in his own way, coordinated effectively the multiple organizations necessary to carry out the conquest. But they met their match in Galdan, Tsewang Rabdan, and Galdan Tseren, who devised daring responses to Qing pressure. Leadership alone did not determine the outcome, but neither was the Zunghar defeat an inevitable result of structural imbalances. The deeds of the Chinese emperors have been well recognized. At the risk of offending Chinese nationalists, I have stressed the foresight and determination of the Zunghar leaders so that their lesser-known story can be told.

The Political Ecology of Frontier Conquest

This account allows us to look at the expansion of the Qing empire on all its frontiers and to compare Qing activities with those of the other states of Eurasia. This model of political ecology brings together four crucial features of Qing military expansion: frontier relations with nomadic state builders, military strategy, logistics, and negotiations with neighboring empires.[1] In each of these areas the Qing followed precedents but went well beyond them.

The term "frontier" has two opposing meanings: it can designate either a broad zone of multiple cultural interactions or a linear border dividing two states. The first usage is predominantly American, the second mainly western European (as in the French *frontière*). The modern Chinese term *bian-jiang* combines both connotations. *Bian* signifies the periphery or borderland zone, while *jiang* (a character made up of a measuring bow and fields with berms separating them) clearly implies territorial separation. Both ideas are embedded in China's history. The Qing project was to eliminate the ambiguous frontier zone and replace it with a clearly defined border through military control, commercial integration, and diplomatic negotiations with border states.

Frontier Relations. Owen Lattimore noted that steppe nomadic empires "follow like a shadow" Chinese centralized regimes, and Thomas Barfield has elaborated upon his thesis.[2] The plausibility of this thesis rests on ecological foundations. The conditions of life in the steppe favor fragmentation. Nomads live off their livestock and move seasonally between pasturelands. If there is enough grazing land, a would-be steppe leader cannot easily establish domination over other tribal leaders because they can simply move away. So tribal rivalries and fragmentation are common. But occasionally great united steppe empires form. Why is this possible? Great empires require both personal charisma and a material basis. The resources for these empires came from outside the steppe, and primarily from China, the richest neighboring settled civilization.

As Chinese dynasties rose and fell, steppe empires rose and fell with them. Contrary to the common Chinese view, it was almost never the ambition of a steppe leader to conquer China itself. Steppe leaders staged raids on the Chinese frontier to plunder it for their own purposes. It took a long time for the Chinese to work out an effective response. Large military campaigns gained brief successes but failed in the long run. The "tribute system" worked as an institutionalized protection racket, in which Chinese traded rich silks, porcelain, jewelry, and money for bad horses, at a loss, in return for nomads' promises to stop raids.

This regular process broke down when a steppe leader lost control of his subordinate Khans, or when a Chinese dynasty at the end of its cycle was too weak to keep up tribute payments. The collapse of a Chinese dynasty threatened the stability of the steppe empire. This relationship explains why, for example, the Uighurs intervened to keep the Tang dynasty alive after the An Lushan rebellion of 755 CE. The Yuan dynasty, which did conquer all of China, is in this perspective the major exception to this pattern, not the rule.

Under the "Manchurian alternative," like the Khitan Liao (907–1124 CE) and Jurchen Jin (1115–1234 CE) dynasties, semi-nomadic leaders conquered part of China and part of the steppe. They set up a kind of dual rule, with one form of administration and army for China and another for their nomad followers. Barfield extends the Manchurian model to cover the Qing dynasty as well.

How closely does Barfield's model of frontier relationships apply to the Qing–Zunghar relationship? The Qing was a "Manchurian" dynasty in origin, and its rulers did establish a dual administrative system, especially in the military realm. They used both the banner system and the Han Green Standard troops for domestic control and frontier expansion. But the Qing rulers did not confine themselves to the North China plain, as the Liao and Jin did, and they did not face any rivals in the Mongolian steppe after the mid-eighteenth century. Like the anomalous Yuan, in Barfield's schema, the Qing rulers expanded far beyond the limits of the steppe–frontier interaction model. Parallels with earlier dynasties are only partial.

Commercial relations on the frontier also display only partial parallels to earlier experiences. We may note especially the continued efforts by the Zunghars to use the tribute system to increase the resources of their state. They requested that more embassies be allowed to go to Beijing, each with as many as two thousand men. Once Qing officials perceived the Zunghars as a threat, they severely restricted the number of tribute embassies. On the one hand, these embassies brought revenue for the Zunghars, as they did for earlier nomadic state builders. On the other hand, the Qing did not have to buy off the nomadic raiders because of their military weakness. Except for a short period in the early eighteenth century, the Qing court kept military pressure on its rivals. Trade was a useful complement to military expansion, not an inadequate substitute for it.

Omeljan Pritsak gives more weight than Barfield to the autonomous activity of traders in forming new states in the steppe. He has argued that an "international trading class" interacting with the nomadic Khazar confederation created the state of Rus' in the tenth century. Barfield, however, tends to examine only relations between nomadic state builders and Chinese officials and merchants, whereas many caravan traders were beyond Chinese state control. In our case, the Zunghars made substantial efforts to draw on commercial resources beyond the Chinese tribute system. They established contacts with "Bukharan" caravan traders, and they aimed to negotiate profitable terms of trade with Russians in Siberia. Our model of frontier state formation needs to incorporate at least four separate actors: nomadic state builders, caravan traders, and both the Chinese and Russian states, instead of only two.

Military Strategy. The classic nomad military response to an approaching Chinese army was the same as Mao Zedong's: withdrawal in the face of superior numbers. Unlike Chinese armies, which depended on supplies from agricultural settlements, the nomads could simply move away until the Chinese had stretched their supply lines too far, then turn around and ambush them. This practice led to numerous Chinese defeats. Han Wudi's long expedition to Central Asia to obtain the "blood-sweating" horses of Ferghana is the classic example. He did get his horses, but only 20 percent of the troops returned. The main cause of losses to the army was inadequate supplies, not combat casualties.[3]

To annihilate nomadic armies, Qing generals had to block their escape routes. They sent three separate armies against Galdan in a pincer attack, hoping to trap Galdan's troops from the rear while the main force attacked in front. This strategy, originated by the Mongols under Chinggis Khan, required difficult feats of coordination of large masses of troops across great distances.[4] It succeeded, but just barely.

Logistics. Massive logistical preparation was the key to such mobilization. The inability of the Chinese to supply large armies in the field for long periods of time created a fundamental barrier to major steppe expeditions. From the Han dynasty up through the end of the seventeenth century, no major military force launched from the core of China could spend much more than ninety days in the steppe. Kangxi's first expedition against Galdan lasted roughly sixty days, his second one ninety-nine days, and his third ninety-one days. In each case he had to turn back because of supply limitations. Until they overcame this logistical barrier, Chinese rulers could never permanently eliminate nomadic autonomy by military means. The Qing only crossed this threshold in the mid-eighteenth century by building a chain of military magazines and supply lines into the steppe.

The resources for these supply routes had to come either from subordinated nomads or from the Chinese peasantry of the northwest, but both of these poor groups could provide only limited amounts. By the mid-eighteenth century, increasing demands for horses, sheep, and human labor touched off the Chingünjav revolt. Military demands on northwestern peasants further increased their suffering from famine and drought. Only the commercialization of the eighteenth-century economy as a whole allowed Qing officials to purchase large supplies on the markets of northwest China and ship them out to Xinjiang. Even though the price of grain in Gansu tripled, the empire-wide civilian granary system, another crucial innovation of the mid-Qing, was able to relieve enough famine-stricken peasants to prevent revolt.

Diplomacy. All Qing efforts would have been in vain if the Zunghars had had unlimited space in which to retreat. Instead, the Sino-Russian treaties constrained their mobility. Both empires agreed to set boundaries and to return refugees who crossed their borders, hindering the Zunghars from recruiting migrants, refugees, or deserters and preventing them from withdrawing out of the reach of Qing troops. Thus the Nerchinsk and Kiakhta treaties, often viewed only as an episode in Sino-Russian relations, made possible the closure of the steppe. The presence of the Russian empire in Siberia rendered Qing—steppe relations radically different from those in any earlier period.

In summary, this model of Qing expansion unites frontier relations, military strategy, logistics, and diplomacy to explain why only in the eighteenth century could a dynasty ruled from Beijing eliminate its nomadic rivals and create the largest empire in Chinese history. Unlike nationalist histories, which view the Qing as the inexorable culmination of earlier imperial projects, this perspective stresses the unpredictability of frontier conquest. Qing emperors, generals, and officials knew well that they were venturing into uncharted terrain, militarily and politically. Only later did they reinterpret all the events as predestined. Before placing the Qing conquests within Chinese and world-historical contexts, we need to recapture the uncertainty that faced the proponents of this unprecedented Great Enterprise.

I turn next to a critique of two comparative historical traditions: political theories that rely primarily on the western European experience, and theories of nomadic state formation. Usually these theories do not address each other's concerns at all. The first focus on the experience of Europe since 1500 and, later, the rest of the modern world; the second address primarily the Middle East and Central Eurasia in the premodern era. The Qing–Zunghar conflict, however, includes elements of both. Here I give only a schematic summary of some of the theoretical perspectives and suggest what can be done with them.

European, Chinese, and Inner Asian Models

Perhaps the most common approach in the first tradition is to deny the relevance of state building at all to most of Asia before the European impact in the nineteenth century. Asian state building, like nation formation, is seen as a derivative phenomenon, driven primarily by the "response to the West." Theorists tend to consider China, India, and the Ottomans as "agrarian empires," under a separate category from European "states." Yet the reasons for distinguishing "empires" from "states" seem unconvincing.

To be sure, obvious differences in scale appear to support this distinction. The Qing at its maximal extent controlled a land area of over 11 million square kilometers, larger than all of Europe to the Urals, and its population of about 300 million in 1800 was approximately the same as Europe's. No European state (except Russia) approached even one-tenth of this size. But this distinction looks only at the end result, not the formation of the Qing state. During its century and a half of creation, from circa 1616 to 1760, the scope of imperial control grew from a few thousand tribal people to a huge empire of hundreds of millions. In the sixteenth to eighteenth centuries, European states also expanded rapidly, either on the continent, as with Sweden, Prussia, and Muscovy, or overseas, like Portugal, Spain, the Netherlands, England, and France. If we take expansion itself as the common element and not simply size at the end, we can find elements of comparison. Rulers seeking to increase their span of control faced similar problems: how to win allies, how to mobilize resources, how to defend against rivals. Less important than ultimate size was the relative rate and direction of expansion. England and France developed more slowly on land than Prussia and Muscovy, but they still shared features with them.

Another political approach, strongly influenced by later nationalist historiography, assumes that western European states incorporated more "homogeneous" populations than either eastern Europeans or the non-Western world. But more recently, many historians have come to realize that national homogeneity in France or England was made, not born.[5] Multiple religious, economic, and social traditions survived within the modern nation. The recent reassertion by regions within European nation-states of their distinctive characteristics reveals the ineradicable multiplicity of state and nation building.[6] In this respect, too, European state and nation building comes to resemble more closely that of empires. We cannot so firmly divide apparently ramshackle empires from streamlined early modern states. European states had more patchwork under the surface, and empires had more homogeneity, than we once thought.

Eric Hobsbawm and David Landes make the opposite argument: that Europe was more diverse than Asia. For Landes, the fragmentation of European states allowed for greater intellectual, commercial, and technological creativity because entrepreneurial and dissident groups could escape oppression by fleeing to a rival prince.[7] Hobsbawm claims that nationalist ideologies originated in nineteenth-century Europe as a homogenizing project, driven by the need to bring together people in political communities unified by common languages and historical traditions. The great conflicts of Europe were a product of its diversity, which created unsolvable tensions when peoples of different languages, religions, and cultures lived as neighbors on the same soil. By contrast, "China, Korea and Japan . . . are indeed among the extremely rare examples of historic states composed of a population that is ethnically almost or entirely homogeneous." These Asian states, in his view, had much less difficulty adopting nationalism because they were already more homogeneous than Europe, and had inherited longstanding bureaucratic state structures.[8] Here the Marxist historian and the worshipper of capitalism both betray their Eurocentric biases. Clearly, we can find just as much diversity within Asian societies as in Europe, and there was no easy transition from premodern to modern nation-states in any East Asian country. Japan, Korea, and Han China each contained many conflicting social and cultural elements. The northwest frontier of China displayed these conflicts in the sharpest, most violent fashion, making it a useful diagnostic for related tensions elsewhere. By this measure, too, Asian empires and kingdoms are not radically distinct from Europe.

Immanuel Wallerstein also sharply divides empires and the "world system" of interacting European states.[9] Wallerstein argues that during the eighteenth century, the expanding European world system drew into its orbit four regions that had previously been unconnected "external arenas": Russia, the Ottoman empire, India, and West Africa.[10] This incorporation of the periphery in the eighteenth century, Wallerstein argues, later characterized the European impact on China in the nineteenth century.

Hobsbawm, Wallerstein, and Landes all find in the fragmentation of Europe the source of the dynamism that led it to conquer the world. Unlike nationalists, they stress the interaction of the state units in Europe *with one another* rather than the distinctive characteristics of a single state. But they limit this dynamic only to Europe. Everywhere else is outside the world system, or subsumed under the term "ancient empires."

Many have disputed these claims for the distinctiveness of the European

state system. Other world system theorists, like Janet Abu-Lughod and Andre Gunder Frank, argue that there has long been only one global economy
encompassing a large portion of the Eurasian continent, not a unique European structure that expanded to the rest of the world.[11] They find Wallerstein's distinction between "external arenas" and "peripheries" to be artificial. Abu-Lughod and Frank differ on the timing of the emergence of a
pan-Eurasian world system—Abu-Lughod finds it emerging in the thirteenth century after the Mongol conquests, while Frank claims that it existed even in prehistoric times—but they agree that Europe had no special
economic features. It was a late and sudden new participant in a well-established exchange network that crisscrossed land and sea routes for many
centuries.

This debate focuses on how state units interact with the larger system.
For Wallerstein, the only significant impacts come from foreign trade, and a
state is part of the world system only when its import-export trade decisively transforms production relations and state structures within it. Before
the eighteenth century, Eastern Eurasia was outside the European world
system because its trade consisted mainly of "luxury" goods which did not
demand a restructuring of institutions and agrarian modes of production.
The "one world system" camp, by contrast, insists that "tributary trade"
relations and other modes of cultural and political interaction before the
European expansion did link the major civilizations and did have effects on
their internal structures. Most notably, the rise and fall of empires depended on flows of goods that supported their ability to resist both domestic and foreign rivals. If military and state power are not directly derived
from trade but have an independent dynamic, and if interaction between
major states strongly affects their military structures, then Wallerstein's exclusion of the Eastern Eurasian empires is based on too narrow a specifica-
tion of what drives historical change.

Wallerstein also does not explore the reasons why the "external" states
allowed the Europeans in. He regards the weakening of the Asian states as
a natural consequence of involvement in export trade, yet at the same time
he admits that commercial revenues from controlled "ports of trade" could
also strengthen central power. This is just what the Qing did with the customs revenues from Guangdong, which went directly into the imperial
household department. If increased trade per se does not weaken central
power, there must be some other factor at work.

I side with those who do not find a strong contrast between the Qing
empire and the European state system until the mid-eighteenth century.
As long as the Qing rulers faced serious rivals, they had to build structures to support substantial, extended military campaigns. The mobiliza-

tion needed for these campaigns had effects well beyond the military: it also transformed the fiscal system, commercial networks, communication technology, and local agrarian society. The need to ship large amounts of military supplies into Central Eurasia constantly put pressure on localities, especially in northwest and North China, but even provinces in South China were indirectly affected through the grain tribute moving up the Grand Canal. Provisioning, military and civilian, became a key concern of the Qing because it was essential to preserve the welfare of the people at the same time the state extracted a surplus from them for security needs. The early Qing empire, then, was not an isolated, stable, united "Oriental empire" but an evolving state structure engaged in mobilization for expansionist warfare.

After the mid-eighteenth century this dynamic changed. Now there were no autonomous armed rivals beyond the reach of imperial control. Every region that was a potential threat had "entered the registers" *(ru bantu)* of administrative and military supervision. Of course, this map was as much mythical as real. The Kazakhs, for example, were autonomous tribes beyond the Qing's reach, but they were treated as loyal "tributaries," quite different from the hostile Zunghars. Changing vocabulary was as important as changing facts on the ground. By defining who was included and who was excluded, and expunging those who had been eliminated, Qing historians worked to stabilize the realm. Our image of a complacent, patronizing regime applies closely only to the late eighteenth century. The empire did not diverge from Europe until this late date.

In sum, the models that argue for distinctive features of a European state system, marked by pluralism, competition, or special core–periphery structures, draw an oversimplified contrast between western Europe and the rest of the Eurasian world. They ignore analogous features found in Eastern Eurasia until 1750, and they fail to assess accurately the interactions between commercial exchange and military force across the continent.

Charles Tilly's model of the formation of the European state system from 990 to 1990 offers more useful comparative insights for the study of Eurasian state building. Unlike many of the world system theorists, he focuses on the twin dynamics of the accumulation of capital and the concentration of coercive force in an environment of nearly unceasing international war. Tilly distinguishes three paths that culminated in the modern national states of Europe. In the *capital-intensive* path, followed mainly by city-states like Venice and Genoa, and by the Dutch republic, "rulers relied on compacts with capitalists . . . to rent or purchase military force, and thereby warred without building vast permanent state structures." In the *coercion-intensive* mode, "rulers squeezed the means of war from their own populations and others they conquered, building massive structures of extraction in the process." Brandenburg-Prussia and Muscovy-Russia illustrate this strategy best. In between lie England and France, whose *capitalized-coercion* mode involved some of each, where "holders of capital and coercion interacted on terms of relative equality."[12]

Tilly's mapping of state formation onto relative concentrations of coercive and capitalist power is, as he recognizes, quite similar to G. William Skinner's discussion of the distribution within the Chinese empire of administrative and commercial resources. Both Europe's state formation and China's imperial formation can be described as the interaction of "the bottom-up building of regional hierarchies based on trade and manufacturing" with "the top-down imposition of political control" or the spatial logic of capital and coercion, respectively.[13] Unlike the world system theorists, Tilly allots considerable autonomy to the state itself. Both trade flows and security demands created by the anarchic international environment shape its interests.

Tilly's account, however, neglects nuances that appear in frontier regions. He treats Russia, for example, as an entirely coercive state, expanding in a region of vast landed resources and very little concentrated capital. In his view, Russian Tsars had little in the way of wealth to offer their followers; instead, they gave out land.[14] This view unduly minimizes the role of mercantile wealth in the building of the Russian state. Under Mongol rule, Russian princes constantly traveled to the Khan's capital at Sarai on tribute missions, which also provided them with valuable connections to the riches of the Byzantine empire. Later, in the seventeenth century, Russian merchants gained valuable privileges from cooperating with the Tsar, who relied on them for essential goods.[15] Moscow delegated the exploitation of the natural resources of Siberia, in particular, to prominent merchant families like the Stroganovs. Military and bureaucratic power still dominated, but with the assistance of a substantial mercantile component—one which is especially visible on the empire's edges.

These considerations suggest how China may fit into Tilly's scheme. At one point he seems to put China "outside the system," dividing it off as an "empire" from the "national states" of Europe. Nevertheless, Tilly also recognizes the salience of warfare in Chinese empire building and the empire's dependence on commercial resources. The "main message" of his book highlights the parallel evolution of urban hierarchies and marketing systems, the construction of state apparatuses of coercion and extraction in both societies.[16]

If the processes are similar enough to be comparable, which path of development fits China best? At first glance, the coercive-intensive mode seems to include both China and Russia. Merchants and imperial officials did not meet on an equal footing; the bureaucratic system clearly had the edge in formally recognized power. When the empire was securely unified, its scale far surpassed that of any individual merchant's wealth.

Yet beneath the orthodox mask of bureaucratic uniformity was a land-mass of astonishing diversity, whose social forms and ecological conditions were just as varied as Europe's. Skinner's model illustrates how the stan-dardized bureaucratic structure accommodated itself to the great range of concentration of commercial and agrarian resources. Different regions of China varied systematically in the relative weight of mercantile, coercive, and redistributive institutions. I have described the problems that impe-rial governance faced in the northwest in allocating limited resources to a region of poor harvests and military vulnerability. Broadly speaking, the northwest had the greatest concentration of coercive force, as the south and southeast coasts had the most powerful merchant classes. Redistributive re-sources represented by the "evernormal" granary system followed that of the military units, with the highest per capita reserves concentrated on the less commercialized peripheries.[17]

If coercion is not the whole story, in Russia or in China, Tilly's three-way division boils down into two: the rather anomalous capital-intensive mode of the Italian city-states and of the Dutch, and the mixed capital-coercive mode of the rest of Eurasia.

Even China's northwest did not totally lack commercial resources. Its trading system bridged China's interior and Central Eurasia, with routes bringing grain from the interior and taking textiles out the Gansu corridor to the Silk Road. The Qing expanded some of these linkages to an unpre-cedented extent and cut off others. Heavy promotion of merchant and of-ficial grain movements from North China to Shaanxi, and from Shaanxi to Gansu, built up a new level of grain flows to the poorest regions, and the promotion of currency circulation and increased copper cash supplies gen-erated greater local market exchange. Coercion and capital supported each other here, but coercion led the way. Military units received primary con-sideration, but the emperor and his officials recognized that they could not allow the military to burden the people excessively.

As long as the frontier expanded, coercive and commercial representa-tives joined in a common cause. The end of expansion, however, allowed other tensions to surface. Each region of the empire then faced distinctive types of social conflict. R. Bin Wong has described the outbreak of grain ri-ots in Hunan province, for example, as a consequence of the extension of market relations to new districts, much as in early modern France. These blockages of grain flows represented protests by local consumers, often backed by local officials, who aimed to protect their own production against outside demands from merchants or higher-level officials.[18] Gansu, by contrast, so far as I can tell, never had any grain riots, despite the fact that external demands on its grain reserves were extremely high. It could be that the active mobilization of granary reserves, as seen in the famine years 1756–1760, successfully staved off resistance, or, just as plausibly, that the heavy military presence in the province provided substantial repressive force.

Gansu still had its own way of sabotaging imperial goals. We have seen two examples: the relief scandal of 1781 and the outbreak of Muslim rebellions from the 1780s to 1820. The first represented collusion between provincial officials and outside merchants against the local peasant producers and urban consumers; the second grew from feuding between different factions of Muslim and Han villagers into protests against Han immigration and Qing rule.[19] These were distinctive forms of resistance to state authority found in frontier regions. Whereas the first represents the victory of capital over bureaucratic control, the second signifies the outbreak of local violence against central coercion. The closing of the Chinese frontier allowed these contradictory impulses to grow large toward the end of the eighteenth century.

Tilly's model, then, although it does not focus on China or on frontiers, helps to orient our discussion toward the interplay of military and commercial forces during the time of Qing expansion. Military considerations were primary, but not exclusive, in defining the empire's identity.

R. Bin Wong also finds many common features between Qing China and early modern European socioeconomic structures. But for him, the vital concern of the imperial regime with provisioning the people derives from a special ethical tradition that has Confucian roots, ever since Mencius urged rulers to act benevolently by ensuring the welfare of their people. This attitude led in practical terms to the concept of "storing wealth among the people" *(cangfu yumin)*, including both lowering levels of taxation and developing an empire-wide structure of evernormal granaries, which sold grain to level prices and provide famine relief.[20]

Broadly speaking, I agree with Wong's description of the Qing imperial structure, but I have a different view of its underlying motivations. In his references to grain provisioning, Wong describes the Chinese imperial ideology as holding the same orientation from classical, pre-imperial times up through the nineteenth century. There certainly was substantial continuity from one dynasty to another, and the classical texts served as reference points for all subsequent discussions, but the evolution of provisioning ideology over time indicates, once again, the prominence of military considerations as much as ethical concerns.

In 81 BCE a defense crisis on the northwest frontier had initiated a discussion of state monopolies and price-leveling sales known as the Salt and Iron Debates. Each side of the argument claimed that only its policies would increase welfare and security. The hard-liners, or statecraft strategists, argued for increased revenues from state monopolies and grain sales. The "soft-liners" *(ru)* argued that the burdens of excessive taxation turned peasants into exhausted soldiers discontented with imperial government. The arguments were both Mencian and strategic.[21] During the policy debates begun by Wang Anshi in 1069–1076 CE, arising from the Song's inability to hold off attack from the Liao, grain provisioning arguments were also closely connected to defense needs.

In short, it is useful but too simple to draw a direct connection between the concern of Mencius for popular welfare and the construction of the vast granary provisioning system in the Qing. Furthermore, we cannot explain the long-term survival of the imperial system solely in terms of a paternalistic interest in the welfare of its subjects. Just as important was the hard-headed realism that recognized military force as the basis of the state, for both internal repression and external war. Wong echoes others who stress China's anti-military orientations by contrast with the aggressive West. But imperial rule relied on both welfare and warfare; each needed the other. The balance between the two shifted over time, but neither disappeared. Imperial China's security concerns, again, were not radically different from those of European states.

Instead of singling out features present in Europe and absent in China, we would do better to think in terms of major and minor themes in both. Like a symphony with several musical themes, each of which over time comes to the fore, both civilian and military provisioning played a role in state policies. Sometimes they complemented each other, and sometimes one was sacrificed to the other. In the relief campaign of 1756–1760, officials struggled mightily to blend both harmoniously, using civilian supplies for military needs and military transport for civilian use.

Grain provisioning aimed both to keep the population healthy and to support the troops in the field. It took a full-court press, mobilizing the resources of nearly the entire empire, to make this policy work. In less happy times, most conspicuously in much of the nineteenth century, grain flows were constantly diverted from civilian to military use. But sometimes the balance tilted the other way, as when Yongzheng deliberately cut back troop concentrations in order to spare resources for the peasantry. Perhaps he even went too far, starving his garrison in Mongolia into defeat. Images of a pendulum swing, or symphonic harmony and disharmony, between military and civilian provisioning put Qing policies more in line with those of European states and give us a richer view of how grain policy worked.

Frontier perspectives enrich our understanding of how empires sustain their core populations.

Theories of Nomadic Empires

Scholars from all the settled civilizations, Middle Eastern, European, and Chinese, have tried to account for the repeated rise and fall of nomadic empires across Central Eurasia. Pride of place perhaps belongs to Ibn-Khaldūn, the Arab scholar whose concept of *ʿasabiyya,* or community solidarity, has been the basis for nearly all analysis of Middle Eastern empires. The "dynastic cycle" theory, created after the first conquest of China from the west by the Zhou in 1045 BCE, does not directly focus attention on the dynamics of nomadic empires but includes nomadic conquest as one of its elements signaling dynastic decline. Modern social scientists and historians, such as Owen Lattimore, have also put special emphasis on the role of the nomadic frontier in the Chinese dynastic experience.[22]

We may broadly classify these theories along two axes. (See Table 15.1.) One way to divide them is according to the relative stress they put on external or internal factors in causing nomad attacks. Nicola Di Cosmo has wittily characterized these as the "needy nomad" and "greedy nomad" stereotypes, respectively. The needy nomad raids because he cannot obtain essential resources from the steppe alone; the greedy nomad raids because of his insatiable avarice.[23]

"Externalists" stress the impact of outside forces, especially invasion and trade. They argue that the resources of the steppe in themselves are too poor and too dispersed to offer the ambitious ruler enough to gather followers and build an army. He must centralize by raiding or trading with the most prosperous settled civilizations around him. Owen Lattimore, Thomas Barfield, and A. M. Khazanov have developed these insights most extensively.[24]

Other analysts tend to focus on dynamics within the nomadic confederations themselves. These may be psychological, economic, or ecological. Ironically, it seems often to be the analysts with the least information about nomadic societies who make the largest claims for internal dynamics. The popular "desiccation" theory, espoused by Ellsworth Huntington in the early twentieth century, for example, explained nomadic invasions as a direct consequence of scarcity of grazing lands caused by climatic change. More primitive psychological arguments, often expressed by Chinese officials, simply claimed that all nomads are fierce, avaricious, and unable to control their desires. This explained their constant raiding of innocent Chi-

Table 15.1 Models of nomadic state formation

	Internalist	Externalist
Structural/cyclical	Environmental/technological/ psychological determinism (greedy nomad, desiccation thesis) (Qing officials, Ibn-Khaldūn, Ellsworth Huntington) Class conflict (Chinese and Soviet Marxists)	Needy nomad (Khazanov, Barfield, Lattimore)
Historical/progressive	Philological (Turks-Mongols-Manchus) (Sinor, Golden)	Technological change; fiscal resources (Di Cosmo)

nese cultivators, who needed to be defended by aggressive military expeditions. Ibn-Khaldūn's *'asabiyya* model, however, based on a much more sensitive understanding of tribal dynamics, essentially reduced the rise and fall of empires to the fluctuations of this crucial socio-psychological component: the feeling of solidarity that inspires warriors and rulers to dedicate themselves to a moral cause. Modern Soviet Marxist discussions invoke more up-to-date internal dynamics, like class conflict, as the driving factor in nomadic society, often combined with the ecological one.[25]

I agree with Di Cosmo that neither the purely internal nor the purely external perspective is adequate.[26] Even though many pastoral peoples do not have all the productive resources of settled societies, creating a large empire is not the only way to obtain them. Trade may often be more attractive than raiding, and nomads do have important products, like horses and sheep, to offer to settled peoples. Furthermore, Di Cosmo and Khazanov point out that nearly all nomads combine at least some agricultural cultivation with pastoral grazing. Contrary to Lattimore's adage that "the pure nomad is the poor nomad," most nomads did not survive exclusively from grazing. What determines whether a tribe will become a confederation, an empire, or a dependency of its neighbors depends as much on personal leadership as on external relations.

A second axis divides structural and historical perspectives. Structural analysts tend to find the same processes repeating themselves. In this view, nomads are seen as particularly static prisoners of nature and psychology, by implicit contrast with more "progressive" settled civilizations. These models make little allowance for technological change, commercial linkages, or population shifts: all nomads simply run on the same tracks. More historical approaches recognize significant differences between time periods. Technologies of warfare changed dramatically from the Xiongnu to the Turks to the Mongols and after. The introduction of the stirrup and compound bow, for example, dramatically expanded the striking power of nomadic forces. Gunpowder weaponry, though not decisive, also changed the character of steppe warfare. Scholars following the Inner Asian philological heritage, which highlights the significance of language and ethnic change, also display a strong historical tendency. They are much more interested in the details of particular shifts in tribal names than in the broader processes of state formation.[27]

Nicola Di Cosmo's model of stages of steppe empire formation combines these historical and external orientations with attention to internal processes.[28] In his model, crises of violent conflict in the steppe produce the general militarization that precedes state formation. One leader then gains victory in battle and names himself Khan, invoking an ideology of sacred investiture to gain legitimacy. He then creates a centralized governmental structure, with his own clan at the top, which requires increased revenue to support the new administration and its followers. Only then does he attack settled societies to obtain these additional resources. The nomadic empire obtains its resources in four different ways, each of which marks a new stage in state formation: tribute, trade partnerships, dual administration of nomadic and settled areas, and regular taxation. Tribute was the main technique used from 209 BCE to 551 CE by the Xiongnu rulers and their successors; trade characterized primarily the period from 551 to 907 CE, seen in relations of the Turks, Khazars, Uighurs, and Tibetans with China's Tang empire; dual administration featured in the Liao and Jin empires of the northeast, the early Mongols, and Tanguts, from around 1000 to 1200 CE; while regular taxation began under Khubilai's Mongol empire and spread to Tamerlane, the Ottomans, and the Manchus. Di Cosmo's historical and externalist model fits well with my analysis of the rise of the Zunghars.

Although decline could have the same causes as growth, explanations of the decline of nomadic power generally follow the internalist and structuralist models. The two most common arguments used to explain the decline of nomadic power after the sixteenth century invoke technological and economic determinism. Many argue that the spread of gunpowder weaponry rendered obsolete the mounted cavalry warrior, thus making nomadic military power no longer the uncontested hegemon of Eurasia. Likewise, world historians from Arnold Toynbee to William McNeill have claimed that the shift of trade from land to sea routes brought down Central Eurasian states by cutting off their commercial resources.

Both of these arguments have long lineages, but their assumptions are questionable. They ignore the role of state power in diverting resources for political use, and they derive political superiority directly from technological and economic change. My own discussion indicates that both technology and commercial exchange strongly affected the encounter between the settled and nomadic regimes, but these resources were available to all the contending parties. The Zunghars made strenuous efforts to forge their own cannon, and they relied heavily on trade to support their state. Their Qing adversaries likewise dragged cannon long distances to engage in battle and mobilized merchants to support their campaigns. When it came to battles, gunpowder added very little military advantage. Most of the Qing cannon were seldom used in battle, and *niaochuang,* or fowling pieces, had nowhere near enough accuracy or power to stop charging horsemen. Even in Europe, whose horsemen were never a match for Central Eurasians, the significance of the gunpowder revolution in the early sixteenth century in giving superiority to infantrymen over cavalry has been highly overrated.[29]

By contrast to these technological and determinist explanations, my discussion of the Zunghar–Qing confrontation supports primarily the historical and externalist perspective. Simply put, the nature of nomadic–settled interactions changed significantly over time, and the interaction of the two conditioned the structures of both. The Zunghar leaders competed and cooperated with the Qing and the Russians to obtain vital technological, commercial, and fiscal resources for their state. They used all four types of resource collection, exacting tribute from the Qing and other Mongols, trading with the Qing and Russians, administering and taxing settled areas in Turkestan. The Manchus likewise employed all four methods on a much bigger scale. The Zunghars lost, in brief, because the Manchus and Russians together deprived them of the critical resources they needed to construct a permanent state.

The Zunghars had to rely even more than the Qing on merchant capital because their agrarian resources were so scarce. They seized the oases in order to control strategic way stations on the trade routes and to tax their agricultural production. They directly deported merchants and artisans and assigned them to state tasks, just as the Manchus, Mongols, and Ottomans had done. They used tribute trade privileges to gather resources for their state and appealed to Russians to increase their trade, offering them access to gold in return for aid. Overpopulation, desiccation, or inherent "greed" were less important than the effort to preserve the state in the face of pressures from rivals.

Qing officials, fully aware of the Zunghar mobilization of capital, moved to cut off these flows. They restricted tribute missions when they knew that the Zunghars were using them to accumulate resources and refusing to submit to Qing control, and they strictly prohibited exports of gunpowder and weaponry while cutting down the silver outflow. They enticed the Russians with access to the vast China market so as to divert them from supporting the Zunghars. The Chinese offered generous conditions for Russian caravan trade so as to cut off aid to the Zunghars, but they could turn off the tap and cancel missions to maintain their diplomatic leverage. Efforts to cut the trade route to Tibet (the "boiled tea" issue) further reveal the Qing plan to isolate the Zunghars commercially and diplomatically.

The Zunghars also suffered from internal instability, seen in the repeated succession crises when their leaders died. Here, too, they were not radically different from their rivals in Russia or the Qing, which also passed through severe succession crises in the seventeenth and eighteenth centuries. Hong Taiji probably usurped power, and the Yongzheng emperor's accession to the throne was particularly controversial, but after him, the Qing rulers regularized their succession to avoid such upheaval. The Zunghars' instability, however, was generated as much by external as by internal factors: they lacked the support of the Chinggisid line because the Qing had captured its symbols and representatives, and they could not build consistently on a Tibetan Buddhist line of legitimacy after the Manchus took over the Khalkhas, including the Jebzongdanba Khutukhtu and the seat of the Panchen Lama in Kokonor.

Joining the historical, externalist model of nomadic state building to our focus on commercial and coercive resources thus allows us to subsume state building across Eurasia under the same model.

Rethinking the Qing in the World

Let us now turn from global models to the paradigms used to explain Qing history alone. Two new trends of interpretation have appeared in recent scholarly studies of the Qing dynasty. We may call them the "Eurasian similarity thesis" and the "Altaic school." The first trend highlights broad comparability of socioeconomic institutions of the Ming–Qing era to those of Europe, while the second stresses the Central Eurasian connections of the Qing conquerors. Both offer provocative, original interpretations of China's imperial institutions, but the two schools are not directly linked. My own focus on expansion and the frontier allows us to connect these two approaches in a more integrated way.[30] What connects them is what both neglect: the security goals of the Qing, expressed in logistics and strategic culture.

Recent research on late imperial China has demonstrated that in most measurable aspects of demographic structure, technology, economic productivity, commercial development, property rights, and ecological pressure, there were no substantial differences between China and western Europe up to around the year 1800. In quantitative demographic data and in family structure, many of China's social practices, as opposed to its ideals, showed marked similarities to those of western Europe. Chinese families did not breed heedlessly, producing a Malthusian situation of population outrunning available resources, but rather limited fertility in response to local economic opportunities.[31] Kenneth Pomeranz has demonstrated by careful estimates that European and Chinese standards of living, agrarian output, and ecological pressure were roughly comparable until 1800.[32]

Qing historians also find no significant differences in the organization of production between the two societies in the preindustrial age. R. Bin Wong argues that "fundamentally similar dynamics of economic expansion via the market took place across Eurasia, and . . . the development of rural industry was also similar in important ways."[33] European industrialism as we know it in the late nineteenth century depended on the combination of three elements: "a market economy driven by Smithian dynamics," the "institutions of commercial capitalism," and "processes of technological change centered on an energy revolution." These three elements were "logically independent" of one another, even though empirically they came together in the late eighteenth century. China possessed the first two elements but, because of geological bad luck, lacked the third.[34]

Cultural distinctions between China and Europe also did not have unequivocally different economic effects. Whether we look at attitudes toward commercial activity, literacy, urbanization, or religious doctrines, for example, we can find in both societies attitudes and institutions favoring and opposing economic growth and technological change. Until 1800 there is no clear balance in favor of Europe promoting economically meaningful activity. In short, Marx, Malthus, Weber, and many other social theorists have been wrong in basing much of their explanations of capitalism on radical distinctions between East and West. The fundamental theoretical flaw is their exclusive focus on internal factors and exaggerated polarities of difference. Better explanations must accept evidence of general comparability and rely more heavily on exogenous intervention and global contexts.

In the light of this recent research, the Industrial Revolution is not a deep, slow evolution out of centuries of particular conditions unique to early modern Europe. It is a late, rapid, unexpected outcome of a fortuitous combination of circumstances in the late eighteenth century. In view of what we now know about imperial China, Japan, and India, among other places, acceptable explanations must invoke a global perspective and allow for a great deal of short-term change.[35]

Yet the European miracle did occur. What were the important factors? Kenneth Pomeranz has argued that global ecological contingencies played a determining role.[36] These included the availability of coal supplies in northern England near to water transport and British access to both the vast "ghost acreage" of the New World and the cotton supplies and domestic market of its colony in India. These are all, in some sense, factors exogenous to the British social system. Imperial China had analogous, but by no means comparable, ecological features. China had coal, but the largest deposits were located in the northwest, far from the textile industries and canals of the lower Yangzi valley. China also had "colonies," new territories conquered by imperial expansion, but these, too, were in the interior of the Eurasian continent, without large arable lands or dense populations. The empire actively promoted the settlement of these regions, but they did not provide the raw materials or commodity demands comparable to those available to the settlers of the New World. Unlike arguments based on proto-industrialization, demographic structures, or commercial culture, where the differences are arguably not large enough to account for major economic change, here the differences in size of resources and transport costs are very large, and thus likely to have large effects.

Before Pomeranz, Rolf Peter Sieferle and Anthony Wrigley had also made a systematic case for the importance of energy supplies, particularly coal, in the Industrial Revolution.[37] The importance of coal is, in fact, an old argument, invoked ever since the Industrial Revolution. No one could miss the polluting effects of the "dark Satanic mills" on the shock cities of northern England.

In short, industrial growth does not have to be an outcome of a centuries-long accumulation of the particular skills found in northwestern Europe; there are numerous paths to economic modernity, and England followed only one of them. Certainly all industrializing societies need vastly increased supplies of energy and raw materials, but they can obtain these from many sources. The much higher costs of transporting coal in China to the coast compared to the cost in Europe, and the different technological demands of mining (pumping out water versus avoiding gas explosions), meant that China in the late eighteenth century would not develop coal- and steam-based industry left to its own devices, but did not preclude China from industrializing later on without creating an English-style agrarian system. Like the models of nomadic state building tabulated earlier, the best approaches to this comparative question are historical (limiting key changes to relatively short time periods, stressing contingencies) and externalist (focusing on the availability of resources from outside the existing socioeconomic system).

And yet this argument ignores the important role of state power in mobilizing natural and economic resources. Unless we include consideration of organized political power, we risk offering excessively reductionist explanations. Even if two countries differ greatly in their energy endowments, it does not necessarily follow that the most favorably endowed one will advance more rapidly. Japan in the late nineteenth century industrialized very rapidly without possessing very large resources in its home islands. (Japan, of course, like England, soon acquired an empire in Taiwan and Korea in order to obtain these resources, including coal, minerals, grain, and *Lebensraum*.) The actions of states, of voluntary and coerced human activity, decisively affected the economic and technological development of societies, even in the early modern period.

A strictly ecological focus omits a crucial question: Why could China not make up for its lack of convenient coal supplies through state action? The ecological thesis of industrialization ultimately relies on a sophisticated form of environmental determinism, since it assumes that the absence of a critical factor doomed the society to a long period of backwardness.

But since humans in general collectively strive to improve their economic situation as much as possible, knowledge of technological advances diffused rapidly across Eurasia. Chinese rulers of the sixteenth to eighteenth centuries were well aware of European advances in military technology and sought to acquire new cannon and guns quickly. The Jesuits, the world's first global arms salesmen, were happy to accommodate them. Both the Ming armies and their enemy Manchu armies used firearms extensively, as did the Japanese during the wars of unification of the early seventeenth century. The eighteenth-century emperors dragged heavy cannon thousands of kilometers into the steppe in pursuit of their Mongol enemies. Asians soon learned of European military technology and adapted it quickly to their purposes.[38]

The Chinese state also had the capability to move bulk goods over long distances. Most of China's copper, which was the basic material for its currency, came from the distant southwest province of Yunnan. Officials carefully tracked the shipment of copper from the mines to the mints.[39] Sometimes they used military escorts for official shipments; sometimes they entrusted shipments to merchant contractors. Filling the evernormal granaries of the empire also required large-scale long-distance transport. Qing officials sometimes shipped grain themselves, under military control, and more often contracted with merchants. There is no reason why the Qing state could not have shipped other bulk goods if it chose to.[40]

Other states that knew of western European advances did mobilize their mineral resources in the eighteenth century. Peter the Great of Russia founded the Mining and Manufactories College and the Commerce College in the 1720s to promote private industrial development with government support. His Siberian Bureau established the first major iron industries in the Ural Mountains in 1701. These industries, located on top of rich mineral deposits, became the primary nucleus of Russian industrial development under state control. Peter also set up state enterprises which were transferred to private owners or created new companies which received special favors. Evgenii V. Anisimov, who criticizes Peter's industrial policies for preventing the emergence of a private capitalist class, nevertheless agrees that Peter created a "powerful economic base, so essential for a developing nation."[41]

Russia's agrarian base was much poorer, and its bureaucracy far more rudimentary, than China's. China had much more commercial capital, and its agriculture was not held back by serfdom. The Russian example indicates that countries without convenient mineral supplies could overcome their disadvantage through energetic state action. Russian industrialization, of course, took a very different path from that of England. It was far more state-directed, coercive, reliant on foreign experts, and directed primarily toward military needs. It was, nevertheless, quite successful, and began quite early.

Thus I would argue that the imperial Chinese state had both the capacity and the experience to transport bulk commodities over long distances. State support, either through direct transport or by contracting with merchants, could overcome enormous barriers. The primary commodities on which Qing officials focused were grain, salt, and copper, because these were crucial to maintaining subsistence for the population and the stability of the currency. They also shipped timber long distances to build palaces, ships, and forts.

In addition, Qing officials invested in the transportation infrastructure by building new roads and dredging rivers. Water conservancy policies aimed to achieve the classic goal of "two birds with one stone" by protecting farmers from flooding and ensuring merchants smooth passage on waterways. The Qing state was neither an "Oriental despotism" that repressed all commerce nor a "laissez-faire" regime taking a hands-off approach to trade. Its officials intervened actively in the trade in some commodities while leaving others alone. Which commodities the state chose to manage depended heavily on the security interests of the state and its attitude toward provisioning its people.

The general capabilities of the state to direct the flows of goods were probably greater in the eighteenth century than in any previous period. The highly elaborated granary system, the reconstructed Grand Canal, the land settlement policies on the frontiers all showed a definite interventionist spirit. The new communication system from the province to the center, using both routine and secret palace memorials, allowed capital officials to keep in close touch with provincial officials. They could also send out special inspectors to make sure that central policies were implemented accurately. The Qing reporting system collected vast amounts of data about the workings of the agrarian economy, including detailed reports on prices, rainfall, grain holdings, and famine relief.

The capabilities of the Qing to manage the economy were powerful enough that we might even call it a "developmental agrarian state." It did not direct resources toward industrialization, but it did encourage the fullest possible exploitation of landed resources, including foodstuffs and minerals. William T. Rowe's biography of the Qing official Chen Hongmou gives impressive examples of one official's activist approach to "managing the world" *(jingshi)*.[42] In his many posts around the empire, Chen directed his energies toward increasing agrarian output, reducing the damage from famines, repairing and expanding waterworks, and developing mining. He did not, however, believe that the state alone should undertake major economic activities; his preference was to allow market forces to induce merchants to transport goods wherever possible. But state regulation and cooperation with merchants was directed toward the common goal of improving the people's welfare while strengthening the resources of the state.

Another example of state activism in the eighteenth century is seen in the activities of Lan Dingyuan in Taiwan. Like Chen Hongmou, he promoted active state direction of economic development, this time in a colonial environment.[43] Lan vigorously promoted the immigration of Han Chinese to the newly conquered island so as to raise its agricultural output and provide grain exports for Fujian province. Taiwan did indeed become a major grain-exporting province in the eighteenth century under the combined impact of official encouragement and mercantile contact.

Much of the earlier literature which contrasted Chinese and European social and economic structures read back China's poverty in the nineteenth century to earlier periods. Both Europeans and Chinese nationalists assumed that China's difficulties in responding to the European industrial impact were rooted in the stagnation bequeathed to it by the stultifying Manchu regime. Now, however, our perspective is different. Seeing the dynamism of China's contemporary market economy, much of which appears to be a revival of the commercial networks of earlier times, alerts us to the significance of those so-called sprouts of capitalism that grew in such fertile soil since at least the tenth century. At the same time, the modern Chinese state has also sponsored major projects to extract its natural resources of energy, like the Three Gorges Dam or the new "Develop the West" plan. The prominence of both state-directed and market-oriented policies in modern China turns our attention back to the similar capacities of the Qing state before the nineteenth century. Eurasian similarities include state action as well as economic structures.

The "Altaic" school stresses the Central Eurasian origins of the Qing state. Pamela Crossley, Mark Elliott, Evelyn Rawski, and Edward Rhoads have reemphasized that the Qing state was controlled by a Manchu elite very conscious of its difference from the subject Han population and constantly concerned to maintain that difference.[44] The Manchus did not assimilate to a "superior" majority Han culture but maintained their distinctiveness, through the banners and imperial rituals, while they collaborated with Han officials to maintain legitimacy and ensure adequate tax collection. Even though they adopted the Chinese language and bureaucratic practices after settling down in China's major cities, they still saw themselves as separate. These scholars may differ over exactly when and how the Manchus constructed their identity, but they agree that they marked themselves off from the Han through the end of the Qing.

The Manchu elite paid particular attention to the empire's peripheries. Under the rubric of "Manchu colonialism," several scholars have examined the special characteristics of Qing rule in Mongolia, Xinjiang, and Tibet.[45] They suggest grounds for comparison of the Qing state to other colonial empires. Like the large agrarian empires of the Ottomans, Russia, or the Mughals, China faced problems with control, expansion, legitimacy, and revenue collection. Contrary to the nationalist narrative, China was not a unique victim of Western imperialism; nor was it unique by virtue of its long-lasting bureaucratic and cultural tradition. China's distinctive characteristics are more like the "special features" of its current "socialist market economy": they are variations within a generic class of market economies, not a radically different type.

The Altaic model, like the Eurasian similarity thesis (EST), invokes comparable structures and processes joining the Qing to Eurasia, but from a perspective focused on the ruling elite, not on socioeconomic structures. Where the EST joins the Ming and Qing dynasties together in a single process, the Altaic model separates them sharply, and where the EST primarily stresses economic development in the core, the Altaic model examines the frontiers. If the EST unduly neglects the potential for state-directed economic change, the Altaic model tends to isolate the Manchus in a separate world from that of the Han official or the majority of the subject population. But we can link these two fruitful perspectives together by looking closely, first, at how military structures drew resources from the mass of the population (logistics) and, second, by examining the Qing's strategic culture. I have discussed logistics extensively; here I briefly address the question of "strategic culture."

Iain Johnston has brilliantly illuminated the coexistence of two strategic cultures in imperial China. He defines "strategic culture" as "ranked grand strategic preferences derived from central paradigmatic assumptions about the nature of conflict and the enemy, and collectively shared by decision makers." He labels one "Confucian," stressing defensive warfare and a preference for negotiation over violence, and the other *"parabellum"* (if you want peace, prepare for war), including assumptions of the inevitability of violent conflict and a preference for preemptive military solutions. He finds China's operational military culture dominated by the *parabellum* culture more than the Confucian one.[46] I have discussed his model in detail elsewhere.[47] Johnston's approach is of great value in placing imperial Chinese strategic reasoning in a comparative framework. Here I point out only that Johnston's model is not sufficiently historical, or externalist. He focuses only on the Ming dynasty, and on earlier military texts, which he takes as emblematic of enduring, relatively unchanging orientations toward the use of force. Instead, we might view the Confucian and *parabellum* paradigms as major and minor themes of imperial discourse, each complementing the other, with one or the other dominant at any given time.

Even during the Ming, themes of military force and moral education varied in salience depending on the frontier. Hard realism certainly prevailed in the late Ming in regard to the Mongols of the northwest frontier, after the horse-and-tea trade failed to tame them. Once it decided on its defensive orientation by investing in a continuous Great Wall, the Ming regarded the tribes of the steppe as alien natural forces who could not be controlled by any appeals to human morality. In this respect, Ming views were not too different from U.S. hard-line attitudes toward the Soviet Union during the cold war. Toward the southwest frontier peoples, however, Ming attitudes were far softer. These peoples, far less threatening or organized, could be enticed into the realm through offers of "civilization," Han-style.

The Qing rulers, because of their Central Eurasian background, blended these two themes in more nuanced fashion. They saw the Mongols of the frontier as humans, not as animals or natural forces. Mongols could respond to ethical appeals, but these did not have to be based in Confucian classical traditions. The Kangxi emperor constantly invoked the similarity between his own principles and those of the Buddhist Dalai Lama. He sought harmony between different religious traditions. At the same time, he never disavowed the use of force.

In fact, Qing ideology could justify even more violent repression than the Ming, because human subjects who rejected a benevolent emperor's appeals for peace were worse than animals: they were traitors who only deserved extermination. I have noted the striking prominence of the term "extermination" in Qing rhetoric; an even more striking contrast with the Ming is that at certain times Qing troops actively carried out atrocities deliberately designed to eliminate a hostile group. In extreme situations the principle of *parabellum* is driven toward eliminationism: the only way to remove the threat of an obdurate enemy is to wipe him out entirely. (This rhetoric, too, we can well recognize from cold war days.) The devastating epigram of Tacitus applies far too often: "They create a desolation and call it peace." The contrary Confucian principle also can be driven toward its extreme of complete assimilation: an effort to remove a people's identity by more peaceful means. Most of the time, however, Qing rulers negotiated flexibly between these poles by conducting an intricate dance of diplomacy, coercion, and exchange.

This special Qing strategic culture shows that the ruling elite saw itself as engaged in a large-scale geopolitical competition and continually sought to maximize the effectiveness of its use of force. Like the European state builders, Qing strategists knew that coercion mattered, but few battles were won by coercion alone. By creating alliance systems among the Mongols, with the Russians also engaged, the Qing aimed to draw as many actors as possible into a Grand Coalition against its rivals. The ultimate goal was a binary division of the steppe, with definite boundaries established to limit expansion, and the removal of ambiguous zones on frontiers.

Their growing focus on territoriality demonstrates further parallels with the European experience of the seventeenth and eighteenth centuries. The balance of power in continental Eastern Eurasia concluded with only two states dividing the huge expanse, leaving no major alternative powers between them. In this sense the Mongol experience was analogous to that of smaller units in Europe, like the Burgundians, for example, absorbed into the larger state of France. Even more similar was the fate of Poland, which was completely eliminated as a state in the eighteenth century, to be revived, like Mongolia, in the twentieth.

The state formation and system analyses I have discussed for the most part ignore symbolic claims by rulers to their subjects' loyalty. Materialist scholars deny that these appeals were anything but hypocritical. Given the power and wealth of the ruling regimes and their predominant focus on revenue collection and war making, what use had they for cultural mobili-

zation? On the other side of the disciplinary spectrum, quite a few historians have discussed the rituals delineating imperial and royal authority
while making almost no reference to the structures of power that backed
them up. For them, rituals and symbols act upon subjects through linguistic
and visual discourse autonomously from the coercive and remunerative incentives of submission to power. These disciplinary flotillas should not always cross in the night. They find a meeting ground in the concerns addressed here about frontier expansion and the incorporation of diverse
peoples into centralized regimes.

As Joseph Conrad and Lu Jia knew, wealth and power alone cannot hold
a regime together for long. Weber's division of legitimate authority into
three categories of "traditional," "charismatic," and "rational" is too stereotyped, but he was correct to stress the role of legitimacy in ensuring that
structures of power last. Warriors, men of wealth, and even foot soldiers
need to be convinced that their cause is just, or at least not futile. Ideologies
are designed at the very least to justify the use of violent sanctions against
others. The Chinese "Mandate of Heaven" theory retrospectively justified
the overthrow of one dynasty by another based on the presumption of in-
curable moral evil in the losers, replaced by the Heaven-supported victors.

Ideologies have other functions as well. They not only justify victories
but also identify who is to be attacked. As Mao Zedong commented, the
central issue in waging revolutionary or any kind of warfare is to determine
who are our enemies and who are our friends. Imperial ideologies are
boundary-definition mechanisms that enable leaders to decide who will be
included and who will be excluded from the stable polity. A shrewd strate-
gist directs the brunt of his forces not at the power that is greatest at the
moment but at the one he expects to be the most enduring threat. Winning
over many potential rivals peacefully can isolate and weaken the most dangerous adversary. As the Chinese phrase puts it, "When the lips are gone,
the teeth get cold" (chunwang chihan). Mao learned his politics of coalition
building from study of ancient Chinese novels of warfare and classic texts
of military strategy, even though he justified his tactical decisions in terms
of the class analysis terminology of Marxism-Leninism.

As certain theorists have begun to recognize, language orients rulers' perceptions of how to form alliances. In Alexander Wendt's phrase, "Anarchy
is what states make of it."[48] I have examined the Qing use of language to
define those to be included and those to be excluded from the "civilized"
realm. Those who submitted, regardless of their ethnicity, received favors;
those who resisted were eliminated. Underlying assumptions of which actors would respond to what kinds of appeals—coercive, monetary, or religious—shaped decisions about frontier policy.

After the conquest, language, ritual, and symbolic action continued to influence the actions of both rulers and ruled. They defined the boundaries of acceptable action, they indicated the degree of inclusiveness of a regime, and they enunciated ideals that directed people's goals. As Catherine Bell and Marshall Sahlins argue, rituals are not merely functional activities that support an inherited structure; each ritual performance reenacts virtually in a contingent manner the conflicts preserved in a society.[49] Qing performances at tribute presentations or on imperial tours played out these tensions arising from the project of embracing diverse peoples under a comprehensive gaze. Their Central Eurasian background gave the Qing emperors the ambition to encompass multitudes; the Han ritual advisers aimed to limit their scope with warnings about a ruler who exceeded proper bounds. They restaged the facts of initial conquest in order to revive and repeat a martial message closely tied to victory in battle. Thus the "Altaic" rituals and institutions of the Manchus spread beyond the ruling elite to the wider audience of their Han subjects.

In short, a frontier perspective on Eurasia focuses on boundary definition and state building through mobilization of culture, commerce, and violence. This frontier culture, designed for expansion, affected the Qing empire's domestic political economy, its governing institutions, its legitimating rituals, and its conception of its place in the world. It not only helps to explain why the Qing grew; it can also explain why the empire fell.

16

Frontier Expansion in the Rise and Fall of the Qing

So far I have stressed the role of expansive warfare in the construction of the Qing state. From the beginning, the Manchu rulers organized their society to make war. The Manchu people were created in 1616 as part of the state formation in Manchuria dedicated to unifying through force the tribes of the Northeast. During the conquest of China proper, continual preparation for military campaigns generated institutional change along with territorial expansion and commercial integration. Until the mid-eighteenth century, the Qing state kept up the momentum of expansion along with institutional transformation. After the borders were fixed and expansion ceased, some energy seems to have seeped out of the imperial structure. The results were not immediately apparent, but by the early nineteenth century, the Qing empire faced new internal challenges, and the glory days were over.

By insisting that militaries mattered to the formation of the Qing state, I aim to balance other works that focus almost exclusively on commercial or cultural integration. Both of these objectives contributed to the cohesion of the empire, but neither could work without effective displays of coercive power. When preaching harmony failed or harvests collapsed in a drought, officials had to summon up whatever police forces they had to prevent banditry or revolt. Balancing coercive, monetary, and cultural appeals was the key to preserving the state and maintaining social order.

The same principles applied to both internal and external relations. Local officials and frontier commanders both had to subdue unruly populations with appropriate mixtures of exhortation, trading incentives, and repression. "Tributaries" and "barbarians" could enjoy the same privileges as inhabitants of the core of the empire if they responded to the imperial carrots and sticks as humans were expected to do. Greedy traders and nomads could transform themselves into civilized people by accepting regulated trade with designated imperial representatives and by making gestures of submission to the emperor. Those who rejected these lures were defined as inhuman, therefore deserving extermination. Just as domestic rebels were divided into treasonous "bandits" and innocent "coerced followers" *(xiecong)*, so external peoples could become either loyal tributaries or alien enemies. A language of civilization defined the identity of these peoples and the treatment they received. Negotiation and incorporation were much more common than repression, but the iron fist always was held in reserve behind the smooth ritual mask.

This frontier expansion project stimulated official mobilization of the empire's economic resources. We have seen how, in Xinjiang, Qing officials promoted large-scale colonial settlement combined with agricultural and mining development. Here they expected extensive immigration of Han Chinese from the interior to raise the productivity of agriculture while binding the region more closely to the center. Xinjiang's experience, like the examples of Taiwan and bulk commodity transport, shows that the Qing officials could carry out significant developmental policies in select regions of the empire. Subsidized settlement thus affected the interior as well as the frontier economically in two ways: by relieving population pressure on marginal lands and by fostering commercial connections. Even if the number of emigrants was a small percentage of the total population and the number of merchants few, their activity had a disproportionate impact in regions of marginal agriculture and limited trade.

Yet despite these powerful capabilities, the Qing state was losing control of many aspects of economic exchange by the end of the eighteenth century. Against many examples of successful projects to relieve famine or settle new lands, we can place equally dramatic evidence of corruption and local oppression. For local officials, the potential for abuse was just as strong as the potential for beneficial action. The outcome depended on the degree of superior official supervision and local political incentives. A powerful provincial governor like Chen Hongmou could crack down on local laxness and abuse, but other governors might be less determined, or less capable. Despite extensive controls, the enormous paper flow of the bureaucracy by its very nature obstructed clear lines of communication and control, leaving the way open for abuse. The 1781 corruption case in Gansu, in which the provincial treasurer exploited the opportunities created by the innovative policy of allowing silver contributions for famine relief, was an ominous indicator of worse to come.

The End of the Qing State

In sum, a key turning point in the effectiveness of the imperial bureaucracy occurred around the middle of the eighteenth century, just as frontier expansion ended. The end to military challenges on the frontier let much dynamism ebb out of the bureaucracy. Its incentive to reform itself declined, and the will to control abuses slackened. There is, therefore, a connection between the completion of frontier expansion in the northwest and China's numerous troubles with social order in the nineteenth century.

If the Qing was a "developmental agrarian state," it was only sporadically, not comprehensively, developmental. Many of its projects were designed to ensure the security of poor regions so that severe attacks of famine would not touch off revolts, and so that military forces could obtain subsistence from local markets. Northwest China was an especially significant site of state intervention because the empire needed to send armies through the region, and gain supplies from it, on their way to battle the Mongols farther west. The northwest, though poor, did generate new policies toward the economy. Chen Hongmou devised innovative methods of agricultural production and mobilization for military needs when he served as governor of Shaanxi, as did other provincial governors and governors-general.

The end of this expansion in the mid-eighteenth century, and the end of the frontier wars, meant that both the incentives for innovation and the means of control slackened. Now there was not such a crying need to press agrarian resources out of the poor peasantry, and conversely, local abuse of the peasantry did not threaten to undermine the security of the entire empire. Paradoxically, the system of price-stabilizing granaries expanded to its greatest extent in the late eighteenth century, but the problems of corruption, peculation of official funds, false reporting, and neglect of grain storage expanded along with it. In the nineteenth century, despite some sporadic exceptions, these endemic weaknesses of the granary system would undermine the entire effectiveness of famine relief, allowing severe outbreaks of peasant revolt.

Many historians have argued that the competitive European state system established in the sixteenth and seventeenth centuries generated the process of state building, military mobilization, and commercial growth that fueled imperial expansion.[1] I would argue here too for plausible similarities between China and Europe during the period of Qing frontier expansion. From the early seventeenth to the mid-eighteenth centuries, the Qing empire also engaged in a competitive state-building process as it pushed its borders outward.

During this expansionary period, the Qing rulers initiated administrative

innovations that built an increasingly centralized and coordinated bureaucracy which used mercantile and agrarian resources actively for economic
development to serve its security needs. These reforms included the establishment of a Grand Council to coordinate secret information flows to the
top level of the state for military decision making; the comprehensive mapping of the empire contracted to the Jesuits, using new geodesic technology
from Europe; collaboration between officials and merchants to promote
commercial penetration of the northwest frontier, which shows some similarities to the European chartered trading companies; and active investment
in agricultural reclamation, including moving large populations and building an infrastructure to support agrarian productivity. In each case the innovations arose from the demand of the frontier regions for security and
the needs of the military commanders for adequate supplies.

Other policy debates of the period did not invoke immediate security
needs but still focused on economic reforms that affected popular subsistence. We can look, for example, at debates in the 1730s and 1740s over
how to use markets to provide grain for the "evernormal" granaries, fiscal
reforms under the Yongzheng emperor (r. 1723–1735) that increased the
rationalization of local tax collection, and continual discussions of water
conservancy.[2] These creative changes improved the ability of the imperial
state to manage flows of information, trade, and commodities in response
to pressures of harvests, populations, and security threats. The contrast between an "agrarian empire" and a "competitive state system" is too over-
drawn, and too static, to capture this dynamic.

European industrialization, in England and even more so on the continent, also depended on a dynamic generated by military competition. John
Brewer points to the fiscal demands created by England's numerous eighteenth-century wars, which led to the establishment of a national debt. Ken
Alder describes the important impact of military engineering in France in
constructing the basis of a standardized system of mass production.[3] We
may find it uncomfortable to accept Werner Sombart's argument that war is
inseparable from capitalism, but a good case can be made that these two
state undertakings are causally, not just casually, linked.[4]

Thus, in their political economy as well as in their ecology, China and
Europe were following parallel lines, at least for a time, in the early modern
period. The delimitation of a fixed border with Russia and the elimination
of the Zunghar Mongol state in the mid-eighteenth century, however, fundamentally changed the Chinese political economy of state building, while
Europeans continued to invest in their wars. David Kaiser, for example, has
shown how European rulers continually used interstate wars from the sixteenth through the twentieth centuries to achieve their political goals of

centralization, homogenization, and simplification.[5] Chinese rulers, in their own eyes, had finished their project by 1760.

The Qianlong emperor could boast that he had achieved something that none of his predecessors had done: ending the two-millennia-long threat from the Central Eurasian steppe. When he met Lord Macartney in 1793 and told him that the empire "possess[ed] all things in prolific abundance and lack[ed] no product within his borders," he was not expressing a deep-seated Chinese sense of xenophobia but boasting of a very recent achievement. He was also not telling the complete truth. Before the mid-eighteenth century, China had lacked two essential products for its security and economy: horses and silver. Now, with the defeat of the Mongols, horses were no longer a problem, but the empire still needed silver.[6]

The docile Mongols and Kazakhs provided huge numbers of mounts from the steppe, while the demands of China's commercializing economy generated the "great sucking sound" that drew in the silver supplies of the world. China was at least equal, if not superior, to Europe in many measures of economic productivity, popular welfare, and social equality. The emperor was indeed complacent, but he had not deluded himself about the state of the world. Yet the flexibility of the empire, its ability to react to external shocks and take advantage of new opportunities, seems to have declined, so that while Japan could react rapidly to the appearance of Western steamships in its harbor in 1854, Chinese officials could not mount a unified response to the Opium War of 1839–1842. But the source of Chinese weakness, complacency, and rigidity, like the Industrial Revolution itself, was late and recent, not deeply rooted in China's traditional culture.

Northwest and Southern Frontiers

Bearing out the prophecy from the Book of Changes, "When the sun is at its peak, it begins to set" *(ri zhong ze ze)*, the balance began to shift just as the Qing project reached its zenith.[7] China's increasing ecological and political difficulties in the early nineteenth century included floods and famine, peasant uprisings on the frontiers, and opium smuggling, in addition to the foreign pressure for trade privileges which culminated in the Opium War. The bureaucracy still had its share of energetic officials, who looked back to Chen Hongmou as a model, but they could not reverse the trend of decline. Wei Yuan, the great historian and advocate of military reform, drew his inspiration for resistance to the West from the eighteenth-century frontier wars of expansion, the "savage wars of peace" that had defined the empire's limits. If only the vigorous spirit of that time could be revived, he felt,

China could ward off the foreign threat. Thus, even after its conclusion, the period of expansion inspired visions of restoration and recovery of the empire's former greatness.

Four processes connected to the frontier conquests played a decisive role in the decline of the Qing empire in the nineteenth century: the accidents of timing of geopolitical relations, the misapplication of northwestern policies to southern environments, the power balance with localities of the Qing "negotiated state," and the impact of commercialization on social solidarity. A combination of logically independent elements, casually but not necessarily causally connected, brought down China's last dynasty. These are, of course, not the whole story of the Qing collapse, but they may help us develop new perspectives on the empire's critical last century.

My explanation for the decline of China and the rise of Europe in the nineteenth century is based first on contingent timing: the British happened to arrive on the South China coast with their demands to expand the opium trade after the 1780s, shortly after Qing troops had achieved their great victories in the northwest and welcomed back the Torghuts. The Qing did not see the British as a serious threat, compared with the Mongols they had just defeated. At the same time, domestic tensions within the empire, expecially exhaustion of cultivable land in frontier peripheries, causing social unrest that demanded the attention of the state, left it unable to respond quickly to the threat from the coast.

A second cause of China's slow reaction to the Western presence also derived from its northwestern experience. Many of the same Qing officials who had been stationed in the northwest attempted to apply the policies that had succeeded against the Mongols to their domestic and south coastal challenges. But strategies designed for Central Eurasian wars were appropriate neither for the mountainous terrain of the interior nor for warding off the sea nomads of the south. Of Qianlong's celebrated Ten Great Campaigns, the three northwestern ones deserved the title of successes, but the others had more dubious claims to greatness. They achieved little gain in security at very high cost.[8] On coastal defense and opium suppression, likewise, the northwestern experience was of little help. Apart from the timing, the kind of military and diplomatic experience gained on the northwestern frontier generated inappropriate responses for the new challenges on different terrain.

Current scholarship has blocked our ability to examine China's frontiers in relation to one another. Discussions of Qing relations with foreign peoples generally consider each relationship in isolation, so that, for example, the Canton trade system on the south coast is viewed as completely separate from the Russian trade in the north.[9] In addition, the use of the term

"Westerners" for Russians and British, for example, but not for Central Eurasians divides these trading and diplomatic relations in a misleading fashion. Lo-Shu Fu's invaluable translation of documents, *A Documentary Chronicle of Sino-Western Relations 1644–1820*, for example, omits many materials related to the Zunghars and considers them only in the context of Qing–Russian relations. Qing policymakers, however, dealt with all the peoples on their frontiers concurrently and applied similar principles to each of them. Many governors and governors-general who served in the northwest also served on the south coast. Continuity of personnel, common policies, and common languages unified frontier policies. The regulated caravan trade with the Zunghars of the early eighteenth century explicitly invoked the Russian precedents, and the south coastal trade with the British of the late eighteenth century built on this experience.

Relations on one frontier with one group altered perceptions of and behaviors toward other groups on other frontiers. We need to include Central Eurasians and Russians as well as Anglo-American traders as part of the same field of frontier relations, and we need to track the shifting influence over time of one experience on another. Here I only suggest some further avenues of research.[10]

Attentive readers will have noticed striking parallels between the pattern of trading relations on the northwest frontier and the well-known Canton trade on China's south coast.[11] From 1760 to 1834 Qing officials controlled British traders using precedents established in the northwest. Designated Han merchant groups obtained monopoly licenses to trade with foreigners; regulations strictly controlled access to ports, times of stay, and goods to be traded. Both frontiers even traded in rhubarb, the medicinal drug in which Lin Zexu placed such faith. Profits from the Jiangnan silk factories which sent goods to Xinjiang went directly to the imperial household department, just like those from the Canton trade.[12]

The Canton trade was, of course, much larger, generating annual exports of $7 million in Chinese goods, and it was quite profitable for the emperor and local officials. The emperor gained 855,000 taels annually for his own imperial household from the Canton trade, giving him a strong financial incentive to continue it. The court also had strong incentives to keep the northwest trade going, but there they were motivated more by strategy than by the lure of profit. One powerful autonomous official from the imperial household, the Hoppo, supervised the Canton trade, while several governors, governors-general, and the Lifanyuan watched over the northwest. These were on the whole, however, differences of scale, not structure.

Although in all of the trades (Zunghar, Xinjiang, Russian, and British) "commercial interests were subordinated to political raisons d'état," state revenue was an equally important consideration.[13] The Qing applied to the south coast the lessons they had learned from the northwest frontier, where close supervision of borders, cooperation with merchants, and restrictions on trade served as useful tools for gaining "barbarian" obedience. Officials applied much the same language to both the Zunghars and the British: they were greedy, unruly people with no sense of shame or ritual who needed to be controlled and softened by imperial grace.

The most important common feature on both frontiers was the constant pressure by outside merchants for larger amounts of trade, which border officials attempted to accommodate by flexibly stretching fixed regulations. Once again, the frontier served as an experimental zone for adapting precedents to local circumstances. Thus officials allowed goods to be sold at the border during tribute missions to the capital, permitted limited amounts of silver to flow beyond the borders, accepted large caravans that arrived unexpectedly, and made provisions for them to stay beyond legal time limits. These practical decisions allowed trade to proceed smoothly and avoided excessively burdening local authorities. All the foreigners astutely took advantage of local flexibility to push their own commercial interests as far as possible, but if they pushed too far, the Qing shut down the trade to bring them in line.

Merchants from China's interior played a vital role in all these trades. On the northwest frontier, they might be Han from Shaanxi and Gansu, Tibetans, Hui Muslims, or Turkic traders experienced in the management of caravan loads. Officials expected them to provide most of the capital for the border trade, but they were willing to supplement mercantile funds when necessary. In the northwest, the state played a larger role in financing the trade through official advances, while in the south, Canton merchants grew increasingly dependent on advances from British traders. Both groups of merchants went into debt, but the northwest merchants owed their capital to the state, while the Canton merchants owed most of it to their trading partners. Financial pressure pulled the merchants in two directions: toward the interior, where they disposed of the goods they bought, and toward the exterior regions, their source of supply.

Officials knew well that money bought allegiance. By intervening to shore up a barter trade in the northwest, they blocked monetary linkages between their own traders and the suspect Zunghars. There they were more effective in drawing the "barbarians" toward the interior economy than on the south coast. The much larger torrent of silver and credit flowing into the south drew Canton merchants into close dependence on their British counterparts. The British Select Committee and the Chinese Cohong became "wedded into a single Anglo-Chinese guild," united against competition from unregulated private traders.[14] Furthermore, although there was substantial private trade across both frontiers, the unregulated smuggling that developed along the south coast, with its many small harbors and fast ships, was far harder to control than the narrow choice of routes across the desert. And Qing military forces, having just completed the conquest of the region, were of course far more dominant in the northwest.

One could cite other similarities and differences, but this sketch suffices to suggest profitable comparisons between the two frontiers. It indicates that the Qing learned from their northwest victories a way of dealing with rival powers, but that they learned the wrong lessons for a very different frontier environment.

The Negotiated State

A third element in nineteenth-century decline was a result of the kind of state the Qing built. By looking at how imperial China defined its relationship with local authorities, especially in frontier environments, we can understand why the issue of when to centralize power and when to allow local autonomy always remained a critical element of state formation.

David Robinson, in an important recent study, has pointed to the prominence of local "men of force" during the early-sixteenth-century Ming dynasty, especially in the region around the capital.[15] Described as "bandits" by official sources, these were not poor peasants driven to rebellion by starvation in remote regions, nor were they would-be Robin Hoods struggling against the state on behalf of local communities. These so-called bandits had powerful patrons, reaching as far as the eunuchs in the imperial court itself. A major rebellion in 1510–1512, leading to an attack on the capital, revealed the deeply rooted local networks of power in communities throughout the capital region. Most local officials had chosen to bargain with, not repress, these local strongmen, allowing them to surround themselves with retinues of armed men who swaggered through the towns.

Repeated use of the terminology of "banditry" concealed the extent to which officials negotiated with influential men in order to stave off open conflict. "Bandit" was not an objective social category but a label used by state officials to mask a fluid, complex social reality. Robinson argues that most historians underestimate the impact of violence on China's history. Even in the relatively peaceful mid-Ming, local control depended precariously on compromises between civil officials and those who controlled military force.

By focusing on the need to negotiate with local men of force in the Ming,

Robinson adds some insight into Qing successes on the frontier. In contrast to their domestic policy, Ming officials never succeeded in negotiating stable defense pacts with the Mongols on the northwest frontier. In general, they regarded the Mongols as an alien, irredeemably violent force with which no compromise was possible.

The Qing rulers, however, realized that negotiation, with coercion held in reserve, could work just as well on distant frontiers as in domestic contexts. Mongol leaders held power in the steppe, but they could be induced to join the imperial cause. From the early period of the state's formation to the dramatic return of the Torghuts, the Manchu leaders gathered in Mongol allies. In each case, Mongol leaders gained official rank, salaries, gifts, and guarantees of subsistence in return for surrendering the right to move or freely designate their successors. As *jasaks* and banner commanders, however, they retained much of their local power, under close Qing supervision. Those who fought determined battles against Qing power, like the Chahars in the 1630s or the Zunghars, faced severe repression. But the Qing could never have defeated all the Mongols united together. The essence of Qing frontier policy was to keep the Mongols divided by constant diplomacy, drawing in allies against other, more dangerous rivals. For many Mongols, other Mongol leaders seemed far more threatening than the Manchu empire itself. Their "fatal individualism" generated tensions among the Mongols, but it would not by itself have brought all the Mongols under Qing sway. Only astute Qing diplomacy prevented unified resistance. Westerners, of course, equally divided among themselves but willing to follow British leadership, included "most-favored nation" clauses in the unequal treaties precisely to prevent this well-known Chinese strategy. Again, what worked in the northwest did not work in the south.

The Qing strategy did construct a centralized state, but by a very different process from that of western Europe. Karen Barkey's study of state formation in the Ottoman empire illuminates the varying paths to centralization in seventeenth-century Eurasia. Barkey calls into question the adequacy of Charles Tilly's simple classification of state-building processes as either "coercion intensive" or "capital intensive" by demonstrating a separate path of state building beyond these two European polarities.[16] She argues that the Ottomans created a centralized state by very different means from western European states like France because they negotiated with their rivals instead of trying to suppress them. While the rigid French centralizers generated strong resistance movements rejecting the right of the state to collect taxes or enforce laws, the Ottomans faced few peasant rebellions or elite revolts. The so-called *celali* bandits who created numerous local disturbances in the seventeenth century were not "social bandits" defending their communities against state impositions; they were mainly demobilized soldiers and vagrant peasants who sought higher positions within the state. Ottoman officials negotiated with these local men of force, granting them official posts and using their military might against other bandit rivals. Here, as in Ming China, *celali* was a state label that constructed a social type for the purpose of increasing state power. The Ottomans also employed force when negotiations broke down, but often they succeeded in bringing the *celali* groups into state structures without repressing them. The Ottoman state stands at the opposite pole from the French example of open defiance of state authorities by coalitions of peasants, nobles, and religious factions, but both represent successful examples of centralization and increased state penetration. Other studies of the Ottoman empire support this concept of the "negotiated state" and suggest comparisons with the Qing.[17]

China stands in between the Ottoman and French examples. Chinese state builders also brought in their rivals through bargaining, but they faced frequent revolts, too. As Barkey recognizes, Chinese local society contained many strong institutions that provided bases for autonomous organization outside the state. Village militia, religious associations, guilds, voluntary associations, marketing hierarchies, gentry literary clubs, native-place associations, and young men's groups proliferated beneath the bureaucratic hierarchy. The autocratic emperor and his officials were suspicious of all of these groups, but they could not eliminate them, only attempt to turn them toward the center. Hence a great deal of authority was delegated to local associations to carry out tasks that served the state. Distributing famine relief, investing in water conservancy, building bridges, operating orphanages, regulating markets, conducting rituals: these were functions performed by local elites under official supervision. If cooperation benefited both sides, local government could be carried out smoothly by flexible interpretation of regulations.[18] But when the state was weak or abusive, or local elites held the balance of power, conflict flared up.

Barkey argues that peasants rarely rebelled in the Ottoman empire because they had few bonds of trust or trade relations outside the household, but Chinese peasants had many more options. China, then, was a negotiated state in its interior, somewhat like the Ottoman empire, but its people had much stronger local social institutions and a greater ability to resist the state when they chose. Nevertheless, the need to balance the use of coercion against other levers of persuasion characterized both empires.

The Yongzheng emperor addressed these questions of negotiation and centralization when he responded to Zeng Jing's call for restoration of the "feudal system" espoused as the ideal form of government in the Confucian classics. Feudalism, in this theory, was in effect a formally recognized division of powers between the center and the localities, allowing local elites hereditary authority under central supervision. Many classical thinkers thought that, before the Qin dynasty unification, the feudal structure had permitted the intimacy between officials and people that produced China's golden age. Some argued for restoring it, while others argued that times had changed, making feudal values irrelevant under a unified empire, and some, like Gu Yanwu, called more modestly for "an infusion of feudal principles into the centralized state in order to cope with the shortcomings" of the bureaucracy.[19] Zeng Jing, however, took the extreme position that just as the Qin emperor had "stolen" power from the people for his own selfish purposes, the Manchus likewise had imposed an oppressive central bureaucracy on their Han subjects. Yongzheng's vigorous rebuttal of Zeng castigated all advocacy of feudalism as a treasonous effort to undermine central authority. With the recent repression of the Three Feudatories fresh in his mind, as well as a disputed succession, and facing powerful military figures like Nian Gengyao and Longkodo in addition to threats from his brothers, Yongzheng had good reason to fear loss of control. He firmly defended the centralized bureaucracy as the only way to ensure order within the empire and defend against threats from outside.

Yet on the frontiers, Yongzheng and his successors enacted precisely the feudalism they despised for the interior. *Begs, jasaks,* and lamas retained a kind of hereditary authority, even though Qing officials approved their posts, and held considerable autonomy in local administration beyond the typical district magistrate. In practice, this form of negotiated, delegated authority added useful flexibility to the administration of the frontier, where elites educated in the Chinese classical tradition were scarce and the population responded to other cultural norms. On China's frontiers, the same decisions faced state makers as in the interior: how to induce rival powers to yield to the expanding empire. Flexible, negotiated local administration, a feature of imperial rule everywhere, revealed itself more openly on the frontier than elsewhere.

Commercialization and Regionalization

Examining the earlier penetration of the Middle Eastern and South Asian "gunpowder empires" by European powers reveals a fourth element of the Qing decline. Christopher Bayly shows how processes within these Eurasian empires made possible the Western imperial intrusion. He argues that political crises rooted in commercialization that shook Muslim empires from North Africa to Java opened the way for European imperialism in the seventeenth and eighteenth centuries. These empires failed "because wealthy and prideful men found less and less reason to support the myth of empire to the disadvantage of their own real local interests."[20]

As the Ottoman historian Suraiya Faroqhi notes, Bayly "combines an Ibn Khaldūnian model of tribes breaking out of their habitats beyond the frontiers of settled civilisation with twentieth-century research on the growth of trade throughout early modern Western and Southern Asia," arguing that "the expansion of the British Empire in the latter half of the eighteenth century became possible because a dynamic generated in England coincided with a crisis caused by political and economic processes particular to the major states of the Islamic world."[21]

The major empires all experienced substantial growth of commercial economies beginning at least as early as the sixteenth century. The influx of silver from the New World played a vital role in increasing the money supply, but at least as important was the spread of New World crops, the turn to cash cropping, the development of local marketing, and the rise of trading classes from peddlers to large urban merchants. These groups were found equally in the Ottoman, Safavid, and Mughal empires, as well as the Ming.

Ultimately, Bayly argues, commercialization challenged the presuppositions on which the empires based their right to rule, which were fundamentally the maintenance of social order and the upholding of moral norms. In the Ottoman and Mughal empires, rising regional powers rivaled the claims of the central state apparatus. The eighteenth century is known as the "age of the local notables [*ayans*]" in Ottoman history, a time when local families were granted significant powers by the central regime. Ottomanists now argue that this should be seen not as the "decline" of Ottoman civilization but as a reorientation of political power toward regions in response to new commercial sources of wealth.[22] The Mughal state faced a more violent process of decentralization, leading to the formation of powerful military regional rulers like the Marathas. They too profited from the new opportunities granted to them by expanding international trading networks.

Bayly's argument points to the corrosive impact of commercialization on social solidarity. The cash nexus challenged bonds based on military loyalty, religious devotion, or kinship, replacing them with considerations of private interest. The state then had to gain the loyalty of its military and official servitors not through appeals to unity but through contractual relationships. In the Ottoman empire in the eighteenth century, the *malikane*, or lifetime tax farm, replaced the *timar*, or military service grant, as the main method of revenue collection for the center. The *timariot* held his land as a condition of military service to the sultan, but the *malikane* holder had nearly unrestricted control of his land grant; he owed in return only a fixed revenue to be delivered to the state. Dina Khoury and others have argued that the rise of *malikane* did not necessarily mean the breakdown of the Ottoman regime, but rather marked its reconstitution on a new, more commercialized and profit-oriented basis.[23]

Qing China had its equivalent to the *timar* in the form of the "feudatories" *(fan)* granted after the conquest to the Han generals who had supported the Manchus. Kangxi's repression of the Three Feudatories marked a more decisive rejection of the military service state than that of the Ottomans or Mughals, and it brought much greater centralization of power.

We can easily recognize how these elements of Bayly's description apply to late Ming China. There, too, concerned scholars and officials debated the social impact of silver and markets. They were most worried about the breakdown of social mores encouraged by the new mobility of wealth and the diffusion of consumer cultures.[24] Ming official discussions of social order, revenue collection, and military defense thus show striking similarities to those of their counterparts in the Hapsburg and Ottoman empires.[25] All of them felt that firm imperial control depended on a land-based economy of stable village settlers who paid revenues in kind. Ming China did, of course, restructure its fiscal system on a monetary basis under the Single Whip reforms, beginning in the fifteenth century. These were among the few major reforms in Chinese institutional history that began from the bottom up, as local officials struggled bit by bit to consolidate the multitudinous fiscal charges into larger units and convert them into sums payable in silver. The monetization of the Ming economy and fiscal system held off the threat of decentralization faced by all these agrarian empires, but it did not resolve the problem of frontier defense. The Manchu takeover was the result of Mongolian raids that exhausted the treasury, combined with rebellion by disaffected soldiers in China's least commercialized and most drought-ridden region, the northwest. The Manchus kept the monetized tax system and individual payment system introduced by the late Ming, removing the burdensome late Ming surcharges. After a short interruption, silver continued to flow into China from the late seventeenth through the eighteenth centuries. As the economy recovered and commercialization spread, many of the same phenomena seen in the late Ming recurred in the eighteenth century: the spread of market towns, the increase in cash crop production, the rise of a vibrant consumer-oriented merchant culture, and the increase in wealth of both small and large merchant classes. But it is notable that, unlike the Mughals and Ottomans, China did not have to contend with strong regional powers or local notables who challenged the power of the center in the eighteenth century.

Suggestions of an answer to the puzzle can be found by looking at Russia, the other vast empire of Eurasia. Russia also experienced considerable growth in markets, commercialization of agriculture, new mobility, and population growth in the eighteenth century. What distinguished China and Russia from the Ottomans and Mughals was that they continued to expand on their frontiers while the others did not. When China and Russia met, they negotiated border treaties and established regulated "ports of trade," which controlled mercantile activities and directed a substantial flow of revenue toward the state coffers. The revenue flow was more important for the Russian state than for China, which had much more productive agricultural lands to draw on. Russia kept expanding across Siberia and into Alaska in the eighteenth century, while China secured its control of Xinjiang. Some wealthy nobles could be bought off by being offered access to the profits of the new frontiers. Finally, frontier expansion offered an outlet for peasant farmers, relieving pressure on the land in the core regions while granting them greater freedom from state burdens. As the Tsars allowed the nobility to grind the serfs down more finely in central Russia, Siberia beckoned as a land without bondage.

Expansion and incorporation of frontier regions diverted pressures that would have forced decentralization on the central states. Merchant elites could benefit from cooperation with state officials in the development of the new regions. We have seen how the Qing promoted the penetration of merchant capital into Mongolia, Gansu, and Xinjiang in the form of investment in agricultural colonies and domination of the cattle trade.[26] Unification of the currency system likewise expanded the market opportunities for traders in the core. Special contracting arrangements allowed Jiangnan merchants to deliver cloth goods on spec to Central Eurasians, who sold them along the Silk Road. Merchants depended on the state to provide the public goods of security and infrastructure, while the state turned to them to relieve food shortages and promote internal trade. Since officials collected taxes in silver, they had a strong interest in making markets available to farmers. Uncommercialized regions only caused trouble for local administrators. In this sense, then, the Qing was not an "agrarian" empire anymore. Although the bulk of its tax revenue came from the land, that revenue itself depended on an extensively monetized agrarian economy, which relied on extensive cooperation with the merchant class.

As it turned out, both Siberia and Central Asia proved disappointing as major sources of revenue. Russia profited more than China because the fur trade yielded much more of value than the oases of Xinjiang, and especially because a large market for Siberian furs existed nearby in Beijing. China had no such equivalent market. Russian state revenues at first gained from the fur trade, but the percentage declined during the eighteenth century. As state-sponsored caravans became increasingly unprofitable, privatization of the trade looked more attractive. China benefited from Xinjiang less in direct revenue flows than in the "forward defense dividend" created by obviating the need to ward off nomadic attacks. No more large military expenditures were necessary against Mongolian states after the mid-eighteenth century, and the lands of Xinjiang did support military garrisons. Heavy subsidies from the interior were, however, still necessary. But even if the region did not pay for itself, Beijing officials could argue that the cost of subsidizing garrisons was less than the cost of extensive campaigns against autonomous nomadic rulers.

Frontier expansion and incorporation could hold off the pressures of regionalization driven by commerce, then, by increasing central revenue or decreasing strategic costs, coopting merchants in the exploitation of new regions, and relieving agrarian pressure in the interior. But these benefits had their limits, and each generated countertendencies. If the new territories yielded relatively little in valuable products but still required heavy military occupation, they would become more drain than gain. This argument was constantly reiterated by lower Yangzi elites opposed to the investment of their tax payments in faraway frontiers. Russia may have generated net profits for itself from Siberia, as its military establishment there was relatively small and mainly self-supporting, and fur revenues were high, even if not as high as expected. The Qing did attempt to reduce the administrative costs of ruling Xinjiang by consolidating military units, reducing troop strength, and vigorously promoting military colonies. At the same time, it increased civilian administration, which also drove up costs.

Private commercial exploitation of the frontier benefited the merchant classes and, by generating more trade, was able to increase the standard of living of the native inhabitants. It did not necessarily benefit the state, unless the state tapped this new wealth or benefited from it indirectly. As long as merchants participated in the grain trade, ensuring stable prices and shoring up peasant taxpayers, state–merchant cooperation facilitated the interests of both sides. But the continual debates over the granary system indicated that merchants did not always help the local people. They could hoard grain and drive up prices in order to make windfall profits; they could tie peasants to them with advance loans, forcing the peasants to deliver the harvest to only one buyer (monopsony); they could corrupt local officials with their wealth and divert official funds to private pockets. Gansu's relief scandal of 1781 illustrates the powerful effects of new commercial wealth in these underdeveloped regions. The merchant–local official nexus was the most threatening to central control because it provided local officials with independent sources of revenue and personal wealth from the central bureaucracy. In this sense, Gansu's scandal foreshadowed the larger problems that would arise in the nineteenth century when the *lijin* tax on commerce was directed into provincial coffers.

Peasant settlement, however, was the most explosive trend, especially for China. As Han migrants penetrated the northwest, they came into contact with diverse populations with alien cultural traditions. The Qing promoted diversity in the region, using the skills of each group for the most appropriate task: Turkic peasants skilled in oasis agriculture dug the canals to water their fields, with Qing backing; Han farmers tilled their own grain fields; Hui and Tibetan merchants transported woolen textiles, clothing, cash, and other products; Mongolians provided horses and, at times, grain. If land was abundant and the climate was favorable, these different peoples could work together for mutual gain; but the northwest was not always so lucky. Xinjiang's ecology was fragile, despite heavy state investment in water conservancy and land clearance. Struggles over water and land could easily generate conflicts, even without the religious factor added in. When new Islamic religious teachings entered Xinjiang in the eighteenth century, they provided foci for community organization. These led to outbreaks of rebellion that required greater military presence at greater expense.

This frontier serves as an early diagnostic of pressures that would strike the rest of the empire in the nineteenth century. The pressures of decentralization driven by commerce and regional elites seen in the Muslim empires did not become apparent in China until the nineteenth century. They had been present, however, as latent tensions ever since the conquest of Xinjiang. While the Qing promoted expansion and incorporation of the frontier, the tense balance between control and fragmentation could be contained, but after 1780, the pieces began to fly apart. At just this point the European traders on the south coast began to promote more vigorously their demands to open China's doors to trade.

Lord Macartney saw a strong but fragile empire in 1793, but he was wrong to attribute the Qing's future troubles to the character of China's leadership alone. The "tensions of empire" had undermined the structures of state power during the previous half century.[27] China's peripheralization occurred despite strenuous resistance by a state that still could mobilize impressive forces. But it was not the state that it had been in the seventeenth and early eighteenth centuries, when it had the largest armies, the richest merchants, and one of the largest territories in the world. This startling shift from strength to weakness was a consequence of the contradictory forces generated by its expansion into Central Eurasia.

R. Bin Wong argues hypothetically that if, say, the successors to Zheng

Chenggong, the powerful mercantile adventurer whose empire briefly occupied Taiwan in the seventeenth century, had created a powerful southeastern merchant empire in China and held out against the Qing through the eighteenth century, Qing officials would have been much more interested in articles of trade, such as weaponry, that the British had to offer. The British, in turn, would not have had to push opium to offset their silver outflow, and China could have resisted pressure to open treaty ports. "In short, a politically powerful China more able to resist militarily the British demands of the 1830s and 1840s could have resulted from a successful southeast Chinese merchant empire."[28] Wong does not claim that this outcome was likely but offers the possibility as a way to envisage alternative futures for China in the nineteenth century.

But one could argue for the same outcome if a Mongolian state had held out in the northwest. (This scenario is more plausible than Wong's, in fact, since such a state did last for nearly a century, while the Zheng regime held Taiwan only from 1661 to 1683.) Then the Qing rulers would also have been interested in getting modern arms for their military expeditions, just as they had contracted for arms production from Jesuits in the seventeenth century. They could have used British military experience, and might even have invited the British to observe their campaigns, like the Jesuits who observed the eighteenth-century wars. Chinese armies had, in fact, come in contact with British arms during their incursions into Burma in the late eighteenth century but failed to borrow any new military technology from the experience.[29] Had there been a strong Mongolian state, it is possible to imagine greater Sino-British military cooperation. The Chinese, aware of the British presence in India, likewise might have realized potential British influence in Tibet, concerned as they were with keeping Tibet out of Mongol hands. This hypothetical argument highlights the openness of China's relations with foreign powers created by its frontier expansion, and points to the possibility of more fluid geopolitical alliances, each of which had effects on military balances, technological reform, and the political economy of trade.

In sum, a view from the frontier shows why the completion of territorial expansion removed dynamics of state building, policy debates, and institutional formation that responded to a competitive geopolitical environment. Four interacting processes opened the Qing to western European penetration in the nineteenth century: new challengers appeared on the south coast shortly after the defeat of the Mongols; policies that were effective against steppe nomads failed in the maritime environment of the south; the negotiated settlements that balanced Qing central interests with local powerholders began to shift toward decentralization; and commercialization under way since the sixteenth century undermined loyalties to the center.

The unprecedented thrust from Beijing into the heart of Eurasia was the product of the conjuncture of a tricultural conquest elite formed in Manchuria, the penetration of a dynamic commercial economy into peripheral regions, and the adroit use of diplomacy. Since no Heavenly will determined the outcome in advance, it is no wonder that the unification of the high Qing did not last. More striking is the fact that over the long term, the modern nation-state has nearly reconstituted the empire of its ancestors of two hundred years past. But the modern nation-state *cum* empire also rests on contingent conjuncture, not on any inevitability. Past experience may offer some guidance to Chinese interested in negotiating a new identity for their nation in the twenty-first century.

APPENDIXES

ABBREVIATIONS

NOTES

BIBLIOGRAPHY

ILLUSTRATION CREDITS

INDEX

Appendix A

Rulers and Reigns

Manchu/Qing Khans and Emperors

Personal name	Chinese reign name	Manchu reign name	Years of reign
Nurhaci	Tianming	Abkai fulingga	1616–1626
Hong Taiji	Tiancong	Abkai sure	1627–1635 (period during which Hong Taiji ruled as Khan of Latter Jin)
Hong Taiji	Chongde	Wesihun erdemungge	1636–1643 (period during which Hong Taiji ruled as emperor of Qing)
Fulin	Shunzhi	Ijishûn dasan	1644–1661
Xuanye	Kangxi	Elhe taifin	1662–1722
Yinzhen	Yongzheng	Hûwaliyasun tob	1723–1735
Hongli	Qianlong	Abkai wehiyehe	1736–1795

Zunghar Mongol Taiji and Khans, with Years of Reign

Khara Khula	died 1635
Batur Hongtaiji	1635–1653
Sengge	1664–1670
Galdan	1671–1697
Tsewang Rabdan	1697–1727
Galdan Tseren	1727–1745
Tsewang Dorji Namjal	1746–1750
Lama Darja	1750–1753
Dawaci	1753–1755
Amursana	1755–1757

Source: I follow the chronology given in Zhungar Shilue Bianxiezu, *Zhungar Shilue;* other sources sometimes differ by one year.

Russian Tsars, with Years of Reign

Michael Romanov	1613–1645
Alexis	1645–1676
Theodore III	1676–1682
Ivan V (co-Tsar with Peter)	1682–1696
Peter I	1689–1725
Catherine I	1725–1727
Peter II	1727–1730
Anne	1730–1740
Ivan VI	1740–1741
Elizabeth	1741–1762
Peter III	1762
Catherine II	1762–1796

Source: Nicholas Riasanovsky, *A History of Russia* (Oxford: Oxford University Press, 1993), p. 631.

Dalai Lamas of Tibet, with Years of Reign

1, 2. Retrospectively given titles in 1578 as father and grandfather of no. 3.
3. bSod-nams-rgya-mts'o (1543–1588): given title by Altan Khan in 1578.
4. Yon-tan-rgya-mts'o (1589–1617): officially recognized in 1601.
5. Nag-dban blo-bzan-rgya-mts'o (1617–1682).
6. Tshangs-dbyangs-rgya-mtsho (1683–1706).
7. Blo-bzan-bskal-bzan-rgya-mts'o, born 1708, r. 1720–1757.

Sources: L. C. Goodrich and Chaoying Fang, *Dictionary of Ming Biography, 1368–1644* (New York: Columbia University Press, 1976), pp. 6–9, 1604; Arthur W. Hummel, ed., *Eminent Chinese of the Ch'ing Period* (Washington, D.C.: U.S. Government Printing Office, 1943–44), pp. 265, 759–761; Luciano Petech, *China and Tibet in the Early Eighteenth Century: History of the Establishment of Chinese Protectorate in Tibet* (Leiden: E. J. Brill, 1950), pp. 8, 9, 267.

Appendix B

The Yongzheng Emperor Reels from the News of Disaster, 1731

In this anguished, rambling, and intimate confession to his premier general, the Yongzheng emperor takes responsibility for the great defeat and tells his general to be cautious, but affirms the dependence of all affairs on the inscrutable will of Heaven.

An edict to Generalissimo Yue Zhongqi: From last year until now, nothing has turned out as I expected. I am really anxious and afraid. Painfully I reflect on my responsibility, and I find that we, ruler and minister, have brought all the blame on ourselves. Military strategists say: Those who show force arrogantly will lose; those who deceive themselves about the enemy will lose; those who do not know the other will lose. Our army has committed all these mistakes. Even worse, with the full blessings of Heaven, the preparations for armies on both routes, all were excessive. I regret it endlessly. I can only confess my sins to Heaven and atone for my crimes. What else can I do? The enemy's power has been far beyond what I had known or expected. As for the plan to advance and annihilate the enemy, not only is our strength and skill dubious, but also, seeing that Heaven does not favor us, do we dare violate Heaven's will? If we, ruler and servant, arouse the troops even further, our crimes will be even more unforgivable. But only the two of us should know these intentions. Not even the Vice Generals must be aware of them, lest the enemy extend his wild ambitions. If we are arrogant about our forces, underestimate the enemy, burden Heaven, and act impatiently, [the vice generals] will certainly move at the wrong time and miss their chance. For now I will respond to circumstances and wait for Heaven's grace. We cannot predict the day when I can wipe away this shame and take revenge. Now the main thing to focus on is to repent our sins and seek Heaven's forgiveness. We certainly cannot think of advancing and annihilating the enemy.

Although you originally proposed this strategy, if I had not agreed to it, how could I have recklessly believed you, or vigorously planned this great action? Furthermore, this frontier situation is an uncompleted goal of my father, and has been a hidden misery for the state. You simply carried out my intentions sincerely and energetically. I really have no one else who can take charge of this matter. I admire and rely on your loyalty, respect, bravery, and sincerity. Truly, my lack of careful examination committed crimes against Heaven and the spirits. How could I desire or bear to hold a grudge or resentment against you? This is my genuine, basic feeling toward you. I am afraid you will not be able to know this, and you won't really know my feelings. If, in the present difficult situation, you are ashamed that your earlier counsel proved unwise or allow some violent agitation to disturb your considered opinions so that I could no longer rely on you, nothing could harm me more than that. If you want to return my favor, the only thing to do is to ensure our security on the frontier. Use carefully the military stratagems that you have relied on before. Now the enemy has defeated us by force, but his forces are not united like ours. Do not neglect military preparations and do not divide our forces; rely on certain victory granted by Heaven to those with adequate plans. It all depends on you to decide when to act.

Absolutely do not try to relieve Turfan, even if the enemy attacks it in full force. My previous instructions and your proposals were all wrong. We must not relieve Turfan. Only you and Generals Yilibu and Chang must know this. Furthermore, Turfan has a city wall to protect it, and ten thousand heroic Turkic soldiers in addition to our three thousand troops there. If the enemy exhausts his forces in attacking it, he will suffer heavy casualties. For now we can only speculate on the consequences. To abandon these three thousand soldiers and the mass of Turfanis does not mean that I am ruthless. The situation simply makes it impossible to rescue them. The results are difficult to bear, but unavoidable. Heaven will understand us. You can decide to move the Turfanis quickly inside the main city wall and merely proclaim to them that our three thousand troops will join forces with them to await relief, calculating that even if the enemy attacks with several myriads of men, he may not take the city easily.

If Heaven bestows pity on the weak and defenseless honest people of Turfan, in the harsh midwinter there will be no supplies for the enemy to plunder. After a long siege, they will run out of provisions, and must then either move on our main camp or head via Yisun Chahan Qilaotu to plunder Kokonor. I leave it up to you to plan the best strategy. Assuming that the enemy clearly knows that our main force is drawn up to await them in the rear, they may not dare to penetrate deeply into Kokonor. They will just bide their time. Last year, when the enemy stole our horses, they lost over one thousand men. In the attack on Turfan, reports are that we killed five hundred of the enemy. Now Furdan reports that in the Northern Route campaigns he killed several thousand. In these reports of enemy casualties there must be some exaggeration, but there must be a total of at least two to three thousand killed in all these battles. Now all we can do is to match our large army against the limited number of Zunghar troops . . . These several thousand enemy casualties are one-tenth of his crack troops. The only strategy to destroy him is to let him come by himself against us. The main point is to kill as many of the enemy as possible, and gradually let Heaven reveal its will. Turfan is one example of this granted by Heaven. We can reinforce our defenses and wait for the opportunity to strike. This is the method for defeating the enemy. We should not expect total victory at present.

We must be sparing in our use of Manchu troops and use them only when appropriate. What do you think of this? It is not that I am stingy, but if we pit our limited number of Manchu troops against the limited number of enemy, it would be unbearable [to have so many losses]. Besides, instead of slaughtering the enemy on horseback, it is better to have foot soldiers kill them at close quarters so that the enemy cannot carry out his stratagems. You must carry this out methodically by yourself, and not let anyone else know, lest we damage the morale of the Green Standard and Banner armies. Conceal your intentions, and let the officers and soldiers think that you despise the Manchu troops' ability but do not dare say so. This is best. But I fear that the Manchu ministers, officials, and troops will disobey your wishes when they do not get special attention, and this will create hostility. Let Yilibu and Chang Ji know my instructions in advance, but they absolutely must not reveal them to anyone else. They will get the point and take care of things.

In general, you should regard the whole situation as if you were me, and make security and seriousness foremost. If you have the slightest thought of taking risky measures to achieve glorious deeds, or sacrificing yourself to repay my favors, not only would this be a mistake, but also you would forget my benevolence and commit an injustice. Nothing is worse than harming me this way. You must follow my orders and consider how to act appropriately. When Aqitu arrives, I will have passed on repeated commands to him orally, instructing him on my intentions of using troops. I am not accusing you of cowardice. We have both received Heavenly favor in many affairs. Heaven will certainly bless us again some day. For now, we must both merely repent of our sins and calmly await Heavenly favor. Emphasize careful defense, absolutely do not advance troops rashly. Hold fast in all things, be farsighted and look at the larger picture. Don't be concerned if you lose a few positions; I will forgive you. If you get so agitated that you lose perspective on the long-term goal, you will disappoint me. Could you bear it? Keep this in mind! Keep this in mind! Strive to follow my earnest instructions and admonishments: do not neglect any opportunity! If you see a completely safe opportunity, act extremely carefully. If Heaven grants us a complete victory, and the enemy flees, you absolutely must not pursue him a long distance. Why is this? Because we cannot gain success in a single engagement. Do not leave the city for more than several hundred *li* in pursuit before having the troops return. You know my intentions; consider them carefully. I am not a coward; I only respect the commands of Heaven and follow Heaven's will. You must take my intentions to your heart. You may take measures on the frontier to rouse up the warrior spirit, and proclaim an advance to exterminate the enemy, stirring up the troops to kill before advancing, but always follow my instructions carefully before you carry them out. Before undertaking a relief expedition, consider all factors carefully. In sum, stay calm and avoid agitation. These are my clear instructions, my most urgent orders about the relief expedition. You should not make a copy of this edict. If you want to read it over several times, you may keep it in your office for a while and return it with a batch of other orders.

I am in good health; please don't be concerned about me. How are you feeling?

Source: Guoli Gugong Bowuyuan, *Gongzhongdang Yongzhengchao Zouzhe* (Taibei: National Palace Museum, 1977–1980). Partial translation in Beatrice S. Bartlett, *Monarchs and Ministers: The Grand Council in Mid-Ch'ing China, 1723–1820* (Berkeley: University of California Press, 1991), p. 62; Shu-hui Wu, "The Imbalance of Virtue and Power in Qing Frontier Policy: The Turfan Campaign of 1731," *Études Mongoles* 27 (1996), pp. 258–261. I am grateful to Professor Bai Qianshen for help in reading the emperor's cursive script.

Appendix C

Haggling at the Border

These amusing excerpts illustrate the frustrating experiences of Qing commanders attempting to control trade at the border and the tenacious efforts of canny Central Eurasian caravan leaders to push as many goods as possible onto Qing markets.

Anxi Provincial Commander-in-Chief Li Shengwu memorializes on reports of barbarian traders arriving at the border:

On May 7, 1748, we received a report from Hami Division Commander Wang Neng'ai saying that from April 28 to May 4 each border post on the mountain ridges sighted from afar men and herds moving eastward on the Leibaquan road. The general received the report and concluded that these were barbarian traders [*maoyi yiren*] heading for East Daban. He immediately sent Captain Chang Qing with troops to East Daban to guard it and wait for the barbarians to arrive at the border. He waited until May 2 without sighting the barbarians. He then took ten crack troops with him to go beyond the palisade to reconnoiter. On May 5 he arrived at Kuisu and saw the barbarians coming.

He asked them, "What are you doing here?"

One of them replied, "This is our trading year. Our chief according to precedent has sent us to do business."

The captain asked, "How many men have come? How many headmen are there? What are their names? How many animals? When did you leave Ili?"

He replied, "There are 136 men, including 46 'Tartars' [Mongols] and 90 'turban heads' [Turkic Muslims]. Of our four headmen, three are Turki. I am Elianhuli; one is called Maimolitihali Bek [given below as Momolitibu], one is called Nasur Haji, and the Mongol is called Dakda. We brought many animals, but we lost many along the road; we don't know exactly how many there are now. There are about 1,300 horses, 600 camels, 900 cattle, and 50,000 sheep. We left last year in December from Ili. Because of heavy snow, the animals moved slowly, and it took five months to get here."

The captain asked, "How many camel loads do you have, and what is in them?"

He replied, "There are over three hundred loads, including a little over ten loads of raisins and sal ammoniac; the rest are hides, furs, and rations."

The captain said, "Nobody here wants to buy raisins or sal ammoniac; you cannot sell them. You know this; why did you bring them anyway?"

He replied, "We can use the sal ammoniac along the way, and we brought the raisins to eat, not to sell."

The captain said, "You traders should report your arrival in advance. We have been watching you from the guard posts for several days. Why didn't you send someone ahead to warn us?"

The headman replied, "If we sent a subordinate to alert you, he might make a mistake in reporting. We four headmen wanted to come directly to report in person. Because Nasur Haji fell ill, we are waiting for him to catch up, and we have brought several servants with us. Now we want to talk with the Hami high official; also our chief has a message to deliver to the general."

The captain said, "By regulation, you traders are allowed to bring only 100 men to Suzhou; why did you bring 136 men?"

Elianhuli said, "The extra men have come to take care of our health and keep accounts. Please wait for two or three days while our men from the rear catch up, and we will leave our servants behind the mountains with the animals. We four headmen want to cross the mountains to see the high official of Hami."

The captain said, "I must report your request to Hami, and I will return with an answer."

They agreed to wait while the captain reported to the general to await orders.

We find, in reference to the traders' statements, that we must wait until they arrive at Hami so that the Brigade General can determine the barbarians' situation, and the Judicial Commissioner can interrogate them. Send these reports to my office. I find that in this year the barbarians are allowed to trade in Suzhou. Even though they have brought extra goods and men, it's not convenient to prevent them from trading, but barbarians are by nature crafty, and their words are not to be trusted. Wait until they meet General Wang Neng'ai, and he will determine the truth.

Anxi Provincial Commander-in-Chief Li Shengwu memorializes on reports of the interrogation of barbarian traders at Hami:

I previously reported on May 10 on the arrival of the barbarian headman Elianhuli and his group at the border. Now, on May 16, I have received the reports of the Hami Division Commander Wang Neng'ai and the Hami Lifanyuan Secretary Nuomuhun. They say: According to the report of Major Hui Maolin, who was sent to East Daban to escort the barbarian headmen to Hami, Elianhuli and the three other headmen, together with twenty-four Tatars and turban heads, carrying five sacks, three fowling pieces, one short sword, leading thirty-six fast horses, forty-eight camels, of which forty-one carried loads, thirty-seven sheep for rations, arrived on May 10 at the palisade. Major Hui escorted them with his troops across the mountains. On this day they stopped at Nanshankou to rest. On the next day he took the barbarians to an open place south of Cai Lake, under the battalion's jurisdiction, to rest, and ordered troops dispatched to take care of them. On May 12 he allowed the barbarian headman to enter the town and submit his list to the Division Commander, telling him to bring his pass to enter the walls according to regulations, and to meet with the Lifanyuan secretary.

Elianhuli, holding the message and a bolt of cloth in his hands, presented them, saying, "This is our chieftain Tsewang Dorji Namjal's message to the Hami general, and a gift of *bolike*[?] brocade. This is Suzhou's trading year. Our chieftain, following regulations, has sent us to do business. The Division Commander asked their names. He replied [same names as above but different characters: Nuoluosu Haji, Momolitibu, Dakdu]. The Division Commander asked, "When you reported north of the mountains, you said there were [the same names with different characters]. Why are three of the names not the same?"

They replied, "The time before we thought the officials did not hear us clearly."

Division Commander: "When did you leave Ili? How long were you on the road?"

They replied, "Last year we left Ili, and we traveled for five months."

Division Commander: "Last time, when Anji Dunduo came to present tribute at Hami, he said you traders would not leave until the grass was fully grown [in the spring]; why do you come now?"

They replied, "When Anji Dunduo left, we were still collecting our animals and hides, and we had not yet named a headman. We had agreed to leave after the grass was fully grown, but after he left, our chief said that was too late, because when we returned it would be too cold. So he sent us four on with a message asking us to leave Ili early. We took our time on the road, and stopped for a while at Ürümchi to collect all the men and animals together. Then we came here."

The Division Commander looked at the message but could not understand it, so he asked the Mongol headman Dakda to read it out loud and have the Lifanyuan secretary write it down in Mongol, make a summary in Manchu, and then translate it into Chinese. The message told the commander that they had received the emperor's edict allowing them to trade in Beijing, but considering that the capital was far away, they could also trade at the border in Suzhou. Following the edict, they traded in the capital and returned. They returned to Hami to do more business. These traders are the same as you people who live on the border. It is a good place to do business in *bolike*[?] brocades. The commander asked them how many men, how many loads of what stuff, they said [same as above].

Division Commander: "Only one hundred men are allowed; why did you bring thirty-six extra, against regulations? You, Elianhuli, have traded here twice before, you know the regulations."

Elianhuli: "The extra thirty-six are bookkeepers, doctors, and cooks. We ask to be allowed to take them to Suzhou. There are only ten or so loads of sal ammoniac and raisins for our own use. We brought so many animals because the road is long and many of them are weak. We beg the commander to graciously sell them for us."

Division Commander: "You are supposed to sell them in Suzhou; how can we possibly do your trading for you? There are only a few official merchants in Hami, and no one wants your goods. You should follow regulations and go to Suzhou."

Elianhuli: "But many of our animals are exhausted and worn out. If we drive them all to Suzhou, many will die in the heat, and the grass and water are scarce along the way. Our common people will suffer."

The Division Commander, scolding them for disobeying regulations, exclaimed: "You barbarians are always joining together to ask for charity! I will discuss your appeals with my superior officers and let you know their response."

The barbarians agreed. We gave them food and drink, and took them to the garrison. [The above requests were reported; a response is to be sent to Tsewang Dorji Namjal.]

We note that in a previous year Elianhuli came to Hami and sold us over ten thousand weak and exhausted animals, after we granted him a special favor of imperial benevolence, but we warned him not to behave this way again. He must follow established regulations. And he agreed. Now again he brings these worn-out animals and asks to sell them at Hami! It's not a good idea to grant his request; it will only stimulate these barbarians' insatiable, illegal demands. I have sent Major Yan Xiangshuai to consult with Wang Neng'ai.

I also have a report from the Suzhou Circuit Intendant Niu Tingcai saying: "Last time we agreed to buy over fifty thousand animals from the barbarians; now they have brought double this number. Suzhou pastures are small and cannot support so many. And we fear that after a while many will die. We request that you cut back the number of barbarian animals by half. Near Hami in the mountains there is water and grass for them. Wait until they recover their strength, then let them move on the roads slowly to Chijin, pasture them there, and let the official merchants buy them and distribute them."

We note that Suzhou's pastures are very small, but Chijin has many Han peasant settlers, and their crops are just sprouting. We cannot let fifty thousand animals disturb them by grazing there. I have thought it over, and told the barbarians to graze their animals north of the mountains, where there is water and grass, let the animals grow stronger there, and then bring them on the road so that not so many may die. This will benefit them, and Suzhou will not suffer. We will manage the interior and exterior lands so that pastoralists do not harass the settled peasantry.

I told the major to tell Wang Neng'ai to discuss the issue with them, and he returned with this report: He received the order to go to Hami to meet Elianhuli et al., telling them that you requested permission to sell animals in Hami. He said, "The high official [Li Shengwu] tells you: perhaps the headman who first came did not understand the regulations or did not know that water and grass were scarce here, but you, Elianhuli, have been here several times, and know that water and grass are scarce in Suzhou. Last time the commander spoke to you personally, when he allowed you to sell your animals at Hami. Because the road was so far and the animals were weak, it was unavoidable. How can you come again bringing so many weak, exhausted animals to sell in Hami? You can't be trusted. Didn't you deliberately intend to violate regulations? Last time it was all right to bring ten extra men; now you bring over thirty men. Why is this? And also, you have their names all mixed up.

Elianhuli: "The commander is correct. We know that the emperor has been deeply gracious to us Zunghars. Formerly we had to go to Beijing to trade, but now we can trade at the border, which saves a great deal of expense. Our chief Tsewang Dorji Namjal and his people are all deeply grateful for the emperor's benevolence. Last time when I asked to sell animals at Hami, the commander told me that I must not bring so many animals next time. I must obey him. I am deeply ashamed. Also, I know that there is very little water and grass on the way to Suzhou, but our Tatars get their living from their animals. We bring these animals not just for our chieftain alone but for all the Zunghar people. There are some households that can sell hides, or can sell at other places, but the poorest people have no hides and rely only on their animals. If they send their animals here, I just cannot prevent them. We cannot treat the rich and poor the same. Since we received the great emperor's benevolence allowing our chief to establish friendly relations, his subjects who used to starve now have something to eat. When the people heard about the chance to trade, every one of them collected his animals to take advantage of the great emperor's benevolence. This is why I had to bring so many animals here again. As for bringing so many men, I really did not know that regulations limited the number of men at Suzhou to one hundred. I thought that bringing these few extra men as bookkeepers, doctors, and cooks would spare you trouble. As for mixing up the names, it is because many Chinese characters have the same sound; the official made this clear last time. As for bringing the extra animals to sell, our chief Tsewang Dorji Namjal certainly does not want to violate the emperor's regulations. I know that water and grass are scarce and these animals were nearly dying. But our poor people are really suffering. I thought this over carefully, and I am sincerely telling you the truth. There really was no choice but to sell them at Hami and depend on the emperor's grace to save our lives."

The major found the barbarian's explanation correct and followed imperial orders, telling Elianhuli, "You have too many animals and many of them are exhausted. You must pasture them north of the mountains where there is water and grass to let them rest. When they recover, you may divide them into groups and proceed. I will return and report your explanation to the commander and tell you his instructions."

The barbarians replied, "This is very helpful for us. We will do as you say. If we can receive the great emperor's grace, it will be very fortunate for us. As for our exhausted animals, there are only about ten thousand sheep, two hundred or three hundred cattle, and two hundred or three hundred horses that cannot move. We ask your indulgence to let us sell them at Hami. Please tell this to the commander."

We reported this situation. We also received a report from Wang Neng'ai that was the same as the major's report.

We note that we must inform Suzhou Circuit Intendant Niu Tingcai to make arrangements for this Elianhuli, who has brought so many more animals than last year, and many of them exhausted, to have them pasture north of the mountains. As for his request to sell the exhausted animals at Hami, we told him the last time that this would not be a precedent, and now he follows in the same tracks. It is difficult to allow it, else this would become a fixed precedent, but if we stick rigidly to the regulations, it will be difficult to keep these ten thousand or more exhausted animals alive. The poor barbarians will be devastated, and this will not carry out our emperor's policy of granting favor to distant peoples. But seeing that Hami is so remote, and since the troop reductions began, there are now only two thousand soldiers there, and merchants are also few, the barbarians coming and going every year asking to sell their animals are very constraining. We have not allocated any extra funds for its defense. If we instruct Hami to buy these ten thousand or more exhausted animals, it will cause them difficulties. I have sent Major Yan to consult with General Wang on how to arrange the sale of these animals without making it a constant rule. We can let the barbarians travel to Suzhou without trouble. As for the thirty extra men, the emperor has stated that we must not be fixated on petty details. We should allow them to come. The sal ammoniac and raisins are for their personal use; we should not prevent them from carrying these with them. We have clarified the question of the discrepancy in barbarian names. We must consult with the Governor-General, but I request imperial approval for the proposed settlement of this affair. Attached is the Mongolian message submitted from Tsewang Dorji Namjal, sent along with the bolt of brocade.

Submitted May 26, 1748, by Anxi tidu Li Shengwu.

Vermilion endorsement: let the Grand Councilors discuss this.

Source: Shiliao Xunkan 25 qi, pp. 481–483.

Appendix D

Gansu Harvests and Yields

(Tables D.1–D.3 follow on pages 584–587.)

Table D.1 Harvests in Gansu

Year	Season	Harvest (on scale of 1–10)	Rainfall (on scale of 1–5)	Source and comment
1738		7.9	3.0	ZPZZ
1747		5–7.5?	3.8	ZPZZ, summer 2–4, fall 6–8; = 7.5; range 6+ to 9+
1748		8.0–8.5	3.0	ZPZZ, overall summer 8, fall 8–9
1749		6.5–8.5	3.25	ZPZZ, 7–10 Hedong only summer; Hexi avg 6.5
1750		9	2.5	ZPZZ, Hedong fall 9.5, Hexi fall 8.5; ZPZZ, "best in several years"
1751		9.5	2.8	GZDQL 1.669
1753		8.5	2.8	ZPZZ
1754		8	3.4	ZPZZ
1755		7.5–8	2.8	ZPZZ
1756		7.5	2.8	GZDQL 15.243, 813
1757		6.5	2.8	ZPZZ
1758		6.5	3.2	ZPZZ
1759	summer	5.5	4.5	ZPZZ
1759	fall	5.5	4.5	ZPZZ
1760		8.5	3.0	ZPZZ
1761		9.5	2.6	ZPZZ
1762	summer	7.5	3.2	ZPZZ
1762	fall	6.5	3.2	ZPZZ
1762		8.5	3.2	ZPZZ
1763	summer	8.5	3.0	ZPZZ
1763		6.5	3.0	GZDQL 18.444;19.332
1766	fall	7.5	2.7	ZPZZ
1766		(drought)	2.7	ZPZZ
1769	summer	7.5	3.4	ZPZZ
1769	fall	7.5	3.4	ZPZZ
1770	summer	6.5	3.6	ZPZZ
1770	fall	6.5	3.6	ZPZZ
1771	summer	6.5 (drought)	2.8	ZPZZ
1771	fall	8.5	2.8	ZPZZ
1772	summer	5–9 (disaster)	3.0	ZPZZ
1772	fall	7.5	3.0	ZPZZ
1773		8.5	3.4	ZPZZ
1774		drought	3.0	ZPZZ
1776		drought	3.3	ZPZZ
1779		8	4.4	ZPZZ
1780		8.5	3.4	ZPZZ

Table D.1 (continued)

Year	Season	Harvest (on scale of 1–10)	Rainfall (on scale of 1–5)	Source and comment
1785		8.5	2.7	ZPZZ
1795		8.5	3.0	LFZZ
1796		7.5	4.3	ZPZZ
Avg.		7.62		
Std. dev.		1.055		
Coeff. of var.		0.138		
No. of yrs. >7		21		
No. of yrs. <7		9		
Total yrs. with data		30		

Source: ZPZZ: *Zhupi Zouzhe* memorials, *cangchu* category; LFZZ: *Lufu Zouzhe* memorials, *nongye tunken* category. Both in Number One Historical Archives, Beijing. GZDQL: Guoli Gugong Bowuyuan, ed., *Gongzhongdang Qianlongchao Zouzhe* (Materials from the Gongzhong Archives, Qianlong Reign). For rainfall sources, see Appendix E.

Note: When different sources give different estimates, the same year is listed twice. If no season is given, the estimate refers to the entire year.

Table D.2 Chinese military colonies

Year	Distributed by state (shi)	Provided by people (shi)	Harvest grade (1–10)	State portion (shi)	Total harvest (shi)	Yield (shi/mou)	Seed yield	Provincial harvest grade (1–10)	Source	Date
1742	21,652	63	3–13	34,032	90,428	2.50	4.18		LFZZ	1743.6.8
1743	23,261	134	3–8	28,867	82,181	2.27	3.53		ZPZZ	1744.6.18
1744	21,730	129	3–8	22,616	67,933	1.88	3.13		LFZZ	1745.4.27
1745	20,222	59	3–10	21,244	64,169	1.78	3.17		LFZZ	1746.4.18
1746				2,779					ZPZZ	1747.6
1746	22,990	106	2–7	23,896	72,737	2.01	3.16		ZPZZ	1747.5.15
1747	21,854	89	3–9	23,986	70,388	1.95	3.22	6.2	ZPZZ	1748.4.4
1749	20,800		2.5–10	15,862	53,924	1.49	2.59	7.5	ZPZZ	1750.4.28
1751	23,841		2–8	26,040	77,215	2.14	3.24	9.5	GZDQL	1752.4.26 2.823
1752	23,456		3–8	25,182	75,108	2.08	3.20		LFZZ	1752.5.4
1753	22,603		3–8	53,489	130,843	3.62	5.79	8.5	GZDQL	1754.4.18 8.57
1754	22,548		3–8	40,084	117,822	3.26	5.23	8.0	LFZZ	1755.2.26
1755	22,493		2–8	35,729	95,130	2.63	4.23	7.7	LFZZ	1756.4.10
1756	21,447	1,112	2–7	30,882	84,439	2.34	3.94	7.5	ZPZZ	1757.5.2
1757	25,528	1,113	1–7	25,741	78,081	2.16	3.06	6.5	ZPZZ	1758.4.27
1758	26,654	1,114	1–8	15,980	88,681	2.45	3.33	6.5	ZPZZ	1759.6.15
1759	26,640	1,110	1.7–7.5	26,141	108,986	3.02	4.09	5.5	ZPZZ	1760.5.22
1761	22,631	1,127	3.1–5.9	29,443	106,083	2.94	4.69	9.5	ZPZZ	1762.4.16
1762	22,583	1,127	1.8–5.9	10,584	66,136	1.83	2.93	7.5	GZDQL	1763.1 16.512; 17.204
1766	3,703		2.2–5.5	6,867	14,377		3.88	7.5	ZPZZ	1766.12.20
1769	3,703		2.1–4.8	2,877	13,247		3.58	7.5	ZPZZ	1769.12.10
1771	3,703		1.8–4.7	2,056	12,614		3.41	6.5	ZPZZ	1771.11.29
1772	3,703		2–5.1	2,696	12,879		3.48	7.5	ZPZZ	1772.11.17
1779	1,499			1,583	6,212		4.14	8.0	ZPZZ	1779.12.20
1780	1,499			1,564	6,176		4.12	8.5	ZPZZ	1780.11.18
1786	1,499			1,681	6,412		4.28		ZPZZ	1786.12.8
Average						2.35	3.74			

Note: Gansu area = 36,131 *mou*, 1742–1762. Seed yield is the ratio of seeds harvested to seeds planted. For sources, see Table D.1. For 1742–1747, author is Huang Tinggui; for 1749, 1752–1754, Echang; for 1756–1759, 1766, Wu Dashan; for 1761, Ming De; for 1762, Yang Yingju; for 1769, Ming Shan; for 1771, Wen Shou; for 1772, 1779–1780, Lerquin; for 1876, Yongbao.

Table D.3 Muslim colonies in Guazhou, Anxi

Year	Seed planted (shi)	Seed yield	Harvest (shi)	Area yield (shi/mou)
1735	1,685			
1747	8,000	6.03	45,265	2.69
1749	8,000	5.47	40,630	2.41
1750	8,000	3.52	25,739	1.53
1751	8,000	6.10	45,345	2.69
1753	8,000	7.43	55,338	3.28
1754	8,000	7.10	52,379	3.11
1755	8,000	7.07	53,241	3.16
Average		6.12	45,420	2.69

Source: Zhupi Zouzhe memorials, *nongye tunken;* for 1751, GZDQL 2.118.

Note: Area = 16,854 *mou* in 1735; 20,400 *mou* in 1757. Total households = 680 *hu* (1757). Seed yield is the ratio of seeds harvested to seeds planted.

Appendix E

Climate and Harvests
in the Northwest

The distinctive climate of the northwest greatly influenced its grain markets. The Climate Research Center has published yearly charts and maps of wet and dry years in China from 1470 to 1979 (Zhongyang Qixiangju Qixiang Kexue Yanjiuyuan [ZQQKY], Zhongguo Wubainian Hanlao Fenbu Tuji [Beijing: Ditu Chubanshe, 1981]). They grade the amount of rainfall in each prefecture into five categories: 1 = "very wet," 2 = "wet," 3 = "normal," 4 = "dry," and 5 = "very dry." The compilers use extensive information from gazetteers all over the empire, although they have not consulted the memorial reports on rainfall in the Beijing archives. If these data are reliable, we may use them to gain a general picture of rainfall conditions over the empire and to examine the impact of years of drought. How plausible are these data? Table D.1 compares harvest reports from Gansu with the rainfall data in this compilation. As it shows, the four driest years do correspond to lower harvest yields across Gansu. Furthermore, we have an extensive report of a relief campaign conducted by Governor General Nayancheng in Gansu in 1810, a year, according to him, of severe drought. This year is indeed classified as a drought year in the *Hanlao* compilation (ZQQKY, map, p. 176). The year 1759, which we know to have been a time of drought, poor harvest, and high prices, is portrayed as a time of major drought in the northwest (ZQQKY, map, p. 150). Broadly speaking, the data in this compilation are usable as indicators of the rainfall conditions across the empire.

Table E.1 Wet and dry years in Gansu, 1725–1810

Wet (1–2)	7
Normal (3)	67
Dry (4–5)	12
Total	86
Average	3.01
Std. dev.	0.57

Note: Years are rated on a scale from 1 to 5, with 1 the wettest and 5 the driest.

Averaging the rainfall grades from the six stations gives annual figures for the overall rainfall in Gansu. From 1724 to 1810 Gansu's average rainfall was "normal" (mean of 3.01 with standard deviation of 0.57; see Table E.1). We may classify as "dry" those years that average over 3.5, and "wet" those years that average under 2.5, each approximately more than one standard deviation away from the mean. Gansu then had seven wet years and twelve dry years during this period. The driest years in Gansu were 1759 (4.5), 1779 (4.4), 1796 (4.33), and 1801 (4.17). The year 1759, the driest of the entire period, also had the lowest harvest yields (5.5). Grain prices soared to unprecedented levels in 1759, while they were generally stable during the rest of the eighteenth century.

There is not necessarily a direct correlation between rainfall and harvests in every year. As local officials often noted, areas with irrigation supplies could withstand temporary droughts, and areas relying on mountain snow-melt could get water in the spring even if no rain fell. Sometimes heavy rain or snowfall was not beneficial to crops. Although floods were rare in Gansu, heavy hailstorms often damaged crops. Most of the time rainfall was distributed unevenly across the region: only in certain rare years, such as 1759, did the rains fail across the entire province. The local variability of rainfall and harvests allowed officials to ship grain between regions to relieve local disasters.

Abbreviations

GZDKX   Guoli Gugong Bowuyuan, ed., *Gongzhongdang Kangxichao Zouzhe*
GZDQL   Guoli Gugong Bowuyuan, ed., *Gongzhongdang Qianlongchao Zouzhe*
GZDYZ   Guoli Gugong Bowuyuan, ed., *Gongzhongdang Yongzhengchao Zouzhe*
HCJSWB   He Changling, comp., *Huangchao Jingshi Wenbian*
LFZZ   *Lufu Zouzhe* memorials, Number One Historical Archives, Beijing
LSDA   Zhongguo Diyi Lishi Dang'anguan, comp., "Qianlong 8 zhi 15 nian
         Zhungar bu zai Suzhou dengdi maoyi"
PDZGFL   Fu Heng, comp., *Pingding Zhungar Fanglue*
QPSF   Zhang Yushu, comp., *Qinzheng Pingding Shuomo Fanglue*
QRZ   *Qingshi Bianweihui*, ed., Qingdai Renwu Zhuan'gao.
QSLKX   *Da Qing Lichao Shilu* (Shengzu: Kangxi reign)
QSLQL   *Da Qing Lichao Shilu* (Gaozong: Qianlong reign)
QSLYZ   *Da Qing Lichao Shilu* (Shizong: Yongzheng reign)
SLXK   *Shiliao Xunkan*
YZHZZ   Zhongguo Diyi Lishi Dang'anguan, comp., *Yongzhengchao Hanwen
         Zhupi Zouzhe Huibian*
ZGSL   Zhungar Shilue Bianxiezu, *Zhungar Shilue*
ZPZZ   *Zhupi Zouzhe*, Number One Historical Archives, Beijing

Notes

Introduction

1. The term "Great Game" usually refers to the geopolitical rivalry over Central Eurasia between the British and Russian empires in the nineteenth century. Rudyard Kipling used it in his novel *Kim*, published in 1901. For recent studies, see Peter Hopkirk, *The Great Game: The Struggle for Empire in Central Asia* (New York: Kodansha, 1992); Karl E. Meyer and Shareen Blair Brysac, *Tournament of Shadows: The Great Game and the Race for Empire in Central Asia* (Washington, D.C.: Counterpoint, 1999).

2. Rein Taagepera lists the Russian and Qing empires as third and fifth among the twenty largest empires in world history, rivaled only by the British, Mongol, and French. Rein Taagepera, "Size and Duration of Empire: Systematics of Size," *Social Science Research* 7 (1978), p. 126.

3. Outer Mongolia proclaimed its independence in 1911 but became a Soviet satellite under Red Army occupation in 1921.

4. For an only partially adequate narrative of these events, based primarily on Russian sources, see Fred W. Bergholz, *The Partition of the Steppe: The Struggle of the Russians, Manchus, and the Zunghar Mongols for Empire in Central Asia, 1619–1758: A Study in Power Politics* (New York: Peter Lang, 1993). Reviews by Elizabeth Endicott-West in *Journal of Asian Studies* 53, no. 2 (May 1994), pp. 527–528, and Robert Montgomery in *Mongolian Studies* 17 (1994), pp. 105–118. Morris Rossabi, *China and Inner Asia: From 1368 to the Present Day* (New York: Pica Press, 1975), contains a brief discussion, as does Thomas J. Barfield, *The Perilous Frontier: Nomadic Empires and China* (Cambridge, Mass.: Basil Blackwell, 1989), pp. 266–296.

5. Denis Sinor, *Introduction à l'Étude de l'Asie Centrale* (Wiesbaden: O. Harrassowitz, 1963).

6. Luc Kwanten, *Imperial Nomads* (Philadelphia: University of Pennsylvania Press, 1979).

7. Halil Inalcik, *The Ottoman Empire: The Classical Age, 1300–1600* (New York: Praeger Publishers, 1973); Huri İslamoğlu and Çaglar Keyder, "Agenda for Ottoman History," in *The Ottoman Empire and the World-Economy*, ed. Huri İslamoğlu-İnan (Cambridge: Cambridge University Press, 1987), pp. 42–62; Peter C. Perdue and Huri İslamoğlu, "Introduction to Special Issue on Qing and Ottoman Empires," *Journal of Early Modern History* 5, no. 4 (December 2001), pp. 271–282.

8. Major Japanese scholars cited throughout this text include Chiba Muneo, Ishihama Yumiko, Katō Naoto, Okada Hidehiro, Miyawaki Junko, Saguchi Tōru, and Wakamatsu Hiroshi. The main Chinese-language survey is Zhungar Shilue Bianxiezu, *Zhungar Shilue* (Outline history of the Zunghars) (Beijing: Renmin Chubanshe, 1985) (abbreviated ZGSL). There are Chinese articles in Zhungar Shilue Bianxiezu, *Zhungarshi Lunwenji* (1981), and excerpted sources in Zhungar Shilue Bianxiezu, ed., *Qingshilu Zhungar Shiliao Zhebian* (Xinjiang: Renmin Chubanshe, 1986).

9. Franz Michael, *The Origin of Manchu Rule in China: Frontier and Bureaucracy as Interacting Forces in the Chinese Empire* (Baltimore: Johns Hopkins University Press, 1942).

10. Peter C. Perdue, "Turning Points: Rise, Crisis, and Decline Paradigms in the Historiography of Two Empires," paper presented at the Conference on Shared Histories of Modernity: State Transformations in the Chinese and Ottoman Contexts, Seventeenth through Nineteenth Centuries, New York University, Kevorkian Center for Middle Eastern Studies, 1999.

11. Fernand Braudel, *A History of Civilizations*, trans. Richard Mayne (New York: Penguin, 1994), p. 164: "The real scourge [of India and China], comparable to the biblical plagues of Egypt, came from the great deserts and steppes . . . which are torrid under the summer sun, and in winter buried under enormous drifts of snow. . . . As soon as [pastoral tribes] appeared in history, they were what they would remain until their decline in the mid-seventeenth century: hordes of violent, cruel, pillaging horsemen full of daredevil courage."

12. William T. Rowe, *Saving the World: Chen Hongmou and Elite Consciousness in Eighteenth-Century China* (Stanford: Stanford University Press, 2001), reviewed by Peter C. Perdue in *China Quarterly* 172 (December 2002), pp. 1096–97; Jack A. Goldstone, "The Problem of the Early Modern World," *Journal of the Economic and Social History of the Orient* 41 (1998), pp. 250–283; Hisayuki Miyakawa, "An Outline of the Naitō Hypothesis and Its Effect on Japanese Studies of China," *Far Eastern Quarterly* 14, no. 8 (1955), pp. 533–552.

13. Di Cosmo, "State Formation"; Thomas J. Barfield, *The Perilous Frontier: Nomadic Empires and China* (Cambridge, Mass.: Basil Blackwell, 1989).

14. Cyril Black et al., *The Modernization of Inner Asia* (Armonk, N.Y.: M. E. Sharpe, 1991).

15. David Christian, "Inner Eurasia as a Unit of World History," *Journal of World History* 5 (1994), pp. 173–213; Andre Gunder Frank, "The Centrality of Central Asia," *Comparative Asian Studies* 8 (1992), pp. 1–57; Owen Lattimore, *Inner Asian Frontiers of China* (Boston: Beacon Press, 1962); Owen Lattimore, *Studies in Frontier History: Collected Papers, 1928–1958* (New York: Oxford University Press, 1962); Halford Mackinder, "The Geographical Pivot of History," *Geographical Journal* 23 (April 1904), pp. 421–444; Halford J. Mackinder, *Democratic Ideals and Reality: A Study in the Politics of Reconstruction* (New York: Henry Holt, 1942). Mackinder's theory is ap-

plied to Russia by John P. LeDonne, *The Russian Empire and the World, 1700–1917: The Geopolitics of Expansion and Containment* (New York: Oxford University Press, 1997).

16. Victor Lieberman, ed., *Beyond Binary Histories: Re-imagining Eurasia to ca. 1830* (Ann Arbor: University of Michigan Press, 1999).

17. John Mack Faragher, "The Frontier Trail: Rethinking Turner and Reimagining the American West," *American Historical Review* 98 (February 1993), pp. 106–117.

18. Morris Rossabi, "The 'Decline' of the Central Asian Caravan Trade," in *The Rise of Merchant Empires*, ed. James D. Tracy (Cambridge: Cambridge University Press, 1990), pp. 351–370.

1. Environments, State Building, and National Identity

1. Charles-Louis de Secondat de Montesquieu, "De L'Esprit des Lois, ou du Rapport que les Lois Doivent Avoir avec la Constitution de Chaque Gouvernement, les Moeurs, le Climat, la Religion, le Commerce, etc.," in *Oeuvres complètes*, (Paris: Gallimard, 1951), pp. 227–995; Denis Sinor, "Montesquieu et le monde altaique," *Études Mongoles* 27 (1996), pp. 51–57; Karl Wittfogel, *Oriental Despotism: A Comparative Study of Total Power* (New Haven: Yale University Press, 1957).

2. Ellsworth Huntington, *The Pulse of Asia: A Journey in Central Asia Illustrating the Geographic Basis of History* (Boston: Houghton Mifflin, 1919), p. 14.

3. "Parts of China have been growing drier and less inhabitable during recent centuries, and if the process continues, we are in danger of being overrun by hungry Chinese in search of bread." Ibid., p. 6.

4. Arnold Toynbee, *A Study of History*, 12 vols. (Oxford: Oxford University Press, 1934), 3:15.

5. Owen Lattimore, *Studies in Frontier History: Collected Papers, 1928–1958* (New York: Oxford University Press, 1962), pp. 62, 116 (quote), 492–500. Mark Elvin endorses the connection between climate change and nomadic invasions, but admits that "we are talking here of pressures operating in contexts that, overall, were much more causally complex." Mark Elvin, *The Retreat of the Elephants: An Environmental History of China* (New Haven: Yale University Press, 2004), pp. 6–7.

6. Jeremy Adelman and Stephen Aron, "From Borderlands to Borders: Empires, Nation-States, and the Peoples in Between in North American History," *American Historical Review* 104 (1999), pp. 814–844, 1221–39, with comments by Haefeli, Schmidt-Nowara, Wunder, and Hämäläinen; John F. Richards, "Land Transformation," in *The Earth as Transformed by Human Action: Global and Regional Changes in the Biosphere over the Past Three Hundred Years*, ed. B. L. Turner et al. (Cambridge: Cambridge University Press, 1990), pp. 163–178; John F. Richards, *The Unending Frontier: An Environmental History of the Early Modern World* (Berkeley: University of California Press, 2003).

7. William Cronon, *Changes in the Land: Indians, Colonists, and the Ecology of New England* (New York: Hill and Wang, 1983); William Cronon, "Kennecott Journey: The Paths Out of Town," in *Under an Open Sky: Rethinking America's Western Past*, ed. William Cronon, George Miles, and Jay Gitlin (New York: Norton, 1992), pp. 28–51; William Cronon, *Nature's Metropolis* (New York: Norton, 1991).

8. Alfred W. Crosby, *Ecological Imperialism: The Biological Expansion of Europe*

(Cambridge: Cambridge University Press, 1986); John R. McNeill, "Of Rats and Men: A Synoptic Environmental History of the Island Pacific," *Journal of World History* 5 (Fall 1994), pp. 299–349.

9. John Mack Faragher, "The Frontier Trail: Rethinking Turner and Reimagining the American West," *American Historical Review* 98 (February 1993), pp. 106–117.

10. Patricia Nelson Limerick, *The Legacy of Conquest: The Unbroken Past of the American West* (New York: Norton, 1987).

11. Charles Tilly, ed., *The Formation of National States in Western Europe* (Princeton, N.J.: Princeton University Press, 1975).

12. Immanuel Wallerstein, *The Modern World-System: Capitalist Agriculture and the Origins of the European World Economy in the Sixteenth Century* (New York: Academic Press, 1974), pp. 1, 57–63.

13. Tilly, *National States*, p. 34.

14. Recent anthologies include Geoff Eley and Ronald Grigor Suny, eds., *Becoming National* (Oxford: Oxford University Press, 1996); John Hutchinson and Anthony D. Smith, eds., *Nationalism* (Oxford: Oxford University Press, 1994). The seminal work is, of course, Benedict Anderson, *Imagined Communities: Reflections on the Origins and Spread of Nationalism* (London: Verso, 1991).

15. Prasenjit Duara, "De-constructing the Chinese Nation," *Australian Journal of Chinese Affairs* 30 (1993), pp. 1–28; Prasenjit Duara, "Historicizing National Identity, or Who Imagines What and When," in Eley and Suny, *Becoming National*, pp. 151–178; Prasenjit Duara, *Rescuing History from the Nation: Questioning Narratives of Modern China* (Chicago: University of Chicago Press, 1995).

16. Eric J. Hobsbawm, "The New Threat to History (Address to the Central European University, Budapest)," *New York Review of Books*, December 16, 1993, pp. 62–64.

17. The term "geobody" comes from Thongchai Winichakul, *Siam Mapped: A History Of The Geo-Body of a Nation* (Honolulu: University of Hawai'i Press, 1994). I thank James Millward for the felicitous phrase "geobody building."

18. William McNeill, *Mythistory and Other Essays* (Chicago: University of Chicago Press, 1986).

19. Cyril Black et al., *The Modernization of Inner Asia* (Armonk, N.Y.: M. E. Sharpe, 1991), p. 3.

20. Joseph Fletcher, "The Mongols: Ecological and Social Perspectives," *Harvard Journal of Asiatic Studies* 46 (1986), p. 12.

21. Denis Sinor, *Introduction a l'Étude de l'Asie Centrale* (Wiesbaden: O. Harrassowitz, 1963).

22. Richard N. Frye, *The Heritage of Central Asia: From Antiquity to the Turkish Expansion* (Princeton: Markus Wiener Publishers, 2001).

23. Denis Sinor, ed., *The Cambridge History of Early Inner Asia* (Cambridge: Cambridge University Press, 1990), p. 29.

24. K. De B. Codrington, "A Geographical Introduction to the History of Central Asia," *Geographical Journal* 104 (1944), p. 28.

25. Justin Jon Rudelson, *Oasis Identities: Uyghur Nationalism along China's Silk Road* (New York: Columbia University Press, 1997), p. 42.

26. Larry Moses, "A Theoretical Approach to the Process of Inner Asian Confederation," *Études Mongoles* 5 (1974), pp. 113–122.

27. Frye, *Heritage,* p. 13.

28. Lattimore, *Studies,* p. 68.

29. Fernand Braudel, *The Mediterranean and the Mediterranean World in the Age of Philip II,* trans. Sian Reynolds (New York: Harper & Row, 1972), p. 25.

30. Codrington, "Geographical Introduction," p. 30.

31. Sinor, *Cambridge History,* p. 37.

32. Robert N. Taaffee, "The Geographic Setting," in Sinor, *Cambridge History,* pp. 32–33.

33. On climate change in eastern Eurasia, see James Reardon-Anderson, "Man and Nature in the West Liao River Basin, during the Past 10,000 Years," unpublished ms. (1994); James Reardon-Anderson, "Reluctant Pioneers: China's Northern Frontier, 1644–1937," unpublished ms. (2002); and Elvin, *Retreat,* pp. 5–8.

34. David Christian, "Inner Eurasia as a Unit of World History," *Journal of World History* 5 (1994), p. 199.

35. Boris A. Litvinskii, "The Ecology of the Ancient Nomads of Soviet Central Asia and Kazakhstan," in *Ecology and Empire: Nomads in the Cultural Evolution of the Old World,* ed. Gary Seaman (Los Angeles: Ethnographics Press, 1989), p. 64.

36. Recent archaeological work in Russia confirms that the first Asian nomads came from the forests. Nicola Di Cosmo, *Ancient China and Its Enemies: The Rise of Nomadic Power in East Asian History* (Cambridge: Cambridge University Press, 2001), pp. 21–43; Nicola Di Cosmo, "Ancient Inner Asian Nomads: Their Economic Basis and Its Significance in Chinese History," *Journal of Asian Studies* 53 (November 1994), pp. 1092–1112. Cf. Lattimore, *Studies,* p. 142.

37. Harold Peake and Herbert Fleure, *The Steppe and the Sown* (New Haven: Yale University Press, 1928).

38. Fletcher, "The Mongols," pp. 15, 40.

39. Thomas J. Barfield, *The Perilous Frontier: Nomadic Empires and China* (Cambridge, Mass.: Basil Blackwell, 1989).

40. Nicola Di Cosmo notes, however, that this sharp distinction of barbarian nomad and civilized settler does not apply to the earliest period of Chinese civilization: it was a product of the wars between the Han dynasty and the Xiongnu confederacy in the second century BCE. Di Cosmo, *Ancient China and Its Enemies.*

41. Moses, "Theoretical Approach."

42. David Anthony, Dimitri Y. Telegin, and Dorcas Brown, "The Origin of Horseback Riding," *Scientific American* (December 1991), pp. 94–100; David W. Anthony and Nikolai B. Vinogradov, "Birth of the Chariot," *Archaeology* (March–April 1995), pp. 36–41.

43. Herrlee G. Creel, "The Role of the Horse in Chinese History," in *What Is Taoism?: And Other Studies in Chinese Cultural History,* ed. Herrlee G. Creel (Chicago: University of Chicago Press, 1970), pp. 160–186.

44. Rudi Paul Lindner, "Nomadism, Horses, and Huns," *Past and Present* 92 (1981), pp. 3–19.

45. Ibid., pp. 14, 19.

46. Herodotus, *Histories,* 4.127.

47. Denis Sinor, "Horse and Pasture in Inner Asian History," *Oriens Extremus* 19 (1972), pp. 171–183.

48. Cited in Sinor, *Cambridge History,* p. 11.

49. Morris Rossabi, "The Tea and Horse Trade with Inner Asia during the Ming," *Journal of Asian History* 4 (1970), pp. 136–168; Henry Serruys, "Sino-Mongol Trade during the Ming," *Journal of Asian History* 9 (1975), pp. 34–56; Paul J. Smith, *Taxing Heaven's Storehouse: Horses, Bureaucrats, and the Destruction of the Sichuan Tea Industry, 1074–1224* (Cambridge, Mass.: Harvard University Press, 1991).

50. See Sinor, *Cambridge History,* p. 11, citing Salvianus of Marseille.

51. Barfield, *The Perilous Frontier.*

52. Creel, "The Role of the Horse," p. 163; Liu Xiang, ed., "Zhanguoce," In *Ershiwu bieshi,* 22 vols. (Jinan: Jilu Shushe, 2000), 6:204–211; *Chan-kuo ts'e,* trans. James I. Crump (Ann Arbor: Center for Chinese Studies, University of Michigan, 1996), pp. 288–294; Sima Qian, "Shiji," *juan* 43, in *Ershiwu shi,* vol. 1 (Shanghai: Shanghai Guji Chubanshe, 1986), p. 215; *Les Mémoires historiques de Se-ma Ts'ien,* trans. Édouard Chavannes, 6 vols. (Paris: Librairie d'Amérique et d'Orient, 1967), 5:72–84.

53. Creel, "The Role of the Horse," p. 170; Burton Watson, *Records of the Grand Historian of China,* 2 vols. (New York: Columbia University Press, 1961), 2:281–287.

54. Christopher I. Beckwith, "The Impact of the Horse and Silk Trade on the Economies of T'ang China and the Uighur Empire," *Journal of the Economic and Social History of the Orient* 34 (1991), pp. 183–198.

55. Owen Lattimore, *Pivot of Asia: Sinkiang and the Inner Asian Frontiers of China and Russia* (Boston: Little, Brown, 1950), p. 155.

56. Litvinskii, "Ecology," p. 64.

57. Thomas J. Barfield, *The Nomadic Alternative* (Englewood Cliffs, N.J.: Prentice-Hall, 1993), p. 20.

58. ZGSL 63.

59. GZDQL 3.710.

60. National Research Council, *Grasslands and Grassland Sciences in Northern China* (Washington, D.C.: National Academy Press, 1992).

61. Arthur de Carle Sowerby, "The Horse and Other Beasts of Burden in China," *China Journal* 26 (1937), pp. 282–287.

62. Edward Schafer, "The Camel in China down to the Mongol Dynasty," *Sinologica* 2 (1950), p. 166.

63. Owen Lattimore, *The Desert Road to Turkestan* (Boston: Little, Brown, 1929), p. 109; Lattimore, *Studies,* p. 43.

64. Jonathan Lipman, "The Border World of Gansu, 1895–1935" (Ph.D. diss., Stanford University, 1981).

65. Morris Rossabi, "The 'Decline' of the Central Asian Caravan Trade," in *The Rise of Merchant Empires,* ed. James D. Tracy (Cambridge: Cambridge University Press, 1990), pp. 351–370.

66. Lattimore, *Studies,* p. 58; Lipman, "The Border World of Gansu," maps 1 and 2, p. xiv.

67. Lai Fushun, *Qianlong Zhongyao Zhanzheng zhi Junxu Yanjiu* (Studies on military supplies in Qianlong's major campaigns) (Taibei: Guoli Gugong Bowuyuan, 1984), pp. 219–221. One *shi* is approximately 103 liters of grain.

68. Braudel, *The Mediterranean,* 1:18; David A. Hollinger, "How Wide the Circle of 'We'? American Intellectuals and the Problem of the Ethnos since World War II," *American Historical Review* 98 (1993), p. 337.

69. Richard White, *The Middle Ground: Indians, Empires, and Republics in the Great Lakes Region, 1650–1815* (Cambridge: Cambridge University Press, 1991).

70. Owen Lattimore, *Inner Asian Frontiers of China* (Boston: Beacon Press, 1962), chap. 1.

71. Lattimore, *Studies,* pp. 165–179; Daniel Power and Naomi Standen, eds., *Frontiers in Question: Eurasian Borderlands, 700–1700* (New York: St. Martin's Press, 1998).

72. Arthur Waldron, *The Great Wall of China: From History to Myth* (Cambridge: Cambridge University Press, 1990).

73. Lattimore, *Studies,* p. 58.

74. On Russian wall building, see Carol B. Stevens, *Soldiers on the Steppe: Army Reform and Social Change in Early Modern Russia* (DeKalb: Northern Illinois University Press, 1995).

75. Lattimore, *Studies,* pp. 113, 117.

76. Arthur Waldron, "Representing China: The Great Wall and Cultural Nationalism in the Twentieth Century," in *Cultural Nationalism in East Asia: Representation and Identity,* ed. Harumi Befu (Berkeley: Institute of East Asian Studies, University of California, 1993), pp. 36–60; Arthur Waldron, "Scholarship and Patriotic Education: The Great Wall Conference," *China Quarterly* 143 (1995), pp. 844–850.

77. Lattimore, *Studies,* pp. 165–179.

78. Christian, "Inner Eurasia."

79. Peake and Fleure, *The Steppe and the Sown.*

80. George Curzon, *Russia in Central Asia and the Anglo-Russian Question* (1889), cited in Denis Sinor, *Inner Asia: History, Civilization, Languages: A Syllabus* (Ann Arbor: University of Michigan Press, 1979), p. 217.

81. McNeill, "Of Rats and Men."

82. Chia-feng Chang, "Disease and Its Impact on Politics, Diplomacy, and the Military: The Case of Smallpox and the Manchus (1613–1795)," *Journal of the History of Medicine and Allied Sciences* 57 (April 2002), pp. 177–197; Henry Serruys, "Smallpox in Mongolia during the Ming and Ch'ing Dynasties," *Zentralasiatische Studien* 14 (1980), pp. 41–63.

83. Li Xinheng, *Jinchuan Suoji* 2.6b, cited in Serruys, "Smallpox," p. 57.

84. Peter Simon Pallas, *Sammlungen Historischer Nachrichten über die Mongolischen Völkerschaften* (Graz: Akademische Druck-u. Verlagsanstalt, 1980), p. 158.

85. James Z. Lee and Wang Feng, *One Quarter of Humanity: Malthusian Mythology and Chinese Realities* (Cambridge, Mass.: Harvard University Press, 1999), pp. 45–46.

86. Hua Li, "Qingdai di Man-Meng lianyin" (Manchu and Mongol connections during the Qing dynasty), *Minzu Yanjiu* (February 1983), pp. 45–54.

87. Chiba Muneo, "Tenzan ni habataku" (Black whirlwind: flags fluttering over the Tianshan Mountains), in *Kara būran: Kuroi suna-arashi* (Tokyo: Kokushokankokai, 1986), p. 89.

88. Okada Hidehiro, *Kōkitei no Tegami* (Letters of the Kangxi emperor) (Tokyo: Chuko Shinsho, 1979), p. 125; QPSF, p. 35, 31b KX36/1 renshen.

89. National Research Council, *Grasslands;* Reardon-Anderson, "Reluctant Pioneers." Elvin, *Retreat,* p. xxvi, defines the logistic curve mathematically and argues for its significance in describing social change.

90. In the United States many are questioning the health of agriculture in this region as environmental degradation worsens. Some well-informed researchers even argue for returning arid fields to a "buffalo commons," which would make better economic and ecological use of the land. In fact, Native Americans are returning to regions of the American West as farms are abandoned. Donald Worster, "Climate and History on the Great Plains," paper presented at the Conference on Humanities and the Environment, MIT, January 9, 1992; Donald Worster, *Rivers of Empire: Water, Aridity, and the Growth of the American West* (New York: Pantheon Books, 1985).

91. Christian, "Inner Eurasia," p. 207.

92. Barfield, *Perilous Frontier*, pp. 164–186.

2. The Ming, Muscovy, and Siberia, 1400–1600

1. Edward L. Farmer, *Early Ming Government: The Evolution of Dual Capitals* (Cambridge, Mass.: Harvard University Press, 1968).

2. "The conqueror of Asia [Timur] expired in the seventieth year of his age, thirty-five years after he had ascended the throne of Zagatai [Chagatai]. His designs were lost; his armies were disbanded; China was saved; and fourteen years after his decease, the most powerful of his children sent an embassy of friendship and commerce to the court of Pekin." Edward Gibbon, *The History of the Decline and Fall of the Roman Empire,* ed. David Womersley, 3 vols. (London: Allen Lane, Penguin Press, 1994), 3:847–850.

3. Okada Hidehiro, "Doruben Oirato no kigen" (Origin of the Derbet Oirats), *Shigaku Zasshi* 83 (1974), pp. 1–44 (English version in *Ural-Altaische Jahrbücher* [1987]); ZGSL, p. 2; David Farquhar, "Oirat-Chinese Tribute Relations, 1408–59," in *Studia Altaica (Festschrift für Nikolaus Poppe)* (1957), pp. 60–68.

4. Paul Ratchnevsky, *Genghis Khan: His Life and Legacy* (Cambridge, Mass.: Basil Blackwell, 1993), pp. 5, 96.

5. Paul Kahn, *The Secret History of the Mongols: The Origin of Chinghis Khan: An Adaptation of the Yuan Chao Pi Shih* (San Francisco: North Point Press, 1984), pp. 60–61. Cf. Francis Cleaves, ed., *The Secret History of the Mongols* (Cambridge, Mass.: Harvard University Press, 1982), p. 70; Ratchnevsky, *Genghis Khan*, p. 62.

6. Okada Hidehiro, "Doruben Oirato"; Ratchnevsky, *Genghis Khan*, p. 117.

7. Ratchnevsky, *Genghis Khan*, p. 96.

8. Morris Rossabi, "The Ming and Inner Asia," in *The Cambridge History of China*, vol. 8, pt. 2, *The Ming Dynasty, 1368–1644,* ed. Denis Twitchett and Frederick Mote (Cambridge: Cambridge University Press, 1998), pp. 221–271.

9. L. C. Goodrich and Chaoying Fang, *Dictionary of Ming Biography, 1368–1644* (New York: Columbia University Press, 1976), pp. 1290–93; Okada Hidehiro, "Doruben Oirato," p. 8.

10. Wolfgang Franke, "Addenda and Corrigenda to Pokotilov," in *History of the Eastern Mongols during the Ming Dynasty,* ed. Dmitrii Pokotilov (Philadelphia: Porcupine Press, 1976), pp. 1–95; Wolfgang Franke, "Chinesische Feldzüge durch die Mongolei im frühen 15. Jahrhundert," *Sinologica* 3 (1951–1953), pp. 81–88; Wolfgang Franke, "Yunglo's Mongolei-Feldzüge," *Sinologische Arbeiten* 3 (1945), pp. 1–54.

11. Goodrich and Fang, *Dictionary*, pp. 531–534.

12. Franke, "Yunglo's Mongolei-Feldzüge," p. 15.

13. Farmer, *Early Ming Government*, pp. 122–123.

14. Goodrich and Fang, *Dictionary*, pp. 416–420.

15. Frederick Mote, "The Tu-Mu Incident of 1449," in *Chinese Ways in Warfare*, ed. Frank Kierman and John K. Fairbank (Cambridge, Mass.: Harvard University Press, 1974), pp. 243–272; Morris Rossabi, "Notes on Esen's Pride and Ming China's Prejudice," *Mongolia Society Bulletin* 17 (1970), pp. 31–39.

16. Goodrich and Fang, *Dictionary*, pp. 854–856 (Li Shi), 1528–31 (Yang Shan).

17. Mote, "The Tu-Mu Incident of 1449"; F. W. Mote, *Imperial China: 900–1800* (Cambridge, Mass.: Harvard University Press, 1999), p. 627.

18. Zhang Tingyu, *Xinjiaoben Mingshi pingfu bianliuzhong* (History of the Ming dynasty), 5th ed. (Taibei: Dingwen shuju, 1991), 171:4565–68 (biography of Yang Shan); translation adapted from Pokotilov, *History*, pp. 54–55. See also Goodrich and Fang, *Dictionary*, pp. 1528–31.

19. Arthur Waldron, *The Great Wall of China: From History to Myth* (Cambridge: Cambridge University Press, 1990), pp. 53–164.

20. Goodrich and Fang, *Dictionary*, pp. 887–892 (Li Ying).

21. Pokotilov, *History*, p. 70.

22. Goodrich and Fang, *Dictionary*, pp. 1455–60 (Wang Yue); Waldron, *The Great Wall*, pp. 91–164.

23. Goodrich and Fang, *Dictionary*, pp. 1620–24 (Yu Zijun); *Mingshilu* (*Changle Liang Hongzhi*, 1940), 108:2120.

24. Goodrich and Fang, *Dictionary*, p. 1344 (Wang Ao); Pokotilov, *History*, pp. 84–85.

25. Goodrich and Fang, *Dictionary*, pp. 17–20 (Batu Möngke), 1516–19 (Yang Yiqing).

26. Ibid., pp. 1303–5 (Zeng Xian). For further discussion of Zeng Xian's strategic thinking, see Peter C. Perdue, "Culture, History, and Imperial Chinese Strategy: Legacies of the Qing Conquests," in *Warfare in Chinese History*, ed. Hans van de Ven (Leiden: Brill, 2000), pp. 252–287.

27. James Geiss, "The Cheng-te Reign, 1506–1521," in *The Cambridge History of China*, vol. 8, pt. 1, *The Ming Dynasty, 1368–1644*, ed. Denis Twitchett and Frederick Mote (Cambridge: Cambridge University Press, 1988), p. 421.

28. Goodrich and Fang, *Dictionary*, pp. 1516–19 (Yang Yiqing).

29. Ibid., pp. 6–9.

30. Waldron, *The Great Wall*, p. 127. For further discussion, see Perdue, "Culture, History, and Imperial Chinese Strategy."

31. Goodrich and Fang, *Dictionary*, pp. 1303–5 (Zeng Xian).

32. Piper Rae Gaubatz, *Beyond the Great Wall: Urban Form and Transformation on China's Frontiers* (Stanford: Stanford University Press, 1996); Paul Hyer, "An Historical Sketch of Koke-Khota City, Capital of Inner Mongolia," *Central Asiatic Journal* 26 (1982), pp. 56–77; Peter C. Perdue, "From Turfan to Taiwan: Trade and War on Two Chinese Frontiers," in *Untaming the Frontier: Interdisciplinary Perspectives on Frontier Studies*, ed. Bradley Parker and Lars Rodseth (Tucson: University of Arizona Press, 2005).

33. Goodrich and Fang, *Dictionary*, p. 55; Ray Huang, "Military Expenditures in Sixteenth-Century Ming China," *Oriens Extremus* 17 (1970), pp. 39–62; Ray Huang,

1587: A Year of No Significance (New Haven: Yale University Press, 1981), pp. 108–112, 181, 231–233.

34. Pokotilov, *History*, pp. 130–131.

35. Goodrich and Fang, *Dictionary*, pp. 1129–31 (Qutughtai).

36. Henry Serruys, "Early Lamaism in Mongolia," *Oriens Extremus* 10 (1963), pp. 181, 214; cf. Goodrich and Fang, *Dictionary*, pp. 9, 23.

37. Pokotilov, *History*, pp. 127–128.

38. Sechin Jagchid and Van Jay Symons, *Peace, War, and Trade along the Great Wall: Nomadic-Chinese Interaction through Two Millennia* (Bloomington: Indiana University Press, 1989), p. 165; Nicola Di Cosmo, "Ancient Inner Asian Nomads: Their Economic Basis and Its Significance in Chinese History," *Journal of Asian Studies* 53 (November 1994), p. 1093.

39. Morris Rossabi, "The Tea and Horse Trade with Inner Asia during the Ming," *Journal of Asian History* 4 (1970), p. 139.

40. Tani Mitsutaka, "Mindai chaba bōeki no kenkyū" (Studies on the Ming horse-tea trade), *Shirin* 49 (September 1966), p. 56.

41. Li Guangbi, "Mingdai Xicha Yima Kao" (The trade of western tea for horses in the Ming dynasty), *Zhongyang Yaxiya* 2 (1943), p. 52.

42. Other markets were briefly established at Ganzhou, abolished in 1443, and re-established in 1563; also at Qinzhou, Minzhou, and Zhuanglang, plus two smaller ones in Sichuan at Diaomen and Yongning.

43. Charles O. Hucker, *A Dictionary of Official Titles in Imperial China* (Stanford: Stanford University Press, 1985), p. 274; Terada Takanobu, *Sansei Shōnin no Kenkyū: Mindai ni okeru shōnin oyobi shōgyō shihon* (Studies on the Shanxi merchants: merchants and merchant capital in the Ming) (Kyoto: Toyoshi Kenkyukai, 1972), pp. 81–89.

44. Goodrich and Fang, *Dictionary*, pp. 1516–19; Rossabi, "Tea and Horse Trade," p. 156; Tani Mitsutaka, "Chaba bōeki," p. 47; Yang Yiqing, *Guanzhong Zouyi*, 18 *juan* (Taibei: Taiwan shangwu yinshuguan, 1983), 3: 1–29.

45. Shimizu Taiji, *Mindai Tochiseidoshi Kenkyū* (Studies on the Ming land system) (Tokyo: Daian 1968), pp. 385–404; Terada Takanobu, *Sansei Shōnin*, pp. 108–118, 199–209; Wang Ch'ungwu, "The Ming System of Merchant Colonization," in *Chinese Social History: Translations of Selected Studies*, ed. E-tu Zen Sun and John De Francis (New York: Octagon Books, 1966), pp. 299–308.

46. Yang Yiqing, *Guanzhong Zouyi*, 3:14a.

47. Timothy Brook, *The Confusions of Pleasure: Commerce and Culture in Ming China* (Berkeley: University of California Press, 1998).

48. Terada Takanobu, *Sansei Shōnin*, pp. 44–60.

49. Huang, "Military Expenditures."

50. Mark Elvin, "The Supremacy of Logistics under the Ming," in *The Pattern of the Chinese Past* (Stanford: Stanford University Press, 1973), pp. 91–110.

51. George Vernadsky, *The Mongols and Russia* (New Haven: Yale University Press, 1953), p. 326.

52. Ibid., pp. 331–332.

53. Vernadsky, *The Mongols and Russia*, p. 333; Donald Ostrowski, "The Mongol

Origins of Muscovite Political Institutions," *Slavic Review* 49 (Winter 1990), pp. 525–542; Donald Ostrowski, *Muscovy and the Mongols: Cross-Cultural Influences on the Steppe Frontier, 1304–1589* (Cambridge: Cambridge University Press, 1998).

54. Ostrowski, "Mongol Origins"; Joseph Fletcher, "Turco-Mongolian Monarchic Tradition in the Ottoman Empire," in *Studies on Chinese and Islamic Inner Asia*, ed. Beatrice Forbes Manz (Brookfield, Vt.: Variorum, 1995), pp. 236–251.

55. Carol B. Stevens, *Soldiers on the Steppe: Army Reform and Social Change in Early Modern Russia* (DeKalb: Northern Illinois University Press, 1995).

56. Vernadsky, *The Mongols and Russia*.

57. Charles Halperin, "Russia in the Mongol Empire in Comparative Perspective," *Harvard Journal of Asiatic Studies* 43 (June 1983), pp. 239–262.

58. Unlike in China and Iran, "in Russia the Mongols chose the geographical isolation of the steppe, not moving into the forest zone. This basic contrast is the key to all comparative analysis of the Golden Horde." Ibid., pp. 247, 250. See also Perry Anderson, *Passages from Antiquity to Feudalism* (London: Verso, 1978), p. 227.

59. Edward Keenan, "Muscovy and Kazan', 1445–1552: Some Introductory Remarks on Steppe Diplomacy," *Slavic Review* 26 (1967), pp. 548–558; Edward Keenan, "Muscovy and Kazan', 1445–1552: A Study in Steppe Politics" (Ph.D. diss., Harvard University, 1965); Jaroslaw Pelenski, *Russia and Kazan: Conquest and Imperial Ideology* (Paris: Mouton, 1974).

60. Keenan, "Muscovy and Kazan'" (1967), p. 552.

61. Ibid.

62. Omeljan Pritsak, "Moscow, the Golden Horde, and the Kazan Khanate from a Polycultural Point of View," *Slavic Review* 26 (1967), pp. 576–583.

63. Vernadsky, *The Mongols and Russia*.

64. Keenan, "Muscovy and Kazan'" (1965), p. 178.

65. Ibid., p. 395.

66. *Kazanskaia Istoriia*, cited in Pelenski, *Russia and Kazan*, p. 117.

67. Ibid., p. 65.

68. Keenan, "Muscovy and Kazan'" (1965), pp. 38–43.

69. For further comparative discussion, see Peter C. Perdue, "The Qing Empire in Eurasian Time and Space: Lessons from the Galdan Campaigns," in *The Qing Formation in World-Historical Time*, ed. Lynn Struve (Cambridge, Mass.: Harvard University Asia Center, 2004), pp. 57–91.

70. Studies include Mark Bassin, "Expansion and Colonialism on the Eastern Frontier: Views of Siberia and the Far East in Pre-Petrine Russia," *Journal of Historical Geography* 14 (1988), pp. 3–21; Mark Bassin, "Inventing Siberia: Visions of the Russian Empire in the Early Nineteenth Century," *American Historical Review* 96 (1991), pp. 763–794; Mark Bassin, "Russia between Europe and Asia: The Ideological Construction of Geographical Space," *Slavic Review* (Spring 1991), pp. 1–17; Fred W. Bergholz, *The Partition of the Steppe: The Struggle of the Russians, Manchus, and the Zunghar Mongols for Empire in Central Asia, 1619–1758: A Study in Power Politics* (New York: Peter Lang, 1993); Yuri Slezkine, *Arctic Mirrors: Russia and the Small Peoples of the North* (Ithaca: Cornell University Press, 1994). Popular accounts include Benson Bobrick, *East of the Sun: The Epic Conquest and Tragic History of Siberia* (New

York: Poseidon Press, 1992); W. Bruce Lincoln, *The Conquest of a Continent: Siberia and the Russians* (New York: Random House, 1994). John F. Richards, *The Unending Frontier: An Environmental History of the Early Modern World* (Berkeley: University of California Press, 2003), pp. 242–273, places Russian expansion in a world historical framework.

71. Janet Martin, *Medieval Russia, 980–1584* (Cambridge: Cambridge University Press, 1995); Janet Martin, "Muscovy's Northeast Expansion: The Context and a Cause," *Cahiers du Monde Russe et Soviétique* 24 (1983), pp. 459–470.

72. Bassin, "Russia between Europe and Asia"; Peter C. Perdue, "Boundaries, Maps, and Movement: The Chinese, Russian, and Mongolian Empires in Early Modern Eurasia," *International History Review* 20 (June 1998), pp. 263–286.

73. Martin, "Muscovy's Northeast Expansion."

74. John Baddeley, *Russia, Mongolia, China, being some record of the relations between them from the beginning of the XVIIth century to the death of the Tsar Alexei Mikhailovich, A.D. 1602–1676*, 2 vols. (London: Macmillan and Company, 1919), 1:69–73; Joseph L. Wieczynski, ed., *The Modern Encyclopedia of Russian and Soviet History* (Gulf Breeze, Fla.: Academic International Press, 1976–), s.v. "Ermak Timofeevich."

75. George V. Lantzeff and Richard Pierce, *Eastward to Empire: Exploration and Conquest on the Russian Open Frontier to 1750* (Montreal: McGill–Queen's University Press, 1973), quote p. 116; see also p. 119; Wieczynski, *Encyclopedia*, s.v. "Kuchum."

76. Raymond H. Fisher, "The Russian Fur Trade, 1550–1700," in *Russia's Eastward Expansion*, ed. George Lensen (Englewood Cliffs, N.J.: Prentice-Hall, 1964), pp. 34–37.

77. V. V. Barthol'd noted: "Almost all the campaigns were undertaken by the Cossacks at their own initiative without any kind of order on the part of the authorities in Moscow. It is only after the completion of the campaign that the Muscovite authorities make their appearance and declare that the new territory was annexed to the possessions of the sovereign." Wieczynski, *Encyclopedia*, s.v. "Siberian Cossacks."

78. Lantzeff and Pierce, *Eastward to Empire*, p. 127.

79. Ibid., p. 159.

80. Ibid., p. 168.

81. Bassin, "Inventing Siberia"; Galya Diment and Yuri Slezkine, *Between Heaven and Hell: The Myth of Siberia in Russian Culture* (New York: St. Martin's, 1993).

82. Alan Wood, ed., *The History of Siberia: From Russian Conquest to Revolution* (London: Routledge, 1991), p. 3.

83. Charles Tilly, *Coercion, Capital, and European States, 990–1992* (Cambridge, Mass.: Basil Blackwell, 1990), p. 30.

84. Wood, *History of Siberia*, pp. 4, 41.

85. Stephen Greenblatt, *Marvelous Possessions: The Wonder of the New World* (Chicago: University of Chicago Press, 1991).

86. Slezkine, *Arctic Mirrors*, pp. 38, 41.

87. Joanna Waley-Cohen, *Exile in Mid-Qing China: Banishment to Xinjiang, 1758–1820* (New Haven: Yale University Press, 1991).

88. David Collins, "Subjugation and Settlement in Seventeenth- and Eighteenth-Century Siberia," in Wood, *History of Siberia*, p. 45.

89. Stevens, *Soldiers on the Steppe*, pp. 122–139.

3. Central Eurasian Interactions and the Rise of the Manchus, 1600–1670

1. The Altyn Khans are not to be confused with Altan Khan (1507–1582), unifier of the Tumed tribes.

2. Sh. B. Chimitdorzhiev, *Vzaimootnosheniia Mongolii i Rossii v 17–18 vekakh* (Relations between Mongolia and Russia in the seventeenth and eighteenth centuries) (Moscow: Nauka, 1978), p. 18; I. Ia. Zlatkin and N. V. Ustiugov, eds., *Materialy po Istorii Russko-Mongol'skikh Otnoshenii: Russko-mongol'skie otnosheniia, 1607–1636: Sbornik Dokumentov* (Materials on the History of Russo-Mongolian relations, 1607–1636) (Moscow: Izdatel'stvo Vostochnoi Literatury, 1959), p. 21.

3. Chimitdorzhiev, *Vzaimootnosheniia*, p. 20; Zlatkin and Ustiugov, eds., *Materialy, 1607–1636*, pp. 24–28.

4. Michael Khodarkovsky, "Ignoble Savages and Unfaithful Subjects: Constructing Non-Christian Identities in Early Modern Russia," in *Russia's Orient: Imperial Borderlands and Peoples, 1700–1917*, ed. Daniel R. Brower and Edward Lazzerini (Bloomington: Indiana University Press, 1997), pp. 12–13.

5. Zlatkin and Ustiugov, *Materialy, 1607–1636*, p. 22.

6. Ibid., p. 53.

7. Chimitdorzhiev, *Vzaimootnosheniia*, p. 26; Zlatkin and Ustiugov, *Materialy, 1607–1636*, p. 99.

8. Michael Khodarkovsky, "Russian Peasant and Kalmyk Nomad: A Tragic Encounter in the Mid-Eighteenth Century," *Russian History* 15 (1988), pp. 43–69; Michael Khodarkovsky, "Uneasy Alliance: Peter the Great and Ayuki Khan," *Central Asian Survey* 7 (1988), pp. 1–45; Michael Khodarkovsky, *Where Two Worlds Met: The Russian State and the Kalmyk Nomads, 1600–1771* (Ithaca: Cornell University Press, 1992).

9. Wakamatsu Hiroshi, "Jungaru Ōkoku no keisei katei" (The formation of the Zunghar empire), *Tōyōshi Kenkyū* 41, no. 4 (1983), pp. 74–117; Wakamatsu Hiroshi, *Qingdai Menggu di Lishi yu Zongjiao* (Mongolian history and religion in the Qing) (Heilongjiang: Heilongjiang Jiaoyu Chubanshe, 1994), pp. 3–43.

10. Dai Yi, *Jianming Qingshi* (A brief history of the Qing dynasty) (Beijing: Renmin Chubanshe, 1984), p. 139.

11. I. Ia. Zlatkin, *Istoriia Dzhungarskogo Khanstvo, 1635–1758* (History of the Zunghar Khanate, 1635–1758) (Moscow: Nauka, 1964), p. 109.

12. Zlatkin and Ustiugov, *Materialy, 1607–1636*, p. 22.

13. Fred W. Bergholz, *The Partition of the Steppe: The Struggle of the Russians, Manchus, and the Zunghar Mongols for Empire in Central Asia, 1619–1758: A Study in Power Politics* (New York: Peter Lang, 1993); Zlatkin, *Istoriia*, p. 138; Zlatkin and Ustiugov, *Materialy, 1607–1636*, pp. 79–80, 114–115.

14. Miyawaki Junko, "The Qalqa Mongols and the Oyirad in the Seventeenth Century," *Journal of Asian History* 18 (1984), p. 157.

15. Ibid., pp. 158–159; Zlatkin, *Istoriia*, pp. 144–147.

16. Khodarkovsky, *Where Two Worlds Met*, p. 80.

17. Excerpts from his biography in K. F. Golstunskii, *Mongolo-oiratskie zakony 1640 goda, dopolnitelnye ukazy Galdan-Khun-Taidzhiia i zakony, sostavlennye dlia volzhskikh kalmykov pri kalmytskom khanie Donduk-Dashi: kalmytskii tekst s russkim perevodom i primiechaniiami* (Mongol-Oirat laws of 1640) (St. Petersburg: Tip. Imperatorskoi akademii nauk, 1880), pp. 121–130; see also A. V. Badmaev, *Zaia-Pandita: Spiski Kalmytskoy Rukopisi "Biografia Zaia-Pandita"* (Description of Kalymyk manuscripts of the biography of Zaia Pandita) (Elista: Kalmytskii nauchno-issledovatel'skii institut iazyka, literatury i istorii pri Sovete Ministrov Kalmytskoi ASSR, 1968); Stephen A. Halkovic, *The Mongols of the West* (Bloomington: Indiana University Press, 1985), p. 37n3; Miyawaki Junko, "Oiratto no kōsō Zaya Pandita denki," (The life of the great Oyirad monk Zaya Pandita), in *Chibetto no Bukkyō to Shakai,* ed. Yamaguchi Zuihō (Tokyo: Shunjusha, 1986), pp. 603–627; Zlatkin, *Istoriia*, p. 156; ZGSL, p. 56.

18. Przewalski quoted in Owen Lattimore, *Studies in Frontier History: Collected Papers, 1928–1958* (New York: Oxford University Press, 1962), p. 62; Karl E. Meyer and Shareen Blair Brysac, *Tournament of Shadows: The Great Game and the Race for Empire in Central Asia* (Washington, D.C.: Counterpoint, 1999), p. 230.

19. Miyawaki Junko, "The Qalqa Mongols"; Miyawaki Junko, *Saigo no Yūboku Teikoku: Jungaru bu no kōbō* (Tokyo: Kodansha, 1995), pp. 163–170.

20. Miyawaki Junko, "Galdan izen no Oiratto: Wakamatsu setsu sai hihan" (The Oyirad before Galdan: Wakamatsu's theory criticized again), *Tōyō Gakuhō* 65 (1984), pp. 91–120; Miyawaki Junko, "Jūnana seiki no Oiratto: Jungar Hankoku ni taisuru gimon" (The Oyirad of the seventeenth century: the "Dzungar Khanate" revisited), *Shigaku Zasshi* 90 (1981), p. 56.

21. Bergholz, *Partition of the Steppe*, p. 55; Zlatkin, *Istoriia*, p. 183.

22. Chimitdorzhiev, *Vzaimootnosheniia*, p. 52n120.

23. Bergholz, *Partition of the Steppe*, pp. 58–59; Chimitdorzhiev, *Vzaimootnosheniia*, p. 45; Sh. B. Chimitdorzhiev, "Iz istorii Russko-Mongol'skikh ekonomicheskikh sviazei" (History of Russian and Mongolian economic ties), *Istoriia SSSR* 2 (1964), pp. 151–156.

24. Chimitdorzhiev, *Vzaimootnosheniia*, pp. 53–54.

25. I. Ia. Zlatkin and N. V. Ustiugov, eds., *Materialy po Istorii Russko-Mongol'skikh Otnoshenii: Russko-mongol'skie otnosheniia, 1636–1654: Sbornik Dokumentov* (Materials on the history of Russo-Mongolian relations, 1636–1654) (Moscow: Izdatel'stvo Vostochnoi Literatury, 1974), pp. 150–151, 176.

26. Chimitdorzhiev, *Vzaimootnosheniia*, p. 42; Chimitdorzhiev, "Iz istorii ekonomicheskikh sviazei."

27. Bergholz, *Partition of the Steppe*, pp. 58–59; Chimitdorzhiev, *Vzaimootnosheniia*, p. 68; Zlatkin, *Istoriia*, pp. 172–178.

28. Golstunskii, *Mongolo-oiratskie zakony;* S. D. Dylykov and Institut vostokovedeniia (Akademiia nauk SSSR), *Ikh tsaaz = "Velikoe ulozhenie": Pamiatnik mongol'skogo feodal'nogo prava XVII v.: Oiratskii tekst* (Moscow, 1981); Tayama Shigeru, *Mōko hōten no kenkyū* (Studies on Mongolian law) (Tokyo: Nihon Gakujutsu Shinkokai, 1967).

29. I avoid the use of "Lamaism," a misleading term created by Westerners and the

Qing to describe Tibetan Buddhism. For a critique of this term, see Donald S. Lopez Jr., *Prisoners of Shangri-La: Tibetan Buddhism and the West* (Chicago: University of Chicago Press, 1998).

30. Miyawaki Junko, "Galdan izen," p. 106; Miyawaki Junko, "Jūnana seiki no Oiratto"; Miyawaki Junko, "Political Organization in the [*sic*] Seventeenth-Century North Asia," *Ajia Afurika Gengo Bunka Kenkyū* 27 (1984), pp. 172–179; Miyawaki Junko, "The Qalqa Mongols," p. 152.

31. Quoted in Mark C. Elliott, *The Manchu Way: The Eight Banners and Ethnic Identity in Late Imperial China* (Stanford: Stanford University Press, 2001), p. 29; Franz Michael, *The Origin of Manchu Rule in China: Frontier and Bureaucracy as Interacting Forces in the Chinese Empire* (Baltimore: Johns Hopkins University Press, 1942), p. 10.

32. Michael, *Origin of Manchu Rule*, p. 119.

33. Elliott, *The Manchu Way*, p. 31; Arthur W. Hummel, ed., *Eminent Chinese of the Ch'ing Period* (Washington, D.C.: U.S. Government Printing Office, 1943–44), p. 685; Bernd-Michael Linke, *Zur Entwicklung des mandjurischen Khanats zum Beamtenstaat: Sinisierung und Burokratisierung der Mandjuren wahrend der Eroberungszeit* (Wiesbaden: Steiner, 1982); Gertraude Roth, "The Manchu-Chinese Relationship, 1618–36," in *From Ming to Ch'ing: Conquest, Region, and Continuity in Seventeenth-Century China*, ed. Jonathan D. Spence and John E. Wills, Jr. (New Haven: Yale University Press, 1979), pp. 1–38.

34. Early Manchu succession customs are unclear. Gertraude Roth-Li states that primogeniture was "an accepted rule" of the early Manchus, but Joseph Fletcher argues that the Manchus followed "the tribal custom of electoral tanistry." Joseph Fletcher, "Ch'ing Inner Asia, c. 1800," in *The Cambridge History of China*, vol. 10, pt. 1, *Late Ch'ing, 1800–1911*, ed. John K. Fairbank (Cambridge: Cambridge University Press, 1978), p. 67; Hummel, *Eminent Chinese*, pp. 212, 594–599, 694; Gertraude Roth-Li, "The Rise of the Early Manchu State: A Portrait Drawn from Manchu Sources to 1636" (Ph.D. diss., Harvard University, 1975), p. 19. Frederic Wakeman Jr., *The Great Enterprise: The Manchu Reconstruction of Imperial Order* (Berkeley: University of California Press, 1985), p. 54, follows Roth.

35. G. V. Melikhov, "The Process of the Consolidation of the Manzhou Tribes under Nuerhaqi and Abahai (1591–1644)," in *Manzhou Rule in China*, ed. S. L. Tikhvinsky (Moscow: Progress Publishers, 1983), pp. 67–87.

36. Elliott, *The Manchu Way*, p. 58. Compare this strategy to the Tokugawa unification in 1603, which preserved *daimyō* autonomy while enforcing shogunal authority across domains.

37. Ibid., p. 62; Wakeman, *Great Enterprise*, p. 55.

38. Hummel, *Eminent Chinese*, pp. 213, 225. Biographies in Linke, *Zur Entwicklung*.

39. Wakeman, *Great Enterprise*, p. 44.

40. Lawrence D. Kessler, *K'ang-hsi and the Consolidation of Ch'ing Rule, 1661–1684* (Chicago: University of Chicago Press, 1976), p. 8.

41. Many texts, including Hummel, *Eminent Chinese* (p. 1) mistakenly call Hong Taiji "Abahai." On the origins of this error, see Giovanni Stary, "The Manchu Emperor 'Abahai': Analysis of an Historiographic Mistake," *Central Asiatic Journal* 28 (1984),

pp. 296–299. Michael, *Origin of Manchu Rule,* following the *Kaiguo Fanglue,* argues that Hong Taiji was chosen by consensus of the senior *beile.* Roth-Li, relying on archival sources, notes great distrust among the *beile* and the superior military power of Hong Taiji to make a case for usurpation, or at least a highly contentious struggle for succession.

42. Roth-Li, "The Rise," p. 118.

43. Robert B. Oxnam, *Ruling from Horseback: Manchu Politics in the Oboi Regency, 1661–69* (Chicago: University of Chicago Press, 1975), pp. 30–31; Wakeman, *Great Enterprise,* pp. 850–851. Elliott, *The Manchu Way,* p. 62, dates the origin of the council to 1615.

44. Roth-Li, "The Rise," p. 134.

45. Oxnam, *Ruling from Horseback,* p. 75.

46. Robert B. Oxnam, "Policies and Institutions of the Oboi Regency, 1661–69," *Journal of Asian Studies* 32 (1972), pp. 265–286; Oxnam, *Ruling from Horseback,* p. 13.

47. Hummel, *Eminent Chinese,* pp. 215–219.

48. Kessler, *K'ang-hsi;* Oxnam, *Ruling from Horseback,* p. 64.

49. Oxnam, *Ruling from Horseback,* pp. 76–81.

50. Victor H. Mair, "Language and Ideology in the Written Popularizations of the Sacred Edict," in *Popular Culture in Late Imperial China,* ed. David Johnson, Andrew J. Nathan, and Evelyn S. Rawski (Berkeley: University of California Press, 1985), p. 326.

51. Hummel, *Eminent Chinese,* p. 215.

52. On the Lifanyuan, see Nicola Di Cosmo, "Qing Colonial Administration in the Inner Asian Dependencies," *International History Review* 20 (1998), pp. 287–309; Oxnam, *Ruling from Horseback,* pp. 31, 69–70; Chia Ning, "The Lifanyuan and the Inner Asian Rituals in the Early Qing," *Late Imperial China* 14, no. 1 (1991), pp. 60–92.

53. Roth, "The Manchu-Chinese Relationship," p. 32.

54. Guoli Gugong Bowuyuan, *Jiu Manzhou Dang* (Old Manchu archives), 10 vols. (Taibei: Guoli Gugong Bowuyuan, 1969), 1:103; Kanda Nobuo et al., eds., *Manbun Rōtō: Tongki Fuka Sindaha Hergen i Dangse* (The Old Manchu archive), 4 vols. (Tokyo: Toyo Bunko, 1955–1959), 1:48.

55. Guoli Gugong Bowuyuan, *Jiu Manzhou Dang,* 1:482–483; Kanda Nobuo et al., *Manbun Rōtō,* 1:189–190.

56. Roth, "The Manchu-Chinese Relationship," p. 9.

57. Guoli Gugong Bowuyuan, *Jiu Manzhou Dang,* 4:1828; Kanda Nobuo et al., *Manbun Rōtō,* 2:906; Roth-Li, "The Rise," p. 56.

58. Guoli Gugong Bowuyuan, *Jiu Manzhou Dang,* 2:586–587; Kanda Nobuo et al., *Manbun Rōtō,* 1:267.

59. Guoli Gugong Bowuyuan, *Jiu Manzhou Dang,* 2:680–681, 684–685, 693–694, 1094; Kanda Nobuo et al., *Manbun Rōtō,* 1:333, 335, 340, 2:584.

60. Guoli Gugong Bowuyuan, *Jiu Manzhou Dang,* 2:856; Kanda Nobuo et al., *Manbun Rōtō,* 1:435.

61. Guoli Gugong Bowuyuan, *Jiu Manzhou Dang,* 2:597, 4:2164; Kanda Nobuo et al., *Manbun Rōtō,* 2:778, 3:1103.

62. Guoli Gugong Bowuyuan, *Jiu Manzhou Dang,* 4:1935–38; Kanda Nobuo et al., *Manbun Rōtō,* 3:991–992.

63. Guoli Gugong Bowuyuan, *Jiu Manzhou Dang,* 3:1439, 1495–97; Kanda Nobuo et al., *Manbun Rōtō,* 2:763–764.

64. Roth-Li, "The Rise," p. 117.

65. Guoli Gugong Bowuyuan, *Jiu Manzhou Dang,* 7:3227–28; Kanda Nobuo et al., *Manbun Rōtō,* 3:1091; *Tiancongchao Chengong Zouyi, juan* 1 (Taibei: Dailian guofeng chubanshe, 1968), pp. 8–9, 22.

66. *Tiancongchao Chengong Zouyi,* 1.16 *juan;* Guoli Gugong Bowuyuan, *Jiu Manzhou Dang,* 9:4151; Roth, "The Manchu-Chinese Relationship," p. 29.

67. Guoli Gugong Bowuyuan, *Jiu Manzhou Dang,* 10:5197; Kanda Nobuo et al., *Manbun Rōtō,* 4:1362–63.

68. Xiao Yishan, *Qingdai Tongshi* (Comprehensive history of the Qing dynasty), 5 vols. (Beijing: Zhonghua shuju, 1986), 1:206.

69. Hummel, *Eminent Chinese,* p. 878; Wakeman, *Great Enterprise,* p. 224; Frederic Wakeman Jr., "The Shun Interregnum of 1644," in Spence and Wills, Jr., *From Ming to Ch'ing,* pp. 39–88.

70. Jack A. Goldstone, "East and West in the Seventeenth Century: Political Crises in Stuart England, Ottoman Turkey, and Ming China," *Comparative Studies in Society and History* (January 1988), pp. 103–142; Jack A. Goldstone, *Revolution and Rebellion in the Early Modern World* (Berkeley: University of California Press, 1991); Charles Tilly, *The Contentious French* (Cambridge, Mass.: Harvard University Press, 1986).

71. Janet Martin, "Muscovy's Northeast Expansion: The Context and a Cause," *Cahiers du Monde Russe et Soviétique* 24 (1983), pp. 459–470.

72. Nicholas Riasanovsky, *A History of Russia* (Oxford: Oxford University Press, 1993), pp. 170–171.

73. David M. Farquhar, "The Origins of the Manchus' Mongolian Policy," in *The Chinese World Order,* ed. John K. Fairbank (Cambridge, Mass.: Harvard University Press, 1968), pp. 198–205; Kanda Nobuo et al., *Manbun Rōtō,* 1:67; Wakeman, *Great Enterprise,* p. 55. For translations of Mongolian documents on this subject, see Nicola Di Cosmo and Dalizhabu Bao, *Manchu-Mongol Relations on the Eve of the Qing Conquest: A Documentary History* (Leiden: Brill, 2003).

74. John D. Langlois, ed., *China under Mongol Rule* (Princeton: Princeton University Press, 1981), pp. 7, 307.

75. Hummel, *Eminent Chinese,* pp. 213, 225; Linke, *Zur Entwicklung,* pp. 112–123; Wakeman, *Great Enterprise,* pp. 43–44.

76. Wakeman, *Great Enterprise,* p. 57.

77. Linke, *Zur Entwicklung,* p. 220; Wakeman, *Great Enterprise,* p. 71.

78. Langlois, *China under Mongol Rule,* pp. 3–5.

79. Farquhar, "Origins of the Manchus' Mongolian Policy," p. 203.

80. Ibid.; Michael, *Origin of Manchu Rule,* p. 65.

81. Romeyn Taylor, "Yuan Origins of the Wei-suo System," in *Chinese Government in Ming Times: Seven Studies,* ed. Charles O. Hucker (New York: Columbia University Press, 1969), pp. 23–40.

82. Farquhar, "Origins of the Manchus' Mongolian Policy," p. 15.

83. To be sure, we could trace the origins of the banners back further, to the Jurchen Jin, for example, and similar organizations are found in other Central Eurasian societies. For the purposes of my argument, the proximate link to the Mongols is sufficient.

84. Roberto M. Unger, *Plasticity into Power: Comparative-Historical Studies on the Institutional Conditions of Economic and Military Success* (Cambridge: Cambridge University Press, 1987), p. 59.

85. Hua Li, "Qingdai di ManMeng lianyin" (Manchu and Mongol connections during the Qing dynasty), *Minzu Yanjiu* (February 1983), pp. 45–54.

86. Cf. Lien-sheng Yang, "Historical Notes on the Chinese World Order," in *The Chinese World Order: Traditional China's Foreign Relations*, ed. John K. Fairbank (Cambridge, Mass.: Harvard University Press, 1968), pp. 20–33; Ying-shih Yu, "Han Foreign Relations," in *The Cambridge History of China, vol. 1, The Ch'in and Han Empires, 221 B.C.–A.D. 220*, ed. Denis Twitchett and Michael Loewe (New York: Cambridge University Press, 1986), pp. 377–462; Ying-shih Yu, *Trade and Expansion in Han China* (Berkeley: University of California Press, 1967). For modern Chinese nationalist invocation of *heqin* as a model of minority peoples' relationships with Han, see Uradyn Erden Bulag, *The Mongols at China's Edge: History and the Politics of National Unity* (Lanham, Md.: Rowman & Littlefield, 2002).

87. QSLKX 143.8, cited in Hua Li, "Qingdai di ManMeng lianyin," p. 54.

88. Kanda Nobuo et al., *Manbun Rōtō*, 7:1403, 1412; Linke, *Zur Entwicklung*, p. 62; Wakeman, *Great Enterprise*, p. 202.

89. Hummel, *Eminent Chinese*, p. 256.

90. Pamela K. Crossley and Evelyn Rawski, "A Profile of the Manchu Language," *Harvard Journal of Asiatic Studies* 53, no. 1 (June 1993), pp. 63–88.

91. *Baqi Tongzhi*, 236:13755, cited in Linke, *Zur Entwicklung*, pp. 121–122.

92. *Qing Taizu Wuhuangdi Shilu* (1599/1), in Pan Zhe, Li Hongbin, and Sun Fangming, eds., *Qing Ruguanqian Shiliao Xuanji*, 3 vols. (Beijing: Renmin Chubanshe, 1984), 1:319.

93. Karen Barkey, *Bandits and Bureaucrats: The Ottoman Route to State Centralization* (Ithaca: Cornell University Press, 1994); Cemal Kafadar, *Between Two Worlds: The Construction of the Ottoman State* (Berkeley: University of California Press, 1995); Rudi Paul Lindner, *Nomads and Ottomans in Medieval Anatolia* (Bloomington: Indiana University Press, 1983).

4. Manchus, Mongols, and Russians in Conflict, 1670–1690

1. Arthur W. Hummel, ed., *Eminent Chinese of the Ch'ing Period* (Washington D.C.: U.S. Government Printing Office, 1943–44), p. 328.

2. Ibid., p. 898; Lawrence D. Kessler, *K'ang-hsi and the Consolidation of Ch'ing Rule, 1661–1684* (Chicago: University of Chicago Press, 1976), p. 56.

3. Kessler, *K'ang-hsi*, p. 54.

4. *Sui* indicates the Chinese year count, in which a person is one *sui* at birth and adds one *sui* on each lunar New Year.

5. Hummel, *Eminent Chinese*, pp. 415, 635–636.

6. Kessler, *K'ang-hsi*, p. 78.

7. Ibid., pp. 167–171.

8. Zhang Yushu comp., *Qinzheng Pingding Shuomo Fanglue* (Chronicle of the emperor's personal expeditions to pacify the northwest frontier) (Beijing: Zhongguo Shudian, 1708), *juan* 1 KX 16/6 *dingwei*, abbreviated QPSF. There are two editions of

this text: one included in the Siku Quanshu Imperial Encyclopedia, and a reprint of the original 1708 edition. The volume *(juan)* numbers are the same, but the page numbers differ, so references are cited by *juan*, year, lunar month, and lunar day. Page numbers that refer to part of one document refer to the 1708 edition. The *Qingshilu* references follow the same format.

9. QPSF j.1 KX 16/10 *jiayin.*

10. QPSF j.1 KX 16/10 *jiayin*; QSLKX j.69 KX16/10 *jiayin.*

11. QPSF j.1 KX 17/8 *jisi*; Hummel, *Eminent Chinese*, p. 266; Cai Jiayi, "Galdan," in *Qingdai Renwu Zhuan Gao* (Draft Qing biographies), ed. Qingshi Bianweihui, pt. 1, 9 vols. (Beijing: Zhonghua Shuju, 1991), 6:173; Miyawaki Junko, "Jūnana seiki no Oiratto: Jungar Hankoku ni taisuru gimon" (The Oyirad of the seventeenth century: the "Dzungar Khanate" revisited), *Shigaku Zasshi* 90 (1981), pp. 40–63.

12. QPSF j.1 KX 17/8 *jisi.*

13. QSLKX j.85 KX 18/10 *renshen.*

14. QPSF j.1 KX 18/7 *jiachen.*

15. QSLKX j.83 KX 18/8 *jichou*; QPSF j.1 KX 18/8 *jichou*; cf. Jonathan D. Spence, *Emperor of China: Self-Portrait of K'ang-hsi* (New York: Knopf, 1974), p. 20.

16. Ferdinand D. Lessing, *Mongolian-English Dictionary* (Bloomington, Ind.: The Mongolia Society, 1995), p. 123. "Mandate of Heaven" *(tianming)* is an ancient Chinese term designating Heavenly approval of the current ruler.

17. QPSF j.2 KX 20/9 *xinwei.*

18. QPSF j.2 KX 22/7 *wuxu*; QSLKX j.111 KX 22/7 *wuxu.*

19. Thomas J. Barfield, *The Perilous Frontier: Nomadic Empires and China* (Cambridge, Mass.: Basil Blackwell, 1989).

20. QPSF j.2 KX 22/7 *wuxu*, p. 29.

21. QSLKX j.112 KX 22/9 *guiwei.*

22. QSLKX j.116 KX 23/9 *yihai.*

23. QSLKX j.127 KX 25/9 *guimao.*

24. QPSF j.5 KX 27/9 *jiashen.*

25. QSLKX j.104 KX 21/8 *yiyou*, j.111 KX 22/7 *jiashen.*

26. QPSF j.3 KX 23/11 *jiazi*, j.3 KX 24/5 *guiwei*; QSLKX j.121 KX 24/5 *guiwei.*

27. QPSF j.3 KX 24/11 *guisi*; QSLKX j.124 KX 25/1 *wuchen, yihai.*

28. The term "wings" for different Mongol confederations derives from the divisions of the army of Chinggis and Khubilai Khan, facing south.

29. Chiba Muneo, "Jungaru no Chōshō," (Black whirlwind: the death knell of the Jungars), in *Kara būran: Kuroi suna-arashi*, 2 vols. (Tokyo: Kokushokankokai, 1986), 1:35; *Qingdai Renwu Zhuan Gao*, 6:174–175; Henry H. Howorth, *History of the Mongols from the Ninth to the Nineteenth Century*, 4 vols. (Taibei: Ch'eng Wen, 1970), p. 470.; Veronika Veit, *Die Vier Qane von Qalqa: ein Beitrag zur Kenntnis der politischen Bedeutung der nordmongolischen Aristokratie in den Regierungsperioden Kang-hsi bis Chien-lung (1661–1796) anhand des biographischen Handbuches Iledkel sastir aus dem Jahre 1795*, 2 vols. (Wiesbaden: O. Harrassowitz, 1990), 2:180.

30. QPSF j.3 KX 23/2 *gengzi*; KX 25/10 *wuwu.*

31. QPSF j.3 KX 25/10 *wuwu.*

32. Ibid.

33. QPSF j.4 KX 26/10 *jisi*; QSLKX j.131 KX 26/9 *gengzi*, KX 26/10 *jisi.*

34. Chiba Muneo, "Jungaru no Chōshō," 1:44; QSLKX j.136 KX 27/7 *renshen;* QPSF KX 27/6 *guichou;* Svat Soucek, *A History of Inner Asia* (Cambridge: Cambridge University Press, 2000), p. 19.

35. QPSF j.4 KX 27/6 *guichou;* QSLKX j.136 KX 27/7 *renshen.*

36. Yanagisawa Akira, "Garudan no Haruha shinkō (1688) kō no Haruha shokō to Roshia" (The Khalkha princes and Russia after Galdan's invasion of 1688), in *Shinchō to Higashi Ajia: Kanda Nobuo Sensei koki kinen ronshū,* ed. Kanda Nobuo Sensei Koki Kinen Ronshū Hensan Iinkai (Tokyo: Yamakawa Shuppansha, 1992), pp. 179–196; Siberian Governors, *Reports* (Moscow: Rossiskiy Gosudarstvennyi Arkhiv Drevnikh Aktov [Russian State Archive of Ancient Acts] and Arkhiv Vneshney Politiki Rossii [Archive of Foreign Relations of Russia], 1680–1800).

37. Jean Baptiste Du Halde, *Description géographique, historique, chronologique, politique, et physique de l'empire de la Chine et de la Tartarie chinoise, enrichie des cartes générales et particulières de ces pays, de la carte générale & des cartes particuliéres du Thibet, & de la Corée; & ornée d'un grand nombre de figures et de vignettes gravées en taille-douce,* vol. 4 (Paris: P. G. Lemercier, 1735), p. 262; quote from Walther Heissig, *Die Familien- und Kirchengeschichtsschreibung der Mongolen,* vol. 1 *16–18 Jhdt.* (Wiesbaden: O. Harrassowitz, 1959), pp. 133–134.

38. Howorth, *History,* p. 478.

39. QSLKX j.136 KX 27/7 *jiaxu.*

40. QSLKX j.136 KX 27/7 *jiashen.*

41. QSLKX j.136 KX 27/8 *jiyou.*

42. QPSF j.5 KX 27/10 *yisi.*

43. QPSF j.5 KX 27/11 *jiashen;* QSLKX j.139 KX 28/1 *dinghai.*

44. Du Halde, *Description,* p. 262.

45. QPSF j.5 KX 28/1 *dinghai,* p. 20b.

46. QPSF j.5 KX 28/5 *guihai,* KX 28/11 *bingchen.*

47. QPSF j.6 KX 29/3 *jiayin.*

48. QPSF j.6 KX 29/4 *jisi.*

49. Hummel, *Eminent Chinese,* pp. 759–760; Zahiruddin Ahmad, *Sino-Tibetan Relations in the Seventeenth Century* (Rome: Istituto italiano per il Medio ed Estremo Oriente, 1970), p. 41.

50. QPSF j.6 KX 29/5 *yiwei.*

51. QPSF j.6 KX 29/6 *renshen.*

52. QSLKX j.146 KX 29/6 *renshen;* Du Halde, *Description,* p. 234; Chen Feng, *Qingdai Junfei Yanjiu* (Military expenses in the Qing dynasty) (Wuhan: Wuhan Daxue Chubanshe, 1991), p. 250.

53. QPSF j.6 KX 29/6 *renshen;* I. Cherepanov, "Sibirskii Letopis" (Manuscript on Siberia), St. Petersburg, 1795.

54. QPSF j.6 KX 29/6 *jiashen.*

55. QPSF j.6 KX 29/6 *dinghai.*

56. QPSF j.7 KX 29/7 *gengyin,* p. 16a; *renyin* p. 21a.

57. QPSF j.7 KX 29/7 *guimao.*

58. QPSF j.7 KX 29/7 *wushen,* p. 37b.

59. Du Halde, *Description,* p. 234. For the location of Ulan Butong, see Yuan Shenbo, "Ulan Butong kao" (A study of Ulan Butong), *Lishi Yanjiu* (1978), pp. 86–91.

60. Maska (Ch. Masiha), "Saibei jicheng" (Account of travels north of the passes), in *Xiaofang Huzhai Yudi Congchao* (Shanghai: Zhuyitang, 1877), pp. 25–29.

61. Du Halde, *Description*, p. 237; Hummel, *Eminent Chinese*, p. 251; Yoshida Kin'ichi, *Roshia no Tōhō Shinshutsu to Nerchinsk Jōyaku* (Russia's advance to the east and the Nerchinsk treaty) (Tokyo: Kindai Chūgoku Kenkyū Sentā, 1984), p. 314; I. Ia. Zlatkin, *Istoriia Dzhungarskogo Khanstva, 1635–1758* (History of the Zunghar Khanate, 1635–1758) (Moscow: Nauka, 1964), p. 282; Joseph Fletcher, "V. A. Aleksandrov on Russo-Ch'ing Relations in the Seventeenth Century: Critique and Résumé," *Kritika* 7, no. 3 (1971), pp. 138–170; V. A. Aleksandrov, *Rossiia na dal'nevostochnykh rubezhakh (vtoraia polovina XVII v.)* (Russia in the Far East in the second half of the seventeenth century) (Moscow: Nauka, 1969), p. 197.

62. QPSF j.8 KX 29/8 *xinyou*.

63. QPSF j.8 KX 29/8 *guiyou*.

64. QPSF j.8 KX 29/8 *bingzi*.

65. Du Halde, *Description*, pp. 242–245.

66. QPSF j.8 KX 29/8/17 *yihai*.

67. QPSF j.8 KX 29/9 *wuzi*.

68. Maska, "Saibei jicheng."

69. Owen Lattimore, in the 1920s, also noticed the nasty taste of tamarisk: "The reason we drank so much tea was because of the bad water . . . The worst water was in tamarisk regions. The tamarisk is a desert tree, or rather shrub, sending down its roots to a great depth to reach water. When the water is near the surface the roots, rotting in the moist earth, turn the water a yellow colour. It is thick, almost sticky, and incredibly bitter and nasty." Owen Lattimore, *Studies in Frontier History: Collected Papers, 1928–1958* (New York: Oxford University Press, 1962), p. 41. On Mongol consumption of marmots, see John Masson Smith Jr., "Mongol Campaign Rations: Milk, Marmots, and Blood?" in *Turks, Hungarians and Kipchaks: A Festschrift in Honor of Tibor Halasi-Kun,* ed. Pierre Oberling (Washington, D.C.: Institute of Turkish Studies, 1984), pp. 223–228.

70. Du Halde, *Description*, p. 234.

71. QPSF j.7 KX 29/7 *guisi*, j.8 KX 29/8/8 *bingyin*.

72. QPSF j.7 KX 29/7 *gengyin*, j.8 KX 29/8 *xinyou*, j.9 KX 30/1 *guisi*, p. 2a.

73. Du Halde, *Description*, p. 250.

74. QPSF j.6 KX 29/4 *jiaxu*, KX 29/6, j.7 KX 29/7 *jiachen*.

75. QPSF j.5 KX 28/4 *jiawu*.

76. Chen Feng, *Junfei*, pp. 251–254.

77. The main English-language studies of Russo-Chinese relations in this period are still Clifford M. Foust, *Muscovite and Mandarin: Russia's Trade with China and Its Setting, 1727–1805* (Chapel Hill: University of North Carolina Press, 1969), and Mark Mancall, *Russia and China: Their Diplomatic Relations to 1728* (Cambridge, Mass.: Harvard University Press, 1971), but both works were written before the publication of many new Russian archival sources in N. F. Demidova and V. S. Miasnikov, eds., *Russko-kitaiskie otnosheniia v XVII veke: Materialy i dokumenty* (Russo-Chinese relations in the seventeenth century), 2 vols. (Moscow: Nauka, 1969–1972); N. F. Demidova, ed., *Materialy po Istorii Russko-Mongol'skikh Otnoshenii: Russko-mongol'skie otnosheniia, 1654–1685 sbornik dokumentov* (Materials on the history of

Russo-Mongolian relations, 1654–1685) (Moscow: Izdatel'skaia Firma Vostochnaia Literatura, 1996); N. F. Demidova, ed., *Materialy po Istorii Russko-Mongol'skikh Otnoshenii: Russko-mongol'skie otnosheniia, 1685–1691: sbornik dokumentov* (Materials on the history of Russo-Mongolian relations, 1685–1691) (Moscow: Izdatel'skaia Firma Vostochnaia Literatura, 2000), cited as RKO 1969, RKO 1996, and RKO 2000, respectively. See Wolfgang Seuberlich, "Review of Russko-Kitajskie Otnoshenija v XVII veke," *Oriens Extremus* 19 (1972), pp. 239–255, for a review of this collection. For a Japanese study, see Yoshida Kin'ichi, *Roshia no Tōhō Shinshutsu to Nerchinsk Jōyaku* (Tokyo: Kindai Chūgoku Kenkyū Sentā, 1984). Gaston Cahen, *Histoire des relations de la Russie avec la Chine sous Pierre le Grand (1689–1730)* (Paris: F. Alcan, 1912); Gaston Cahen, *Some Early Russo-Chinese Relations* (Shanghai: National Review Office, 1912); and John Baddeley, *Russia, Mongolia, China, being some record of the relations between them from the beginning of the XVIIth century to the death of the Tsar Alexei Mikhailovich,* A.D. *1602–1676,* 2 vols. (London: Macmillan and Company, 1919), also provide translations of many Russian documents. The French edition of Cahen includes notes and commentary omitted from the English translation. (French edition citations are given as F plus page, English citations as E plus page.)

78. Baddeley, *Russia, Mongolia, China,* 1:69.

79. Ibid., 2:35.

80. Ibid., p. 66.

81. Mancall, *Russia and China,* pp. 20–29.

82. Ibid., p. 58.

83. Peter C. Perdue, "Boundaries, Maps, and Movement: The Chinese, Russian, and Mongolian Empires in Early Modern Eurasia," *International History Review* 20, no. 2 (1998), pp. 263–286; Wakamatsu Hiroshi, "Ganchimūru no Roshia bōmei jiken o meguru Shin, Roshia Kōshō" (Sino-Russian negotiations concerning Gantimur's flight to Russia), *Kyōto Furitsu Daigaku Gakujutsu Hōkoku: Jimbun* 25 (1973), pp. 25–39; 26 (1974), pp. 1–12; Wakamatsu Hiroshi, "Ganchimūru no Roshia bōmei jiken o megutte" (Gantimur's flight to Russia), *Yūboku Shakaishi* 46 (1973–74), pp. 8–13.

84. Cahen, *Histoire,* pp. E13–14, F43–47; Hummel, *Eminent Chinese,* pp. 442–443, 630, 663–666, 794; Mancall, *Russia and China,* pp. 153–162; Yanagisawa Akira, "Garudan."

85. RKO 1969, 2:514.

86. RKO 1969, 2:516.

87. Mancall believes the Jesuit pretext that "the Mongolian translators on each side were so poor that the negotiations reverted to Latin immediately," but Cahen demonstrates by referring to Golovin's report that the Russians were capable of communicating with the Manchus but were prevented from doing so by Jesuit interference. Mancall, *Russia and China,* p. 156; Cahen, *Histoire,* pp. E14, F47; RKO, 1969, 2:514, 516, 521, 523, 528, 544.

88. "Kissinger's penchant for secrecy and his personalized diplomacy with China served his own purposes by augmenting his power . . . Kissinger worked assiduously to ensure that nothing and no one should interfere with his own dominance over diplomacy with Beijing." James Mann, *About Face: The History of America's Relationship with China* (New York: Vintage, 1998), p. 67.

89. RKO 1969, 2:620–632.

90. Mancall, *Russia and China*, p. 159; Cahen, *Histoire*, pp. E29, F76; Fu Lo-shu, *A Documentary Chronicle of Sino-Western Relations (1644–1820)*, 2 vols. (Tucson: University of Arizona Press, 1966), 1:104.

91. RKO 1969, 2:5–54; Yoshida Kin'ichi, *Roshia*, p. 345.

5. Eating Snow

1. "Through the entire history of the Mongols [runs] a red thread of fatal individualism, which gives personal loyalty precedence over loyalty to politically or ideologically founded institutions." Veronika Veit, *Die Vier Qane von Qalqa: ein Beitrag zur Kenntnis der politischen Bedeutung der nordmongolischen Aristokratie in den Regierungsperioden Kang-hsi bis Chien-lung (1661–1796) anhand des biographischen Handbuches Iledkel sastir aus dem Jahre 1795*, 2 vols. (Wiesbaden: O. Harrassowitz, 1990), 1:10.

2. QPSF j.9 KX 30/3 *gengzi*.

3. QPSF j.9 KX 30/4 *renxu*.

4. QPSF j.10 KX 30/5 *wuzi*.

5. Jean Baptiste Du Halde, *Description géographique, historique, chronologique, politique, et physique de l'empire de la Chine et de la Tartarie chinoise, enrichie des cartes générales et particulières de ces pays, de la carte générale & des cartes particuliéres du Thibet, & de la Corée; & ornée d'un grand nombre de figures et de vignettes gravées en taille-douce*, 4 vols. (Paris: P. G. Lemercier, 1735), 4:252, 266.

6. Veit, *Die Vier Qane*, 2:181; QPSF j.10 KX 30/5 *dinghai, wuzi*.

7. QPSF j.10 KX 30/6 *yimao*.

8. QPSF j.9 KX 30/2 *dingmao*.

9. QPSF j.13 KX 32/9 *jiyou*.

10. See, e.g., QPSF j.9 KX 30/3 *gengzi*, j.12 KX 31/9 *gengzi*.

11. QPSF j.14 KX 33/5 *jiayin*.

12. QPSF j.12 KX 31/9 *wushen*.

13. Henry H. Howorth, *History of the Mongols from the Ninth to the Nineteenth Century*, 4 vols. (Taibei: Ch'eng Wen, 1970), 1:630.

14. QPSF j.12 KX 31/12 *jiachen*.

15. QPSF j.11 KX 30/9 *dingmao*.

16. Zahiruddin Ahmad, *Sino-Tibetan Relations in the Seventeenth Century* (Rome: Istituto italiano per il Medio ed Estremo Oriente, 1970), p. 295

17. QPSF j.15 KX 34/4 *gengzi*.

18. QPSF j.14 KX 33/11 *guiwei*.

19. QPSF j.16 KX 34/8 *xinchou*.

20. QPSF j.16 KX 34/8 *jiyou*.

21. QPSF j.16 KX 34/8 *jiyou*.

22. QPSF j.17 KX 34/11 *wuchen*, j.16 KX 34/9 *jisi*.

23. QPSF j.17 KX 34/11 *wuzi*.

24. QPSF j.16 KX 34/10/ *gengzi, dingwei*.

25. QPSF j.19 KX 35/1 *jiachen*.

26. QPSF j.17 KX 34/11 *renxu*.

27. QPSF j.17 KX 34/11 *bingzi*.

28. "Yu Chenglong Nianpu," in Wei Yuan, *Shengwuji* (Record of sacred military victories) (Beijing: Zhonghua Shuju, 1984), pp. 134–135; QPSF j.17 KX 34/11 *wuyin.*

29. QPSF j.18 KX 34/12 *jiawu.*

30. QPSF j.18 KX 34/12 *jihai, wuxu.*

31. Yin Huaxing, *Xizheng Jilue* (An account of the western expedition) (Taibei: Guangwen Shuju, 1968), p. 5b.

32. QPSF j.15 KX 34/7 *yiyou,* j.18 KX 34/12 *wushen.*

33. QPSF j.19 KX 35/1 *guihai;* Du Halde, *Description,* p. 307.

34. QPSF j.19 KX 35/1 *renshen.*

35. QPSF j.18 KX 34/12 *dingyou.*

36. QPSF j.20 KX 35/2 *jihai.*

37. QPSF j.18 KX 34/12 *jihai.*

38. QPSF j.10 KX 30/5 *wuzi,* j.17 KX 34/11 *gengchen,* j.18 KX 34/12 *jihai.*

39. QPSF j.20 KX 35/2 *gengxu, renchen.*

40. QPSF j.20 KX 35/2 *xinchou,* j.22 KX 35/4 *renchen, bingxu.*

41. QPSF j.21 KX 35/3 *gengshen.*

42. Wei Yuan, *Shengwuji,* pp. 134–135; QPSF j.21 KX 35/3 *jiaxu,* j.22 KX 35/4 *bingwu, xinmao.*

43. Du Halde, *Description,* p. 304.

44. Manchu originals in GZDKX, vols 8, 9; selected translations in Jaqa Cimeddorji, *Die Briefe des Kang-Hsi-Kaisers aus den Jahren 1696–97 an den Kronprinzen Yin-Cheng aus mandschurischen Geheimdokumenten: ein Beitrag zum ersten Dsungarenkrieg der Ching, 1690–1697* (Wiesbaden: Otto Harrassowitz, 1991); Okada Hidehiro, "Outer Mongolia through the Eyes of Emperor Kangxi," *Ajia Afurika Gengo Bunka Kenkyū* 18 (1979), pp. 1–11, and Okada Hidehiro, *Kōkitei no Tegami* (Letters of the Kangxi emperor) (Tokyo: Chuko Shinsho, 1979).

45. QPSF j.23 KX 35/5 *renxu.*

46. Du Halde, *Description,* p. 315; Okada Hidehiro, "Outer Mongolia," p. 4.

47. Cimeddorji, *Die Briefe,* p. 80, letter no. 6, KX 35/3/18.

48. Arthur W. Hummel, ed., *Eminent Chinese of the Ch'ing Period* (Washington, D.C.: U.S. Government Printing Office, 1943–44), pp. 663, 795; QPSF j.22 KX 35/4 *yiwei;* Cimeddorji, *Die Briefe,* pp. 96–97.

49. QPSF j.24 KX 35/5 *jisi.*

50. QPSF j.21 KX 35/3 *yihai.*

51. QPSF j.22 KX 35/4 *guichou.*

52. Du Halde, *Description,* p. 318.

53. QPSF j.22 KX 35/4 *jiayin;* Cimeddorji, *Die Briefe,* p. 116, letter no. 15, KX 35/5/10.

54. Du Halde, *Description,* pp. 318–322.

55. Yin Huaxing, *Xizheng Jilue,* p. 7b.

56. QPSF j.22 KX 35/4 *xinhai;* Cimeddorji, *Die Briefe,* p. 123, letter no. 16, KX 35/5/18.

57. QPSF j.23 KX 35/5 *jiwei.*

58. QPSF j.23 KX 35/5 *renxu;* Cimeddorji, *Die Briefe,* p. 127, letter no. 17, KX 35/5/13.

59. Du Halde, *Description,* p. 324.

60. Cimeddorji, *Die Briefe*, pp. 148–152, letter no. 21, KX 35/5/26.

61. Du Halde, *Description*, p. 330; Ferdinand D. Lessing, *Mongolian-English Dictionary* (Bloomington, Ind.: The Mongolia Society, 1995), p. 1024; Yin Huaxing, *Xizheng Jilue*, p. 10a.

62. QPSF j.24 KX 35/5 *renshen*, p. 17; Cimeddorji, *Die Briefe*, pp. 161–165; Du Halde, *Description*, pp. 328–331.

63. Cimeddorji, *Die Briefe*, p. 161, letter no. 25, KX 35/5/22 (written 5/18); QPSF j.24 KX 35/5 *renshen, guiyou*.

64. Du Halde, *Description*, p. 334; Cimeddorji, *Die Briefe*, p. 176, letter no. 29, KX 35/5/18.

65. Cimeddorji, *Die Briefe*, pp. 141–143, letter no. 19, KX 35/5/15.

66. QPSF j.25 KX 35/5 *bingzi*.

67. QPSF j.25 KX 35/5 *guiyou*.

68. QPSF j.25 KX 35/5 *guiyou*, p. 18a.

69. QPSF j.25 KX 35/5 *jiashen*. On the concept of *shi*, see François Jullien, *The Propensity of Things: Toward a History of Efficacy in China* (New York: Zone Books, 1995).

70. QPSF j.26 KX 35/6 *guisi*; Wei Yuan, *Shengwuji*; Hummel, *Eminent Chinese*, p. 851.

71. William McNeill, *Mythistory and Other Essays* (Chicago: University of Chicago Press, 1986).

72. The Qing term "Huizi" does not clearly distinguish between Turkic and Chinese Muslims.

73. Ahmad, *Sino-Tibetan Relations*, pp. 41–52.

74. QPSF j.28 KX 35/8 *jiawu*, p. 28a.

75. QPSF j.26 KX 35/6 *xinhai*.

76. QPSF j.28 KX 35/8 *jiawu*.

77. QPSF j.28 KX 35/8 *jiawu*, p. 37a.

78. QPSF j.27 KX 35/7 *wuwu*.

79. QPSF j.27 KX 35/7 *xinyou*.

80. QPSF j.27 KX 35/7 *jiaxu*, p. 48a.

81. QPSF j.28 KX 35/8 *renchen*, p. 13b.

82. QPSF j.28 KX 35/8 *renchen*.

83. QPSF j.28 KX 35/8 *jiawu*, p. 38b.

84. QPSF j.28 KX 35/8 *jiawu*.

85. Ahmad, *Sino-Tibetan Relations*, p. 318.

86. QPSF j.33 KX 35/11 *jiaxu*, p. 44b.

87. QPSF j.29 KX 35/9 *bingchen*.

88. Du Halde, *Description*, p. 346.

89. QPSF j.30 KX 35/9 *xinsi*.

90. QPSF j.30 KX 35/9 *renwu*.

91. Cimeddorji, *Die Briefe*, p. 198, letter no. 35 KX 35/11/6; QPSF j.33 KX 35/11 *bingchen*.

92. QPSF j.32 KX 35/10 *wushen*.

93. QPSF j.33 KX 35/11 *wushen*, p. 20b.

94. Cimeddorji, *Die Briefe*, pp. 218–19; QPSF j.33 KX 35/11 *jiaxu*.

95. QPSF j.33 KX 35/11 *wuyin.*

96. Cimeddorji, *Die Briefe*, p. 230.

97. Ibid., p. 232; QPSF j.33 KX 35/11 *gengchen.*

98. Chiba Muneo, "Jungaru no Chōshō" (Black whirlwind: the death knell of the Jungars), in *Kara būran: Kuroi suna-arashi* (Tokyo: Kokushokankokai, 1986), p. 183; QPSF j.36 KX 36/2 *dinghai.*

99. QPSF j.35 KX 36/1 *gengwu*, j.38 KX 36/3 *yimao.*

100. QPSF j.43 KX 36/4 *dingsi.*

101. Okada Hidehiro, *Tegami*, p. 151; QPSF j.38 KX 36/3 *wuwu*, pp. 21b–23a; On the Chengde emperor, see L. C. Goodrich and Chaoying Fang, *Dictionary of Ming Biography, 1368–1644* (New York: Columbia University Press, 1976), p. 307; David Robinson, *Bandits, Eunuchs, and the Son of Heaven* (Honolulu: University of Hawai'i Press, 2001).

102. Du Halde, *Description*, p. 364; QPSF j.38 KX 36/3 *yimao.*

103. QPSF j.40 KX 36/3* *guiwei.*

104. QPSF j.42 KX 36/3* *yisi.*

105. Cimeddorji, *Die Briefe*, p. 256, letter no. 50 KX 36/3*/13.

106. QPSF j.36 KX 36/2 *jichou.*

107. Du Halde, *Description*, p. 372.

108. QPSF j.40 KX 36/3* *yiyou.*

109. Okada Hidehiro, *Tegami*, p. 160.

110. QPSF j.37 KX 36/2 *renyin.*

111. Arthur Waldron, *The Great Wall of China: From History to Myth* (Cambridge: Cambridge University Press, 1990), p. 106.

112. Du Halde, *Description*, p. 364.

113. QPSF j.39 KX 36/3 *wuchen.*

114. Chiba Muneo, "Jungaru no Chōshō," p. 195; Du Halde, *Description*, p. 373; QPSF j.39 KX 36/3 *dingchou.*

115. Wei Yuan, *Shengwuji*, p. 135.

116. Cimeddorji, *Die Briefe*, p. 259, letter no. 51, p. 266, letter no. 53.

117. QPSF j.41 KX 36/3* *jiawu.*

118. QPSF j.41 KX 36/3* *guisi.*

119. Okada Hidehiro, *Tegami*, p. 174.

120. QPSF j.39 KX 36/3 *gengchen.*

121. QPSF j.43 KX 36/4 *jiazi*, KX 36/4 *jiaxu*, Cimeddorji, *Die Briefe*, p. 66.

122. Cimeddorji, *Die Briefe*, p. 274, letter no. 55, KX 36/4/22; QPSF j.43 KX 36/4 *gengwu.* I have found no record of the doctor's interrogation.

123. Cimeddorji, *Die Briefe*, p. 277. In the mid-nineteenth century, the sudden death of the Turkestani "holy warrior" Yakub beg, who occupied Xinjiang for thirteen years, produced the same debate: poison, suicide, or brain seizure? See Hodong Kim, *Holy War in China: The Muslim Rebellion and State in Chinese Central Asia, 1864–1877* (Stanford: Stanford University Press, 2004), p. 168.

124. Okada Hidehiro, "Galdan's Death: When and How," *Memoirs of the Research Department of the Toyo Bunko* 37 (1979), pp. 91–97; Okada Hidehiro, *Tegami*; Borjigidai Oyunbilig, *Zur Überlieferungsgeschichte des Berichts über den persönlichen Feldzug des Kangxi Kaisers gegen Galdan (1696–1697)* (Wiesbaden: Harrassowitz, 1999).

125. QPSF j.43 KX 36/4 *jiazi*, p. 37b.

126. QSLKX j.183 KX 36/5 *guimao*; QPSF j.45 KX 36/7 *dingyou*.

127. QPSF j.45 KX 36/7 *yisi*, j.45 KX 36/8 *xinmao*, j.46 KX 36/10 *bingchen*, j.46 KX 36/10 *guihai*, j.47 KX 36/11 *jiashen*, j.47 KX 36/12 *jiyou*, j.48 KX 37/3 *jimao*, j.48 KX 37/6 *wuwu*.

128. Thomas Metzger, *The Internal Organization of Ch'ing Bureaucracy* (Cambridge, Mass.: Harvard University Press, 1973).

129. QPSF j.47 KX 36/12 *gengwu*.

130. QPSF j.43 KX 36/4 *gengwu*.

131. QPSF j.46 KX 36/9 *guihai*; Howorth, *History,* 1:642.

132. QPSF j.46 KX 36/9 *guihai*, p. 32b.

133. QPSF j.48 KX 37/09 *guiwei*, p. 32b.

134. Evelyn S. Rawski, *The Last Emperors: A Social History of Qing Imperial Institutions* (Berkeley: University of California Press, 1998), pp. 197–294.

6. Imperial Overreach and Zunghar Survival, 1700–1731

1. Henry H. Howorth, *History of the Mongols from the Ninth to the Nineteenth Century,* 4 vols. (Taibei: Ch'eng Wen, 1970), 1:640; ZGSL 91, 121.

2. I. Ia. Zlatkin, *Istoriia Dzhungarskogo Khanstvo, 1635–1758* (History of the Zunghar Khanate, 1635–1758) (Moscow: Nauka, 1964), p. 299.

3. Miyawaki Junko, "Oiratto Han no tanjō" (The birth of the Oirat Khanship), *Shigaku Zasshi* 100 (1991), p. 63.

4. ZGSL 123.

5. Zlatkin, *Istoriia,* p. 323.

6. PDZGFL *qian* 4.3a KX 54/6 *yiyou*; Howorth, *History,* 1:567.

7. ZGSL 148; Gaston Cahen, *Histoire des relations de la Russie avec la Chine sous Pierre le Grand (1689–1730)* (Paris: F. Alcan, 1912), pp. E63, F135.

8. ZGSL 149; Cahen, *Histoire,* pp. E64, F143; Howorth, *History,* 1:647; Gerard Fridrikh Miller, *Sammlung russischer Geschichte,* 4 vols. (St. Petersburg: Kayserliche academie der wissenschaften, 1760), 4:183–247.

9. Sh. B. Chimitdorzhiev, *Vzaimootnosheniia Mongolii i Rossii v 17–18 vekakh* (Relations between Mongolia and Russia in the seventeenth and eighteenth centuries) (Moscow: Nauka, 1978).

10. Zlatkin, *Istoriia,* p. 347.

11. Clifford M. Foust, *Muscovite and Mandarin: Russia's Trade with China and Its Setting, 1727–1805* (Chapel Hill: University of North Carolina Press, 1969).

12. Bell on Tulisen: "The 24th, arrived an officer from the court of Pekin, sent on purpose to discover the number and quality of the embassy. This gentleman, whose name was Tulishin, was a Mantshu Tartar by birth, and a member of the tribunal for western affairs, with which he was very well acquainted . . . He pretended to have been employed on some business with the Tush-du-Chan at Urga; and, hearing of the ambassador's arrival, had come to pay his respects to him. It was however well known that he was sent to enquire whether the ambassador came on a friendly errand. He was received very kindly; and after he had stayed three days, and made his observations, returned very well satisfied . . . This wise and cautious nation, jealous of all the world, suffer none to enter their territories, but such as bring friendly messages." Tulisen refers to Bell only

as a "physician" accompanying the Izmailov embassy. John Bell, *A Journey from St. Petersburg to Peking, 1719–1722*, ed. J. L. Stevenson (Edinburgh: Edinburgh University Press, 1965), pp. 15, 97–98.

13. Michael Khodarkovsky, "Russian Peasant and Kalmyk Nomad: A Tragic Encounter in the Mid-Eighteenth Century," *Russian History* 15 (1988), pp. 43–69; Michael Khodarkovsky, "Uneasy Alliance: Peter the Great and Ayuki Khan," *Central Asian Survey* 7 (1988), pp. 1–45; Michael Khodarkovsky, *Where Two Worlds Met: The Russian State and the Kalmyk Nomads, 1600–1771* (Ithaca: Cornell University Press, 1992).

14. Cahen, *Histoire*, pp. F115–133, E51–59.

15. Tulisen, *Lakcaha Jecende takûraha ejehe bithe (Kōchū Iikiroku: Tulisen's I-yu-lu)*, ed. Imanishi Shunju (Tenri: Tenri Daigaku Oyasato Kenkyujo, 1964), p. 6a (cited as *Kōchū Iikiroku*); cf. Tulisen (Too-le-Shin), *Narrative of the Chinese Embassy to the Khan of the Tourgouth Tartars in the Years 1712–1715*, trans. Sir George Staunton (London, 1821), pp. 10–11; my translation from the Manchu edition of Imanishi. Note that Staunton's translation of 1821 is only from the Chinese text: "Should Ayuki express to you a wish for our assistance in any hostile operations against Tsewang Rabdan, you are by no means to make any promises or to listen to any proposals of that nature, but are thus to reply: 'Tsewang Rabdan is on very friendly terms with his Imperial Majesty. He frequently sends envoys with complimentary enquiries, and they are always received at court, and honored with presents and other marks of imperial favor. As to his strength and resources, he, no doubt, is weak, straitened, and helpless in the extreme, but our most excellent master does not therefore desire to make war against him and subdue him . . . [I]t is our opinion that our Emperor, desiring nothing more than that all nations under heaven should enjoy peace and tranquility, has no intention whatever of occasioning to Tsewang Rabdan any disturbance.'"

16. Tulisen, *Kōchū Iikiroku*, p. 8a.

17. Ibid., p. 10a, b.

18. Cahen, *Histoire*, p. F131.

19. Tulisen, *Narrative*, p. 94.

20. Ma. "Ceni da banin uttu, ainaha seme halame muterakū. Tsewang Rabdan i weile be fonjibume dailabume unggimbi"; Ch. "Gai qi tianxing shi ran, zhong mo neng quan. Sheng zui zhi tao."

21. Tulisen, *Kōchū Iikiroku*, pp. 180–181, 337; Tulisen, *Narrative*, pp. 216–219.

22. Staunton translates the Chinese only as "upon the occasion of hostilities being commenced against the wicked and rebellious Tsewang Rabdan," obscuring the moral force of *zhengjiao*. Tulisen, *Narrative*, p. 213.

23. Tulisen, *Kōchū Iikiroku*, pp. 151, 347; Tulisen, *Narrative*, p. 171.

24. Stephen A. Halkovic, *The Mongols of the West* (Bloomington: Indiana University Press, 1985); Zhang Weihua, "Tuerhute Xixi yu Tulisen zhi Chushi" (The Torghut westward migration and the appearance of Tulisen), *Bianzheng Gonglu* 2, nos. 3–5 (1943), pp. 26–35.

25. Bell, *A Journey*, p. v.

26. Ibid., p. 51.

27. Ibid., p. 88.

28. Ibid., pp. 52–53.

29. Contrary to the note by the editor of Bell's text, who interprets it as a reference

to Kangxi's wars against Galdan in 1696 and 1697. The figure of 300,000 men seems, however, to come from the Qing invasion of Tibet from Xining in 1718.

30. Ibid., p. 53.

31. Chiba Muneo, "Tenzan ni habataku" (Black whirlwind: flags fluttering over the Tianshan Mountains), in *Kara būran: Kuroi suna-arashi* (Tokyo: Kokushokankokai, 1986), p. 43; PDZGFL *qian* j.5 KX57/1 *bingwu*.

32. Bell, *A Journey*, p. 53.

33. William C. Fuller, *Strategy and Power in Russia, 1600–1914* (New York: Free Press, 1992), p. 30.

34. John Baddeley, *Russia, Mongolia, China, being some record of the relations between them from the beginning of the XVIIth century to the death of the Tsar Alexei Mikhailovich, A.D. 1602–1676,* 2 vols. (London: Macmillan and Company, 1919), 1:184; Cahen, *Histoire*, pp. F150, E67–68.

35. N. I. Veselovskii, "Posolstvo k zyungarskomu khun-taichzhi Tsevan Rabtanu kapitana ot artillerii Ivana Unkovskago i putevoy zhurnal ego za 1722–1724 godu: dokumenty, izdannye s predisloviem i primechaniami" (The embassy of Artillery Captain Ivan Unkovski to the Zunghar Khan-Taiji Tsewang Rabdan and his travel journal of 1722–1724: documents with a preface and annotations), *Zapiski imperatorskago russkago geograficheskago obshchestva* 10 (1887), pp. iii, 53. The *zaisang*'s second question refers to statements made by Ivan Cheredov, who had visited Tsewang Rabdan two years earlier with the same mission.

36. Ibid., pp. 120–124, 56, 113.

37. Ibid., p. 60.

38. Richard White, *The Middle Ground: Indians, Empires, and Republics in the Great Lakes Region, 1650–1815* (Cambridge: Cambridge University Press, 1991), p. 359.

39. Qingshi Bianwei Hui, ed., *Qingdai Renwu Zhuangao* (Draft Qing biographies) (Beijing: Zhonghua Shuju, 1992), 12 vols., *shang* 6.189–194.

40. Giuseppe Tucci, *Tibetan Painted Scrolls,* 2 vols. (Rome: Libreria dello Stato, 1949), 1:65.

41. Ibid., p. 74.

42. Arthur W. Hummel, ed., *Eminent Chinese of the Ch'ing Period* (Washington, D.C.: U.S. Government Printing Office, 1943–44), pp. 759–761.

43. Ippolito Desideri, *An Account of Tibet: The Travels of Ippolito Desideri of Pistoia, S. J., 1712–1727,* ed. Filippo de Filippi (London: Routledge, 1932), p. 150.

44. Desideri's eyewitness account is clearly biased in favor of Lazang Khan, whom he describes as "gay, joyous, and affable . . . by nature kindly and unsuspicious," and against the Dalai Lama and the regent. Ibid., pp. 149, 152.

45. PDZGFL *qian* j.1 KX45/10 *yiji*; Desideri, *An Account of Tibet,* p. 132; Luciano Petech, *China and Tibet in the Early Eighteenth Century: History of the Establishment of Chinese Protectorate in Tibet* (Leiden: E. J. Brill, 1950), p. 13.

46. PDZGFL *qian* j.1 KX54/4 *jiashen*; Veselovskii, "Posolstvo," pp. 180–193.

47. PDZGFL *qian* j.1 KX54/4 *yiwei*.

48. Qingshi Bianwei Hui, *Qingdai Renwu, shang* 5.29–45.

49. PDZGFL *qian* j.4 KX56/7 *xinwei*; cf. Jonathan D. Spence, *Emperor of China: Self-Portrait of K'ang-hsi* (New York: Knopf, 1974), pp. 143–151.

50. PDZGFL *qian* j.3 KX55/3 *xinchou*.

51. Hummel spells his Manchu name as Funninggan, but I follow Kraft's version, Funninga, based on her transcription of his Manchu memorials. Hummel, *Eminent Chinese*, p. 263; Eva S. Kraft, *Zum Dsungarenkrieg im 18 Jahrhundert: Berichte des Generals Funingga* (Leipzig: Harrassowitz, 1953), p. 7; Qingshi Bianwei Hui, *Qingdai Renwu*, shang 5.253.

52. PDZGFL *qian* j.2 KX54/8 *renchen*; Fuller, *Strategy and Power in Russia*, p. 18.

53. PDZGFL *qian* j.4 KX56/10 *bingwu*, j.7 KX58/10 *bingyin*.

54. PDZGFL *qian* j.3 KX55/10 *guisi*, j.4 KX56/2 *yiwei*.

55. PDZGFL *qian* j.3 KX57/1 *renshen*.

56. PDZGFL *qian* j.3 KX55/12 *bingwu*.

57. PDZGFL *qian* j.3 KX55/10 *guisi*, j.4 KX56/3 *wuyin*.

58. PDZGFL *qian* j.4 KX56/5 *gengyin*.

59. PDZGFL *qian* j.5 KX57/6 *renwu*.

60. Judy Bonavia, *The Silk Road: From Xi'an to Kashgar* (Hong Kong: Odyssey, 2002), pp. 234–235.

61. James A. Millward, *Beyond the Pass: Economy, Ethnicity, and Empire in Qing Central Asia, 1759–1864* (Stanford: Stanford University Press, 1998), pp. 50–52; Peter C. Perdue, "The Agrarian Basis of Qing Expansion into Central Asia," in *Papers from the Third International Conference on Sinology: History Section* (Zhongyang Yanjiuyuan Disanzhou Guoji Hanxue Huiyi Lunwenji Lishizu) (Taibei: Institute of History and Philology, Academia Sinica, 2002), pp. 181–223; Xu Bofu, "Qingdai qianqi Xinjiang diqu di bingtun" (Military agricultural colonies in Xinjiang in the early Qing), *Xinjiang Shehui Kexue Yanjiu* 13 (July 1984), pp. 1–20; Xu Bofu, "Qingdai qianqi Xinjiang diqu di mintun" (Civilian agricultural colonies in Xinjiang in the early Qing), *Zhongguoshi Yanjiu* 2 (February 1985), pp. 85–95.

62. Joanna Waley-Cohen, *Exile in Mid-Qing China: Banishment to Xinjiang, 1758–1820* (New Haven: Yale University Press, 1991).

63. PDZGFL *qian* j.5 KX57/8* *yimao*, j.6 KX58/1 *wuxu*.

64. C. R. Bawden, *The Modern History of Mongolia* (New York: Praeger, 1968), pp. 55–56; Paul Hyer, "An Historical Sketch of Koke-Khota City, Capital of Inner Mongolia," *Central Asiatic Journal* 26 (1982), pp. 56–77, 63.

65. PDZGFL *qian* j.6 KX58/5 *xinmao*.

66. PDZGFL *qian* j.3 KX55/3* *gengchen*.

67. Desideri, *An Account of Tibet*, p. 151.

68. Petech, *China and Tibet*, p. 28.

69. Desideri, *An Account of Tibet*, p. 153; PDZGFL *qian* j.4 KX56/8 *dingwei*. Luciano Petech finds him less admirable: "Tsering Dondup had not shown, nor was to show in the future, any outstanding qualities as a general, as far as we can judge; but he had faithfully and successfully carried out the difficult task allotted to him." Petech, *China and Tibet*, p. 42.

70. PDZGFL *qian* j.4 KX56/11 *jiaxu*, KX57/1 *renshen*, KX57/2 *gengyin*; Kraft, *Zum Dsungarenkrieg*, pp. 34–35, 128.

71. PDZGFL *qian* j.4 KX56/9 *renzi*, KX56/10 *yisi*.

72. Desideri, *An Account of Tibet*, p. 158; Kraft, *Zum Dsungarenkrieg*, pp. 18, 44–45, 134–135; Petech, *China and Tibet*, p. 56.

73. Hummel, *Eminent Chinese*, p. 930; Qingshi Bianwei Hui, *Qingdai Renwu*, shang 9.36–42. This Yinti (14) is not to be confused with Kangxi's eldest son Yinti (1).

74. PDZGFL *qian* j.6 KX58/6 *dingwei*.

75. Petech, *China and Tibet*, p. 59; PDZGFL *qian* j.7 KX59/1 *renshen*, KX59/2 *guichou*.

76. PDZGFL *qian* j.8 KX60/1 *guiwei*; Hummel, *Eminent Chinese*, pp. 759, 908; Qingshi Bianwei Hui, *Qingdai Renwu*, *shang* 9.36–42.

77. Evelyn S. Rawski, *The Last Emperors: A Social History of Qing Imperial Institutions* (Berkeley: University of California Press, 1998), p. 298.

78. The main official sources on the Tibetan campaigns, contained in the *Pingding Shuomo Fanglue* and *Qingshilu,* are noticeably abbreviated by comparison with the wealth of detail on other campaigns. The *Qingshilu* for the Kangxi reign contains only 4.9 *juan* per year, compared to 8 for the Shunzhi reign, 12 for Yongzheng, and 25 for Qianlong. Because Yinti became the foremost rival of Yongzheng for succession to the throne, it is suspected that Yongzheng deliberately contrived to minimize his contributions. Fortunately, other materials, including the handwritten Manchu memorials of Yinti to the throne, reveal in much greater detail the complexities of the Tibetan campaign. Hummel, *Eminent Chinese*, p. 588; Xu Zengzhong, "Qing Shizong Yinzhen jicheng huangwei wenti xintan" (A new discussion of the question of the succession of Yinzhen to the throne), in *KangYong Qian Sandi Pingyi*, ed. Zuo Buqing (Beijing: Zijincheng Chubanshe, 1986), p. 255; Ishihama Yumiko, "The Attitude of Qing-hai Qoshot toward the Ch'ing Dynasty's Subjugation of Tibet," *Nihon Chibetto* 34 (1988), pp. 1–7; Ishihama Yumiko, "Gushi Han Ōka no Chibetto Ōken sōshitsu katei ni kansuru ichi kōsatsu: Ropusan Danjin no hanran saikō" (The process by which the Gusi Khan family lost its authority over Tibet: a reconsideration of the Lobzang Danjin "rebellion"), *Tōyō Gakuhō* 69, nos. 3, 4 (March 1988), pp. 151–171.

79. Ishihama Yumiko, "Tōyō Bunko shozō shahon 'Fuyuan Dajiangjun zouzhe' to 'Qingshi Ziliao' Daisanki shoshū 'Fuyuan Dajiangjun zouyi' ni tsuite" (An introduction to the newly discovered manuscripts on the Chinese conquest of Tibet in 1720), *Mongoru Kenkyū* 18 (1987), p. 10; Yinti, "Fuyuan Dajiangjun zouyi" (Memorials of the Generalissimo Who Pacifies the Frontiers), *Qingshi Ziliao* 3 (1982), pp. 185–186.

80. Yinti, "Fuyuan Dajiangjun zouyi," KX59/5/21, cited in Ishihama Yumiko, "Tōyō Bunko shozō shahon," p. 14; Kraft, *Zum Dsungarenkrieg*, p. 19.

81. PDZGFL *qian* j.9 KX60/9 *dingsi*.

82. Kraft, *Zum Dsungarenkrieg*, pp. 49, 63.

83. PDZGFL *qian* j.7 KX59/3 *bingshen*; Kraft, *Zum Dsungarenkrieg*, p. 45.

84. Kraft, *Zum Dsungarenkrieg*, p. 84, Manchu text p. 159.

85. PDZGFL *qian* j.10 KX61/2 *renshen*.

86. PDZGFL *qian* j.10 KX61/5 *guisi*.

87. See, e.g., Beatrice S. Bartlett, *Monarchs and Ministers: The Grand Council in Mid-Ch'ing China, 1723–1820* (Berkeley: University of California Press, 1991), pp. 25–27; Feng Erkang, "Kangxi chao di zhuwei zhi zheng he Yinzhen di shengli" (The struggle of the princes in the Kangxi reign and the victory of Yinzhen), in *Kang Yong Qian Sandi Pingyi*, ed. Zuo Buqing (Beijing: Zijin Chubanshe, 1986), pp. 262–286; Hummel, *Eminent Chinese*, pp. 552, 588, 916, 924, 926, 929–930; Huang Pei, *Autocracy at Work: A Study of the Yung-cheng Period, 1723–1735* (Bloomington: Indiana University Press, 1974), pp. 51–80; Silas Wu, *Passage to Power: K'ang-hsi and His Heir Apparent, 1661–1722* (Cambridge, Mass.: Harvard University Press, 1979); Xu Zengzhong, "Qing Shizong."

88. Pei, *Autocracy at Work*, p. 69.

89. Hummel, *Eminent Chinese*, p. 927.

90. Feng Erkang, "Kangxi chao," p. 273.

91. Xu Zengzhong, "Qing Shizong," p. 233.

92. Pei, *Autocracy at Work*, p. 59.

93. PDZGFL *qian* j.11 YZ1/1 *bingwu*.

94. Bartlett, *Monarchs and Ministers*; Madeleine Zelin, *The Magistrate's Tael: Rationalizing Fiscal Reform in Eighteenth-Century Ch'ing China* (Berkeley: University of California Press, 1984).

95. PDZGFL *qian* j.11 YZ1/3 *jiashen*.

96. In 1724 the Yongzheng emperor had demanded that all his father's high officials return every scrap of official documentation which contained the emperor's vermilion rescripts. The disgruntled Funingga returned all his documents, but fortunately for the historian, he still retained the manuscript drafts of his memorials, many of which were never published. Kraft, *Zum Dsungarenkrieg*, pp. 94, 165.

97. PDZGFL *qian* j.15 YZ3/2 *jisi*.

98. Shu-hui Wu, "The Imbalance of Virtue and Power in Qing Frontier Policy: The Turfan Campaign of 1731," *Études Mongoles* 27 (1996), pp. 241–264.

99. Hummel, *Eminent Chinese*, p. 395; Petech, *China and Tibet*; Luciano Petech, "Notes on Tibetan History of the Eighteenth Century," *T'oung Pao* 52 (1965–66), p. 281.

100. Petech, *China and Tibet*, p. 68; Petech, "Notes," p. 280, corrects the misidentification of Kancennas as chief minister to Lazang Khan.

101. Katō Naoto, "Lobzang Danjin's Rebellion of 1723: With a Focus on the Eve of the Rebellion," *Acta Asiatica* 64 (1993), p. 60; Petech, *China and Tibet*, p. 74.

102. Katō Naoto, "Lobzang Danjin's Rebellion," p. 65.

103. Ma Ruheng and Ma Dazheng, *Elute Menggushi Lunji* (Essays on the history of the Oirat Mongols) (Xining: Qinghai renmin chubanshe, 1984), pp. 35–51; Petech, *China and Tibet*, p. 82; Rawski, *The Last Emperors*, pp. 250–251.

104. Katō Naoto, "Lobzang Danjin's Rebellion," p. 72; Nian Gengyao, *Nian Gengyao Zouzhe Zhuanji* (Collected memorials of Nian Gengyao), 3 vols. (Taibei: Guoli Gugong Bowuyuan, 1971), 1:89–94 (Manchu text).

105. PDZGFL *qian* j.11 YZ1/7 *jimao*.

106. Ishihama Yumiko, "Gushi Han," p. 157.

107. PDZGFL *qian* j.12 YZ1/10 *wushen*.

108. Katō Naoto, "Robuzan Danjin no hanran to Shinchō: hanran no keikō o chūshin to shite" (The rebellion of Lobzang Danjin and the Qing dynasty), *Tōyōshi Kenkyū* 45 (1986), pp. 46–47; PDZGFL *qian* j.13 YZ2/1 *jiawu*, YZ2/2 *dingmao*.

109. PDZGFL *qian* j.13 YZ2/3 *dinghai*.

110. PDZGFL *qian* j.14 YZ2/6 *yiyou*. Chinese traditionally considered the owl to be a wicked bird which eats its own young.

111. PDZGFL *qian* j.14 YZ2/5 *renxu*; Satō Hisashi, "Lobzan Danjin no hanran ni tsuite" (On Lobzan Danjin's rebellion), *Shirin* 55 (1972), pp. 26–30.

112. Qingshi Bianwei Hui, *Qingdai Renwu, shang* 9.251–255.

113. Ishihama Yumiko, "Gushi Han"; Katō Naoto, "Lobzang Danjin's Rebellion"; Katō Naoto, "Robuzan Danjin"; Satō Hisashi, "Lobzan Danjin."

114. Hummel, *Eminent Chinese*, pp. 589, 958; Qingshi Bianwei Hui, *Qingdai Renwu, shang* 9.50–59; Xu Zengzhong, "Qing Shizong," pp. 253–261.

115. PDZGFL *qian* j.23 YZ9/6 *dingwei, wuwu*; Satō Hisashi, *Chūsei Chibetto shi kenkyū* (Kyoto: Dohosha, 1986), pp. 757–768.

116. PDZGFL *qian* j.24 YZ9/6 *gengxu*.

117. PDZGFL *qian* j.14 YZ2/9 *guimao*.

118. Hummel, *Eminent Chinese*, p. 395; Petech, *China and Tibet*, pp. 99–141, 244–251; Wu Shu-hui, "How the Qing Army Entered Tibet in 1728 after the Tibetan Civil War," *Zentralasiatische Studien* 26 (1996), pp. 122–138.

119. Petech, *China and Tibet*, p. 101, erroneously gives the date as August 6; Hummel, *Eminent Chinese*, p. 395, is correct.

120. PDZGFL *qian* j.17 YZ6/7 *yichou*.

121. Wu Shu-hui, "Qing Army," p. 137.

122. Petech, *China and Tibet*, p. 132.

123. Ibid., pp. 134–135; Wei Yuan, *Shengwuji* (Record of sacred military victories) (Beijing: Zhonghua Shuju, 1984), p. 213.

124. GZDYZ 10.634, cited in Wu Shu-hui, "Qing Army," p. 138.

125. Quote from Fu Lo-shu, *A Documentary Chronicle of Sino-Western Relations (1644–1820)*, 2 vols. (Tucson: University of Arizona Press, 1966), 1:150–152; PDZGFL YZ5/8 *jiachen*; Foust, *Muscovite and Mandarin*, chap. 2; Peter C. Perdue, "Boundaries, Maps, and Movement: The Chinese, Russian, and Mongolian Empires in Early Modern Eurasia," *International History Review* 20, no. 2 (1998), pp. 263–286; Peter C. Perdue, "Military Mobilization in Seventeenth- and Eighteenth-Century China, Russia, and Mongolia," *Modern Asian Studies* 30, no. 4 (1996), pp. 757–793.

126. Petech, *China and Tibet*, pp. 135–136, citing QSL j.64 YZ5/12 *jiawu*; cf. PDZGFL *qian* j.17 YZ5/12 *jiawu*.

127. PDZGFL *qian* j.17 YZ5/8 *dingwei*.

128. PDZGFL *qian* j.18 YZ7/2 *guisi*, j.22 YZ9/4 *gengzi*.

129. For further discussion, see Peter C. Perdue, "Culture, History, and Imperial Chinese Strategy: Legacies of the Qing Conquests," in *Warfare in Chinese History*, ed. Hans van de Ven (Leiden: Brill, 2000), pp. 252–287.

130. Cf. Emmanuel Todd, *Après l'empire: essai sur la décomposition du système américain* (Paris: Gallimard, 2002), p. 9: "[The United States] asks the entire planet to recognize that certain minor states constitute an 'axis of evil' which must be fought and annihilated."

131. PDZGFL *qian* j.17 YZ5/12 *jiawu*; Wu, "The Imbalance," p. 244.

132. PDZGFL *qian* j.18 YZ7/3 *renzi*.

133. Bartlett, *Monarchs and Ministers*, pp. 64–79; Wu, "The Imbalance," p. 246.

134. PDZGFL *qian* j.18 YZ8/5 *dingchou*.

135. PDZGFL *qian* j.21 YZ9/1 *guiyou*, YZ9/2 *guichou*; Wu, "The Imbalance," p. 252.

136. PDZGFL *qian* j.21 YZ9/2 *guichou*.

137. PDZGFL *qian* j.22 YZ9/3 *yihai*.

138. PDZGFL *qian* j.22 YZ9/4 *gengzi, bingwu*.

139. PDZGFL *qian* j.23 YZ9/6 *jiawu*.

140. PDZGFL *qian* j.23 YZ9/6 *gengwu*.

141. PDZGFL *qian* j.24 YZ9/7 *yihai*.

142. PDZGFL *qian* j.24 YZ9/7 *jiashen*.

143. PDZGFL *qian* j.25 YZ9/8 *guimao*.

144. ZGSL 175, citing QSLYZ j.111, p. 27.

145. ZGSL 176; Hummel, *Eminent Chinese*, pp. 265, 756; Qingshi Bianwei Hui, *Qingdai Renwu, shang* 8.312; Zhang Yuxin, "Suzhou maoyi kaolue" (A study of Suzhou trade), *Xinjiang Daxue Xuebao* 1 (1986), pp. 67–76; 3 (1986), pp. 24–32; 4 (1986), pp. 48–54.

7. The Final Blows, 1734–1771

1. Cai Jiayi, "Shiba shiji zhongye Zhungar tong Zhongyuan diqu di maoyi wanglai lueshu" (A summary of trade between the Zunghars and China in the eighteenth century), *Qingshi Luncong* 4 (1983), p. 242.

2. Ye Zhiru, "Cong maoyi aocha kan Qianlong qianqi dui Zhungar bu di minzu zhengce" (The nationality policy toward the Zunghars in the early Qianlong period viewed from the boiled tea issue), *Xinjiang Daxue Xuebao* 1 (1986), p. 63.

3. Zhang Yuxin, "Suzhou maoyi kaolue" (A study of Suzhou trade), *Xinjiang Daxue Xuebao* 1 (1986), pp. 67–76, fn5.

4. Ibid., 3 (1986), p. 25.

5. Ma Lin, "Qianlong chunian Zhungar bu shouci ruzang aocha" (The first entry of the Zunghars to Tibet for boiled tea in the early Qianlong reign), *Xizang Yanjiu* 1 (1988), pp. 62–69.

6. The main sources for this section are Ye Zhiru, "Cong maoyi aocha"; Zhang Yuxin, "Suzhou maoyi"; Zhongguo Diyi Lishi Dang'anguan, comp., "Qianlong 8 zhi 15 nian Zhungar bu zai Suzhou dengdi maoyi" (Suzhou trade with the Zunghars from 1743 to 1750), *Lishi Dang'an* 2 (1984), pp. 21–34; 3 (1984), pp. 12–20 (cited as LSDA by document number); QSLQL; PDZGFL; *Shiliao Xunkan* (1930) (cited as SLXK). There are additional archival materials which I have not seen.

7. LSDA 13; QSLQL QL5/2 *yimao* j.110.

8. The exact numbers of men specified in regulations varied. Ma Lin, "Qianlong chunian," p. 64, and Cai Jiayi, "Shiba shiji zhongye Zhungar," say two hundred men, citing the *Donghualu* and QSLQL j.110; Zhang Yuxin, "Suzhou maoyi," says there were three hundred men at Beijing.

9. LSDA 1.

10. LSDA 18.

11. LSDA 2, 12, 13.

12. SLXK 19.364–367, 20.386–390.

13. SLXK 20.387.

14. SLXK 25.481–484.

15. SLXK 26.504–507.

16. SLXK 27.523–524.

17. Zhang Yuxin, "Suzhou maoyi," p. 29.

18. SLXK 25.481.

19. LSDA 13.

20. LSDA 2; SLXK 24.456.

21. LSDA 17.

22. Ye Zhiru, "Cong maoyi aocha," p. 65; LSDA 1, 11, 13.

23. LSDA 20, 21.

24. Cai Jiayi, "Shiba shiji zhongye Zhungar," p. 250; QSLQL j.380 QL16/1 *wushen*.

25. LSDA 28.

26. Cai Jiayi, "Shiba shiji zhongye Zhungar"; Ma Lin, "Qianlong chunian"; James A. Millward, *Beyond the Pass: Economy, Ethnicity, and Empire in Qing Central Asia, 1759–1864* (Stanford: Stanford University Press, 1998), p. 29; Ye Zhiru, "Cong maoyi aocha"; archival materials in ZPZZ Minzu Shiwu nos. 147–154, 166–168.

27. Luciano Petech, *China and Tibet in the Early Eighteenth Century: History of the Establishment of Chinese Protectorate in Tibet* (Leiden: E. J. Brill, 1950), p. 134, calls it a "collective tea-party to the monks."

28. ZGSL 57; Henry H. Howorth, *History of the Mongols from the Ninth to the Nineteenth Century*, 4 vols. (Taibei: Ch'eng Wen, 1970), 1:517.

29. QSLQL QL4/2 *gengzi* j.87; QSLQL QL5/2 *yimao* j.110.

30. Cai Jiayi, "Shiba shiji zhongye Zhungar," p. 245.

31. SLXK 19.364, 20.386, 24.455–456a.

32. Cai Jiayi, "Shiba shiji zhongye Zhungar," p. 246; Petech, *China and Tibet*, p. 166.

33. Petech, *China and Tibet*, pp. 169–170.

34. Cai Jiayi, "Shiba shiji zhongye Zhungar," p. 248; Petech, *China and Tibet*, p. 183.

35. Ma Lin, "Qianlong chunian," p. 67.

36. Ibid., p. 68.

37. Cai Jiayi, "Qingdai Zhongwanqi Jinzang Aocha Gaishu" (A survey of the boiled tea trade to Tibet in the middle and late Qing), *Minzu Yanjiu* 6 (1986), pp. 42–47.

38. LSDA 14, 28. On the language of tribute relations, see James L. Hevia, *Cherishing Men from Afar: Qing Guest Ritual and the Macartney Embassy of 1793* (Durham: Duke University Press, 1995), and a critique of Hevia by Joseph W. Esherick in *Modern China* 24, no. 2 (April 1998), pp. 135–161, also in *21 Shiji* 44 (December 1997), pp. 105–117. For other discussions, see replies by Hevia and Esherick in *Modern China* 24, no. 3 (July 1998), pp. 319–332; rebuttal of Esherick by Benjamin Elman and Theodore Huters in *21 Shiji* 44 (December 1997), pp. 118–130; further discussion by Zhang Longxi in *21 Shiji* 45 (February 1998), pp. 56–63; Ge Jianxiong in *21 Shiji* 46 (April 1998), pp. 135–139; and Luo Zhitian in *21 Shiji* 49 (October 1998), pp. 138–145.

39. Sechin Jagchid and Van Jay Symons, *Peace, War, and Trade along the Great Wall: Nomadic–Chinese Interaction through Two Millennia* (Bloomington: Indiana University Press, 1989); Ye Zhiru, "Cong maoyi aocha," p. 69; Ying-shih Yu, "Han Foreign Relations," in *The Cambridge History of China*, vol. 1, *The Ch'in and Han Empires, 221 B.C.–A.D. 220*, ed. Denis Twitchett and Michael Loewe (New York: Cambridge University Press, 1986), pp. 377–462; Ying-shih Yu, *Trade and Expansion in Han China* (Berkeley: University of California Press, 1967).

40. Susan Naquin, Pamela K. Crossley, and Nicola Di Cosmo, "Rethinking Tribute: Concept and Practice," papers presented at the Association of Asian Studies Annual

Meeting, 1995, Boston; John E. Wills, Jr., *Pepper, Guns, and Parleys: The Dutch East India Company and China, 1622–1681* (Cambridge: Harvard University Press, 1974); John E. Wills, Jr., "Maritime Asia, 1500–1800: The Interactive Emergence of European Domination," *American Historical Review* 98, no. 1 (February 1993), pp. 83–105.

41. Nicola Di Cosmo, "Kirghiz Nomads on the Qing Frontier: Tribute, Trade, or Gift-Exchange?" in *Political Frontiers, Ethnic Boundaries, and Human Geographies in Chinese History*, ed. Nicola Di Cosmo and Don J. Wyatt (London: Curzon Press, 2003); James A. Millward, "Qing Silk–Horse Trade with the Qazaqs in Yili and Tarbaghatai, 1758–1853," *Central and Inner Asian Studies* 7 (1992), pp. 1–42.

42. Hamashita Takeshi, "The Intra-regional System in East Asia in Modern Times," in *Network Power: Japan and Asia*, ed. Peter Katzenstein and Takashi Shiraishi (Ithaca: Cornell University Press, 1997), pp. 113–135; Hamashita Takeshi, *Kindai chūgoku no kokusaiteki keiki: chōkō bōeki shisutemu to kindai Ajia* (Modern China's international moment: the tribute trade system and modern Asia) (Tokyo: Tokyo Daigaku Shuppankai, 1990); Hamashita Takeshi, "The Tribute Trade System and Modern Asia," *Memoirs of the Research Department of the Toyo Bunko* 46 (1988), pp. 7–26.

43. Thomas J. Barfield, *The Perilous Frontier: Nomadic Empires and China* (Cambridge, Mass.: Basil Blackwell, 1989).

44. Nicola Di Cosmo, *Ancient China and Its Enemies: The Rise of Nomadic Power in East Asian History* (Cambridge: Cambridge University Press, 2001), pp. 217–227.

45. Chiba Muneo, "Tenzan ni habataku" (Black whirlwind: flags fluttering over the Tianshan Mountains), in *Kara būran: Kuroi suna-arashi* (Tokyo: Kokushokankokai, 1986), p. 96; ZGSL 180–183.

46. ZGSL 191.

47. Chiba Muneo, "Tenzan ni habataku," p. 108; PDZGFL *zheng* 4.15b QL19/9 *jiaxu.*

48. I. Ia. Zlatkin, "Russkie arkhivnye materialy ob Amursane" (Russian archival material on Amursana), in *Filologia I istoriia Mongol'skikh Narodov: Pamiati Akademika Borisa Yakovlevicha Vladimirtsova*, ed. Akademiia Nauk SSSR Institut Vostokovedeniia (Moscow: Izdatelstvo Vostochnoí Literatury, 1958), p. 292.

49. Erich Haenisch, "Der Chinesische Feldzug in Ili im Jahre 1755" (The Chinese campaign in Ili [Sinkiang] in 1755), *Ostasiatische Zeitschrift* 7 (April–September 1918), pp. 57–86.

50. Chiba Muneo, "Tenzan ni habataku," chap. 5; I. Ia. Zlatkin, *Istoriia Dzhungarskogo Khanstvo, 1635–1758* (History of the Zunghar Khanate, 1635–1758) (Moscow: Nauka, 1964), chap. 6.

51. C. R. Bawden, *The Modern History of Mongolia* (New York: Praeger, 1968), pp. 101–132; C. R. Bawden, "The Mongol Rebellion of 1756–1757," *Journal of Asian History* 2 (1968), pp. 1–31; C. R. Bawden, "Some Documents Concerning the Rebellion of 1756 in Outer Mongolia," *Guoli Zhengzhi Daxue Bianzheng Yanjiusuo Nianbao* 1 (1970), pp. 1–23; Morikawa Tetsuo, "Chinggunjabu no ran ni tsuite" (On Chingünjav's rebellion), *Rekishigaku Chirigaku Nenpō (Kyūshū Daigaku)* 3 (1979), pp. 73–103; Alynn Nathanson, "Ch'ing Policies in Khalkha Mongolia and the Chingünjav Rebellion of 1756" (Ph.D. diss., University of London, 1983).

52. Joseph Fletcher, "Ch'ing Inner Asia c. 1800," in *The Cambridge History of China*, vol. 10, pt. 1, *Late Ch'ing, 1800–1911*, ed. John K. Fairbank (Cambridge: Cam-

bridge University Press, 1978), p. 51; Nathanson, "Ch'ing Policies," p. 25; M. Sanjdorj, *Manchu Chinese Colonial Rule in Northern Mongolia,* trans. Urgunge Onon (New York: St. Martin's Press, 1980), p. 31.

53. Bawden, *Modern History,* p. 101.

54. "It is the poor nomad who is the pure nomad: by stripping themselves of the accessories and luxuries that a prosperous nomadism acquires they establish afresh the possibility of survival under strictly steppe conditions, and even in the harshest parts of the steppe, and thus attain once more the extreme phase of departure from the edge of the steppe . . . Where a "true" nomad from the far steppe might have understood only plunder and tribute, a border nomad knew how to handle different kinds of men." Owen Lattimore, *Inner Asian Frontiers of China* (Boston: Beacon Press, 1962), pp. 522, 546; cf. Nathanson, "Ch'ing Policies," pp. 85–89.

55. Bawden, "Some Documents," pp. 4, 21.

56. Ibid., p. 10.

57. Bawden, *Modern History,* p. 112.

58. Ibid., p. 115; Morikawa Tetsuo, "Chinggunjabu no ran."

59. QSLQL j.512 QL21.5/1; PDZGFL *zheng* j.27 QL21/5 *wuchen.*

60. QSLQL j.519/16b; *zheng* PDZGFL *zheng* j.30/43a QL21/8/29 *yichou;* QSLQL j.512(QL21.5) 7a *renshen;* PDZGFL *zheng* j.27 QL21/5 *renshen.*

61. QSLQL j.529 (QL21.12.21) 9b *jiashen.*

62. PDZGFL *zheng* j.43 QL22/8 *dinghai.*

63. QSLQL j.539 (QL22.5) *dingwei;* PDZGFL *zheng* j.39, p. 26b.

64. Zuo Shu'e, "Cong PingZhun zhanzheng kan Qianlong dui Zhunbu zhengce di zhuanbian" (Qianlong's changes in policy in the wars against the Zunghars), *Xibei Shidi* 2 (1985), pp. 58–63; QSLQL j.532.13b; PDZGFL *zheng* j.37 QL22/2 *renwu.*

65. QSLQL j.532.8a QL22/2/4 *bingyin,* j.534 QL22/3/10, j.536.11b QL22/4 *xinchou;* PDZGFL j.36 QL22/2 *bingyin,* j.37 QL22/3 *xinchou,* j.38 QL22/4 *bingyin.*

66. QSLQL j.535 QL22/3 *gengxu;* PDZGFL j.38/9a.

67. PDZGFL *zheng* j.42 QL22/8 *guihai;* QSLQL j.544.13a QL22/8 *guihai.*

68. QSLQL 510.2–3; PDZGFL j.37 QL22/3 *yiwei;* QSLQL j.534 QL22/3/4 *yiwei.*

69. QSLQL j.539.1a QL22/5 *bingwu;* PDZGFL j.39/23a QL22/5 *bingwu.*

70. QSLQL j.539.20A QL22/5 *yimao;* QSLQL j.540/22b QL22/6 *jisi;* PDZGFL j.40 QL22/6 *jisi.*

71. Zlatkin, "Russkie arkhivnye materialy," p. 312.

72. Zuo Shu'e, "Cong PingZhun zhanzheng."

73. PDZGFL j.42 QL22/8 *guiyou;* QSLQL j.544.34B QL22/8 *guiyou.*

74. QSLQL j.541 QL22/6 *dinghai,* j.543 QL22/7 *jiwei;* PDZGFL j.42 QL22/7 *jiwei.*

75. Hummel says merely, "Many Eleuths were put to the sword and a large number were removed to different localities." Dai Yi, however, writes: "We must point out that, although the Qing government's wars against the Zunghars had extremely great significance for the restoration of national unity and the protection of the northwest frontier, this very progressive achievement from the perspective of objective history must be offset by the recognition that the Qing's methods of unification were extremely cruel. Because of the long-lasting autonomy of the Zunghars and their repeated submission and rebellion, the Qing rulers regarded them with deep-rooted hostility and lack of

trust. The Qing armies took advantage of internal divisions in Zungharia to penetrate deep into the territory, and to burn, kill, and plunder the innocent. The scale of killing exceeded that of ordinary warfare. 'All remote mountains and water margins, wherever one could hunt or fish a living thing, were scoured out, leaving no traces'; 'there was not a trace of a living thing, whether grass, bird, or animal' [from Zhaolian, *Xiaoting zalu*]. The Qing troops were even suspicious of some tribes that surrendered to them, and massacred them in large numbers. The Zunghar people suffered a severe disaster. We must expose and criticize the Qing government for adopting such cruel methods." He criticizes Qing brutality but ultimately justifies it as serving the progress of history—like the Stalinist omelette metaphor turned to nationalist ends. Dai Yi, *Jianming Qingshi* (A brief history of the Qing dynasty) (Beijing: Renmin Chubanshe, 1984), p. 181; Arthur W. Hummel, ed., *Eminent Chinese of the Ch'ing Period* (Washington, D.C.: U.S. Government Printing Office, 1943–44), p. 16.

76. C. R. Bawden does not find this to be too strong a word. Bawden, *Modern History*, p. 132.

77. Wei Yuan, *Shengwuji* (Record of sacred military victories) (Beijing: Zhonghua Shuju, 1984), p. 156.

78. The classic description of the massacre at Yangzhou is translated in Lynn A. Struve, *Voices from the Ming–Qing Cataclysm: China in Tigers' Jaws* (New Haven: Yale University Press, 1993), pp. 28–48.

79. PDZGFL j.34 QL21/11/27 *gengshen*; QSL j.527 QL21/11/27 *gengshen*.

80. PDZGFL j.34 QL21/11/27 *gengshen*; QSL j.527 QL21/11/27 *gengshen*.

81. Ma Ruheng, "Lun Amuersa'na de (Fandong) Yisheng" (On Amursana's Reactionary Life), in *Elute Menggushi Lunji*, ed. Ma Ruheng and Ma Dazheng (Xining: Qinghai Renmin Chubanshe, 1979), pp. 107–120; Zlatkin, "Russkie arkhivnye materialy," pp. 296, 307.

82. Morikawa Tetsuo, "Amursana o meguru RoShin Kôshô Shimatsu" (Sino-Russian relations on the problem of Amursana), *Rekishigaku Chirigaku Nenpō (Kyūshū Daigaku)* 7 (1983), pp. 75–105; Zlatkin, "Russkie arkhivnye materialy," p. 312.

83. Morikawa Tetsuo, "Amursana o meguru RoShin Kōshō Shimatsu," p. 91; PDZGFL j.48 QL23/1/19 *bingwu*.

84. There is no evidence in the *Pingding* source material, or in the studies by Zlatkin, Morikawa, or Chiba, that Amursana's body was ever returned.

85. Ma Ruheng, "Lun Amuersa'na," p. 23; Zlatkin, "Russkie arkhivnye materialy," p. 312.

86. English language sources on these campaigns are brief. See Joseph Fletcher, "The Biography of Khwush Kipäk Beg (d. 1781) in the Wai-fan Meng-ku Hui-pu Wang Kung Piao Chuan," in *Studies on Chinese and Islamic Inner Asia*, ed. Beatrice Forbes Manz (Brookfield, Vt.: Variorum, 1995), pp. 167–172; Hummel, *Eminent Chinese*, pp. 72–74; Millward, *Beyond the Pass*, pp. 30–32. Fletcher translates the Manchu text given in Gertraude Roth Li, *Manchu: A Textbook for Reading Documents* (Honolulu: University of Hawaii Press, 2000), pp. 50–71. The most extended secondary account is Chiba Muneo, "Tenzan ni habataku," chaps. 6–9. In Chinese, see Dai Yi, *Jianming Qingshi*, 2:182–185; Wei Yuan, *Shengwuji*, pp. 161–169; PDZGFL *Zhengbian, Xubian*; Zhaolian, *Xiaoting Zalu* (1880), *juan* 6.

87. Wei Yuan, *Shengwuji*, p. 163; Fletcher, "Ch'ing Inner Asia," p. 74.

88. Fletcher, "Khwush Kipäk Beg," p. 170.

89. Chiba Muneo, "Tenzan ni habataku," pp. 271–277; PDZGFL *juan* 80 QL24/10 *dinghai*.

90. PDZGFL j.81 QL24/10 *gengzi*.

91. Millward, *Beyond the Pass*, p. 31.

92. Chiba Muneo, "Tenzan ni habataku," chap. 11; Millward, *Beyond the Pass*, pp. 124–125; Joanna Waley-Cohen, *Exile in Mid-Qing China: Banishment to Xinjiang, 1758–1820* (New Haven: Yale University Press, 1991), p. 175; Wei Yuan, *Shengwuji*, pp. 179–180; PDZGFL *xubian* j.28–32.

93. David Anthony Bello, *Opium and the Limits of Empire: The Opium Problem in the Chinese Interior, 1729–1850* (Cambridge, Mass.: Harvard University Asia Center, 2005); Waley-Cohen, *Exile*, pp. 184–185; Wei Yuan, *Shengwuji*, p. 180.

94. Thomas De Quincey, *Revolt of the Tartars* (New York: Longmans, Green, and Co., 1896), p. 3.

95. Benjamin Bergmann, *Nomadische Streifereien unter den Kalmuken in den Jahren 1802 und 1803* (Riga: E. J. G. Hartmann, 1804). For short, more recent English accounts, see C. D. Barkman, "The Return of the Torghuts from Russia to China," *Journal of Oriental Studies* 2 (1955), pp. 89–115; James A. Millward, "Qing Inner Asian Empire and the Return of the Torghuts," in *New Qing Imperial History: The Making of Inner Asian Empire at Qing Chengde*, ed. James A. Millward and Ruth Dunnell (New York: Routledge Curzon, 2004), 91–105. James A. Millward, "The Qing Formation, the Mongol Legacy, and the 'End of History' in Early Modern Central Eurasia," in *The Qing Formation in World-Historical Time*, ed. Lynn Struve (Cambridge, Mass.: Harvard University Asia Center, 2004), pp. 92–120. An older account in Howorth, *History*, 1:561–589, is based on Benjamin Bergmann, *Nomadische Streifereien*, and Peter Simon Pallas, *Sammlungen Historischer Nachrichten über die Mongolischen Völkerschaften* (Graz: Akademische Druck-u. Verlagsanstalt, 1980). Khodarkovsky's excellent studies focus only on Kalmyk relations with Russia, and discuss the decision to return very briefly. See Michael Khodarkovsky, "Russian Peasant and Kalmyk Nomad: A Tragic Encounter in the Mid-Eighteenth Century," *Russian History* 15 (1988), pp. 43–69; Michael Khodarkovsky, "Uneasy Alliance: Peter the Great and Ayuki Khan," *Central Asian Survey* 7 (1988), pp. 1–45; Michael Khodarkovsky, "War and Politics in Seventeenth-Century Muscovite and Kalmyk Societies as Viewed in One Document: Reinterpreting the Image of the 'Perfidious Nomad,'" *Central and Inner Asian Studies* 3 (1989), pp. 36–56; Michael Khodarkovsky, *Where Two Worlds Met: The Russian State and the Kalmyk Nomads, 1600–1771* (Ithaca: Cornell University Press, 1992). He does not use Chinese sources. The best Chinese accounts still suffer from Sinocentric nationalism as much as the Russian accounts suffer from Russocentrism. Cf. Ma Ruheng and Ma Dazheng, *Piaoluo Yiyu di Minzu: 17 zhi 18 shiji di Turhute Menggu* (The people who drifted to a faraway land: the Torghut Mongols in the seventeenth and eighteenth centuries) (Beijing: Zhongguo Shehui kexueyuan, 1991); Ren Shijiang, "Shixi Tuerhute huigui zuguo di yuanyin" (An analysis of the causes of the Torghut return to the motherland), *ShehuiKexue(Gansu)* (February 1983), pp. 107–111; ZGSL, pp. 216–240.

96. Khodarkovsky, *Two Worlds*, p. 232.

97. Ibid., p. 230.

98. Ibid., p. 228.

99. Bergmann, *Nomadische Streifereien*, 1:181–183. See also Khodarkovsky, *Two Worlds*, p. 230.

100. Howorth, *History*, p. 575; Hummel, *Eminent Chinese*, pp. 659–661; Khodarkovsky, *Two Worlds*, p. 232.

101. ZGSL 234.

102. Barkman, "The Return," 104.

103. Khodarkovsky, *Two Worlds*, p. 235.

104. Zhongguo Shehui Kexueyuan Minzu Yanjiusuo et al., *Manwen Tuerhute Dang'an Yibian* (The translated Manchu Torghut archive) (Beijing: Minzu Chubanshe, 1988). This volume contains Chinese translations of 145 documents out of a total of 409 items in the Manchu *Turhutedang* and 70 items in the Manchu *Yuezhedang*. How these documents were selected is not clear. The entire archival corpus still awaits study. Cited as *Turhute Dang'an* with document number.

105. Khodarkovsky, *Two Worlds*, p. 235.

106. *Turhute Dang'an*, nos. 4, 10.

107. *Turhute Dang'an*, no. 9.

108. *Turhute Dang'an*, no. 4.

109. *Turhute Dang'an*, no. 8.

110. *Turhute Dang'an*, no. 22.

111. *Turhute Dang'an*, no. 35; QSLQL 36/6 *dinghai*.

112. Copies of the two Potala inscriptions in Joseph Amiot, "Monument de la transmigration des tourgouths des bords de la mer caspienne, dans l'Empire de la Chine," in *Mémoires concernant l'histoire, les sciences, les arts, les moeurs, etc. des chinois, par les Missionaires de Pekin* (Paris: Chez Nyon, 1776–), pp. 401–431. Berthold Laufer and Otto Franke, *Epigraphisches Denkmäler aus China*, vol. 1 (Berlin: Dietrich Reimer, 1914), plates 63–70, translates the Manchu text of the Ili inscription, which is close to that of the *Turhute Quanbu Guishunji*; partial translation in Millward, "Torghuts"; excerpts from the Chinese text in Qi Jingzhi, *Waibamiao beiwen zhushi* (Annotated stelae of the Outer Eight Temples) (Beijing: Zijincheng Chubanshe, 1985). Zhang Weihua, "Tuerhute Xixi yu Tulisen zhi Chushi" (The Torghut westward migration and the appearance of Tulisen), *Bianzheng Gonglu* 6 (1943), p. 29, cites an excerpt from *Donghualu*.

113. Amiot, "Monument," p. 420.

114. Laufer and Franke, *Epigraphisches Denkmäler*, plate 63.

115. Barkman, "The Return," p. 108; Ma Ruheng and Ma Dazheng, *Piaoluo Yiyu*.

116. Barkman, "The Return," p. 110.

117. Millward, "Torghuts."

118. By 2004 the president of Kalmykia, Kirsan Ilyumzhinov, had, however, invested tens of millions of dollars of his impoverished republic's resources in building a glittering complex to host international chess tournaments. Seth Mydans, "Where Chess Is King and the People Are the Pawns," *New York Times*, June 20, 2004, p. 3.

8. Cannons on Camelback

1. This section draws on Peter C. Perdue, "The Agrarian Basis of Qing Expansion into Central Asia," in *Papers from the Third International Conference on Sinology:*

History Section (Zhongyang Yanjiuyuan Disanzhou Guoji Hanxue Huiyi Lunwenji Lishizu) (Taibei: Institute of History and Philology, Academia Sinica, 2002), pp. 181–223.

2. I. Ia. Zlatkin, *Istoriia Dzhungarskogo Khanstvo, 1635–1758* (History of the Zunghar Khanate, 1635–1758) (Moscow: Nauka, 1964), p. 179.

3. Ibid., p. 182.

4. Ibid., p. 222.

5. Liang Fen, *Qinbian Jilue* (Qinghai: Qinghai Renmin Chubanshe, 1987); Naitō Konan, "'Qinbian Jilue' no 'Gardan zhuan,'" in *Naitō Konan Zenshū,* 14 vols. (Tokyo: Chikuma Shobo, 1970), 7:380–425.

6. Liang Fen, *Qinbian Jilue,* 421.

7. Ibid., 401.

8. ZGSL 91–92.

9. Zlatkin, *Istoriia,* pp. 323, 381.

10. Ibid., p. 361; ZGSL 127.

11. John Baddeley, *Russia, Mongolia, China, being some record of the relations between them from the beginning of the XVIIth century to the death of the Tsar Alexei Mikhailovich, A.D. 1602–1676* (London: Macmillan and Company, 1919), p. 176; Sven Hedin, *Southern Tibet: Discoveries in Former Times Compared with My Own Researches in 1906–1908,* 11 vols. (Stockholm: Lithographic Institute of the General Staff of the Swedish Army, 1917), 1:246–259; Arthur W. Hummel, ed., *Eminent Chinese of the Ch'ing Period* (Washington, D.C.: U.S. Government Printing Office, 1943–44), p. 759; Paul Pelliot, "Notes critiques d'histoire kalmouke," in *Oeuvres posthumes* (Paris: Librairie d'Amerique et d'Orient, 1960), pp. 2, 81.

12. A. I. Andreev, *Ocherki po Istochnikovedeniiu Sibiri* (Studies on the sources of Siberian history), 2 vols. (Leningrad: Izd-vo Akademii Nauk SSSR, 1960–), 2:32.

13. Baddeley, *Russia, Mongolia, China,* p. 166.

14. Zlatkin, *Istoriia,* p. 361.

15. Baddeley, *Russia, Mongolia, China,* p. 168.

16. Ibid., p. 166; A. Maksheev, "Karta Zhungarii sostav. Renatom," *Zapiski imperatorskago russkago geograficheskago obshchestva* 11 (1888), pp. 105–145.

17. For further discussion, see Peter C. Perdue, "Boundaries, Maps, and Movement: The Chinese, Russian, and Mongolian Empires in Early Modern Eurasia," *International History Review* 20, no. 2 (1998), pp. 263–286. G. Henrik Herb, "Mongolian Cartography," in *The History of Cartography: Cartography in the Traditional East and Southeast Asian Societies,* ed. J. B. Harley and David Woodward (Chicago: University of Chicago Press, 1994), pp. 682–685, mentions Renat's maps but argues that there is "little Mongolian contribution" to them. Also see Walther Heissig, "Über Mongolische Landkarten," *Monumenta Serica* 9 (1944), pp. 123–173; Nicholas Poppe, "Renat's Kalmuck Maps," *Imago Mundi* 12 (1955), pp. 157–160.

18. Zlatkin, *Istoriia,* p. 361.

19. This discussion draws on Peter C. Perdue, "Empire and Nation in Comparative Perspective," *Journal of Early Modern History* 5, no. 4 (2001), pp. 282–304.

20. Manchu text in Nian Gengyao, *Nian Gengyao Zouzhe Zhuanji* (Collected memorials of Nian Gengyao), 3 vols. (Taibei: Guoli Gugong Bowuyuan, 1971), 3:855–876; Chinese text in YZHZZ 3:27–43. Citations to Chinese text, 3:864a.

21. YZHZZ 3:33a.

22. YZHZZ 3:33b.

23. For a discussion of the role of Kham in Tibetan history, see Carole McGranahan, "Arrested Histories: Between Empire and Exile in 20th Century Tibet" (Ph.D. diss., University of Michigan, 2001).

24. YZHZZ 3:34b.

25. Ishihama Yumiko, "Gushi Han Ōka no Chibetto Ōken sōshitsu katei ni kansuru ichi kōsatsu: Ropusan Danjin no hanran saikō" (The process by which the Gusi Khan family lost its authority over Tibet: a reconsideration of the Lobzang Danjin 'rebellion'), Tōyō Gakuhō 69, nos. 3, 4 (1988), pp. 151–171.

26. "From 1699 forward . . . the whole bureaucratic apparatus of diplomacy in Istanbul moved to strategies of peace which involved mediation and fixed borders . . . [In Russia] [a] new fortress line was built in the northern Caucasus, further closing the ill-defined border between Russian and nomad, between Orthodoxy and Islam." Virginia H. Aksan, "Locating the Ottomans among Early Modern Empires," Journal of Early Modern History 3 (1999), pp. 123, 128.

27. Matthew H. Edney, Mapping an Empire: The Geographical Construction of British India, 1765–1843 (Chicago: University of Chicago Press, 1997).

28. Nian Gengyao, Zouzhe, 3:21a.

29. Joseph K. Fletcher, "The Heyday of the Ch'ing Order in Mongolia, Sinkiang, and Tibet," in The Cambridge History of China, vol. 10, pt. 1, Late Ch'ing, 1800–1911, ed. John K. Fairbank (Cambridge: Cambridge University Press, 1978), p. 378.

30. For further discussion, see Peter C. Perdue, "Identifying China's Northwest: For Nation and Empire," in Locating China: Space, Place, and Popular Culture, ed. Jing Wang and David Goodman (London: Routledge, 2005).

31. See also R. Kent Guy, "Inspired Tinkering: The Qing Creation of the Province," unpublished ms., 2003, chap. 5.

32. Gilbert Rozman, Urban Networks in Ch'ing China and Tokugawa Japan (Princeton: Princeton University Press, 1973); William G. Skinner, ed., The City in Late Imperial China (Stanford: Stanford University Press, 1977), pp. 301–336.

33. Charles O. Hucker, A Dictionary of Official Titles in Imperial China (Stanford: Stanford University Press, 1985), p. 534, no. 7158. Hucker notes that the Governor-General was an "ad hoc trouble shooter" in the Ming, but it became a regular post in the Qing.

34. Guy, "Inspired Tinkering," chap. 5.

35. In 1977 Skinner defined eight macroregions of imperial China, based on water-sheds and mountain ranges. Skinner, The City, pp. 214–215. In 1985, by splitting Jiangxi from Huguang to create a ninth macroregion, Skinner fit the central Yangzi macroregion quite closely to the Huguang Governor-Generalship. G. William Skinner, "Presidential Address: The Structure of Chinese History," Journal of Asian Studies 44 (February 1985), pp. 271–292. I use the 1985 macroregional division here.

36. QSLQL j.593.28b QL24/7.

37. QSLQL 597.5b QL24/9.

38. QSLQL 597.12b.

39. Hucker, Dictionary, p. 391, no. 4770; Niu Pinghan, ed., Qingdai Zhengqu Yange Zongbiao (Comprehensive chart of administrative changes in the Qing) (Beijing: Zhongguo Ditu Chubanshe, 1990), p. 453.

40. Niu Pinghan, *Qingdai Zhengqu,* pp. 453–477.

41. Skinner, *The City,* p. 305.

42. Wang Shaoguang and Hu Angang, *The Political Economy of Uneven Development: The Case of China* (Armonk, N.Y.: M. E. Sharpe, 1999), p. 45.

43. Span of control (county-level units per prefecture) varied from 1 to 18 across the empire, with an average of 5 to 6. Skinner, *The City,* p. 305.

44. Niu Pinghan, *Qingdai Zhengqu,* p. 435. "A critical feature of that radical overhaul [by the Yongzheng emperor] was the creation of new prefectural-level units outside the regional cores, thereby reducing the span of control in peripheral areas and facilitating supervision of remote county-level units." Skinner, *The City,* p. 270.

9. Land Settlement and Military Colonies

1. Huan K'uan, *Discourses on Salt and Iron: A Debate on State Control of Commerce and Industry in Ancient China,* trans. Esson Gale (Leiden: E. J. Brill, 1931).

2. Judy Bonavia, *The Silk Road: From Xi'an to Kashgar* (Hong Kong: Odyssey, 2002); Albert von Le Coq, *Buried Treasures of Chinese Turkestan* (London: G. Allen and Unwin, 1928).

3. On Ming military colonies, see Cong Peiyuan, "Mingdai Liaodong juntun" (Military colonies in Liaodung in the Ming dynasty), *Zhongguoshi Yanjiu* 3 (1985), pp. 93–107; L. C. Goodrich and Chaoying Fang, *Dictionary of Ming Biography, 1368–1644* (New York: Columbia University Press, 1976), pp. 220, 488, 496, 655, 716, 1099, 1114, 1250, 1294, 1341, 1621; Terada Takanobu, *Sansei Shōnin no Kenkyū: Mindai ni okeru shōnin oyobi shōgyō shihon* (Studies on the Shanxi merchants: merchants and merchant capital in the Ming) (Kyoto: Toyoshi Kenkyukai, 1972); Arthur Waldron, *The Great Wall of China: From History to Myth* (Cambridge: Cambridge University Press, 1990); Wang Yuquan, *Mingdai di Juntun* (Military colonies in the Ming dynasty) (Beijing: Zhonghua Shuju, 1965); Wang Yuquan, "Mingdai juntun zhidu di lishi yuanyuan ji qi tedian" (The historical sources of the Ming military colony system and its special characteristics), *Lishi Yanjiu* 6 (1959), pp. 45–55; Yi Baozhong, "Guanyu mingdai juntun zhidu pohuai guocheng zhong di jige wenti" (On several issues regarding the decline of the Ming military colonies), *Songliao Xuekan* 3 (1984), pp. 41–46; Zuo Shu'e, "Mingdai Gansu tungtian shulue" (A survey of military colonies in Ming Gansu), *Xibei Shidi* 2 (1987), pp. 81–90.

4. Waldron, *The Great Wall,* p. 83.

5. Ibid., p. 187.

6. QPSF KX31/12 j.12 *renyin.*

7. PDZGFL KX54/7 *xinyou* YZ3/4 *wuzi.*

8. Joanna Waley-Cohen, *Exile in Mid-Qing China: Banishment to Xinjiang, 1758–1820* (New Haven: Yale University Press, 1991).

9. PDZGFL KX57/2 *gengyin.*

10. PDZGFL KX56/5 *gengyin,* KX60/10 *yihai,* KX61/10 *xinwei.*

11. PDZGFL KX58/1.

12. PDZGFL KX56/10.

13. PDZGFL KX55/7, KX61/4, KX63/3 *renzhen.*

14. PDZGFL YZ7/11 *yiwei.*

15. Peter C. Perdue, "Empire and Nation in Comparative Perspective," *Journal of Early Modern History* 5, no. 4 (2001), pp. 282–304; Saguchi Tōru, "The Formation of the Turfan Principality under the Qing Empire," *Acta Asiatica* 41 (1981), pp. 76–94.

16. PDZGFL KX60/6.

17. PDZGFL KX61/1 *gengzi*.

18. PDZGFL YZ3/4.

19. PDZGFL YZ9/6 *jiawu*, YZ9/11.

20. GZDYZ 17.601–612; YZHZZ 19.990; Saguchi Tōru, "Shinchō shihaika no Turfan" (Turfan under Qing administration), *Tōyō Gakuhō* 60, no. 3 (1979), p. 9.

21. One *shi* of grain weighs approximately 60 kilograms.

22. PDZGFL YZ9/2 *guichou*.

23. Hua Li, "Qianlong nianjian yimin chuguan yu Qing qianqi Tianshan Beilu nongye di fazhan" (Migration of people beyond the wall in early Qianlong and the development of agriculture in northern Tianshan in the early Qing), *Xibei Shidi* 4 (1987), pp. 119–131; Hua Li, *Qingdai Xinjiang Nongye Fazhanshi* (History of the development of agriculture in Xinjiang in the Qing) (Heilongjiang: Heilongjiang Jiaoyu Chubanshe, 1995); James A. Millward, *Beyond the Pass: Economy, Ethnicity, and Empire in Qing Central Asia, 1759–1864* (Stanford: Stanford University Press, 1998); Waley-Cohen, *Exile.*

24. Pamela Kyle Crossley, *A Translucent Mirror: History and Identity in Qing Imperial Ideology* (Berkeley: University of California Press, 1999), pp. 99–100.

25. This section draws on Peter C. Perdue, "The Agrarian Basis of Qing Expansion into Central Asia," in *Papers from the Third International Conference on Sinology: History Section* (Zhongyang Yanjiuyuan Disanzhou Guoji Hanxue Huiyi Lunwenji Lishizu) (Taibei: Institute of History and Philology, Academia Sinica, 2002), pp. 181–223.

26. Dorothy V. Borei, "Beyond the Great Wall: Agricultural Development in Northern Xinjiang, 1760–1820," in *To Achieve Security and Wealth: The Qing Imperial State and the Economy, 1644–1911*, ed. Jane K. Leonard and John Watt (Ithaca: Cornell University Press, 1991), pp. 21–46; Chen Tsu-yuen, "Histoire du défrichement de la province de Sin-Kiang sous la dynastie Ts'ing" (Ph.D. diss., University of Paris, 1932); Lazar' Isaevich Duman, *Agrarnaia politika tsinskogo (Man'chzhurskogo) pravitel'stva v Sin'tsziane v kontse 18 veka* (Agrarian policies of the Manchu Qing dynasty in Xinjiang at the end of the eighteenth century) (Moscow: Izd-vo Akademii nauk SSSR, 1936); Lazar' Isaevich Duman, "The Qing Conquest of Junggariye and Eastern Turkestan," in *Manzhou Rule in China*, ed. S. L. Tikhvinsky (Moscow: Progress Publishers, 1983), pp. 235–256; Fang Yingkai, *Xinjiang Tunkenshi* (History of clearance in Xinjiang) (Ürümchi: Xinjiang Qingshaonian Chubanshe, 1989); Joseph Fletcher, "Ch'ing Inner Asia, c. 1800," in *The Cambridge History of China*: vol. 10, pt. 1, *Late Ch'ing, 1800–1911*, ed. John K. Fairbank (Cambridge: Cambridge University Press, 1978), pp. 35–106; Ma Dongyu, "Qingdai tuntian tantao" (An analysis of Qing military colonies), *Liaoning Shifan Daxue Xuebao* (January 1985), pp. 62–67; Ma Ruheng and Cheng Chongde, eds., *Qingdai Bianjiang Kaifa* (The opening of borders in the Qing) (Taiyuan: Shanxi Renmin Chubanshe, 1998); Ma Zhenglin, "Xibei kaifa yu shuili" (Water conservancy and the opening of the northwest), *Shaanxi Shifan Daxue Xuebao* 3 (1987), pp. 66–73; Millward, *Beyond the Pass*, pp. 50–52; Waley-Cohen, *Exile*, pp. 27–32,

170–174; Wang Xilong, "Qingdai Shibian Xinjiang Shulue" (Qing dynasty administration of Xinjiang), *Xibei Shidi* 4 (1985), pp. 62–71; Wang Xilong, "Qingdai Wulumuqi Tuntian Shulun" (Military colonies in Qing dynasty Ürümchi), *Xinjiang Shehui Kexue* 5 (1989), pp. 101–108; Wang Xilong, *Qingdai Xibei Tuntian Yanjiu* (Studies on military colonies in the Qing northwest) (Lanzhou: Lanzhou Daxue Chubanshe, 1990); Wang Xilong, "Qingdai Xinjiang di Huitun" (Hui agricultural colonies in Qing dynasty Xinjiang), *Xibei Minzu Xueyuan Xuebao* 1 (1985), pp. 44–53; Xu Bofu, "Qingdai qianqi Xinjiang diqu di bingtun" (Military agricultural colonies in Xinjiang in the early Qing), *Xinjiang Shehui KexueYanjiu* 13 (July 1984), pp. 1–20; Xu Bofu, "Qingdai qianqi Xinjiang diqu di mintun" (Civilian agricultural colonies in Xinjiang in the early Qing), *Zhongguoshi Yanjiu* 2 (February 1985), pp. 85–95; Zeng Wenwu, *Zhongguo Jingying Xiyushi* (A history of China's management of the western regions), 2 vols. (Shanghai: Shangwu Yinshuguan, 1936).

27. Chen Tsu-yuen, "Histoire du défrichement," p. 5.

28. More recently, however, as part of a new focus on "sustainable development," the PRC has promoted the return of arable fields to grassland and forest.

29. Nicola Di Cosmo, "Qing Colonial Administration in the Inner Asian Dependencies," *International History Review* 20 (1998), pp. 287–309; Peter C. Perdue, "Comparing Empires: Manchu Colonialism," *International History Review* 20, no. 2 (1998), pp. 255–262.

30. Sabine Dabringhaus, *Das Qing-Imperium als Vision und Wirklichkeit: Tibet in Laufbahn und Schriften des Song Yun (1752–1835)* (Stuttgart: Franz Steiner Verlag, 1994); William T. Rowe, *Saving the World: Chen Hongmou and Elite Consciousness in Eighteenth-Century China* (Stanford: Stanford University Press, 2001).

31. Tan Qixiang, *Zhongguo lishi dituji*, 1st ed., 8 vols. (Shanghai: Ditu chuban she, 1982); Tan Qixiang and Zhongguo shehui kexueyuan, *The Historical Atlas of China* (Hong Kong: Joint Publishing, 1991); Jeremy Black, *Maps and History: Constructing Images of the Past* (New Haven: Yale University Press, 1997).

32. Peter C. Perdue, *Exhausting the Earth: State and Peasant in Hunan, 1500–1850* (Cambridge, Mass.: Harvard University Press, 1987), p. 74; Madeleine Zelin, *The Magistrate's Tael: Rationalizing Fiscal Reform in Eighteenth-Century Ch'ing China* (Berkeley: University of California Press, 1984).

33. Yeh-chien Wang, *Land Taxation in Imperial China, 1750–1911* (Cambridge, Mass.: Harvard University Press, 1973), p. 7.

34. Peter C. Perdue, "Official Goals and Local Interests: Water Control in the Dongting Lake Region during the Ming and Qing Periods," *Journal of Asian Studies* 41, no. 4 (1982), pp. 747–765.

35. Millward, *Beyond the Pass*, p. 110.

36. Julia Clancy-Smith and Frances Gouda, *Domesticating the Empire: Race, Gender, and Family Life in French and Dutch Colonialism* (Charlottesville: University Press of Virginia, 1998); Frederick Cooper and Ann Stoler, eds., *Tensions of Empire: Colonial Cultures in Bourgeois Worlds* (Berkeley: University of California Press, 1997).

37. Stevan Harrell, ed., *Cultural Encounters on China's Ethnic Frontiers* (Seattle: University of Washington Press, 1995), intro.; Rowe, *Saving the World,* p. 417.

38. C. Patterson Giersch, "Qing China's Reluctant Subjects: Indigenous Communities and Empire along the Yunnan Frontier" (Ph.D. diss., Yale University, 1998);

Emma Jinhua Teng, *Taiwan's Imagined Geography: Chinese Colonial Travel Writing and Pictures, 1683–1895* (Cambridge, Mass.: Harvard University Asia Center, 2004).

39. Ping-ti Ho, "In Defense of Sinicization: A Rebuttal of Evelyn Rawski's Reenvisioning the Qing," *Journal of Asian Studies* 57 (1998), pp. 123–155.

40. Pamela Kyle Crossley, *Orphan Warriors: Three Manchu Generations and the End of the Qing World* (Princeton: Princeton University Press, 1990); Pamela Kyle Crossley, "Thinking about Ethnicity in Early Modern China," *Late Imperial China* 11 (1990), pp. 1–35; Mark C. Elliott, *The Manchu Way: The Eight Banners and Ethnic Identity in Late Imperial China* (Stanford: Stanford University Press, 2001); Evelyn S. Rawski, *The Last Emperors: A Social History of Qing Imperial Institutions* (Berkeley: University of California Press, 1998); Evelyn S. Rawski, "Reenvisioning the Qing: The Significance of the Qing Period in Chinese History," *Journal of Asian Studies* 55 (November 1996), pp. 829–850; Edward J. Rhoads, *Manchus and Han: Ethnic Relations and Political Power in Late Qing and Early Republican China, 1861–1928* (Seattle: University of Washington Press, 2000).

41. "Sinkiang's overall administration was in essence nothing more than a huge garrison under the command of the military governor." Fletcher, "Ch'ing Inner Asia," p. 59. See also Niu Pinghan, ed., *Qingdai Zhengqu Yange Zongbiao* (Comprehensive chart of administrative changes in the Qing) (Beijing: Zhongguo Ditu Chubanshe, 1990), pp. 503–510.

42. Recent studies of the Ottoman empire have likewise replaced older notions of "Oriental despotism" with the concept of "negotiated settlements" between the center and elites. Peter C. Perdue and Huri İslamoğlu, "Introduction to Special Issue on Qing and Ottoman Empires," *Journal of Early Modern History* 5, no. 4 (2001), pp. 271–282.

43. Wang Xilong, "Guanyu Qingdai Ili Huitun shouhuo jisuan danwei 'fen' di bianxi" (An analysis of the harvest measure "fen" in Qing dynasty Ili Hui colonies), *Lanzhou Daxue Xuebao* 4 (1986), pp. 39–44.

44. Waldron, *The Great Wall*, p. 83; Wang Xilong, *Xibei Tuntian*, p. 3.

45. Hua Li, "Qianlong nianjian yimin chuguan."

46. "The idea was to combine military service with farming and thus reduce drastically the cost of the army and enable its men to lead a normal family life . . . Alexander I's and Arakcheev's scheme failed principally because of the extreme regimentation and minute despotism that it entailed, which became unbearable and resulted in revolts and most cruel punishments." Nicholas Riasanovsky, *A History of Russia* (Oxford: Oxford University Press, 1993), pp. 318–319.

47. Waley-Cohen, *Exile*; reviewed by Peter C. Perdue in *Pacific Affairs* 65, no. 4 (Winter 1992), pp. 558–559.

48. Peter C. Perdue, "The Qing State and the Gansu Grain Market, 1739–1864," in *Chinese History in Economic Perspective*, ed. Thomas G. Rawski and Lillian M. Li (Berkeley: University of California Press, 1992), pp. 100–125.

49. Duman, *Agrarnaia politika*; Duman, "Qing Conquest"; Fang Yingkai, *Xinjiang Tunkenshi*; Wang Xilong, *Xibei Tuntian*, pp. 48–49.

50. Wang Xilong, *Xibei Tuntian*, pp. 73–75.

51. Ibid., p. 78.

52. For a major study of the civilian granaries, see Pierre-Étienne Will, R. Bin Wong et al., *Nourish the People: The State Civilian Granary System in China, 1650–1850* (Ann Arbor: University of Michigan Press, 1991).

53. Hua Li, "Daoguang nianjian Tianshan Nanlu Bingtun di yanbian" (Changes in military colonies south of the Tianshan in the Daoguang reign), *Xinjiang Shehui Kexue* 2 (1988), pp. 99–105.

54. Wang Xilong, *Xibei Tuntian*, p. 84.

55. Duman, *Agrarnaia politika*, pp. 136–155; Wang Xilong, *Xibei Tuntian*, pp. 86–104.

56. *Qinding Xinjiang Shilue*, 6/11–13, cited in Duman, *Agrarnaia politika*, pp. 142–145.

57. Qi Qingshun, "Shilun Qingdai Xinjiang tunbing di fazhan he yanbian" (On the development and transformation of military colonies in Qing Xinjiang), *Xinjiang Daxue Xuebao* 2 (1988), pp. 46–53.

58. Wang Xilong, *Xibei Tuntian*, p. 99.

59. Ibid., chap. 4.

60. Ibid., p. 124.

61. Ibid., p. 130.

62. Qi Qingshun, "1767 nian Changji qianfan baodong bu ying kending" (The rebellion in 1767 by the convicts sent to Changji should not be regarded positively), *Xinjiang Daxue Xuebao* 4 (1986), pp. 63–65; Qi Qingshun, "Qingdai Xinjiang qianfan yanjiu" (A study of criminal rebellions in Qing Xinjiang), *Zhongguoshi Yanjiu* 2 (1988), pp. 45–57; Waley-Cohen, *Exile*, p. 156; Wang Xilong, *Xibei Tuntian*, p. 132; Wei Yuan, *Shengwuji* (Record of sacred military victories) (Beijing: Zhonghua Shuju, 1984), p. 180; Ji Yun, "Ji Xinjiang bianfang erze" (Two principles of border defense in Xinjiang), HCJSWB 81.32b–33a.

63. Waley-Cohen, *Exile*, p. 112, gives the text of tattoos in Manchu and Chinese.

64. Ibid., p. 29; Wang Xilong, *Xibei Tuntian*, pp. 144–145.

65. Waley-Cohen, *Exile*, pp. 84–85.

66. Ibid., p. 89.

67. Wang Xilong, *Xibei Tuntian*, pp. 152–163.

68. Wu Yuanfeng, "Qing Qianlong nianjian Yili tuntian shulue" (A survey of military colonies in Ili during the Qing dynasty), *Minzu Yanjiu* 5 (1987), p. 98.

69. Wang Xilong, *Xibei Tuntian*, p. 174.

70. Ibid., p. 179.

71. Wen Shou, "Chen Jiayuguan Wai Qingxingshu" (A report on conditions beyond Jiayuguan), HCJSWB, *juan* 81.12a.

72. Wang Xilong, "Qingdai Shibian Xinjiang Shulue"; Wang Xilong, *Xibei Tuntian*, p. 176; Duman, *Agrarnaia politika*, pp. 166–168, 171.

73. Jiang Qixiang, "Luelun Qingdai Ili huitun" (A discussion of Muslim colonies in Ili), *Xinjiang Daxue Xuebao* 3 (March 1984), pp. 82–89; Wang Xilong, *Xibei Tuntian*, pp. 194–230; Wang Xilong, "Qingdai Xinjiang di Huitun"; Wu Yuanfeng, "Ili tuntian."

74. Millward, *Beyond the Pass*, p. 271n18.

75. ZGSL 145.

76. Wang Xilong, *Xibei Tuntian*, p. 215.

77. Wu Yuanfeng, "Ili tuntian," p. 98.

78. The quota was raised to 17.2 *shi* in 1789. Wang Xilong, *Xibei Tuntian*, p. 216.

79. The *patman*, a Turkestani land and grain measure, was equal to 26.5 *mou*; 200 *patman* = 5,300 *mou*, or 352 hectares.

80. On the mid-nineteenth-century rebellion in Xinjiang, see Hodong Kim, *Holy War in China: The Muslim Rebellion and State in Chinese Central Asia, 1864–1877* (Stanford: Stanford University Press, 2004). On the Dung'an (Dongans), see Svetlana Rimsky-Korsakov Dyer, "The Dungans: Some Aspects of the Culture of Chinese Muslims in the Soviet Union," paper presented at The Legacy of Islam in China: An International Symposium in Memory of Joseph F. Fletcher, Harvard University, April 14–16, 1989.

81. Wang Xilong, *Xibei Tuntian,* p. 234.

82. Xu Bofu, "18–19 shiji Xinjiang diqu di guanyin xumuye" (Official pastures in eighteenth- and nineteenth-century Xinjiang), *Xinjiang Shehui Kexue* 5 (1987), pp. 101–112.

83. Wang Xilong, *Xibei Tuntian,* p. 235.

84. Ibid., p. 249.

85. Kim, *Holy War.*

10. Harvests and Relief

1. "The centralization of knowledge requires facts . . . to justify features and forms of policy. The facts relate to what we may call the statistical idea . . . [and are] key instruments of the moral revolution of the nineteenth century." Philip Corrigan and Derek Sayer, *The Great Arch: English State Formation as Cultural Revolution* (New York: Blackwell, 1985), p. 124; Paul Rabinow, *French Modern: Norms and Forms of the Social Environment* (Cambridge, Mass.: MIT Press, 1989).

2. Pierre-Étienne Will, R. Bin Wong et al., *Nourish the People: The State Civilian Granary System in China, 1650–1850* (Ann Arbor: University of Michigan Press, 1991), p. 25. See also James C. Scott, *Seeing Like a State: How Certain Schemes to Improve the Human Condition Have Failed* (New Haven: Yale University Press, 1998).

3. For discussion of the harvest scale, see Robert B. Marks, *Tigers, Rice, Silk, and Silt: Environment and Economy in Late Imperial South China* (Cambridge: Cambridge University Press, 1998), pp. 206–210.

4. ZPZZ *tunken* QL37/10/24 Lerqin.

5. Peter C. Perdue, "The Qing State and the Gansu Grain Market, 1739–1864," in *Chinese History in Economic Perspective,* ed. Thomas G. Rawski and Lillian M. Li (Berkeley: University of California Press, 1992), pp. 100–125; hereafter Perdue, "Gansu Grain."

6. Harold Fullard, ed., *China in Maps* (Chicago: Denoyer-Geppert, 1968), p. 14.

7. GZDQL 13.447.

8. See, e.g., GZDQL 1.152, 8.17, 8.346.

9. Perdue, "Gansu Grain," p. 101.

10. Li Bozhong, *Agricultural Development in Jiangnan, 1620–1850* (New York: St. Martin's Press, 1998), pp. 120, 124.

11. Philip C. C. Huang, *The Peasant Economy and Social Change in North China* (Stanford: Stanford University Press, 1985), pp. 59, 141.

12. ZPZZ Yang Yingju, QL25/6/8; Yang Yingju, QL26/8/9; Huang Tinggui, QL23/10/17.

13. Will et al., *Nourish the People,* pp. 298, 433n3.

14. In my essay I reduced the official reported figures for Gansu grain reserves by 30 percent because it seemed that the reports used a different size unit from the imperial standard. I am now convinced by Pierre-Étienne Will's argument that the reported figures do conform to the standard grain measure. Ibid., pp. 237–238. The figures in the chart on p. 108 of Perdue, "Gansu Grain," are thus too small, and the correct numbers are given in Will et al., *Nourish the People,* table A.1.

15. Will et al., *Nourish the People,* p. 61. Pierre-Étienne Will in *Bureaucratie et famine en Chine au 18e siècle* (Paris: Mouton, 1980), p. 174, and *Bureaucracy and Famine in Eighteenth-Century China* (Stanford: Stanford University Press, 1990), pp. 193, 196, gives 1.8 million *shi,* following Ma Duanlin, ed., *Wenxian Tonglao* (Beijing: Zhonghua Shuju, 1986); I use the figure in GZDQL 19.63.

16. Will et al., *Nourish the People,* p. 9.

17. Ibid., pp. 89, 91, 101, 168.

18. Ibid., p. 61.

19. Ibid., p. 464.

20. Ibid., pp. 298, 439, 465, 482. Estimates of annual per capita consumption are 2.5 to 3.6 *shi* of husked grain for each adult.

21. Ibid., p. 467.

22. Ibid., pp. 116, 469, 471.

23. GZDQL 12.27; QSLQL j.513.12.

24. Will et al., *Nourish the People,* p. 477.

25. William T. Rowe, *Saving the World: Chen Hongmou and Elite Consciousness in Eighteenth-Century China* (Stanford: Stanford University Press, 2001), pp. 256–259; Will, *Bureaucracy,* p. 133; R. Bin Wong and Peter C. Perdue, "Famine's Foes in Ch'ing China (Review of Pierre-Étienne Will, *Bureaucratie et Famine . . .*)," *Harvard Journal of Asiatic Studies* 43 (June 1983), pp. 291–332.

26. Melissa Macauley, *Social Power and Legal Culture: Litigation Masters in Late Imperial China* (Stanford: Stanford University Press, 1998); William T. Rowe, *Hankow: Commerce and Society in a Chinese City, 1796–1889* (Stanford: Stanford University Press, 1984).

27. *Qingchao Wenxian Tongkao* (Hangzhou: Zhejiang guji chubanshe, 2000), 36.5187a; Will et al., *Nourish the People,* pp. 113, 143.

28. GZDQL 8.366.

29. ZPZZ *cangchu* Wu Dashan, QL22/7/15. These figures assume average prices of 1.5 to 2.2 taels per *shi* of unhusked grain in Anxi. See Will et al., *Nourish the People,* p. 49, for the standard rate.

30. Xu Daling, *Qingdai Juanna Zhidu* (The Qing contributions system) (Beijing: Hafo Yanjing Xueshe, 1950).

31. Ibid., pp. 27, 34, 35, 73.

32. Ibid., p. 32.

33. Will et al., *Nourish the People,* p. 439.

34. GZDQL 19.63.

35. Ping-ti Ho, *The Ladder of Success in Imperial China: Aspects of Social Mobility, 1368–1911* (New York: Columbia University Press, 1962), pp. 188, 236.

36. ZPZZ *cangchu* Wu Dashan, QL22/6/24.

37. Will, *Bureaucratie,* p. 173n43; Ma Duanlin, *Wenxian Tongkao,* 37.5201.

38. QSLQL 527/16, 528/8b, 532/26a.

39. QSLQL 561/33b; ZPZZ *cangchu* Wu Dashan, QL24/5/6.

40. *Huangchao Wenxian Tongkao* (Taibei: Shangwu Yinshuguan, 1983), 37.5205.

41. For discussion of this case, see Perdue, "Gansu Grain"; Will et al., *Nourish the People*, pp. 78, 226–232; R. Kent Guy, "Inspired Tinkering: The Qing Creation of the Province," unpublished ms., 2003; Muhammad Usiar Huaizhong Yang, "The Eighteenth-Century Gansu Relief Fraud Scandal," paper presented at The Legacy of Islam in China: An International Symposium in Memory of Joseph F. Fletcher, Harvard University, April 1989.

42. See graph in Perdue, "Gansu Grain," pp. 115, 118–119.

43. QSLQL 529/9b.

44. QSLQL 528/14b.

45. QSLQL 530/10, 530/20.

46. QSLQL 528/12.

47. QSLQL 541/2b.

48. QSLQL 554/2b.

49. QSLQL 572/16a.

50. QSLQL 573/18.

51. QSLQL 579/12a.

52. QSLQL 545/33b, 550/9b.

53. QSLQL 565/20.

54. QSLQL 565/15, 566/6b, 578/2.

55. QSLQL 541/40, 544/26a, 551/29, 566/7b.

56. QSLQL 565/20b, 567/27a.

57. QSLQL 569/11, 587/17a, 594/22a, 601/4b.

58. QSLQL 571/21.

59. QSLQL 581/21a; ZPZZ Jiang Bing, QL24/7/21.

60. QSLQL 569/12b, 584/32, 587/33a, 591/8a, 599/9b, 602/16a. By 1777, because of administrative changes, there were only sixty-two units, as listed in Chapter 8.

61. QSLQL 576/30.

62. ZPZZ Yong Chang, QL14/12/24.

63. QSLQL 578/7a, 584/20.

64. QSLQL 579/3a.

65. QSLQL 578/12a.

66. QSLQL 579/11a, 587/17a.

67. QSLQL 586/2b, 587/17a, 587/24; Will et al., *Nourish the People*, p. 61.

68. QSLQL 579/11a.

69. QSLQL 588/21a.

70. R. Bin Wong, *China Transformed: Historical Change and the Limits of European Experience* (Ithaca: Cornell University Press, 1997), chap. 9; R. Bin Wong, "Food Riots in the Qing Dynasty," *Journal of Asian Studies* 41, no. 8 (1982), pp. 767–797.

71. QSLQL 587/17a.

72. QSLQL 591/24b.

73. QSLQL 593/37a.

74. QSLQL 587/16b. On the 1744 famine, see Will, *Bureaucracy;* Will, *Bureaucratie;* Wong and Perdue, "Famine's Foes."

75. QSLQL 585/3a.

76. QSLQL 603/11a, 25a.

77. Peter C. Perdue, *Exhausting the Earth: State and Peasant in Hunan, 1500–1850* (Cambridge, Mass.: Harvard University Press, 1987); QSLQL 601/5b.

78. ZPZZ Wu Dashan, QL24/2/17; Wu Dashan, QL24/5/16.

79. ZPZZ Yang Yingju, QL26/8/9. One *jin* = ca. 0.6 kg or 1.3 pounds.

80. ZPZZ Huang Tinggui, QL22/10/27; ZPZZ *nongye tunken* Chen Xisi 1772.

81. ZPZZ Wu Dashan, QL24/12/10.

82. ZPZZ Huang Tinggui, QL22/4/13.

83. QSLQL 579/12a; GZDQL 19.63.

11. Currency and Commerce

1. Susan Mann, *Local Merchants and the Chinese Bureaucracy, 1750–1950* (Stanford: Stanford University Press, 1987); R. Bin Wong, *China Transformed: Historical Change and the Limits of European Experience* (Ithaca: Cornell University Press, 1997); Madeleine Zelin, *The Magistrate's Tael: Rationalizing Fiscal Reform in Eighteenth-Century Ch'ing China* (Berkeley: University of California Press, 1984).

2. Robert Marks, "Rice Prices, Food Supply, and Market Structure in Eighteenth-Century South China," *Late Imperial China* 12 (December 1991), pp. 64–116; Robert B. Marks, *Tigers, Rice, Silk, and Silt: Environment and Economy in Late Imperial South China* (Cambridge: Cambridge University Press, 1998); Wang Yeh-chien, "Food Supply in Eighteenth-Century Fukien," *Late Imperial China* 7 (December 1986), pp. 80–117; R. Bin Wong and Peter C. Perdue, "Grain Markets and Food Supplies in Eighteenth-Century Hunan," in *Chinese History in Economic Perspective,* ed. Thomas G. Rawski and Lillian M. Li (Berkeley: University of California Press, 1992), pp. 126–144.

3. Richard von Glahn, *Fountain of Fortune: Money and Monetary Policy in China, 1000–1700* (Berkeley: University of California Press, 1996).

4. Ibid., p. 251; Harriet T. Zurndorfer, "Another Look at China, Money, Silver, and the Seventeenth-Century Crisis (Review of Richard von Glahn, *Fountain of Fortune*)," *Journal of the Economic and Social History of the Orient* 42 (1999), pp. 396–412.

5. Dennis O. Flynn and Arturo Giraldez, "Cycles of Silver: Global Economic Unity through the Mid-Eighteenth Century," *Journal of World History* 13 (Fall 2002), pp. 391–427; von Glahn, *Fountain of Fortune.*

6. Timothy Brook, *The Confusions of Pleasure: Commerce and Culture in Ming China* (Berkeley: University of California Press, 1998), frontispiece.

7. Dennis O. Flynn and Arturo Giraldez, "Money and Growth without Development: The Case of Ming China," in *Asia Pacific Dynamism, 1550–2000,* ed. A. J. H. Latham and Kawakatsu Heita (London: Routledge, 2000), pp. 199–215; Andre Gunder Frank, *ReOrient: Global Economy in the Asian Age* (Berkeley: University of California Press, 1998); Peter C. Perdue, "The Shape of the World: Asian Continents and the Scraggy Isthmus of Europe," *Bulletin of Concerned Asian Scholars* 30, no. 4 (1998), pp. 53–62.

8. Miyazawa Tomoyuki, "HokuSō no zaisei to kahei keizai" (Northern Song fiscal policy and the money economy), in *Chūgoku sensei kokka to shakai tōgō*, ed. Chūgokushi Kenkyūkai (Kyoto: Bunrikaku, 1990), pp. 279–332.

9. Von Glahn, *Fountain of Fortune*, p. 148.

10. William De Bary, *Waiting for the Dawn: A Plan for the Prince: Huang Tsunghsi's Ming-I Tai-fang lu* (New York: Columbia University Press, 1993), p. 152.

11. Gu Jiegang, *Xibei Kaocha Riji* (Diary of an investigation of the northwest) (Lanzhou: Lanzhou guji shudian, 1983); Laurence Schneider, *Ku Chieh-kang and China's New History: Nationalism and the Quest for Alternative Traditions* (Berkeley: University of California Press, 1971), p. 153.

12. Von Glahn, *Fountain of Fortune*, pp. 211–233.

13. Amartya K. Sen, *Poverty and Famines: An Essay on Entitlement and Deprivation* (Oxford: Clarendon Press, 1981).

14. Wong, *China Transformed*, pp. 92–101; Alexander B. Woodside, "From Mencius to Amartya Sen: East Asian Welfare States," paper presented at the Reischauer Lecture, Harvard University, March 10, 2001.

15. Qingchao Wenxian Tongkao (Qing dynasty encyclopedia of institutions) (Hangzhou: Zhejiang Guji Chubanshe, 2000), 36:5187a.

16. William T. Rowe, "State and Market in mid-Qing Economic Thought," *Études Chinoises* 12 (1993), pp. 7–40.

17. Hans Ulrich Vogel, "Chinese Central Monetary Policy and Yunnan Copper Mining in the Early Qing (1644–1800)" (Ph.D. diss., University of Zurich, 1983); Hans Ulrich Vogel, "Chinese Central Monetary Policy, 1644–1800," *Late Imperial China* 8 (December 1987), pp. 1–52.

18. Von Glahn, *Fountain of Fortune*, p. 109.

19. GZDYZ 11.782 YZ 6/11/16. Also cited in Kuroda Akinobu, *Chūka Teikoku no kōzō to sekai keizai* (The structure of the Chinese empire and the world economy) (Nagoya-shi: Nagoya Daigaku Shuppankai, 1994), p. 43n3.

20. GZDYZ 5.231.

21. Kuroda Akinobu, *Chūka Teikoku*, pp. 40–61; von Glahn, *Fountain of Fortune*, pp. 253–255; Wang Hongbin, "QianJia shiqi yingui qianjian wenti tanyuan" (A discussion of the causes of the high silver-copper ratio in the Qianlong and Jiaqing periods), *Zhongguo Shehui Jingjishi Yanjiu* 2 (1987), pp. 86–92; Yuan Yitang, "Qingdai Qianhuang Yanjiu" (On the scarcity of copper in the Qing dynasty), *Shehui Kexue Zhanxian* 2 (1990), pp. 182–188.

22. Kuroda Akinobu, *Chūka Teikoku*, p. 87, graph 2.

23. QSLQL 5.790.

24. Yeh-chien Wang, *An Estimate of the Land Tax Collection in China, 1753 and 1908* (Cambridge, Mass.: Harvard University Press, 1973), table 27; excludes estimated surcharges.

25. Ibid., table 9. Straw accounted for an additional 70,000 taels of tax.

26. Kuroda Akinobu, *Chūka Teikoku*, English abstract, pp. 1–3; Kuroda Akinobu, "Another Money Economy: The Case of Traditional China," in Latham and Heita, *Asia Pacific Dynamism*, pp. 187–215.

27. Yuan Yitang, "Qingdai Qianhuang."

28. Marks, "Rice Prices, Food Supply, and Market Structure"; Peter C. Perdue,

"The Qing State and the Gansu Grain Market, 1739–1864," in Rawski and Li, *Chinese History in Economic Perspective*, pp. 100–125; Wang Yeh-chien, "Food Supply."

29. Sucheta Mazumdar, *Sugar and Society in China: Peasants, Technology, and the World Market* (Cambridge, Mass.: Harvard University Press, 1998); Peter C. Perdue, "China in the World Economy: Exports, Regions, and Theories (Review of Sucheta Mazumdar, *Sugar and Society in China: Peasants, Technology, and the World Market*)," *Harvard Journal of Asiatic Studies* 60 (June 2000), pp. 259–275; Kenneth Pomeranz, *The Making of a Hinterland: State, Society, and Economy in Inland North China, 1853–1937* (Berkeley: University of California Press, 1993).

30. Kenneth Pomeranz, *The Great Divergence: China, Europe, and the Making of the Modern World Economy* (Princeton: Princeton University Press, 2000), pp. 242–253; Wong and Perdue, "Grain Markets."

31. Kenneth Pomeranz, "Local Interest Story: Political Power and Regional Differences in the Shandong Capital Market, 1900–1937," in Rawski and Li, *Chinese History in Economic Perspective*, pp. 295–318.

32. James A. Millward, *Beyond the Pass: Economy, Ethnicity, and Empire in Qing Central Asia, 1759–1864* (Stanford: Stanford University Press, 1998), pp. 64, 74.

33. Ibid., p. 58n44; Qi Qingshun, "Qingdai Xinjiang di xiexiang gongying he caizheng weiji" (Supplementary funding and the fiscal crisis in Qing Xinjiang), *Xinjiang Shehui Kexue* 3 (1987), pp. 74–85.

34. Millward, *Beyond the Pass,* pp. 59–61.

35. Ibid., pp. 64–65.

36. Ibid., p. 66.

37. Ibid., p. 70, Table 3.

38. Joseph Fletcher, "Ch'ing Inner Asia, c. 1800," in *The Cambridge History of China*, vol. 10, pt. 1, *Late Ch'ing, 1800–1911,* ed. John K. Fairbank (Cambridge: Cambridge University Press, 1978), pp. 35–106; M. Sanjdorj, *Manchu Chinese Colonial Rule in Northern Mongolia*, trans. Urgunge Onon (New York: St. Martin's Press, 1980).

39. Owen Lattimore, *Studies in Frontier History: Collected Papers, 1928–1958* (New York: Oxford University Press, 1962); Sanjdorj, *Colonial Rule;* B. Ia. Vladimirtsov, *Le Régime social des Mongoles: Le Féodalisme nomade* (Paris: A. Maisonneuve, 1948), pp. 243–252; I. Ia. Zlatkin, *Istoriia Dzhungarskogo Khanstvo, 1635–1758* (History of the Zunghar Khanate, 1635–1758) (Moscow: Nauka, 1964), p. 464.

40. Fan Jinmin, "Qingdai Jiangnan yu Xinjiang diqu di sichou maoyi" (Jiangnan and the silk textile trade with Xinjiang in the Qing period), in *Qingdai Quyu Shehui Jingji Yanjiu*, ed. Ye Xian'en (Beijing: Zhonghua, 1992), pp. 715–728; Lin Yongkuang, "Cong yijian dangan kan Xinjiang yu neidi di sizhou maoyi" (A look at trade between Xinjiang and the interior from an archival document), *Qingshi Yanjiu Tongxun* 1 (1983), pp. 23–26; Lü Xiaoxian and Li Shouju, "Qianlongchao neidi yu Xinjiang sichou maoyi gaishu" (An outline of the silk trade from the interior to Xinjiang in the Qianlong reign), in *Qingdai Quyu Shehui Jingji Yanjiu*, ed. Ye Xian'en (Beijing: Zhonghua, 1992), pp. 742–755; Millward, *Beyond the Pass*, pp. 45–49; James A. Millward, "Qing Silk–Horse Trade with the Qazaqs in Yili and Tarbaghatai, 1758–1853," *Central and Inner Asian Studies* 7 (1992), pp. 1–42; Tang Cheng'en and Chen Baosheng, *Gansu Minzu Maoyi Shigao* (History of Gansu trade) (Lanzhou: Gansu

renmin chubanshe, 1986); Wang Xi and Lin Yongkuang, "Qingdai Jiangning Zhizao yu Xinjiang di Sichou Maoyi" (The Jiangning textile factories and the Xinjiang silk trade), *Zhongyang Minzu Xueyuan Xuebao* 3 (1987), pp. 76–78; Wang Xi and Lin Yongkuang, *Qingdai Xibei Minzu Maoyishi* (History of trade in the Qing dynasty northwest) (Beijing: Zhongyang Minzu Xueyuan Chubanshe, 1991); and many other articles by Wang Xi and Lin Yongkuang.

41. Lü Xiaoxian and Li Shouju, "Qianlongchao neidi yu Xinjiang."

42. Wang Xi and Lin Yongkuang, "Qingdai Jiangning Zhizao."

43. Fan Jinmin, "Qingdai Jiangnan."

44. QSLQL j.550, cited in Lü Xiaoxian and Li Shouju, "Qianlongchao neidi yu Xinjiang," p. 743.

45. John K. Fairbank, ed., *The Chinese World Order* (Cambridge, Mass.: Harvard University Press, 1968).

46. Millward, "Qing Silk–Horse Trade"; Millward, *Beyond the Pass*, pp. 45–49. See also John E. Wills, Jr., *Pepper, Guns, and Parleys: The Dutch East India Company and China, 1622–1681* (Cambridge, Mass.: Harvard University Press, 1974).

47. Nicola Di Cosmo, "Kirghiz Nomads on the Qing Frontier: Tribute, Trade, or Gift-Exchange?" in *Political Frontiers, Ethnic Boundaries, and Human Geographies in Chinese History,* ed. Nicola Di Cosmo and Don J. Wyatt (London: Curzon Press, 2003); Nicola Di Cosmo, "A Set of Manchu Documents Concerning a Khokand Merchant," *Central Asian Journal* 41 (1997), pp. 160–199; Nicola Di Cosmo, *Reports from the Northwest: A Selection of Manchu Memorials from Kashgar (1806–1807)* (Bloomington, Ind.: Research Institute for Inner Asian Studies, 1993). For a related perspective, see Hamashita Takeshi, "The Tribute Trade System and Modern Asia," *Memoirs of the Research Department of the Tōyō Bunko* (1988): 7–26.

48. On the multiplicity of practices encompassed by ritual language, see Catherine M. Bell, *Ritual Theory, Ritual Practice* (New York: Oxford University Press, 1992), p. 191: "Ideology is not a coherent set of ideas, statements, or attitudes imposed on people who dutifully internalize them. Nor are societies themselves a matter of unitary social systems or totalities that act as one. Any ideology is always in dialogue with, and thus shaped and constrained by, the voices it is suppressing, manipulating, echoing." Also see James L. Hevia, *Cherishing Men from Afar: Qing Guest Ritual and the Macartney Embassy of 1793* (Durham: Duke University Press, 1995); Angela Zito, *Of Body and Brush: Grand Sacrifice as Text/Performance in Eighteenth-Century China* (Chicago: University of Chicago Press, 1997).

49. Tang Cheng'en and Chen Baosheng, *Gansu Maoyi*, pp. 43–46.

50. Andrea McElderry, "Frontier Commerce: An Incident of Smuggling," *American Asian Review* 5 (1987), pp. 47–82; Millward, *Beyond the Pass*, pp. 180–191; Preston Torbert, *The Ch'ing Imperial Household Department: A Study of Its Organization and Principal Functions, 1662–1796* (Cambridge, Mass.: Harvard University Press, 1977), pp. 136–171.

51. Millward, "Qing Silk–Horse Trade," p. 3; Morris Rossabi, "Notes on Esen's Pride and Ming China's Prejudice," *Mongolia Society Bulletin* 17 (1970), pp. 31–39; Morris Rossabi, "The Tea and Horse Trade with Inner Asia during the Ming," *Journal of Asian History* 4 (1970), p. 145.

52. Millward, "Silk–Horse Trade," p. 2.

53. Ibid., pp. 6–7.

54. Fan Jinmin, "Qingdai Jiangnan."

55. Torbert, *Imperial Household*, pp. 136–171.

56. Immanuel C. Y. Hsu, *The Rise of Modern China* (New York: Oxford University Press, 2000), map on inside front cover.

12. Moving through the Land

1. Charles Maier, "Consigning the Twentieth Century to History: Alternative Narratives for the Modern Era," *American Historical Review* 105 (June 2000), p. 808.

2. Derek Croxton, however, denies that there was conscious recognition of sovereignty as an ideal in 1648: it was an unintended consequence of political and religious conflict. Derek Croxton, "The Peace of Westphalia of 1648 and the Origins of Sovereignty," *International History Review* 21 (1999), pp. 569–591.

3. Maier, "Consigning the Twentieth Century to History," p. 817.

4. Jerry Norman, *A Concise Manchu-English Lexicon* (Seattle: University of Washington Press, 1978), pp. 210, 279.

5. Chandra Mukerji, *Territorial Ambitions and the Gardens of Versailles* (Cambridge: Cambridge University Press, 1997), pp. 39–97; James C. Scott, *Seeing Like a State: How Certain Schemes to Improve the Human Condition Have Failed* (New Haven: Yale University Press, 1998), pp. 11–52; James C. Scott, "State Simplifications: Nature, Space, and People," *Journal of Political Philosophy* 3 (September 1995), pp. 191–233.

6. Benjamin Elman, *A Cultural History of Civil Examinations in Late Imperial China* (Berkeley: University of California Press, 2000); Madeleine Zelin, "The Yung-cheng Reign," in *The Cambridge History of China*, vol. 9, pt. 1, *The Ch'ing Empire to 1800,* ed. Willard J. Peterson (Cambridge: Cambridge University Press, 2002), pp. 220–221; Alexander Woodside, "The Ch'ien-lung Reign," in *The Cambridge History of China,* pp. 252–268.

7. James Z. Lee and Cameron Campbell, *Fate and Fortune in Rural China: Social Organization and Population Behavior in Liaoning, 1774–1873* (Cambridge: Cambridge University Press, 1997), p. 215; reviewed by Peter C. Perdue in *Journal of Asian Studies* 57, no. 3 (August 1998), pp. 854–856.

8. Cited in Isaiah Berlin, *The Crooked Timber of Humanity: Chapters in the History of Ideas* (New York: Vintage, 1990).

9. James C. Scott, *Domination and the Arts of Resistance: Hidden Transcripts* (New Haven: Yale University Press, 1990).

10. Ranajit Guha, *Elementary Aspects of Peasant Insurgency in Colonial India* (Oxford: Oxford University Press, 1983); Ranajit Guha, "The Prose of Counter-insurgency," *Subaltern Studies* 2 (1983), pp. 1–43.

11. Richard Strassberg, *Inscribed Landscapes: Travel Writing from Imperial China* (Berkeley: University of California Press, 1994).

12. Ibid., p. 5.

13. Ibid., p. 6.

14. James Buzard, *The Beaten Track: European Tourism, Literature, and the Ways to Culture, 1800–1918* (Oxford: Oxford University Press, 1993); James Buzard, "Any-

where's Nowhere": *Bleak House* as Autoethnography," *Yale Journal of Criticism* 12, no. 1 (Spring 1999), pp. 7–39.

15. Emma Jinhua Teng, *Taiwan's Imagined Geography: Chinese Colonial Travel Writing and Pictures, 1683–1895* (Cambridge, Mass.: Harvard University Asia Center, 2004).

16. The Palace Museum in Taiwan has published copies of the Manchu text of 125 letters in GZDKX, vols. 8 and 9. Okada Hidehiro, *Kōkitei no Tegami* (Letters of the Kangxi emperor) (Tokyo: Chuko Shinsho, 1979), and Okada Hidehiro, "Mongoru shinseiji no Shōso no Manbun shoken" (Emperor Kangxi's Manchu letters on his Mongolian campaigns), in *Nairiku Ajia no Shakai to Bunka,* ed. Mori Masao (Tokyo: Yamakawa Shuppansha, 1983), pp. 303–321, discuss the letters and their background. Okada Hidehiro, "Outer Mongolia through the eyes of Emperor Kangxi," *Ajia Afurika Gengo Bunka Kenkyū* 18 (1979), pp. 1–11, is a shorter English version. Jaqa Cimeddorji, *Die Briefe des Kang-Hsi-Kaisers aus den Jahren 1696–97 an den Kronprinzen Yin-Cheng aus mandschurischen Geheimdokumenten: ein Beitrag zum ersten Dsungarenkrieg der Ching, 1690–1697* (Wiesbaden: Otto Harrassowitz, 1991), transcribes and translates into German fifty-six of the documents. Borjigidai Oyunbilig, *Zur Überlieferungsgeschichte des Berichts über den persönlichen Feldzug des Kangxi Kaisers gegen Galdan (1696–1697)* (Wiesbaden: Harrassowitz, 1999), translates excerpts from other letters. Also see Jonathan D. Spence, *Emperor of China: Self-Portrait of K'ang-hsi* (New York: Knopf, 1974), Appendix A, pp. 156–166.

17. Strassberg, *Inscribed Landscapes,* p. 10.

18. Ezra Pound, trans., *Shih-ching: The Classic Anthology Defined by Confucius* (Cambridge, Mass.: Harvard University Press, 1982), p. ix.

19. Strassberg, *Inscribed Landscapes,* p. 15.

20. James Legge, *The Chinese Classics,* 5 vols. (Taibei: Wenshizhe chubanshe, 1971), 5:641; Zheng Dekun, trans., "The Travels of Emperor Mu *(Mu Tianzi Zhuan),*" *Journal of the North China Branch of the Royal Asiatic Society* 64 (1933–34), p. 140.

21. Strassberg, *Inscribed Landscapes,* p. 15.

22. Angela Zito, *Of Body and Brush: Grand Sacrifice as Text/Performance in Eighteenth-Century China* (Chicago: University of Chicago Press, 1997).

23. Jean-François Gerbillon, "Voyages en Tartarie du Père Gerbillon," in *Description géographique, historique, chronologique, politique, et physique de l'empire de la Chine et de la Tartarie chinoise . . . ,* ed. Jean Baptiste Du Halde, 4 vols. (Paris: P. G. Lemercier, 1735), 4:250.

24. Michael Chang, "A Court on Horseback: Constructing Manchu Ethno-Dynastic Rule in China, 1751–84" (Ph.D. diss., University of California, San Diego, 2001), pp. 293–420.

25. Joseph Fletcher, "Turco-Mongolian Monarchic Tradition in the Ottoman Empire," in *Studies on Chinese and Islamic Inner Asia,* ed. Beatrice Forbes Manz (Brookfield, Vt.: Variorum, 1995), pp. 236–251.

26. Cimeddorji, *Die Briefe.* p. 254; GZDKX 8.839–841, no. 175, dated KX36/3*/5.

27. Zhongguo Diyi Lishi Dang'anguan, ed., *Kangxichao Manwen Zhupi Zouzhe Quanyi* (Complete translations of Manchu memorials of the Kangxi reign) (Beijing: Zhongguo Shehui Kexue Chubanshe, 1996), p. 161 no. 317 KX 36 3*/7.

28. Ibid., p. 159 no. 312 KX 36/3*/5; p. 172 no. 336 KX 36/3*/17; Okada Hidehiro, *Kōkitei no Tegami*, p. 174.

29. Arthur W. Hummel, ed., *Eminent Chinese of the Ch'ing Period* (Washington, D.C.: U.S. Government Printing Office, 1943–44), p. 924; Spence, *Emperor of China*, pp. 125–139.

30. R. Bin Wong, *China Transformed: Historical Change and the Limits of European Experience* (Ithaca: Cornell University Press, 1997), p. 121.

31. Cimeddorji, *Die Briefe*, no. 21, pp. 148–152, dated 1696/5/26 (actually sent 5/13); GZDKX 9.82–85, no. 218.

32. Catherine M. Bell, *Ritual Theory, Ritual Practice* (New York: Oxford University Press, 1992); Peter Burke, *The Fabrication of Louis XIV* (New Haven: Yale University Press, 1992); Takashi Fujitani, *Splendid Monarchy: Power and Pageantry in Modern Japan* (Berkeley: University of California Press, 1996); James L. Hevia, *Cherishing Men from Afar: Qing Guest Ritual and the Macartney Embassy of 1793* (Durham: Duke University Press, 1995); Chandra Mukerji, *Territorial Ambitions and the Gardens of Versailles* (Cambridge: Cambridge University Press, 1997); Richard S. Wortman, *Scenarios of Power: Myth and Ceremony in Russian Monarchy*, vol. 1, *From Peter the Great to the Death of Nicholas I* (Princeton: Princeton University Press, 1995); Zito, *Of Body and Brush*.

33. Wortman, *Scenarios of Power*, p. 122.

34. Burke, *Fabrication of Louis XIV*, p. 160.

35. Dorinda Outram, "Chariots of the Sun: Ritual Travel, Territory, and Monarchy in Eighteenth-Century France," paper presented at the Workshop on Pomp and Circumstance: Political Uses of Public Culture, MIT, May 1, 1992.

36. Ray Huang, *1587: A Year of No Significance* (New Haven: Yale University Press, 1981).

37. Cimeddorji, *Die Briefe*, no. 49, p. 254; GZDKX 8.839–841, no. 175, dated 1697/3*/5.

38. Chang, "Court on Horseback," pp. 127–133.

39. Ibid., Appendix B.

40. Ibid., p. 232; Harold Kahn, *Monarchy in the Emperor's Eyes: Image and Reality in the Chien-lung Reign* (Cambridge, Mass.: Harvard University Press, 1971).

41. Chang, "Court on Horseback," p. 3; Ma Dongyu, *Xiongshi Sifang: Qingdi xunshou huodong* (Qing emperors' touring activities) (Shenyang: Liaohai chubanshe, 1997).

42. Philip A. Kuhn, *Soulstealers: The Chinese Sorcery Scare of 1768* (Cambridge, Mass.: Harvard University Press, 1990).

43. Tulisen (Too-le-Shin), *Narrative of the Chinese Embassy to the Khan of the Tourgouth Tartars in the Years 1712–1715*, trans. Sir George Staunton (London, 1821), pp. 57, 58.

44. Teng, *Taiwan's Imagined Geography*.

45. John Robert Shepherd, *Statecraft and Political Economy on the Taiwan Frontier, 1600–1800* (Stanford: Stanford University Press, 1993); reviewed by Peter C. Perdue, *Harvard Journal of Asiatic Studies* 55, no. 1 (June 1995), pp. 261–269.

46. Stevan Harrell, ed., *Cultural Encounters on China's Ethnic Frontiers* (Seattle: University of Washington Press, 1995). In the southwest, however, the main focus of

Harrell's work, the civilizing mission was more uniform and uncompromising than elsewhere. Cf. William T. Rowe, *Saving the World: Chen Hongmou and Elite Consciousness in Eighteenth-Century China* (Stanford: Stanford University Press, 2001), p. 417.

47. Joanna Waley-Cohen, *Exile in Mid-Qing China: Banishment to Xinjiang, 1758–1820* (New Haven: Yale University Press, 1991).

48. Hummel, *Eminent Chinese*, p. 120; Ji Yun, *Wulumuqi Zashi* (Assorted poems from Ürümchi) (Shanghai: Shangwu Yinshuguan, 1937); excerpts translated in James A. Millward, *Beyond the Pass: Economy, Ethnicity, and Empire in Qing Central Asia, 1759–1864* (Stanford: Stanford University Press, 1998), p. 135 and passim; Waley-Cohen, *Exile*, pp. 148, 155, 214.

49. Ji Yun, *Wulumuqi Zashi*, pp. 2, 4.

50. Ibid., p. 4.

51. Ibid., p. 1.

52. Jing Wang, *The Story of Stone: Intertextuality, Ancient Chinese Stone Lore, and the Stone Symbolism in "Dream of the Red Chamber," "Water Margin," and "The Journey to the West"* (Durham: Duke University Press, 1992), pp. 66–70.

53. Ibid., pp. 251–268.

54. Edward Tabor Linenthal, *Sacred Ground: Americans and Their Battlefields* (Champaign-Urbana: University of Illinois Press, 1991).

55. Berthold Laufer and Otto Franke, *Epigraphisches Denkmäler aus China*, 2 vols. (Berlin: Dietrich Reimer, 1914).

56. Arthur Waldron, *The Great Wall of China: From History to Myth* (Cambridge: Cambridge University Press, 1990), p. 146. In this inscription, Sanskrit and Tibetan replaced Arabic and Persian.

57. Laufer, *Epigraphisches Denkmaler*, plates 1–4. The languages are Chinese, Manchu, Mongolian, Tibetan, Oirat Mongolian, and East Turkish. The stone is now located outside the entrance to the Confucian temple.

58. Ibid., plates 4–81.

59. Texts quoted in this section can be found in QPSF 48.36–42b.

60. On this phrase, see Morohashi Tetsuji, *Dai Kanwa Jiten* (Great Chinese-Japanese dictionary) (Tokyo: Taishukan shoten, 1960), nos. 15500.11, 7445.130.

61. Chang, "Court on Horseback," Appendix B.

62. PDZGFL *qianbian shou*, 6a, *zhengbian*, 12.24b. Erich Haenisch, "Zwei Viersprachige Inschriften zum Dsungarenkrieg aus den Jahren 1755 und 1758," *Miscellanea Academica Berolinensis* 2 (1950), pp. 224–247, translates the Chinese text; John Krueger, "The Ch'ien-lung Inscriptions of 1755 and 1758 in Oirat-Mongolian," *Central Asiatic Journal* 18, no. 11 (1974), pp. 214–226, translates the Mongolian text; originals in Laufer, *Epigraphisches Denkmäler*, plates 44–47. Cf. Joanna Waley-Cohen, "Commemorating War in Eighteenth-Century China," *Modern Asian Studies* 30 (1996), pp. 880–882.

63. Jin Liang, *Yonghegong Zhilue* (Outline of the Yonghegong temple) (Beijing: Zhongguo Zangxue Chubanshe, 1994), p. 312; Laufer, *Epigraphisches Denkmäler*, plates 2–7; F. D. Lessing, *Yung-ho-kung: An Iconography of the Lamaist Cathedral*, Publication 18 (Stockholm: Sino-Swedish Expedition, 1942), pp. 7–13.

64. Lessing, *Yung-ho-kung*, p. 12.

65. Ibid., p. 12.

66. Ibid., p. 62.

67. Jin Liang, *Yonghegong Zhilue*, pp. 316–322; Laufer, *Epigraphisches Denk-mäler*, plates 4–7; Lessing, *Yung-ho-kung*, pp. 57–61.

68. Sarat Chandra Das, *A Tibetan-English Dictionary* (Delhi: Motilal Banarsidass Publishers, 1995), confirms this etymology.

69. Hummel, *Eminent Chinese*, p. 254.

70. Modified from Jin Liang, *Yonghegong Zhilue*, p. 321; Lessing, *Yung-ho-kung*, p. 61.

71. See James Hevia, "Lamas, Emperors, and Rituals: Political Implications in Qing Imperial Ceremonies," *Journal of the International Association of Buddhist Studies* 16 (1993), pp. 243–278.

72. Jonathan Mirsky, "A Lamas' Who's Who," *New York Review of Books*, April 27, 2000, p. 15; Peter C. Perdue, "Identifying China's Northwest: For Nation and Empire," in *Locating China: Space, Place, and Popular Culture*, ed. Jing Wang and David Goodman (London: Routledge, 2005).

73. Waley-Cohen, "Commemorating War in Eighteenth-Century China"; Joanna Waley-Cohen, "God and Guns in Late Imperial China: Jesuit Missionaries and the Military Campaigns of the Qianlong Emperor (1736–1795)," in *Proceedings of the Thirty-third Conference of the International Congress of Asian and North African Studies*, ed. Bernard Hung-kay Luk (Lewiston, Me.: F. Mellen Press, 1991); Joanna Waley-Cohen, "Military Ritual and the Qing Empire," in *Warfare in Inner Asian History*, ed. Nicola Di Cosmo (Leiden: Brill, 2002), pp. 405–444.

74. Wang Hongjun and Liu Ruzhong, "Qingdai pingding Jungeer guizu panluan di lishi huajuan" (Historical paintings of the Qing suppression of the Zunghar rebellion), *Wenwu* 12 (1976), pp. 68–74.

75. Isidore Stanislas Helman, *Suite des seize estampes représentant les Conquêtes de l'Empereur de la Chine* (Paris, 1788); Paul Pelliot, "Les 'Conquêtes de l'empereur de la Chine,'" *T'oung Pao* 20, nos. 3–4 (August 1920–21), pp. 183–274; Michèle Pirazzoli-t'Serstevens, *Gravures des conquêtes de l'empereur de Chine Kien-Long au Musée Guimet* (Paris: Musée Guimet, 1969). Copies of the engravings are available on-line from the Library of Congress Web site *www.loc.gov/rr/print*; search by negative numbers USZ62–44389, etc.

76. Piper Rae Gaubatz, *Beyond the Great Wall: Urban Form and Transformation on China's Frontiers* (Stanford: Stanford University Press, 1996).

77. This discussion draws on Peter C. Perdue, "Boundaries, Maps, and Movement: The Chinese, Russian, and Mongolian Empires in Early Modern Eurasia," *International History Review* 20 (June 1998), pp. 263–286.

78. Cao Wanru et al., *Zhongguo Gudai Dituji* (An atlas of ancient maps in China), 3 vols. (Beijing: Wenwu Chubanshe, 1990–1997); Richard J. Smith, *Chinese Maps: Images of "All under Heaven"* (New York: Oxford University Press, 1996); Richard J. Smith, "Mapping China's World: Cultural Cartography in Late Imperial China," in *Landscape, Culture, and Power in Chinese Society*, ed. Wen-hsin Yeh (Berkeley: Institute of East Asian Studies, University of California, Berkeley, Center for Chinese Studies, 1998), pp. 52–109; Cordell D. K. Yee, "Traditional Chinese Cartography and the Myth of Westernization," in *The History of Cartography: Cartography in the Traditional East*

and Southeast Asian Societies, ed. J. B. Harley and David Woodward (Chicago: University of Chicago Press, 1994), pp. 170–201.

79. Leo Bagrow, *A History of Russian Cartography up to 1800*, ed. Henry W. Castner (Wolfe Island, Ont.: Walker Press, 1975).

80. Perdue, "Boundaries, Maps," p. 273 and references cited there; Jeremy Black, *Maps and History: Constructing Images of the Past* (New Haven: Yale University Press, 1997); Thongchai Winichakul, *Siam Mapped: A History Of The Geo-Body of a Nation* (Honolulu: University of Hawai'i Press, 1994).

81. Mario Biagioli, *Galileo Courtier: The Practice of Science in the Culture of Absolutism* (Chicago: University of Chicago Press, 1993); Black, *Maps and History*; Jeremy Black, *Maps and Politics* (Chicago: University of Chicago Press, 1997); J. B. Harley, "Deconstructing the Map," in *Writing Worlds: Discourse, Text, and Metaphor in the Representation of Landscape*, ed. Trevor J. Barnes and James S. Duncan (London: Routledge, 1992), pp. 231–247; J. B. Harley, "Meaning and Ambiguity in Tudor Cartography," in *English Map-Making, 1500–1650: Historical Essays*, ed. Sarah Tyacke (London: British Library, 1983), pp. 23–45; J. B. Harley, "Silences and Secrecy: The Hidden Agenda of Cartography in Early Modern Europe," *Imago Mundi* 40 (1988), pp. 57–76; J. B. Harley, "Maps, Knowledge, and Power," in *The Iconography of Landscape*, ed. Denis E. Cosgrove and Stephen Daniels (Cambridge: Cambridge University Press, 1988), pp. 277–312; J. B. Harley and David Woodward, eds., *The History of Cartography: Cartography in the Traditional East and Southeast Asian Societies*, vol. 2, bk. 2 (Chicago: University of Chicago Press, 1994); Joseph Needham, "Geography and Cartography," in *Science and Civilisation in China* (Cambridge: Cambridge University Press, 1959), 7 vols., 3:497–590; Steven Shapin and Simon Schaffer, *Leviathan and the Air-Pump: Hobbes, Boyle, and the Experimental Life* (Princeton: Princeton University Press, 1985).

82. Mark Elliott, "The Limits of Tartary: Manchuria in Imperial and National Geographies," *Journal of Asian Studies* 59 (August 2000), pp. 603–646; Benjamin A. Elman, "Geographical Research in the Ming-Ch'ing Period," *Monumenta Serica* 35 (1981–1983), pp. 1–18; Laura Hostetler, *Qing Colonial Enterprise: Ethnography and Cartography in Early Modern China* (Chicago: University of Chicago Press, 2001); Laura Hostetler, "Qing Connections to the Early Modern World: Ethnography and Cartography in Eighteenth-Century China," *Modern Asian Studies* 34 (July 2000), pp. 623–662; James A. Millward, "Coming onto the Map: The Qing Conquest of Xinjiang," *Late Imperial China* 20 (1999), pp. 61–98; Emma Jinhua Teng, "An Island of Women: The Discourse of Gender in Qing Travel Accounts of Taiwan," *International History Review* 20 (June 1998), pp. 353–370; Teng, *Taiwan's Imagined Geography*.

83. Scott, *Seeing Like a State*.

84. David Buisseret, ed., *Monarchs, Ministers, and Maps: The Emergence of Cartography as a Tool of Government in Early Modern Europe* (Chicago: University of Chicago Press, 1992); Josef Konvitz, *Cartography in France, 1660–1848: Science, Engineering, and Statecraft* (Chicago: University of Chicago Press, 1987).

85. Yee, "Traditional Chinese Cartography."

86. Walter Fuchs, *Der Jesuiten-Atlas der Kanghsi-Zeit; seine Entstehungsgeschichte nebst Namensindices fur die Karten der Mandjurei, Mongolei, Ostturkestan und Tibet,*

mit Wiedergabe der Jesuiten-Karten in Original Grosse (Beijing: Fu-Jen University, 1943); Walter Fuchs, "Materialen zur Kartographie der Mandju-Zeit," *Monumenta Serica* 1 (1935–36, 1938), pp. 386–427.

87. Chang, "Court on Horseback," Appendix A.

88. QSLKX cited in Fuchs, *Jesuiten-Atlas,* pp. 29–30.

89. Theodore N. Foss, "A Western Interpretation of China: Jesuit Cartography," in *East Meets West: The Jesuits in China, 1582–1773,* ed. Charles E. Ronan, S.J., and Bonnie B. C. Oh (Chicago: Loyola University Press, 1988), pp. 209–251.

90. Joseph-Anne-Marie de Moyriac de Mailla, *Histoire générale de la Chine, ou Annales de cet empire,* 13 vols. (Taibei: Ch'eng-wen Publications, 1967–1969), 11:313–317; Foss, "Jesuit Cartography," p. 234; Fuchs, "Materialen," p. 398.

91. John Baddeley, *Russia, Mongolia, China, being some record of the relations between them from the beginning of the XVIIth century to the death of the Tsar Alexei Mikhailovich, A.D. 1602–1676,* 2 vols. (London: Macmillan and Company, 1919), 2:328; Fuchs, "Materialen," p. 412.

92. Henri Bernard, "Les Étapes de la cartographie scientifique pour la Chine et les pays voisins," *Monumenta Serica* 1 (1935–36), pp. 428–477; Elman, "Geographical Research."

93. Strahlenberg's longitude lines are quite close to modern ones, but zero degrees longitude is not centered on Greenwich. England did not dominate cartographic practice, and Greenwich had not made itself the world center of time.

94. Waldron, *The Great Wall.*

95. Millward, "Coming onto the Map."

96. Matthew H. Edney, *Mapping an Empire: The Geographical Construction of British India, 1765–1843* (Chicago: University of Chicago Press, 1997).

97. Such discrepancy between ideal and practice is "the core of the epistemological dilemma of modern mapping: no matter how accurately and precisely the world's structure is measured, that structure is created through the surveyor's and geographer's experiential perception. This perception is initially personal." Ibid., pp. 95–96.

98. With the survey, "the British thought they might reduce India to a rigidly coherent, geometrically accurate, and uniformly precise imperial space, a rational space within which a systematic archive of knowledge about the Indian landscapes and people might be constructed. India, in all of its geographic aspects, would be made knowable to the British." Ibid., p. 319.

99. Ibid., p. 325.

100. Ibid., pp. 332–333, emphasis added.

101. Ibid., p. 143.

102. "The Atlas embodied the British view of India in the 1820s: fixed, eternal, imperial, and known (or knowable) to the British through scientific observation . . . With the Atlas, the British shed their belief that India was defined as the realm of the Mughal empire and recast their conception of India as the realm of British imperial interest in southern Asia." Ibid., pp. 202, 220, 230, quotation p. 235. Such a gap between secret precision and public approximation persists today. Until very recently, images from U.S. Landsat satellites were deliberately degraded in precision when made available to the public so as to protect militarily sensitive sites.

103. Bagrow, *History of Russian Cartography,* pp. 116–119.

104. Fuchs, *Jesuiten-Atlas;* Fuchs, "Materialen." For recent notes on its publication history, see Elliott, "The Limits of Tartary"; Millward, "Coming onto the Map."

105. Yee, "Traditional Chinese Cartography," p. 183.

106. Needham, "Geography and Cartography"; Smith, "Mapping China's World"; Yee, "Traditional Chinese Cartography."

107. Jean Baptiste du Halde, *Description géographique, historique, chronologique, politique, et physique de l'empire de la Chine et de la Tartarie chinoise, enrichie des cartes générales et particulières de ces pays, de la carte générale & des cartes particuliéres du Thibet, & de la Corée; & ornée d'un grand nombre de figures et de vignettes gravées en taille-douce* (Paris: P. G. Lemercier, 1735).

108. G. Henrik Herb, "Mongolian Cartography," in Harley and Woodward, *History of Cartography,* pp. 682–685.

109. Baddeley, *Russia, Mongolia, China,* 1:166–176.

110. Millward, "Coming onto the Map."

111. Elliott, "The Limits of Tartary."

112. Wortman, *Scenarios of Power.*

113. Fujitani, *Splendid Monarchy.*

114. Chang, "Court on Horseback," p. 156.

13. Marking Time

1. Paul Pellisson-Fontanier, *Project for the History of Louis XIV,* cited in Louis Marin, *Portrait of the King* (Minneapolis: University of Minnesota Press, 1988), p. 40.

2. This discussion draws on Peter C. Perdue, "The Qing Empire in Eurasian Time and Space," in *The Qing Formation in World-Historical Time,* ed. Lynn Struve (Cambridge, Mass.: Harvard University Asia Center, 2004), pp. 57–91.

3. QSLKX j.174 1696/7/*wuwu;* Jaqa Cimeddorji, *Die Briefe des Kang-Hsi-Kaisers aus den Jahren 1696–97 an den Kronprinzen Yin-Cheng aus mandschurischen Geheimdokumenten: ein Beitrag zum ersten Dsungarenkrieg der Ching 1690–1697* (Wiesbaden: Otto Harrassowitz, 1991), p. 21; Borjigidai Oyunbilig, *Zur Überlieferungsgeschichte des Berichts über den persönlichen Feldzug des Kangxi Kaisers gegen Galdan (1696–1697)* (Wiesbaden: Harrassowitz, 1999), p. 35; cf. Arthur W. Hummel, ed., *Eminent Chinese of the Ch'ing Period* (Washington, D.C.: U.S. Government Printing Office, 1943–44), pp. 66, 309, 489.

4. Oyunbilig, *Zur Überlieferungsgeschichte,* p. 2; Xia Hongtu, "Qingdai Fanglueguan Sheli Shijian juzheng" (An analysis of the time of establishment of the Qing Fanglueguan), *Lishi Dang'an* 2 (1997), p. 134, corrects Beatrice S. Bartlett, *Monarchs and Ministers: The Grand Council in Mid-Ch'ing China, 1723–1820* (Berkeley: University of California Press, 1991), pp. 225–228, who says that the Office of Military Archives was established in 1749 to chronicle the Jinchuan campaigns.

5. Hummel, *Eminent Chinese,* pp. 253, 271, 275, 327, 494, 616, 685. Hummel omits the important characters *qinzheng* in his references to the title. Erich Hauer, ed., *Huang-ts'ing k'ai-kuo fang-lueh: Die grundung des mandschurischen kaiserreiches* (Berlin: W. de Gruyter, 1926), is a translation of the *Kaiguo Fanglue.*

6. On its compilation, see Bartlett, *Monarchs and Ministers,* pp. 4, 11, 188; Cimeddorji, *Die Briefe,* p. 21; Oyunbilig, *Zur Überlieferungsgeschichte.*

7. Lionel Gossman, *The Empire Unpossess'd: An Essay on Gibbon's "Decline and Fall"* (Cambridge: Cambridge University Press, 1981), p. 75.

8. Mark Edward Lewis, *Writing and Authority in Early China* (Albany: State University of New York Press, 1999).

9. For this reason it is rather misleading to translate "Fanglueguan" as "Office of Military Archives," as Beatrice Bartlett does, but I have followed her terminology for consistency.

10. Gertraude Roth-Li, "The Rise of the Early Manchu State: A Portrait Drawn from Manchu Sources to 1636" (Ph.D. diss., Harvard University, 1975).

11. Oyunbilig, *Zur Überlieferungsgeschichte*.

12. Ibid., p. 84.

13. Ibid., pp. 84–91.

14. Oyunbilig used the 1778 *Siku Quanshu* edition, claiming that the 1710 edition is unavailable. A reprint of the 1710 edition has recently been published, however. It would be worthwhile to check differences between the two editions.

15. Oyunbilig, *Zur Überlieferungsgeschichte*, p. 96.

16. As the modern capital of Inner Mongolia, it has now recovered its Mongolian name, Hohhot (Ch. Huhehaote).

17. Oyunbilig, *Zur Überlieferungsgeschichte*, p. 109.

18. On the Lifanyuan, see Sabine Dabringhaus, *Das Qing-Imperium als Vision und Wirklichkeit: Tibet in Laufbahn und Schriften des Song Yun (1752–1835)* (Stuttgart: Franz Steiner Verlag, 1994), pp. 23–28; Nicola Di Cosmo, "Qing Colonial Administration in the Inner Asian Dependencies," *International History Review* 20 (1998), pp. 287–309; Chia Ning, "The Lifanyuan and the Inner Asian Rituals in the Early Qing," *Late Imperial China* 14 (1991), pp. 60–92.

19. See Okada Hidehiro, "Doruben Oirato no kigen" (Origin of the Derbet Oirats), *Shigaku Zasshi* 83 (1974), pp. 1–44, and discussion in Chapter 2.

20. Oyunbilig, *Zur Überlieferungsgeschichte*, p. 108.

21. Pamela Kyle Crossley, *A Translucent Mirror: History and Identity in Qing Imperial Ideology* (Berkeley: University of California Press, 1999), p. 270.

22. Cf. comments by Mark Elliott, "The Manchu Language Archives of the Qing Dynasty and the Origins of the Palace Memorial System," *Late Imperial China* 22 (2001), pp. 1–70.

23. Hummel, *Eminent Chinese*, p. 917.

24. The best discussion of the implications of the Zeng Jing case is Min Tuki, "Ch'ŏngcho ŭi hwangche sasang t'ongche ŭi silche (Imperial thought control and practice in the Qing dynasty)," in *Chungkuk Kûntaesa Yônku*, ed. Min Tuki (Seoul: Ichokak, 1973), pp. 2–53. See also Crossley, *Translucent Mirror*, pp. 253–260; Feng Erkang, Xu Shengheng, and Yan Aimin, *Yongzheng Huangdi Quanzhuan* (Complete biography of the Yongzheng emperor) (Beijing: Xueyuan Chubanshe, 1994), pp. 132–147; Hummel, *Eminent Chinese*, pp. 747–749, 918, 957. Jonathan Spence, *Treason by the Book* (New York: Viking, 2001), is an entertaining recent account.

25. Thomas Fisher, "Lü Liuliang and the Zeng Jing Case" (Ph.D. diss., Princeton University, 1974).

26. The text itself comprises several imperial edicts and a detailed record of Zeng and his disciples' interrogation, followed by a copy of a book by Zeng, the *Guirenlu,* in

which he asserts his acceptance of imperial orthodoxy. The first *juan* contains two edicts, in the first of which the emperor outlines his general views on the justification of Manchu rule; in the second, he answers in detail the charges of personal immorality leveled at him by Zeng. Yongzheng, *Dayi Juemilu* (Record of how Great Righteousness Awakens the Misguided), in *Qingshi Ziliao*, ed. Zhongguo Shehui Kexueyuan Lishi Yanjiusuo Qingshi Yanjiushi (Beijing: Zhonghua Shuju, 1983), pp. 1–170; Yongzheng, *Dayi Juemilu* (Wenhai, 1730).

27. For discussion of this contrast, see George M. Frederickson, *Racism: A Short History* (Princeton: Princeton University Press, 2002).

28. Yongzheng, *Dayi Juemilu*, p. 3.

29. Ho Ping-ti has referred to Chinese civilization in very similar terms, praising its "open-mindedness and large-heartedness." Yet he ascribes this capaciousness to the sinicization of Manchus by Chinese culture, while Yongzheng argues just the opposite: that only because the Manchus remain distinct can they fulfill the ideals of civilization. Ping-ti Ho, "In Defense of Sinicization: A Rebuttal of Evelyn Rawski's Reenvisioning the Qing," *Journal of Asian Studies* 57 (1998), p. 151.

30. Here I differ from Pamela Crossley, who finds that Qianlong deviated radically from Yongzheng's ideology. She relies on the *Dayi Juemilu* as a "central text" for her discussion of imperial legitimation. Crossley argues that the term *xianghua* (transformation), as used by Yongzheng, implies that the Manchus evolved from a barbarian to a civilized state, a notion that Qianlong rejected. In the *Dayi Juemilu*, however, Yongzheng asserts that the Manchus already were civilized as soon as their state formed in the Northeast. The term *xianghua* is applied not to the Manchus but only to Ming officials who converted to serve the Qing. Crossley also creates an original explanation of why the Qianlong emperor suppressed the *Dayi Juemilu*. She claims that Qianlong suppressed it because he disliked its ideological message. I find the ideologies of Yongzheng and Qianlong much more compatible, and prefer the conventional explanation that Qianlong suppressed the *Dayi Juemilu* because it exonerated Zeng Jing, who had insulted the emperor's father, and it revealed embarrassing rumors about the troubled succession of Yongzheng to the throne. Crossley, *Translucent Mirror*, pp. 46n94, 253–260.

31. Yongzheng, *Dayi Juemilu*, p. 25; page numbers from *Qingshi Ziliao* edition.

32. "Those who understand the great righteousness of respect for their kin, and are clear about the fixed distinctions between superior and inferior, may be called human. Those who destroy the constancy of Heaven and devastate the human order are animals." Ibid., p. 22.

33. Ibid., p. 8.

34. Bruce E. Brooks and Taeko Brooks, eds., *The Original Analects: Sayings of Confucius and His Successors, 0479–0249* (New York: Columbia University Press, 1998); Arthur Waley, trans., *The Analects of Confucius* (New York: Vintage Books, 1938), p. 95; emphasis added in both. Confucius, *Yizhu Lunyu Zixiu Duben* (Analects) (Taibei: Yiwen Yinshuguan, 1967), 3.5.

35. Yongzheng, *Dayi Juemilu*, p. 21.

36. Ibid.

37. Cf. François Jullien, *The Propensity of Things: Toward a History of Efficacy in China* (New York: Zone Books, 1995).

38. Yongzheng, *Dayi Juemilu*, p. 9.

39. Min Tuki, "Ch'ôngcho ûi Hwangche Sasang," p. 262.

40. Yongzheng, *Dayi Juemilu*, p. 24.

41. *Iledkel Shastir* is a short version of the Mongolian title *Jarligh-iyar toghtaghaghsan ghadaghadu muji-yin mongghol qotong ayimagh-un wang güng-üd-ün iledkel shastir*. The Chinese title is *Qinding Waifan menggu huibu wang gong biao zhuan* (Imperially commissioned biographies of the outer dependencies' Mongolian and Turkestani kings and princes). There are partial translations by Veronika Veit, *Die Vier Qane von Qalqa: ein Beitrag zur Kenntnis der politischen Bedeutung der nordmon-golischen Aristokratie in den Regierungsperioden Kang-hsi bis Chien-lung (1661–1796) anhand des biographischen Handbuches Iledkel sastir aus dem Jahre 1795*, 2 vols. (Wiesbaden: O. Harrassowitz, 1990), and Joseph Fletcher, "The Biography of Khwush Kipäk Beg (d. 1781) in the Wai-fan Meng-ku Hui-pu wang kung piao chuan," in *Studies on Chinese and Islamic Inner Asia*, ed. Beatrice Forbes Manz (Brookfield, Vt.: Vario-rum, 1995), pp. 167–172. On the *Zhigongtu*, see Zhuang Jifa, *Xiesui Zhigongtu Manwen tushuo jiaozhu* (The annotated Manchu pictures of tributary peoples) (Taibei: Guoli gugong bowuyüan, 1989).

42. Hummel, *Eminent Chinese*, p. 763.

43. Translation by Paul Pelliot, "Notes critiques d'histoire kalmouke," in *Oeuvres posthumes* (Paris: Librairie d'Amerique et d'Orient, 1960), p. 8, from *Qinding Huangyu Xiyu tuzhi*, *Siku Quanshu* edition, pp. 22b–23a.

44. Ibid., pp. 13–14, from *Qinding Huangyu Xiyu tuzhi*, p. 31a. On the Han scholar Jia Yi, see Herbert Allen Giles, *A Chinese Biographical Dictionary* (Taibei: Cheng-wen, 1968), p. 128.

45. R. Kent Guy, *The Emperor's Four Treasuries: Scholars and the State in the Late Ch'ien-lung Era* (Cambridge, Mass.: Harvard University Press, 1987), p. 50; Hummel, *Eminent Chinese*, pp. 121, 198, 253.

46. Fu Heng, ed., *Pingding Zhungar Fanglue* (Beijing: Xinhua Shudian, 1990), pref-ace.

47. Crossley, *Translucent Mirror*, p. 27.

48. Qishiyi, *Xiyu Wenjianlu* (A record of things seen and heard in the western re-gions) (Taibei: Wenhai Chubanshe, 1777). Pelliot, "Notes critiques," translates the sec-tion on the Torghuts' return from the Volga. Also see Dorothy V. Borei, "Images of the Northwest Frontier: A Study of the *Hsiyu Wenchianlu*," *American Asian Review* 5 (1989), pp. 26–46. Biographies of Qishiyi in Sheng Yu and Yang Zhongxi, *Baqi Wen-jing*, 60 juan (Taibei: Huawen Shuju, 1969), j.58/16; and He Qiutao, *Shuofang beisheng* (Defense of the North) (Zhongguo Lanzhou: Lanzhou gu ji shu dian, 1990), j.56.

49. Qishiyi, *Xiyu Wenjianlu*, p. 51a–b.

50. Michael Khodarkovsky, *Where Two Worlds Met: The Russian State and the Kalmyk Nomads, 1600–1771* (Ithaca: Cornell University Press, 1992), p. 228.

51. "Konggar" probably comes from the Turkish word Hünkâr, for "sultan." I am grateful to Matthew Mosca for this information.

52. Qishiyi, *Xiyu Wenjianlu*, p. 56b.

53. Ibid., p. 66a.

54. Ibid., p. 69a. Wei Yuan's figure of a Zunghar population of 600,000 appears to be based on Qianlong's estimate of 200,000 tents, multiplied by three. Since the typical

Mongol household size was probably larger, closer to the Chinese average of five, Qishiyi's figure may well be more accurate.

55. Ibid., p. 69a.

56. Ibid., p. 89a.

57. Francis Cleaves, ed., *The Secret History of the Mongols* (Cambridge, Mass.: Harvard University Press, 1982); Walther Heissig, *Die Familien- und Kirchengeschichtsschreibung der Mongolen*, vol. 1, *16–18 Jhdt.* (Wiesbaden: O. Harrassowitz, 1959); Paul Kahn, *The Secret History of the Mongols: The Origin of Chinghis Khan: An Adaptation of the Yuan Chao Pi Shih* (San Francisco: North Point Press, 1984); David Morgan, *The Mongols* (Cambridge, Mass.: Basil Blackwell, 1986).

58. Heissig, *Geschichtsschreibung der Mongolen*, p. 11.

59. Ibid., pp. 16, 22, 57, and map p. 9.

60. Veit, *Die Vier Qane*, 1:67; M. Sanjdorj, *Manchu Chinese Colonial Rule in Northern Mongolia*, trans. Urgunge Onon (New York: St. Martin's Press, 1980).

61. Heissig, *Geschichtsschreibung der Mongolen*, pp. 121–134; Walther Heissig and Charles Bawden, eds., *Mongol borjigid obogh-un teüke von Lomi* (Wiesbaden: O. Harrassowitz, 1957).

62. Heissig, *Geschichtsschreibung der Mongolen*, p. 129; Veit, *Die Vier Qane*, 1:67.

63. Christopher Atwood, "Worshiping Grace: The Language of Loyalty in Qing Mongolia," *Late Imperial China* 21, no. 2 (December 2000), p. 99.

64. Ibid., p. 128. Cf. David M. Farquhar, "Emperor as Bodhisattva in the Governance of the Ch'ing Empire," *Harvard Journal of Asiatic Studies* 38 (1978), pp. 5–34; Crossley, *Translucent Mirror*.

65. Heissig, *Geschichtsschreibung der Mongolen*, p. 134.

66. Partial translation in Veit, *Die Vier Qane*, 1:75.

67. Joseph Fletcher, "A Neglected Source of Erdeni-yin Erike," *Harvard Journal of Asiatic Studies* 24 (1962), pp. 229–233.

68. Original text and translation in Stephen A. Halkovic, *The Mongols of the West* (Bloomington: Indiana University Press, 1985).

69. Ibid., p. 50.

70. Ibid., p. 72.

71. Ibid., p. 77.

72. Ibid., p. 70.

73. B. Ia. Vladimirtsov, "Mongol'skie skazaniia ob Amursane" (Mongolian tales of Amursana), *Vostochnie Zapiski* 1 (1927), pp. 271–282.

74. Vladimirtsov, "Mongol'skie skazaniia," pp. 280–282; C. R. Bawden, *The Modern History of Mongolia* (New York: Praeger, 1968), p. 192.

75. James C. Scott, *Domination and the Arts of Resistance: Hidden Transcripts* (New Haven: Yale University Press, 1990).

14. Writing the National History of Conquest

1. Jane Kate Leonard, "Qing History, Wei Yuan, and Contemporary Political Dialogue," in *New Directions in the Social Sciences and Humanities in China*, ed. Michael B. Ahead (London: Macmillan, 1987), pp. 28–45; Jane Kate Leonard, *Wei Yuan and China's Rediscovery of the Maritime World* (Cambridge, Mass.: Harvard University

Press, 1984); Judith Whitbeck, "Kung Tzu-chen and the Redirection of Literati Commitment in Early Nineteenth-Century China," *Ch'ing-shih Wèn'-t'i* 4 (1983), pp. 1–32; Shirleen S. Wong, *Kung Tzu-chen* (Boston: Twayne, 1975).

2. Philip A. Kuhn, *Origins of the Modern Chinese State* (Stanford: Stanford University Press, 2002), p. 31.

3. Gong Zizhen, "Xiyu zhi xingsheng yi," in *Gong Ding'an Quanji Leibian* (Complete works of Gong Zizhen), ed. Gong [Zizhen] (Shanghai: Shijie shuju, 1937), pp. 164–172; He Changling, *Huangchao Jingshi Wenbian* (Collected essays on statecraft) (Shanghai: Zhongxi shuju, 1899), j.80:17a–23a. See also James A. Millward, *Beyond the Pass: Economy, Ethnicity, and Empire in Qing Central Asia, 1759–1864* (Stanford: Stanford University Press, 1998), pp. 241–243.

4. Gong Zizhen, "Xiyu zhi xingsheng yi," pp. 164–165.

5. Millward, *Beyond the Pass*, pp. 41–42.

6. Wei Yuan, "Da renwen Xibei bianyu shu," in He, *Huangchao*, j.80:1a–4b.

7. Ibid., 3b.

8. Kuhn, *Origins*, p. 31.

9. Philip A. Kuhn, "Ideas behind China's Modern State," *Harvard Journal of Asiatic Studies* 55 (1995), p. 301; Wei Yuan, *Shengwuji* (Record of sacred military victories) (Beijing: Zhonghua Shuju, 1984), preface.

10. Hummel, *Eminent Chinese*, p. 851.

11. Quinton G. Priest, "Portraying Central Government Institutions: Historiography and Intellectual Accommodation in the High Ching," *Late Imperial China* 7 (January 1986), p. 39. On "historical analogism," see Robert M. Hartwell, "Historical Analogism, Public Policy, and Social Science in Eleventh- and Twelfth-Century China," *American Historical Review* 76 (June 1971), pp. 690–728.

12. Wei Yuan, *Shengwuji*, preface, p. 1.

13. Jane Kate Leonard, "Wei Yuan and Images of the Nanyang," *Ch'ing Shih Wen-T'i* 4 (1979), pp. 23–57.

14. Xiao Yishan, *Qingdai Tongshi* (Comprehensive history of the Qing dynasty) (Beijing: Zhonghua shuju, 1986); Millward, *Beyond the Pass*, pp. 76, 286–287. Earlier, Naitō Konan also exposed inaccuracies in Wei Yuan's account; see Naitō Konan, "'Qinbian Jilue' no 'Gardan zhuan,'" in *Naitō Konan Zenshū*, 14 vols. (Tokyo: Chikuma Shobo, 1970), 7:380–425.

15. Peter C. Perdue, "The Qing Empire in Eurasian Time and Space: Lessons from the Galdan Campaigns," in *The Qing Formation in World-Historical Time*, ed. Lynn Struve (Cambridge, Mass.: Harvard University Asia Center, 2004), pp. 57–91.

16. Wei Yuan, *Shengwuji*, p. 121.

17. Jean-François Gerbillon, "Voyages en Tartarie du Père Gerbillon," in *Description géographique, historique, chronologique, politique, et physique de l'empire de la Chine et de la Tartarie chinoise . . .* ed. Jean Baptiste du Halde, 4 vols. (Paris: P. G. Lemercier, 1735), 4:87–422.

18. J. L. Cranmer-Byng, ed., *An Embassy to China: Being the journal kept by Lord Macartney during his embassy to the Emperor Ch'ien-lung, 1793–1794* (London: Longmans, 1962), pp. 212–213.

19. Ibid., p. 211.

20. Halford Mackinder, "The Geographical Pivot of History," *Geographical Jour-*

nal 23 (April 1904), pp. 421–444; Halford J. Mackinder, *Democratic Ideals and Reality: A Study in the Politics of Reconstruction* (New York: Henry Holt, 1942), originally published 1919; Alfred T. Mahan, *The Influence of Sea Power upon History, 1660–1783* (Boston: Little & Brown, 1890).

21. Zbigniew K. Brzezinski, *The Grand Chessboard: American Primacy and Its Geostrategic Imperatives* (New York: Basic Books, 1997).

22. Peter Hopkirk, *The Great Game: The Struggle for Empire in Central Asia* (New York: Kodansha, 1992); Rudyard Kipling, *Kim* (1901; Oxford: Oxford University Press, 1987); Karl E. Meyer and Shareen Blair Brysac, *Tournament of Shadows: The Great Game and the Race for Empire in Central Asia* (Washington, D.C.: Counterpoint, 1999).

23. John Baddeley, *Russia, Mongolia, China, being some record of the relations between them from the beginning of the XVIIth century to the death of the Tsar Alexei Mikhailovich, A.D. 1602–1676* (London: Macmillan and Company, 1919); Henry H. Howorth, *History of the Mongols from the Ninth to the Nineteenth Century,* 4 vols. (Taibei: Ch'eng Wen, 1970), originally published 1876; Gaston Cahen, *Histoire des relations de la Russie avec la Chine sous Pierre le Grand (1689–1730)* (Paris: F. Alcan, 1912); Maurice Courant, *L'Asie centrale aux 17e et 18e siècles: empire kalmouk ou empire mantchou?* (Paris: Librairie A. Picard et fils, 1912).

24. Liu Ge and Huang Xianyang, eds., *Xiyu shidi lunwen ziliao suoyin* (Index to materials and articles on the history and lands of the western regions) (Ürümchi: Xinjiang, 1988); Zhongguo Renmin Daxue Qingshi Yanjiusuo, Zhongguo Shehui Kexueyuan, and Zhongguo Bianjiang Shidi Yanjiu Zhongxin, eds., *Qingdai Bianjiang Shidi Lunzhuo Suoyin* (Index to articles on the history of Qing dynasty borderlands) (Beijing: Zhongguo Renmin Chubanshe, 1987).

25. Cf. Joan Scott: "'Man' and 'woman' are at once empty and overflowing categories. Empty because they have no ultimate, transcendent meaning. Overflowing because even when they appear to be fixed, they still contain within them alternative, denied, or suppressed definitions." Joan W. Scott, *Gender and the Politics of History* (New York: Columbia University Press, 1988), p. 49.

26. This discussion draws on Perdue, "The Qing Empire in Eurasian Time and Space."

27. Wei Yuan, *Shengwuji,* p. 3.

28. Dai Yi, *Jianming Qingshi* (A brief history of the Qing dynasty) (Beijing: Renmin Chubanshe, 1984). For lack of space, I do not consider here Chinese historical writings since the 1990s, which have somewhat changed the perspective.

29. Ma Ruheng, "Lun Amuersa'na de [Fandong] Yisheng" (On Amursana's reactionary life)," *Xinjiang Daxue Xuebao* (1979), p. 23; Ma Ruheng and Ma Dazheng, *Elute Menggushi Lunji* (Essays on the history of the Oirat Mongols) (Xining: Qinghai renmin chubanshe, 1984), p. 107. The title of the 1984 version lacks the adjective "reactionary" (a significant change of tone?).

30. Ma Ruheng and Ma Dazheng, *Elute Menggushi,* p. 120.

31. Joseph Fletcher, "Review of I. Ia. Zlatkin, *Istoriia Dzhungarskogo Khanstvo (1635–1758),*" *Kritika* 2 (Spring 1966), pp. 19–28; I. Ia. Zlatkin, *Istoriia Dzhungarskogo Khanstvo, 1635–1758* (History of the Zunghar Khanate, 1635–1758) (Moscow: Nauka, 1964). For a similar perspective and critique, see V. A. Aleksandrov,

Rossiia na dal'nevostochnykh rubezhakh (vtoraia polovina XVII v.) (Moscow: Nauka, 1969); Joseph Fletcher, "V. A. Aleksandrov on Russo-Ch'ing Relations in the Seventeenth Century: Critique and Résumé," *Kritika* 7, no. 3 (1971): pp. 138–170.

32. Miyawaki Junko provides the most cogent critique of the views of Zlatkin and his followers. See Miyawaki Junko, "Galdan izen no Oiratto: Wakamatsu setsu sai hihan" (The Oyirad before Galdan: Wakamatsu's theory criticized again), *Tōyō Gakuhō* 65 (1984), pp. 91–120; Miyawaki Junko, "Jūnana seiki no Oiratto: Jungar Hankoku ni taisuru gimon" (The Oyirad of the seventeenth century: the "Dzungar Khanate" revisited), *Shigaku Zasshi* 90 (1981), pp. 40–63; Miyawaki Junko, "Political organization in the [sic] Seventeenth-Century North Asia," *Ajia Afurika Gengo Bunka Kenkyū* 27 (1984), pp. 172–179; Miyawaki Junko, *Saigo no Yūboku Teikoku: Jungaru bu no kōbō* (The last nomad empire: the rise and fall of the Jungar tribe) (Tokyo: Kodansha, 1995).

33. Sh. Bira, N. Ishzhamts et al., *The Maoist Falsification of the History of the Mongolian People's Republic and the Historical Truth* (Ulaan Baatar: State Publishing House, 1981).

34. C. R. Bawden, *The Modern History of Mongolia* (New York: Praeger, 1968), p. 40.

35. Lucien Paul Victor Febvre, "Frontière, the Word and the Concept," in *A New Kind of History and Other Essays*, ed. Peter Burke (New York: Harper & Row, 1973), pp. 208–218.

36. Michel Foucault, *Madness and Civilization: A History of Insanity* (New York: Vintage, 1965); Barrington Moore, *Reflections on the Causes of Human Misery and upon Certain Proposals to Eliminate Them* (Boston: Beacon Press, 1972); Hayden White, *Tropics of Discourse: Essays in Cultural Criticism* (Baltimore: Johns Hopkins University Press, 1978).

37. Edward Said, *Orientalism* (New York: Vintage, 1994). On China, see Chen Xiaomei, *Occidentalism: A Counter-discourse in Post-Mao China* (New York: Oxford University Press, 1995).

38. Benedict Anderson, *Imagined Communities: Reflections on the Origins and Spread of Nationalism,* (London: Verso, 1991); Liah Greenfeld, *Nationalism: Five Roads to Modernity* (Cambridge, Mass.: Harvard University Press, 1992); Erich S. Gruen, *Culture and National Identity in Republican Rome* (Ithaca: Cornell University Press, 1992), p. 51.

39. Edward Friedman, "Reconstructing China's National Identity," in *National Identity and Democratic Prospects in Socialist China*, ed. Edward Friedman (Armonk, N.Y.: M. E. Sharpe, 1995), pp. 87–114; Dru C. Gladney, "Representing Nationality in China: Refiguring Majority/Minority Identities," *Journal of Asian Studies* 53 (February 1994), pp. 92–123.

15. State Building in Europe and Asia

1. For use of the term "political ecology," see Thomas J. Barfield, *The Perilous Frontier: Nomadic Empires and China* (Cambridge, Mass.: Basil Blackwell, 1989), p. 167; John Robert Shepherd, *Statecraft and Political Economy on the Taiwan Frontier, 1600–1800* (Stanford: Stanford University Press, 1993).

2. "Following the rule that the organization of states among pastoral nomads follows like a shadow the formation of neighboring civilized states, there arose in the steppe, in this period [Tang], a series of 'tribal' nations: the Orkhon Turks in Mongolia, the Uighur and other Turkish nations in Inner Asia, and the Khazar, Bulgar, and Pecheneg states in the Caspian–Black Sea steppe." Owen Lattimore, *Pivot of Asia: Sinkiang and the Inner Asian Frontiers of China and Russia* (Boston: Little, Brown, 1950), p. 11. Omeljan Pritsak also has noted this phenomenon: "One can even say that a nomadic pax [empire] always developed in response to the challenge of a sedentary society. For instance, the moment a given agricultural empire (Iran, China, Rome) developed economic stability and achieved a measure of prosperity [by establishing international commercial ties], the 'nomadic' charismatic clans were tempted to try their luck in obtaining a portion of the El Dorado." Omeljan Pritsak, *The Origin of Rus*, vol. 1, *Old Scandinavian Sources* (Cambridge, Mass.: Harvard University Press, 1981), p. 13.

3. Barfield, *Perilous Frontier*, p. 57.

4. Denis Sinor, "The Inner Asian Warriors," *Journal of the American Oriental Society* 101 (1981), pp. 133–144.

5. Linda Colley, *Britons: Forging the Nation, 1707–1837* (New Haven: Yale University Press, 1992); Eugen Joseph Weber, *Peasants into Frenchmen: The Modernization of Rural France, 1870–1914* (London: Chatto & Windus, 1979).

6. Celia Applegate, "A Europe of Regions: Reflections on the Historiography of Subnational Places," *American Historical Review* 104, no. 10 (1999), pp. 1157–82.

7. "To be sure, kings could, and did, make or break the men of business; but the power of the sovereign was constrained by the requirements of state (money was the sinews of war) and international competition. Capitalists could take their wealth and enterprise elsewhere; and even if they could not leave, the capitalists of other realms would not be slow to profit from their discomfiture. Because of this crucial role as midwife and instrument of power *in a context of multiple, competing polities* (the contrast is with the all-encompassing empires of the Orient or the Ancient World), private enterprise in the West possessed a social and political vitality without precedent or counterpart." David Landes, *The Unbound Prometheus* (Cambridge: Cambridge University Press, 1969), p. 15.

8. Eric J. Hobsbawm, *Nations and Nationalism since 1780* (Cambridge: Cambridge University Press, 1990), p. 66.

9. "[In] a world-economy . . . the basic linkage between the parts of the system is economic . . . An empire, by contrast, is a political unit . . . Political empires are a primitive means of economic domination." Immanuel Wallerstein, *The Modern World-System: Capitalist Agriculture and the Origins of the European World Economy in the Sixteenth Century* (New York: Academic Press, 1974), p. 15.

10. Immanuel Wallerstein, *The Modern World-System III: The Second Era of Great Expansion of the Capitalist World-Economy, 1730s–1840s* (San Diego: Academic Press, 1989), p. 129.

11. Janet Abu-Lughod, *Before European Hegemony: The World System, A.D. 1250–1350* (Oxford: Oxford University Press, 1989); Janet Abu-Lughod, "Discontinuities and Persistence: One World System or a Succession of Systems?" in *The World System: Five Hundred Years or Five Thousand?*, ed. Andre Gunder Frank and Barry K. Gills (London: Routledge, 1993), pp. 278–291. On Frank, see Peter C. Perdue, "The

Shape of the World: Asian Continents and the Scraggy Isthmus of Europe," *Bulletin of Concerned Asian Scholars* 30, no. 4 (1998), pp. 53–62.

12. Charles Tilly, *Coercion, Capital, and European States, 990–1992* (Cambridge, Mass.: Basil Blackwell, 1990), p. 30.

13. Ibid., p. 128.

14. Ibid., p. 140, citing Jerome Blum, *Lord and Peasant in Russia from the Ninth to the Nineteenth Century* (Princeton: Princeton University Press, 1961).

15. Paul Bushkovitch, *The Merchants of Moscow, 1580–1650* (Cambridge: Cambridge University Press, 1980); Charles Halperin, *Russia and the Golden Horde: The Mongol Impact on Medieval Russia* (Bloomington: Indiana University Press, 1985); George V. Lantzeff and Richard Pierce, eds., *Eastward to Empire: Exploration and Conquest on the Russian Open Frontier to 1750* (Montreal: McGill–Queen's University Press, 1973), chap. 5; Janet Martin, *Medieval Russia, 980–1584* (Cambridge: Cambridge University Press, 1995), chap. 9; Donald Ostrowski, *Muscovy and the Mongols: Cross-Cultural Influences on the Steppe Frontier, 1304–1589* (Cambridge: Cambridge University Press, 1998).

16. Tilly, *Coercion, Capital*, pp. 71–72, 130.

17. Pierre-Étienne Will and R. Bin Wong et al., *Nourish the People: The State Civilian Granary System in China, 1650–1850* (Ann Arbor: University of Michigan Press, 1991).

18. R. Bin Wong, *China Transformed: Historical Change and the Limits of European Experience* (Ithaca: Cornell University Press, 1997), pp. 224–226; R. Bin Wong, "Food Riots in the Qing Dynasty," *Journal of Asian Studies* 41, no. 8 (1982), pp. 767–797.

19. Jonathan Lipman, *Familiar Strangers: A Muslim History in China* (Seattle: University of Washington Press, 1997).

20. William T. Rowe, *Saving the World: Chen Hongmou and Elite Consciousness in Eighteenth-Century China* (Stanford: Stanford University Press, 2001), pp. 251–252, 262, 264; Will et al., *Nourish the People*; Wong, *China Transformed*; R. Bin Wong, "Confucian Agendas for Material and Ideological Control in Modern China," in *Culture and State in Chinese History: Conventions, Accommodations, and Critiques,* ed. Theodore Huters, Pauline Yu, and R. Bin Wong (Stanford: Stanford University Press, 1997), pp. 303–325.

21. "The chief motive was not price support and famine prevention but rather large and easy profit for the treasury." John K. Fairbank and Edwin O. Reischauer, *East Asia: The Great Tradition*, vol. 1 (Boston: Houghton Mifflin, 1960), p. 119.

22. Cornell Fleischer, "Royal Authority, Dynastic Cyclism, and "Ibn Khaldūnism" in Sixteenth-Century Ottoman Letters," *Journal of Asian and African Studies* 18 (1983), pp. 198–220; Ibn-Khaldūn, *The Muqaddimah: An Introduction to History,* vol. 1, trans. Franz Rosenthal (New York: Pantheon Books, 1958); Muhsin Mahdi, *Ibn Khaldūn's Philosophy of History* (London: G. Allen and Unwin, 1957); Gordon D. Newby, "Ibn Khaldūn and Frederick Jackson Turner: Islam and the Frontier Experience," *Journal of Asian and African Studies* 18 (1983), pp. 274–285. On the dynastic cycle theory, see Benjamin Schwartz, *The World of Thought in Ancient China* (Cambridge, Mass.: Harvard University Press, 1985), pp. 47, 53.

23. Nicola Di Cosmo, "Ancient Inner Asian Nomads: Their Economic Basis and Its

Significance in Chinese History," *Journal of Asian Studies* 53 (November 1994), pp. 1092–1112.

24. Barfield, *Perilous Frontier;* A. M. Khazanov, *Nomads and the Outside World* (Cambridge: Cambridge University Press, 1984); Owen Lattimore, *Inner Asian Frontiers of China* (Boston: Beacon Press, 1962).

25. Ellsworth Huntington, *The Pulse of Asia: A Journey in Central Asia Illustrating the Geographic Basis of History* (Boston: Houghton Mifflin Company, 1919). See Nicola Di Cosmo, *Ancient China and Its Enemies: The Rise of Nomadic Power in East Asian History* (Cambridge: Cambridge University Press, 2001).

26. Also see Caroline Humphrey and David Sneath, *The End of Nomadism? Society, State, and the Environment in Inner Asia* (Durham: Duke University Press, 1999).

27. Peter B. Golden, *An Introduction to the History of the Turkic Peoples* (Wiesbaden: Otto Harrassowitz, 1992); Denis Sinor, *Inner Asia: History, Civilization, Languages: A Syllabus* (Ann Arbor: University of Michigan Press, 1979); Denis Sinor, *Introduction à l'étude de l'Asie Centrale* (Wiesbaden: O. Harrassowitz, 1963).

28. Nicola Di Cosmo, "State Formation and Periodization in Inner Asian History," *Journal of World History* 10 (1999), pp. 1–40.

29. On the European military revolution and its effects, see Geoffrey Parker, *The Military Revolution: Military Innovation and the Rise of the West* (Cambridge: Cambridge University Press, 1988). Bert Hall questions the effect of early gunpowder weaponry in "Early Modern Ballistics and Tactical Change in Sixteenth-Century Warfare," paper presented at the Conference on Colonels and Quartermasters: War and Technology during the Old Regime, Dibner Institute, MIT, April 1996.

30. What I call here the "Eurasian similarity thesis" has sometimes been called the "(Southern?) California school" of Chinese history (because its most forceful promoters, like R. Bin Wong, Kenneth Pomeranz, James Z. Lee, Robert Marks, and Jack Goldstone, are all in California), or the "early modern thesis." There are problems with both names, since, for example, others outside California, like A. G. Frank, endorse the general "California" argument, and some within California, like Philip Huang, reject it. For further discussion, see Andre Gunder Frank, *ReOrient: Global Economy in the Asian Age* (Berkeley: University of California Press, 1998); Jack A. Goldstone, "Neither Late Imperial nor Early Modern: Efflorescences and the Qing Formation in World History," in *The Qing Formation in World-Historical Time,* ed. Lynn Struve (Cambridge, Mass.: Harvard University Asia Center, 2004), pp. 242–302; Jack A. Goldstone, "The Problem of the Early Modern World," *Journal of the Economic and Social History of the Orient* 41 (1998), pp. 250–283; Philip C. C. Huang, "Development or Involution in Eighteenth-Century Britain and China? A Review of Kenneth Pomeranz's *The Great Divergence: China, Europe, and the Making of the Modern World Economy,*" *Journal of Asian Studies* 61 (May 2002), pp. 501–538; Peter C. Perdue, "China in the Early Modern World: Shortcuts, Myths, and Realities," *Education about Asia* 4, no. 1 (1999), pp. 21–26; Perdue, "The Shape of the World"; Kenneth Pomeranz, "Beyond the East–West Binary: Resituating Development Paths in the Eighteenth-Century World," *Journal of Asian Studies* 61 (May 2002), pp. 539–590.

31. James Z. Lee and Cameron Campbell, *Fate and Fortune in Rural China: Social Organization and Population Behavior in Liaoning, 1774–1873* (Cambridge: Cambridge University Press, 1997); James Z. Lee and Wang Feng, *One Quarter of Human-*

ity: Malthusian Mythology and Chinese Realities (Cambridge, Mass.: Harvard University Press, 1999), reviewed by Peter C. Perdue in *Journal of Asian Studies* 57, no. 3 (1998), pp. 854–856, 59, no. 2 (2000), pp. 410–412.

32. Kenneth Pomeranz, *The Great Divergence: China, Europe, and the Making of the Modern World Economy* (Princeton: Princeton University Press, 2000), reviewed by Peter C. Perdue in H-World listserve, *www.h-net.msu.edu/~world*, August 2000.

33. Wong, *China Transformed*, p. 52.

34. Ibid., p. 58.

35. Critics of this kind of argument often respond by insisting that such a major transformation cannot be just an "accident." They misunderstand the argument. I am not claiming that Europe's miracle is inexplicable, only that it cannot be explained either by long-term causes purportedly unique to Europe or solely by internal characteristics of European societies. For further discussion, see Peter C. Perdue, "How Different Was China? Or, Bringing the Army Back In: Coercion and Ecology in the Comparative Sociology of Europe and China," in *Agriculture, Population, and Economic Development in China and Europe*, ed. Rolf Peter Sieferle and Helga Breuniger (Stuttgart: Breuniger Stiftung, 2003), pp. 311–330.

36. Pomeranz, *Great Divergence*.

37. Rolf Peter Sieferle, *The Subterranean Forest: Energy Systems and the Industrial Revolution* (Cambridge: White Horse Press, 2001); E. A. Wrigley, *Continuity, Chance, and Change: The Character of the Industrial Revolution in England* (Cambridge: Cambridge University Press, 1988).

38. Joanna Waley-Cohen, "China and Western Technology in the Eighteenth Century," *American Historical Review* 98 (December 1993), pp. 1525–44.

39. See Helen Dunstan, "Safely Supping with the Devil: The Qing State and Its Merchant Suppliers of Copper," *Late Imperial China* 13 (December 1992), pp. 42–81; Hans Ulrich Vogel, "Chinese Central Monetary Policy, 1644–1800," *Late Imperial China* 8 (December 1987), pp. 1–52.

40. Will et al., *Nourish the People*.

41. Evgenii V. Anisimov, *The Reforms of Peter the Great* (Armonk, N.Y.: M. E. Sharpe, 1993), pp. 73, 171, quote p. 183.

42. Rowe, *Saving the World*, reviewed by Peter C. Perdue, *China Quarterly* 172 (December 2002), pp. 1096–97.

43. Shepherd, *Statecraft and Political Economy*, pp. 17, 138–142, 185–190, reviewed by Peter C. Perdue, *Harvard Journal of Asiatic Studies* 55, no. 1 (June 1995), pp. 261–269; Chen Qiukun, "From Aborigines to Landed Proprietors: Taiwan Aboriginal Land Rights, 1690–1850," in *Remapping China: Fissures in Historical Terrain*, ed. Gail Hershatter et al. (Stanford: Stanford University Press, 1996), pp. 130–142; Chen Qiukun, *Qingdai Taiwan Tuzhu Diquan: Guanliao, Handian yu Anli sheren di Tudi Bianqian, 1700–1895* (Land rights in Qing dynasty Taiwan: changes in landownership by Han tenants, officials, and Anli aborigines, 1700–1895) (Taibei: Zhongyang Yanjiuyuan Jindaishi Yanjiusuo, 1994); Emma Jinhua Teng, *Taiwan's Imagined Geography: Chinese Colonial Travel Writing and Pictures, 1683–1895* (Cambridge, Mass.: Harvard University Asia Center, 2003), pp. 93–96, 128–136.

44. Pamela Kyle Crossley, *Orphan Warriors: Three Manchu Generations and the End of the Qing World* (Princeton: Princeton University Press, 1990); Pamela Kyle

Crossley, *A Translucent Mirror: History and Identity in Qing Imperial Ideology* (Berkeley: University of California Press, 1999); Mark C. Elliott, *The Manchu Way: The Eight Banners and Ethnic Identity in Late Imperial China* (Stanford: Stanford University Press, 2001); Evelyn S. Rawski, *The Last Emperors: A Social History of Qing Imperial Institutions* (Berkeley: University of California Press, 1998); Evelyn S. Rawski, "Reenvisioning the Qing: The Significance of the Qing Period in Chinese History," *Journal of Asian Studies* 55 (November 1996), pp. 829–850; critique by Ping-ti Ho, "In Defense of Sinicization: A Rebuttal of Evelyn Rawski's Reenvisioning the Qing," *Journal of Asian Studies* 57 (1998), pp. 123–155; discussion in Ann Waltner and Thomas A. Wilson, "Forum: Four Books on the Manchus in China and in Greater Asia," *Journal of Asian Studies* 61 (February 2002), pp. 149–177. This section draws on Peter C. Perdue, "A Frontier View of Chineseness," in *The Resurgence of East Asia: 500, 150, and 50-Year Perspectives,* ed. Giovanni Arrighi, Takeshi Hamashita, and Mark Selden (London: Routledge, 2003), pp. 51–77.

45. Nicola Di Cosmo, "Qing Colonial Administration in the Inner Asian Dependencies," *International History Review* 20 (1998), pp. 287–309; Dorothea Heuschert, "Legal Pluralism in the Qing Empire: Manchu Legislation for the Mongols," *International History Review* 20 (June 1998), pp. 310–324; James A. Millward, *Beyond the Pass: Economy, Ethnicity, and Empire in Qing Central Asia, 1759–1864* (Stanford: Stanford University Press, 1998); Peter C. Perdue, "Comparing Empires: Manchu Colonialism," *International History Review* 20, no. 2 (1998), pp. 255–262; Elliot Sperling, "Awe and Submission: A Tibetan Aristocrat at the Court of Qianlong," *International History Review* 20 (June 1998), pp. 325–335; Emma Jinhua Teng, "An Island of Women: The Discourse of Gender in Qing Travel Accounts of Taiwan," *International History Review* 20 (June 1998), pp. 353–370; Joanna Waley-Cohen, "Religion, War, and Empire in Eighteenth-Century China," *International History Review* 20 (June 1998), pp. 336–352.

46. Alastair Iain Johnston, *Cultural Realism: Strategic Culture and Grand Strategy in Ming China* (Princeton: Princeton University Press, 1995), p. ix.

47. Peter C. Perdue, "Culture, History, and Imperial Chinese Strategy: Legacies of the Qing Conquests," in *Warfare in Chinese History,* ed. Hans van de Ven (Leiden: Brill, 2000), pp. 252–287.

48. Alexander Wendt, "Anarchy Is What States Make of It: The Social Construction of Power Politics," *International Organization* 46, no. 2 (1992), pp. 391–425.

49. Catherine M. Bell, *Ritual Theory, Ritual Practice* (New York: Oxford University Press, 1992); Marshall Sahlins, *Islands of History* (Chicago: University of Chicago Press, 1987).

16. Frontier Expansion in the Rise and Fall of the Qing

1. William H. McNeill, *The Pursuit of Power: Technology, Armed Force, and Society since A.D. 1000* (Chicago: University of Chicago Press, 1982); Charles Tilly, ed., *The Formation of National States in Western Europe* (Princeton: Princeton University Press, 1975).

2. On the granary debate, see Helen Dunstan, "The Autocratic Heritage and China's Political Future: A View from the Qing," *East Asian History* 12 (1996), pp. 79–

104. On frontier trade, see Wang Xi and Lin Yongkuang, *Qingdai Xibei Minzu Maoyishi* (History of trade in the Qing dynasty northwest) (Beijing: Zhongyang Minzu Xueyuan Chubanshe, 1991). On the Grand Council, see Beatrice S. Bartlett, *Monarchs and Ministers: The Grand Council in Mid-Ch'ing China, 1723–1820* (Berkeley: University of California Press, 1991). On the Yongzheng tax reforms, see Madeleine Zelin, *The Magistrate's Tael: Rationalizing Fiscal Reform in Eighteenth-Century Ch'ing China* (Berkeley: University of California Press, 1984). On water conservancy, see Michael Chang, "A Court on Horseback: Constructing Manchu Ethno-Dynastic Rule in China, 1751–84" (Ph.D. diss., University of California, San Diego, 2001), chap. 5; Jane Kate Leonard, *Controlling from Afar: The Daoguang Emperor's Management of the Grand Canal Crisis, 1824–26* (Ann Arbor: University of Michigan Press, 1996); Pierre-Étienne Will, "Clear Waters versus Muddy Waters: The Zheng-Bai Irrigation System of Shaanxi Province in the Late-Imperial Period," in *Sediments of Time: Environment and Society in Chinese History*, ed. Mark Elvin and Ts'ui-jung Liu (Cambridge: Cambridge University Press, 1998), pp. 283–343; Pierre-Étienne Will, "State's Interest in the Administration of a Hydraulic Infrastructure: The Example of Hubei," in *The Scope of State Power*, ed. Stuart Schram (Hong Kong: Chinese University of Hong Kong Press, 1985), pp. 295–349.

3. Ken Alder, *Engineering the Revolution: Arms and Enlightenment in France, 1763–1815* (Princeton: Princeton University Press, 1997); John Brewer, *The Sinews of Power: War, Money, and the English State, 1688–1783* (Cambridge, Mass.: Harvard University Press, 1990).

4. Werner Sombart, *Krieg und Kapitalismus* (1913; New York: Arno Press, 1975).

5. David Kaiser, *Politics and War: European Conflict from Philip II to Hitler* (Cambridge, Mass.: Harvard University Press, 1990).

6. Robert B. Marks, *The Origins of the Modern World: A Global and Ecological Narrative* (Lanham, Md.: Rowman & Littlefield, 2002), p. 114; Joanna Waley-Cohen, "China and Western Technology in the Eighteenth Century," *American Historical Review* 98, no. 5 (1993), pp. 1525–44.

7. Cited in Jonathan Spence, *The Search for Modern China* (New York: Norton, 1990), p. 137.

8. The Ten Great Campaigns, celebrated in Qianlong's essay of this name in 1792, were the two Zunghar campaigns, one in Turkestan, two against the Jinchuan rebels, one in Taiwan, one in Burma, one in Annam, and two against the Gurkhas of Nepal. Arthur W. Hummel, ed., *Eminent Chinese of the Ch'ing Period* (Washington, D.C.: U.S. Government Printing Office, 1943–44), p. 369. On the Burmese and Annam campaigns, see Dai Yingcong, "A Disguised Defeat: The Myanmar Campaign of the Qing Dynasty," *Modern Asian Studies* 38, no. 1 (2004), pp. 145–188; and Alexander Woodside, "The Ch'ien-lung Reign," in *The Cambridge History of China*, vol. 9, pt. 1, *The Ch'ing Empire to 1800*, ed. Willard J. Peterson (Cambridge: Cambridge University Press, 2002), pp. 260–268, 276–278. On Jinchuan, see Joanna Waley-Cohen, "Religion, War, and Empire in Eighteenth-Century China," *International History Review* 20, no. 3 (1998), pp. 336–352.

9. In the *Cambridge History of China*, two authors discuss these trades separately but neither refers to the other; only the kowtow issue links the two frontiers. See Joseph K. Fletcher, "The Heyday of the Ch'ing Order in Mongolia, Sinkiang, and Tibet," in

The Cambridge History of China, vol. 10, pt. 1, *Late Ch'ing, 1800–1911*, ed. John K. Fairbank (Cambridge: Cambridge University Press, 1978), pp. 351–408; Joseph K. Fletcher, "Sino-Russian Relations, 1800–1862," ibid., p. 323; and Frederic Wakeman Jr., "The Canton Trade and the Opium War," ibid., pp. 163–212.

10. See Peter C. Perdue, "From Turfan to Taiwan: Trade and War on Two Chinese Frontiers," in *Untaming the Frontier: Interdisciplinary Perspectives on Frontier Studies*, ed. Bradley J. Parker and Lars Rodseth (Tucson: University of Arizona Press, 2005), for a preliminary exploration of these themes.

11. Basic accounts include John K. Fairbank, "The Creation of the Treaty System," in *Cambridge History of China*, vol. 10, pt. 1, pp. 213–263; John King Fairbank, *Trade and Diplomacy on the China Coast: The Opening of the Treaty Ports, 1842–1854* (Stanford: Stanford University Press, 1969); Michael Greenberg, *British Trade and the Opening of China* (Cambridge: Cambridge University Press, 1951); Wakeman, "Canton Trade"; Frederic Wakeman Jr., *Strangers at the Gate: Social Disorder in South China, 1839–61* (Berkeley: University of California Press, 1966).

12. Wang Xi and Lin Yongkuang, "Hangzhou zhizao yu Qingdai Xinjiang di Sichou maoyi" (The Hangzhou textile factory and the Qing silk trade with Xinjiang), *Hangzhou Daxue Xuebao* 16 (June 1986), pp. 108–115.

13. Wakeman, "Canton Trade," p. 163.

14. Ibid., p. 169.

15. David Robinson, *Bandits, Eunuchs, and the Son of Heaven* (Honolulu: University of Hawai'i Press, 2002).

16. Karen Barkey, *Bandits and Bureaucrats: The Ottoman Route to State Centralization* (Ithaca: Cornell University Press, 1994).

17. Dina Rizk Khoury, "Administrative Practice between Religious Law (Shari'a) and State Law (Kanun) on the Eastern Frontiers of the Ottoman Empire," *Journal of Early Modern History* 5 (December 2001), pp. 305–330; Melissa Macauley, "A World Made Simple: Law and Property in the Ottoman and Qing Empires," ibid., pp. 331–352; Peter C. Perdue, "Empire and Nation in Comparative Perspective," ibid., pp. 282–304; Peter C. Perdue and Huri Islamoglu, "Introduction to Special Issue on Qing and Ottoman Empires," ibid., pp. 271–282; Huri Islamoglu, "Modernities Compared: State Transformations and Constitutions of Property in the Qing and Ottoman Empires," ibid., pp. 353–386; R. Bin Wong, "Formal and Informal Mechanisms of Rule and Economic Development: The Qing Empire in Comparative Perspective," ibid., pp. 387–408.

18. Jane Kate Leonard and Robert Antony, *Dragons, Tigers, and Dogs: Qing Crisis Management and the Boundaries of State Power* (Ithaca: Cornell University Press, 2002).

19. See Min Tu-ki, *National Polity and Local Power: The Transformation of Late Imperial China* (Cambridge, Mass.: Harvard University Press, 1989), p. 93.

20. Christopher Bayly, *Imperial Meridian: The British Empire and the World, 1780–1830* (London: Longman, 1989), p. 34.

21. Suraiya Faroqhi, "In Search of Ottoman History," in *New Approaches to State and Peasant in Ottoman History*, ed. Halil Berktay and Suraiya Faroqhi (London: Frank Cass, 1992), p. 218.

22. Thomas Naff and Roger Owen, *Studies in Eighteenth-Century Islamic History*

(Carbondale: Southern Illinois University Press, 1977); Ariel Salzman, "An Ancien Regime Revisited: 'Privatization' and Political Economy in the Eighteenth-Century Ottoman Empire," *Politics and Society* 21 (December 1993), pp. 393–423.

23. Dina Rizk Khoury, *State and Provincial Society in the Ottoman Empire: Mosul, 1540–1834* (Cambridge: Cambridge University Press, 1997).

24. Zhang Han (1511–1593), in Timothy Brook, *The Confusions of Pleasure: Commerce and Culture in Ming China* (Berkeley: University of California Press, 1998), frontispiece (quoted in Chapter 11).

25. William S. Atwell, "Ming Observers of Ming Decline: Some Chinese Views on the Seventeenth-Century Crisis," *Journal of the Royal Asiatic Society* 2 (1988), pp. 316–348.

26. M. Sanjdorj, *Manchu Chinese Colonial Rule in Northern Mongolia,* trans. Urgunge Onon (New York: St. Martin's Press, 1980).

27. This phrase comes from Frederick Cooper and Ann Stoler, eds., *Tensions of Empire: Colonial Cultures in Bourgeois Worlds* (Berkeley: University of California Press, 1997).

28. R. Bin Wong, "The Search for European Differences and Domination in the Early Modern World: A View from Asia," *American Historical Review* 107, no. 2 (2002), pp. 447–469, at 460.

29. Dai Yingcong, "A Disguised Defeat."

Bibliography

1. Archival and Manuscript Sources

Cherepanov, I. "Sibirskii Letopis" (Manuscript on Siberia). St. Petersburg, 1795. In Lenin Library, Moscow.

Gongzhongdang Zhupi Zouzhe (Palace memorials and vermilion rescripts). Number One Historical Archives, Beijing. Categories: *tudi kaiden* (land clearance); *xiaoshu minzu* (minority peoples); *caizheng cangchu* (taxation and granaries); *junxu* (military supply); *hukou liangjia* (population and grain price reports). (ZPZZ)

Siberian governors. "Reports." Moscow: Rossiskiy Gosudarstvennyi Arhiv Drevnikh Aktov (Russian State Archive of Ancient Acts) and Arhiv Vneshney Politiki Rossii (Archive of Foreign Relations of Russia), 1680–1800.

2. Published Primary Sources

Baddeley, John. *Russia, Mongolia, China, being some record of the relations between them from the beginning of the XVIIth century to the death of the Tsar Alexei Mikhailovich, A.D. 1602–1676.* London: Macmillan and Company, 1919.

Badmaev, A. V. *Zaia-Pandita: Spiski Kalmytskoy Rukopisi "Biografia Zaia-Pandita."* Elista: Kalmytskii nauchno-issledovatel'skii institut iazyka, literatury i istorii pri Sovete Ministrov Kalmytskoi ASSR, 1968.

Bawden, C. R. "Some Documents Concerning the Rebellion of 1756 in Outer Mongolia." *Guoli Zhengzhi Daxue Bianzheng Yanjiusuo Nianbao*, no. 1 (1970): 1–23.

Bell, John. *A Journey from St. Petersburg to Peking, 1719–1722.* Edited by J. L. Stevenson. Edinburgh: Edinburgh University Press, 1965.

Cao Wanru et al. *Zhongguo Gudai Dituji* (An atlas of ancient maps in China). 3 vols. Beijing: Wenwu Chubanshe, 1990–1997.

Cimeddorji, Jaqa. *Die Briefe des Kang-Hsi-Kaisers aus den Jahren 1696–97 an den*

Kronprinzen Yin-Cheng aus mandschurischen Geheimdokumenten: Ein Beitrag zum ersten Dsungarenkrieg der Ching, 1690–1697. Wiesbaden: Otto Harrassowitz, 1991.

Cleaves, Francis, ed. *The Secret History of the Mongols.* Cambridge, Mass.: Harvard University Press, 1982.

Confucius. *Yizhu Lunyu Zixiu Duben* (Analects). Taibei: Yiwen Yinshuguan, 1967.

Cranmer-Byng, J. L., ed. *An Embassy to China: Being the journal kept by Lord Macartney during his embassy to the Emperor Ch'ien-lung, 1793–1794.* London: Longmans, 1962.

Da Qing Lichao Shilu (Historical records of the Qing dynasty). Kangxi, Yongzheng, Qianlong reigns. Taibei: Huawen Shuju, 1970. (QSLKX, QSLQL, QSLYZ)

De Bary, William. *Waiting for the Dawn: A Plan for the Prince: Huang Tsung-hsi's Ming-I Tai-fang lu.* New York: Columbia University Press, 1993.

Demidova, N. F., ed. *Materialy po Istorii Russko-Mongol'skikh Otnoshenii: Russko-mongol'skie otnosheniia, 1654–1685, sbornik dokumentov.* Moscow: Izdatel'skaia Firma Vostochnaia Literatura, 1996.

Demidova, N. F., ed. *Materialy po Istorii Russko-Mongol'skikh Otnoshenii: Russko-mongol'skie otnosheniia, 1685–1691, sbornik dokumentov.* Moscow: Izdatel'skaia Firma Vostochnaia Literatura, 2000.

Demidova, N. F., and V. S. Miasnikov, eds. *Russko-kitaiskie otnosheniia v XVII veke: Materialy i dokumenty.* 2 vols. Moscow: Nauka, 1969–1972.

Desideri, Ippolito. *An Account of Tibet: The Travels of Ippolito Desideri of Pistoia, S.J., 1712–1727.* Edited by Filippo de Filippi. London: Routledge, 1932.

Di Cosmo, Nicola. "A Set of Manchu Documents Concerning a Khokand Merchant . . ." *Central Asian Journal* 41, no. 2 (1997): 160–199.

Di Cosmo, Nicola. *Reports from the Northwest: A Selection of Manchu Memorials from Kashgar (1806–1807).* Bloomington, Ind.: Research Institute for Inner Asian Studies, 1993.

Dylykov, S. D., and Institut vostokovedeniia (Akademiia nauk SSSR). *Ikh tsaaz = "Velikoe ulozhenie": pamiatnik mongol'skogo feodal'nogo prava XVII v.: oiratskii tekst.* Moskva: Izd-vo "Nauka" Glav. red. vostochnoi lit-ry, 1981.

Fletcher, Joseph. "The Biography of Khwush Kipäk Beg (d. 1781) in the Wai-fan Meng-ku Hui-pu wang kung piao chuan." In *Studies on Chinese and Islamic Inner Asia,* edited by Beatrice Forbes Manz, 167–172. Brookfield, Vt.: Variorum, 1995.

Fu Heng, comp. *Pingding Zhungar Fanglue* (Record of pacification of the Zunghars). Beijing: Xinhua Shudian, 1990. (PDZGFL)

Fu Lo-shu, comp. *A Documentary Chronicle of Sino-Western Relations (1644–1820).* 2 vols. Tucson: University of Arizona Press, 1966.

Gerbillon, Jean-François. "Voyages en Tartarie du Père Gerbillon." In *Description géographique, historique, chronologique, politique, et physique de l'empire de la Chine et de la Tartarie chinoise . . .* edited by Jean Baptiste du Halde. 4 vols. Paris: P. G. Lemercier, 1735. 4:87–422.

Golstunskii, K. F. *Mongolo-oiratskie zakony 1640 goda, dopolnitelnye ukazy Galdan-Khun-Taidzhiia i zakony, sostavlennye dlia volzhskikh kalmykov pri kalmytskom khanie Donduk-Dashi: kalmytskii tekst s russkim perevodom i primiechaniiami.* St. Petersburg: Tip. Imperatorskoi akademii nauk, 1880.

Gong Zizhen. *Gong Ding'an Quanji Leibian*. Edited by Gong [Zizhen]. Shanghai: Shijie shuju, 1937.

Gu Jiegang. *Xibei Kaocha Riji*. Lanzhou: Lanzhou guji shudian, 1983.

Guoli Gugong Bowuyuan, comp. *Gongzhongdang Kangxichao Zouzhe* (Memorials from the Gongzhong Archives, Kangxi reign). 9 vols. Taibei: National Palace Museum Press, 1977. (GZDKX)

Guoli Gugong Bowuyuan, comp. *Gongzhongdang Qianlongchao Zouzhe* (Memorials from the Gongzhong Archives, Qianlong reign). 75 vols. Taibei: National Palace Museum Press, 1982–1988. (GZDQL)

Guoli Gugong Bowuyuan, comp. *Gongzhongdang Yongzhengchao Zouzhe* (Memorials from the Gongzhong Archives, Yongzheng reign). 32 vols. Taibei: National Palace Museum Press, 1977–1980. (GZDYZ)

Guoli Gugong Bowuyuan, comp. *Jiu Manzhou Dang* (Old Manchu Archives). 10 vols. Taibei: Guoli Gugong Bowuyuan, 1969.

Haenisch, Erich. "Zwei Viersprachige Inschriften zum Dsungarenkrieg aus den Jahren 1755 und 1758." *Miscellanea Academica Berolinensis* 2, no. 2 (1950): 224–247.

Hauer, Erich, ed. *Huang-ts'ing k'ai-kuo fang-lueh: Die Gründung des Mandschurischen Kaiserreiches*. Berlin: W. de Gruyter, 1926.

He Changling, comp. *Huangchao Jingshi Wenbian* (Collected imperial essays on statecraft). Shanghai: Zhongxi shuju, 1899. (HCJSWB)

He Qiutao. *Shuofang beisheng* (Defense of the north). Lanzhou: Lanzhou guji shudian, 1990.

Hedin, Sven. *Southern Tibet: Discoveries in Former Times Compared with My Own Researches in 1906–1908*. Vol. 1. Stockholm: Lithographic Institute of the General Staff of the Swedish Army, 1917.

Heissig, Walther, and Charles Bawden, eds. *Mongol borjigid obogh-un teüke von Lomi*. Wiesbaden: Otto Harrassowitz, 1957.

Helman, Isidore Stanislas. *Suite des seize estampes représentant les Conquêtes de l'Empereur de la Chine*. Paris, 1788.

Herodotus. *The Histories*. Translated by Aubrey de Selincourt. Baltimore: Penguin Books, 1954.

Huan K'uan. *Discourses on Salt and Iron: A Debate on State Control of Commerce and Industry in Ancient China*. Translated by Esson Gale. Leiden: E. J. Brill, 1931.

Huangchao Wenxian Tongkao (Encyclopedia of imperial institutions). Taibei: Taiwan Shangwu Yinshuguan, 1983.

Ibn-Khaldūn. *The Muqaddimah: An Introduction to History*. Translated by Franz Rosenthal. Vol. 1. New York: Pantheon Books, 1958.

Kanda Nobuo et al., eds. *Manbun Rōtō: Tongki Fuka Sindaha Hergen i Dangse* (The old Manchu Archive). 7 vols. Tokyo: Toyo Bunko, 1955.

Kraft, Eva S. *Zum Dsungarenkrieg im 18 Jahrhundert: Berichte des Generals Funingga*. Leipzig: Harrassowitz, 1953.

Krueger, John. "The Ch'ien-lung Inscriptions of 1755 and 1758 in Oirat-Mongolian." *Central Asiatic Journal* 18 (1974): 214–226.

Laufer, Berthold, and Otto Franke. *Epigraphisches Denkmäler aus China*. 2 vols. Berlin: Dietrich Reimer, 1914.

Lin Yongkuang. "Cong yijian dangan kan Xinjiang yu neidi di sizhou maoyi" (A look at trade between Xinjiang and the interior from an archival document). *Qingshi Yanjiu Tongxun* 1 (1983): 23–26.

Ma Duanlin, ed., *Wenxian Tongkao*. Beijing: Zhonghua Shuju, 1986. (WXTK)

Maska [Masiha]. "Saibei jicheng" (Account of travels north of the passes). In *Xiaofang Huzhai Yudi Congchao*, 25–29. Shanghai: Zhuyitang, 1877.

Mingshilu (Ming Dynasty Veritable Records) 500 *juan*. Changle Liang Hongzhi, 1940.

Nian Gengyao. *Nian Gengyao Zouzhe Zhuanji* (Collected memorials of Nian Gengyao). 3 vols. Taibei: Guoli Gugong Bowuyuan, 1971.

Pallas, Peter Simon. *Sammlungen Historischer Nachrichten über die Mongolischen Völkerschaften*. Graz: Akademische Druck-u. Verlagsanstalt, 1980.

Pan Zhe, Li Hongbin, and Sun Fangming, eds. *Qing Ruguanqian Shiliao Xuanji*. Beijing: Renmin Chubanshe, 1984.

Qi Jingzhi. *Waibamiao beiwen zhushi* (Annotated stelae of the outer eight temples). Beijing: Zijincheng, 1985.

Qingchao Wenxian Tongkao (Qing dynasty general history of institutions). Hangzhou: Zhejiang guji chubanshe, 2000.

Qishiyi. *Xiyu Wenjianlu* (A record of things seen and heard in the western regions). Taibei: Wenhai Chubanshe, 1966 [1777].

Sheng Yu and Yang Zhongxi. *Baqi Wenjing* (Documents of the eight banners). 60 *juan*. Taibei: Huawen Shuju, 1969.

Shiliao Xunkan (Archival documents series). Beijing: Gugong bowuyuan wenxian guan, 1930–. (SLXK)

Tulisen. *Lakcaha Jecende takûraha ejehe bithe* (Kōchū Iikiroku: Tulisen's I-yu-lu). Edited by Imanishi Shunju. Tenri: Tenri Daigaku Oyasato Kenkyujo, 1964.

Tulisen [Too-le-Shin]. *Narrative of the Chinese Embassy to the Khan of the Tourgouth Tartars in the Years 1712–1715*. Translated by Sir George Staunton. London, 1821.

Veit, Veronika. *Die Vier Qane von Qalqa: Ein Beitrag zur Kenntnis der politischen Bedeutung der nordmongolischen Aristokratie in den Regierungsperioden Kang-hsi bis Chien-lung (1661–1796) anhand des biographischen Handbuches Iledkel šastir aus dem Jahre 1795*. 2 vols. Wiesbaden: O. Harrassowitz, 1990.

Veselovskii, N. I. "Posolstvo k zyungarskomu khun-taichzhi Tsevan Rabtanu kapitana ot artillerii Ivana Unkovskago i putevoy zhurnal ego za 1722–1724 godu: Dokumenty, izdannye s predisloviem i primechaniami." *Zapiski imperatorskago russkago geograficheskago obshchestva* 10, no. 2 (1887), 1–276.

Yin Huaxing. *Xizheng Jilue* (An account of the western expedition). Taibei: Guangwen Shuju, 1968.

Yongzheng. "Dayi Juemilu" (Record of how great righteousness awakens the misguided). In *Qingshi Ziliao*, ed. Zhongguo Shehui Kexueyuan Lishi Yanjiusuo Qingshi Yanjiushi, 1–170. Beijing: Zhonghua Shuju, 1983.

Zhang Tingyu. *Xinjiaoben Mingshi pingfu bianliuzhong* (History of the Ming dynasty). 5th ed. Taibei: Dingwen shuju, 1991.

Zhang Yushu, comp. *Qinzheng Pingding Shuomo Fanglue* (Chronicle of the emperor's personal expeditions to pacify the frontier). Beijing: Zhongguo Shudian, 1708. (QPSF)

Zhaolian. *Xiaoting Zalu* (Miscellaneous notes). Beijing: Zhonghua Shuju, 1980.

Zhongguo Diyi Lishi Dang'anguan, comp. *Kangxichao Manwen Zhupi Zouzhe Quanyi* (Complete translations of Manchu memorials of the Kangxi reign). Beijing: Zhongguo Shehui Kexue Chubanshe, 1996.

Zhongguo Diyi Lishi Dang'anguan, comp. "Qianlong 8 zhi 15 nian Zhungar bu zai Suzhou dengdi maoyi" (Suzhou trade with the Zunghars from 1743 to 1750). *Lishi Dang'an* 2 (1984): 21–34; 3 (1984): 12–20. (LSDA)

Zhongguo Diyi Lishi Dang'anguan, comp. *Yongzhengchao Hanwen Zhupi Zouzhe Huibian* (Chinese vermilion endorsement memorials of the Yongzheng reign). Nanjing: Jiangsu Guji Chubanshe, 1986. (YZHZZ)

Zhungar Shilue Bianxiezu. *Zhungar Shilue.* Beijing: Renmin Chubanshe, 1985. (ZGSL)

Zhungar Shilue Bianxiezu, comp. *Qingshilu Zhungar Shiliao Zhebian* (Collected materials from the Qingshilu on the Zunghars). Ürümchi: Xinjiang Renmin Chubanshe, 1986.

Zhupi Yuzhi (Yongzheng emperor's edicts and vermilion endorsements). Neifuzhu Motaoyinben, 1738.

Zlatkin, I. Ia. "Russkie arkhivnye materialy ob Amursane." In *Filologia I istoriia Mongol'skikh Narodov: Pamiati Akademika Borisa Yakovlevicha Vladimirtsova,* edited by Akademiia Nauk SSSR Institut Vostokovedeniia, 289–313. Moscow: Izdatel'stvo Vostochnoi Literatury, 1958.

Zlatkin, I. Ia., and N. V. Ustiugov, eds. *Materialy po Istorii Russko-Mongol'skikh Otnoshenii: Russko-mongol'skie otnosheniia, 1607–1636: Sbornik Dokumentov.* Moscow: Izdatel'stvo Vostochnoi Literatury, 1959.

Zlatkin, I. Ia., and N. V. Ustiugov, eds. *Materialy po Istorii Russko-Mongol'skikh Otnoshenii: Russko-mongol'skie otnosheniia, 1636–1654: Sbornik Dokumentov.* Moscow: Izdatel'stvo Vostochnoi Literatury, 1974.

3. Secondary Sources

Abu-Lughod, Janet. *Before European Hegemony: The World System, A.D. 1250–1350.* Oxford: Oxford University Press, 1989.

Abu-Lughod, Janet. "Discontinuities and Persistence: One World System or a Succession of Systems?" In *The World System: Five Hundred Years or Five Thousand?* edited by Andre Gunder Frank and Barry K. Gills, 278–291. London: Routledge, 1993.

Adelman, Stephen, and Jeremy Aron. "From Borderlands to Borders: Empires, Nation-States, and the Peoples in Between in North American History." *American Historical Review* 104, no. 3 (1999): 814–844; no. 4 (1999): 1221–39.

Ahmad, Zahiruddin. *Sino-Tibetan Relations in the Seventeenth Century.* Rome: Istituto italiano per il Medio ed Estremo Oriente, 1970.

Aksan, Virginia H. "Locating the Ottomans among Early Modern Empires." *Journal of Early Modern History* 3, no. 2 (1999): 103–134.

Alder, Ken. *Engineering the Revolution: Arms and Enlightenment in France, 1763–1815.* Princeton: Princeton University Press, 1997.

Aleksandrov, V. A. *Rossiia na dal'nevostochnykh rubezhakh (vtoraia polovina XVII v.).* Moscow: Nauka, 1969.

Amiot, Joseph. "Monument de la transmigration des tourgouths des bords de la mer caspienne, dans l'Empire de la Chine." In *Mémoires concernant l'histoire, les sciences, les arts, les moeurs, etc. des chinois, par les Missionaires de Pekin*, 401–431. Paris: Chez Nyon, 1776–.

Anderson, Benedict. *Imagined Communities: Reflections on the Origins and Spread of Nationalism*. London: Verso, 1991.

Anderson, Perry. *Passages from Antiquity to Feudalism*. London: Verso, 1978.

Andreev, A. I. *Ocherki po Istochnikovedeniiu Sibiri*. Vol. 2. Pt. 1. Leningrad: Izd-vo Akademii Nauk SSSR, 1960–.

Anisimov, Evgenii V. *The Reforms of Peter the Great*. Armonk, N.Y.: M. E. Sharpe, 1993.

Anthony, David, Dimitri Y. Telegin, and Dorcas Brown. "The Origin of Horseback Riding." *Scientific American* (December 1991): 94–100.

Anthony, David W., and Nikolai B. Vinogradov. "Birth of the Chariot." *Archaeology* (March–April 1995): 36–41.

Applegate, Celia. "A Europe of Regions: Reflections on the Historiography of Subnational Places." *American Historical Review* 104, no. 4 (1999): 1157–82.

Atwell, William S. "Ming Observers of Ming Decline: Some Chinese Views on the Seventeenth-Century Crisis." *Journal of the Royal Asiatic Society* 2 (1988): 316–348.

Atwood, Christopher. "Worshiping Grace: The Language of Loyalty in Qing Mongolia." *Late Imperial China* 21, no. 2 (2000): 86–139.

Bagrow, Leo. *A History of Russian Cartography up to 1800*. Edited by Henry W. Castner. Wolfe Island, Ont.: Walker Press, 1975.

Barfield, Thomas J. *The Nomadic Alternative*. Englewood Cliffs, N.J.: Prentice-Hall, 1993.

Barfield, Thomas J. *The Perilous Frontier: Nomadic Empires and China*. Cambridge, Mass.: Basil Blackwell, 1989.

Barkey, Karen. *Bandits and Bureaucrats: The Ottoman Route to State Centralization*. Ithaca: Cornell University Press, 1994.

Barkman, C. D. "The Return of the Torghuts from Russia to China." *Journal of Oriental Studies* 2 (1955): 89–115.

Bartlett, Beatrice S. *Monarchs and Ministers: The Grand Council in Mid-Ch'ing China, 1723–1820*. Berkeley: University of California Press, 1991.

Bassin, Mark. "Expansion and Colonialism on the Eastern Frontier: Views of Siberia and the Far East in Pre-Petrine Russia." *Journal of Historical Geography* 14, no. 1 (1988): 3–21.

Bassin, Mark. "Inventing Siberia: Visions of the Russian Empire in the Early Nineteenth Century." *American Historical Review* 96, no. 3 (1991): 763–794.

Bassin, Mark. "Russia between Europe and Asia: The Ideological Construction of Geographical Space." *Slavic Review* (Spring 1991): 1–17.

Bawden, C. R. *The Modern History of Mongolia*. New York: Praeger, 1968.

Bawden, C. R. "The Mongol Rebellion of 1756–1757." *Journal of Asian History* 2, no. 3 (1968): 1–31.

Bayly, Christopher. *Imperial Meridian: The British Empire and the World, 1780–1830*. London: Longman, 1989.

Beckwith, Christopher I. "The Impact of the Horse and Silk Trade on the Economies of T'ang China and the Uighur Empire." *Journal of the Economic and Social History of the Orient* 34, no. 2 (1991): 183–198.

Bell, Catherine M. *Ritual Theory, Ritual Practice*. New York: Oxford University Press, 1992.

Bello, David Anthony. *Opium and the Limits of Empire: The Opium Problem in the Chinese Interior, 1729–1850*. Cambridge, Mass.: Harvard University Press, 2005.

Bergholz, Fred W. *The Partition of the Steppe: The Struggle of the Russians, Manchus, and the Zunghar Mongols for Empire in Central Asia, 1619–1758: A Study in Power Politics*. New York: Peter Lang, 1993.

Bergmann, Benjamin. *Nomadische Streifereien unter den Kalmuken in den Jahren 1802 und 1803*. Riga: E. J. G. Hartmann, 1804.

Berlin, Isaiah. *The Crooked Timber of Humanity: Chapters in the History of Ideas*. New York: Vintage, 1990.

Bernard, Henri. "Les Étapes de la Cartographie Scientifique pour la Chine et les Pays Voisins." *Monumenta Serica* 1 (1935–36): 428–477.

Biagioli, Mario. *Galileo Courtier: The Practice of Science in the Culture of Absolutism*. Chicago: University of Chicago Press, 1993.

Bira, Sh., Ishjamts, N., et al. *The Maoist Falsification of the History of the Mongolian People's Republic and the Historical Truth*. Ulaan Baatar: State Publishing House, 1981.

Black, Cyril, et al. *The Modernization of Inner Asia*. Armonk, N.Y.: M. E. Sharpe, 1991.

Black, Jeremy. *Maps and History: Constructing Images of the Past*. New Haven: Yale University Press, 1997.

Black, Jeremy. *Maps and Politics*. Chicago: University of Chicago Press, 1997.

Blum, Jerome. *Lord and Peasant in Russia from the Ninth to the Nineteenth Century*. Princeton: Princeton University Press, 1961.

Bobrick, Benson. *East of the Sun: The Epic Conquest and Tragic History of Siberia*. New York: Poseidon Press, 1992.

Bonavia, Judy. *The Silk Road: From Xi'an to Kashgar*. Hong Kong: Odyssey, 2002.

Borei, Dorothy V. "Beyond the Great Wall: Agricultural Development in Northern Xinjiang, 1760–1820." In *To Achieve Security and Wealth: The Qing Imperial State and the Economy, 1644–1911*, edited by Jane K. Leonard and John Watt, 21–46. Ithaca: Cornell University Press, 1991.

Borei, Dorothy V. "Ethnic Conflict and Qing Land Policy in Southern Xinjiang, 1760–1840." In *Dragons, Tigers, and Dogs: Qing Crisis Management and the Boundaries of State Power*, edited by Jane Kate Leonard and Robert Antony, 273–301. Ithaca: Cornell University Press, 2002.

Borei, Dorothy V. "Images of the Northwest Frontier: A Study of the Hsiyu Wenchianlu." *American Asian Review* 5, no. 2 (1989): 26–46.

Braudel, Fernand. *The Mediterranean and the Mediterranean World in the Age of Philip II*. Translated by Sian Reynolds. New York: Harper & Row, 1972.

Brewer, John. *The Sinews of Power: War, Money, and the English State, 1688–1783*. Cambridge, Mass.: Harvard University Press, 1990.

Brook, Timothy. *The Confusions of Pleasure: Commerce and Culture in Ming China*. Berkeley: University of California Press, 1998.

Brooks, Bruce E., and Taeko Brooks, eds. *The Original Analects: Sayings of Confucius and His Successors, 0479–0249*. New York: Columbia University Press, 1998.

Brunnert, I. S., and V. V. Hagelstrom. *Present Day Political Organization of China.* Taibei: Book World Co., 1911.

Brzezinski, Zbigniew K. *The Grand Chessboard: American Primacy and Its Geostrategic Imperatives.* New York: Basic Books, 1997.

Buisseret, David, ed. *Monarchs, Ministers, and Maps: The Emergence of Cartography as a Tool of Government in Early Modern Europe.* Chicago: University of Chicago Press, 1992.

Bulag, Uradyn Erden. *The Mongols at China's Edge: History and the Politics of National Unity.* Lanham, Md.: Rowman & Littlefield, 2002.

Burke, Peter. *The Fabrication of Louis XIV.* New Haven: Yale University Press, 1992.

Bushkovitch, Paul. *The Merchants of Moscow, 1580–1650.* Cambridge: Cambridge University Press, 1980.

Buzard, James. "Anywhere's Nowhere": *Bleak House* as Autoethnography." *Yale Journal of Criticism* 12, no. 1 (Spring 1999): 7–39.

Buzard, James. *The Beaten Track: European Tourism, Literature, and the Ways to Culture, 1800–1918.* Oxford: Oxford University Press, 1993.

Cahen, Gaston. *Histoire des relations de la Russie avec la Chine sous Pierre le Grand (1689–1730).* Paris: F. Alcan, 1912.

Cahen, Gaston. *Some Early Russo-Chinese Relations.* Shanghai: National Review Office, 1912.

Cai Jiayi. "Galdan." In *Qingdai Renwu Zhuangao,* edited by Qingshi Bianweihui, pt. 1, 9 vols., 6:173–184. Beijing: Zhonghua Shuju, 1991.

Cai Jiayi. "Qingdai zhongwanqi jinzang aocha gaishu." *Minzu Yanjiu* 6 (1986): 42–47.

Cai Jiayi. "Shiba shiji zhongye Zhungar tong Zhongyuan diqu di maoyi wanglai lueshu." *Qingshi Luncong* 4 (1983): 241–255.

Chang, Chia-feng. "Disease and Its Impact on Politics, Diplomacy, and the Military: The Case of Smallpox and the Manchus (1613–1795)." *Journal of the History of Medicine and Allied Sciences* 57, no. 2 (2002): 177–197.

Chang, Michael. "A Court on Horseback: Constructing Manchu Ethno-Dynastic Rule in China, 1751–84." Ph.D. dissertation, University of California, San Diego, 2001.

Chen Feng. *Qingdai Junfei Yanjiu.* Wuhan: Wuhan Daxue Chubanshe, 1991.

Chen Qiukun. "From Aborigines to Landed Proprietors: Taiwan Aboriginal Land Rights, 1690–1850." In *Remapping China: Fissures in Historical Terrain,* edited by Gail Hershatter et al., 130–142. Stanford: Stanford University Press, 1996.

Chen Qiukun. *Qingdai Taiwan Tuzhu Diquan: Guanliao, Handian yu Anli sheren di Tudi Bianqian, 1700–1895.* Taibei: Zhongyang Yanjiuyuan Jindaishi Yanjiusuo, 1994.

Chen Tsu-yuen. "Histoire du défrichement de la province de Sin-Kiang sous la dynastie Ts'ing." Ph.D. dissertation, University of Paris, 1932.

Chen Xiaomei. *Occidentalism: A Counter-discourse in Post-Mao China.* New York: Oxford University Press, 1995.

Cheng Chongde. *18 shiji di Zhongguo yu shijie: Bianjiang minzu juan.* Shenyang: Liaohai chubanshe, 1999.

Chiba Muneo. "Jungaru no Chōshō." In *Kara būran: Kuroi suna-arashi,* 2 vols. Tokyo: Kokushokankokai, 1986. Vol. 1.

Chiba Muneo. "Tenzan ni habataku." In *Kara būran: Kuroi suna-arashi*, 2 vols. Tokyo: Kokushokankokai, 1986. Vol. 2.

Chimitdorzhiev, Sh. B. "Iz istorii Russko-Mongol'skikh ekonomicheskikh sviazei." *Istoriia SSSR* 2 (1964): 151–156.

Chimitdorzhiev, Sh. B. *Vzaimootnosheniia Mongolii i Rossii v 17–18 vekakh*. Moscow: Nauka, 1978.

Christian, David. "Inner Eurasia as a Unit of World History." *Journal of World History* 5, no. 2 (1994): 173–213.

Clancy-Smith, Julia, and Frances Gouda. *Domesticating the Empire: Race, Gender, and Family Life in French and Dutch Colonialism*. Charlottesville: University Press of Virginia, 1998.

Colley, Linda. *Britons: Forging the Nation, 1707–1837*. New Haven: Yale University Press, 1992.

Cong Peiyuan. "Mingdai Liaodong juntun." *Zhongguoshi Yanjiu* (March 1985): 93–107.

Cooper, Frederick, and Ann Stoler, eds. *Tensions of Empire: Colonial Cultures in Bourgeois Worlds*. Berkeley: University of California Press, 1997.

Corrigan, Philip, and Derek Sayer. *The Great Arch: English State Formation as Cultural Revolution*. New York: Blackwell, 1985.

Courant, Maurice. *L'Asie Centrale aux 17e et 18e siècles: Empire Kalmouk ou Empire Mantchou?* Paris: Librairie A. Picard and fils, 1912.

Creel, Herrlee G. "The Role of the Horse in Chinese History." In *What Is Taoism? and Other Studies in Chinese Cultural History*, edited by Herrlee G. Creel, 160–186. Chicago: University of Chicago Press, 1970.

Cronon, William. *Changes in the Land: Indians, Colonists, and the Ecology of New England*. New York: Hill and Wang, 1983.

Cronon, William. "Kennecott Journey: The Paths Out of Town." In *Under an Open Sky: Rethinking America's Western Past*, edited by William Cronon, George Miles, and Jay Gitlin, 28–51. New York: Norton, 1992.

Cronon, William. *Nature's Metropolis: Chicago and the Great West*. New York: Norton, 1991.

Crosby, Alfred W. *Ecological Imperialism: The Biological Expansion of Europe*. Cambridge: Cambridge University Press, 1986.

Crossley, Pamela Kyle. *Orphan Warriors: Three Manchu Generations and the End of the Qing World*. Princeton: Princeton University Press, 1990.

Crossley, Pamela Kyle. "Thinking about Ethnicity in Early Modern China." *Late Imperial China* 11 (1990): 1–35.

Crossley, Pamela Kyle. *A Translucent Mirror: History and Identity in Qing Imperial Ideology*. Berkeley: University of California Press, 1999.

Crossley, Pamela K., and Evelyn Rawski. "A Profile of the Manchu Language." *Harvard Journal of Asiatic Studies* 53, no. 1 (June 1993): 63–88.

Croxton, Derek. "The Peace of Westphalia of 1648 and the Origins of Sovereignty." *International History Review* 21, no. 3 (1999): 569–591.

Dabringhaus, Sabine. *Das Qing-Imperium als Vision und Wirklichkeit: Tibet in Laufbahn und Schriften des Song Yun (1752–1835)*. Stuttgart: Franz Steiner Verlag, 1994.

Daffinà, Paolo. *Il Nomadismo centrasiatico.* [Rome]: Istituto di studi dell'India e dell'Asia orientale Università di Roma, 1982.

Dai Yi. *Jianming Qingshi.* Beijing: Renmin Chubanshe, 1984.

Dai Yingcong. "A Disguised Defeat: The Myanmar Campaign of the Qing Dynasty." *Modern Asian Studies* 38, no. 1 (2004): 145–188.

Das, Sarat Chandra. *A Tibetan-English Dictionary.* Delhi: Motilal Banarsidass Publishers, 1995.

De B. Codrington, K. "A Geographical Introduction to the History of Central Asia." *Geographical Journal* 104 (1944): 27–40, 73–91.

De Mailla, Joseph-Anne-Marie de Moyriac. *Histoire générale de la Chine, ou Annales de cet empire.* Taibei: Ch'eng-wen Publications, 1967–1969.

De Quincey, Thomas. *Revolt of the Tartars.* New York: Longmans, Green, and Co., 1896.

Di Cosmo, Nicola. *Ancient China and Its Enemies: The Rise of Nomadic Power in East Asian History.* Cambridge: Cambridge University Press, 2001.

Di Cosmo, Nicola. "Ancient Inner Asian Nomads: Their Economic Basis and Its Significance in Chinese History." *Journal of Asian Studies* 53, no. 4 (1994): 1092–1112.

Di Cosmo, Nicola. "Kirghiz Nomads on the Qing Frontier: Tribute, Trade, or Gift-Exchange?" In *Political Frontiers, Ethnic Boundaries, and Human Geographies in Chinese History,* edited by Nicola Di Cosmo and Don J. Wyatt, pp. 351–372. New York: Routledge, Curzon, 2003.

Di Cosmo, Nicola. "Qing Colonial Administration in the Inner Asian Dependencies." *International History Review* 20, no. 2 (1998): 287–309.

Di Cosmo, Nicola. "Rethinking Tribute: Concept and Practice." Paper presented at the Association of Asian Studies Annual Meeting, Boston, 1995.

Di Cosmo, Nicola. "State Formation and Periodization in Inner Asian History." *Journal of World History* 10, no. 1 (1999): 1–40.

Diment, Galya, and Yuri Slezkine. *Between Heaven and Hell: The Myth of Siberia in Russian Culture.* New York: St. Martin's, 1993.

Du Halde, Jean Baptiste. *Description géographique, historique, chronologique, politique, et physique de l'empire de la Chine et de la Tartarie chinoise, enrichie des cartes générales et particulières de ces pays, de la carte générale & des cartes particuliéres du Thibet, & de la Corée; & ornée d'un grand nombre de figures et de vignettes gravées en taille-douce.* Paris: P. G. Lemercier, 1735.

Duara, Prasenjit. "De-constructing the Chinese Nation." *Australian Journal of Chinese Affairs* 30 (1993): 1–28.

Duara, Prasenjit. "Historicizing National Identity, or Who Imagines What and When." In *Becoming National,* edited by Geoff Eley and Ronald Grigor Suny, 151–178. Oxford: Oxford University Press, 1996.

Duara, Prasenjit. *Rescuing History from the Nation: Questioning Narratives of Modern China.* Chicago: University of Chicago Press, 1995.

Duman, Lazar' Isaevich. *Agrarnaia politika tsinskogo (Man'chzhurskogo) pravitel'stva v Sin'tsziane v kontse 18 veka.* Moscow: Izd-vo Akademii nauk SSSR, 1936.

Duman, Lazar' Isaevich. "The Qing Conquest of Junggariye and Eastern Turkestan." In *Manzhou Rule in China,* edited by S. L. Tikhvinsky, 235–256. Moscow: Progress Publishers, 1983.

Dunstan, Helen. "The Autocratic Heritage and China's Political Future: A View from the Qing." *East Asian History* 12 (1996): 79–104.

Dunstan, Helen. "Safely Supping with the Devil: The Qing State and Its Merchant Suppliers of Copper." *Late Imperial China* 13, no. 2 (1992): 42–81.

Edney, Matthew H. *Mapping an Empire: The Geographical Construction of British India, 1765–1843.* Chicago: University of Chicago Press, 1997.

Eley, Geoff, and Ronald Grigor Suny, eds. *Becoming National.* Oxford: Oxford University Press, 1996.

Elliott, Mark. "The Limits of Tartary: Manchuria in Imperial and National Geographies." *Journal of Asian Studies* 59, no. 3 (2000): 603–646.

Elliott, Mark. "The Manchu Language Archives of the Qing Dynasty and the Origins of the Palace Memorial System." *Late Imperial China* 22, no. 1 (2001): 1–70.

Elliott, Mark C. *The Manchu Way: The Eight Banners and Ethnic Identity in Late Imperial China.* Stanford: Stanford University Press, 2001.

Elman, Benjamin. *A Cultural History of Civil Examinations in Late Imperial China.* Berkeley: University of California Press, 2000.

Elman, Benjamin. "Geographical Research in the Ming-Ch'ing Period." *Monumenta Serica* 35 (1981–83): 1–18.

Elvin, Mark. *The Pattern of the Chinese Past.* Stanford: Stanford University Press, 1973.

Fairbank, John K. "The Creation of the Treaty System." In *The Cambridge History of China.* Volume 10. Part 1. *Late Ch'ing, 1800–1911,* edited by John K. Fairbank, 213–263. Cambridge: Cambridge University Press, 1978.

Fairbank, John K., ed. *The Chinese World Order.* Cambridge, Mass.: Harvard University Press, 1968.

Fairbank, John K., and Edwin O. Reischauer. *East Asia: The Great Tradition.* Volume 1. Boston: Houghton Mifflin, 1960.

Fairbank, John King. *Trade and Diplomacy on the China Coast: The Opening of the Treaty Ports, 1842–1854.* Stanford: Stanford University Press, 1969.

Fan Jinmin. "Qingdai Jiangnan yu Xinjiang diqu di sichou maoyi." In *Qingdai Quyu Shehui Jingji Yanjiu,* edited by Ye Xian'en, 715–728. Beijing: Zhonghua, 1992.

Fang Yingkai. *Xinjiang Tunkenshi.* Ürümchi: Xinjiang Qingshaonian Chubanshe, 1989.

Faragher, John Mack. "The Frontier Trail: Rethinking Turner and Reimagining the American West." *American Historical Review* 98, no. 1 (1993): 106–117.

Farmer, Edward L. *Early Ming Government: The Evolution of Dual Capitals.* Cambridge, Mass.: Harvard University Press, 1968.

Faroqhi, Suraiya. "In Search of Ottoman History." In *New Approaches to State and Peasant in Ottoman History,* edited by Halil Berktay and Suraiya Faroqhi, 212–241. London: Frank Cass, 1992.

Farquhar, David M. "Emperor as Bodhisattva in the Governance of the Ch'ing Empire." *Harvard Journal of Asiatic Studies* 38 (1978): 5–34.

Farquhar, David M. "Oirat-Chinese Tribute Relations, 1408–59." *Studia Altaica (Festschrift für Nikolaus Poppe)* (1957): 60–68.

Farquhar, David M. "The Origins of the Manchus' Mongolian Policy." In *The Chinese World Order,* edited by John K. Fairbank, 198–205. Cambridge, Mass.: Harvard University Press, 1968.

Febvre, Lucien Paul Victor. "Frontière, the Word and the Concept." In *A New Kind of History and Other Essays,* edited by Peter Burke, 208–218. New York: Harper & Row, 1973.

Feng Erkang. "Kangxi chao di zhuwei zhi zheng he Yinzhen di shengli." In *Kang Yong Qian Sandi Pingyi,* edited by Zuo Buqing, 262–286. Beijing: Zijin Chubanshe, 1986.

Feng Erkang, Xu Shengheng, and Yan Aimin. *Yongzheng Huangdi Quanzhuan.* Beijing: Xueyuan Chubanshe, 1994.

Fisher, Thomas. "Lü Liuliang and the Zeng Jing Case." Ph.D. dissertation, Princeton University, 1974.

Fleischer, Cornell. "Royal Authority, Dynastic Cyclism, and "Ibn Khaldūnism" in Sixteenth-Century Ottoman Letters." *Journal of Asian and African Studies* 18, no. 3–4 (1983): 198–220.

Fletcher, Joseph. "Ch'ing Inner Asia c. 1800." In *The Cambridge History of China.* Volume 10. Part 1. *Late Ch'ing, 1800–1911,* edited by John K. Fairbank, 35–106. Cambridge: Cambridge University Press, 1978.

Fletcher, Joseph. "The Heyday of the Ch'ing Order in Mongolia, Sinkiang, and Tibet." In *The Cambridge History of China.* Volume 10. Part 1. *Late Ch'ing, 1800–1911,* edited by John K. Fairbank, 351–408. Cambridge: Cambridge University Press, 1978.

Fletcher, Joseph. "The Mongols: Ecological and Social Perspectives." *Harvard Journal of Asiatic Studies* 46, no. 1 (1986): 11–50.

Fletcher, Joseph. "A Neglected Source of Erdeni-yin Erike." *Harvard Journal of Asiatic Studies* 24 (1962): 229–33.

Fletcher, Joseph. "Review of I. Ia. Zlatkin, *Istoriia Dzhungarskogo Khanstvo (1635–1758)." Kritika* 2, no. 3 (1966): 19–28.

Fletcher, Joseph. "Sino-Russian Relations, 1800–1862." In *The Cambridge History of China.* Volume 10. Part 1. *Late Ch'ing, 1800–1911,* edited by John K. Fairbank, 318–350. Cambridge: Cambridge University Press, 1978.

Fletcher, Joseph. "Turco-Mongolian Monarchic Tradition in the Ottoman Empire." In *Studies on Chinese and Islamic Inner Asia,* edited by Beatrice Forbes Manz, 236–251. Brookfield, Vt.: Variorum, 1995.

Fletcher, Joseph. "V. A. Aleksandrov on Russo-Ch'ing Relations in the Seventeenth Century: Critique and Résumé." *Kritika* 7, no. 3 (1971): 138–170.

Flynn, Dennis O., and Arturo Giraldez. "Cycles of Silver: Global Economic Unity through the Mid-Eighteenth Century." *Journal of World History* 13, no. 2 (2002): 391–427.

Foss, Theodore N. "A Western Interpretation of China: Jesuit Cartography." In *East Meets West: The Jesuits in China, 1582–1773,* edited by Charles E. Ronan, S.J., and Bonnie B. C. Oh, 209–251. Chicago: Loyola University Press, 1988.

Foucault, Michel. *Madness and Civilization: A History of Insanity in the Age of Reason.* New York: Vintage, 1965.

Foust, Clifford M. *Muscovite and Mandarin: Russia's Trade with China and Its Setting, 1727–1805.* Chapel Hill: University of North Carolina Press, 1969.

Frank, Andre Gunder. *ReOrient: Global Economy in the Asian Age.* Berkeley: University of California Press, 1998.

Franke, Wolfgang. "Addenda and Corrigenda to Pokotilov." In Dmitrii Pokotilov, *History of the Eastern Mongols during the Ming Dynasty*. Part 2, 1–95. Philadelphia: Porcupine Press, 1976.

Franke, Wolfgang. "Chinesische Feldzüge durch die Mongolei im frühen 15. Jahrhundert." *Sinologica* 3 (1951–1953): 81–88.

Franke, Wolfgang. "Yunglo's Mongolei-Feldzüge." *Sinologische Arbeiten* 3 (1945): 1–54.

Frederickson, George M. *Racism: A Short History*. Princeton: Princeton University Press, 2002.

Friedman, Edward. "Reconstructing China's National Identity." In *National Identity and Democratic Prospects in Socialist China*, edited by Edward Friedman, 87–114. Armonk, N.Y.: M. E. Sharpe, 1995.

Frye, Richard N. *The Heritage of Central Asia: From Antiquity to the Turkish Expansion*. Princeton: Markus Wiener Publishers, 2001.

Fuchs, Walter. *Der Jesuiten-Atlas der Kanghsi-Zeit: Seine Entstehungsgeschichte nebst Namensindices für die Karten der Mandjurei, Mongolei, Ostturkestan und Tibet, mit Wiedergabe der Jesuiten-Karten in Original Grosse*. Beijing: Fu-Jen-Universität, 1943.

Fuchs, Walter. "Materialen zur Kartographie der Mandju-Zeit." *Monumenta Serica* l (1935–36, 1938): 386–427.

Fujitani, Takashi. *Splendid Monarchy: Power and Pageantry in Modern Japan*. Berkeley: University of California Press, 1996.

Fullard, Harold, ed. *China in Maps*. Chicago: Denoyer-Geppert, 1968.

Fuller, William C. *Strategy and Power in Russia, 1600–1914*. New York: Free Press, 1992.

Gaubatz, Piper Rae. *Beyond the Great Wall: Urban Form and Transformation on China's Frontiers*. Stanford: Stanford University Press, 1996.

Geiss, James. "The Cheng-te Reign, 1506–1521." In *The Cambridge History of China*. Volume 8. Part 1. *The Ming Dynasty, 1368–1644*, edited by Denis Twitchett and Frederick Mote, 403–439. Cambridge: Cambridge University Press, 1988.

Gibbon, Edward. *The History of the Decline and Fall of the Roman Empire*. Edited by David Womersley. London: Allen Lane, Penguin Press, 1994.

Giersch, Patterson C. "Qing China's Reluctant Subjects: Indigenous Communities and Empire along the Yunnan Frontier." Ph.D. dissertation, Yale University, 1998.

Giles, Herbert Allen. *A Chinese Biographical Dictionary*. Taibei: Cheng-wen, 1968.

Gladney, Dru C. "Representing Nationality in China: Refiguring Majority/Minority Identities." *Journal of Asian Studies* 53, no. 1 (1994): 92–123.

Golden, Peter B. *An Introduction to the History of the Turkic Peoples*. Wiesbaden: Otto Harrassowitz, 1992.

Goldstone, Jack A. "East and West in the Seventeenth Century: Political Crises in Stuart England, Ottoman Turkey, and Ming China." *Comparative Studies in Society and History* (1988): 103–142.

Goldstone, Jack A. "Neither Late Imperial nor Early Modern: Efflorescences and the Qing Formation in World History." In *The Qing Formation in World-Historical Time*, edited by Lynn Struve, 242–302. Cambridge, Mass.: Harvard University Asia Center, 2004).

Goldstone, Jack A. "The Problem of the Early Modern World." *Journal of the Economic and Social History of the Orient* 41, no. 3 (1998): 250–283.

Goldstone, Jack A. *Revolution and Rebellion in the Early Modern World*. Berkeley: University of California Press, 1991.

Goodrich, L. C., and Chaoying Fang. *Dictionary of Ming Biography, 1368–1644*. New York: Columbia University Press, 1976.

Gossman, Lionel. *The Empire Unpossess'd: An Essay on Gibbon's "Decline and Fall."* Cambridge: Cambridge University Press, 1981.

Greenberg, Michael. *British Trade and the Opening of China*. Cambridge: Cambridge University Press, 1951.

Greenblatt, Stephen. *Marvelous Possessions: The Wonder of the New World*. Chicago: University of Chicago Press, 1991.

Greenfeld, Liah. *Nationalism: Five Roads to Modernity*. Cambridge, Mass.: Harvard University Press, 1992.

Gruen, Erich S. *Culture and National Identity in Republican Rome*. Ithaca: Cornell University Press, 1992.

Guha, Ranajit. *Elementary Aspects of Peasant Insurgency in Colonial India*. Oxford: Oxford University Press, 1983.

Guha, Ranajit. "The Prose of Counter-insurgency." *Subaltern Studies* 2 (1983): 1–43.

Guy, R. Kent. *The Emperor's Four Treasuries: Scholars and the State in the Late Ch'ien-lung Era*. Cambridge, Mass.: Harvard University Press, 1987.

Guy, R. Kent. "Inspired Tinkering: The Qing Creation of the Province." Unpublished, 2003.

Haenisch, Erich. "Der Chinesische Feldzug in Ili im Jahre 1755." *Ostasiatische Zeitschrift* 7, no. 1–2 (1918): 57–86.

Halkovic, Stephen A. *The Mongols of the West*. Bloomington: Indiana University Press, 1985.

Hall, Bert. "Early Modern Ballistics and Tactical Change in Sixteenth-Century Warfare." Paper presented at the Conference on Colonels and Quartermasters: War and Technology during the Old Regime, Dibner Institute, MIT, April 1996.

Halperin, Charles. *Russia and the Golden Horde: The Mongol Impact on Medieval Russia*. Bloomington: Indiana University Press, 1985.

Halperin, Charles. "Russia in the Mongol Empire in Comparative Perspective." *Harvard Journal of Asiatic Studies* 43, no. 1 (1983): 239–262.

Hamashita Takeshi. "The Intra-regional System in East Asia in Modern Times." In *Network Power: Japan and Asia*, edited by Peter Katzenstein and Takashi Shiraishi, 113–135. Ithaca: Cornell University Press, 1997.

Hamashita Takeshi. *Kindai chūgoku no kokusaiteki keiki: chōkō bōeki shisutemu to kindai Ajia*. Tokyo: Tokyo Daigaku Shuppankai, 1990.

Hamashita Takeshi. "The Tribute Trade System and Modern Asia." *Memoirs of the Research Department of the Toyo Bunko* 46 (1988): 7–26.

Harley, J. B. "Deconstructing the Map." In *Writing Worlds: Discourse, Text, and Metaphor in the Representation of Landscape*, edited by Trevor J. Barnes and James S. Duncan, 231–247. London: Routledge, 1992.

Harley, J. B. "Maps, Knowledge, and Power." In *The Iconography of Landscape*, edited by Denis E. Cosgrove and Stephen Daniels, 277–312. Cambridge: Cambridge University Press, 1988.

Harley, J. B. "Meaning and Ambiguity in Tudor Cartography." In *English Map-Making, 1500–1650: Historical Essays,* edited by Sarah Tyacke, 23–45. London: British Library, 1983.

Harley, J. B. "Silences and Secrecy: The Hidden Agenda of Cartography in Early Modern Europe." *Imago Mundi* 40 (1988): 57–76.

Harley, J. B., and David Woodward, eds. *The History of Cartography: Cartography in the Traditional East and Southeast Asian Societies.* Vol. 2. Book 2. Chicago: University of Chicago Press, 1994.

Harrell, Stevan, ed. *Cultural Encounters on China's Ethnic Frontiers.* Seattle: University of Washington Press, 1995.

Hartwell, Robert M. "Historical Analogism, Public Policy, and Social Science in Eleventh- and Twelfth-Century China." *American Historical Review* 76, no. 3 (1971): 690–727.

Heissig, Walther. *Die Familien- und Kirchengeschichtsschreibung der Mongolen.* Volume 1. *16–18 Jhdt.* Wiesbaden: O. Harrassowitz, 1959.

Heissig, Walther. "Über Mongolische Landkarten." *Monumenta Serica* 9 (1944): 123–173.

Herb, G. Henrik. "Mongolian Cartography." In *The History of Cartography: Cartography in the Traditional East and Southeast Asian Societies,* edited by J. B. Harley and David Woodward, 682–685. Chicago: University of Chicago Press, 1994.

Heuschert, Dorothea. "Legal Pluralism in the Qing Empire: Manchu Legislation for the Mongols." *International History Review* 20, no. 2 (1998): 310–24.

Hevia, James L. *Cherishing Men from Afar: Qing Guest Ritual and the Macartney Embassy of 1793.* Durham: Duke University Press, 1995.

Hevia, James. "Lamas, Emperors, and Rituals: Political Implications in Qing Imperial Ceremonies." *Journal of the International Association of Buddhist Studies* 16, no. 2 (1993): 243–278.

Ho, Ping-ti. "In Defense of Sinicization: A Rebuttal of Evelyn Rawski's Reenvisioning the Qing," *Journal of Asian Studies* 57, no. 1 (1998): 123–155.

Hobsbawm, Eric J. *Nations and Nationalism since 1780: Programme, Myth, Reality.* Cambridge: Cambridge University Press, 1990.

Hobsbawm, Eric J. "The New Threat to History (Address to the Central European University, Budapest)." *New York Review of Books,* December 16, 1993, 62–64.

Hollinger, David A. "How Wide the Circle of 'We'? American Intellectuals and the Problem of the Ethnos since World War II." *American Historical Review* 98, no. 2 (1993): 317–338.

Hopkirk, Peter. *The Great Game: The Struggle for Empire in Central Asia.* New York: Kodansha, 1992.

Hostetler, Laura. *Qing Colonial Enterprise: Ethnography and Cartography in Early Modern China.* Chicago: University of Chicago Press, 2001.

Hostetler, Laura. "Qing Connections to the Early Modern World: Ethnography and Cartography in Eighteenth-Century China." *Modern Asian Studies* 34, no. 3 (2000): 623–662.

Howorth, Henry H. *History of the Mongols from the Ninth to the Nineteenth Century.* 4 volumes. Taibei: Ch'eng Wen, 1970.

Hsu, Immanuel C. Y. *The Rise of Modern China.* New York: Oxford University Press, 2000.

Hua Li. "Daoguang nianjian Tianshan Nanlu Bingtun di yanbian." *Xinjiang Shehui Kexue* 2 (1988), 99–105.

Hua Li. "Qianlong nianjian yimin chuguan yu Qing qianqi Tianshan Beilu nongye di fazhan." *Xibei Shidi* 4 (1987): 119–131.

Hua Li. "Qingdai di ManMeng lianyin." *Minzu Yanjiu* (1983): 45–54.

Hua Li. *Qingdai Xinjiang Nongye Fazhanshi.* Heilongjiang: Heilongjiang Jiaoyu Chubanshe, 1995.

Huang, Philip C. C. "Development or Involution in Eighteenth-Century Britain and China? A Review of Kenneth Pomeranz's *The Great Divergence: China, Europe, and the Making of the Modern World Economy.*" *Journal of Asian Studies* 61, no. 2 (2002): 501–538.

Huang, Philip C. C. *The Peasant Economy and Social Change in North China.* Stanford: Stanford University Press, 1985.

Huang, Ray. *1587: A Year of No Significance.* New Haven: Yale University Press, 1981.

Huang, Ray. "Military Expenditures in Sixteenth-Century Ming China." *Oriens Extremus* 17 (1970): 39–62.

Huangchao Wenxian Tongkao. Taibei: Taiwan shangwu yinshuguan, 1983.

Hucker, Charles O. *A Dictionary of Official Titles in Imperial China.* Stanford: Stanford University Press, 1985.

Hummel, Arthur W., ed. *Eminent Chinese of the Ch'ing Period.* Washington, D.C.: U.S. Government Printing Office, 1943–44.

Humphrey, Caroline, and David Sneath. *The End of Nomadism? Society, State, and the Environment in Inner Asia.* Durham: Duke University Press, 1999.

Huntington, Ellsworth. *The Pulse of Asia: A Journey in Central Asia Illustrating the Geographic Basis of History.* Boston: Houghton Mifflin, 1919.

Hutchinson, John, and Anthony D. Smith, eds. *Nationalism.* Oxford: Oxford University Press, 1994.

Hyer, Paul. "An Historical Sketch of Koke-Khota City, Capital of Inner Mongolia." *Central Asiatic Journal* 26, no. 1–2 (1982): 56–77.

Inalcik, Halil. *The Ottoman Empire: The Classical Age, 1300–1600.* New York: Praeger Publishers, 1973.

Ishihama Yumiko. "The Attitude of Qing-hai Qoshot toward the Ch'ing Dynasty's Subjugation of Tibet." *Nihon Chibetto* 34 (1988): 1–7.

Ishihama Yumiko. "Gushi Han Ōka no Chibetto Ōken sōshitsu katei ni kansuru ichi kōsatsu: Ropusan Danjin no hanran saikō." *Tōyō Gakuhō* 69, nos. 3, 4 (1988): 151–171.

Ishihama Yumiko. "Tōyō Bunko shozō shahon 'Fuyuan Dajiangjun zouzhe' to 'Qingshi Ziliao' Daisanki shoshū 'Fuyuan Dajiangjun zouyi' ni tsuite," *Mongoru Kenkyū* 18 (1987): 3–17.

İslamoğlu, Huri. "Modernities Compared: State Transformations and Constitutions of Property in the Qing and Ottoman Empires." *Journal of Early Modern History* 5, no. 4 (2001): 353–386.

İslamoğlu, Huri, and Çaglar Keyder. "Agenda for Ottoman History." In *The Ottoman Empire and the World-Economy,* edited by Huri Islamoglu-Inan, 42–62. Cambridge: Cambridge University Press, 1987.

Jagchid, Sechin, and Van Jay Symons. *Peace, War, and Trade along the Great Wall: No-madic–Chinese Interaction through Two Millennia*. Bloomington: Indiana University Press, 1989.

Ji Yun. *Wulumuqi Zashi*. Shanghai: Shangwu Yinshuguan, 1937.

Jiang Qixiang. "Luelun Qingdai Ili huitun." *Xinjiang Daxue Xuebao* 3 (1984): 82–89.

Jin Liang. *Yonghegong Zhilue*. Beijing: Zhongguo Zangxue Chubanshe, 1994.

Johnston, Alastair Iain. *Cultural Realism: Strategic Culture and Grand Strategy in Ming China*. Princeton: Princeton University Press, 1995.

Jullien, François. *The Propensity of Things: Toward a History of Efficacy in China*. New York: Zone Books, 1995.

Kafadar, Cemal. *Between Two Worlds: The Construction of the Ottoman State*. Berkeley: University of California Press, 1995.

Kahn, Harold. *Monarchy in the Emperor's Eyes: Image and Reality in the Chien-lung Reign*. Cambridge, Mass.: Harvard University Press, 1971.

Kahn, Paul. *The Secret History of the Mongols: The Origin of Chinghis Khan: An Adaptation of the Yuan Chao Pi Shih*. San Francisco: North Point Press, 1984.

Kaiser, David. *Politics and War: European Conflict from Philip II to Hitler*. Cambridge, Mass.: Harvard University Press, 1990.

Katō Naoto. "Lobzang Danjin's Rebellion of 1723: With a Focus on the Eve of the Rebellion." *Acta Asiatica* 64 (1993): 57–80.

Katō Naoto. "Robuzan Danjin no hanran to Shinchō: Hanran no keikō o chūshin to shite." *Tōyōshi Kenkyū* 45, no. 3 (1986): 28–54.

Keenan, Edward. "Muscovy and Kazan', 1445–1552: Some Introductory Remarks on Steppe Diplomacy." *Slavic Review* 26, no. 4 (1967): 548–558.

Keenan, Edward. "Muscovy and Kazan', 1445–1552: A Study in Steppe Politics." Ph.D. dissertation, Harvard University, 1965.

Kessler, Lawrence D. *K'ang-hsi and the Consolidation of Ch'ing Rule, 1661–1684*. Chicago: University of Chicago Press, 1976.

Khazanov, A. M. *Nomads and the Outside World*. Cambridge: Cambridge University Press, 1984.

Khodarkovsky, Michael. "Ignoble Savages and Unfaithful Subjects: Constructing Non-Christian Identities in Early Modern Russia." In *Russia's Orient: Imperial Borderlands and Peoples, 1700–1917*, edited by Daniel R. Brower and Edward Lazzerini, 9–26. Bloomington: Indiana University Press, 1997.

Khodarkovsky, Michael. "Russian Peasant and Kalmyk Nomad: A Tragic Encounter in the Mid-Eighteenth Century." *Russian History* 15, no. 1 (1988): 43–69.

Khodarkovsky, Michael. "Uneasy Alliance: Peter the Great and Ayuki Khan." *Central Asian Survey* 7, no. 4 (1988): 1–45.

Khodarkovsky, Michael. "War and Politics in Seventeenth-Century Muscovite and Kalmyk Societies as Viewed in One Document: Reinterpreting the Image of the 'Perfidious Nomad.'" *Central and Inner Asian Studies* 3 (1989): 36–56.

Khodarkovsky, Michael. *Where Two Worlds Met: The Russian State and the Kalmyk Nomads, 1600–1771*. Ithaca: Cornell University Press, 1992.

Khoury, Dina Rizk. "Administrative Practice between Religious Law (Shari'a) and State Law (Kanun) on the Eastern Frontiers of the Ottoman Empire." *Journal of Early Modern History* 5, no. 4 (2001): 305–330.

Khoury, Dina Rizk. *State and Provincial Society in the Ottoman Empire: Mosul, 1540–1834*. Cambridge: Cambridge University Press, 1997.

Kim, Hodong. *Holy War in China: The Muslim Rebellion and State in Chinese Central Asia, 1864–1877*. Stanford: Stanford University Press, 2004.

Kipling, Rudyard. *Kim*. Oxford: Oxford University Press, 1987.

Konvitz, Josef. *Cartography in France, 1660–1848: Science, Engineering, and Statecraft*. Chicago: University of Chicago Press, 1987.

Kuhn, Philip A. "Ideas behind China's Modern State." *Harvard Journal of Asiatic Studies* 55, no. 2 (1995): 295–337.

Kuhn, Philip A. *Origins of the Modern Chinese State*. Stanford: Stanford University Press, 2002.

Kuhn, Philip A. *Soulstealers: The Chinese Sorcery Scare of 1768*. Cambridge, Mass.: Harvard University Press, 1990.

Kuroda Akinobu. "Another Money Economy: The Case of Traditional China." In *Asia Pacific Dynamism, 1550–2000*, edited by A. J. H. Latham and Kawakatsu Heita, pp. 187–215. London: Routledge, 2000.

Kuroda Akinobu. *Chūka Teikoku no kōzō to sekai keizai*. Nagoya-shi: Nagoya Daigaku Shuppankai, 1994.

Lai Fushun. *Qianlong Zhongyao Zhanzheng zhi Junxu Yanjiu*. Taibei: Gugong, 1984.

Landes, David. *The Unbound Prometheus*. Cambridge: Cambridge University Press, 1969.

Langlois, John D., ed. *China under Mongol Rule*. Princeton: Princeton University Press, 1981.

Lantzeff, George V., and Richard Pierce, eds. *Eastward to Empire: Exploration and Conquest on the Russian Open Frontier to 1750*. Montreal: McGill–Queen's University Press, 1973.

Lattimore, Owen. *The Desert Road to Turkestan*. Boston: Little, Brown, 1929.

Lattimore, Owen. *Inner Asian Frontiers of China*. Boston: Beacon Press, 1962.

Lattimore, Owen. *Pivot of Asia: Sinkiang and the Inner Asian Frontiers of China and Russia*. Boston: Little, Brown, 1950.

Lattimore, Owen. *Studies in Frontier History: Collected Papers, 1928–1958*. New York: Oxford University Press, 1962.

Lee, James Z., and Cameron Campbell. *Fate and Fortune in Rural China: Social Organization and Population Behavior in Liaoning, 1774–1873*. Cambridge: Cambridge University Press, 1997.

Lee, James Z., and Wang Feng. *One Quarter of Humanity: Malthusian Mythology and Chinese Realities*. Cambridge, Mass.: Harvard University Press, 1999.

Legge, James. *The Chinese Classics*. Taibei: Wenshizhe chubanshe, 1971.

Lensen, George, ed. *Russia's Eastward Expansion*. Englewood Cliffs, N.J.: Prentice-Hall, 1964.

Leonard, Jane Kate. *Controlling from Afar: The Daoguang Emperor's Management of the Grand Canal Crisis, 1824–26*. Ann Arbor: University of Michigan Press, 1996.

Leonard, Jane Kate. "Qing History, Wei Yuan, and Contemporary Political Dialogue." In *New Directions in the Social Sciences and Humanities in China*, edited by Michael B. Yahuda, 28–45. London: Macmillan, 1987.

Leonard, Jane Kate. *Wei Yuan and China's Rediscovery of the Maritime World*. Cambridge, Mass.: Harvard University Press, 1984.

Leonard, Jane Kate. "Wei Yuan and Images of the Nanyang." *Ch'ing Shih Wen-t'i* 4, no. 1 (1979): 23–57.

Leonard, Jane Kate, and Robert Antony, eds. *Dragons, Tigers, and Dogs: Qing Crisis Management and the Boundaries of State Power.* Ithaca: Cornell University Press, 2002.

Lessing, F. D. *Yung-ho-kung: An Iconography of the Lamaist Cathedral.* Publication 18. Stockholm: Sino-Swedish Expedition, 1942.

Lessing, Ferdinand D. *Mongolian-English Dictionary.* Bloomington, Indiana: Mongolia Society, 1995.

Lewis, Mark Edward. *Writing and Authority in Early China.* Albany: State University of New York Press, 1999.

Li Bozhong. *Agricultural Development in Jiangnan, 1620–1850.* New York: St. Martin's, 1998.

Li, Gertraude Roth. *Manchu: A Textbook for Reading Documents.* Honolulu: University of Hawai'i Press, 2000.

Li Guangbi. "Mingdai Xicha Yima Kao." *Zhongyang Yaxiya* 2, no. 2 (1943): 47–53.

Lieberman, Victor B., ed. *Beyond Binary Histories: Re-imagining Eurasia to ca. 1830.* Ann Arbor: University of Michigan Press, 1999.

Limerick, Patricia Nelson. *The Legacy of Conquest: The Unbroken Past of the American West.* New York: Norton, 1987.

Lincoln, W. Bruce. *The Conquest of a Continent: Siberia and the Russians.* New York: Random House, 1994.

Lindner, Rudi Paul. "Nomadism, Horses, and Huns." *Past and Present* 92 (1981): 3–19.

Lindner, Rudi Paul. *Nomads and Ottomans in Medieval Anatolia.* Bloomington: Indiana University Press, 1983.

Linenthal, Edward Tabor. *Sacred Ground: Americans and Their Battlefields.* Champaign-Urbana: University of Illinois Press, 1991.

Linke, Bernd-Michael. *Zur Entwicklung des mandjurischen Khanats zum Beamtenstaat: Sinisierung und Burokratisierung der Mandjuren wahrend der Eroberungszeit.* Wiesbaden: Steiner, 1982.

Lipman, Jonathan. "The Border World of Gansu, 1895–1935." Ph.D. dissertation, Stanford University, 1981.

Lipman, Jonathan. *Familiar Strangers: A Muslim History in China.* Seattle: University of Washington Press, 1997.

Litvinskii, Boris A. "The Ecology of the Ancient Nomads of Soviet Central Asia and Kazakhstan." In *Ecology and Empire: Nomads in the Cultural Evolution of the Old World,* edited by Gary Seaman, 61–72. Los Angeles: Ethnographics Press, 1989.

Liu Ge and Huang Xianyang, eds. *Xiyu shidi lunwen ziliao suoyin.* Ürümchi: Xinjiang, 1988.

Lopez, Donald S. Jr. *Prisoners of Shangri-La: Tibetan Buddhism and the West.* Chicago: University of Chicago Press, 1998.

Lü Xiaoxian and Li Shouju. "Qianlongchao neidi yu Xinjiang sichou maoyi gaishu." In *Qingdai Quyu Shehui Jingji Yanjiu,* edited by Ye Xian'en, 742–755. Beijing: Zhonghua, 1992.

Ma Dongyu. "Qingdai tuntian tantao." *Liaoning Shifan Daxue Xuebao* (January 1985): 62–67.

Ma Dongyu. *Xiongshi Sifang: Qingdi xunshou huodong*. Shenyang: Liaohai chubanshe, 1997.

Ma Lin. "Qianlong chunian Zhungar bu shouci ruzang aocha." *Xizang Yanjiu* 1 (1988): 62–69.

Ma Ruheng. "Lun Amuersa'na de (Fandong) Yisheng." In *Elute Menggushi Lunji*, edited by Ma Ruheng and Ma Dazheng, 107–120. Xining: Qinghai Renmin Chubanshe, 1979.

Ma Ruheng and Cheng Chongde, eds. *Qingdai Bianjiang Kaifa*. 2 vols. Taiyuan: Shanxi Renmin Chubanshe, 1998.

Ma Ruheng and Ma Dazheng. *Elute Menggushi Lunji*. Xining: Qinghai renmin chubanshe, 1984.

Ma Ruheng and Ma Dazheng. *Piaoluo Yiyu di Minzu: 17 zhi 18 shiji di Turhute Menggu*. Beijing: Zhongguo Shehui kexueyuan, 1991.

Ma Zhenglin. "Xibei kaifa yu shuili." *Shaanxi Shifan Daxue Xuebao* (March 1987): 66–73.

Macauley, Melissa. *Social Power and Legal Culture: Litigation Masters in Late Imperial China*. Stanford: Stanford University Press, 1998.

Macauley, Melissa. "A World Made Simple: Law and Property in the Ottoman and Qing Empires." *Journal of Early Modern History* 5, no. 4 (2001): 331–352.

Mackinder, Halford J. *Democratic Ideals and Reality: A Study in the Politics of Reconstruction*. New York: Henry Holt, 1942.

Mackinder, Halford. "The Geographical Pivot of History." *Geographical Journal* 23, no. 4 (1904): 421–444.

Mahan, Alfred T. *The Influence of Sea Power upon History, 1660–1783*. Boston: Little & Brown, 1890.

Mahdi, M. *Ibn Khaldun's Philosophy of History*: London: G. Allen and Unwin, 1957.

Maier, Charles. "Consigning the Twentieth Century to History." *American Historical Review* 105, no. 3 (2000): 807–831.

Mair, Victor H. "Language and Ideology in the Written Popularizations of the Sacred Edict." In *Popular Culture in Late Imperial China*, edited by David Johnson, Andrew J. Nathan, and Evelyn S. Rawski, 325–359. Berkeley: University of California Press, 1985.

Maksheev, A. "Karta Zhungarii sostav. Renatom." *Zapiski imperatorskago russkago geograficheskago obshchestva* 11 (1888): 105–145.

Mancall, Mark. *Russia and China: Their Diplomatic Relations to 1728*. Cambridge, Mass.: Harvard University Press, 1971.

Mann, James. *About Face: The History of America's Relationship with China*. New York: Vintage, 1998.

Mann, Susan. *Local Merchants and the Chinese Bureaucracy, 1750–1950*. Stanford: Stanford University Press, 1987.

Marks, Robert. "Rice Prices, Food Supply, and Market Structure in Eighteenth-Century South China." *Late Imperial China* 12, no. 2 (1991): 64–116.

Marks, Robert B. *The Origins of the Modern World: A Global and Ecological Narrative*. Lanham, Md.: Rowman & Littlefield, 2002.

Marks, Robert B. *Tigers, Rice, Silk, and Silt: Environment and Economy in Late Imperial South China*. Cambridge: Cambridge University Press, 1998.

Martin, Janet. *Medieval Russia, 980–1584*. Cambridge: Cambridge University Press, 1995.

Martin, Janet. "Muscovy's Northeast Expansion: The Context and a Cause." *Cahiers du Monde Russe et Soviétique* 24, no. 4 (1983): 459–470.

Mazumdar, Sucheta. *Sugar and Society in China: Peasants, Technology, and the World Market*. Cambridge, Mass.: Harvard University Press, 1998.

McElderry, Andrea. "Frontier Commerce: An Incident of Smuggling." *American Asian Review* 5, no. 2 (1987): 47–82.

McGranahan, Carole. "Arrested Histories: Between Empire and Exile in Twentieth-Century Tibet." Ph.D. dissertation, University of Michigan, 2001.

McNeill, John R. "Of Rats and Men: A Synoptic Environmental History of the Island Pacific." *Journal of World History* 5, no. 2 (1994): 299–349.

McNeill, William. *Mythistory and Other Essays*. Chicago: University of Chicago Press, 1986.

McNeill, William H. *The Pursuit of Power: Technology, Armed Force, and Society since A.D. 1000*. Chicago: University of Chicago Press, 1982.

Melikhov, G. V. "The Process of the Consolidation of the Manzhou Tribes under Nuerhaqi and Abahai (1591–1644)." In *Manzhou Rule in China*, edited by S. L. Tikhvinsky, 67–87. Moscow: Progress Publishers, 1983.

Metzger, Thomas. *The Internal Organization of Ch'ing Bureaucracy*. Cambridge, Mass.: Harvard University Press, 1973.

Meyer, Karl E., and Shareen Blair Brysac. *Tournament of Shadows: The Great Game and the Race for Empire in Central Asia*. Washington, D.C.: Counterpoint, 1999.

Michael, Franz. *The Origin of Manchu Rule in China: Frontier and Bureaucracy as Interacting Forces in the Chinese Empire*. Baltimore: Johns Hopkins University Press, 1942.

Miller, Gerard Fridrikh. *Sammlung russischer Geschichte*. Vol. 4. St. Petersburg: Kayserliche academie der wissenschaften, 1760.

Millward, James A. *Beyond the Pass: Economy, Ethnicity, and Empire in Qing Central Asia, 1759–1864*. Stanford: Stanford University Press, 1998.

Millward, James A. "Coming onto the Map: The Qing Conquest of Xinjiang." *Late Imperial China* 20, no. 2 (1999): 61–98.

Millward, James A. "The Qing Formation, the Mongol Legacy, and the 'End of History' in Early Modern Central Eurasia." In *The Qing Formation in World-Historical Time*, edited by Lynn Struve, 92–120. Cambridge, Mass.: Harvard Asia Center, 2004.

Millward, James A. "Qing Silk–Horse Trade with the Qazaqs in Yili and Tarbaghatai, 1758–1853." *Central and Inner Asian Studies* 7 (1992): 1–42.

Millward, James A. "Qing Inner Asian Empire and the Return of the Torghuts." In *New Qing Imperial History: The Making of Inner Asian Empire at Qing Chengde*, edited by James A. Millward and Ruth Dunnell, 91–105. New York: Routledge Curzon, 2004.

Min Tu-ki. "Ch'ôngcho ûi hwangche sasang t'ongche ûi silche." In *Chungkuk Kûntaesa Yônku*, 2–53. Seoul: Ichokak, 1973.

Min Tu-ki. *National Polity and Local Power: The Transformation of Late Imperial China*. Cambridge, Mass.: Harvard University Press, 1989.

Mirsky, Jonathan. "A Lamas' Who's Who." *New York Review of Books*, April 27, 2000, 15.

Miyawaki Junko. "Galdan izen no Oiratto: Wakamatsu setsu sai hihan." *Tōyō Gakuhō* 65, no. 1.2 (1984): 91–120.

Miyawaki Junko. "Jūnana seiki no Oiratto: Jungar Hankoku ni taisuru gimon." *Shigaku Zasshi* 90, no. 10 (1981): 40–63.

Miyawaki Junko. "Oiratto Han no tanjō." *Shigaku Zasshi* 100, no. 1 (1991): 36–73.

Miyawaki Junko. "Oiratto no kōsō Zaya Pandita denki." In *Chibetto no Bukkyō to Shakai*, edited by Yamaguchi Zuihô, 603–627. Tokyo: Shunjusha, 1986.

Miyawaki Junko. "Political Organization in the [sic] Seventeenth-Century North Asia." *Ajia Afurika Gengo Bunka Kenkyū* 27 (1984): 172–179.

Miyawaki Junko. "The Qalqa Mongols and the Oyirad in the Seventeenth Century." *Journal of Asian History* 18, no. 2 (1984): 136–173.

Miyawaki Junko. *Saigo no Yūboku Teikoku: Jungaru bu no kōbō*. Tokyo: Kodansha, 1995.

Miyazawa Tomoyuki. "HokuSō no zaisei to kahei keizai." In *Chōgoku sensei kokka to shakai tōgō*, edited by Chūgokushi Kenkyūkai, 279–332. Kyoto: Bunrikaku, 1990.

Montesquieu, Charles-Louis de Secondat de. "De l'Esprit des Lois, ou du Rapport que les Lois Doivent Avoir avec la Constitution de Chaque Gouvernement, les Moeurs, le Climat, la Religion, le Commerce, etc." In *Oeuvres complètes*, 227–995. Paris: Gallimard, 1951.

Moore, Barrington. *Reflections on the Causes of Human Misery and upon Certain Proposals to Eliminate Them*. Boston: Beacon Press, 1972.

Morgan, David. *The Mongols*. Cambridge, Mass.: Basil Blackwell, 1986.

Morikawa Tetsuo. "Amursana o meguru RoShin Kōshō Shimatsu." *Rekishigaku Chirigaku Nenpō [Kyūshū Daigaku]* 7 (1983): 75–105.

Morikawa Tetsuo. "Chinggunjabu no ran ni tsuite." *Rekishigaku Chirigaku Nenpō [Kyūshū Daigaku]* 3 (1979): 73–103.

Morohashi Tetsuji. *Dai Kanwa Jiten*. Tokyo: Taishukan shoten, 1960.

Moses, Larry. "A Theoretical Approach to the Process of Inner Asian Confederation." *Études Mongoles* 5 (1974): 113–122.

Mote, F. W. *Imperial China: 900–1800*. Cambridge, Mass.: Harvard University Press, 1999.

Mote, Frederick. "The Tu-mu Incident of 1449." In *Chinese Ways in Warfare*, edited by Frank A. Kierman Jr. and John K. Fairbank, 243–272. Cambridge, Mass.: Harvard University Press, 1974.

Mukerji, Chandra. *Territorial Ambitions and the Gardens of Versailles*. Cambridge: Cambridge University Press, 1997.

Mydans, Seth. "Where Chess Is King and the People Are the Pawns." *New York Times*, June 20, 2004, 3.

Naff, Thomas, and Roger Owen. *Studies in Eighteenth-Century Islamic History*. Carbondale: Southern Illinois University Press, 1977.

Naitō Konan. "'Qinbian Jilue' no 'Gardan zhuan.'" In *Naitō Konan Zenshū*, 14 vols., 7:380–425. Tokyo: Chikuma Shobo, 1970.

Nathanson, Alynn. "Ch'ing Policies in Khalkha Mongolia and the Chingünjav Rebellion of 1756." Ph.D. dissertation, University of London, 1983.

National Research Council. *Grasslands and Grassland Sciences in Northern China.* Washington, D.C.: National Academy Press, 1992.

Needham, Joseph. "Geography and Cartography." In *Science and Civilisation in China,* 7 vols., 3:497–590. Cambridge: Cambridge University Press, 1959.

Newby, Gordon D. "Ibn Khaldun and Frederick Jackson Turner: Islam and the Frontier Experience." *Journal of Asian and African Studies* 18, no. 3–4 (1983): 274–285.

Ning, Chia. "The Lifanyuan and the Inner Asian Rituals in the Early Qing." *Late Imperial China* 14, no. 1 (1991): 60–92.

Niu Pinghan, ed. *Qingdai Zhengqu Yange Zongbiao.* Beijing: Zhongguo Ditu Chubanshe, 1990.

Norman, Jerry. *A Concise Manchu-English Lexicon.* Seattle: University of Washington Press, 1978.

Okada Hidehiro. "Doruben Oirato no kigen." *Shigaku Zasshi* 83, no. 6 (1974): 1–44.

Okada Hidehiro. "Galdan's Death: When and How." *Memoirs of the Research Department of the Toyo Bunko* 37 (1979): 91–97.

Okada Hidehiro. *Kōkitei no Tegami.* Tokyo: Chuko Shinsho, 1979.

Okada Hidehiro. "Mongoru shinseiji no Shōso no Manbun shoken." In *Nairiku Ajia no Shakai to Bunka,* edited by Mori Masao, 303–321. Tokyo: Yamakawa Shuppansha, 1983.

Okada Hidehiro. "Outer Mongolia through the Eyes of Emperor Kangxi." *Ajia Afurika Gengo Bunka Kenkyû* 18 (1979): 1–11.

Ostrowski, Donald. "The Mongol Origins of Muscovite Political Institutions." *Slavic Review* 49, no. 4 (1990): 525–542.

Ostrowski, Donald. *Muscovy and the Mongols: Cross-Cultural Influences on the Steppe Frontier, 1304–1589.* Cambridge: Cambridge University Press, 1998.

Outram, Dorinda. "Chariots of the Sun: Ritual Travel, Territory, and Monarchy in Eighteenth-Century France." Paper presented at the Workshop on Pomp and Circumstance: Political Uses of Public Culture, MIT, May 1, 1992.

Oxnam, Robert B. "Policies and Institutions of the Oboi Regency, 1661–69." *Journal of Asian Studies* 32 (1972): 265–286.

Oxnam, Robert B. *Ruling from Horseback: Manchu Politics in the Oboi Regency, 1661–69.* Chicago: University of Chicago Press, 1975.

Oyunbilig, Borjigidai. *Zur Überlieferungsgeschichte des Berichts über den persönlichen Feldzug des Kangxi Kaisers gegen Galdan (1696–1697).* Wiesbaden: Harrassowitz, 1999.

Parker, Geoffrey. *The Military Revolution: Military Innovation and the Rise of the West.* Cambridge: Cambridge University Press, 1988.

Peake, Harold, and Herbert Fleure. *The Steppe and the Sown.* New Haven: Yale University Press, 1928.

Pei, Huang. *Autocracy at Work: A Study of the Yung-cheng Period, 1723–1735.* Bloomington: Indiana University Press, 1974.

Pelenski, Jaroslaw. *Russia and Kazan: Conquest and Imperial Ideology.* Paris: Mouton, 1974.

Pelliot, Paul. "Les Conquêtes de l'empereur de la Chine." *Toung Pao* 20 no. 3–4 (1921), 183–274.

Pelliot, Paul. *Notes critiques d'histoire kalmouke*. Paris: Librairie d'Amerique et d'Orient, 1960.

Perdue, Peter C. "The Agrarian Basis of Qing Expansion into Central Asia." In *Papers from the Third International Conference on Sinology: History Section* (Zhongyang Yanjiuyuan Disanzhou Guoji Hanxue Huiyi Lunwenji Lishizu), 181–223. Taibei: Institute of History and Philology, Academia Sinica, 2002.

Perdue, Peter C. "Boundaries, Maps, and Movement: The Chinese, Russian, and Mongolian Empires in Early Modern Eurasia." *International History Review* 20, no. 2 (1998): 263–286.

Perdue, Peter C. "China in the Early Modern World: Shortcuts, Myths, and Realities." *Education about Asia* 4, no. 1 (1999): 21–26.

Perdue, Peter C. "China in the World Economy: Exports, Regions, and Theories (Review of Sucheta Mazumdar, *Sugar and Society in China: Peasants, Technology, and the World Market*)." *Harvard Journal of Asiatic Studies* 60, no. 1 (2000): 259–275.

Perdue, Peter C. "Comparing Empires: Manchu Colonialism." *International History Review* 20, no. 2 (1998): 255–262.

Perdue, Peter C. "Culture, History, and Imperial Chinese Strategy: Legacies of the Qing Conquests." In *Warfare in Chinese History*, edited by Hans van de Ven, 252–287. Leiden: Brill, 2000.

Perdue, Peter C. "Empire and Nation in Comparative Perspective." *Journal of Early Modern History* 5, no. 4 (2001): 282–304.

Perdue, Peter C. *Exhausting the Earth: State and Peasant in Hunan, 1500–1850*. Cambridge, Mass.: Harvard University Press, 1987.

Perdue, Peter C. "From Turfan to Taiwan: Trade and War on Two Chinese Frontiers." In *Untaming the Frontier: Interdisciplinary Perspectives on Frontier Studies*, edited by Bradley Parker and Lars Rodseth. Tucson: University of Arizona Press, 2005.

Perdue, Peter C. "A Frontier View of Chineseness." In *The Resurgence of East Asia: 500, 150, and 50-Year Perspectives*, edited by Giovanni Arrighi, Takeshi Hamashita, and Mark Selden, 51–77. London: Routledge, 2003.

Perdue, Peter C. "How Different Was China? Or, Bringing the Army Back In: Coercion and Ecology in the Comparative Sociology of Europe and China." In *Agriculture, Population, and Economic Development in China and Europe*, edited by Rolf Peter Sieferle and Helga Breuniger, 311–330. Stuttgart: Breuniger Stiftung, 2003.

Perdue, Peter C. "Identifying China's Northwest: For Nation and Empire." In *Locating China: Space, Place, and Popular Culture*, edited by Jing Wang and David Goodman. London: Routledge, 2005.

Perdue, Peter C. "Military Mobilization in Seventeenth- and Eighteenth-Century China, Russia, and Mongolia." *Modern Asian Studies* 30, no. 4 (1996): 757–793.

Perdue, Peter C. "Official Goals and Local Interests: Water Control in the Dongting Lake Region during the Ming and Qing Periods." *Journal of Asian Studies* 41, no. 4 (1982): 747–765.

Perdue, Peter C. "The Qing Empire in Eurasian Time and Space: Lessons from the Galdan Campaigns." In *The Qing Formation in World-Historical Time*, edited by Lynn Struve, 57–91. Cambridge, Mass.: Harvard University Asia Center, 2004.

Perdue, Peter C. "The Qing State and the Gansu Grain Market, 1739–1864." In *Chi-*

nese History in Economic Perspective, edited by Thomas G. Rawski and Lillian M. Li, 100–125. Berkeley: University of California Press, 1992.

Perdue, Peter C. "The Shape of the World: Asian Continents and the Scraggy Isthmus of Europe." *Bulletin of Concerned Asian Scholars* 30, no. 4 (1998): 53–62.

Perdue, Peter C. "Turning Points: Rise, Crisis, and Decline Paradigms in the Historiography of Two Empires." Paper presented at the Conference on Shared Histories of Modernity: State Transformations in the Chinese and Ottoman Contexts, Seventeenth through Nineteenth Centuries, New York University, Kevorkian Center for Middle Eastern Studies, 1999.

Perdue, Peter C., and Huri İslamoğlu. "Introduction to Special Issue on Qing and Ottoman Empires." *Journal of Early Modern History* 5, no. 4 (2001): 271–282.

Petech, Luciano. *China and Tibet in the Early Eighteenth Century: History of the Establishment of Chinese Protectorate in Tibet.* Leiden: E. J. Brill, 1950.

Petech, Luciano. "Notes on Tibetan History of the Eighteenth Century." *T'oung Pao* 52 (1965–66): 261–292.

Pirazzoli-t'Serstevens, Michele. *Gravures des conquêtes de l'empereur de Chine Kien-Long au Musée Guimet.* Paris: Musée Guimet, 1969.

Pokotilov, Dmitrii. *History of the Eastern Mongols during the Ming Dynasty.* Philadelphia: Porcupine Press, 1976.

Pomeranz, Kenneth. "Beyond the East-West Binary: Resituating Development Paths in the Eighteenth-Century World." *Journal of Asian Studies* 61, no. 2 (2002): 539–590.

Pomeranz, Kenneth. *The Great Divergence: China, Europe, and the Making of the Modern World Economy.* Princeton: Princeton University Press, 2000.

Pomeranz, Kenneth. "Local Interest Story: Political Power and Regional Differences in the Shandong Capital Market, 1900–1937." In *Chinese History in Economic Perspective,* edited by Thomas G. Rawski and Lillian Li, 295–318. Berkeley: University of California Press, 1988.

Pomeranz, Kenneth. *The Making of a Hinterland: State, Society, and Economy in Inland North China, 1853–1937.* Berkeley: University of California Press, 1993.

Poppe, Nicholas. "Renat's Kalmuck Maps." *Imago Mundi* 12 (1955): 157–160.

Pound, Ezra. *Shih-ching: The Classic Anthology Defined by Confucius.* Translated by Ezra Pound. Cambridge: Harvard University Press, 1982.

Power, Daniel, and Naomi Standen, eds. *Frontiers in Question: Eurasian Borderlands 700–1700.* New York: St.Martin's Press, 1998.

Priest, Quinton G. "Portraying Central Government Institutions: Historiography and Intellectual Accommodation in the High Ching." *Late Imperial China* 7 (1986): 27–49.

Pritsak, Omeljan. "Moscow, the Golden Horde, and the Kazan Khanate from a Polycultural Point of View." *Slavic Review* 26, no. 4 (1967): 576–583.

Pritsak, Omeljan. *The Origin of Rus. Vol. 1. Old Scandinavian Sources.* Cambridge, Mass.: Harvard University Press, 1981.

Qi Qingshun. "Qingdai Xinjiang di xiexiang gongying he caizheng weiji." *Xinjiang Shehui Kexue* 3 (1987): 74–85.

Qi Qingshun. "Qingdai Xinjiang qianfan yanjiu." *Zhongguoshi Yanjiu* 2 (1988): 45–57.

Qi Qingshun. "1767 nian Changji qianfan baodong bu ying kending." *Xinjiang Daxue Xuebao* 4 (1986): 63–65.

Qi Qingshun. "Shilun Qingdai Xinjiang tunbing di fazhan he yanbian." *Xinjiang Daxue Xuebao* 2 (1988): 46–53.

Qingshi Bianweihui, ed. *Qingdai Renwu Zhuan'gao.* 19 vols. Beijing: Zhonghua Shuju, 1992. (QRZ)

Rabinow, Paul. *French Modern: Norms and Forms of the Social Environment.* Cambridge, Mass.: MIT Press, 1989.

Ratchnevsky, Paul. *Genghis Khan: His Life and Legacy.* Cambridge, Mass.: Basil Blackwell, 1993.

Rawski, Evelyn S. *The Last Emperors: A Social History of Qing Imperial Institutions.* Berkeley: University of California Press, 1998.

Rawski, Evelyn S. "Reenvisioning the Qing: The Significance of the Qing Period in Chinese History." *Journal of Asian Studies* 55, no. 4 (1996): 829–850.

Reardon-Anderson, James. "Man and Nature in the West Liao River Basin during the Past 10,000 Years." Unpublished. 1994.

Reardon-Anderson, James. "Reluctant Pioneers: China's Northern Frontier, 1644–1937." Unpublished. 2002.

Ren Shijiang. "Shixi Tuerhute huigui zuguo di yuanyin." *ShehuiKexue(Gansu)* (February 1983), 107–111.

Rhoads, Edward J. *Manchus and Han: Ethnic Relations and Political Power in Late Qing and Early Republican China, 1861–1928.* Seattle: University of Washington Press, 2000.

Riasanovsky, Nicholas. *A History of Russia.* Oxford: Oxford University Press, 1993.

Richards, John. "Land Transformation." In *The Earth as Transformed by Human Action: Global and Regional Changes in the Biosphere over the Past Three Hundred Years,* edited by B. L. Turner et al., 163–178. Cambridge: Cambridge University Press, 1990.

Rimsky-Korsakov Dyer, Svetlana. "The Dungans: Some Aspects of the Culture of Chinese Muslims in the Soviet Union." Paper presented at "The Legacy of Islam in China: An International Symposium in Memory of Joseph F. Fletcher," Harvard University, April 14–16, 1989.

Robinson, David. *Bandits, Eunuchs, and the Son of Heaven.* Honolulu: University of Hawai'i Press, 2001.

Rossabi, Morris. *China and Inner Asia: From 1368 to the Present Day.* New York: Pica Press, 1975.

Rossabi, Morris. "The 'Decline' of the Central Asian Caravan Trade." In *The Rise of Merchant Empires,* edited by James D. Tracy, 351–370. Cambridge: Cambridge University Press, 1990.

Rossabi, Morris. "The Ming and Inner Asia." In *The Cambridge History of China.* Vol. 8. Part 2. *The Ming Dynasty, 1368–1644,* edited by Denis Twitchett and Frederick Mote, 221–271. Cambridge: Cambridge University Press, 1998.

Rossabi, Morris. "Notes on Esen's Pride and Ming China's Prejudice." *Mongolia Society Bulletin* 17 (1970): 31–39.

Rossabi, Morris. "The Tea and Horse Trade with Inner Asia during the Ming." *Journal of Asian History* 4, no. 2 (1970): 136–168.

Roth, Gertraude. "The Manchu-Chinese Relationship, 1618–36." In *From Ming to*

Ch'ing: Conquest, Region, and Continuity in Seventeenth-Century China, edited by Jonathan D. Spence and John E. Wills, Jr., 1–38. New Haven: Yale University Press, 1979.

Roth-Li, Gertraude. "The Rise of the Early Manchu State: A Portrait Drawn from Manchu Sources to 1636." Ph.D. dissertation, Harvard University, 1975.

Rowe, William T. *Hankow: Commerce and Society in a Chinese City, 1796–1889.* Stanford: Stanford University Press, 1984.

Rowe, William T. *Saving the World: Chen Hongmou and Elite Consciousness in Eighteenth-Century China.* Stanford: Stanford University Press, 2001.

Rowe, William T. "State and Market in mid-Qing Economic Thought." *Études Chinoises* 12, no. 3 (1993): 7–40.

Rozman, Gilbert. *Urban Networks in Ch'ing China and Tokugawa Japan.* Princeton: Princeton University Press, 1973.

Rudelson, Justin Jon. *Oasis Identities: Uyghur Nationalism along China's Silk Road.* New York: Columbia University Press, 1997.

Saguchi Tōru. "The Formation of the Turfan Principality under the Qing Empire." *Acta Asiatica* 41 (1981): 76–94.

Saguchi Tōru. "Shinchō shihaika no Turfan." *Tōyō Gakuhō* 60, no. 3–4 (1979): 1–31.

Sahlins, Marshall. *Islands of History.* Chicago: University of Chicago Press, 1987.

Said, Edward. *Orientalism.* New York: Vintage, 1994.

Salzman, Ariel. "An Ancien Regime Revisited: 'Privatization' and Political Economy in the Eighteenth-Century Ottoman Empire." *Politics and Society* 21, no. 4 (1993): 393–423.

Sanjdorj, M. *Manchu Chinese Colonial Rule in Northern Mongolia.* Translated by Urgunge Onon. New York: St. Martin's, 1980.

Satō Hisashi. *Chūsei Chibetto shi kenkyū.* Kyoto: Dohosha, 1986.

Satō Hisashi. "Lobzan Danjin no hanran ni tsuite." *Shirin* 55, no. 6 (1972): 1–32.

Schafer, Edward. "The Camel in China down to the Mongol Dynasty." *Sinologica* 2 (1950): 165–194, 263–282.

Schneider, Laurence. *Ku Chieh-kang and China's New History: Nationalism and the Quest for Alternative Traditions.* Berkeley: University of California Press, 1971.

Schwartz, Benjamin. *The World of Thought in Ancient China.* Cambridge, Mass.: Harvard University Press, 1985.

Scott, James C. *Domination and the Arts of Resistance: Hidden Transcripts.* New Haven: Yale University Press, 1990.

Scott, James C. *Seeing Like a State: How Certain Schemes to Improve the Human Condition Have Failed.* New Haven: Yale University Press, 1998.

Scott, James C. "State Simplifications: Nature, Space, and People." *Journal of Political Philosophy* 3, no. 3 (1995): 191–233.

Sen, Amartya K. *Poverty and Famines: An Essay on Entitlement and Deprivation.* Oxford: Clarendon Press, 1981.

Serruys, Henry. "Early Lamaism in Mongolia." *Oriens Extremus* 10 (1963): 181–216.

Serruys, Henry. "Sino-Mongol Trade during the Ming." *Journal of Asian History* 9 (1975): 34–56.

Serruys, Henry. "Smallpox in Mongolia during the Ming and Ch'ing Dynasties." *Zentralasiatische Studien* 14 (1980): 41–63.

Seuberlich, Wolfgang. "Review of *Russko-Kitajskie Otnoshenija v XVII veke*." *Oriens Extremus* 19, no. 1–2 (1972): 239–255.

Shapin, Steven, and Simon Schaffer. *Leviathan and the Air-Pump: Hobbes, Boyle, and the Experimental Life*. Princeton: Princeton University Press, 1985.

Shepherd, John Robert. *Statecraft and Political Economy on the Taiwan Frontier, 1600–1800*. Stanford: Stanford University Press, 1993.

Shimizu Taiji. *Mindai Tochiseidoshi Kenkyū*. Tokyo: Daian, 1968.

Sieferle, Rolf Peter. *The Subterranean Forest: Energy Systems and the Industrial Revolution*. Cambridge: White Horse Press, 2001.

Sinor, Denis. "Horse and Pasture in Inner Asian History." *Oriens Extremus* 19 (1972): 171–183.

Sinor, Denis. *Inner Asia: History, Civilization, Languages: A Syllabus*. Ann Arbor: University of Michigan Press, 1979.

Sinor, Denis. "The Inner Asian Warriors." *Journal of the American Oriental Society* 101 (1981): 133–144.

Sinor, Denis. *Introduction a l'étude de l'Asie centrale*. Wiesbaden: O. Harrassowitz, 1963.

Sinor, Denis. "Montesquieu et le monde altaique." *Études Mongoles* 27 (1996): 51–57.

Sinor, Denis, ed. *The Cambridge History of Early Inner Asia*. Cambridge: Cambridge University Press, 1990.

Skinner, G. William. "Presidential Address: The Structure of Chinese History." *Journal of Asian Studies* 44, no. 2 (1985): 271–292.

Skinner, G. William, ed. *The City in Late Imperial China*. Stanford: Stanford University Press, 1977.

Slezkine, Yuri. *Arctic Mirrors: Russia and the Small Peoples of the North*. Ithaca: Cornell University Press, 1994.

Smith, John Masson Jr. "Mongol Campaign Rations: Milk, Marmots, and Blood?" In *Turks, Hungarians, and Kipchaks: A Festschrift in Honor of Tibor Halasi-Kun*, edited by Pierre Oberling, 223–228. Washington, D.C.: Institute of Turkish Studies, 1984.

Smith, Paul J. *Taxing Heaven's Storehouse: Horses, Bureaucrats, and the Destruction of the Sichuan Tea Industry, 1074–1224*. Cambridge, Mass.: Harvard University Press, 1991.

Smith, Richard J. *Chinese Maps: Images of "All under Heaven."* New York: Oxford University Press, 1996.

Smith, Richard J. "Mapping China's World: Cultural Cartography in Late Imperial China." In *Landscape, Culture, and Power in Chinese Society*, edited by Wen-hsin Yeh, 52–109. Berkeley: Institute of East Asian Studies, University of California, Center for Chinese Studies, 1998.

Sombart, Werner. *Krieg und Kapitalismus*. New York: Arno Press, 1975 [1913].

Soucek, Svat. *A History of Inner Asia*. Cambridge: Cambridge University Press, 2000.

Sowerby, Arthur de Carle. "The Horse and Other Beasts of Burden in China." *China Journal* 26 (1937): 282–287.

Spence, Jonathan. *The Search for Modern China*. New York: Norton, 1990.

Spence, Jonathan. *Treason by the Book*. New York: Viking, 2001.

Spence, Jonathan D. *Emperor of China: Self-Portrait of K'ang-hsi*. New York: Knopf, 1974.

Sperling, Elliot. "Awe and Submission: A Tibetan Aristocrat at the Court of Qianlong." *International History Review* 20, no. 2 (1998): 325–335.

Stary, Giovanni. "The Manchu Emperor 'Abahai': Analysis of an Historiographic Mistake." *Central Asiatic Journal* 28, no. 3–4 (1984): 296–299.

Stevens, Carol B. *Soldiers on the Steppe: Army Reform and Social Change in Early Modern Russia.* DeKalb: Northern Illinois University Press, 1995.

Strassberg, Richard. *Inscribed Landscapes: Travel Writing from Imperial China.* Berkeley: University of California Press, 1994.

Struve, Lynn A. *Voices from the Ming-Qing Cataclysm: China in Tigers' Jaws.* New Haven: Yale University Press, 1993.

Taaffee, Robert N. "The Geographic Setting." In *The Cambridge History of Early Inner Asia,* edited by Denis Sinor, 19–40. Cambridge: Cambridge University Press, 1990.

Taagepera, Rein. "Size and Duration of Empire: Systematics of Size." *Social Science Research* 7 (1978): 108–127.

Tan Qixiang. *Zhongguo lishi dituji.* First edition. 8 volumes. Shanghai: Ditu chubanshe, 1982.

Tan Qixiang and Zhongguo shehui kexueyuan. *The Historical Atlas of China.* Hong Kong: Joint Publishing, 1991.

Tang Cheng'en and Chen Baosheng. *Gansu Minzu Maoyi Shigao.* Lanzhou: Gansu renmin chubanshe, 1986.

Tani Mitsutaka. "Mindai chaba bōeki no kenkyū." *Shirin* 49, nos. 5, 6 (1966): 83–101, 41–59.

Tayama Shigeru. *Mōko hōten no kenkyū.* Tokyo: Nihon Gakujutsu Shinkokai, 1967.

Taylor, Romeyn. "Yuan Origins of the Wei-suo System." In *Chinese Government in Ming Times: Seven Studies,* edited by Charles O. Hucker, 23–40. New York: Columbia University Press, 1969.

Teng, Emma Jinhua. "An Island of Women: The Discourse of Gender in Qing Travel Accounts of Taiwan." *International History Review* 20, no. 2 (1998): 353–370.

Teng, Emma Jinhua. *Taiwan's Imagined Geography: Chinese Colonial Travel Writing and Pictures, 1683–1895.* Cambridge, Mass.: Harvard University Asia Center, 2004.

Terada Takanobu. *Sansei Shōnin no Kenkyō: Mindai ni okeru shōnin oyobi shōgyō shihon.* Kyoto: Toyoshi Kenkyukai, 1972.

Tilly, Charles. *Coercion, Capital, and European States, 990–1992.* Cambridge, Mass.: Basil Blackwell, 1990.

Tilly, Charles. *The Contentious French.* Cambridge, Mass.: Harvard University Press, 1986.

Tilly, Charles, ed. *The Formation of National States in Western Europe.* Princeton: Princeton University Press, 1975.

Torbert, Preston. *The Ch'ing Imperial Household Department: A Study of Its Organization and Principal Functions, 1662–1796.* Cambridge, Mass.: Harvard University Press, 1977.

Toynbee, Arnold. *A Study of History.* 12 vols. Oxford: Oxford University Press, 1934.

Tucci, Giuseppe. *Tibetan Painted Scrolls.* 2 vols. Rome: Libreria dello Stato, 1949.

Unger, Roberto M. *Plasticity into Power: Comparative-Historical Studies on the Institutional Conditions of Economic and Military Success.* Cambridge: Cambridge University Press, 1987.

Vernadsky, George. *The Mongols and Russia*. New Haven: Yale University Press, 1953.

Vladimirtsov, B. Ia. "Mongol'skie skazaniia ob Amursane." *Vostochnie Zapiski* 1 (1927): 271–282.

Vladimirtsov, B. Ia. *Le Régime social des Mongoles: Le Féodalisme nomade*. Paris: A. Maisonneuve, 1948.

Vogel, Hans Ulrich. "Chinese Central Monetary Policy, 1644–1800." *Late Imperial China* 8, no. 2 (1987): 1–52.

Vogel, Hans Ulrich. "Chinese Central Monetary Policy and Yunnan Copper Mining in the Early Qing (1644–1800)." Ph.D. dissertation, University of Zurich, 1983.

von Glahn, Richard. *Fountain of Fortune: Money and Monetary Policy in China, 1000–1700*. Berkeley: University of California Press, 1996.

von Le Coq, Albert. *Buried Treasures of Chinese Turkestan*. London: G. Allen and Unwin, 1928.

Wakamatsu Hiroshi. "Ganchimūru no Roshia bōmei jiken o meguru Shin, Roshia Kōshō." *Kyōto Furitsu Daigaku Gakujutsu Hōkoku: Jimbun* 25 (1973): 25–39; 26 (1974): 1–12.

Wakamatsu Hiroshi. "Ganchimūru no Roshia bōmei jiken o megutte." *Yūboku Shakaishi* 46 (1973–74): 8–13.

Wakamatsu Hiroshi. "Jungaru Ōkoku no keisei katei." *Tōyōshi Kenkyū* 41, no. 4 (1983): 74–117.

Wakamatsu Hiroshi. *Qingdai Menggu di Lishi yu Zongjiao*. Heilongjiang: Heilongjiang Jiaoyu Chubanshe, 1994.

Wakeman, Frederic Jr. "The Canton Trade and the Opium War." In *The Cambridge History of China*. Vol. 10. Part 1. *Late Ch'ing, 1800–1911*, edited by John K. Fairbank, 163–212. Cambridge: Cambridge University Press, 1978.

Wakeman, Frederic Jr. *The Great Enterprise: The Manchu Reconstruction of Imperial Order*. Berkeley: University of California Press, 1985.

Wakeman, Frederic Jr. "The Shun Interregnum of 1644." In *From Ming to Ch'ing: Conquest, Region, and Continuity in Seventeenth-Century China*, edited by Jonathan Spence and John E. Wills, Jr., 39–88. New Haven: Yale University Press, 1979.

Wakeman, Frederic Jr. *Strangers at the Gate: Social Disorder in South China, 1839–61*. Berkeley: University of California Press, 1966.

Waldron, Arthur. *The Great Wall of China: From History to Myth*. Cambridge: Cambridge University Press, 1990.

Waldron, Arthur. "Representing China: The Great Wall and Cultural Nationalism in the Twentieth Century." In *Cultural Nationalism in East Asia: Representation and Identity*, edited by Harumi Befu, 36–60. Berkeley: Institute of East Asian Studies, University of California, 1993.

Waldron, Arthur. "Scholarship and Patriotic Education: The Great Wall Conference." *China Quarterly* 143 (1995): 844–850.

Waley, Arthur, trans. *The Analects of Confucius*. New York: Vintage Books, 1938.

Waley-Cohen, Joanna. "China and Western Technology in the Eighteenth Century." *American Historical Review* 98, no. 5 (1993): 1525–44.

Waley-Cohen, Joanna. "Commemorating War in Eighteenth-Century China." *Modern Asian Studies* 30, no. 4 (1996): 869–899.

Waley-Cohen, Joanna. *Exile in Mid-Qing China: Banishment to Xinjiang, 1758–1820.* New Haven: Yale University Press, 1991.

Waley-Cohen, Joanna. "God and Guns in Late Imperial China: Jesuit Missionaries and the Military Campaigns of the Qianlong Emperor (1736–1795)." In *Proceedings of the Thirty-third Conference of the International Congress of Asian and North African Studies,* edited by Bernard Hung-kay Luk. Lewiston, Me.: E. Mellen Press, 1991.

Waley-Cohen, Joanna. "Military Ritual and the Qing Empire." In *Warfare in Inner Asian History,* edited by Nicola Di Cosmo, 405–444. Leiden: Brill, 2002.

Waley-Cohen, Joanna. "Religion, War, and Empire in Eighteenth-Century China." *International History Review* 20, no. 3 (1998): 336–352.

Wallerstein, Immanuel. *The Modern World System.* Vol. 3. *The Second Era of Great Expansion of the Capitalist World-Economy, 1730s–1840s.* San Diego: Academic Press, 1989.

Waltner, Ann, and Thomas A. Wilson. "Forum: Four Books on the Manchus in China and in Greater Asia." *Journal of Asian Studies* 61, no. 1 (2002): 149–177.

Wang Ch'ungwu. "The Ming System of Merchant Colonization." In *Chinese Social History: Translations of Selected Studies,* edited by E-tu Zen Sun and John De Francis, 299–308. New York: Octagon Books, 1966.

Wang Hongbin. "QianJia shiqi yingui qianjian wenti tanyuan." *Zhongguo Shehui Jingjishi Yanjiu* 2 (1987): 86–92.

Wang Hongjun and Liu Ruzhong. "Qingdai pingding Zhungar guizu panluan di lishi huajuan." *Wenwu* (December 1976): 68–74.

Wang Shaoguang and Hu Angang. *The Political Economy of Uneven Development: The Case of China.* Armonk: M. E. Sharpe, 1999.

Wang Xi and Lin Yongkuang. "Qingdai Jiangning Zhizao yu Xinjiang di Sichou Maoyi." *Zhongyang Minzu Xueyuan Xuebao,* 3 (1987): 76–78.

Wang Xi and Lin Yongkuang. *Qingdai Xibei Minzu Maoyishi.* Beijing: Zhongyang Minzu Xueyuan Chubanshe, 1991.

Wang Xilong. "Guanyu Qingdai Ili Huitun shouhuo jisuan danwei 'fen' di bianxi." *Lanzhou Daxue Xuebao* (April 1986): 39–44.

Wang Xilong. "Qingdai Shibian Xinjiang Shulue." *Xibei Shidi* 4 (1985): 62–71.

Wang Xilong. "Qingdai Wulumuqi Tuntian Shulun." *Xinjiang Shehui Kexue* 5 (1989): 101–108.

Wang Xilong. *Qingdai Xibei Tuntian Yanjiu.* Lanzhou: Lanzhou Daxue Chubanshe, 1990.

Wang Xilong. "Qingdai Xinjiang di Huitun." *Xibei Minzu Xueyuan Xuebao,* no. 1 (1985): 44–53.

Wang Yuquan. *Mingdai di Juntun.* Beijing: Zhonghua Shuju, 1965.

Wang Yuquan. "Mingdai juntun zhidu di lishi yuanyuan ji qi tedian." *Lishi Yanjiu* 6 (1959): 45–55.

Wang, Jing. *The Story of Stone: Intertextuality, Ancient Chinese Stone Lore, and the Stone Symbolism in "Dream of the Red Chamber," "Water Margin," and "The Journey to the West."* Durham: Duke University Press, 1992.

Wang, Yeh-chien. *An Estimate of the Land-Tax Collection in China, 1753 and 1908.* Cambridge, Mass.: Harvard University Press, 1973.

Wang, Yeh-chien. "Food Supply in Eighteenth-Century Fukien." *Late Imperial China* 7, no. 2 (1986): 80–117.

Wang, Yeh-chien. *Land Taxation in Imperial China, 1750–1911.* Cambridge, Mass.: Harvard University Press, 1973.

Watson, Burton, trans. *Records of the Grand Historian of China.* 2 vols. New York: Columbia University Press, 1961.

Weber, Eugen Joseph. *Peasants into Frenchmen: The Modernization of Rural France, 1870–1914.* London: Chatto & Windus, 1979.

Wei Yuan. *Shengwuji.* Beijing: Zhonghua Shuju, 1984.

Weiers, Michael. "Die historische Dimension des Jade-Siegels zur Zeit des Mandschuherrschers Hongtaiji." *Zentralasiastische Studien* 24 (1994): 119–145.

Wendt, Alexander. "Anarchy Is What States Make of It: The Social Construction of Power Politics." *International Organization* 46, no. 2 (1992): 391–425.

Whitbeck, Judith. "Kung Tzu-chen and the Redirection of Literati Commitment in Early-Nineteenth-Century China." *Ch'ing-shih Wen-t'i* 4, no. 10 (1983): 1–32.

White, Hayden. *Tropics of Discourse: Essays in Cultural Criticism.* Baltimore: Johns Hopkins University Press, 1978.

White, Richard. *The Middle Ground: Indians, Empires, and Republics in the Great Lakes Region, 1650–1815.* Cambridge: Cambridge University Press, 1991.

Wieczynski, Joseph L., ed. *The Modern Encyclopedia of Russian and Soviet History.* 60 vols. Gulf Breeze, Fla.: Academic International Press, 1976–.

Will, Pierre-Étienne. *Bureaucracy and Famine in Eighteenth-Century China.* Stanford: Stanford University Press, 1990.

Will, Pierre-Étienne. *Bureaucratie et famine en Chine au 18e siècle.* Paris: Mouton, 1980.

Will, Pierre-Étienne. "Clear Waters versus Muddy Waters: The Zheng-Bai Irrigation System of Shaanxi Province in the Late-Imperial Period." In *Sediments of Time: Environment and Society in Chinese History,* edited by Mark Elvin and Ts'ui-jung Liu, 283–343. Cambridge: Cambridge University Press, 1998.

Will, Pierre-Étienne. "State's Interest in the Administration of a Hydraulic Infrastructure: The Example of Hubei." In *The Scope of State Power,* edited by Stuart Schram, 295–349. Hong Kong: Chinese University of Hong Kong Press, 1985.

Will, Pierre-Étienne, R. Bin Wong et al. *Nourish the People: The State Civilian Granary System in China, 1650–1850.* Ann Arbor: University of Michigan Press, 1991.

Wills, John E., Jr. "Maritime Asia, 1500–1800: The Interactive Emergence of European Domination." *American Historical Review* 98, no. 1 (1993): 83–105.

Wills, John E., Jr. *Pepper, Guns, and Parleys: The Dutch East India Company and China, 1622–1681.* Cambridge, Mass.: Harvard University Press, 1974.

Winichakul, Thongchai. *Siam Mapped: A History of the Geo-Body of a Nation.* Honolulu: University of Hawai'i Press, 1994.

Wittfogel, Karl. *Oriental Despotism: A Comparative Study of Total Power.* New Haven: Yale University Press, 1957.

Wong, R. Bin. *China Transformed: Historical Change and the Limits of European Experience.* Ithaca: Cornell University Press, 1997.

Wong, R. Bin. "Confucian Agendas for Material and Ideological Control in Modern China." In *Culture and State in Chinese History: Conventions, Accommodations, and Critiques,* edited by Theodore Huters, Pauline Yu, and R. Bin Wong, 303–325. Stanford: Stanford University Press, 1997.

Wong, R. Bin. "Food Riots in the Qing Dynasty," *Journal of Asian Studies* 41, no. 4 (1982): 767–797.

Wong, R. Bin. "Formal and Informal Mechanisms of Rule and Economic Development: The Qing Empire in Comparative Perspective." *Journal of Early Modern History* 5, no. 4 (2001): 387–408.

Wong, R. Bin. "The Search for European Differences and Domination in the Early Modern World: A View from Asia." *American Historical Review* 107, no. 2 (2002): 447–469.

Wong, R. Bin, and Peter C. Perdue. "Famine's Foes in Ch'ing China (Review of Pierre-Étienne Will, *Bureaucratie et Famine* . . .)." *Harvard Journal of Asiatic Studies* 43, no. 1 (1983): 291–332.

Wong, R. Bin, and Peter C. Perdue. "Grain Markets and Food Supplies in Eighteenth-Century Hunan." In *Chinese History in Economic Perspective,* edited by Thomas G. Rawski and Lillian M. Li, 126–144. Berkeley: University of California Press, 1992.

Wong, Shirleen S. *Kung Tzu-chen.* Boston: Twayne, 1975.

Wood, Alan, ed. *The History of Siberia: From Russian Conquest to Revolution.* London: Routledge, 1991.

Woodside, Alexander. "The Ch'ien-lung Reign." In *The Cambridge History of China.* Volume 9. Part 1. *The Ch'ing Empire to 1800,* edited by Willard J. Peterson, 230–309. Cambridge: Cambridge University Press, 2002.

Woodside, Alexander B. "From Mencius to Amartya Sen: East Asian Welfare States." Paper presented at the Reischauer Lecture, Harvard University, March 10, 2001.

Worster, Donald. "Climate and History on the Great Plains." Paper presented at the Conference on Humanities and the Environment, MIT, January 9, 1992.

Worster, Donald. *Rivers of Empire: Water, Aridity, and the Growth of the American West.* New York: Pantheon Books, 1985.

Wortman, Richard S. *Scenarios of Power: Myth and Ceremony in Russian Monarchy.* Vol. 1. *From Peter the Great to the Death of Nicholas I.* Princeton: Princeton University Press, 1995.

Wrigley, E. A. *Continuity, Chance, and Change: The Character of the Industrial Revolution in England.* Cambridge: Cambridge University Press, 1988.

Wrigley, E. A. "The Limits to Growth: Malthus and the Classical Economists." In *Population and Resources in Western Intellectual Traditions*, edited by Michael S. Teitelbaum and Jay M. Winter, 30–48. Cambridge: Cambridge University Press, 1989.

Wu, Shu-hui. *Die Eroberung von Qinghai unter Berücksichtigung von Tibet und Khams, 1717–1727: Anhand der Throneingaben des Grossfeldherrn Nian Gengyao.* Wiesbaden: Harrassowitz, 1995.

Wu, Shu-hui. "How the Qing Army Entered Tibet in 1728 after the Tibetan Civil War." *Zentralasiatische Studien* 26 (1996): 122–138.

Wu, Shu-hui. "The Imbalance of Virtue and Power in Qing Frontier Policy: The Turfan Campaign of 1731." *Études Mongoles* 27 (1996): 241–264.

Wu, Silas. *Passage to Power: K'ang-hsi and His Heir Apparent, 1661–1722.* Cambridge, Mass.: Harvard University Press, 1979.

Wu Yuanfeng. "Qing Qianlong nianjian Yili tuntian shulue." *Minzu Yanjiu* 5 (1987): 92–100.

Xia Hongtu. "Qingdai Fanglueguan Sheli Shijian juzheng." *Lishi Dang'an* 2 (1997): 134.

Xiao Yishan. *Qingdai Tongshi.* 5 vols. Beijing: Zhonghua shuju, 1986.

Xu Bofu. "18–19 shiji Xinjiang diqu di guanyin xumuye." *Xinjiang Shehui Kexue* 5 (1987): 101–112.

Xu Bofu. "Qingdai qianqi Xinjiang diqu di bingtun." *Xinjiang Shehui Kexue Yanjiu* 13 (1984): 1–20.

Xu Bofu. "Qingdai qianqi Xinjiang diqu di mintun." *Zhongguoshi Yanjiu* 2 (1985): 85–95.

Xu Daling. *Qingdai Juanna Zhidu.* Beijing: Hafo Yanjing Xueshe, 1950.

Xu Zengzhong. "Qing Shizong Yinzhen jicheng huangwei wenti xintan." In *KangYongQian Sandi Pingyi*, edited by Zuo Buqing, 227–261. Beijing: Zijincheng Chubanshe, 1986.

Yanagisawa Akira. "Garudan no Haruha shinkō (1688) kō no Haruha shokō to Roshia." In *Shinchō to Higashi Ajia: Kanda Nobuo Sensei koki kinen ronshū*, edited by Kanda Nobuo Sensei Koki Kinen Ronshū Hensan Iinkai, 179–196. Tokyo: Yamakawa Shuppansha, 1992.

Yang, Lien-sheng. "Historical Notes on the Chinese World Order." In *The Chinese World Order: Traditional China's Foreign Relations*, edited by John K. Fairbank, 20–33. Cambridge, Mass.: Harvard University Press, 1968.

Yang, Muhammad Usiar Huaizhong. "The Eighteenth-Century Gansu Relief Fraud Scandal." Conference paper presented at "The Legacy of Islam in China: An International Symposium in Memory of Joseph F. Fletcher," Harvard University, April 1989.

Yang Yiqing. *Guanzhong Zouyi.* 18 juan. Taibei: Taiwan shangwu yinshuguan, 1983.

Ye Zhiru. "Cong maoyi aocha kan Qianlong qianqi dui Zhungar bu di minzu zhengce." *Xinjiang Daxue Xuebao* 1 (1986), 62–71.

Yee, Cordell D. K. "Traditional Chinese Cartography and the Myth of Westernization." In *The History of Cartography: Cartography in the Traditional East and Southeast Asian Societies*, edited by J. B. Harley and David Woodward, 170–201. Chicago: University of Chicago Press, 1994.

Yi Baozhong. "Guanyu Mingdai juntun zhidu pohuai guocheng zhong dijige wenti." *SongliaoXuekan* 3 (1984): 41–46.

Yinti. "Fuyuan Dajiangjun zouyi." *Qingshi Ziliao* 3 (1982): 159–196.

Yoshida Kin'ichi. "Langdan no 'Jilin Jiuhetu' to Nerchinsk jōyaku." *Tōyō Gakuhō* 62, nos. 1–2 (1980): 31–70.

Yoshida Kin'ichi. *Roshia no Tōhō Shinshutsu to Nerchinsk Jōyaku.* Tokyo: Kindai Chūgoku Kenkyū Senta-, 1984.

Yu, Ying-shih. "Han Foreign Relations." In *The Cambridge History of China.* Vol. 1. *The Ch'in and Han Empires, 221 B.C.–A.D. 220*, edited by Denis Twitchett and Michael Loewe, 377–462. New York: Cambridge University Press, 1986.

Yu, Ying-shih. *Trade and Expansion in Han China.* Berkeley: University of California Press, 1967.

Yuan Shenbo. "Ulan Butong kao." *Lishi Yanjiu* 8 (1978): 86–91.

Yuan Yitang. "Qingdai Qianhuang Yanjiu," *Shehui Kexue Zhanxian* 2 (1990): 182–188.

Zelin, Madeleine. *The Magistrate's Tael: Rationalizing Fiscal Reform in Eighteenth-Century Ch'ing China*. Berkeley: University of California Press, 1984.

Zelin, Madeleine. "The Yung-cheng Reign." In *The Cambridge History of China*. Volume 9. Part 1. *The Ch'ing Empire to 1800*, edited by Willard J. Peterson, 183–229. Cambridge: Cambridge University Press, 2002.

Zeng Wenwu. *Zhongguo Jingying Xiyushi*. 2 vols. Shanghai: Shangwu Yinshuguan, 1936.

Zhang Weihua. "Tuerhute Xixi yu Tulisen zhi Chushi." *Bianzheng Gonglu* 2, nos. 3–5 (1943), 26–35.

Zhang Yuxin. "Suzhou maoyi kaolue." *Xinjiang Daxue Xuebao*, nos. 1 (1986): 67–76; 3 (1986): 24–32; 4 (1986): 48–54.

Zheng Dekun, trans. "The Travels of Emperor Mu (Mu Tianzizhuan)." *Journal of the North China Branch of the Royal Asiatic Society* 64 (1933–34): 124–142.

Zhongguo Renmin Daxue Qingshi Yanjiusuo, Zhongguo Shehui Kexueyuan, and Zhongguo Bianjiang Shidi Yanjiu Zhongxin, eds. *Qingdai Bianjiang Shidi Lunzhuo Suoyin*. Beijing: Zhongguo Renmin Chubanshe, 1987.

Zhongguo Shehui Kexueyuan Minzu Yanjiusuo et al. *Manwen Tuerhute Dang'an Yibian*. Beijing: Minzu Chubanshe, 1988.

Zhuang Jifa, *Xiesui Zhigongtu Manwen tushuo jiaozhu*. Taibei: Guoli gugong bowuyuan, 1989.

Zito, Angela. *Of Body and Brush: Grand Sacrifice as Text/Performance in Eighteenth-Century China*. Chicago: University of Chicago Press, 1997.

Zlatkin, I. Ia. *Istoriia Dzhungarskogo Khanstvo, 1635–1758*. Moscow: Nauka, 1964.

Zuo Shu'e. "Cong PingZhun zhanzheng kan Qianlong dui Zhunbu zhengce di zhuanbian." *Xibei Shidi* 2 (1985): 58–63.

Zuo Shu'e. "Mingdai Gansu tuntian shulue." *Xibei Shidi* 2 (1987): 81–90.

Zurndorfer, Harriet T. "Another Look at China, Money, Silver, and the Seventeenth-Century Crisis (Review of Richard von Glahn, *Fountain of Fortune*)." *Journal of the Economic and Social History of the Orient* 42, no. 3 (1999): 396–412.

Illustration Credits

162   Ides, *Three Years Travels,* p. 42. By permission of the Houghton Library, Harvard University.

163   National Palace Museum, Taiwan: Junjichu dang #104546 (detail).

170   Julius von Klaproth, *Mémoires relatifs à l'Asie, contenant des recherches historiques, géographiques et philologiques sur les peuples de l'Orient,* 3 vols. (Paris: Librairie orientale de Dondey-Dupré, 1826), 1:26–27.

171   National Palace Museum, Taiwan.

179   Military Museum of China. Photograph by author.

207   Library of Congress, Prints and Etching division. LC USZ62-44357.

242   Palace Museum, Beijing.

244   Palace Museum, Beijing.

246   Wulsin photographic collection, Peabody Museum.

257   Wulsin photographic collection, Peabody Museum.

258   Palace Museum, Beijing.

270   National Palace Museum, Taiwan.

271   Staatliche Museen zu Berlin–Ethnologisches Museum.

277   National Palace Museum, Taiwan.

305   Library of Congress, Prints and Etching division. LC USZ62-44377.

308–309   John Baddeley, *Russia, Mongolia, China . . . ,* 2 vols. (London: Macmillan and Company, 1919).

326–327   Judy Bonavia, *The Silk Road: From Xi'an to Kashgar* (Hong Kong: Odyssey Publications, 2002), pp. 234–235. Photograph by How Man Wong.

330   Judy Bonavia, *The Silk Road: From Xi'an to Kashgar* (Hong Kong: Odyssey Publications, 2002), p. 193. Photograph by Peter Fredenburg.

334   National Palace Museum, Taiwan, #074261 (detail).

371   Zhongyang Qixiangju Qixiang Kexue Yanjiuyuan, *Zhongguo Wubainian Hanlao Fenbu Tuji* (Charts of Droughts and Floods over 500 Years in China) (Beijing: Ditu Chubanshe, 1981), p. 150.

393   (a) Okudaira Masahiro, *Tōa senshi* (History of East Asian Coins) (Tokyo: Iwanami Shoten, 1938), *juan* 13, p. 45; (b, c) Shanghai bowuguan, *Shanghai bowuguan cang qianbi* (Coins in the Shanghai Museum) (Shanghai: Shanghai Shuhua Chubanshe, 1994), *xia,* pp. 37, 47.

398–399   Réunion des Musées Nationaux/Art Resource, NY.

410   By author.

420–421   Palace Museum, Beijing.

430–431   Photograph by author.

438   Photograph by author.

444   Library of Congress, Prints and Etching division. LC USZ62-44408.

445   Library of Congress, Prints and Etching division. LC USZ62-44377.

448   Walter Fuchs, *Der Jesuiten-Atlas der Kanghsi-Zeit* (Beijing: Fu-Jen-Universität, 1943), pl. 11. Harvard Map Collection, Harvard University.

450–451   Harvard Map Collection, Harvard University.

455   Jiang Tingxi and Chen Menglei, eds., *Gujin tushu jicheng kaozheng,* 79 vols. (1726; Shanghai: Zhonghua shu ju, 1934), 11:4431.

458   Bildarchiv Preussischer Kulturbesitz/Art Resource, NY.

477   National Palace Museum, Taiwan.

492   Palace Museum, Beijing.

498   Ye Yanlan and Ye Gongchuo, *Qingdai xuezhe xiangzhuan* (Portraits and Biographies of Qing Scholars), 2 vols. (Shanghai: Shanghai shudian chubanshe, 2001), 2:361.

390, 391, 395   Data source for Maps 8a, 8b, and 9: Grain price memorials *(liangjiadan)* in First Historical Archives, Beijing, and Palace Museum, Taiwan.

Index

Page numbers in *italics* refer to illustrations.